S0-BSW-399

# ANNUAL REVIEW OF
# ANTHROPOLOGY

# EDITORIAL COMMITTEE (1998)

ELIZABETH M. BRUMFIEL
E. VALENTINE DANIEL
ALESSANDRO DURANTI
WILLIAM H. DURHAM
FAYE V. HARRISON
JANE H. HILL
SHIRLEY LINDENBAUM
BAMBI B. SCHIEFFELIN
KENNETH M. WEISS

International Correspondents
RAJEND MESTHRIE
DON ROBOTHAM
ANDREW SHERRATT

Responsible for organization of Volume 27
(Editorial Committee, 1996)

ELIZABETH M. BRUMFIEL
E. VALENTINE DANIEL
WILLIAM H. DURHAM
FAYE V. HARRISON
JANE H. HILL
LOUISE A. LAMPHERE
SHIRLEY LINDENBAUM
MICHAEL A. LITTLE
BAMBI B. SCHIEFFELIN
MARILYN IVY (Guest)
JOHN PEMBERTON (Guest)
ERIC SMITH (Guest)

Production Editor        LISA DEAN
Subject Indexer          KYRA KITTS
Indexing Coordinator     MARY A. GLASS

# ANNUAL REVIEW OF ANTHROPOLOGY

VOLUME 27, 1998

WILLIAM H. DURHAM, *Editor*
Stanford University

E. VALENTINE DANIEL, *Associate Editor*
University of Michigan

BAMBI B. SCHIEFFELIN, *Associate Editor*
New York University

http://www.AnnualReviews.org          science@annurev.org                    650-493-4400
ANNUAL REVIEWS       4139 EL CAMINO WAY      P.O. BOX 10139      PALO ALTO, CALIFORNIA 94303-0139

ANNUAL REVIEWS
Palo Alto, California, USA

COPYRIGHT © 1998 BY ANNUAL REVIEWS, PALO ALTO, CALIFORNIA, USA, ALL RIGHTS RESERVED. The appearance of the code at the bottom of the first page of an article in this serial indicates the copyright owner's consent that copies of the article may be made for personal or internal use, or for the personal or internal use of specific clients. This consent is given on the condition, however, that the copier pay the stated per-copy fee of $8.00 per article through the Copyright Clearance Center, Inc. (222 Rosewood Drive, Danvers, MA 01923) for copying beyond that permitted by Section 107 or 108 of the US Copyright Law. The per-copy fee of $8.00 per article also applies to the copying, under the stated conditions, of articles published in any *Annual Review* serial before January 1, 1978. Individual readers, and nonprofit libraries acting for them, are permitted to make a single copy of an article without charge for use in research or teaching. This consent does not extend to other kinds of copying, such as copying for general distribution, for advertising or promotional purposes, for creating new collective works, or for resale. For such uses, written permission is required. Write to Permissions Dept., Annual Reviews, 4139 El Camino Way, P.O. Box 10139, Palo Alto, CA 94303-0139 USA.

*International Standard Serial Number: 0084-6570*
*International Standard Book Number: 0-8243-1927-3*
*Library of Congress Catalog Card Number: 72-821360*

Annual Review and publication titles are registered trademarks of Annual Reviews.

The paper used in this publication meets the minimum requirements of American National Standards for Information Sciences—Permanence of Paper for Printed Library Materials, ANZI Z39.48-1992

Annual Reviews and the Editors of its publications assume no responsibility for the statements expressed by the contributors to this *Review.*

Typesetting by Ruth McCue Saavedra and the Annual Reviews Editorial Staff

PRINTED AND BOUND IN THE UNITED STATES OF AMERICA

# PREFACE

One of the topics that always comes up at annual meetings of the Editorial Committee of the *Annual Review of Anthropology* is the workload and general "busy-ness" of anthropologists today. The consensus view of Committee members is that most, if not all, anthropologists are experiencing a relentless, continuing acceleration of demands upon our time. The trend is reported across continents, subfields, and type of employment, though it may well apply with particular force to academic anthropologists. While surely every generation must feel this way to an extent, data and observations from the 27 years of the ARA suggest that the correlation is not imaginary. In preparing chapters for publication, more authors are asking for more lead-time than ever before.

Naturally, there is no shortage of theories to explain the perceived speedup. People have argued that there has been an inflation of expectations on the part of universities and other employers; that there is a greater "need" for anthropology in the world these days and that we (or our employers) are simply responding to these increased demands and opportunities; that there is an intrinsic increase in the marginal time and effort required for new anthropological knowledge; that students see greater relevance of anthropology in their lives and are thus eager for more, and more intensive, training; and that the personal computer revolution has, in some sense, backfired—giving us more to do (e.g. email, web-surfing, etc.), not just more efficient ways to do the same things.

Whatever the reasons, we at ARA could not ignore the trend. No one likes to be in the business of hassling already busy people on tight deadlines. So we have decided to reorganize our production schedule, and thus to move our annual planning meeting (as described in the Preface to V. 25, for example) 6 months earlier, increasing the average lead time for authors from 16 to 22 months. Our planning meetings henceforth will take place in early March, leaving authors until the second January thereafter to submit invited chapters. Lead-time is always a balancing act between preparation and timeliness. We hope this new schedule will preserve the timeliness of published reviews, while promoting a higher on-time completion rate and a fuller, more balanced coverage of our special themes (where we have sometimes, in the past, had to go to press without certain chapters). We also hope that, in this era of accelerating demands, the advantages to our readers of high-quality, comprehensive reviews will only increase—especially once they are electronically available (as expected later this year). Let me thus encourage potential authors to take note of our new lengthened production cycle. And, as always, I would be delighted to hear from readers and authors alike with further suggestions on coping with, or combating, the speedup problem.

In the volume before you, we continue with two special theme sections (Human Genetic Diversity and Demographic Anthropology) and with the new series, announced last year, on anthropology and philosophy (see Veena Das's chapter on "Wittgenstein and Anthropology.") We are gratified by readers' enthusiastic responses to these recent innovations. Joining us this year on the Editorial Committee is Dr. Alessandro Duranti (UCLA) who brings with him a wealth of experience in anthropological linguistics; meanwhile, we convey our mighty thanks to Dr. Jane Hill (Arizona) for committed enthusiasm during her rotation on the Committee. Likewise we thank Drs. Veena Das (Delhi) and Alcida Rita Ramos (Brasilia) for their able assistance these last few years as International Correspondents and welcome Raj Mesthrie (Capetown) and Don Robotham (West Indies) who take their places. We also welcome Lisa Dean to our throng as Production Editor. Lisa takes the place of Noël Thomas who leaves us for graduate study at Harvard University. I especially thank Lisa and Noël for their efforts to help all of us on the Editorial Committee contend with our share of anthropology's more general speedup.

William H. Durham
Editor

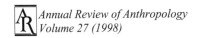
*Annual Review of Anthropology*
*Volume 27 (1998)*

# CONTENTS

SOME RELATED ARTICLES IN OTHER *ANNUAL REVIEWS*

From the *Annual Review of Ecology and Systematics*, Volume 29 (1998)

*Roads and Their Major Ecological Effects*, Richard T. T. Forman and Lauren E. Alexander

From the *Annual Review of Political Science*, Volume 1 (1998)

*The Causes of War and the Conditions of Peace*, Jack S. Levy
*Social Science and Scientific Change: A Note on Thomas S. Kuhn's Contribution*, Nelson W. Polsby

From the *Annual Review of Psychology*, Volume 49 (1998)

*Psychology and the Study of Marital Processes*, John Mordechai Gottman
*Models of the Emergence of Language*, Brian MacWhinney
*Theories Linking Culture and Psychology: Universal and Community-Specific Processes*, Catherine R. Cooper and Jill Denner

From the *Annual Review of Sociology*, Volume 24 (1998)

*Using Computers to Analyze Ethnographic Field Data: Theoretical and Practical Considerations*, Daniel Dohan and Martin Sánchez-Jankowski
*Narrative Analysis—or Why (and How) Sociologists Should be Interested in Narrative*, Roberto Franzosi
*Fundamentalism Et Al: Conservative Protestants in America*, Christian S. Smith and Robert D. Woodberry
*Globalization and Democracy*, Kathleen C. Schwartzman
*Ethnic and Nationalist Violence*, Rogers Brubaker and David D. Laitin

ANNUAL REVIEWS is a nonprofit scientific publisher established to promote the advancement of the sciences. Beginning in 1932 with the *Annual Review of Biochemistry,* the Company has pursued as its principal function the publication of high-quality, reasonably priced *Annual Review* volumes. The volumes are organized by Editors and Editorial Committees who invite qualified authors to contribute critical articles reviewing significant developments within each major discipline. The Editor-in-Chief invites those interested in serving as future Editorial Committee members to communicate directly with him. Annual Reviews is administered by a Board of Directors, whose members serve without compensation.

## 1998 Board of Directors, Annual Reviews

Richard N. Zare, Chairman of Annual Reviews
  *Marguerite Blake Wilbur Professor of Chemistry, Stanford University*
Peter F. Carpenter, *Founder, Mission and Values Institute*
W. Maxwell Cowan, *Vice President and Chief Scientific Officer, Howard Hughes Medical Institute, Bethesda*
Sandra M. Faber, *Professor of Astronomy and Astronomer at Lick Observatory, University of California at Santa Cruz*
Eugene Garfield, *Publisher,* The Scientist
Samuel Gubins, *President and Editor-in-Chief, Annual Reviews*
Daniel E. Koshland, Jr., *Professor of Biochemistry, University of California at Berkeley*
Joshua Lederberg, *University Professor, The Rockefeller University*
Gardner Lindzey, *Director Emeritus, Center for Advanced Study in the Behavioral Sciences, Stanford University*
Sharon R. Long, *Professor of Biological Sciences, Stanford University*
Michael Peskin, *Professor of Theoretical Physics, Stanford Linear Accelerator Ctr.*
Peter H. Raven, *Director, Missouri Botanical Garden*
Harriet A. Zuckerman, *Vice President, The Andrew W. Mellon Foundation*

## Management of Annual Reviews

Samuel Gubins, President and Editor-in-Chief
Patricia D. Kassner, Chief Financial Officer and Business Manager
Richard L. Burke, Technology Applications Manager
John W. Harpster, Marketing Manager
Gwen Larson, Director of Production

ANNUAL REVIEWS OF

| | | |
|---|---|---|
| Anthropology | Fluid Mechanics | Phytopathology |
| Astronomy and Astrophysics | Genetics | Plant Physiology and Plant |
| Biochemistry | Immunology | Molecular Biology |
| Biomedical Engineering | Materials Science | Political Science |
| Biophysics and Biomolecular | Medicine | Psychology |
| Structure | Microbiology | Public Health |
| Cell and Developmental Biology | Neuroscience | Sociology |
| Computer Science | Nuclear and Particle Science | |
| Earth and Planetary Sciences | Nutrition | SPECIAL PUBLICATIONS |
| Ecology and Systematics | Pharmacology and Toxicology | Excitement and Fascination of |
| Energy and the Environment | Physical Chemistry | Science, Vols. 1, 2, 3, |
| Entomology | Physiology | and 4 |
| | | Intelligence and Affectivity, |
| | | by Jean Piaget |

For the convenience of readers, a detachable order form/envelope is bound into the back of this volume.

Harold C. Conklin

*Annu. Rev. Anthropol. 1998. 27:xiii–xxx*
*Copyright © 1998 by Annual Reviews. All rights reserved*

# LANGUAGE, CULTURE, AND ENVIRONMENT: My Early Years

*Harold C. Conklin*

Department of Anthropology, Yale University, New Haven, Connecticut 06520

KEY WORDS: anthropology, ethnography, linguistics, ecology, field work

---

ABSTRACT

In this brief account of my childhood introduction to anthropology and the subsequent ways I began acquiring a more intimate and analytical understanding of languages, cultures, societies, and impinging relevant surroundings, I acknowledge my indebtedness to the people and institutions that have facilitated this enduring process and note how informal influences and associations—some from nonanthropological domains—may be of invaluable assistance to the field-oriented ethnologist. First educated in public schools on eastern Long Island, I went for my undergraduate and graduate work to Berkeley and Yale, respectively. Since then, I have been on the anthropology faculties at Columbia (1954–1962) and Yale (1962 to the present). Since World War II, my principal ethnographic, linguistic, and ecological field sites have been on Mindoro (Hanunóo) and Luzon (Ifugao), in the Philippines.

---

## FIRST STEPS

My enthusiasm for things anthropological was sparked on a hot August afternoon in a dusty arena at the 1933 Chicago World's Fair. I was seven years old and entranced by the performance of a large, well-outfitted group of Plains Indian singers, drummers, and dancers. My father, who had brought me along on a week's trip by train from the East Coast, suggested I go down from our seats in the bleachers for a closer look. Delighted, I did not hesitate. A few minutes later a Dakota woman beckoned, and I joined my first Native American friends and, for the next hour, followed their lead and instructions. Their hospitality,

xiii

0084-6570/98/1015-xiii$08.00

rhythms, voices, songs, trappings, colors—even the smell of buckskin and rawhide—I found extremely appealing.

Of all the events we had attended and exhibitions we had viewed, this one made the most unforgettable impression by far on me. I wanted to find out more about these and other Amerindian groups. During the next five years I became an Indian buff, cutting tepee poles, making percussion instruments, beading moccasins, and reading everything I could find on related topics. My curiosity about and attraction to unknown languages and practices became a passion. I learned that specialists who studied or worked seriously with such peoples were called anthropologists and I decided I wanted to be one. In what follows, I trace briefly and selectively the way this childhood enthusiasm developed into a career.

## LONG ISLAND

Although born in Easton, Pennsylvania, where my father was an instructor at Lafayette College, I grew up in his hometown, Patchogue (and in the nearby hamlets of Bluepoint and East Patchogue), a small incorporated village on Long Island, 65 miles east of New York City. We moved there before I was one so that my father could take over the stationery, sporting goods, and camera store his recently deceased father had started and managed since the 1880s.

Father's roots on the island were deep, especially on the South Fork. Relatives were mostly descendants of English settlers—farmers, millers, fishermen, and whalers out of Sag Harbor—like my great grandfather, who "removed as far west" as East Patchogue after the Civil War. Despite my father's struggle to keep the family store afloat, and despite other Depression-related financial hardships that led to his becoming—among other things—a life insurance underwriter, he always found time to share with those around him (my younger sister, me, our mother, and often one of our grandmothers) his enthusiasm for books, music, photography, canoeing, camping, hiking, scouting, and travel. A pilot during World War I, he worked abroad through 1919 in various capacities, including that of overseas representative of the Community Motion Picture Bureau and the YMCA in France, Great Britain, Norway, and Russia. Such experiences left an indelible mark and resulted in a remarkable and—for our family and community at large—atypical tolerance for, sympathy with, and curiosity about different societies and cultures. In spite of our modest means, our dinner fare was often shared with foreign visitors Father brought home from the International House in the city.

My mother, of Dutch ancestry, was born at the other end of Long Island, in Brooklyn, but spent much of her youth in Patchogue living with cousins. After high school, she joined her mother and brother, who had moved to southern California. There she attended the California State Normal School at Los Angeles, which would later be known as UCLA, and became a marvelous, innovative elementary school teacher. Mother's talents made our home a wonderful learning environment, where even in the very early years a well-lit blackboard, a rapidly filling bookcase, and a portable typewriter were as important as toys, scrapbooks, and sports equipment.

My paternal great-uncle, Frank Overton, was considered by many of my kin an enigmatic eccentric, but my father and I were drawn to him. A physician, author, medical-journal editor, and avid naturalist, he counted among his friends not only medical colleagues, museum-based ornithologists, and herpetologists but also a colorful mix of farmers, bird banders, and baymen. Some of these people I met when I accompanied him on his frequent, and highly rewarding, day trips to ocean beaches, salt marshes, and freshwater lakes to observe and photograph regional avifauna and other forms of wildlife. He shared with me a deep respect for the knowledge possessed by people who lived close to the land.

My interest in Indians and anthropology grew with each year, and my family encouraged me. Our trips into New York City often included visits to museums, and if my father learned that a powwow or similar performance was going to be held within driving distance of Patchogue, he would put us all in the car to attend. By the summer of 1939, just before entering eighth grade, I had gotten to know a number of Indians personally, including William J Cook, a Mohawk counselor at a nearby state health camp. He visited and stayed with us often. That fall, through him and his kin, I was adopted by the Akwesasne (St. Regis) Mohawk into the Turtle clan and was given the name Ionkwatahron, "Our Friend." Two years later, Bill Cook, Ray Fadden, and Ernie Benedict, as well as some others, arranged to have me invited as the only non-Indian to the last pre-war National Youth Association Indian Counselor Training encampment held at Old Forge in the Adirondacks, from which all of us (more than 100 Iroquois from five reservations) went off to be counselors and Indian lore directors at summer camps in New York and neighboring states. I did this for each of the next three summers.

While in high school, I was given a part-time volunteer position (1941–1943) in anthropology at the American Museum of Natural History by the curator and department chairman, Clark Wissler (whom I first met in 1940). That job was fabulous. It included (*a*) checking catalog information on Northwest Coast and Philippine carvings stored in the seventh-floor southwest corner attic; (*b*) learning about the workings of various fire-producing devices; (*c*) being introduced by Wissler to such regular denizens or visitors as Bella Weitzner, Harry Shapiro, Gregory Bateson, and George Valliant (and later, Margaret Mead and Junius Bird); (*d*) a pass to enter the museum before and after hours; and (*e*) a large work space adjacent to the North American ethnology storerooms. I was given access to the library, where I read LH Morgan's

*League of the Ho-dé-no-sau-nee, or Iroquois* (1901[1851]) and other works not available in school or at the public library at home. Wissler would often check on my progress, offer me advice on colleges and universities, and comment on my drawings, sketch maps, and notes based on museum exhibits, stored materials, and North American cultural areas and languages.

During this period I had also begun a long-term special friendship with Jesse J Cornplanter, artist, craftsman, singer, World War I veteran, author, and Seneca intellectual (Cornplanter 1938). At the Cornplanters' home in 1942, within sight of the Tonawanda longhouse that I would not visit again until 1996, Jesse treated me like a nephew. Our wide-ranging conversations—regarding everything from reservation politics and longhouse religion to his family genealogy and the writing and pronunciation of Seneca—and his expert tutelage in the proper use of water drum and horn rattle to accompany his strong singing voice went far into the nights. We continued to discuss such matters by mail for more than a decade (Fenton 1978, p. 178). He often supplemented his long, typed, ethnographically rich responses to my queries with miniature sketches in pencil or ink. In this way, I learned more from him about dozens of topics in Seneca culture than I had from Morgan.

Arthur C Parker, director of the new Rochester Museum of Arts and Sciences, and William N Fenton, then ethnologist at the Bureau of American Ethnology, opened doors and generously answered questions and sent reprints, as did others from such offices as the Bureau of Indian Affairs. *Indians at Work* and *América Indígena* came in regularly, and for a fee of $6.00 (AAA membership in 1943), so did the *American Anthropologist*.

It should be no surprise that I worked Indian themes into as much of my schoolwork as possible. At the beginning of my second year in high school, I was in English class, eagerly awaiting my turn to present my essay to the class, when a new transfer student whom I had not yet met stood up and gave a detailed report on exactly the same topic as mine—the Iroquois confederacy. This explained why so many of the books I had been looking for in the public library had been checked out! I was delighted to meet William T Sanders, another anthropologist-to-be who had as strong an interest in nuclear American archeology as I did in North American ethnology. From that day on, we traded bibliographies and sharpened each other's wits in long discussions of mutual anthropological interests.

In high school, biology, history, mathematics, and languages were my favorite subjects. In track I ran and pole-vaulted, and clubs I joined included math, biology, archery, and Spanish (which was not offered as a course). Outside of school, I pursued scouting and woodcraft and learned how to handle a spinning rope. I studied Latin and French and found the latter more to my liking than the former, partly because of the greater stress on pronunciation and conversation. In class, I also learned the relevant parts of the International Phonetic Alphabet at the same time that I was trying to sort out the multiple orthographies missionaries and anthropologists had used to record Iroquoian languages. I wrote a term paper in English on Indian (mostly Algonquian) contributions to the American language. As far as real comprehension and fluency were concerned, however, I was still living in a largely monolingual universe. That would change.

# WEST COAST

After correspondence with ten or so colleges and universities beginning as early as my freshman year in high school, I decided—for a number of reasons, not the least of which was the advice Wissler and others had given me and the warm letters I had received from Robert H Lowie in reply to my questions about preparation for a career in anthropology and his department's offerings—to apply only to Berkeley. Such plans were problematic during the war, but my goal was to graduate from high school at 17 the next spring and to complete one year of college before ending up in the army. It worked.

On the three-week journey by train to Berkeley, in the fall of 1943, my first trip west of the Mississippi, I met and discussed my plans with anthropologists I had corresponded with or had known of from having read some of their work. These included Frank Speck, in his marvelous fourth-floor walk-up office at the Department of Anthropology at the University of Pennsylvania, and others in Washington DC, Chicago, and Los Angeles. I also visited museums, government offices, and Indian rights organizations and made new Indian friends along the way.

In my freshman year at Berkeley, aside from history, German, English, and some required subjects, I took two courses with Carl O Sauer in geography and took or audited six courses in anthropology with Ronald Olson, Robert H Lowie, Alfred L Kroeber, and Edward W Gifford (the entire department then). I also took a seminar in Oriental languages. Olson's introductory anthropology sequence had an enrollment of 725, but at tea in the student center after each lecture, anyone could discuss the day's presentation or other issues with him, and five or six of us usually did. In addition, although I had an assigned freshman advisor from the French department, Lowie discussed my academic program with me and followed my progress closely. Gifford, at the Anthropology Museum, then housed in a former chemistry building and "guarded" by a wonderful Papago elder, Juan Dolores, helped plan a field trip I made during the Christmas break to several Pomo communities in the Clear Lake area 100 miles north of the Bay Area. Attending an all-night Bole Maru ceremony in honor of a returned veteran, which was held in a Southeastern Pomo roundhouse, was an unexpectedly vivid introduction to California Indian ethnography. Gifford encouraged me to write up my notes, and Kroeber read and commented in a most constructive and supportive fashion on that report (Meighan & Riddell 1972, pp. 3, 22, 36–37, 62, 68, 131) and on one of my English papers on Northeastern Indian art. On the environmental side, Sauer's courses were eye-openers. Conversations with him, which continued over the years, were always rewarding, especially on topics like agricultural regimes, vegetatively reproduced crops, technology, and the Tropics (Sauer 1952).

As helpful as these developments were for me, the most unanticipated benefit from this period was my accidental introduction to Austronesian languages and linguistics. It happened this way. Almost all dormitories and dining facilities had been taken over by the military for the duration. As a result, boarding places for others were few, overcrowded, and—for my appetite—inadequate. So, when one of my coworkers at the Berkeley Cyclotron, where I had a part-time defense job, told me of an opening for a hasher at the Gamma Phi Beta sorority house, I took it. Only a week earlier an extremely capable and likable young cook from Gresik, East Java, had jumped the Dutch ship he was working on in San Francisco and landed a job as live-in cook's assistant at the sorority house. His four languages—Javanese, Madurese, Dutch, and what he told us at first was "Maleis"—did not include ours. Eventually, of course, Moehammad Oesman Pa' Ma'moer would learn English, but in the meantime, he convinced us that our learning a bit of Malay might be the quickest route to a mutually understood lingo. It also enabled us to exchange our—even in those days—politically incorrect opinions of the sorority members without their understanding us. Those daily three to four hours together flew by. Not only did I get three square meals a day, I also had the opportunity to learn Malay in a relaxing, refreshing environment. Progress was fun and fast. By the end of the first semester I was able to converse with Ozzie on many topics, and he had begun teaching two of us to read and write as he did, in *gundul*, a form of Arabic script modified for Malay.

The second semester, through the kindness of Peter Boodberg, a professor in the Oriental languages department and a former Kroeber student, I enrolled in his exploratory seminar on Indonesian and Malay. There were five others in the class, mostly graduate students. Our main task was to transcribe and translate disk recordings of programs recently broadcast from Australia and the United States for Indonesians in the then-Japanese-occupied archipelago. Although Boodberg was not a Malay specialist, his guidance in Malay grammatical analysis and with Malay script was my first chance to see a linguist at work.

Between the end of that semester and my induction into the army in July 1944, one of the other hashers and I took Ozzie on a Sierra pack trip above Yosemite Valley. For a week the three of us spoke only Malay. I had no idea when we parted that, four years later, before he saw them himself, I would see Ozzie's family in Java.

# SOUTHWEST PACIFIC

My participation in World War II led to my living in the Philippine Islands for most of the next four years. Beginning the summer of 1944, for more than two years I was on active duty in the army. After basic training at Fort Bliss, Texas, in anti-aircraft artillery, and after brief periods in New Guinea and Leyte, I served as a replacement ground artilleryman and foot soldier with the 158th Regimental Combat Team on Luzon, north of Subic in Zambales, and in the Bicol peninsula of southern Luzon, from Legaspi to Iriga. Following the Bicol Operation, we returned to Zambales and began preparing for landings in Japan. That was soon stopped by the end of the war. We then moved our encampments: to Alabang, to Los Baños, to quarters on the war-torn Escolta in downtown Manila, and finally to tents and quonset huts behind Rizal Stadium, also in Manila. I was scheduled to be shipped back to the States in August 1946, soon after the Commonwealth became a Republic, but I arranged instead to be discharged in the Philippines in order to carry out at least one stint of serious, uninterrupted field work before returning to California. Lowie, Kroeber, and Gifford supported the plan, though the proposed additional six months turned into a year and a half.

In each of the rural and urban locations in which we had been stationed, I had almost daily contact with Filipinos of many backgrounds. They all spoke Philippine languages distantly related to Malay, and they manifested a resilience, vigor, and rich cultural diversity that I found most attractive. Even during infantry patrols in the Iriga hills, for example, our Negrito guides demonstrated amazing engineering and survival skills, with lianas and boulders and only the simplest of tools but with a wealth of jungle know-how. It irked me that I could not adequately converse with them.

By constantly questioning, watching, listening, note-taking, and practicing, I learned the language of Manila and surrounding provinces well enough to be persuaded, in late 1945 while bivouacked in Los Baños, to offer an informal class on Tagalog to fellow GIs. A few months later, while teaching a course in anthropology at the Philippine Institute for the Armed Forces (PIFTAF; located in buildings now forming part of De La Salle University in Manila), I was asked to take the place of the Filipina instructor of a regularly scheduled Tagalog course who had left suddenly.

On my first visit to the city, I sought out the Sampaloc home of Guillermo E Tolentino, sculptor, poet, and professor of fine arts at the University of the Philippines (UP) (Tolentino 1937, Paras-Perez & Capistrano 1976). From the moment we met, we conversed only in Tagalog. He and his wife were exceedingly hospitable. They made me an adopted member of their growing family (five, later seven, children) and insisted that I stay with them whenever I could. Not only then but during many trips to the Philippines in the following years, my family and I could drop in on Amang and Inang at any time. Indeed we are family.

Within a few days I also located H Otley Beyer, Iowa-born geologist-teacher-anthropologist-professor, who had lived and traveled widely in the archipelago since 1905 (Manuel 1978, Conklin 1967) and had founded the Department of Anthropology at UP in 1916. He was at his living quarters and library in the UP Museum and Institute of Archeology and Ethnology, housed on the second floor of the Watson Building near Malacañang, in Manila. Unlike the Bureau of Science and Beyer's two houses south of the Pasig River, the Watson Building, on the north side, had miraculously escaped damage during the war. Tadao Kano—Japanese cultural attaché, zoologist, and prehistorian-ethnographer (Kano & Segawa 1956 [1945])—had arranged for a major portion of Beyer's library and other collections to be well installed there before his internment in Santo Tomás. An endless office-kitchen-Chinese-restaurant-Jai-Alai-roundtable Philippine tutorial and anthropological seminar began immediately and continued for years whenever I was in Manila. At the Watson Building, I met Natividad Noriega, Beyer's secretary, and William Gambuk Beyer, his son. They provided special and timely research assistance in Manila and Ifugao, respectively. Doc invited me to use the Institute as my research headquarters, and for the two years during this period that I was based in Manila, his and the Tolentinos's places served as ideal office-lab and home.

My other mentors and close friends in Manila during this time came to include local scholars: Gabriel Bernardo, UP librarian with strong interests in Tagalog and Philippine paleography (1953); E Arsenio Manuel, language specialist (1971), bibliophile, folklorist, ethnologist, and assistant to Beyer; Cecilio Lopez, student of Otto Scheerer and Otto Dempwolff and UP professor of Oriental languages who introduced me to comparative Philippine grammar (cf. Lopez 1940); Jose V Panganiban, Tagalog lexicographer; Lope K Santos, Tagalista, poet; and authors such as NVM Gonzalez and Hernando J Abaya.

Robert B Fox, an officer in the US Navy who already had an MA in Anthropology from the University of Texas, was the only other serviceman I knew at the time who planned to stay on to do field work (Fox 1952, 1982; Conklin 1986). We met, of course, at Beyer's place and became buddies. He headed and taught anthropology and sociology at PIFTAF for a while, and together we took students on short field trips to fishing, farming, and foraging communities in nearby provinces, mostly within sight of Laguna de Bay or Manila Bay. On one occasion, Fox and I visited Ilongot settlements north of Baler on the Tayabas side of the Sierra Madre (and were subsequently rebuffed by the Bureau of Non-Christian Tribes when we volunteered to teach school among those people if they would give us minimum subsistence support; "too dangerous"). On another leave I visited Benguet, Bontoc, and Ifugao, and made somewhat shorter trips to Bataan and northern Mindoro.

In Manila, I also recorded musical and linguistic material in a preliminary but systematic fashion from speakers of 14 Philippine languages. Many of these people traveled long distances to the city to expedite claims for war damages. Occasionally, I was able to augment my handwritten notes by recordings made in the United States Information Service (USIS) sound studios. The resulting disks are now at the Library of Congress. Even portable wire recorders were not yet available in Manila.

In 1947 I surveyed the linguistic and cultural landscape on Mindoro and Palawan, two islands where the continued use of pre-Hispanic Indic writing systems had been reported as still flourishing (Gardner & Maliwanag 1939–1940). My reception in southern Mindoro by the Hanunóo was so warm and their literacy so pervasive despite the lack of any formal instruction that I decided to spend the most time with them and with the Tagbanuwa of central Palawan.

During three and a half months of one of the most concentrated and rewarding ethnographic experiences I have ever had, Lūyun, his wife Apih, and her father and brother, Yadnis and Dag'ud, together with many of their kinsmen and neighbors in Tarubung, Yāgaw, gave me a crash course on Hanunóo language, culture, and local ecological relations. I was unprepared for the volume of information they provided me, especially about the local flora. No money changed hands, but I did have a stock of highly valued red and white seed beads and a large quantity of Australian post-war relief clothing and medicines to distribute for the governor of the province, who felt that through me some of the goods might actually reach the interior. It was inconceivable to most people in the region that I would be giving things away, so for each item distributed, some local woven, carved, or useful craft product would be left for me. When I ran out of space and containers, I suggested that they bring in plant leaves and cuttings for identification later in Manila. I was overwhelmed but continued to accept whatever was offered.

On a trip to Manila with Lūyun to make some disk recordings, I found that the accumulated artifacts made a fine collection for the ethnological division of the Philippine National Museum, but I was told that the bags of tagged plant parts were a total disaster. At Beyer's table that night, however, we were joined by a visitor from Ann Arbor, MI. HH Bartlett—Filipinist, Indonesianist, and distinguished tropical plant scientist—was in town to give a talk at UP. He was captivated by Lūyun and his bamboo inscriptions. Being very interested in Southeast Asian vernaculars and ethnobotany (Bartlett 1929, 1939, 1940), he proceeded, completely unexpectedly, to solve my botanical problems. He spent the next morning teaching me how to make proper herbarium vouchers by uprooting exemplars of all the flowering weeds that we found growing around the Walled City near his accommodations at the Manila Hotel. We arranged duplicates of each specimen in folded newspapers and used the mattress of his bed for a press. Within the next two days he arranged for one of his pre-war Philippine plant collectors, Liborio Ebalo from Zambales, to be released from a government job to accompany me for the next three months among the Tagbanuwa. As if this were not enough, he gave me a copy of ED Merrill's *Plant Life of the Pacific World* (1945) and my first research grant, of $300, from the University of Michigan Herbarium funds, to make an annotated ethnobotanical collection from Palawan. With that incentive, my next months in Palawan and my introduction to Malesian botany, and to Sulu Sea ecology in particular, sped by.

After a visit to the Batak in northern Palawan and several weeks in Mindoro, I spent the last part of 1947 and early 1948 writing up preliminary field reports and transferring my Mindoro and Palawan collections to the Philippine National Museum and the Philippine National Herbarium. Both of these establishments were then directed by the botanist Eduardo Quisumbing (1951), an ebullient, dynamic, and effective scientific advocate of original field research in many, fields who would prove to be of great help to me later on in my ethnographic and ecological studies among the Hanunóo.

My trip home and back to Berkeley began with an exciting first lap aboard a tramp steamer that took me from Manila and Butuan to Shanghai, several China-coast ports, and Malaya, with several-day to week-long stopovers at each port of call. I had time to roam at will while shipments were being unloaded and loaded. In Singapore, I spent three or four days at the Raffles Museum, where anthropologists met regularly, and took a brief trip with Dennis Collings to a Riau Island fishing community before boarding a smaller Dutch ship for Batavia (Jakarta).

During the following six weeks, on Java, Bali, and Celebes (Sulawesi), I discussed common regional and anthropological interests and exchanged news and publications with Dutch and Indonesian friends in museums, botanical gardens, and other government offices and mountain rest houses. More importantly, I got to meet and visit with farmers, traders, weavers, and school teachers while hiking through the more rural areas of these islands. Robert van Heekering in Makassar (Udung Pandang) was most helpful in interpreting physical and cultural landscapes, and P Voorhoeve in Jakarta was a gold mine of information on Indonesian languages, linguistics, writing systems, and Dutch scholarly bibliography—as he continued to be long afterward.

The third leg of the journey, from Jakarta to Southampton, England, was enlivened by three Mill Hill fathers from Jesselton (Kota Kinabalu), who sat at the same table as I. Each knew a different North Bornean language and was eager to compare Bornean and Philippine linguistic structures. While in Europe, I talked with scholars in England, Wales, France, Holland, and Switzerland whose regional and topical interests were related to mine. For example, Ifor B Powell, reader in history at the University of Wales in Cardiff and, as I was to learn later on, probably the most well-informed Filipinist in the United Kingdom, insisted on my coming out to stay with him and his wife as soon as I called from London. We talked continuously for a week about early Philippine history, more recent social history, anthropology, Doc Beyer, and our respective field experiences: his lasted three years, in the mid-1920s, when he traveled, often by foot, across Mindanao and Panay and all over Luzon while studying local government at various levels. He encouraged me to get in touch with the anthropologists at the London School of Economics (LSE) because of their interest in Southeast Asia. Several days later I phoned the LSE anthropology department, and Raymond Firth urged me to come over immediately. He was most cordial, and after we had exchanged news about Manila, Berkeley, Chicago, and his own and others' recent or proposed field work in Malaya and Borneo, he introduced me to Edmund Leach, in an adjacent office, for what would be the first of many discussions. Later we all attended and participated in Firth's weekly seminar, where I met graduate students and additional faculty from LSE and other London universities. Firth's treating me—a visiting college undergraduate who had been away from college for four years—just like he did everyone else in the room was a most generous gesture.

I made very helpful research contacts with anthropologists and area specialists at the British Museum and in Cambridge, Oxford, Leiden, Amsterdam, Paris, and Basel and Fribourg, Switzerland. At each place, I found Philippine and other Southeast Asian materials of special interest, exchanged news and messages, took notes and photographs, and established collegial friendships.

## BERKELEY AND YALE

From 1948 to 1950, I finished my undergraduate work at Berkeley. These were Lowie's last teaching years. Kroeber had retired, but we saw each other often when he was in Berkeley, at his home or office, and discussed many topics: writing systems, languages, technology, Philippine ethnography and ethnographers (John Garvan, Roy F Barton, and Beyer).

I took or audited courses with Lowie, Gifford (who offered me a work space next to Clement W Meighan and a part-time job in the Museum), John Howland Rowe, Ann Gayton, Theodore McCown, Robert F Heizer, and David Mandelbaum, as well as with visiting faculty members Daryll Forde, Melville Herskovits, Loren C Eiseley, and Katharine Luomala. On several occasions during these two years I met and conferred with a number of senior anthropologists who had previously carried out field work in the Philippines. These included David Prescott Barrows, Fay-Cooper Cole, Felix M Keesing, and Fred Eggan. Along with other Southeast Asianists Raymond Kennedy and Robert Heine-Geldern, Eggan had gotten in touch with me by phone soon after I arrived in New York for news of Philippine anthropology. Pre-jet travel at midcentury affected path-crossing in many ways. In Berkeley, field workers in the Pacific arriving and departing from Oakland in sea planes or from San Francisco by ship often stopped over in Berkeley or were met at the airport or dock. By 1949, there was, it seemed, a constant flow of such visitors. Fellow anthropology students included Eugene Hammel, Catherine McClellan, and Donald W Lathrap.

Professor Boodberg proudly introduced me to Mary R Haas as a significant addition to a new department of linguistics in the making, and I took and audited courses with her as well as with Murray B Emeneau, Denzel Carr (who also taught me Dutch, in an Oriental languages department course), and Yuen Ren Chao. Fellow students included Samuel Martin, RB Jones, Jesse Sawyer, William Bright, and William Samarin.

Of my teachers in anthropology and linguistics at this time, Kroeber, Haas, Rowe, Lowie, Emeneau, and Gifford probably influenced me most. Others who gave important advice and support included Sauer and the entomologist and naturalist Edward Ross, of the California Academy of Sciences. Ross had frequently visited westernmost Hanunóo settlements during the war when stationed in San Jose in southwestern Mindoro.

By the time I left for graduate school at Yale in the fall of 1950, I had cataloged the bamboo manuscripts I had brought back from Mindoro and Palawan and had written several articles (Conklin 1949a,b) and typed up a 600-page Hanunóo-English dictionary that began as a semantically arranged glossary to go with my Hanunóo field notes. Shortly thereafter, Kroeber and Haas suggested that I submit the manuscript to the recently inaugurated *University of California Publications in Linguistics,* which in 1951 I did (Conklin 1953a).

The following two years at Yale I studied with Floyd G Lounsbury (who became my close mentor and dissertation advisor), Bernard Bloch, Isidore Dyen (with whom in Berkeley I had already had some detailed discussions about Tagalog), Karl J Pelzer, Wendell C Bennett, Cornelius Osgood, George Peter Murdock, Ralph Linton, Irving Rouse, Clellan S Ford, Sidney Mintz, John Embree, and Paul Fejos. (Raymond Kennedy would have been in this group had he not been killed in Java the spring before I arrived; Embree died at the end of that year, and Bennett and Linton died two years later.) Frequently on campus, at monthly Yale Linguistic Club meetings and for other events, were Joseph H Greenberg, Henry A Gleason, and Charles F Hockett. Visitors included JG Held, SF Nadel, Meyer Fortes, and Peter Buck (Te Rangi Hiroa). In addition, Paul B Sears (botany, ecology, and conservation) and ED Merrill [dean of Philippine and Pacific botanists (1922–1926, 1946)] were important mentors on campus and at the Harvard Arnold Arboretum, respectively. On the basis of what he had seen of our herbarium sheets from Palawan, Merrill transferred a substantial subvention to me from his Guggenheim funds to make a similar collection in the Hanunóo area. Later he gave me a portion of his personal annotated Philippine botanical library.

Equally if not more important were fellow graduate students and visiting scholars in anthropology, linguistics, and other departments centered around the Hall of Graduate Studies (HGS) and at nearby eateries. These people included, most significantly for me, William C Sturtevant and Charles O Frake. The three of us for decades have shared deep interests in language, culture, environment, classification, history, and cognition (Sturtevant 1964, 1966, 1969; Frake 1962a,b, 1994). Sturtevant and I proctored Linton's introductory course together for a semester or two. We also managed to take an 11-day field trip at the beginning of my fourth semester—accepting an invitation from Albert and Geneva Jones, Allegany Seneca friends Fenton had introduced to me in 1948 and to both of us at a Red House Iroquoian conference in 1951—to attend their annual Midwinter longhouse ceremonies. Our absence from classes was not looked on favorably by the faculty, except for Lounsbury, but we saw to it that it resulted in a joint paper accepted for publication before I left for the field in the Philippines the following summer (Conklin & Sturtevant 1953). Frake and I have continued our HGS discussions and mutual enthusiasms in the Philippines and in many other contexts over the decades as well.

Other anthropology graduate students whom I associated with frequently at HGS or elsewhere on campus during the five semesters I was taking courses included William H Davenport, Jacob Fried, Paul W Friedrich, Thomas R Gladwin, Peter R Goethals, Rufus S Hendon, Joanna Kirkpatrick, Ruth H Landman, Frank LeBar, William P Mangin, Thomas W Maretzki, Leopold J Pospisil, Abraham Rosman, Richard P Schaedel, Douglas W Schwartz, Annemarie Anrod Shimony, Donald C Simmons, Councill S Taylor, and Stephen Williams. Among other close friends at that time were visiting fellows, young faculty members, postdocs, or graduate students in other departments: Stephan F Borhegyi, Johannes Wilbert, Cecilio Lopez, Samuel Martin, Rulon Wells, David L Olmsted, Donald C Robertson, Alexander M Schenker, Niels Ege, and Laurence L Thompson.

For my dissertation field work with the Hanunóo, I returned to Yágaw from 1952 to early 1954 (Conklin 1954a, 1957, 1960). Lúyun had died, but I was able to settle in nearby Parína with his younger brother, Badu' (ca 1920–1994), who also proved to be an exceptional host, a creative artist, and an untiring tutor. I am greatly indebted to him and his immediate family and kin, including especially Balik, Nū'an, Ayakan, Alis, Hagnay, Lig'um, Sigmay, Uming, Maling, and Bining. During this period, Wilhelm G Solheim II urged me to look at Buhíd technology (Conklin 1953b); ethnomusicologist Jose Maceda visited my mountainside base and provided valuable expertise on the recordings I was making with a first generation Magnemite tape recorder that Moe Asch of Folkways Records and Service Corporation in New York had lent me (Conklin 1955b, Conklin & Maceda 1971); and I completed a paper on betel chewing, written in Yágaw and delivered at the Eighth Pacific Science Congress in Manila in 1953 (Conklin 1958). In early 1954 I returned to Yale for my last semester and accepted Columbia's offer of a regular teaching position with an annual salary of $3600. I turned in my Yale dissertation the day before I met my first class at Columbia in New York.

# FROM MINDORO TO IFUGAO

My main Hanunóo field work on Mindoro (four trips, from 1947 to 1958) and post-fieldwork analysis in New York concluded in 1961, close to the end of my eight years at Columbia. Almost immediately thereafter, I began my first main stretch of Ifugao field work in northern Luzon (six trips, from 1961 to 1973) and subsequent research, mostly in New Haven, which extended to 1980.

This shift in focus from Mindoro to Ifugao around 1961 resulted from a survey I made in 1958 to locate another, distinct Philippine field site that would provide significant environmental, linguistic, and other cultural contrasts with the Hanunóo area. As great as those differences were (e.g. a new and phonetically and morphologically much more challenging language, a ten-fold increase in population density, and a move from an economy based entirely on shifting cultivation to an agrarian landscape dominated by permanent-field, irrigated terracing), one thing was similar: the availability of exceptional informants among our neighbors, without whom my Ifugao research could not have been accomplished. Special recognition must go to Puggūwon Lupāih, gifted field cartographer and superb general assistant, his wife, Malīngay, and daughters, Inhaybung and Nolma; and to Buwāya Tindūngan, Būgan Doyog, Libdan Dātong, Malīngay and Ottēngan Bihtul, and Nanguddi Buwāya and his daughter, Immayya.

Simultaneously, at the American Geographical Society in New York City, OM Miller and, especially, Miklos Pinther provided the technical cartographic genius that was crucial to the production of the *Ethnographic Atlas of Ifugao* (Conklin 1980b; cf Conklin & Pinther 1976).

During my years at Columbia (1954–1962), continuing and expanding my research interests in cognition, kinship, language use, and folk classification (Conklin 1955a, 1959a, 1962a,b; 1964, pp. 39–41; 1980a, 1991), I got to know and benefitted greatly from informal discussions and exchanges with Ward H Goodenough (1957), Anthony FC Wallace, Claude Lévi-Strauss (1962), John Lotz, Roman Jakobson, and George A Miller, as well as with Einar Haugen (1957), Robert Austerlitz, Uriel Weinreich, Aert Kuipers, Noam Chomsky, Dell V Hymes, Sydney Lamb, and others. On related matters but with less direct concern with linguistics or ethnography, Paul F Lazersfeld (Sociology), Arthur C Danto (Philosophy), and Meyer Shapiro (History of Art) offered valued insights.

With respect to my interests in more concrete aspects of ethnobiological classification, ecology and tropical agricultural systems (Conklin 1954b, 1959b, 1963), I learned much from conversations and discussions with IH Burkill, author of the great "dictionary" (1935; cf 1960) of Malesian economic resources; George Gaylord Simpson on animal taxonomy (1961); Ernst Mayr on zoological systematics (1953); George HM Lawrence on plant taxonomy (1951); Edgar Anderson on tropical ethnobotany (1952); PW Richards, author of the classic work on tropical rain-forest ecology (1952, 1996); and the younger-generation scholars Jacques Barrau and Douglas E Yen, both Oceanic ethnobotanists (Yen spent two mutually very helpful stints with us in Ifugao working on sweet potato, taro, and medicinal plants). With Hugh Popenoe, soil scientist and tropical agriculturist, we exchanged useful field-site visits on Mindoro and in Guatemala among the Polochic K'ekchi.

During this period, some of my main discussions on ecologically related topics in anthropology were with Karl G Izikowitz from Göteborg, Fredrik Barth from Bergen, Derek Freeman in Bangkok and Rumah Nyala (Sarawak), Georges Condominas in Paris, William Henry Scott (1958, 1974; Conklin 1994) from Sagada in the Philippines, and Eric Wolf and Marshall Sahlins, who were often at Columbia in the mid-1950s.

In bringing this review to a close, and in terms similar to those I have expressed elsewhere (Conklin 1988), I would like to add several general observations that derive directly from the kinds of field-work experience and anthropological inquiry to which I have been referring: (*a*) Most contrastive forms of human behavior, including language use, reflect cultural variation rather than profound psychological differences in cognitive capacities. (*b*) To avoid the premature homogenization of knowledge that may mask this variation, the prodigious problems of translation and observation must be seriously addressed and the analysis of internal cultural structures advanced. (*c*) Many peoples possess remarkable amounts of information about their physical as well as social surroundings. To be able to interpret the ethnoecological relationships linking these phenomena may often require considerable knowledge of material and environmental substance. (*d*) In the analysis of specific systems of shared understandings it is essential to distinguish between sensory reception and cultural perception. Acknowledging these views, and with the guidance of talented informants, it is indeed difficult to escape the beauty of the internal logic of many complex cultural systems and the universality of human creativity.

In the field I have been inspired repeatedly by the intelligence, patience, and enduring friendship of many neighbors and friends, from small children to toothless elders. They have all served not just as respondents but as close coinvestigators of other cultural worlds. Often accompanied by zest, humor, and wit, their conduct, words, and shared understandings of ecological and cultural relations have made ethnographic field work a challenging and intellectually exciting enterprise.

## SPECIAL ACKNOWLEDGMENTS

It goes without saying that during more than four decades of teaching and research at Columbia and Yale (1954–1962, 1962–present), I have also learned much from many exceptional colleagues and students (both graduate and undergraduate) in anthropology, and from other special friends. I wish to thank them all and to acknowledge in particular a few of those who, although not named previously, have provided me extraordinary research assistance or information directly related to my continuing field-work efforts: Leonard E Newell, Alan Harwood, Michiko Takaki, Maria Angelina Esquivel, Allen R Maxwell, Antonio S Buangan, Hamako A McIlroy, Patricia O Afable, Yoshiko Yamamoto, Brian Fegan, Elizabeth O Kyburg, Leticia Vicente, Myrdene Anderson, Rosemary Gianno, Joel Kuipers, and Paul M Taylor.

My deepest appreciation goes to my wife, Jean Mieko Conklin, whose insight and unfailing support have no parallel. We have made three year-long field trips together, two of them with our sons, Bruce Robert and Mark William, who, in turn, have also provided invaluable perspectives.

---

Visit the *Annual Reviews home page* at
http://www.AnnualReviews.org.

---

## Literature Cited

Anderson E. 1952. *Plants, Man and Life.* Boston: Little, Brown. 245 pp.

Bartlett HH. 1929. Color nomenclature in Batak and Malay. *Pap. Mich. Acad. Sci. Arts Lett.* 10:1–52

Bartlett HH. 1939. The geographic distribution, migration, and dialectical mutation of certain plant names in the Philippines and Netherlands India, with special reference to the materia medica of a Mangyan [Iráya] Mediquillo. *Proc. Pac. Sci. Congr. 6th Berkeley*, 4:85–109

Bartlett HH. 1940. The concept of genus: I. History of the generic concept in botany. *Bull. Torrey Bot. Club* 67(5):349–62

Bernardo GA. 1953. *A Bibliography of the Old Philippine Syllabaries.* Quezon City: Univ. Philipp. Libr.

Burkill IH. 1935. *A Dictionary of the Economic Products of the Malay Peninsula*, 2 Vols. London: Crown Agents for the Colonies. 2402 pp.

Burkill IH. 1960. The organography and evolution of *Dioscoreaceae*, the family of yams. *J. Linn. Soc. London Bot.* 56: 319–412

Conklin HC. 1949a. Preliminary report of field work on the islands of Mindoro and Palawan, Philippines. *Am. Anthropol.* 51(2):268–73

Conklin HC. 1949b. Bamboo literacy on Mindoro. *Pac. Discov.* 2(4):4–11

Conklin HC. 1953a. Hanunóo-English vocabulary. *Univ. Calif. Publ. Linguist.* 9: 1–290

Conklin HC. 1953b. Buhíd pottery. *Univ. Manila J. East Asiat. Stud.* 3(1):1–12

Conklin HC. 1954a. *The relation of Hanunóo culture to the plant world.* PhD thesis. Yale Univ., New Haven, CT. 471 pp. (Univ. Microfilms International [No. 67-4119])

Conklin HC. 1954b. An ethnoecological approach to shifting agriculture. *Trans. NY Acad. Sci.* 17(2):133–42

Conklin HC. 1955a. Hanunóo color categories. *Southwest. J. Anthropol.* 11(4):339–44

Conklin HC. 1955b. *Hanunóo music from the Philippines. Ethn. Folkways Libr. Album P466* [later: FE4466; 04466]. New York: Folkways Rec. Serv. Corp.

Conklin HC. 1957. *Hanunóo agriculture, a report on an integral system of shifting cultivation in the Philippines. FAO For. Dev. Pap. No. 12.* Rome: Food Agric. Org. UN. 209 pp.

Conklin HC. 1958. *Betel Chewing Among the Hanunóo.* Quezon City: Natl. Res. Counc. Philipp. 41 pp.

Conklin HC. 1959a. Linguistic play in its cultural context. *Language* 35(4):631–36

Conklin HC. 1959b. Ecological interpretations and plant domestication. *Am. Antiq.* 25(2):260–62

Conklin HC. 1960. Maling, a Hanunóo girl from the Philippines; A day in Parina. In *In the Company of Man: Twenty Portraits by Anthropologists,* ed. JE Casagrande, pp. 101–25. New York: Harper

Conklin HC. 1962a. Ethnobotanical problems in the comparative study of folk taxonomy. *Proc. Pac. Sci. Congr. 9th, 1957,* 4:299–301

Conklin HC. 1962b. Lexicographical treatment of folk taxonomies. *Int. J. Am. Linguist.* 28(2):119–41

Conklin HC. 1963. *El estudio del cultivo de roza—The Study of Shifting Cultivation.* Washington, DC: Union Panam. 185 pp.

Conklin HC. 1964. Ethnogenealogical method. In *Explorations in Cultural Anthropology: Essays in Honor of George Peter Murdock,* ed. WH Goodenough, pp. 25–55. New York: McGraw-Hill

Conklin HC. 1967. Ifugao ethnobotany 1905–1965: the 1911 Beyer-Merrill report in perspective. *Econ. Bot.* 21(3):243–71

Conklin HC. 1980a. *Folk Classification: A Topically Arranged Bibliography of Contemporary and Background References Through 1971.* Revised edition, with index. New Haven, CT: Yale Univ. Dep. Anthropol. 521 pp.

Conklin HC. 1980b. *Ethnographic Atlas of Ifugao: A Study of Environment, Culture, and Society in Northern Luzon.* With the special assistance of Puggūwon Lupāih and Miklos Pinther. New Haven, CT: Yale Univ. Press. 116 pp.

Conklin HC. 1986. A bibliography of the works of Robert B. Fox. *Pilipinas: J. Philipp. Stud.* 7:75–85

Conklin HC. 1988. Des orientements, des vents, des riz... Pour une étude lexicologique des savoirs traditionnels. *J. Agric. Tradit. Bot. Appl.* 33:3–10

Conklin HC. 1991. Doctrina Christiana, en lengua española y tagala. Manila 1593. Collection 1302. In *Vision of a Collector: The Lessing J. Rosenwald Collection in the Library of Congress/Rare Book and Special Collections Division,* ed. K Mang, P VanWingen, pp. 36–40, 119. Washington, DC: Libr. Congr.

Conklin HC. 1994. A biobibliography of William Henry Scott. *Pilipinas J. Philipp. Stud.* 22:62–91

Conklin HC, Maceda J. 1971. Hanunóo music from the Philippines. In *Readings in Ethnomusicology,* ed. DP McAllester, pp. 186–214. New York/London: Johnson Repr. Corp.

Conklin HC, Pinther M. 1976. Pseudoscopic illusion. *Science* 194:374

Conklin HC, Sturtevant WC. 1953. Seneca Indian singing tools at Coldspring Longhouse: musical instruments of the modern Iroquois. *Proc. Am. Philos. Soc.* 97(3):262–90

Cornplanter JJ. 1938. *Legends of the Longhouse.* Philadelphia, PA: Lippincott. 217 pp.

Fenton WN. 1978. "Aboriginally yours" Jesse J. Cornplanter, Ha-yonh-wonh-ish, the Snipe, Seneca 1889–1957. In *American Indian Intellectuals,* ed. M Liberty, pp. 176–95. St. Paul, MN: West

Fox RB. 1952. The Pinatubo Negritos: their useful plants and material culture. *Philipp. J. Sci.* 81(3–4):173–414

Fox RB. 1982. *Religion and Society Among the Tagbanuwa of Palawan Island, Philippines.* Natl. Mus. Monogr. No. 9, Manila. 262 pp.

Frake CO. 1962a. The ethnography of cognitive systems; Comment by HC Conklin. In *Anthropology and Human Behavior,* ed. T Gladwin, WC Sturtevant, pp. 72–93. Washington, DC: Anthropol. Soc. Wash.

Frake CO. 1962b. Cultural ecology and ethnography. *Am. Anthropol.* 64(1):54–59

Frake CO. 1994. Dials: a study in the physical representation of cognitive systems. In *The Ancient Mind: Elements of Cognitive Archaeology,* ed. C Renfrew, EBW Zubrow, pp. 119–32. Cambridge, UK: Cambridge Univ. Press

Gardner F, Maliwanag I. 1939–1940. *Indic Writings of the Mindoro-Palawan axis,* Vols. 1, 2. San Antonio, TX: Witte Mem. Mus. 88 pp. 71 pp.

Goodenough WH. 1957. Cultural anthropology and linguistics. *Georgetown Univ. Monogr. Ser. Lang. Linguist.* 9:167–73

Haugen E. 1957. The semantics of Icelandic orientation. *Word* 13(3):447–59

Kano T, Segawa K. (1945) 1956. *An Illus-*

trated Ethnography of Formosan Aborigines, Vol. 1. The Yami. Tokyo: Maruzen

Lawrence GHM. 1951. Taxonomy of Vascular Plants. New York: Macmillan. 823 pp.

Lévi-Strauss C. 1962. La Pensée Sauvage. Paris: Plon. 395 pp.

Lopez C. 1940. A Manual of the Philippine National Language. Manila: Bur. Print. 327 pp. 3rd ed.

Manuel EA. 1971. A lexicographic study of Tayabas Tagalog. Diliman Rev. 19(1–4): 1–420

Manuel EA. 1978. H. Otley Beyer, 1883–1966, anthropologist. In Scientists in the Philippines, Vol. II. Manila: Natl. Sci. Dev. Board

Mayr E, Linsley EG, Usinger RL. 1953. Methods and Principles of Systematic Zoology. New York: McGraw-Hill. 328 pp.

Meighan CW, Riddell FA. 1972. The Maru Cult of the Pomo Indians: a California Ghost Dance Survival. Southwest Mus. Pap. No. 23. Los Angeles: Southwest Mus. 134 pp.

Merrill ED. 1922–1926. An enumeration of Philippine flowering plants. Bur. Sci. Publ. No. 18, Manila. 4 Vols.

Merrill ED. 1945. Plant Life of the Pacific World. New York: Macmillan. 295 pp.

Merrill ED. 1946. Merrilleana: a selection from the general writings of Elmer Drew Merrill. Chron. Bot. 10(3–4):127–394

Morgan LH. (1851) 1901. League of the Ho-dé-no-sau-nee, or Iroquois, ed. H Lloyd. New York: Dodd, Mead. 2 Vols.

Paras-Perez R, Capistrano FH. 1976. Tolentino. Malolos, RP: Natl. Art Found. Malolos. 209 pp.

Quisumbing E. 1951. Medicinal Plants of the Philippines. Dep. Agric. Nat. Res. Tech. Bull. 16, Manila. 1238 pp.

Richards PW. 1952. The Tropical Rain Forest: An Ecological Study. Cambridge, UK: Cambridge Univ. Press. 450 pp.

Richards PW. 1996. The Tropical Rain Forest: An Ecological Study. Cambridge UK: Cambridge Univ. Press. 575 pp. 2nd ed.

Sauer CO. 1952. Agricultural Origins and Dispersals. New York: Am. Geog. Soc.

Scott WH. 1958. A preliminary report on upland rice in northern Luzon. Southwest. J. Anthropol. 14(1):87–105

Scott WH. 1974. The Discovery of the Igorots: Spanish Contacts with the Pagans of Northern Luzon. Foreword by HC Conklin. Quezon City, Philipp.: New Day. 374 pp.

Simpson GG. 1961. Principles of Animal Taxonomy. Columbia Biol. Ser., No. 20. New York: Columbia Univ. Press. 247 pp.

Sturtevant WC. 1964. Studies in ethnoscience. Am. Anthropol. 66(3, Pt. 2):99–113

Sturtevant WC. 1966. Anthropology, history and ethnohistory. Ethnohistory 13:1–51

Sturtevant WC. 1969. Does anthropology need museums? Proc. Biol. Soc. Wash. 82: 559–762

Tolentino GE. 1937. Ang Wika at Baybaying Tagalog. Maynila, RP: Sariling Limbag. 202 pp.

*Annu. Rev. Anthropol. 1998. 27:1–23*
*Copyright © 1998 by Annual Reviews. All rights reserved*

# GENETICS OF MODERN HUMAN ORIGINS AND DIVERSITY

*John H. Relethford*

Department of Anthropology, State University of New York, College at Oneonta, Oneonta, New York 13820; e-mail: relethjh@oneonta.edu

KEY WORDS: population genetics, DNA, population size, gene flow, genetic diversity, genetic distance

---

ABSTRACT

A major and continuing debate in anthropology concerns the question of whether modern *Homo sapiens* emerged as a separate species roughly 200,000 years ago in Africa (recent African origin model) or as the consequence of evolution within a polytypic species spread across several regions of the Old World (multiregional model). Genetic data have been used to address this debate, focusing on the analysis of gene trees, genetic diversity within populations, and genetic differences between populations. Although the genetic data do provide support for the recent African origin model, they also are compatible with the multiregional model. The genetic evidence provides little direct inference regarding phylogeny, but it can tell us a great deal about ancient demography. Currently, neither model of modern human origins is unequivocally supported to the exclusion of the other.

---

## INTRODUCTION

During the last decade, the question of modern human origins has been addressed more and more often using genetic data. The motivation behind this research is that genetic variation in the world today is a reflection of the past. Combined with inferences from fossil and archaeological records, genetic data may supply answers to some basic questions about human population history. The primary, and most controversial, focus of such research has been the debate over modern human origins.

1

0084-6570/98/1015-0001$08.00

This paper outlines current understanding of the anthropological implications of genetic variation for models of modern human origins. A quick review of recent literature might suggest that the basic question is solved and that there is no further controversy. Numerous genetics papers indicate the genetic data come down firmly in favor of an African replacement model. Most often, however, the data can be interpreted in several ways. Genetics can tell us a great deal about our species' history, but it is not always the information we expect.

## MODELS OF MODERN HUMAN ORIGINS

The question of modern human origins is concerned with the evolutionary relationship of anatomically modern humans to hominids that appear earlier in the fossil record. Which populations (both spatially and temporally) contributed to later humanity? Did any become extinct without issue? Did the contributions vary across both time and space? Did the evolutionary transitions take place within a single evolutionary lineage or are they associated with speciation events? The modern human origins debate goes beyond the basic question of reconstructing our family tree. It is also concerned with tempo and mode of evolution, different concepts of species, and the extent to which hominids are (or are not) unique in their evolutionary history.

Before considering how genetic data and analyses contribute to this debate, it is first necessary to summarize the basic models of modern human origins. This is not a simple task. A variety of different models have been proposed, and though many are similar, they have different emphases (Smith & Harrold 1997). This article takes the simple approach of distinguishing between two basic views—recent African origin and multiregional evolution. Other variants, such as Bräuer's (1984) "Afro-European hybridization model" and Smith et al's (1989) "assimilation model" are considered within this general framework.

### The Recent African Origin Model

The recent African origin model proposes that anatomically modern humans emerged in Africa roughly 200,000 years ago and then dispersed throughout the Old World, replacing preexisting archaic hominids with little or no admixture (e.g. Cann et al 1987, Stringer & Andrews 1988, Stringer 1990, Stringer & McKie 1996). Implicit in many discussions of the recent African origin model is the idea that anatomically modern *Homo sapiens* are a separate species from archaic *Homo sapiens*. The origin of modern humans is, therefore, often seen as resulting from cladogenesis, the formation of a new lineage.

### The Multiregional Evolution Model

The multiregional evolution model is not a specific model of modern human origins but rather a general model focusing on evolutionary process within a polytypic species (e.g. Wolpoff et al 1984, Wolpoff 1989, Thorne & Wolpoff 1992, Wolpoff & Caspari 1997). Multiregional evolution views all hominid evolution since the origin of *Homo erectus* as taking place within a single evolutionary lineage. Multiregional evolution is a general evolutionary model that attempts to account for species-wide change while allowing for local and regional continuity. It is important to note that despite arguments to the contrary (e.g. Waddle 1994), multiregional evolution does not necessarily argue that the primary genetic input into any region of modern humans came from within the same geographic region. Other models are also possible within the general multiregional framework, including major genetic changes originating within Africa and mixing, through gene flow, with non-African populations. A good example of the range of models accommodated under the general model can be found in Wolpoff et al (1994).

## Intermediate Models

The recent African origin and multiregional evolution models are often portrayed as two extremes within a range of possible models dealing with modern human origins. As a result, several "intermediate" models have been proposed. One such is the assimilation model of Smith et al (1989). It views modern humans as resulting from an initial genetic change occurring within Africa, which then spread throughout the rest of the Old World through gene flow and mixture with archaic non-African populations. This model is often labeled intermediate because it appears to combine the initial appearance of modern morphology in Africa with regional continuity outside of Africa. In actuality, this is one of several specific models possible under the general multiregional framework (Wolpoff et al 1994).

Another example is the Afro-European model proposed by Bräuer (1984). In it, modern humans are thought to arise in Africa and from there spread throughout the remainder of the Old World, as suggested by the recent African origin model. However, Bräuer also acknowledges some admixture between the modern humans and preexisting archaic humans outside of Africa. At the most general level, this is similar to the views of Smith et al, even though Bräuer argues that his model is a variant of the recent African origin model (Stringer & Bräuer 1994). The difficulty the newcomer (or professional) faces is clear—at what point do the various specific models labeled as "recent African origin" or "multiregional evolution" overlap with one another? The literature suggests that the same terms are frequently used to mean different things.

A further complication is the frequent dichotomy between models that propose a single region of origin versus those that propose more than one. On this point, multiregional models are often portrayed as implying that all major geographic regions (Europe, Africa, Middle East, East Asia, Australasia) are involved in the transition. Although this is one possible model within the general multiregional framework, it is not the only one. To be multiregional in the most general sense, all that is required is genetic contributions from at least two geographic regions. As a result, many possible specific models can be subsumed under the general multiregional model.

## Genetic Perspectives—Phylogenetic Branching or Population Structure?

Population genetics can be brought to bear on the issue of modern human origins by analyzing patterns of genetic variation within and among living populations. These present-day patterns can be interpreted in terms of the likelihood of different past evolutionary patterns giving rise to contemporary variation. This is not as clear cut as it might seem. To start with, there are two different perspectives that can be applied to analyzing patterns of genetic variation.

One perspective is a phylogenetic branching model. Here, genetic differences between populations are thought to have arisen from a series of bifurcating splits. A typical scenario sees modern humans arising as a single population in Africa. At some later time, this parental population splits, giving rise to a non-African daughter population. Later, the non-African population splits further, giving rise to separate regional populations in Europe, Asia, and Australia. Under a phylogenetic branching model, genetic distances between regional populations result from the accumulation of mutations and the action of genetic drift along each branch, such that genetic distance is proportional to time. Also, mutations will accumulate within populations, such that the oldest populations will show the greatest accumulation and, hence, the greatest within-group genetic diversity.

This phylogenetic perspective corresponds to the recent African origin model, which sees a series of population splits over time. As reviewed below, there is ample evidence that sub-Saharan Africans today have the greatest levels of within-group diversity and are generally the most distant regional population in genetic distance analyses. On the surface, the close fit between observed data and the predictions of a phylogenetic branching process would seem to argue for a recent African origin model.

The situation, however, is more complex. The fact that the genetic evidence is compatible with the recent African origin model does not prove it true. The fit of data and theory would be proof only if a phylogenetic branching process was the only way to generate the observed patterns of genetic variation. The fact that data can be fit by a tree does not make it a tree. An alternative is the population structure approach, which focuses on the evolution of populations connected by gene flow. Genetic variation within and among populations is seen as resulting from the balance between gene flow and genetic drift (note that this discussion assumes that the traits in question are selectively neutral, an assumption also shared by the phylogenetic branching model).

The conflict between these approaches arises because of the indeterminate nature of the results of genetic analyses. As Felsenstein (1982) points out, migration can mimic a phylogenetic branching process and vice versa. This point has also been emphasized by Relethford (1995), Relethford & Harpending (1994, 1995), and Sherry & Batzer (1997). Since phylogenetic branching models and population structure (gene flow-drift) models can give the same results, this means that our analyses are not often likely to tell us which underlying model is correct!

An additional, and often ignored, problem is due to the nature of our units of analysis—living human populations. Many evolutionary questions are directly interpretable from a phylogenetic branching model because we start with living groups that are separate species, such as humans and the living great apes. Because these groups have been separate evolutionary entities (species) for a long time, the issue of gene flow between them is meaningless, and the only appropriate model is based on a phylogenetic branching process. Genetic distances between living hominoids can be taken as an index of the pattern and timing of cladogenesis.

The situation with modern human origins is more problematic. Regardless of the number of species in the past, all living human populations belong to the same species. Any attempt to force data from regional populations (races) into a phylogenetic branching model is invalid because they are not separate evolutionary entities. Regional populations are all interconnected via gene flow and, as far as we can tell, have been so for some time. Even if regional differences began only 100,000 years ago as the result of dispersal from Africa and subsequent branching, the continued action of gene flow makes the reconstruction of phylogenetic trees and the dating of population splits difficult at best (Weiss & Maruyama 1976, Weiss 1988).

## GENETIC EVIDENCE FOR MODERN HUMAN ORIGINS

Several lines of genetic evidence bear on the modern human origins debate. Each must be looked at from both the phylogenetic branching model and the alternative population structure approach based on migration-drift models.

### Gene Trees and Coalescence

Much of the debate has focused on the genealogical relations between genes rather than populations. Such gene trees describe the process of coalescence (Hudson 1990, Donnelly & Tavaré 1995, Harding 1997, Marjoram & Donnelly 1997). The objective is to determine how and when the genes from any two individuals join together in a common ancestor (coalescence) at some point in the past. Given knowledge of the mutation rate for a given genetic trait, the date of coalescence can be estimated.

MITOCHONDRIAL DNA    Much of the discussion of coalescence theory and gene trees in the modern human origins debate has focused on mitochondrial DNA (mtDNA), a small amount of DNA in the mitochondria of cells that is inherited maternally (Stoneking 1993). The first significant application of mtDNA to the question of modern human origins was in a study by Cann et al (1987). mtDNA for 133 distinct types was collected from 147 people representing ancestry in Africa, Europe, Asia, and Australasia. Their gene tree had two major branches: One consisted entirely of individuals with African ancestry, and the other contained individuals of all different ancestries (including Africa). From this it was concluded that the common mtDNA ancestor of all living humans ("mitochondrial Eve") lived in Africa. By itself, this conclusion was not controversial because proponents of both recent African origin and multiregional evolution models acknowledge an African origin of humanity. The controversy is over timing—the multiregional model claims that the common African ancestor was *Homo erectus*, who lived close to two million years ago, whereas the recent African origin model postulates the origin of modern humans as a separate species whose existence came about within the past 200,000 years.

The controversial point of the paper was the estimate of the age of coalescence. Using a mutation divergence rate of 2–4% per million years, the authors estimated that mtDNA coalescence took place between 140,000 and 290,000 years ago. In their view, this was too recent to be detecting the African origin of *Homo erectus*. In addition, they noted the higher mtDNA diversity within their African sample, which they argued was consistent with a greater age for African populations. Some of the initial criticisms (Spuhler 1988, Excoffier & Langaney 1989, Wolpoff 1989) included discussion of problems in estimating the mutation rate, methods used to derive the genealogical tree, and the use of African Americans to represent African ancestry. A number of these criticisms were addressed in a subsequent study by Vigilant et al (1991), who also found an African root for the genealogical tree and estimated a coalescent date of 166,000–249,000 years ago. Since these papers, numerous studies have dealt with the analysis and interpretation of mtDNA variation. Rather than review these studies extensively, this article focuses on two key findings that have been used to argue for a recent African origin—the African root of the gene tree and the date of coalescence.

*An African root*    The African location of the common mtDNA ancestor has been questioned by several studies that found that the initial application of the computer algorithm used to find the best-fitting tree was flawed (Maddison 1991, Templeton 1992, Hedges et al 1992). Sometimes the best-fitting trees showed an African origin, but sometimes they did not. However, a newer method that has since been applied to the mtDNA data also argues for an African origin (Penny et al 1995).

A problem that remains is the exact interpretation of such results. Many researchers suggest that the geographic pattern of mtDNA variation is best described by the recent African origin model, but not everyone agrees. Excoffier & Langaney (1989) critiqued the methodology of Cann et al (1987) and suggested that there was no clear support for an African origin. Templeton (1993, 1994, 1996b, 1997) argued that the geographic distribution of mtDNA types is also compatible with recurrent gene flow under a multiregional model. Templeton (1997) further notes that although a non-African root for a gene tree could reject the recent African origin model, the reverse is not true: An African root could be explained by either replacement out of Africa or by low levels of gene flow between geographic regions since the time of coalescence. As Templeton (1997:330) points out, "Under the gene flow hypothesis, the common ancestor could have lived anywhere in the Old World, including Africa."

*The date of the mtDNA coalescent*   Much debate has focused on the initial estimate by Cann et al (1987) of roughly 200,000 years for the date of the common mtDNA ancestor. Many subsequent studies have also argued for a relatively recent date of coalescence, though there are some differences, depending on the specific date used for the human-chimpanzee split, which is used to calibrate estimates of the mutation rate. Vigilant et al (1991) estimated a date of 166,000–249,000 years based on a 4- to 6-million-year date for the human-chimpanzee divergence. Ruvolo et al (1993) used a 6-million-year calibration time and estimated the coalescence to human mtDNA at 298,000 years, with a 95% confidence interval (CI) of 129,000–536,000 years. Horai et al (1995) used a 4.9-million-year divergence to estimate 143,000 years (95% CI = 107,000–179,000 years). Stoneking et al (1992) estimated the date of coalescence with a method that used estimates of the peopling of New Guinea for calibration and obtained a date of 137,000 years (95% CI = 63,000–416,000 years).

Several problems in estimation have been addressed. Templeton (1993) reviewed problems in potential error due to the large variance of such estimates and the choice of calibration date for the human-chimpanzee divergence. Based on the data from Cann et al (1987) and Vigilant et al (1991), Templeton argued that the upper bound for the date of coalescence could be as high as 473,000–844,000 years ago. Wills (1995) pointed out that the failure to adjust for variable mutation rates across mtDNA sites tends to underestimate the date of coalescence. After correction, he suggested a range of 436,000–806,000 years ago, depending on the specific human-chimpanzee calibration date used. Additional problems with mtDNA coalescent dates include the fact that the influence of selection has not been ruled out (Hey 1997, Loewe & Scherer 1997) and new work suggests a wide range of possible mutation rates (Gibbons 1997).

In addition to continued debate over the specific date of coalescence, the whole relevance of coalescent dates has been questioned. Templeton (1994, 1997) questioned the frequent assumption that a mtDNA coalescence prior to 1 million years ago rejects the multiregional model and pointed out that any of the dates estimated so far are compatible with both the recent African origin and the multiregional models. Rogers & Jorde (1995) suggested that such estimates tell us nothing about age per se but rather are an indication that average population size has been small since the time of coalescence (the date of coalescence and population size are both proportional to mtDNA diversity).

THE Y CHROMOSOME   Y chromosome polymorphisms provide the male analogue to mtDNA because the Y chromosome is paternally inherited and, excluding a small section, does not recombine (Hammer & Zegura 1996). Although Y chromosome variation is relatively low, several attempts have been made to estimate a coalescence date. Dorit et al (1995) estimated this date to be 270,000 years (95% CI = 0–800,000 years). Using different polymorphisms, Hammer (1995) derived an estimate of 188,000 years (95% CI = 51,000–411,000 years). Both estimates fall within the range of estimates from mtDNA and are consistent with a recent African origin. However, Whitfield et al (1995) came up with a much lower estimate, roughly 40,000 years, using the same polymorphisms. Hammer & Zegura (1996) noted that this difference may reflect differences in sample size (small in both studies) and that revised calculations support Hammer's initial estimate. More recently, Underhill et al (1997) detected 22 Y chromosome polymorphisms in numerous samples of chromosomes. Using two different subsets of their data, they estimated the date of coalescence to be 162,000 (95% CI = 69,000–316,000) years or 186,000 (95% CI = 77,000–372,000) years. The geographic structure of the variation was less clear and suggested the possibility of relatively deep non-African roots.

OTHER GENE TREES   Although the mtDNA and Y chromosome data are frequently cited as support for a recent African origin, it has been suggested that the same patterns are expected under a multiregional model (Templeton 1993, 1997). In addition, the application of coalescent theory to nuclear genes has often resulted in different interpretations. Klein et al (1993) and Ayala et al (1994) examined variation in the major histocompatibility complex and concluded that either origin model could be supported and that the major histocompatibility complex (as well as mtDNA) tells us primarily about ancient population size (see below). Harding et al (1997) examined the gene tree for the beta-globin gene and estimated coalescence in Africa roughly 800,000 years ago. However, they also found evidence for an ancient Asian influence, dating back more than 200,000 years. They argued that this evidence does not support a recent African origin model where modern humans dispersed from Africa 100,000 years ago and replaced all preexisting non-African populations. Rather, their data suggest that there is significant Asian ancestry well before that time. A recent analysis of *Alu* insertion polymorphisms estimated a date of approximately 1.4 million years ago for the human coalescent (Sherry et al 1997). Considering the likely standard error, this date is not incompatible with the origin of *Homo erectus*.

## Genetic Diversity Within Populations

In addition to an estimate of the location and age of coalescence from mtDNA, Cann et al (1987) also noted that mtDNA sequence diversity was greatest within their African sample. A higher level of diversity within Africa was felt to be consistent with the recent African origin model under the assumption that the older a population is, the more mutations have accumulated. Stoneking & Cann (1989:22) note: "If one accepts that mtDNA mutations are largely neutral, then their occurrence and accumulation are mostly a function of time: the more variability a population possesses, the older it is." Since Africa had the greatest level of mtDNA diversity, it was therefore the oldest, in agreement with the prediction from the recent African origin model that modern humans arose in Africa and only later dispersed into other parts of the Old World.

Subsequent analysis has confirmed higher levels of mtDNA diversity (measured in several ways) in sub-Saharan Africa (e.g. Vigilant et al 1991, Bowcock et al 1994, Jorde et al 1995), although the statistical significance has been questioned (Templeton 1993). In any case, excess African diversity has also been observed for microsatellite DNA (Bowcock et al 1994, Deka et al 1995, Jorde et al 1995, 1997; Tishkoff et al 1996; JH Relethford, LB Jorde, unpublished data), craniometric data (Relethford & Harpending 1994), and *Alu* insertion polymorphisms (Stoneking et al 1997).

In general, most of the genetic data to date shows the highest levels of within-group variation in sub-Saharan African populations. There are two exceptions: classic genetic markers and restriction fragment length polymorphisms (RFLPs) (Bowcock et al 1994, Jorde et al 1995). One possible explanation is ascertainment bias (Rogers & Jorde 1996): Because both classic genetic markers and RFLPs were first detected in European populations, the loci that were polymorphic among Europeans were those applied most often elsewhere in the world. As a result, European heterozygosity is biased upwards. Another contributing factor is mutation rate. Both classic genetic markers and RFLPs have low mutation rates relative to mtdna, microsatellite DNA, and cranio-metrics and will therefore not show excess African diversity (Relethford 1997).

Apart from these exceptions, the pattern of within-group diversity appears to be consistent with the recent African origin model. However, a critical assumption is made relating a population's diversity and its age (Relethford 1995). A new daughter population must experience a severe and long-lasting reduction in population size (bottleneck) in order to reduce its level of within-group diversity to zero. Although new founding populations are generally small, the actual reduction must be large and long lasting in order to reduce the initial level of diversity significantly. In addition, as a daughter population increases in size (required by the recent African origin model), the level of within-group diversity will increase. The actual impact of a founding event on within-group diversity in a daughter population depends on the sizes of the parent and daughter population(s) and the extent and duration of the bottleneck. Rogers & Jorde (1995) showed that to produce a strong correlation between age and diversity, such bottlenecks would have to have been much more severe and long lasting than is realistic.

The arguments linking population diversity and age are clearly within the phylogenetic branching framework discussed above. An alternative view, stemming from a population structure perspective, is that the level of within-group diversity is to a large extent a function of population size. Relethford & Harpending (1994) showed that higher levels of craniometric variation in sub-Saharan Africans is most likely the consequence of the long-term population in Africa being more numerous than in any other geographic region. This same finding has also been observed with microsatellite DNA data (JH Relethford, LB Jorde, unpublished data). These results suggest that during recent human evolution, the bulk of our ancestors (estimated between 50% and 70%) lived in sub-Saharan Africa (Relethford & Harpending 1994; JH Relethford, LB Jorde, unpublished data). Using a similar method applied to a worldwide analysis of *Alu* insertion polymorphisms, Stoneking et al (1997) also found evidence for a more numerous African population, although they did not estimate relative population size. It is important to note that a more numerous African population is also expected based on its larger landmass (Thorne et al 1993, Wolpoff & Caspari 1997).

A larger long-term African population size fits the recent African origin model because the non-African daughter populations would initially be small in number and later grow. Because the long-term effective size of a population is closer to the minimum than to the arithmetic average, the demographic history suggested by the recent African origin model would result in a large African size. However, a more numerous African population is also expected by, and is consistent with, the multiregional evolution model, where Africa serves as the center of the species' distribution and the peripheries are smaller in population (Wolpoff & Caspari 1997).

## Genetic Differences Between Populations

The focus of gene trees and coalescent theory is on the relationships of individual genes. Another approach is to examine genetic relationships among populations. Most typically, genetic data are aggregated at a regional level (e.g. sub-Saharan Africa, East Asia, Europe, and so forth). Genetic differences between populations are then computed and used to generate insight into past evolutionary events. Genetic differences may be simply reported or more formally compared using one of a variety of genetic distance measures. The focus of such studies is the reconstruction of population history. On a global level, this reconstruction relates directly to the issue of modern human origins.

GENETIC DISTANCES BETWEEN HUMAN POPULATIONS    A variety of genetic data have been examined at the populational level with a consistent result: Sub-Saharan African populations tend to be the most genetically distant, and non-African regional populations tend to be more similar to one another than any are to Africa. This pattern has been found for mtDNA (Vigilant et al 1991, Jorde et al 1995), Y chromosomes (Underhill et al 1997), *Alu* insertion polymorphisms (Batzer et al 1994, Stoneking et al 1997), microsatellite DNA (Bowcock et al 1994, Deka et al 1995, Jorde et al 1995, Tishkoff et al 1996), RFLPs (Bowcock et al 1991, Mountain & Cavalli-Sforza 1994, Jorde et al 1995), classic genetic markers (Nei 1978, Nei & Livshits 1989, Cavalli-Sforza et al 1994, Relethford & Harpending 1995), and craniometrics (Lynch 1989, Relethford & Harpending 1994, 1995).

The greater divergence of Africa is compatible with the recent African origin model, which predicts that the first split is between Africa and a non-African population, with a later split that populates the rest of the Old World. As such, the genetic distances between regional populations (which are often expressed graphically by a cluster analysis tree) are a record of these past splits. Under this view, Europe and Asia are more similar genetically to each other than either is to Africa because they share a more recent common ancestor.

However, the fact that the genetic distances between populations can be represented by a tree structure does not mean that an underlying tree model is correct (Relethford & Harpending 1994, Relethford 1995, Sherry & Batzer 1997). An alternative is that the genetic distances are instead a reflection of varying rates of gene flow. Relethford & Harpending (1994, 1995) have used genetic marker and craniometric data to show that the pattern of genetic distances among living human populations could just as easily be explained by variation in population size and rates of gene flow (see also Relethford 1995).

LEVELS OF GENETIC MICRODIFFERENTIATION   Another type of genetic distance analysis focuses on the degree of among-group variation relative to total variation. A number of studies have shown that the relative proportion of among-group variation, $F_{ST}$ (Wright 1951), is low for the human species. The values of $F_{ST}$ as computed among major geographic regions clusters around 0.10–0.15, showing that roughly 10–15% of total genetic variation is between groups and 85–90% is within groups. Estimates in this range have been found in analyses of classic genetic markers (Lewontin 1974, Latter 1980, Nei & Roychoudhury 1982, Ryman et al 1983, Livshits & Nei 1990, Cavalli-Sforza et al 1994), nuclear DNA restriction site polymorphisms (Bowcock et al 1991, Jorde et al 1995, Barbujani et al 1997), microsatellite DNA (Deka et al 1995, Barbujani et al 1997), *Alu* insertion polymorphisms (Batzer et al 1994, Stoneking et al 1997), and craniometrics (Relethford 1994). Lower values of $F_{ST}$ have been found for some microsatellite loci (Jorde et al 1995) and for mtDNA (Whittam et al 1986, Jorde et al 1995, Harpending et al 1996), perhaps reflecting higher mutation rates for these traits.

These $F_{ST}$ values are generally considered low relative to many other animals (Relethford 1995), and they have often been taken as evidence for a recent African origin. Under this model, the relatively low among-group variation of modern humans is a direct reflection of a fairly recent common ancestry where there has not been sufficient time for larger genetic distances to evolve. Again, while such evidence is compatible with a recent African origin, it is also compatible with a migration-based alternative. Perhaps these relatively low $F_{ST}$ values reflect relatively higher rates of migration? Since multiregional evolution requires migration among groups throughout the species, then perhaps all we are seeing is a genetic index of the rate of such migration.

## Genetic Demography and Modern Human Origins

In recent years the debate over modern human origins has, to some extent, moved from phylogenetic questions to demographic questions. The specific focus of interest has been on estimating changes in ancient population size from genetic data. Population size figures into virtually every equation relating to genetic variation, and it is therefore of interest to use various population genetic models to estimate species and regional population size during recent human evolution. Such estimates do not focus on phylogenetic history directly but can perhaps indirectly provide us with insight into questions of population relationships (Relethford 1995, Rogers & Jorde 1995).

Central to much of population genetics theory is the concept of effective population size (Wright 1969, Crow & Kimura 1970), or the size of the population needed to explain a given pattern of genetic variation. Effective population size $N_e$ is not the same as census population size ($N_c$), the total number of individuals in a population. For one thing, not everyone in a population is of reproductive age. Counting the number of reproductive-age individuals in a population is a first approximation to the genetic size of a population, but it is not the only one. A variety of factors—including sex ratio, differential fertility, age structure, temporal changes, level of differentiation among groups, and others—can affect the genetic size of a population. Effective population size is a concept that adjusts for such factors and provides an estimate of the genetic size of a population under ideal conditions.

THE EFFECTIVE POPULATION SIZE OF THE HUMAN SPECIES    The concept of effective population size has been used in several analyses of genetic variation of living humans. Here, levels of genetic variation at equilibrium are used to estimate long-term effective population size of the entire species. The results across traits are surprisingly similar and cluster around an approximate long-term average effective size of roughly 10,000. These estimates have been based on variation in classic genetic polymorphisms (Nei & Graur 1984), mtDNA (Wilson et al 1985, Rogers & Jorde 1995), Y chromosome data (Hammer & Zegura 1996), the beta-globin gene (Harding et al 1997), and nuclear DNA sequences (Takahata 1993, Takahata et al 1995). Using *Alu* insertion polymorphisms, Sherry (1996) and Sherry et al (1997) estimated a slightly higher value of $N_e$ (18,000). A higher value of roughly 100,000 was obtained by Ayala (1995) in his analysis of the DRB1 HLA gene (see Erlich et al 1996 and Ayala 1996 for discussion of this estimate). Differences in long-term effective size are in part related to differences in time frame, most often defined by coalescence dates. The mtDNA and Y chromosome estimates relate back to the time period defined by the past 200,000 years or so, whereas Ayala's (1995) estimate refers back to an initial primate ancestor roughly 60 million years ago. Some estimates refer back to a population ancestral to all hominids, whereas others refer back to recent populations ancestral to modern humans (Ayala 1996).

GENETIC EVIDENCE FOR A PLEISTOCENE POPULATION EXPLOSION    Estimates of long-term effective size are useful, but it would be better to have a more specific knowledge of possible changes in population size over time. A long-term average value of $N_e \approx 10,000$ over the past 200,000 years could theoretically arise from a variety of different demographic scenarios, including constancy, growth, or decline in overall population size. We are better able to interpret the estimate of $N_e$ if we know even approximately the underlying demographic history.

A major breakthrough in studying the genetic signature of ancient demographic events came with the mismatch analysis of Rogers & Harpending (1992). Their method relies on the comparison of mtDNA sequences between all pairs of individuals in a sample. For each comparison, the number of nucleotide differences (or restriction site differences) is counted and tallied in a histogram. For worldwide human mtDNA data, the resulting histogram (called a mismatch distribution) resembles a bell-shaped curve and is completely different from the distribution expected under a model of constant population size. Instead, the observed mismatch distribution is the same as that expected under a model of rapid population growth. Further, Rogers & Harpending (1992) developed methods to allow estimation of the time of growth and the size of the initial population prior to growth.

The results to date support a rapid population explosion in the Late Pleistocene from a small initial population size (Rogers 1992, Rogers & Harpending 1992, Harpending et al 1993, Harpending 1994, Sherry et al 1994, Rogers 1995, 1997, Rogers et al 1996; see also Marjoram & Donnelly 1994). Estimates of the timing of population expansion vary across populations (as well as by the specific mutation rate used for calibration) but generally fall within the past 100,000 years or so, clustering at around 50,000 years (Sherry et al 1994). Although tentative, preliminary work suggests that the African population expanded earlier than those of other regions (Sherry et al 1994, Relethford 1998) and that prior to the expansion it was more numerous (Relethford 1998).

Of greater potential significance to the modern human origins debate is the finding of expansion from a very small initial population size, usually estimated at no more than several thousand females. Growth at the time of expansion is estimated to be on the order of 100-fold or more (Rogers 1995, 1997, Rogers & Jorde 1995). The small pre-expansion population size is similar to a somewhat larger ($\approx$10,000) long-term effective size. If the human species had an initial pre-expansion population of several thousand individuals and then later reproduced rapidly, the long-term effective population size would be much closer to the minimum number than the maximum. Thus, our species' relatively low effective population size, compared with our relatively large census size even in the past 10,000 years or so (Weiss 1984), appears to be the result of rapid expansion from a small initial effective size.

IMPLICATIONS FOR MODERN HUMAN ORIGINS   The studies noted above suggest that the effective species size of human ancestors was low (10,000) at the start of the Late Pleistocene. This estimate is much lower than the usual (although crude) estimates of total population size obtained from archaeological and ethnographic inference, which typically are about one million during the Middle Pleistocene (Howell 1996). The low estimated species size has most often been interpreted as support for the recent African origin model, which predicts that the Late Pleistocene ancestors of living humans were all from a single region. The multiregional model, on the other hand, predicts that our

Late Pleistocene ancestors were spread out over at least two geographic regions, and perhaps across the entire Old World. A number of papers have suggested that any such widespread distribution is incompatible with a low species population size, and therefore it is more reasonable to interpret the genetic evidence in terms of a localized ancestral population, as predicted by the recent African origin model (Harpending et al 1993, 1996, Rogers & Jorde 1995, Harpending & Relethford 1997).

Templeton (1997) has argued against this interpretation for several reasons. First, the problems in estimating coalescence dates also apply to estimates of species effective size. There is variation due to evolutionary stochasticity and variation due to the specific mutation rate used for inference. As a result, the true long-term effective size of our species could be higher than suggested by the point estimate of $N_e = 10,000$.

Templeton (1997) also noted that effective size is usually much lower than census size, often by several orders of magnitude. This point is also clear from a review by Nei & Graur (1984). They examined estimates of long-term effective size versus total census size for a variety of organisms. They found that the effective size is often a small proportion of the census size, often by one or more orders of magnitude. According to their data, the median ratio of effective size to census size among 43 mammalian species (excluding humans) is 0.003. The range is 0.0–0.9, with most ratios less than 0.1. What accounts for such low ratios? One common explanation is a population increase from a small initial size because the long-term effective size will tend to remain low in such cases. This is consistent with Rogers & Harpending's finding of rapid Late Pleistocene population growth from a small initial population size (see above).

A recent African origin could produce a small long-term effective population size. Does low effective species size necessarily support only a recent African origin model? The possibility of a small effective species size being compatible with a multiregional model must also be considered. Is the low long-term effective size compatible with estimated census sizes of several hundred thousands? One possibility is a worldwide reduction in population size prior to the Late Pleistocene. If recent human evolution were multiregional, and if population sizes decreased rapidly across much or all of the Old World, then the net result would be a relatively low long-term effective size over the last 200,000 years or so. If so, then the human species was numerous, shrank in number, and then expanded again later. Given the major climatic shifts that have occurred within the last half a million years or more, this is not that unlikely. However, recent work by Sherry and colleagues (1997) argues against this interpretation; their analysis of *Alu* insertion polymorphisms suggested that the population size of the line ancestral to modern humans has been small over the past 500,000 years or so. Rather than a pattern of population decline and recovery, their work suggests a pattern of continued small size over time.

Another possibility is the frequent extinction and recolonization of local populations over time. Wright (1940) noted that if local populations that were small in size are prone to frequent extinction and recolonization by founders from elsewhere, then the effective population size of a species could be very small even though the census size might be in the millions. Several theoretical treatments suggest that such a demographic history could easily result in a low, long-term effective species size (Slatkin 1977, Maruyama & Kimura 1980, Takahata 1994, 1995, Whitlock & Barton 1997). This model might be appropriate for considering recent hominid evolution. The many climatic shifts throughout most of the Pleistocene suggest the possibility of fairly high rates of local population extinction. Estimates based on simulation of hunting and gathering demographic schedules suggest that the rate of extinction for local bands could have been substantial (Wobst 1974, Gaines & Gaines 1997).

The exact ratio of effective size to census size depends on a number of factors, including local group size, the number of new founders, local extinction rate, and local and long-range migration rates. The critical parameter is the ratio of the local migration rate to the local extinction rate (Maruyama & Kimura 1980). When migration rate is low relative to extinction, the ratio of effective size to census size can be quite low. Thus, the extinction/recolonization process would have its greatest impact when migration rates were low and/or extinction rates were high.

One argument against this model is the fact that low migration rates means greater among-group variation. Several studies have argued that an increase in among-group variation (higher values of $F_{ST}$) actually inflates the effective population size of a species (Nei & Takahata 1993, Rogers & Jorde 1995). As such, our genetic estimates of effective size might be overestimates, and any reduction because of local population extinction might be offset by such inflation. Recently, however, Whitlock & Barton (1997) found that although this expectation applies to a simple island model of population structure, under more realistic models, increased subdivision acts to decrease effective size. Thus, a general model of relative isolation and frequent extinction of local populations would produce a relatively low effective species size.

It is tempting to suggest that such a scenario actually occurred in the past, but all we can really do is suggest the general conditions under which a small effective species population size is compatible with a multiregional model. Currently, we lack sufficient estimates of the parameters of subdivision and extinction. All we can say is that such a model points to the possibility that low effective species population size is compatible with a multiregional model. Perhaps further simulation and modeling will help narrow the range of likely parameter values such that more definitive statements can be made.

Of course, all such arguments about ancient population size derived from mtDNA are based on the assumption that it is selectively neutral. If this is not the case, as suggested by several studies (e.g. Templeton 1996a, Hey 1997, Loewe & Scherer 1997, Wise et al 1997), then estimates of both coalescent dates and species effective size from mtDNA diversity will not be reliable. A "selective sweep" might be mimicking a low effective species size.

## Neandertal DNA

Until recently, all genetic data pertaining to the question of modern human origins came from living humans. This situation changed with the sequencing of a section of mtDNA from a Neandertal fossil (Krings et al 1997). Because extraction of ancient DNA is fraught with problems, this study stands as a milestone of technical achievement. A 378-bp sequence was extracted from the humerus of the Neandertal type specimen and compared with the same sequence from samples of numerous living humans.

Compared with living humans, the Neandertal specimen is different at 27 positions, considerably more than the average of 8 differences among living humans. However, there is some slight overlap: The number of mtDNA differences between living humans and the Neandertal specimen ranges from 22 to 36 substitutions, whereas the number of mtDNA differences among living humans ranges from 1 to 24 substitutions. The authors suggested that these results support the view that Neandertals did not contribute any mtDNA to living humans, although they noted that the possibility that Neandertals contributed other genes could not be ruled out.

Krings et al (1997) further estimated coalescent dates using a 4- to 5-million-year human-chimpanzee divergence date for calibration. They estimated that the common mtDNA ancestor of the Neandertal specimen and living humans lived between 550,000 and 690,000 years ago. These dates are consistent with the view that the ancestor of Neandertals and living humans diverged roughly 600,000 years ago and that Neandertals are a separate species from modern *Homo sapiens*. Again, however, this is not the only possible scenario. As noted above, coalescent dates often tell us more about ancient demography than about phylogeny. It might simply be that the effective species size 600,000 years ago was slightly larger than in more recent times. Given the relationship between long-term effective population size and coalescent date (e.g. Ayala 1995), a coalescent date of 600,000 years would correspond to an effective size of 30,000. Given the large evolutionary and statistical variance of such estimates (Templeton 1993, 1997) and the sample size of $n = 1$ for the Neandertals, there is little point in trying to read too much into such an estimate. Also, if mtDNA is conclusively shown to be affected by natural selection, then the relevance of the Neandertal specimen is less clear.

Krings et al (1997) conducted an additional analysis by comparing the Neandertal mtDNA sequence with different groups of living humans. There was no tendency for Neandertals to more closely resemble modern Europeans than people other from geographic regions. This finding might be taken by some as a rejection of the multiregional model because it is widely assumed that the European Neandertals would be most closely related to living Europeans under the multiregional model. This assumption, however, misrepresents the multiregional model. If living Europeans derive some of their ancestry from the Neandertals, it is not necessary that the majority of their ancestry do so. Under the multiregional model, people from every region have multiple ancestors and multiple descendants (Wolpoff & Caspari 1997). Furthermore, even if additional evidence shows conclusively that Neandertals were a separate species, this does not automatically rule out a multiregional perspective unless the same case could be made for every region other than Africa.

The Neandertal mtDNA sequence data is exciting but not conclusive. Additional specimens are needed to place the 27-bp difference in perspective. Is this specimen different because he belonged to a different species, because he lived many tens of thousands of years ago, because of demographic shifts over time, or because of recent natural selection? Additional sequence data, particularly with definite early European moderns (e.g. Cro-Magnon), would be most informative.

## CONCLUSIONS

The use of genetic data for addressing questions of modern human origins is an exciting area and one that serves potentially to unite researchers in the disparate fields of molecular genetics, population genetics, and paleoanthropology. In the past, the genetic evidence for modern human origins has most often been portrayed as support for a recent African origin model of near-complete replacement (e.g. Lewin 1993). All the pieces seemed to fit, ranging from greater African diversity to greater African divergence to the estimates of when "Eve" lived.

Although it is tempting to stick to this interpretation (which might be correct), it is useful to step back and consider possible alternatives. The fact that the genetic evidence suggests compatibility with the recent African origin model does not necessarily rule in its favor unless it can be shown unequivocally that the same evidence is not compatible with a multiregional model. For the bulk of the genetic data discussed here, a multiregional model is also compatible. Each type of evidence can be interpreted from either a phylogenetic branching perspective or a population structure perspective. Patterns of within-group diversity, for example, can be explained by a process of bifurcations or by variation in long-term effective population size.

Of all the genetic evidence analyzed to date, the result that most strongly supports a recent African origin model is the consistent finding across several loci of a small long-term effective species size over at least the last 200,000 years (and perhaps longer). Even here, however, the evidence is not as conclusive as we might think. We need to look much more closely at factors that could affect the relationship between effective population size and census population size and determine if they are likely to have operated in recent human evolution, and further explore the assumption of selective neutrality for mtDNA. We also need more loci, further work on the possible role of selection, and additional fossil specimens. I suspect that the pace of discovery and analysis will soon render this review out of date.

ACKNOWLEDGMENTS

I thank numerous colleagues who have talked with me, and inspired me, regarding the subject of modern human origins. I am particularly indebted for assistance and good conversation over the past few years to Rachel Caspari, Mike Hammer, John Hawks, Roz Harding, Henry Harpending, Lynn Jorde, Lyle Konigsberg, Ken Korey, Andy Kramer, Alan Rogers, Steve Sherry, Fred Smith, Mark Stoneking, Chris Stringer, Sarah Tishkoff, and Milford Wolpoff. Obviously, any errors in interpretation or fact are my own.

> Visit the *Annual Reviews home page* at
> http://www.AnnualReviews.org.

## Literature Cited

Ayala FJ. 1995. The myth of Eve: molecular biology and human origins. *Science* 270: 1930–36

Ayala FJ. 1996. HLA sequence polymorphism and the origin of humans. *Science* 274: 1554

Ayala FJ, Escalante A, O'Huigin C, Klein J. 1994. Molecular genetics of speciation and human origins. *Proc. Natl. Acad. Sci. USA* 91:6787–94

Barbujani G, Magagni A, Minch E, Cavalli-Sforza LL. 1997. An apportionment of human DNA diversity. *Proc. Natl. Acad. Sci. USA* 94:4516–19

Batzer MA, Stoneking M, Alegria-Hartman M, Bazan H, Kass DH, et al. 1994. African origin of human-specific polymorphic *Alu* insertions. *Proc. Natl. Acad. Sci. USA* 91: 12288–92

Bowcock AM, Kidd JR, Mountain JL, Hebert JM, Carstenuto L, et al. 1991. Drift, admixture, and selection in human evolution: a study with DNA polymorphisms. *Proc. Natl. Acad. Sci. USA* 88:839–43

Bowcock AM, Ruiz-Linares A, Tomfohrde J, Minch E, Kidd JR, Cavalli-Sforza LL. 1994. High resolution of human evolutionary trees with polymorphic microsatellites. *Nature* 368: 455–57

Bräuer G. 1984. A craniological approach to the origin of anatomically modern *Homo sapiens* in Africa and implications for the appearance of modern Europeans. See Smith & Spencer 1984, pp. 327–410

Cann RL, Stoneking M, Wilson AC. 1987. Mitochondrial DNA and human evolution. *Nature* 325:31–36

Cavalli-Sforza LL, Menozzi P, Piazza A.

1994. *The History and Geography of Human Genes*. Princeton: Princeton Univ. Press

Clark GA, Willermet CM, eds. 1997. *Conceptual Issues in Modern Human Origins Research*. New York: Adline de Gruyter

Crow JF, Kimura M. 1970. *An Introduction to Population Genetics Theory*. Minneapolis: Burgess

Deka R, Jin L, Shriver MD, Yu LM, DeCroo S, et al. 1995. Population genetics of dinucleotide $(dC-dA)_n \bullet (dG-dT)_n$ polymorphisms in world populations. *Am. J. Hum. Genet.* 56:461–74

Donnelly P, Tavaré S. 1995. Coalescents and genealogical structure under neutrality. *Annu. Rev. Genet.* 29:401–21

Donnelly P, Tavaré S, eds. 1997. *Progress in Population Genetics and Human Evolution*. New York: Springer-Verlag

Dorit RL, Akashi H, Gilbert W. 1995. Absence of polymorphism at the ZFY locus on the human Y chromosome. *Science* 268:1183–85

Erlich HA, Bergström TF, Stoneking M, Gyllensten U. 1996. HLA sequence polymorphism and the origin of humans. *Science* 274:1552–54

Excoffier L, Langaney A. 1989. Origin and differentiation of human mitochondrial DNA. *Am. J. Hum. Genet.* 44:73–85

Felsenstein J. 1982. How can we infer geography and history from gene frequencies? *J. Theor. Biol.* 96:9–20

Gaines SW, Gaines WM. 1997. Simulating success or failure: another look at small-population dynamics. *Am. Antiq.* 62: 683–97

Gibbons A. 1997. Calibrating the mitochondrial clock. *Science* 279:28–29

Hammer MF. 1995. A recent common ancestor for human Y chromosomes. *Nature* 378:376–78

Hammer MF, Zegura SL. 1996. The role of the Y chromosome in human evolutionary studies. *Evol. Anthropol.* 5:116–34

Harding RM. 1997. Lines of descent from mitochondrial Eve: an evolutionary look at coalescence. See Donnelly & Tavaré 1997, pp. 15–31

Harding RM, Fullerton SM, Griffiths RC, Bond J, Cox MJ, et al. 1997. Archaic African and Asian lineages in the genetic ancestry of modern humans. *Am. J. Hum. Genet.* 60:772–89

Harpending HC. 1994. Signature of ancient population growth in a low-resolution mitochondrial DNA mismatch distribution. *Hum. Biol.* 66:591–600

Harpending HC, Relethford JH. 1997. Population perspectives on human origins research. See Clark & Willermet 1997, pp. 361–68

Harpending HC, Relethford JH, Sherry ST. 1996. Methods and models for understanding human diversity. In *Molecular Biology and Human Diversity*, ed. AJ Boyce, CGN Mascie-Taylor, pp. 283–99. Cambridge, UK: Cambridge Univ. Press

Harpending HC, Sherry ST, Rogers AR, Stoneking M. 1993. The genetic structure of ancient human populations. *Curr. Anthropol.* 34:483–96

Hedges SB, Kumar S, Tamura K, Stoneking M. 1992. Human origins and analysis of mitochondrial DNA sequences. *Science* 255:737–38

Hey J. 1997. Mitochondrial and nuclear genes present conflicting portraits of human origins. *Mol. Biol. Evol.* 14:166–72

Horai S, Hayasaka K, Kondo R, Tsugane K, Takahata N. 1995. Recent African origin of modern humans revealed by complete sequences of hominoid mitochondrial DNAs. *Proc. Natl. Acad. Sci. USA* 92: 532–36

Howell FC. 1996. Thoughts on the study and interpretation of the human fossil record. In *Contemporary Issues in Human Evolution*, ed. WE Meikle, FC Howell, NG Jablonski, pp. 1–45. San Francisco: Calif. Acad. Sci.

Hudson RR. 1990. Gene genealogies and the coalescent process. *Oxford Surv. Evol. Biol.* 7:1–44

Jorde LB, Bamshad MJ, Watkins WS, Zenger R, Fraley AE, et al. 1995. Origins and affinities of modern humans: a comparison of mitochondrial and nuclear genetic data. *Am. J. Hum. Genet.* 57:523–38

Jorde LB, Rogers AR, Bamshad M, Watkins WS, Krakowiak P, Paabo S. 1997. Microsatellite diversity and the demographic history of modern humans. *Proc. Natl. Acad. Sci. USA* 94:3100–3

Klein J, Takahata N, Ayala FJ. 1993. MHC polymorphism and human origins. *Sci. Am.* 269(12):78–83

Krings M, Stone A, Schmitz RW, Krainitzki H, Stoneking M, et al. 1997. Neandertal DNA sequences and the origin of modern humans. *Cell* 90:19–30

Latter BDH. 1980. Genetic differences within and between populations of the major human groups. *Am. Nat.* 116:220–37

Lewin R. 1993. *The Origin of Modern Humans*. New York: Freeman

Lewontin RC. 1974. The apportionment of human diversity. *Evol. Biol.* 6:381–98

Livshits G, Nei M. 1990. Relationships between intrapopulational and interpopulational genetic diversity in man. *Ann. Hum. Biol.* 6:501–13

Loewe L, Scherer S. 1997. Mitochondrial Eve: the plot thickens. *Trends Ecol. Evol.* 12:422–23

Lynch M. 1989. Phylogenetic hypotheses under the assumption of neutral quantitative-genetic variation. *Evolution* 43:1–17

Maddison DR. 1991. African origin of human mitochondrial DNA reexamined. *Syst. Zool.* 40:355–63

Marjoram P, Donnelly P. 1994. Pairwise comparisons of mitochondrial DNA sequences in subdivided populations and implications for early human evolution. *Genetics* 136:673–83

Marjoram P, Donnelly P. 1997. Human demography and the time since mitochondrial Eve. See Donnelly & Tavaré 1997, pp. 107–31

Maruyama T, Kimura M. 1980. Genetic variability and effective population size when local extinction and recolonization of subpopulations are frequent. *Proc. Natl. Acad. Sci. USA* 77:6710–14

Mellars PA, Stringer CB, eds. 1989. *The Human Revolution: Behavioral and Biological Perspectives on the Origin of Modern Humans.* Princeton: Princeton Univ. Press

Mountain JL, Cavalli-Sforza LL. 1994. Inference of human evolution through cladistic analysis of nuclear DNA restriction polymorphisms. *Proc. Natl. Acad. Sci. USA* 91:6515–19

Nei M. 1978. The theory of genetic distance and the evolution of human races. *Jpn. J. Hum. Genet.* 23:341–69

Nei M, Graur D. 1984. Extent of protein polymorphism and the neutral mutation theory. *Evol. Biol.* 27:73–118

Nei M, Livshits G. 1989. Genetic relationships of Europeans, Asians and Africans and the origin of modern *Homo sapiens. Hum. Hered.* 39:276–81

Nei M, Roychoudhury AK. 1982. Genetic relationship and evolution of human races. *Evol. Biol.* 14:1–59

Nei M, Takahata N. 1993. Effective population size, genetic diversity, and coalescence time in subdivided populations. *J. Mol. Evol.* 37:240–44

Penny D, Steel M, Waddell PJ, Hendy MD. 1995. Improved analyses of human mtDNA sequences support a recent African origin for Homo sapiens. *Mol. Biol. Evol.* 12:863–82

Relethford JH. 1994. Craniometric variation among modern human populations. *Am. J. Phys. Anthropol.* 95:53–62

Relethford JH. 1995. Genetics and modern human origins. *Evol. Anthropol.* 4:53–63

Relethford JH. 1997. Mutation rate and excess African heterozygosity. *Hum. Biol.* 69:785–92

Relethford JH. 1998. Mitochondrial DNA and ancient population growth. *Am. J. Phys. Anthropol.* 105:1–7

Relethford JH, Harpending HC. 1994. Craniometric variation, genetic theory, and modern human origins. *Am. J. Phys. Anthropol.* 95:249–70

Relethford JH, Harpending HC. 1995. Ancient differences in population size can mimic a recent African origin of modern humans. *Curr. Anthropol.* 36:667–74

Rogers AR. 1992. Error introduced by the infinite-sites model. *Mol. Biol. Evol.* 9:1181–84

Rogers AR. 1995. Genetic evidence for a Pleistocene population explosion. *Evolution* 49:608–15

Rogers AR. 1997. Population structure and modern human origins. See Donnelly & Tavaré 1997, pp. 55–79

Rogers AR, Fraley AE, Bamshad MJ, Watkins WS, Jorde LB, et al. 1996. Mitochondrial mismatch analysis is insensitive to the mutational process. *Mol. Biol. Evol.* 13:895–902

Rogers AR, Harpending H. 1992. Population growth makes waves in the distribution of pairwise genetic differences. *Mol. Biol. Evol.* 9:552–69

Rogers AR, Jorde LB. 1995. Genetic evidence on modern human origins. *Hum. Biol.* 67:1–36

Rogers AR, Jorde LB. 1996. Ascertainment bias in estimates of average heterozygosity. *Am. J. Hum. Genet.* 58:1033–41

Ruvolo M, Zehr S, von Dornum M, Pan D, Chang B, Lin J. 1993. Mitochondrial COII sequences and modern human origins. *Mol. Biol. Evol.* 10:1115–35

Ryman N, Chakraborty R, Nei M. 1983. Differences in the relative distribution of human gene diversity between electrophoretic and red and white cell antigen loci. *Hum. Hered.* 33:93–102

Sherry ST. 1996. *Estimating human effective population sizes with genetic models incorporating demographic fluctuation.* PhD thesis. Penn. State Univ., University Park. 146 pp.

Sherry ST, Batzer MA. 1997. Modeling human evolution—To tree or not to tree? *Genome Res.* 7:947–49

Sherry ST, Harpending HC, Batzer MA, Stoneking M. 1997. *Alu* evolution in human populations: using the coalescent to estimate effective population size. *Genetics* 147:1977–82

Sherry ST, Rogers AR, Harpending H, Soodyall H, et al. 1994. Mismatch distributions of mtDNA reveal recent human population expansions. *Hum. Biol.* 66:761–75

Slatkin M. 1977. Gene flow and genetic drift in a species subject to frequent local extinctions. *Theor. Popul. Biol.* 12:253–62

Smith FH, Falsetti AB, Donnelly SM. 1989. Modern human origins. *Yearb. Phys. Anthropol.* 32:35–68

Smith FH, Spencer F, eds. 1984. *The Origins of Modern Humans: A World Survey of the Fossil Evidence.* New York: Liss

Smith SL, Harrold FB. 1997. A paradigm's worth of difference? Understanding the impasse over modern human origins. *Yearb. Phys. Anthropol.* 40:113–38

Spuhler JN. 1988. Evolution of mitochondrial DNA in monkeys, apes, and humans. *Yearb. Phys. Anthropol.* 31:15–48

Stoneking M. 1993. DNA and recent human evolution. *Evol. Anthropol.* 2:60–73

Stoneking M, Cann RL. 1989. African origin of human mitochondrial DNA. See Mellars & Stringer 1989, pp. 17–30

Stoneking M, Fontius JJ, Clifford SL, Soodyall H, Arcot SS, et al. 1997. *Alu* insertion polymorphisms and human evolution: evidence for a larger population size in Africa. *Genome Res.* 7:1061–71

Stoneking M, Sherry ST, Vigilant L. 1992. Geographic origin of human mitochondrial DNA revisited. *Syst. Biol.* 41:384–91

Stringer CB. 1990. The emergence of modern humans. *Sci. Am.* 263(6):98–104

Stringer CB, Andrews P. 1988. Genetic and fossil evidence for the origin of modern humans. *Science* 239:1263–68

Stringer CB, Bräuer G. 1994. Methods, misleading, and bias. *Am. Anthropol.* 96: 416–24

Stringer CB, McKie R. 1996. *African Exodus: The Origins of Modern Humanity.* New York: Holt

Takahata N. 1993. Allelic genealogy and human evolution. *Mol. Biol. Evol.* 10:2–22

Takahata N. 1994. Repeated failures that led to the eventual success in human evolution. *Mol. Bol. Evol.* 11:803–5

Takahata N. 1995. A genetic perspective on the origin and history of humans. *Annu. Rev. Ecol. Syst.* 26:343–72

Takahata N, Satta Y, Klein J. 1995. Divergence time and population size in the lineage leading to modern humans. *Theor. Popul. Biol.* 48:198–221

Templeton AR. 1992. Human origins and analysis of mitochondrial DNA sequences. *Science* 255:737

Templeton AR. 1993. The "Eve" hypothesis: a genetic critique and reanalysis. *Am. Anthropol.* 95:51–72

Templeton AR. 1994. "Eve": hypothesis compatibility versus hypothesis testing. *Am. Anthropol.* 96:141–47

Templeton AR. 1996a. Contingency tests of neutrality using intra/interspecific gene trees: the rejection of neutrality for the evolution of the mitochondrial cytochrome oxidase II gene in the hominoid primates. *Genetics* 144:1263–70

Templeton AR. 1996b. Gene lineages and human evolution. *Science* 272:1363

Templeton AR. 1997. Testing the Out of Africa replacement hypothesis with mitochondrial DNA data. See Clark & Willermet 1997, pp. 329–60

Thorne AG, Wolpoff MH. 1992. The multiregional evolution of humans. *Sci. Am.* 266 (4):76–83

Thorne AG, Wolpoff MH, Eckhardt RB. 1993. Genetic variation in Africa. *Science* 261: 1507–8

Tishkoff SA, Dietzsch E, Speed W, Pakstis AJ, Kidd JR, et al. 1996. Global patterns of linkage disequilibrium at the CD4 locus and modern human origins. *Science* 271: 1380–87

Underhill PA, Jin L, Lin AA, Mehdi SQ, Jenkins T, et al. 1997. Detection of numerous Y chromosome biallelic polymorphisms by denaturing high-performance liquid chromatography. *Genome Res.* 7: 996–1005

Vigilant L, Stoneking M, Harpending H, Hawkes K, Wilson AC. 1991. African populations and the evolution of human mitochondrial DNA. *Science* 253:1503–7

Waddle DM. 1994. Matrix correlation tests support a single origin for modern humans. *Nature* 368:452–54

Weiss KM. 1984. On the number of members of the genus *Homo* who have ever lived, and some evolutionary implications. *Hum. Biol.* 56:637–49

Weiss KM. 1988. In search of times past: gene flow and invasion in the generation of human diversity. In *Biological Aspects of Human Migration*, ed. CGN Mascie-Taylor, GW Lasker, pp. 130–66. Cambridge, UK: Cambridge Univ. Press

Weiss KM, Maruyama T. 1976. Archeology, population genetics and studies of human racial ancestry. *Am. J. Phys. Anthropol.* 44:31–50

Whitfield LS, Sulston JE, Goodfellow PN. 1995. Sequence variation of the human Y chromosome. *Nature* 378:379–80

Whitlock MC, Barton NH. 1997. The effective size of a subdivided population. *Genetics* 146:427–41

Whittam TS, Clark AG, Stoneking M, Cann RL, Wilson AC. 1986. Allelic variation in human mitochondrial genes based on patterns of restriction site polymorphism. *Proc. Natl. Acad. Sci. USA* 83:9611–15

Wills C. 1995. When did Eve live? An evolutionary detective story. *Evolution* 49:593–607

Wilson AC, Cann RL, Carr SM, George M, Gyllensten UB, et al. 1985. Mitochondrial DNA and two perspectives on evolutionary genetics. *Biol. J. Linn. Soc.* 26:375–400

Wise CA, Sraml M, Rubinsztein DC, Easteal S. 1997. Comparative nuclear and mitochondrial genome diversity in humans and chimpanzees. *Mol. Biol. Evol.* 14:707–16

Wobst HM. 1974. Boundary conditions for Paleolithic social systems: a simulation approach. *Am. Antiq.* 39:147–78

Wolpoff MH. 1989. Multiregional evolution: the fossil alternative to Eden. See Mellars & Stringer 1989, pp. 62–108

Wolpoff MH, Caspari R. 1997. *Race and Human Evolution.* New York: Simon & Schuster

Wolpoff MH, Thorne AG, Smith FH, Frayer DW, Pope GG. 1994. Multiregional evolution: a world-wide source for modern human populations. In *Origins of Anatomically Modern Humans,* ed. MH Nitecki, DV Nitecki, pp. 175–99. New York: Plenum

Wolpoff MH, Wu X, Thorne AG. 1984. Modern *Homo sapiens* origins: a general theory of hominid evolution involving the fossil evidence from East Asia. See Smith & Spencer 1984, pp. 411–83

Wright S. 1940. Breeding structure of populations in relation to speciation. *Am. Nat.* 74:232–48

Wright S. 1951. The genetical structure of populations. *Ann. Eugen.* 15:323–54

Wright S. 1969. *Evolution and the Genetics of Populations.* Vol. 2: *The Theory of Gene Frequencies.* Chicago: Univ. Chicago Press

*Annu. Rev. Anthropol. 1998. 27:25–62*
*Copyright 1998 by Annual Reviews. All rights reserved*

# MISSION ARCHAEOLOGY

*Elizabeth Graham*

Department of Anthropology, York University, North York, Ontario, Canada M3J
1P3; e-mail: egraham@rom.on.ca; egraham@yorku.ca

KEY WORDS: historical archaeology, Spanish borderlands, conversion, religion, Maya

### ABSTRACT

"Mission archaeology" is a novel conjunction of terms devised to focus attention on an archaeology of mission sites, and thereby on the light that can be shed on the process of the Christianization of the Americas by examining the material culture of missions. Discussion centers on a summary of mission research in the Spanish-occupied territories of North America and Mayan Mesoamerica. I then draw conclusions from these data, and from anthropological and historical analyses of mission encounters, to suggest where mission studies should be headed and the role that archaeology can play in expanding our knowledge of the mission transformation.

## GUIDING QUESTIONS

### What Is Mission Archaeology?

"Mission archaeology" is not a recognized subfield of anthropology. In order to synthesize and assess its practices and progress, first I ascribe meaning to mission archaeology, and second, I explain how archaeology has contributed to a general understanding of the role that Christian missions and missionaries played in the European displacement of indigenous peoples in the Americas.

DEFINING MISSION    The colonizing process, the spread of the Christian faith, and the enculturation of the Indians are common to all missionizing efforts, and this commonality at first led me to consider a rather tight definition of missions:

0084-6570/98/1015-0025$08.00

> A mission is an ecclesiastical unit of area of sufficient size, within which all activities (such as construction, farming, handicrafts, herding, recreation, etc) are administered by a ministry commissioned by, and dependent upon, a larger religious organization for direction or financial support. (Snow 1967:59)

Although this definition has the advantage of situating missions globally, it privileges a mission ideal only nearly achieved in Alta California (Jackson 1994:37) and Paraguay (Whigham 1995:157–159), and it represents only a facet of the mission experience. In-depth knowledge is better achieved by broad research that extends beyond the ideal mission community to communities with only *visita* churches; to mission communities with limited resources and permeable boundaries; to the full range of Indian settlements, both Christian and non-Christian; and to colonial communities as well, with the understanding that local conditions are critical in explaining the diversity of mission encounters.

DEFINING ARCHAEOLOGY   Having thus defined the mission component of mission archaeology, what about the archaeology component? Does it refer only to excavations, or to studies of material culture as well? Is all historical or ethnohistorical research relevant, or only that bearing on the location of the mission site? I take the broadest view possible and consider a range of research that not only helps to locate and excavate mission sites, but also illuminates the historical, demographic, or sociocultural context of mission encounters.

## What Areas Will Be Covered, and What Is the Rationale for Selection?

My coverage is spotty and perforce dominated by North American material, where so much mission research has been carried out and published. I consider a limited range of work on missions and church-period sites carried out in Mexico, but much of it, like my own work in Belize, is relatively recent or adjunct to architectural survey or to prehistoric work, leaving full excavation reports and syntheses yet unpublished. I do not explore the Caribbean encounter or South America. I hope, however, that the conclusions I draw from a review of mission archaeology will be useful to scholars in other areas. For example, a comparison of the North American-Mesoamerican missionizing experiences suggests that, for the Spanish church, the conversion of urbanized peoples was logistically and perhaps structurally a less daunting task than the conversion of nonagriculturalists or foragers. Christianity was a religion well rooted in urban traditions, and an outgrowth of societies that were highly specialized and hierarchical (Herrin 1987:20–23; Pagden 1982:21–22). Complex social and economic structures of Mesoamerica and the Andes could readily be adjusted to support, and be supported by, Christianity. Ironically, this meant that "the most powerful polities were the least able to resist the Spanish *conquista*" (McGuire & Villalpando 1989:160–161).

## Who Is Interested in Mission Research, and Why?

Those with an interest in missions come from a variety of backgrounds and disciplines. Anthropologists target the role of Christian missionaries in the transformation of non-Western societies (Peel 1995:581). In New World mission histories, Catholic historians have generally chronicled missionary expansion for its success in Christianizing the Indians (Arias 1994; Engelhardt 1908–1915; Geiger 1937, 1969; Shea 1855) and for information on friars and priests who were martyred (Harkins 1990).

Archaeologists interested in missions include those focused specifically on the contact experience (e.g. Deagan 1983, Deagan & Cruxent 1993, Thomas 1993, South 1988), as well as those who examine mission documents for the information they contain on indigenous groups at the time of contact (Latta 1985). In California, where extant mission buildings are seen as idealized representations of California's Spanish-period past, standing architecture has become a focus of study for its own sake (Baer 1958), and archaeology is used to recover information for the reconstruction of mission buildings for tourists. In Mesoamerica, the concern with missionizing efforts and the location of churches grows from an interest in the politics of conquest and colonization.

Sturtevant once suggested (1962:42) that anthropologists attribute differences in the course of Indian-European relations in colonial Latin America to the variety in responses of differing Indian cultures (Service 1955), while historians attribute the course of colonial relations to differing European policies, actions, and institutions. Historians now include native policies and institutions in their scope (Jackson 1995, Langer & Jackson 1995, Weber 1990), but anthropological writing has still not explored European Christian religious roots and practices with a critical eye for difference and contradiction.

Most researchers are united by an interest in the role of the missionaries and the church in transforming native American societies and in the structuring of new societies in the Americas. The differences lie in methods of investigation (documentary vs material cultural) and methods of inquiry (historical vs anthropological). Ethnohistorians' focus on documents perforce privileges European narratives, and archaeologists' focus on material culture highlights native responses, but cooperation and interchange are widespread, so that a good balance of perspectives is being achieved (Thomas 1989a, 1990a, 1991b).

The next section lays out a theoretical context for understanding mission archeology. This is followed by a survey of regional patterns in mission archaeology. The final section expands on investigations in the Maya area, and highlights theoretical issues.

# WHERE SHOULD MISSION STUDIES BE HEADED, AND WHAT ROLE DOES ARCHAEOLOGY HAVE IN EXPANDING OUR KNOWLEDGE OF THE MISSION ENCOUNTER?

## Christianity and the Cultural Imagination

In both history and anthropology, missionaries are generally depicted as agents of imperialism (Farnsworth & Jackson 1995, McGuire & Villalpando 1989). Underplayed in these analyses is the impact on what has been called the cultural imagination of the proselytized. (See Ranger n.d. in Comaroff & Comaroff 1986:1.) The idea of an evolving or changing cultural imagination as the result of the mission encounter can be taken in two directions, and both lines of inquiry can benefit from archaeological input.

## The Native American Cultural Imagination

The first direction is suggested by the Comaroffs' (1986) insights into the African experience. They examine the cultural implications of the mission and specifically how these affect political processes, with a focus on the interplay of power and meaning (Comaroff & Comaroff 1986:1). They consider the role of the missionary in terms of his power to impose "conditions of being" on others. These conditions have been generally recognized as institutional and political, but the Comaroffs draw attention to the spheres of "aesthetics and religion, built form and bodily presentation, medical knowledge and the mundane habits of everyday life" (Comaroff & Comaroff 1986:2).

The Comaroffs contrast what might be called the variable role of the missionary in the political domain with the decisive role the missionary played in imposing new modes of perception and practice on Africans. Like the missions in the New World, the missions in Africa failed to create a unified ideal society built on Christian principles (Phelan 1970), but both continental enterprises succeeded in generating the restructuring of the native conceptual universe. This restructuring indeed helped to underpin the new order, but also exposed its contradictions (Comaroff & Comaroff 1986:2; Comaroff 1989:661; Sweet 1995:40).

In the New World as in Africa, such contradictions made protest not only possible but effective. Protest in the political sphere is the most easily documented, and such manifestations, especially outright revolt, are most likely to surface in European accounts [e.g. the 1597 Guale Revolt in Florida (de Oré 1936), the Pueblo Revolt in 1680 (Hackett & Shelby 1942), the lowland Maya rebellion in 1638 (Jones 1989:19), or the Tzeltal Revolt in 1712–1713 (MacLeod 1991:384–385)]. However, where protest is manifested in more mundane aspects of life such as religious expression, aesthetics, built form, or representation—although potentially more effective than rebellion (MacLeod 1991:376–377)—it is more difficult to detect from documents and ethnohistoric accounts alone.

I suggest that the material record—built form, representation, etc—be examined as a reflection of the idea of changing cultural imagination and reordering of a conceptual universe.

The bias in archaeology has been to emphasize the political role of Christianity as a religion of the state, and thereby to interpret pre-Columbian elements in religious material culture as resistance phenomena. But this interpretation plays on reactive rather than proactive imagery. Responses to mission encounters are not only efforts to thwart domination, but also efforts to "fashion an understanding of, and gain conceptual mastery over, a changing world" (Comaroff & Comaroff 1991:31). Resistance and protest occur alongside active reexamination of former values, together with the development of new concepts about the world that indeed receive European input, but are the product of indigenous minds. Of the many aspects of the material record that might reflect native conceptual gains, the most revealing is the record of the Christianization process. Archaeologists must be careful not to adopt the simplistic approach of colonial Catholic priests and interpret the material culture of mission sites as manifestations of either acceptance or rejection of Christianity.

## The Cultural Imagination of Europeans

As individuals adopt new beliefs, practice old rituals, and consider new shared experiences as part of becoming Christian, Christianity undergoes conversion by being continually transformed. The Christianity that reached the New World in the sixteenth century had undergone changes of varying intensity since its inception; recognizing New World transformations as part of this continuum is a key to understanding the process of Christianization in missions. Mission research, then, should also be headed toward a more critical stance regarding European Christianity and its historical contradictions.

The overwhelming impression derived from mission archaeology is that Christianity is both monolithic and genetically European. Even in complex treatments of native responses (Brown 1996, Comaroff & Comaroff 1986, Furniss 1995), the practice has been to consider incoming Christianity as a colonial package, and to view native responses as the forces that unwrap, disassemble, and re-sort the package's contents. Christianity is not represented as an ongoing process that began long before European expansion. We could say, reflecting Wolf (1984), that what we have here is European Christianity without history.

In addition, Christianity is regarded as always having been part of the European character. Yet Europeans have no more claim to the roots of Christianity than do native Americans. Neither produced Jesus of Nazareth, and the history of the adaptive and often sponge-like process of the Christianization of the New World closely parallels the history of the Christianization of Europe in terms of the interaction between changing beliefs and traditional rituals. Christian ritual and imagery in Europe were, after all, heavily influenced by the pre-Christian religions of indigenous Europeans. By the time Christianity was brought to the New World, it was already syncretic, although by then, syncretic imagery had been internalized by proselytizers as Christian. Given this scenario, it is easy to see that any view of European Christianity as monolithic would mask recognition of the sources of contradictions exposed as European conditions of being were required of the Indians.

Therefore the first thing we must do in mission archaeology is let doubt creep in regarding Europeans' claims to knowing Christianity any better than native Americans, or to experiencing Christianity in any superior way. The idea of European Christianity as genuine or authentic is not an explicit stance, but it underlies studies of syncretism (Thompson 1954), partial conversion (Klor de Alva 1982), and otherwise detailed and insightful studies of indigenous belief systems (Burkhart 1989). These studies imply that indigenous peoples never quite understood Christianity; but, as Ricard (1966:278) pointed out, many so-called Indian superstitions are European in origin. And as for the Indians' so-called weak grasp of doctrine, it would be interesting to know how many Spaniards counted knowledge of church doctrine as one of their great strengths. The direction of culture, too, is always seen as being *from* Europe *to* the New World, and the Indians either accept or reject Christianity as European. This is not the venue to list the ways in which the culture of the New World affected the Old (in food, architecture, art, design, for example), but it should be noted that religion and culture in the New World deeply affected and altered Christianity, not only as it has come to be practiced in the New World, but also as it came to be practiced in Europe (Kehoe 1979).

## THE STUDY REGIONS

The study regions comprise what has come to be known as the Spanish Borderlands (Bolton 1921), more recently proposed as el Gran Norte Español (Jiménez 1996). Because my own experience has been in Mesoamerica, I include recent work on missions in the Maya lowlands.

For each of the study regions, I ask the following questions:

1. What is distinctive about the research?
2. What is distinctive about the region?
3. What has been learned through archaeology about the mission layout and material culture change?

## La Florida and the Southeastern United States

DISTINCTIVE RESEARCH CONTEXT   No one interested in the archaeology and ethnohistory of missions anywhere in the New World should neglect to read the literature on the missions of La Florida, an area that includes the present-day state of Florida, the Georgia coast, and the southeastern coast of South Carolina (Thomas 1990b:357). The cohesiveness with which research on the Spanish mission enterprise has proceeded in La Florida is, in my view, unmatched elsewhere. I have therefore devoted more space to the context of inquiry in this region than in others, and I use the discussion as a vehicle for general comments on mission research.

The distinctive qualities of La Florida mission research derive from the history of archaeological work, the lack of standing mission architecture, and the nature of the research community.

*History of archaeological work and the lack of standing mission architecture*
Archaeology in Florida has not been preoccupied with pre-Columbian cultures to the exclusion of post-contact remains. Florida's post-contact remains, in turn, lack the standing architecture that captured the late nineteenth- and twentieth-century imagination of Californians with regard to their missions (James 1973, Baer 1958). Concerted effort to locate and study missions in Florida began with Boyd (1939, 1948), who first used primary Spanish accounts methodically to illuminate Florida's mission period. Although he worked with documents, his interest in locating missions led inevitably to collaboration with archaeologists. He and his colleagues laid the foundations of long-term cooperation between historians and archaeologists in 1951 with a publication in which a range of important documents were assembled and translated; excavations of mission sites, whose location was aided by the documents, were reported for the first time (Boyd et al 1951), as were the initial guidelines for the location of mission and other Spanish-period sites in Florida. Boyd's contribution lies not only in his efforts to make the information from early Spanish and English documents widely available, but also in his lively narrative and rich contextual presentation of documentary details.

Subsequent historians and ethnohistorians have enriched the tradition by drawing on documentary research to assess various facets of the mission and colonization process (Lyon 1976, Sturtevant 1962, Weber 1990), and by using documents to reconstruct contact-period or pre-Hispanic social, political, and material cultural conditions (e.g. Hann 1988, Hudson et al 1985, Jones 1978, Widmer 1988). Primary documents continue to be translated and/or made more widely accessible (Hann 1993a, Thomas 1991a), or used to reconstruct mission locations and encounters (Hann 1990, 1991, 1993b). In addition, broader treatments and analyses are available (Marquardt 1987, 1988; Milanich & Proctor 1978).

*Nature of the research community*    The La Florida research community was, until recently, relatively small, with two institutions, the University of Florida and Florida State University, providing the bulk of academic scholars. Notable exceptions are the research carried out by the American Museum of Natural History (Thomas 1993) and by the University of South Carolina (South 1988). These scholars have worked closely with researchers based in government departments, such as the National Park Service and the Florida Bureau of Archaeological Research.

Reports on excavations in Florida are generally accessible. Although knowledge of Spanish is necessary to read documents, English is the dominant language of publication. This contrasts with Canada, where the French-speaking scholarly community and the English-speaking scholarly community, both working on the Jesuit missions, maintain relatively discrete enterprises. Where Florida research does not appear in national journals or books, it can be found in a range of academic publications focused on Florida research in history, anthropology, and archaeology.

DISTINCTIVE REGIONAL CONTEXT    The Jesuits were the first to missionize Florida; they were replaced in 1604 by the Franciscans, who remained until 1704 (Deagan 1990:304). In Spanish eyes, Florida was resource-poor, largely owing to the lack of minerals and metals (Deagan 1990:301), but the Spaniards also had difficulties in adjusting to Florida's subtropical environment. Soil that could support sustained agriculture existed only in the area of Apalachee, in west Florida, and this led to problems in furnishing Spanish settlers, particularly in St. Augustine, with food (Matter 1990:7; Thomas 1990b:367–369). Florida's native peoples were highly mobile; although most practiced agriculture, they readily turned to hunting and gathering when stored food ran low (Matter 1990:9). The *entradas* of Narváez and DeSoto encountered complex chiefdoms and large populations (1513–1561) in northwest Florida, but by the time the Spaniards returned to settle and missionize Florida, disease had taken its toll, populations had declined, and these complex sociopolitical systems had fragmented (Milanich 1990:10–17; Fairbanks 1985: 133–134,139 in Thomas 1990b:367). Ultimately, British and Indian attacks resulted in the burning of St. Augustine in 1702, and in the destruction of the mission communities in North Florida in 1704 (Deagan 1983:26). Recent syntheses of documentary evidence on Florida missions and native cultures are listed in Thomas 1990a and McEwan 1993a.

ARCHAEOLOGY    The best-known mission sites occur in the areas of the Apalachee, Timucua, and Guale Indians. The chiefdoms of the nonagricultural but sedentary Calusa, farther south, were never successfully missionized (Hann 1988:226). Some of the better-known sites that have been excavated and reported are St. Augustine (Deagan 1978, 1983, 1990, 1993), San Luis de Talimali (McEwan 1991, 1993b; McEwan & Larsen 1996), Mission Santa Catalina de Guale in Georgia (Thomas 1987, 1988, 1993; Thomas et al 1978), Fig Springs Mission (Weisman 1992, 1993), Mission Patale (Marrinan 1993), Missions Santa María and Santa Catalina de Amelia (Saunders 1993), Mission Santa Fé de Toloca (Johnson 1993), and Baptizing Spring (Loucks 1993). Of these, St. Augustine was not a mission but a Spanish residential town with a church and fortifications; San Luis was a mission but had resident Spanish families as well as Christianized Apalachees (McEwan 1993b:297) and was also fortified; the remaining sites were missions with exclusively native residents and a friar or friars to administer to the community.

MISSION LAYOUT   The general mission model proposes a complex of church, convento or friary, and cocina or kitchen/storage structure (McAndrew 1965: 133). These exist in La Florida but vary in size, in relation to one another, and in their individual features. Church and burial orientation is east-west or a near variation, and churches are likely to have subfloor burials. Altars are at the west end, which is at variance with the European tradition (McEwan 1991:47, Saunders 1990:528), yet church proportions, at least at the site of San Luis, were dictated by the Golden Rectangle (McEwan & Larsen 1996). The feet of burials point toward the altar end (Marrinan 1993). Burial goods are generally sparse or nonexistent in Florida missions and in the Spanish settlements, with the exception of Santa Catalina de Guale, on St. Catherine's Island, which contained a wide variety of grave goods, and the Florida sites of Patale I, San Damian de Escambi (Thomas 1990b:384; 1993), and San Luis (McEwan & Larsen 1996). The evidence from both Santa Catalina de Guale and San Luis indicates that higher-status burials were placed near the altar (Thomas 1990b:384; McEwan & Larsen 1996).

Mission buildings were constructed of either vertical boards or wattle and daub with thatched roofs, and depending on the area could reflect either Hispanic or Guale traditions (McEwan 1993b:314; Saunders 1990:529). Although archaeology has revealed the dimensions and character of some native residences (Shapiro & Hann 1990), native settlements or pueblos of mission sites have not been excavated (Marrinan 1993:283), nor have Indian town sites in St. Augustine (Deagan 1990:307) or San Luis (McEwan 1993b).

MATERIAL CULTURE   Indian pottery forms persist largely unchanged through the mission period at St. Augustine, whereas at mission sites the Indian ceramic assemblage displays European formal elements (Deagan 1990:307). It seems that at sites of Hispanic settlement the Spaniards did not try to make local pottery conform to Spanish tastes, and the indications are, coupled with documentary evidence, that Spanish men frequently married Indian, and particularly Guale, women. This evidence also reflects the adoption of aboriginal foodways and ceramic functions by the Spaniards (Deagan 1978:33). With regard to life in the missions, it is possible that the friars required Indian pottery substitutes for Spanish tablewares (Deagan 1990:307–309).

Locally made pottery, olive jars, and majolica ware from Spain and Mexico and other European wares, as well as some indigenous ceramics from Yucatan and other areas of Mexico, occur in Florida contexts (Deagan 1978, 1987). Other kinds of artifacts, too varied to detail here (Deagan 1987), include brass (rings, shoebuckles), iron (nails, locks), glass beads, jet, buttons, household items, and jewelry, often found in middens (McEwan 1991:47) rather than in burials. Ceramic analysis reveals that aboriginal influence was strongest in kitchen areas, indicating, as do the documents, that Indian women dominated the domestic sphere in Spanish households and were paired with Spanish men (Deagan 1983:122; 1990:309).

## The American Southwest, or the Mexican Northwest

This area includes the modern Mexican states of Sonora and Chihuahua, and the US states of Arizona, New Mexico, southwestern Colorado, southeastern Utah, and a portion of western Texas. Prior to Anglo-American expansion into Mexican territories in the nineteenth century and the formation of the modern boundaries of the United States, this region was part of Mexico. Therefore the term Northwest is used by some scholars (McGuire & Villalpando 1989). When the term Northwest is used, it includes the mining frontier of Chichimeca.

DISTINCTIVE RESEARCH CONTEXT   Most archaeological research on the early historic period in the Southwest was carried out earlier in this century (Lycett 1989:117), when the goal was often to stabilize ruins to promote tourism (Hewett & Fisher 1943). Excavations were often extensive, but with some exceptions (Montgomery et al 1949), little was published and/or analyzed at the time. Cordell (1989:33), however, following Wilcox & Masse (1981), cites a number of individuals whose analyses or reporting since then have illuminated historic material (e.g. Dutton 1985; Stubbs 1959; Toulouse & Stephenson 1960; Vivian 1964).

In the Southwest, pre-Columbian archaeology still captures the lion's share of attention. Research designed specifically to focus on missions or on the transformation of communities that became part of the mission system is relatively underdeveloped in comparison to Florida or Texas. But the Park Service, the Bureau of Land Management, and the Forest Service have extended cultural resource management activities to archaeological sites with historic components, and these agencies have produced invaluable reports on archaeological and historical research (e.g. Hayes 1981 and Hayes et al 1981 for the National Park Service; Marshall & Walt 1984 for state historic preservation interests; or Tainter & Gillio 1980 and Tainter & Levine 1987 for the Bureau of Land Management). Although reports by state and federal agencies are not as widely accessible as museum or standard press outlets (e.g. Hayes 1974), the body of work is becoming better known and is contributing to a range of recent archaeological and documentary endeavors, such as those represented in the landmark *Columbian Consequences* volumes (Thomas 1989a).

Historical and documentary research in the Southwest is characterized by intensive and sustained interest in the mission and contact experience (Thomas 1989a). Research has been carried out both by historians and ethnohistorians working within a larger-scale Spanish colonial framework (e.g. Bolton 1921; Scholes 1929, 1936–1937; Weber 1979, 1988), and by local institutions with regional interests, such as the Documentary Relations of the Southwest project (DRSW), begun in 1974 at the Arizona State Museum, and the wealth of Spanish colonial documentary literature sponsored by the Quivira Society (Polzer 1989:181–182).

One criticism of this research context is that there is too much emphasis on institutional history: the mission, the presidio, the hacienda, the real de minas (Polzer 1989:181). According to Polzer, historians and archaeologists should be examining development and change in mission dependence on social systems in the interior of New Spain. This criticism is certainly apposite, but when relatively little mission work has been undertaken, it is quite an achievement, *pace* Polzer (1989:181), to "dig up a mission." At Awatovi, no descriptions of the mission buildings are known from archives. Thus the size and design of some of the mission buildings, particularly the foundations for a grandiose second church and a substantial military barrack and stable revealed by excavation, came as quite a surprise to the archaeologists, who had expected humbler architecture (Brew 1994:31,45–46).

DISTINCTIVE REGIONAL CONTEXT   The Southwest/Northwest environment is varied, comprising mountains, mesas, broad valleys, desert, plateaus, and wooded mountains (Cordell 1989:17). However, because the friars depended on irrigation, and irrigation depended on water availability, it is the region's aridity more than any other environmental feature that affected the agricultural productivity of the missions (Adams 1989:82).

The Southwest/Northwest region formed a cohesive cultural area from about A.D. 1400 to 1700 (Cordell 1989:17,18). Most groups were sedentary agriculturalists who cultivated corn, beans, and squash and also hunted and gathered. They had permanent architecture and storage facilities. There was some unification of villages but no state-level organization. Nonetheless, groups were united by sociopolitical, religious, and economic interaction (Cordell 1989:18; Riley 1987).

Although the region lacked mineral wealth worthy of exploitation, areas were tapped for Indian labor and food supplies for the mines farther south in Nuevo Leon and Zacatecas. Ultimately, though, Christianization of the Indians became the main colonizing force. Unlike Texas, California, or Florida, where settlement was initiated in order to forestall colonization by other colonial powers, the Southwest was not settled to defend the empire. The region is distinctive in that it attracted a substantial number of Spanish colonists. By 1820 there were fewer than 2500 colonists in Texas and only about 3000 in California, whereas there were about 28,000 in New Mexico and Arizona; these were people of Spanish origin, mestizos, and hispanicized Indians (Cordell 1989:18–19).

The Jesuit mission program began in the 1590s in the Pimeria Alta, which included Sonora and southern Arizona, and was epitomized by Fray Eusebio Francisco Kino, the dominant figure here of Jesuit expansion (Cordell 1989: 30). The Franciscans concerned themselves with the Hopi, the Zuni, and the Pueblo peoples in New Mexico; their missionizing began in the seventeenth century when about 40 mission churches were built in New Mexico (Cordell 1989:27–28). The missionary effort in Arizona and Sonora produced highly variable responses, from the complete withdrawal of the Hopi to Pima agricultural transformation. New Mexico became the focus of colonial settlement, and after the Pueblo Revolt of 1680, Puebloans and hispanos (descendants of Spanish settlers who could be of mixed ancestry) frequently served as godparents for each other's children (Kessell 1989:133). Therefore the archaeology of missions and related communities ought to reflect the complexity of acculturation strategies on both sides that led to the varied communities in existence today, from Indian Pueblos to the hispanic/hispano communities that maintain a tradition of Spanish language, law, and custom.

What distinguished resistance in the Southwest/Northwest? Many of the Indian leaders, specifically among Pueblo groups, were strongly anti-Spaniard. They closely guarded Pueblo beliefs and religious practices, and their political leadership remains in place today (Cordell 1989:23; Dozier 1970). Only a few Franciscans learned Pueblo languages well, because Puebloans guarded their language to preserve their culture (Kessell 1989:133). Among the Arizona Hopi, Christian beliefs were internalized only at Awatovi, as indicated by burials placed in the nave of the ruined church after Awatovi was burned in the Pueblo Revolt (Brew 1994:31,38).

Archaeology might tell us more about how Hopi leadership remained strong. Was Christianity rejected totally, with all its material cultural representations and rituals, or was there appropriation of sacred places or imagery or ritual paraphernalia (Farriss 1993, Graham 1995) that does not surface in the documents or in Hopi accounts? What effect did the arrival of apostate groups from the eastern Pueblos have on the Hopi? Why did this strengthen their resistance rather than weaken their defenses by intergroup rivalry? In this light, the Pueblo Revolt of 1680 is itself remarkable, because it is the only time in history when the traditionally independent Pueblo entities have ever acted in concert (Brew 1994:42). The archaeology of mission and *visita* sites could be investigated with a view toward distinguishing how the details of mission life impinged on pan-Pueblo values and minimized the effects of Spaniards' cooptation of powerful leaders.

The Southwest/Northwest region is also distinguished by the presence of non-Christianized Plains Indians, mainly Apache and Comanche, who preyed on Spanish and Christianized Indian settlements with increasing ferocity in the colonial period. The Pueblo had a long-standing trade relationship with the Apache, but the nature of trade changed with Spanish colonization and missionization. Archaeological data from excavations at Gran Quivira Pueblo show that both long-distance hunting and acquisition of bison meat became problematic for the Pueblo, and in response, they increased their dependence on small mammals (Spielmann 1989).

The Pimeria Alta was occupied by Piman-speaking groups who practiced a range of subsistence strategies from nomadic hunting and gathering to partial reliance on floodwater agriculture to irrigation (Doyel 1989:139–141). Although the documentary and ethnographic literature has been analyzed for information on the hispanic acculturation of some groups, such as the Gila River Pima (Ezell 1961), not enough archaeological work on missions has been carried out to indicate the historical processes involved in countering and/or accommodating the Spaniards and their Christian message. The introduction of wheat and the horse transformed local economies (Doyel 1989:145). Nonetheless, populations were reduced as the result of epidemics (Jackson 1981) and Apache attacks. The only people whose population increased were the Gila Pima, who had not been missionized. The Gila selectively adopted subsistence and technology-related items, but their native religion is interpreted by anthropologists as intact (Doyel 1989:146).

Archaeological excavation of Gila Pima historic sites might reveal details of the selective process and serve as a comparison to cases in which material culture was altered within the mission system. Only archaeological excavation of missions, mission ranches, and non-mission sites can provide the details of adoption, accommodation, and rejection that resulted in Indian survival or extinction.

ARCHAEOLOGY AND MISSION LAYOUT  The typical southwestern mission complex (drawn from Bunting 1976; Kubler 1972; Marrinan 1993:282–283) is made up of two components: the core of religious-use buildings and the general occupation area. The core comprises the church and *convento* and these are often a single unit joined by a common wall, or they are separated by an alleyway. The *convento* is usually situated on the same site as the sacristy, which is the room off the sanctuary where the priest dresses for mass and where altar paraphernalia are stored. The church has a single nave, and the sanctuary or altar area can be raised or level with the nave floor. There is sometimes a clerestory. Burials, as was the case in Florida, are beneath the floor of the church, and they are oriented with the feet toward the sanctuary.

One of the more revealing comparisons of indigenous vs Spanish European manipulation and use of space is evident in the Awatovi excavations (Montgomery et al 1949), where the Franciscans placed their church and one of the schoolrooms over a kiva (Brew 1994:30,41) and where in turn there is considerable evidence of Hopi reuse and remodeling of Franciscan buildings after the mission was abandoned as a result of the Pueblo Revolt. For example, the Hopi subdivided friary spaces into two to four rooms. Doorways were also materially reduced in width and height (Brew 1994:39).

Awatovi is interesting in other ways. Although its friary did not have two stories as did the wealthier missions of Mexico, Father Porras' church was a startling undertaking. The foundations indicated that it was to have been a cruciform building with a nave well over 100 ft in length and 30 ft wide, with a transept in the range of 30 ft by 45 ft (Brew 1994:31). Father Porras died in 1633, however, and the building was never completed. The friary consisted of 16 rooms of various sizes surrounding the garden. A number of other buildings and features were also identified, among them a kitchen, portico, workyard, military barrack, stable, shops, storage rooms, shelters for animals, a corral, and facilities for industrial activities, such as soap-making (Brew 1994:42,45). The sequence of use at Awatovi is uniquely documented and reveals much about Hopi vs Spanish concepts of ritual and domestic space (Fletcher 1977: 111–139), and about power and manipulation of space in hegemonic circumstances.

MATERIAL CULTURE   Material culture change is well documented at Walpi (Adams 1982, 1989:85) where, during the mission period, the Hopi were encouraged to adopt Spanish pottery designs such as flowers. Forms were also introduced that reflected Spanish tastes, such as candlesticks and everted rims of serving bowls (Adams 1989:85). Since supplies to missions arrived infrequently, as was the case in Florida, the friars encouraged local manufacture of styles reminiscent of Spain. Post-missionary Walpi is quite different. The form and design of bowls and jars were influenced by the Tanoan people, who moved into the area in the late 1690s (Adams 1989:85). All forms of Spanish design were eliminated, and ceramics found in burials again reflected native preferences, although not just Hopi preferences this time. This is similar to the situation at Lamanai, in Belize (Pendergast 1993), where, after a Maya rebellion, pre-Columbian–style ceramic censers reappear and are found cached in church destruction debris.

Corn remained the center of the diet, although European domesticates such as peaches and melons were added. The major impact on the eighteenth-century Hopi economy was the introduction of sheep, and wool replaced cotton as the most popular textile (Adams 1989:85).

## Texas/Northeast Mexico

DISTINCTIVE RESEARCH CONTEXT   Hester (1989a:202–203) summarizes the history of archaeological research on the missions of Texas, and a good cross-section of the archaeological work appears in the same volume. Archaeology was initiated in the 1930s, but the fieldwork was poor by modern standards and irreparable damage was done to mission buildings. Museums carried out work on mission sites in the 1950s and 1960s at Fort St. Louis, at an Apache mission site, and at the San Antonio missions that had undergone restoration programs in the 1930s. Publication of results was fairly consistent (Gilmore 1967, 1969; Greer 1967; Schuetz 1966, 1968, 1969; Tunnell & Ambler 1967; Tunnell & Newcomb 1969). In the 1970s, archaeological research at mission and other Spanish colonial sites expanded, with more focus on the Indian inhabitants. The Center for Archaeological Research at the University of Texas at San Antonio (CAR-UTSA) and the Texas Historical Commission initiated the research, which resulted in the establishment of the San Antonio Mission National Historical Park for the protection of mission resources. Work continued in the late 1970s at missions, mission ranches, and other colonial sites: e.g. Fox (1989) at Rancho de las Cabras; Ivey (1981) at Mission Espada ranch on the Rio Grande; the missions of San Juan Bautista and San Bernardo in Coahuila (Campbell 1979; Eaton 1981, 1989); Corbin (1989) on the missions of eastern Texas; and Gilmore (1984, 1989) on the Karankawa Mission Rosario. In the 1980s, Fox (e.g. 1985, 1988) directed mission archaeological investigations in San Antonio.

Almost all of the excavation reporting has been in state or state university publications, such as those of the University of Texas at San Antonio, the Texas Archaeological Research Laboratory at Austin, the CAR-UTSA, the State Building Commission in Austin, the Texas Parks and Wildlife Department in Austin, and the Texas Historical Survey Committee. The reporting of Texas mission work has been notably consistent, and it is a model for how effectively state or provincially supported archaeology can proceed. This is partly due to the fact that most missions are located on public land (AA Fox, personal communication). A permit from the Texas Historical Commission is required to investigate a historic monument or site on public land, and the permit requires that a report not only be produced but published by the Historical

Commission. Much of this research is cited and synthesized in more widely circulated contexts (Fox 1991, Thomas 1989a).

DISTINCTIVE REGIONAL CONTEXT Prior to the time of Spanish contact, most Indians in the Texas-Mexico borderlands followed hunting and gathering strategies. Major linguistic groups included the Coahuiltecans in the lower Rio Grande Valley (Campbell 1988) and the Karankawans (Newcomb 1983) along the south Texas coast. The Caddoan peoples in east Texas were settled agriculturalists. Texas and the area of northeast Mexico did not attract large numbers of Spanish settlers. There were fewer than 2500 people of European descent in Texas by 1820 (Cordell 1989:19). Spanish settlement in this region was initially prompted by French military and commercial activity near Matagorda Bay and in Louisiana (Cordell 1989:19).

The Caddoans of eastern Texas were first approached in 1690–1691, but the missions failed. A renewed effort was made in 1714–1716, with the establishment of missions and presidios that extended into Louisiana. Once hostilities ceased between Spaniards and French in 1763, the eastern missions were abandoned and the civilian population was ordered to move to San Antonio. However, most eventually returned to the area and settled at Nacogdoches near an abandoned mission (Corbin 1989: 269–270).

Missions to the Caddo failed for a number of reasons. The Caddo were involved in trade with the French, and this gave them economic clout outside relationships with the Spaniards. Their dispersed pattern of residence, an adaptation to an environment of patchy resources, made them a poor military target (Corbin 1989:270). The missions themselves were poorly situated—sites seem to have been selected more for defense than to facilitate cultivation. The friars often did not have enough food for themselves, let alone enough to attract the Indians (Corbin 1989:271–277).

In central and southern Texas, major mission efforts began between 1699 and 1703, when missions were established on the middle to lower Rio Grande. These first missions served as gateway communities that sent missionaries and settlers to other areas of Texas. Some missions in this area succeeded for a time. They ministered to the many hunting and gathering groups (Eaton 1989:250) but suffered from problems of water supply and crop failures. The mobile lifestyle of the Indians made it easy to leave the missions at any time. San Juan Bautista and its Presidio del Rio Grande operated until 1823–1824, when secularization and the Mexican independence movement brought about a number of changes. In theory, secularization meant replacement of state-supported missionaries from religious orders by parish priests who were obedient to the ecclesiastical hierarchy (Rausch 1987:340), but such a transfer entailed break-up and dispersal of mission lands to non-Indians and disintegration of the community that had been held together by the mission. Excavations have been carried out at the sites of San Juan Bautista and the nearby mission site of San Bernardo (Eaton 1989).

Beginning in 1718, the mission effort shifted eastward to the area of present-day San Antonio along the San Antonio River. The missions prospered here, at least for a time (Hester 1989a:200). They were characterized by major buildings, and the communities were supplied with cattle and food from ranches in outlying areas. One of the outlying ranches, Rancho de las Cabras at San Antonio (Fox 1989), has been excavated. The Indians of the San Antonio missions were Coahuiltecans and Karankawans as well as groups from outside. Both diseases and Apache attacks threatened the missions. In the 1750s in central Texas and the 1760s in south-central Texas, the missions tried to provide protection to the Indians, including the Apaches, from the increasing threats posed by the Comanches, but they apparently did not succeed (Hester 1989a: 200–201). The missions waned in importance by the 1780s and 1790s, but their ultimate demise was the result of secularization that began in 1793 (Hester 1989a:201).

The last of the Indians of the Texas-Mexico borderlands to be missionized were the Karankawans of the south Texas coast (Gilmore 1984, Newcomb 1983). Mission Rosario was established for the Karankawa in 1754 in present-day Goliad County, about 48 km from the coast. But the Karankawa felt that the mission restricted their liberty, and they continued to practice their seasonal rounds, visiting the mission only when food supplies were short (Gilmore 1989: 233–234). In 1779–1781 they left for the coast and never returned (Gilmore 1984:165).

Mission Rosario was abandoned in 1805 and the remaining Indians moved to Mission Refugio, established in 1794 and the last of the missions in Texas. Still, the Karankawans resisted mission life and continued to move between the two mission sites and from the woods to the sea. Land-hungry Anglo-American settlers moved into Karankawa territory in the 1820s, and by 1858 the Karankawa were exterminated (Gilmore 1989:182, 237).

MISSION LAYOUT    In the area of the middle and lower Rio Grande and the Texas-Mexico borderlands, missions were often situated near Indian camps to ease the transition to mission life (Eaton 1989:248). Defense against marauding Apaches was a consideration, and mission buildings generally formed an inward-facing compound with restricted access to the inner courts and, in some cases, high enclosing walls (Eaton 1989:248). As elsewhere, the complex consisted of a church, friary, granary, workshops, storerooms, and housing. The church and *convento* (friary) formed the religious core, with the workshops and housing as the center of industrial and social activities (Eaton 1989:249). Agriculture and stock-raising were carried out, and a major first activity was the digging of a ditch system to bring water from its nearest source to the mission. Eaton (1989:249) notes that no two missions were exactly alike, although the basic architectural components were much the same.

Rancho de las Cabras on the San Antonio River was run entirely independently by the Indian acolytes. Ranch residents were left on their own as long as livestock were tended and the proper number of animals were supplied weekly to one of the San Antonio missions for slaughter (Leutenegger 1976:19). As Fox (1989:261) has pointed out, the site offers an unusual opportunity to examine the extent to which acculturation had taken place.

In east Texas, the Caddo missions investigated show wall alignments running northeast/southwest, which suggests that standard mission building practices were followed (Corbin 1989:273).

MATERIAL CULTURE   Most details on material culture come from the excavation of Indian residential quarters in missions. Overall, Indians took well-developed lithic and ceramic technologies with them into the mission context. Introduced items of Spanish manufacture include crucifixes, rosaries, scissors, knives, and of course trade beads (Hester 1989b:218, Miroir et al 1975). Inventories of Indian households on missions show that the Indians also used grinding stones, grills, and copper pans; excavations have revealed iron comales, copper kettles, iron spurs, copper jewelry, lead-glazed pottery, Spanish military buttons, gun flints, ceramics from Mexico, Chinese porcelain, English earthenware, needles, buttons, buckles, knives, spoons and finger rings. On the whole, however, metal artifacts are scarce and there seems to have been recycling of metal scraps (Hester 1989b:218–219).

Not surprisingly, mission documents say little about Indian technology and material culture. Hunting and gathering remained important throughout the mission experience in Texas and northeast Mexico. Although this may not be representative, the observations quoted by Hester (1989b:219) from Almaráz (1979) and Leutenegger (1976) suggest that the friars in Texas were more tolerant of this wandering lifestyle than those in Florida (Bushnell 1990), although this could be due to their recognition that the missions often could not supply the Indians with enough foodstuffs.

Hester notes that in addition to "Guerrero points" used for hunting in the absence of guns (Hester 1989b:220–222), a variety of other stone tools were used at the missions. The association of chert flakes and debris with Spanish colonial domestic trash indicates that chert tools were made either by Spaniards, or by Indians linked to Spanish households (Hester 1989b:223). Non-Indians are known to have made gun flints when they could not be imported (Fox 1977), and Indians on missions made gun flints to supply Spaniards (Hester 1989b: 223).

The most common pottery on mission sites is a bone-tempered ware that was first made in A.D. 1200–1300 and persisted through the mission period.

There also occurs less frequently a sandy-paste pottery with asphaltum designs that is believed to be a part of the Karankawa tradition. Two missions in Coahuila lack the bone-tempered ware, but this may relate to the fact that groups from northeastern Mexico populated these missions. Bone-tempered ware is also found in Spanish household debris in San Antonio in the early nineteenth century. The pervasiveness of Indian pottery may reflect a shortage of Spanish ceramics from Mexico, or, as in Florida, Indian women may have married into Spanish households and brought their pottery-making skills with them (Fox 1977; Hester 1989b:224).

Locally made native pottery is found in Spanish residential areas, Indian residential areas, and missions. In Florida and the Southwest, Indian pottery made on missions for the friars reflects some attempt to conform to Spanish styles; in Texas, this phenomenon occurs only at missions in the east, where plate rims and ring-footed flatware indicate that local potters were creating European forms (Corbin 1989:274). Sherds of French faience and Chinese porcelain outnumber Mexican majolica in east Texas, which indicates that the friars were obtaining trade items from the French, either directly or through the Indians. Officially, missions were allowed to obtain only food items from the French (Corbin 1989:274).

Majolica and other European wares seem to have occurred more commonly in Spanish residential sites in Florida and the Southwest than in Texas/northeastern Mexico. This seems odd given the proximity to Mexican manufacturing areas. However, not as much has been reported in Texas of Spanish material from Spanish residences.

## The Californias

DISTINCTIVE RESEARCH CONTEXT    The mission institution had been operative in the New World for more than two centuries before the first missions were established in California in 1769. The mission and presidio were tried and tested institutions, and in California they persisted until secularization in 1832. After secularization, the mission lands were divided and sold, mostly to non-Indians; when California became a state in 1850, President Lincoln returned at least the central mission buildings to the Catholic church. Where there was an active parish, churches were preserved, although other unused buildings often fell into ruin (Costello & Hornbeck 1989:321). Nonetheless, mission buildings dot the California landscape, and the mission period has been an important part of California consciousness.

In the 1890s, a move arose from several quarters to preserve and restore mission buildings as part of California's romantic historical past. Private benefactors made funds available to the Catholic church to renovate missions, but the early reconstructions were not often based on accurate information derived from archaeology. Larger scale, systematic reconstructions were carried out by state and local authorities, with some archaeological work, in the 1940s and 1950s, and in the 1960s many university field schools focused on mission research (Costello & Hornbeck 1989:321–322). There was a shift from a sole concern with architecture to an interest in the cultural record, but it was not until the 1970s that the culture of the missions became the main research aim (Deetz 1978).

The reports produced by contract archaeological projects remain largely unpublished, or are limited in circulation (Dietz et al 1983). The reports resulting from university field school excavations appear in local and state journals such as *Masterkey, Pacific Coast Archaeological Society Quarterly,* and *Journal of San Diego History,* and the California Department of Parks and Recreation publishes archaeological reports (Felton & Schulz 1983). Other data from excavations, often combined with historical research, are more widely published (Hoover & Costello 1985, Farnsworth 1989, and the papers in Thomas 1989a).

On a rather different note, California research is distinctive in the extent to which pollen, opal phytolith, and macrobotanical studies have documented environmental change brought about by the introduction of European plants and grazing animals (e.g. Bartolomé et al 1986, Burcham 1981, Heizer & Hester 1973, West 1989). Recent years have also seen publication of a considerable amount of material on the demographics and health of the California native population as the result of missionization (Farnsworth 1989, Farnsworth & Jackson 1995, Jackson 1994, Walker et al 1989).

DISTINCTIVE REGIONAL CONTEXT   California had the highest population density in North America at the time of Contact, with about 300,000 people who spoke approximately 90 different languages (Costello & Hornbeck 1989:305). Indian groups in California were complex hunter-gatherers with hierarchical social organization and villages that ranged in size from 20 to 1000 people. Agriculture was practiced by only a few groups in the south, but all groups harvested tobacco, grapes, mesquite, and wild seeds. They are perhaps best known for their skills at basket-making. Some groups, such as the Chumash, were heavily oriented toward coastal subsistence and trade, and made ocean-going plank canoes. Trade networks were widespread within California, and between California and the Southwest, and the Sierra Nevada. Animosities and warfare among Californian groups were common (Costello & Hornbeck 1989: 307).

In Baja California, now-extinct hunter-gatherers once numbered about 25,000. They traveled in extended family groups rarely larger than 20 people, although they came together seasonally in larger groups to harvest wild food after a successful hunt. The Indians of Baja had become familiar with at least some Spanish goods and aspects of Spanish culture before missionization as the result of irregular contact (Mathes 1989:409,419). When missions were established in 1697, they developed in relative isolation because populations were low and missions spread widely (Mathes 1989:409, Weber 1968). Partly due to dearth of agricultural land, missions could not be self-supporting and were integrated with existing outlying settlements, some of which were *visita* sites with a chapel; in these the Indians continued traditional hunting and gathering practices (Jackson 1994:34). By the time of secularization and collapse of the mission system in the late 1830s, the gathering of all Indians into mission settlements was almost complete (Jackson 1994:34,36).

Like Florida and Texas, settlement of Alta California was stimulated by the presence of other colonial powers in the area, in this case, the Russians and English (Costello & Hornbeck 1989:303). Along with the 21 missions founded by the Franciscans between 1769 and 1823 were four presidios and three pueblos or communities with colonists from New Spain.

It has been said that the missionaries knew from past experience that the Indian populations brought into missions would experience drastic decline as the result of diseases, but the Franciscans' sense of the superiority of Iberian culture and their focus on economic imperatives meant that they proceeded with missionization in any case (Jackson 1994:166). To this extent, the Alta California mission heritage is tinged with irony—the area with the greatest consciousness of missions as remnants of a romantic era is the one area in which missionizers had the experience to know better.

At first, the missions did not work well and converts were few. Agriculture was new to most of the converts and crop production was low. Soldiers seem to have been generally available to control the frontier. In 1776 there were three presidios, seven missions, 300–350 Hispanic colonists, 19 missionaries, 160 soldiers, and 2000 resident Indians. By 1805 there were more missions and 20,000 resident Indians. Agricultural and irrigation systems had developed and small-scale industries were in operation. The peak of Indian population was reached in 1822 at 21,000, after which populations declined (Costello & Hornbeck 1989:310,313; Webb 1982). During the mission period, civilian and military populations grew slowly. By 1815 all presidios except San Diego had populations of 300 to 600. The three pueblo communities that had been established, San José, Los Angeles, and what is present-day Santa Cruz, had a population of about 1800 at this time. By 1820 the number of settlers totaled only 3000, and it was not until 1834, after secularization, that new communities were founded and settlement expanded (Costello & Hornbeck 1989: 317,318).

The civilian communities never provided the agricultural supplies that were expected, mainly because there was no economic incentive to do so, due to low prices set by the military (Costello & Hornbeck 1989:317; Mosk 1938). Civilians and military became dependent on the missions and by 1815, the missions were "the sole supporters of Spain's program to colonize its California frontier" (Costello & Hornbeck 1989:318). Thus the mission in Alta California developed from an institution of acculturation into a commercial operation. By the end of the period, missions were supplying food and products to civilian and military populations, and were also supplying a commercial international market with tallow and hides (Hornbeck 1989:431–432). The mission period ended with secularization. Between 1834 and 1836 all 8,000,000 acres of mission land became available for civilian settlement. Provisions were made for tools and lands to be distributed to the Indians, but in reality all mission lands went to the civilian and military population. Some of the Indians remained at the missions but most left to work on ranches owned by settlers (Costello & Hornbeck 1989:319,320).

How the native population accommodated to mission life in California is judged differently by different people. One extreme sees benefits to mission life in terms of Christianization and acculturation (Engelhardt 1908–1915); but most evidence points to cruelty, punishments, and death (Castillo 1989, Cook 1976, Jackson 1994). The extent to which native practices and traditions continued seems to have depended on the intensity of local resistance and the approaches of individual missionaries. At some missions, but not at others, religious ceremonies such as ceremonial dances continued. Traditional ceremonies associated with subsistence practices were kept, such as rituals associated with fishing among the Chumash, because the Indians were encouraged to continue their traditional procurement patterns during the mission period. Sweat lodges, also with a ritual component, were prohibited by friars, but not by all. Some adults were buried in their local village cemetery rather than at the mission (Costello & Hornbeck 1989:313,316). Native decorative elements were incorporated into paintings on churches (Lee & Neuerburg 1989).

Resistance is difficult to characterize accurately because documentary evidence is biased toward Spanish views. There is, nonetheless, evidence from the documents that abortion and infanticide were practiced as a response to rape (Castillo 1989:379), and very likely to keep children from being born into a world that the Indians could not call their own. Fugitivism was resorted to but was sometimes difficult to sustain because the environment had changed so drastically with the introduction of European plants and grazing animals (Castillo 1989:381–382; Johnson 1989:368). Armed resistance was also practiced and was a threat to church and civilian authorities, with the result that the interior of California became a haven for refugees from missions along the coast (Castillo 1989).

ARCHEOLOGY AND MISSION LAYOUT   The physical layout was similar in all missions. The central mission buildings enclosed a quadrangle or courtyard that included the church, friars' apartments, shops, storage areas, and a sleeping area for unmarried women. Indian family dwellings were an adjacent complex; the houses were first built of traditional materials and later of adobe. Soldiers' quarters stood on the opposite side of the quadrangle from the Indians' residences (Costello & Hornbeck 1989:310).

Outside the mission core, many facilities existed but have not survived. Where archaeological excavations have recovered information, we know that some of the activities carried on included tanning, milling, tile making, and lime production. Corrals were also situated outside the mission center, as were complex aqueduct systems to carry water to fields, gardens, activity areas, and residences (e.g. Greenwood & Gessler 1968). Archaeology also reveals that building maintenance and renovation were regular activities, and the effects of earthquakes resulted in building redesign (Costello & Hornbeck 1989:311–312).

Ranchos or estancias were established to keep livestock and to grow crops for the missions. Archaeological excavation of these mission stations is important to an understanding of the mission system. Although sites of ranchos are largely unknown (Costello & Hornbeck 1989:313), a number have been located and investigated (e.g. Chace 1966, Greenwood & Browne 1968).

The diet of the Indians on missions changed as the result of the introduction of European crops and animals. Beef came to be the primary meat consumed, then mutton, and occasionally pork. Spanish butchering practices were adopted as well (Gust 1982). From archaeological remains we know that deer and rabbit continued to be hunted. Native wild plants continued to be collected, but wheat and corn made up the bulk of the diet, and secondarily barley, beans, fruits and vegetables (Costello & Hornbeck 1989:315). European plants spread rapidly (Burcham 1981) as revealed through recovery of seeds and pollen from plants preserved in adobe bricks and cultural deposits (Hendry 1931; West 1989:336,337).

MATERIAL CULTURE  Generally speaking, stone tools, glass and shell beads, and floor hearths are distinctive of native populations, whereas imported ceramics and bottle glass, raised hearths, musket balls, and gun flints are distinctive of areas occupied by friars and/or soldiers (Costello 1989, Costello & Hornbeck 1989:316, Hoover & Costello 1985). As in Florida, European artifacts are often associated with males, whereas native-produced goods are part of the female sphere (Deetz 1978). Archaeology has shown that later in mission history—first with illegal and then legalized international trade in hides and tallow—English ceramics, French wine, champagne, English gin, and whiskey were the main exchange items (Costello & Hornbeck 1989:319).

Because pottery production was known only in the extreme southern part of California, most neophytes learned to make and fire pottery at the mission, and they were also taught a range of European crafts (Costello & Hornbeck 1989:314; Engelhardt 1908–1915:2:235). Archaeological analysis of brick and tile kilns and cement production sites indicates that the skills may not have been completely mastered (see Costello 1989).

Metal tools were used for labor-intensive tasks such as shell bead manufacture and heavy woodworking. Iron knives were used for a variety of tasks such as butchering, and axes and adzes to work wood (Bamforth 1993). Generally, however, metal tools were in short supply, so that stone tools and flakes were common. Cow hides were processed with bone and stone scrapers (Deetz 1978:169); stone continued to be used in fishhook production and fish processing; and flakes used in pre-Columbian times for woodworking were put to a range of applications (Bamforth 1993). There is evidence from one Chumash site to suggest that on-site tool production increased because specialized production was very probably disrupted and communities were thrown back on their own resources. Obsidian also drops in frequency (Bamforth 1993). That traditional rituals and beliefs persisted is indicated by the presence of shaman's whistles and crystals in Indian residences (Costello & Hornbeck 1989: 315,316 and also Greenwood 1976:170).

Interesting data have come from an analysis of a number of mission sites by Farnsworth (1989). Artifact analyses show basically that differences in wealth of assemblages reflect a mission's general access to Spanish goods, rather than greater access to Spanish goods by certain classes or strata of people. Also, although higher status was in one sense related to acquisition of Spanish goods, such goods were sometimes used to reinforce native traditional values. Conversely, native goods could be fashioned according to Spanish tastes. Higher status was displayed in different ways at different missions and reflected individual taste and cultural traditions (Farnsworth 1989:195–204).

## Yucatan in Mesoamerica

I use the term Yucatan to refer to the entire Yucatan Peninsula and therefore to the area of the Maya southern and northern lowlands that includes Guatemala, Belize, and portions of Mexico. There are times, however, when the term Yucatan refers specifically to the Mexican state, and in this case I will use the term state to avoid confusion.

DISTINCTIVE RESEARCH CONTEXT   In Mexico and Guatemala, as in California, standing colonial monuments received attention because their restoration stimulated the tourist industry (Andrews 1981:1; Yadeun 1978). A good descriptive foundation exists for historic archaeology in Yucatan. There is a registry of colonial monuments in Mexico (Fernández 1945) and a number of other valuable architectural studies (see Andrews 1991). A proposed model for historic sites classification in Yucatan includes extensive references to architectural, regional, and community studies of value to archaeologists (Andrews 1981). The most comprehensive studies of the immediate pre-Hispanic and post-Contact period in Yucatan are those of Roys (1943, 1957), who draws information from colonial documents—particularly from a kind of early Maya ethnography undertaken by the Bishop of Yucatan, Diego de Landa (Tozzer 1941). These documents supply information on the pre-Hispanic location of Maya towns, on Maya political, social, and religious systems, and on continuity and change once the *cacique* system is established by the Spaniards.

Of interest to mission archaeology are the Contact-period sites with churches where Christianization of the Maya was first attempted. Churches are surveyed in Artigas Hernández 1983, Bretos 1987, Castells 1904, Cortes de Brasdefer 1996, Escalona Ramos 1946, Fernández 1945, and McAndrew 1965. Particular church descriptions exist for Ecab, Quintana Roo (Benavides Castillo & Andrews 1979); open chapels in Campeche (Messmacher 1966); Dzibilchaltun, Yucatan (Folan 1970); Xcaret (Andrews & Andrews 1975, Hanson 1990), Ek Balam (Hanson 1995, 1996, 1997), and Xlacah (Gallareta Negrón et al 1990) in the state of Yucatan; Tancah (Miller & Farriss 1979) and Oxtankah (Cortes de Brasdefer 1992, 1995) in Quintana Roo; and farther south, Lamanai (Pendergast 1986, 1991, 1993) and Tipu (Graham 1991, Graham & Bennett 1989, Graham et al 1985, Graham et al 1989, Jones et al 1986) in Belize. Some work has also been done by Luis Millet at Tecoh and by Jorge Victoria Ojedo at Tihosuco.

Historic-sites archaeology in Yucatan remains sadly underdeveloped. This is partly because archaeological resources are limited and focused on pre-Columbian remains, and partly because archaeologists have traditionally left historical research to ethnohistorians and historians. Where projects have been carried out, they have been concerned with colonial architecture and its restoration, and reporting is generally descriptive and superficial. Analysis of recovered artifacts is rare, although there are important exceptions that grew out of an initial focus on Central Mexico (for example, Lister & Lister 1974, 1987). In addition, the interest in past social processes that might lead to historic research has not been a concern (Fournier-Garcia & Miranda-Flores 1992; Andrews 1981:2). This is not too far from the situation as it stood with regard to Spanish colonial archaeology in North America until almost the time of the quincentenary (Farnsworth & Williams 1992:1).

North American and Mexican archaeologists often collaborate on archaeological projects. But North Americans lack easy access to Mexican or other Middle American publications in which research results are disseminated (Fournier-Garcia & Miranda-Flores 1992:75). By the same token, Mexican and other Middle American scholars have limited access to reports on historic sites in US state or Canadian provincial publications or in contract archaeology reports. In general then, there is a need for better ways to report and share results.

DISTINCTIVE REGIONAL CONTEXT    Missionization in Yucatan proceeded under the direction of Franciscan friars. An initial mission in Campeche is dated to about 1536 (Hanson 1995:17), but other records show that the Franciscans did not officially arrive until 1544 (Andrews 1991:357), when the brutal conquest of the area that includes Belize was undertaken by Melchor and Alonso Pacheco (Jones 1989:41–45). In the next 30 years, Franciscan friars established convents (residences for the friars) and small churches in both urban and rural areas of Yucatan. From these convents, the friars traveled to more remote native communities to proselytize, and in many of these communities they built small chapels or churches (Andrews 1991:357). Towns such as Lamanai and Tipu, however, unlike Ecab, were probably not served by resident friars, and would be considered *visita* missions—those served only part-time by visiting priests.

In 1552, Tomás Lopez, one of the judges of the superior court in Guatemala, inaugurated the practice of concentrating or congregating the rural inhabitants in towns near convents in Yucatan (Roys 1943:134). Along with resettlement went the economic integration of the Maya into Spanish colonial society. *Repartimiento* in Yucatan—that is, the production of items for resale by merchants as commodities—took the form of the production of salt, indigo, and lime (Farriss 1984, Hanson 1997) in the north and very likely cacao in the south in Belize (Jones 1989:41–42,104,121). In addition to the tribute paid to the *encomendero*—usually in salt, honey, chickens, wax, cotton, or, in Belize, cacao—households were encouraged to produce commodities to be sold to the *encomendero*, who himself resold the items. Producers often had to abandon other activities, including aspects of subsistence activities, to produce the commodity (Hanson 1997).

Archaeological evidence from the site of Ek Balam in the vicinity of Valladolid (Hanson 1997) has revealed the presence of a probable lime kiln, the Iberian-influenced construction of which suggests local production of lime for sale to the Spanish community. Other unexcavated kilns suggest further commodity production, possibly in ceramics. No archaeological evidence for commodity production was recovered from Lamanai or Tipu.

ARCHAEOLOGY AND MISSION LAYOUT   Mission layout conforms to the general pattern for missions in areas of predominantly native settlement. There is a church and *convento* (on a small scale) for the friar or friars, usually at one side of a plaza. Important community residential and/or civic structures can also border the plaza, with other residences grouped nearby. At Ek Balam, the Franciscan chapel and friary complex lay east of the monumental site center, with pre-Hispanic platforms that supported occupation into the historic period surrounding the chapel complex (Hanson 1996). Likewise, at Lamanai and Tipu, the church complex was placed within or adjacent to active community buildings, with the church at Lamanai placed directly over a fifteenth century temple (Pendergast 1993:121).

The churches in Yucatan and Belize consistently have altar ends facing east, a pre-seventeenth century pattern (Saunders 1990:528). At both Lamanai and Tipu, the probable friar's residence stands north of the church (Graham 1991:Figure 15–1; Pendergast 1993).

The churches at Lamanai and Tipu were European in design in terms of dimensions, organization of interior space, and perhaps the apsidal ends of the early churches, but construction techniques were local in that limestone blocks like those used in pre-Hispanic construction were used, along with mortar, plaster, pole, clay daub, and thatched roofs. The second church at Lamanai saw some changes; wall core of the masonry sanctuary of the second church was fully cemented, not a Maya practice, and the facings were of undressed spalls and cobbles capped with heavy plaster, whereas the Maya would have used dressed facing stones with a thinner coating of plaster (Pendergast 1993:346).

Burials at Lamanai occur beneath the nave floor of the first church within the platform core of a pre-Hispanic building, and in a cemetery on the east side of the second church. At Tipu, the burials occur within the nave, and on the north, south, and west sides. Bedrock close to the surface at Lamanai made burial within the nave of the second church impossible. The implication in any case is that custom could be important but that expediency ruled.

MATERIAL CULTURE  Very little is known about historic artifacts in Yucatan in comparison with central and northern Mexico (Andrews 1981:13; Cohen-Williams 1992, Lister & Lister 1982, López Cervantes 1976; Noguera 1934; Seifert 1975). However, continuing work in Yucatan coupled with a focus on the potteries in Spain itself (McEwan 1992) will go far in filling this gap. The kinds of majolica ware and olive jars found at Ek Balam, Lamanai, and Tipu are the same (Hanson 1996, Pendergast 1993), which suggests how tightly integrated the mission and colonization effort was in the region. Regarding local pottery, my impression is that change was more rapid at Ek Balam and Lamanai. Both sites, and Tipu as well, produce ceramics during this period with wash-like slips. Hanson ties this change to historic times, Pendergast to the immediate preconquest period. The same ceramics do not appear at Tipu until the historic period, and we seem to see more stable precontact to postcontact local pottery production there. Some change is quite distinctive, such as the Spanish-style censer of local manufacture found in one of the burials within the nave of the church at Tipu (Graham et al 1989:Figure 3). At Lamanai, some effigy censers show no change (Pendergast 1991:Figure 16–3, 1993:Figure 5), whereas others may be distinctive of the historic period (Pendergast 1993:Figure 9). An unslipped jar form found in the cemetery at Tipu, for example, is indistinguishable from pre-Hispanic jars. This makes sense if we assume that exchange in slips, like exchange in chert, was disrupted in historic times, and the artifacts least affected would be those dependent only on local materials.

A range of other European materials occurs, although not in large quantities. At Lamanai glass beads occur predominantly in middens, and at Tipu predominantly in burials, mostly with children (Smith et al 1994). Other objects—bells, rings, earrings, needles, locks, nails—are few, but their contexts and, in some cases, chemical sourcing tell us a great deal about the dynamics of the colonial setting (see Graham 1991; Graham & Wayman 1989; Lambert et al 1994; Pendergast 1991, 1993). Formal chert tools also undergo some significant changes. At Tipu, the formal tools are dominated by small, side-notched points (arrowheads), and small, bipointed bifaces (Simmons 1991, 1995). The arrowheads were manufactured quickly with minimal retouch, and Simmons (1995:144–145) interprets this and other evidence as suggestive of increased warfare. Ongoing analysis of informal tools also points to greater on-site production and re-use of informal chert tools, a possible consequence of the disruption of trade that supplied chert and obsidian (Hilborn, personal communication; see also Bamforth 1993:67–68).

Burials from within and outside of the churches at Lamanai and Tipu provide a wealth of information on the health of the early-colonial-period Maya (Cohen et al 1994; Danforth et al 1997; White 1986, 1989; White et al 1994). The results from Tipu indicate that adults and children enjoyed relatively good health (Danforth et al 1997:20). Along with information from ceramic and faunal analysis, considerable continuity from pre-Hispanic times seems to have been maintained, despite disruption owing to Tipu's function as a congregation center and resultant changes to community layout and organization. At Lamanai, the burial and faunal data reflect greater disruption of pre-Hispanic patterns and generally lower health than at Tipu (Graham 1991:333; Emery 1990; White et al 1994). The lesson to be learned from this example is that we cannot generalize about the effects of contact.

Maya groups in Belize rebelled in 1638 (Jones 1989), during which the church and other buildings at Lamanai were burned and abandoned (Pendergast 1991:346; Jones 1989:214–224). Archaeological investigations revealed that a stela was erected outside the church sanctuary after the uprising, and several offerings were also interred nearby (Pendergast 1991:346). Although we originally interpreted these actions as apostasy, evidence for continuing use of the Christian cemetery at Tipu and the locus for offerings within Christian sacred space suggest more complex processes of transformation.

## PATTERN, SUCCESS, AND FAILURE OF MISSIONS IN YUCATAN AND FUTURE IMPLICATIONS FOR MISSION ARCHAEOLOGY

Missionization was most successful in the northern and western portions of the Yucatan peninsula because it was here that the Spaniards established a secure presence (Andrews 1991:357). The far-eastern and southern interior portions of the peninsula were more difficult to secure and administer. Ek Balam (Hanson 1995), one of the communities undergoing investigation, falls within a fully administered region, whereas Lamanai and Tipu are clearly frontier missions (Jones 1989).

Maya resistance culminated in rebellion in Belize in 1638, which paved the way for British incursion into Spanish territory. During the rest of the century, most of the missions in the eastern and southern zones were abandoned (Clendinnen 1987, Farriss 1984, Jones 1989). Only the Itzá Maya of Lake Peten remained staunchly anti-Christian as well as anti-Spaniard, however. At Tipu and Lamanai, and presumably other communities as well, the Maya became Christian and remained Catholic, at least in some form, until exposed to the Protestant evangelizing sects of the present day. Given the Spaniards' neglect of the Maya in the more remote areas of Campeche and Quintana Roo, and their complete withdrawal from Belize, the Christianization phenomenon in this region is worthy of interest.

Studies of nativism and syncretism (e.g. Edmonson et al 1960) are important to any future studies of the mission encounter. Generally, however, these studies adopt the concept of syncretism uncritically, and interpret the retention of traditional imagery and ritual as a conservative and not a transformative process for Maya and Spaniard, acolyte and friar alike. Treatments of nativism and syncretism also assess Maya behavior against an ideal of true or real conversion that goes unquestioned (Thompson 1954).

Roys (1943) states that the Spaniards governed through existing native hierarchies; thus, it was in the new caciques' best interests to be Christian. Here we see that the complex sociopolitical systems of the Maya facilitated conversion, and to this extent, the dichotomy Jackson (1995) draws between missionizing sedentary and non-sedentary societies is extremely significant. It has been suggested that the native societies that were culturally Mesoamerican and thereby more complex sociopolitically were more vulnerable to Spanish conquest and conversion than were other groups, who were less hierarchical and never made reliable subjects (Carmack 1991:404–405).

Not all Maya, despite their pre-Hispanic engagement in state society, however, accommodated rapidly to Christianity. The Itzá of Lake Peten consistently resisted both Spanish secular and religious authority (Jones 1989), and the Quiche Maya of highland Guatemala initially strongly and persistently resisted Spanish conquest efforts (Carmack 1981, 1991). The most powerful groups stood to lose the most and put up the staunchest resistance, whereas groups that were in subordinate positions during the pre-conquest period had less to lose by switching overlords. The Momostecans, for example, also of highland Guatemala, accepted peace from the Spaniards, and their leaders became caciques and maintained rights to authority, as was the case for Maya nobles in Yucatan (Carmack 1991:397). Although we do not know for certain, the willingness of Tipuans to capitulate to Christianity may reflect pre-Hispanic subordination to the powerful Itza of the Peten, so that alliance with the Spaniards was seen as a move to limit Itza hegemony.

Thus I have added support for the argument that conversion to Christianity was related to political expediency, or at least to relations of political power (Farriss 1993). On the other hand, political maneuvering cannot explain Christianity's staying power in remote areas of the frontier such as Lamanai and Tipu, places that the Spaniards ultimately abandoned. I have made the case elsewhere that the longevity of Christianity, even in remote communities such as Lamanai and Tipu, can be explained by the fact that sincere and complete conversion (Klor de Alva 1982) was indeed effected in the Maya area (Graham 1992, 1995). This runs counter to scholars' claims that the Maya never quite got it. The staying power of Christianity is undoubtedly the result of the incorporation of pre-Hispanic religious elements, but this has always been part of the Christian experience, and indeed characterizes Christianity rather than demonstrates that the Maya, or other Indians, never became true Christians.

At the start of this chapter I suggested that the New World mission experience is interpreted by scholars as if Europeans had a special claim to Christianity; on this point, Spaniards, priests, and modern scholars all seem to agree. It is partly because such authenticity goes unchallenged that social and cultural change for the Indians continues to be measured in increments of retention of traditional practices. Here, directly as the result of my knowledge of the complexity of the Mesoamerican mission experience, I add the idea that the Indians anywhere in the Americas, in undergoing proselytization, could not help but be aware of the historical and ritual patchwork that made Christianity what it was and therefore responded, not to an elusive Christian ideal, but to a Christian reality. There are indications that at least a few friars realized this. It may not have undermined their faith, but perhaps made them aware of the flaws and tears in the fabric of Christian ritual, which would explain the tolerance exhibited in at least some Mesoamerican contexts (e.g. Carmack 1991:393). In Central Mexico, Ingham (1986:35) observed that priests were often loyal to the folk customs of their native villages but adopted the received standards when they worked in alien parishes!

This rich and varied evolution of Christianity in Mesoamerica, often seen to be entirely separate from and irrelevant to what was happening in North America, can indeed be mined for information if the idea of a monolithic European Christianity is rejected and each region or zone or town or village is studied in terms of its contribution to an ongoing and worldwide process of religious transformation.

Visit the *Annual Reviews home page* at
http://www.annualreviews.org.

# Literature Cited

Adams EC. 1982. *Walpi Archaeological Project: Synthesis and Interpretation.* Flagstaff: Mus. North. Ariz.

Adams EC. 1989. Passive resistance: Hopi responses to Spanish contact and conquest. See Thomas 1989a, pp. 77–91

Almaraz FD Jr. 1979. *Crossroad of Empire: The Church and State on the Rio Grande Frontier of Coahuila and Texas, 1700–1821.* Archaeol. Hist. San Juan Bautista Mission Area, Coahuila and Texas. Rep. No. 2. San Antonio: Univ. Tex., Cent. Archaeol. Res.

Andrews AP. 1981. Historical archaeology in the Yucatan: a preliminary framework. *Hist. Archaeol.* 15(1):1–18

Andrews AP. 1991. The rural chapels and churches of Early Colonial Yucatan and Belize: an archaeological perspective. See Thomas 1991b, pp. 355–74

Andrews EW IV, Andrews AP. 1975. *A Preliminary Study of the Ruins of Xcaret, Quintana Roo.* New Orleans: Middle Am. Res. Inst., Publ. No. 40. Tulane Univ. Press

Arias D. 1994. *Spanish Cross in Georgia.* Lanham, MD: Univ. Press Am.

Artigas Hernández JB. 1983. *Capillas Abiertas Aisladas de México.* México, DF: Univ. Nac. Autón. Méx.

Baer K. 1958. *Architecture of California Missions.* Berkeley: Univ. Calif. Press

Bamforth DB. 1993. Stone tools, steel tools: Contact Period household technology at Helo'. In *Ethnohistory and Archaeology: Approaches to Postcontact Change in the Americas,* ed. JD Rogers, SM Wilson, pp. 49–72. New York: Plenum

Bartolomé JW, Klukkert SE, Barry WJ. 1986. Opal phytoliths as evidence for displacement of native California grassland. *Madrono* 33:217–22

Benavides Castillo A, Andrews AP. 1979. *Ecab: Poblado y Provincia del Siglo XVI en Yucatán.* Cuad. Cent. Reg. México DF: INAH

Bolton HE. 1921. *Spanish Borderlands: A Chronicle of Old Florida and the Southwest.* New Haven, CT: Yale Univ. Press

Boyd MF. 1939. Spanish mission sites in Florida. *Fla. Hist. Q.* 17:254–80

Boyd MF. 1948. Enumeration of Florida Spanish missions in 1675. *Fla. Hist. Q.* 27(2):181–88

Boyd MF, Smith HG, Griffin JW. 1951. *Here They Once Stood: The Tragic End of the Apalachee Missions.* Gainesville: Univ. Fla. Press

Bray W, ed. 1993. *The Meeting of Two Worlds, Europe and the Americas 1492–1650.* Oxford: Oxford Univ. Press

Bretos MA. 1987. Capillas de Indios Yucatecas del siglo XVI: notas sobre un complejo formal. *Cuad. Arquit. Yucatán* 1:1–12. Merida: Fac. Arquit., Univ. Autón. Yucatán

Brew JO. 1994. St. Francis at Awatovi. In *Pioneers in Historical Archaeology, Breaking New Ground,* ed. S South, pp. 27–47. New York: Plenum

Brown JS. 1996. Reading beyond the missionaries, dissecting responses. *Ethnohistory* 43(4):713–19

Bunting B. 1976. *Early Architecture in New Mexico.* Albuquerque: Univ. NM Press

Burcham LT. 1981. California rangelands in historical perspective. *Rangelands* 3:95–104

Burkhart LM. 1989. *The Slippery Earth: Nahua-Christian Moral Dialogue in Sixteenth-Century Mexico.* Tucson: Univ. Ariz. Press

Bushnell AT. 1990. The sacramental imperative: Catholic ritual and Indian sedentism in the provinces of Florida. See Thomas 1990b, pp. 475–90

Campbell TN. 1979. Ethnohistoric notes on Indian groups associated with three Spanish missions at Guerrero, Coahuila. In *Archaeology and History of the San Juan Bautista Mission Area, Coahuila and Texas,* Rep. No. 3. San Antonio: Univ. Tex., Cent. Archaeol. Res.

Campbell TN. 1988. *The Indians of Southern Texas and Northeastern Mexico. Selected Writings of Thomas N. Campbell.* Austin: Univ. Tex., Archaeol. Res. Lab.

Carmack RM. 1981. *The Quiché Mayas of Utatlán.* Norman: Univ. Okla. Press

Carmack RM. 1991. The Spanish conquest of Central America: comparative cases from Guatemala and Costa Rica. See Thomas 1991b, pp. 389–409

Carrico RL. 1973. The identification of two

burials at the San Diego Presidio. *J. San Diego Hist.* 19(4):51–55

Castells F de P. 1904. The ruins of Indian Church in British Honduras. *Am. Antiq. Orient. J.* 26(1):32–37

Castillo ED. 1989. The native response to the colonization of Alta California. See Thomas 1989a, pp. 377–94

Chace PG. 1966. A summary report of the Costa Mesa Estancia. *Pac. Coast Archaeol. Soc. Q.* 2(3):30–37

Clendinnen I. 1987. *Ambivalent Conquests: Maya and Spaniard in Yucatan, 1517–1570.* Cambridge: Cambridge Univ. Press

Cohen MN, O'Connor K, Danforth M, Jacobi K, Armstrong C. 1994. Health and diet at Tipu. See Larsen & Milner 1994, pp. 121–33

Cohen-Williams AG. 1992. Common maiolica types of northern New Spain. *Hist. Archaeol.* 26(1):119–30

Comaroff JL. 1989. Images of empire, contests of conscience: models of colonial domination in South Africa. *Am. Ethnol.* 16:661–85

Comaroff J, Comaroff J. 1986. Christianity and colonialism in South Africa. *Am. Ethnol.* 13(1):1–22

Comaroff J, Comaroff J. 1991. *Of Revelation and Revolution: Christianity, Colonialism, and Consciousness in South Africa,* Vol. 1. Chicago: Univ. Chicago Press

Cook SF. 1976. *The Conflict Between the California Indian and White Civilization.* Berkeley: Univ. Calif. Press

Corbin JE. 1989. Spanish-Indian interaction on the eastern frontier of Texas. See Thomas 1989a, pp. 269–76

Cordell LS. 1989. Durango to Durango: an overview of the Southwest heartland. See Thomas 1989a, pp. 17–40

Cortés de Brasdefer F. 1992. Oxtankah: la villa real de Chetumal. *Antropología.* Bol. Of. Inst. Nac. Antropol. Hist. Nueva Epoca No. 38. April/June. México D.F.: INAH

Cortés de Brasdefer F. 1995. *Oxtankah: El Uso del Espacio y su Entorno.* Quintana Roo: Cent. INAH

Cortés de Brasdefer F. 1996. *Los Monumentos Históricos de Quintana Roo y La Villa Real de Chetumal.* Quintana Roo: Cent. INAH

Costello JG. 1989. *Santa Inés Mission Excavation 1986–1988.* Hist. Archaeol. Calif. No. 10. Salinas, CA: Coyote Press

Costello JG, Hornbeck D. 1989. Alta California: an overview. See Thomas 1989a, pp. 303–31

Danforth ME, Jacobi KP, Cohen MN. 1997. Gender and health among the Colonial

Maya of Tipu, Belize. *Anc. Mesoam.* 8(1): 13–22

Deagan KA. 1978. The material assemblage of 16th century Spanish Florida. *Hist. Archaeol.* 12:25–50

Deagan KA. 1983. *Spanish St. Augustine: The Archaeology of a Colonial Creole Community.* New York: Academic

Deagan KA. 1987. *Artifacts of the Spanish Colonies of Florida and the Caribbean, 1500–1800.* Vol. 1: *Ceramics, Glassware, and Beads.* Washington, DC: Smithson. Inst.

Deagan KA. 1990. Accommodation and resistance: the process and impact of Spanish colonization in the Southeast. See Thomas 1990b, pp. 297–314

Deagan KA. 1993. St. Augustine and the mission frontier. See McEwan 1993a, pp. 87–110

Deagan KA, Cruxent JM. 1993. From contact to *Crillos*: the archaeology of Spanish colonization in Hispaniola. See Bray 1993, pp. 67–104

Deetz J. 1978. Archaeological investigations at La Purisima Mission. In *Historical Archaeology: A Guide to Substantive and Theoretical Contributions,* ed. RL Schuyler, pp. 160–90. Farmingdale, NY: Baywood

de Oré LG. 1936. The martyrs of Florida (1513–1616). In *Franciscan Studies,* 19:iii-xx, 1–145. Transl. and ed. M Geiger. New York: Joseph W. Wagner

Dietz SA, West GJ, Costello J, Needles HL, Cassman V. 1983. *Final Rep. Archaeol. Invest. Mission San Jose (CA-Ala-1).* Mission San Jose, CA

Doyel DE. 1989. The transition to history in Northern Pimeria Alta. See Thomas 1989a, pp. 139–58

Dozier EP. 1970. *The Pueblo Indians of North America.* New York: Holt, Rinehart & Winston

Dutton BP. 1985. Excavation tests at the pueblo ruins of Abo, Part II. In *Prehistory and History in the Southwest, Collected Papers in Honor of Alden C. Hayes,* ed. N Fox, pp. 91–104. Pap. No. 11. Santa Fe: Archaeol. Soc. NM

Eaton JD. 1981. *Guerrero, Coahuila, Mexico. A Guide to the Town and Missions.* Archaeol. Hist. San Juan Bautista Mission Area, Coahuila and Texas. Rep. No. 4. San Antonio: Univ. Tex., Cent. Archaeol. Res.

Eaton JD. 1989. The gateway missions of the Lower Rio Grande. See Thomas 1989a, pp. 245–58

Edmonson MS, Correa G, Thompson DE, Madsen W. 1960. *Nativism and Syncre-*

*tism.* New Orleans: Middle Am. Res. Inst., Publ. 19, Tulane Univ. Press

Emery K. 1990. *Colonial period dietary strategies in the southern Maya lowlands.* MA thesis. Dep. Anthropol., Univ. Toronto

Engelhardt Z. 1908–1915. *The Missions and Missionaries of California.* San Francisco: James H. Barry. 4 Vols.

Escalona Ramos A. 1946. Algunas ruinas prehispánicas en Quintana Roo. *Bol. Soc. Mex. Geogr. Estad.* 61(3):513–628

Ezell PH. 1961. *The Hispanic Acculturation of the Gila River Pimas.* Mem. No. 90. Menasha: Am. Anthropol. Assoc.

Ezell PH, Ezell GS. 1980. Bread and barbecues at San Diego Presidio. In *Spanish Colonial Frontier Research*, compiled ed. HF Dobyns. Albuquerque: Cent. Anthropol. Stud., Spanish Borderlands Res. No. 1

Fairbanks CH. 1985. From exploration to settlement: Spanish strategies for colonization. In *Alabama and the Borderlands: From Prehistory to Statehood*, ed. RR Badger, LA Clayton, pp. 128–39. Tuscaloosa: Univ. Ala. Press

Farnsworth P. 1989. Native American acculturation in the Spanish colonial empire: the Franciscan missions of Alta California. In *Centre and Periphery*, ed. TC Champion, pp. 186–206. London: Unwin Hyman

Farnsworth P, Jackson RH. 1995. Cultural, economic, and demographic change in the missions of Alta California: the case of Nuestra Señora de Soledad. See Langer & Jackson 1995, pp. 109–29

Farnsworth P, Williams JS, eds. 1992. The archaeology of the Spanish colonial and Mexican Republic periods: introduction. *Hist. Archaeol.* 26(1):1–6

Farriss NM. 1984. *Maya Society under Colonial Rule: The Collective Enterprise of Survival.* Princeton, NJ: Princeton Univ. Press

Farriss NM. 1993. Sacred power in Colonial Mexico: The case of sixteenth century Yucatan. See Bray 1993, pp. 145–62

Felton DL, Schulz PD. 1983. *The Diaz Collection: Material Culture and Social Change in Mid-Nineteenth-Century Monterey.* Calif. Archaeol. Rep. No. 23. Sacramento: Calif. Dep. Parks Recreat.

Fernández J, ed. 1945. *Catálogo de Construcciones Religiosas del Estado de Yucatán.* México, DF: Talleres Gráf. Nac. 2 Vols.

Fletcher R. 1977. Settlement studies (micro and semi-micro). In *Spatial Archaeology*, ed. DL Clarke, pp. 47–162. London: Academic

Folan WJ. 1970. *The Open Chapel of Dzibilchaltun, Yucatan.* New Orleans: Middle Am. Res Inst., Publ. No. 26, Tulane Univ. Press

Fournier-Garcia P, Miranda-Flores FA. 1992. Historic sites archaeology in Mexico. *Hist. Archaeol.* 26(1):75–83

Fox AA. 1977. *The Archaeology and History of the Spanish Governor's Palace Park.* Archaeol. Surv. Rep. No. 31. San Antonio: Univ. Tex. Cent. Archaeol. Res.

Fox AA. 1985. *Testing for the Location of Alamo Acequia (41BX8) at Hemisfair Plaza, San Antonio, Texas.* Archaeol. Surv. Rep. No. 142. San Antonio: Univ. Tex. Cent. Archaeol. Res.

Fox AA. 1988. *Archaeological Investigations at Mission Concepcion, Fall of 1986.* Archaeol. Surv. Rep. No. 172. San Antonio: Univ. Tex. Cent. Archaeol. Res.

Fox AA. 1989. The Indians at Rancho de las Cabras. See Thomas 1989a, pp. 259–67

Fox AA, ed. 1991. *Spanish Borderlands Sourcebooks 21: Archaeology of the Spanish Missions of Texas*, ed. AA Fox. New York: Garland

Furniss E. 1995. Resistance, coercion, and revitalization: The Shuswap encounter with Roman Catholic missionaries, 1860–1900. *Ethnohistory* 42(2):231–63

Gallareta Negrón T, Andrews AP, Schmidt PJ. 1990. A 16th century church at Xlacah, Panaba, Yucatan. *Mexicon* 12:33–36

Geiger M. 1937. The Franciscan conquest of Florida. In *Studies in Hispanic-American History 1.* Washington, DC: Cathol. Univ. Am. Press

Geiger M. 1969. *Franciscan Missionaries in Hispanic California, 1769–1848.* San Marino, CA: Huntington Lib.

Gilmore K. 1967. *A Documentary and Archeological Investigation of Presidio San Luis de las Amarillas and Mission Santa Cruz de San Saba, Menard County, Texas.* Archeol. Program Rep. No. 16. Austin: State Build. Comm.

Gilmore K. 1969. *The San Xavier Missions: A Study in Historical Site Identification.* Archeol. Program Rep. No. 9. Austin: State Build. Comm.

Gilmore K. 1984. The Indians of Mission Rosario. In *The Scope of Historical Archaeology*, ed. DG Orr, DG Crozier, pp. 163–91. Philadelphia: Temple Univ., Lab. Anthropol.

Gilmore K. 1989. The Indians of Mission Rosario: from the books and from the ground. See Thomas 1989a, pp. 231–44

Graham E. 1991. Archaeological insights into Colonial Period Maya life at Tipu, Belize. See Thomas 1991b, pp. 319–35

Graham E. 1992. *Idol speculation: the spirit world of pagans and priests.* Presented at

Annu. Meet. Soc. Hist. Archaeol., 25th, Kingston, Jamaica

Graham E. 1995. A spirited debate. *Rotunda* 28(2):18–23

Graham E, Bennett S. 1989. The 1986–1987 Excavations at Negroman-Tipu, Belize. *Mexicon* 11(6):114–17

Graham E, Jones GD, Kautz RR. 1985. Archaeology and history on a Spanish colonial frontier: the Macal-Tipu Project in western Belize. In *The Lowland Maya Postclassic*, ed. AF Chase, PM Rice, pp. 206–14. Austin: Univ. Tex. Press

Graham E, Pendergast DM, Jones GD. 1989. On the fringes of conquest: Maya-Spanish contact in colonial Belize. *Science* 246:1254–59

Graham E, Wayman M. 1989. Maya Material Culture at Conquest: Copper and Other Artifacts from Colonial Tipu, Belize. Annu. Meet. Am. Anthropol. Assoc., 88th, Washington, DC.

Greenwood RS, ed. 1976. *The Changing Faces of Main Street*. Greenwood & Assoc. Submitted to Redev. Agency, City of Buenaventura, CA

Greenwood RS, Browne RW. 1968. The chapel of Santa Gertrudis. *Pac. Coast Archaeol. Soc. Q.* 4(4):1–59

Greenwood RS, Gessler N. 1968. The Mission San Buenaventura aqueduct with particular reference to the fragments at Weldon Canyon. *Pac. Coast Archaeol. Society Q.* 4(4):61–87

Greer JW. 1967. *A Description of the Stratigraphy, Features and Artifacts from Archeological Excavation at the Alamo*. Archeol. Program Rep. No. 3. Austin: State Build. Comm.

Griffin JW. 1993. Foreword. See McEwan 1993a, pp. xv-xvii

Gust SM. 1982. Faunal analysis and butchering. In *The Ontiveros Adobe: Early Rancho Life in Alta California*, ed. JD Frierman, pp. 101–44. Greenwood & Assoc. Submitted to Redev. Agency, Santa Fe Springs, CA

Hackett CW, Shelby C. 1942. *Revolt of the Pueblo Indians of New Mexico and Otermin's Attempted Reconquest, 1680–1682*. Albuquerque: Univ. NM Press

Hann JH. 1988. *Apalachee: The Land Between the Rivers*. Gainesville: Univ. Fla. Press

Hann JH. 1990. Summary guide to Spanish Florida missions and *visitas* with churches in the sixteenth and seventeenth centuries. *The Americas* 46(4):417–514

Hann JH, ed. 1991. *Missions to the Calusa*. Gainesville: Univ. Fla./Fla. Mus. Nat. Hist.

Hann JH. 1993a. Document: 1630 Memorial of Fray Francisco Alonso de Jesus on Spanish Florida's missions and natives. *The Americas* 50(1):85–105

Hann JH. 1993b. The Mayaca and Jororo and missions to them. See McEwan 1993a, pp. 111–40

Hanson CA. 1990. *The Spanish Chapel at Xcaret, Quintana Roo*. Ms., New Orleans: Middle Am. Res. Inst., Tulane Univ.

Hanson CA. 1995. The Hispanic horizon in Yucatan: a model of Franciscan missionization. *Anc. Mesoam.* 6:15–28

Hanson CA. 1996. *The Postclassic Xtabay and Early Hispanic Cizin Ceramic Complexes at Ek Balam, Yucatan*. Ms., New Orleans: Middle Am. Res. Inst., Tulane Univ.

Hanson CA. 1997. *Incorporating the Sixteenth Century Periphery: From Tributary to Capitalist Production in the Yucatecan Maya Cuchcabal of Tiquibalón*. Presented at Annu. Conf. Hist. Underw. Archaeol., 30th, Corpus Christi, Tex.

Harkins C. 1990. On Franciscans, archeology, and old missions. See Thomas 1991b, pp. 459–73

Hayes AC. 1974. *The Four Churches of Pecos*. Albuquerque: Univ. NM Press

Hayes AC. 1981. *Contributions to Gran Quivira Archeology: Gran Quivira National Monument, New Mexico*. Washington, DC: Publ. Archaeol. No. 17, Natl. Park Serv.

Hayes AC, Young JN, Warren AH. 1981. *Excavations of Mound 7 Gran Quivira National Monument, New Mexico*. Washington, DC: Publ. Archaeol. No. 17, Natl. Park Serv.

Hefner RW, ed. 1993. *Conversion to Christianity: Historical and Anthropological Perspectives on a Great Transformation*. Berkeley: Univ. Calif. Press

Heizer RF, Hester TR. 1973. *The Archaeology of Bamert Cave, Amador County, California*. Berkeley: Univ. Calif. Archaeol. Res. Facil.

Hendry GW. 1931. The adobe brick as a historical source. *Agric. Hist.* 5:110–27

Herrin J. 1987. *The Formation of Christiandom*. Princeton, NJ: Princeton Univ. Press

Hester TR. 1989a. Texas and northeastern Mexico: an overview. See Thomas 1989a, pp. 191–211

Hester TR. 1989b. Perspectives on the material culture of the mission Indians of the Texas-northeastern Mexico borderlands. See Thomas 1989a, pp. 213–29

Hewett EL, Fisher RG. 1943. *Mission monuments of New Mexico*. Handbooks of Archaeological History, ed. EL Hewett. Albuquerque: Univ. NM Press

Hoover RL, Costello JG, eds. 1985. *Excava-*

*tions at Mission San Antonio 1976–1978*. Los Angeles: Univ. Calif., Inst. Archaeol. Monogr. No. 26

Hornbeck D. 1989. Economic growth and change at the missions of Alta California, 1769–1846. See Thomas 1989a, pp. 423–33

Horton R. 1975. On the rationality of conversion. *Africa* 45:219–35, 373–99

Hudson C, Smith M, Hally D, Polhemus R, DePratter C. 1985. Coosa: a chiefdom in the sixteenth century southeastern United States. *Am. Antiq.* 50:723–37

Ingham JM. 1986. *Mary, Michael and Lucifer: Folk Catholicism in Central Mexico*. Austin: Univ. Tex. Press

Ivey JE. 1981. *Archaeological Investigations at Rancho de las Cabras, Wilson County, Texas*. Archaeol. Surv. Rep. No. 104. San Antonio: Univ. Tex., Cent. Archaeol. Res.

Jackson RH. 1981. The last Jesuit censuses of the Pimeria Alta missions, 1761 and 1766. *Kiva* 46:243–72

Jackson RH. 1994. *Indian Population Decline: The Missions of Northwest New Spain 1687–1840*. Albuquerque: Univ. NM Press

Jackson RH. 1995. Introduction. See Langer & Jackson 1995, pp. vii–xviii

James GW. 1973. *The Old Franciscan Missions of California*. Boston: Milford House. (Originally publ. 1913)

Jiménez A. 1996. El Lejano Norte español: cómo escapar del "American West" y las "Spanish Borderlands". *Colon. Lat. Am. Hist. Rev.* 5(4):381–412

Johnson JR. 1989. The Chumash and the missions. See Thomas 1989a, pp. 365–76

Johnson KW. 1993. Mission Santa Fé de Toloca. See McEwan 1993a, pp. 141–64

Jones GD. 1978. The ethnohistory of the Guale Coast through 1684. See Thomas et al 1978, pp. 178–210

Jones GD. 1989. *Maya Resistance to Spanish Rule: Time and History on a Colonial Frontier*. Albuquerque: Univ. NM Press

Jones GD, Kautz RR, Graham E. 1986. Tipu: a Maya town on the Spanish colonial frontier. *Archaeology* 39(1):40–47

Kehoe A. 1979. The scared heart: a case study for stimulus diffusion. *Am. Ethnol.* 6: 763–71

Kessell JL. 1989. Spaniards and pueblos: from crusading intolerance to pragmatic accommodation. See Thomas 1989a, pp. 127–38

Klor de Alva JJ. 1982. Spiritual conflict and accommodation in New Spain: toward a typology of Aztec responses to Christianity. In *The Inca and Aztec States, 1400–1800*, ed. GA Collier, RI Rosaldo,

JD Wirth, pp. 345–66. New York: Academic

Kubler G. 1973. *The Religious Architecture of New Mexico in the Colonial Period and since the American Occupation*. Albuquerque: Univ. NM Press

Lambert JB, Graham E, Smith MT, Frye JS. 1994. Amber and jet from Tipu, Belize. *Anc. Mesoam.* 5:55–60

Langer E, Jackson RH, eds. 1995. *The New Latin American Mission History*. Lincoln: Univ. Nebr. Press

Larsen CS, Milner GR, eds. 1994. *In the Wake of Contact: Biological Responses to Conquest*. New York: Wiley-Liss

Latta MA. 1985. Identification of the 17th century French missions in Eastern Huronia. *Can. J. Archaeol.* 9(2):147–71

Lee G, Neuerberg N. 1989. The Alta California Indians as artists before and after contact. See Thomas 1989a, pp. 467–80

Leutenegger B. (Transl.) 1976. *Guidelines for a Texas Mission. Instructions for the Missionary of a Mission Concepcion in San Antonio*. San Antonio: Old Span. Missions Res. Libr., San Jose Mission

Lister FC, Lister RH. 1974. Maiolica in colonial Spanish America. *Hist. Archaeol.* 8: 17–52

Lister FC, Lister RH. 1982. *Sixteenth century maiolica pottery in the Valley of Mexico*. Anthropol. Pap. Univ. Ariz. 39. Tucson: Univ. Ariz. Press

Lister FC, Lister RH. 1987. *Andalusian Ceramics in Spain and New Spain*. Tucson: Univ. Ariz. Press

López Cervantes G. 1976. *Cerámica colonial en la Ciudad de México*. México DF: INAH

Loucks LJ. 1993. Spanish-Indian interaction on the Florida missions: the archaeology of Baptizing Spring. See McEwan 1993a, pp. 193–216

Lycett MT. 1989. Spanish contact and pueblo organization: long-term implications of European colonial expansion in the Rio Grande Valley, New Mexico. See Thomas 1989a, pp. 115–25

Lyon E. 1976. *The Enterprise of Florida*. Gainesville: Univ. Fla. Press

MacLeod MJ. 1991. Indian riots and rebellions in colonial Central America, 1530–1720: causes and categories. See Thomas 1991b, pp. 375–87

Marquardt WH. 1987. The Calusa formation in protohistoric South Florida. In *Power Relations and State Formations*, ed. TC Patterson, CW Gailey, pp. 98–116. Washington, DC: Archaeol. Sect., Am. Anthropol. Assoc.

Marquardt WH. 1988. Politics and production

## 60  GRAHAM

among the Calusa of South Florida. In *Hunters and Gatherers*. Vol. 1: *History, Environment, and Social Change among Hunting and Gathering Societies*, ed. D Riches, T Ingold, J Woodburn, pp. 161–88. London: Berg

Marrinan RA. 1993. Archaeological investigations at Mission Patale, 1984–1992. See McEwan 1993a, pp. 244–94

Marshall MP, Walt HJ. 1984. *Rio Abajo, Prehistory and History of a Rio Grande Province*. Santa Fe: NM Hist. Preserv. Program, Hist. Preserv. Div.

Mathes WM. 1989. Baja California: a special area of contact and colonization, 1535–1697. See Thomas 1989a, pp. 407–22

Matter RA. 1990. *Pre-Seminole Florida: Spanish Soldiers, Friars, and Indian Missions, 1513–1763*. New York: Garland

McAndrew J. 1965. *The Open-Air Churches of Sixteenth-Century Mexico: Atrios, Posas, Open Chapels, and Other Studies*. Cambridge: Harvard Univ. Press

McEwan BG. 1991. San Luis de Talimali: the archaeology of Spanish-Indian relations at a Florida mission. *Hist. Archaeol.* 25: 36–60

McEwan BG. 1992. The role of ceramics in Spain and Spanish America during the 16th century. *Hist. Archaeol.* 26(1): 92–108

McEwan BG, ed. 1993a. *The Spanish Missions of La Florida*. Gainesville: Univ. Fla. Press

McEwan BG. 1993b. Hispanic life on the seventeenth-century Florida frontier. See McEwan 1993a, pp. 295–321

McEwan BG, Larsen CS. 1996. *Archaeological Investigations in the Church at San Luis*. Presented at Soc. Hist. Archaeol. Conf., Cincinnati, OH

McGuire RH, Villalpando ME. 1989. Prehistory and the making of history in Sonora. See Thomas 1989a, pp. 159–77

Messmacher M. 1966. Capilla aberta en el Camino Real de Campeche. *Bol. INAH* 24: 13–21

Milanich JT. 1990. The European Entrada into La Florida. See Thomas 1990b, pp. 3–29

Milanich JT, Proctor S, eds. 1978. *Tacachale: Essays on the Indians of Florida and Southeastern Georgia during the Historic Period*. Gainesville: Univ. Fla. Press

Miller AG, Farriss NM. 1979. Religious syncretism in colonial Yucatan: the archaeological and ethnohistorical evidence from Tancah, Quintana Roo. In *Maya Archaeology and Ethnohistory*, ed. N Hammond, GR Willey, pp. 223–40. Austin: Univ. Tex. Press

Miroir MP, Harris RH, Blaine JC, McVay J, Book DC, et al. 1975. Benard de La Harpe and the Nassonite Post. *Bull. Tex. Archeol. Soc.* 44:113–68

Montgomery RG, Smith W, Brew JO. 1949. *Franciscan Awatovi, The Excavation and Conjectural Reconstruction of a 17th-century Spanish Mission Establishment at a Hopi Indian Town in Northeastern Arizona*. Pap. Peabody Mus. Am. Archaeol. Ethnol., Harvard Univ., Vol. 36. Rep. Awatovi Exped., No. 3. Cambridge, MA: Peabody Mus.

Mosk SA. 1938. Price fixing in Spanish California. *Calif Hist. Q.* 17(2):118–22

Newcomb WW Jr. 1983. The Karankawa. In *Southwest*, ed. A Ortiz, pp. 359–67. *Handb. North Am. Indians*, Vol. 10, ed. WC Sturtevant. Washington, DC: Smithson. Inst.

Noguera E. 1934. Estudio de la cerámica encontrada en el sitio donde estaba el Templo Mayor de México. *An. Mus. Nac. Arqueol., Hist. Etnogr., Epoca* 5(2):267–82

Pagden A. 1982. *The Fall of Natural Man: The American Indian and the Origins of Comparative Ethnology*. Cambridge: Cambridge Univ. Press

Peel JD. 1995. For who hath despised the day of small things?: missionary narratives and historical anthropology. *Comp. Stud. Soc. Hist.* 37:581

Pendergast DM. 1986. Stability through change: Lamanai, Belize, from the ninth to the seventeenth century. In *Late Lowland Maya Civilization: Classic to Postclassic*, ed. JA Sabloff, EW Andrews IV, pp. 223–49. Albuquerque: Univ. NM Press, Sch. Am. Res.

Pendergast DM. 1991. The southern Maya lowlands contact experience: the view from Lamanai, Belize. See Thomas 1991b, pp. 337–54

Pendergast DM. 1993. Worlds in collision: the Maya/Spanish encounter in sixteenth and seventeenth century Belize. See Bray 1993, pp. 105–43

Phelan JL. 1970. *The Millennial Kingdom of the Franciscans*. Berkeley: Univ. Calif. Press. (Originally publ. 1956)

Polzer CW. 1989. The Spanish colonial southwest: new technologies for old documents. See Thomas 1989a, pp. 179–88

Rausch JM. 1987. Frontiers in crisis: the breakdown of the missions in far northern Mexico and New Granada, 1821–1849. *Comp. Stud. Soc. Hist.* 29:340–59

Ricard R. 1966. *The Spiritual Conquest of Mexico*. Transl. LB Simpson. Berkeley: Univ. Calif. Press

Riley CL. 1987. *The Frontier People, The*

*Greater Southwest in the Protohistoric Period.* Albuquerque: Univ. NM Press

Roys RL. 1943. *The Indian Background of Colonial Yucatan.* Washington, DC: Carnegie Inst. Washington Publ. 548

Roys RL. 1957. *The Political Geography of the Yucatan Maya.* Washington, DC: Carnegie Inst. Washington Publ. 613

Saunders R. 1990. Ideal and innovation: Spanish mission architecture in the southeast. See Thomas 1990b, pp. 527–42

Saunders R. 1993. Architecture of the missions Santa Maria and Santa Catalina de Amelia. See McEwan 1993a, pp. 35–61

Scholes FV. 1929. Documents for the history of the New Mexican missions in the seventeenth century. *NM Hist. Rev.* 4(1):45–48, 4(2):195–201

Scholes FV. 1936–1937. Church and state in New Mexico, 1610–1650. *NM Hist. Rev.* 11(1):9–76; (2):145–78; (3):283–94; (4): 297–349; 12(1):78–106

Schuetz MK. 1966. *Historic Background of the Mission San Antonio de Valero.* Archeol. Program Rep. No. 1. Austin: State Build. Comm.

Schuetz MK. 1968. *The History and Archeology of Mission San Juan Capistrano, San Antonio, Texas,* Vol. 1: *Historical Documentation and Description of the Structures.* Archaeol. Program Rep. No. 10. Austin: State Build. Comm.

Schuetz MK. 1969. *The History and Archeology of Mission San Juan Capistrano, San Antonio, Texas,* Vol. 2: *Description of the Artifacts and Ethno-History of the Coahuiltecan Indians.* Archaeol. Program Rep. No. 11. Austin: State Build. Comm.

Seifert DJ. 1975. Archaeological majolicas of the Teotihuacán Valley. *Actas XLI Congr. Int. Am.* 1:238–51

Service ER. 1955. Indian-European relations in colonial Latin America. *Am. Anthropol.* 57(3):411–25

Shapiro GN, Hann JH. 1990. The documentary image of the council houses of Spanish Florida tested by excavations at the Mission of San Luis de Talimali. See Thomas 1990b, pp. 511–26

Shea JG. 1855. *History of the Catholic Missions among the Indian Tribes of the United States 1529–1854.* New York: Edward Dunigan & Brother

Simmons SE. 1991. *Arrows of Consequence: Contact Period Maya Tool Technology at Tipu, Belize.* MA thesis. Dep. Anthropol., Univ. Mass., Boston

Simmons SE. 1995. Maya resistance, Maya resolve: the tools of autonomy from Tipu, Belize. *Anc. Mesoam.* 6(2):135–46

Smith MT, Graham E, Pendergast DM. 1994.

European beads from Spanish-Colonial Lamanai and Tipu, Belize. *Beads* 6:21–47

Snow DH. 1967. Archaeology and nineteenth century missions. *Hist. Archaeol.* 1:57–59

South S. 1988. Santa Elena: threshold of conquest. In *The Recovery of Meaning: Historical Archaeology in the Eastern United States,* ed. MP Leone, PB Potter Jr, pp. 27–71. Washington, DC: Smithson. Inst.

Spielmann KA. 1989. Colonists, hunters, and farmers: plains-pueblo interaction in the seventeenth century. See Thomas 1989a, pp. 101–13

Stubbs S. 1959. "New" old churches found at Quarai and Tabira (Pueblo Blanco). *El Palacio* 66(5):162–69

Sturtevant WC. 1962. Spanish-Indian relations in southeastern North America. *Ethnohistory* 9:41–94

Sweet D. 1995. The Ibero-American frontier mission in native American history. See Langer & Jackson 1995, pp. 1–48

Tainter JA, Gillio DA. 1980. *Cultural Resources Overview: Mt. Taylor Area, New Mexico.* USDA For. Serv., Southwest Reg., Albuquerque/USDI, Bur. Land Manage., Santa Fe

Tainter JA, Levine F. 1987. *Cultural Resources Overview: Central New Mexico.* USDA For. Serv., Southwest Reg., Albuquerque/USDI, Bur. Land Manage., Santa Fe

Thomas DH. 1987. *The Archaeology of Mission Santa Catalina de Guale: 1. Search and Discovery,* Anthropol. Pap. Vol. 63, Part 2. New York: Am. Mus. Nat. Hist.

Thomas DH. 1988. Saints and soldiers at Santa Catalina: Hispanic designs for colonial America. In *The Recovery of Meaning: Historical Archaeology in the Eastern United States,* ed. MP Leone, PB Potter Jr, pp. 73–140. Washington, DC: Smithson. Inst.

Thomas DH, ed. 1989a. *Columbian Consequences Vol. 1: Archaeological and Historical Perspectives on the Spanish Borderlands West,* Washington, DC: Smithson. Inst.

Thomas DH. 1989b. Columbian consequences: the Spanish borderlands in Cubist perspective. See Thomas 1989a, pp. 1–14

Thomas DH, ed. 1990a. *Columbian Consequences Vol. 2: Archaeological and Historical Perspectives on the Spanish Borderlands East,* Washington, DC: Smithson. Inst.

Thomas DH. 1990b. The Spanish Missions of La Florida: an overview. See Thomas 1990a, pp. 357–97

Thomas DH, ed. 1991a. *Spanish Borderlands*

*Sourcebooks 23: The Missions of Spanish Florida.* New York: Garland

Thomas DH, ed. 1991b. *Columbian Consequences: The Spanish Borderlands in Pan-American Perspective,* Vol. 3. Washington, DC: Smithson. Inst.

Thomas DH. 1993. The archaeology of Mission Santa Catalina de Guale: our first 15 years. See McEwan 1993a, pp. 1–34

Thomas DH, Jones GD, Durham RS, Larsen CS, eds. 1978. *The Anthropology of St. Catherines Island: 1. The Natural and Cultural History,* Anthropol. Pap. Vol. 55, Part 2. New York: Am. Mus. Nat. Hist.

Thompson DE. 1954. Maya paganism and Christianity. See Edmonson et al 1954, pp. 1–36

Toulouse JH Jr, Stephenson RL. 1960. *Excavations at Pueblo Pardo.* Pap. Anthropol. No. 2. Santa Fe: Mus. NM

Tozzer AM, (Transl.). 1941. *Landa's Relación de las Cosas de Yucatan.* Pap. Peabody Mus. Am. Archaeol. Ethnol., Harvard Univ., Vol. 18. Cambridge, MA: Peabody Mus.

Tunnell CD, Ambler JR. 1967. *Archaeological Excavations at Presidio San Augustín de Ahumada, with a Historical Background by J.V. Clay.* Archaeol. Program Rep. No. 6. Austin: State Build. Comm.

Tunnell CD, Newcomb WW Jr. 1969. *A Lipan Apache Mission, San Lorenzo de la Santa Cruz, 1762–1771.* Austin: Tex. Mem. Mus., Bull. No. 14

Vivian RG. 1964. *Excavations in a 17th Century Jumano Pueblo, Gran Quivira.* Archaeol. Res. Ser. 8. Washington, DC: Natl. Park Ser.

Walker PL, Lambert P, DeNiro MJ. 1989. The effects of European contact on the health of Alta California Indians. See Thomas 1989a, pp. 349–64

Webb EB. 1982. *Indian Life at the Old Missions.* Lincoln: Univ. Nebr. Press

Weber DJ. 1968. *The Missions and Missionaries of Baja California.* Los Angeles: Dawson's Book Shop

Weber DJ. 1988. *Myth and the History of the Hispanic Southwest: Essays by David J. Weber.* Albuquerque: Univ. NM Press

Weber DJ. 1990. Blood of martyrs, blood of Indians: toward a more balanced view of Spanish missions in seventeenth-century North America. See Thomas 1990b, pp. 429–48

Weber FJ. 1979. Introduction. In *New Spain's Far Northern Frontier, Essays on Spain in the American West, 1540–1821,* ed. FJ Weber, pp. vii-xvii. Albuquerque: Univ. NM Press

Weisman BR. 1992. *Excavations on the Franciscan Frontier—Archaeology at the Fig Springs Mission.* Gainesville: Univ. Press Fla./Fla. Mus. Nat. Hist.

Weisman BR. 1993. Archaeology of Fig Springs Mission, Ichetucknee Springs State Park. See McEwan 1993a, pp. 165–92

West GJ. 1989. Early historic vegetation change in Alta California: the fossil evidence. See Thomas 1989a, pp. 333–48

Whigham T. 1995. Paraguay's pueblos de Indios: echoes of a missionary past. See Langer & Jackson 1995, pp. 157–85

White CD. 1986. *Paleodiet and nutrition of the ancient Maya at Lamanai, Belize: a study of trace elements, stable isotopes, nutritional and dental pathologies.* MA thesis. Dep. Anthropol., Trent Univ., Peterborough, Ont.

White CD. 1989. Ancient Maya diet: as inferred from isotopic and elemental analysis of human bone. *J. Archaeol. Sci.* 16: 451–74

White CD, Wright LE, Pendergast DM. 1994. Biological disruption in the early Colonial period at Lamanai. See Larsen & Milner 1994, pp. 135–45

Widmer RJ. 1988. *The Evolution of the Calusa: A Non-agricultural Chiefdom on the Southwest Florida Coast.* Tuscaloosa: Univ. Ala. Press

Wilcox DR, Masse WB. 1981. A history of protohistoric studies in the North American southwest. In *The Protohistoric Period in the North American Southwest, A.D. 1450–1700,* ed. DR Wilcox, WB Masse, pp. 1–27. Anthropol. Res. Pap. No. 24. Tempe: Ariz. State Univ.

Wolf ER. 1984. *Europe and the People without History.* Berkeley: Univ. Calif. Press

Yadeun J. 1978. Arqueología de la arqueología. *Rev. Mex. Estud. Antropol.* 24(2): 152–91

*Annu. Rev. Anthropol. 1998. 27:63–82*
*Copyright © 1998 by Annual Reviews. All rights reserved*

# THE ARCHAEOLOGY OF THE AFRICAN DIASPORA

## C. E. Orser, Jr.

Anthropology Program, Illinois State University, Normal, Illinois 61790-4640;
e-mail ceorser@ilstu.edu

KEY WORDS:   post-Columbian archaeology, transcontinental African culture, maroons, race and racism, archaeological interpretation

### ABSTRACT

Archaeologists currently studying the African diaspora generally examine three broad issues, in decreasing order of prominence: the material identification of African identity, the archaeology of freedom at maroon sites, and race and racism. While conducting this research, several scholars have learned that many nonarchaeologists are deeply interested in their interpretations. At the present time, the archaeology of the African diaspora is not a truly global pursuit and the New World is overrepresented. This situation should change as archaeologists around the world discover post-Columbian archaeology and take up diasporic investigations.

## INTRODUCTION

The archaeology of the post-Columbian African diaspora has the potential to become one of the most important kinds of archaeology in the world. Archaeologists working on small portions of the African diaspora are conducting research that is often the driving force behind much of today's most interesting and intellectually satisfying historical archaeology. The archaeologists' advances and refinements in this area of research generally have application throughout post-Columbian archaeology because the topics they are pursuing reach into every corner of archaeological thought and practice. In this essay, I explore three prominent areas of research: the archaeology of cultural identity, the material aspects of freedom from enslavement, and the archaeological examination of race. I also explore a practical matter in the archaeology of the African diaspora, namely the idea that the archaeologists' interpretations have an impact that reaches far beyond the often narrow confines of professional archaeology.

0084-6570/98/1015-0063$08.00

Given the rapidly expanding nature of the archaeology of the African diaspora, I cannot provide an exhaustive overview in this brief essay. Instead, I seek only to present my perspective on the most far-reaching aspects of this archaeology and to explore some of the key issues that are central to the archaeological investigation of the spread of Africans across the globe. My focus is specifically on the archaeology of the transcontinental diaspora of African peoples rather than on the internal movements of peoples within the African continent.

Before beginning, I must address the issue of coverage. Some historians argue that the post-Columbian slave trade is largely responsible for the African presence in locales around the globe (e.g. Harris 1996). Many of these same historians, however, also point out that African peoples settled outside Africa at least 1,500 years before the commencement of the post-Columbian slave trade. Arab traders regularly took African slaves—usually identified as non-Muslim infidels—to the Middle East, India, and Asia, and Africans who were not enslaved traveled the globe as sailors, explorers, missionaries, and merchants. Without question, the African diaspora has deep roots in history and is a truly global phenomenon.

Regrettably, archaeologists have not kept pace with historians in examining the global nature of the diaspora, and our knowledge is unrealistically skewed toward the New World. The reason for the unfair representation of post-Columbian, New World Africans in the archaeological examination of the African diaspora has to do with the slow worldwide development of an archaeology dedicated to the study of the modern world. At the same time, a great deal of the world's archaeology has been focused on the application of its results to nation building and nationalism. For example, in Spain, where we may reasonably expect to see clear, early evidence of an African presence, Islamic archaeology has been slow to develop, and its precise character is still being formulated (Díaz-Andreu 1996). By the same token, archaeologists in much of Southeast Asia have ignored their region's African history in favor of an archaeology directed toward prehistoric and European colonial history (Proust 1993). As a result, the archaeology of the African diaspora as presently constructed focuses on the New World, the region where the archaeology of the Africa diaspora is most advanced. So, while my coverage cannot be as global as I might wish, the issues I explore have wide application, and it is likely that archaeologists around the world will eventually confront them at numerous sites related to the African diaspora.

## BEGINNINGS

Everyone with even a passing knowledge of world history knows that diverse African peoples were dispersed outside their homelands by numerous historical forces, led most visibly by Europe's postmedieval search for global wealth, power, and political domination. Historians have been piecing together the diverse historical strands of the African diaspora for years, but it has been only recently that archaeologists have understood the importance of this massive population movement. The immaturity of historical archaeology is undoubtedly part of the reason for the archaeologists' late acknowledgment of the historical and cultural importance of diasporic studies, and it has been only within recent years that archaeologists have even begun to use the word "diaspora" in their writings.

The roots of historical archaeology as a field designed specifically to investigate post-Columbian history extend only to the 1930s. From then until the late 1960s, historical archaeologists directed their excavations almost exclusively toward sites and properties associated with the wealthy and the famous (Orser & Fagan 1995, pp. 25–32). In the American South, this interest translated into the study of plantation mansions, while in the North, archaeologists generally directed their excavations toward colonial settlements or sites associated with the birth of the nation. Such research often had the tangible goal of physical restoration or reconstruction of buildings and monuments intended to promote the American national ideology. These reconstruction projects in turn fed a growing interest in historical tourism and the telling of history through the homes, workplaces, and settlements of history's elites. Despite the disciplinary urge to study high society, many archaeologists were inspired by the ethnic pride movements that appeared around the globe, and many followed their colleagues in the social sciences and the humanities in turning their attention to the oppressed, ill-used, or forgotten. As part of their awakening, archaeologists developed a "subordinate perspective" as a way of examining culture and history from the bottom up (Orser 1990, pp. 122–29). This shift in focus from the elite minority to the subordinate majority inspired many archaeologists to investigate the lives of men and women who up until then had been largely erased from traditional history. Relying for the most part on their anthropological training, American archaeologists sought ways to understand these men and women on their own terms.

Before the 1980s, when archaeologists first combined their interest in subordinate lifeways with African diasporic history, they overwhelmingly turned, with some notable exceptions (e.g. Bullen & Bullen 1945; Deetz 1977, pp. 138–154; Schuyler 1974), to the slaves of the American South and the Caribbean. As a result, the archaeology of the African diaspora began and largely remains to this day an archaeology of New World slavery (but see Cabak et al 1995; Schuyler 1980), a situation many archaeologists find especially frustrating given the richness and variety of the African experience outside Africa, particularly in places like colonial New England and early modern Europe, where the African presence has been often overlooked (Garman 1994, pp. 89–90). (Useful historical overviews of plantation archaeology appear in Fairbanks 1983, 1984; Orser 1984, 1990; Samford 1996; Singleton 1991, 1995.) The unequal distribution of archaeological research in the New World tends to foreground the United States and the Caribbean while downplaying or even ignoring important African contributions in Asia, the Middle East, and Europe (e.g. Saunders 1982).

Several historians have recently illustrated the diasporic nature of African cultural history, and many of them have diligently worked to prove the African contribution to New World history (e.g. Curtin 1990; Gilroy 1993; Harris 1993; Jalloh & Maizlish 1996; Lemelle & Kelley 1994; Solow 1991). Today, many historical archaeologists freely acknowledge that the history they study is inexorably entangled with global capitalism, imperialism, and colonialism (Orser 1996). For the most part, their research on the African diaspora has always contained a tacit understanding of the worldwide nature of post-Columbian African life, a transcontinental conceptualization that began with the search for African identity at archaeological sites outside Africa.

## THE ARCHAEOLOGY OF AFRICAN IDENTITY

When historical archaeologists first turned to the study of people of African heritage outside Africa, they were encouraged by their anthropological training to examine them as members of displaced cultures. As initially established, the archaeologists' contribution to African diasporic studies would be to provide tangible evidence for the continuation of African cultural traits beyond the borders of Africa. In beginning this program of study, archaeologists situated themselves within the famous Herskovits-Frazier debate over whether enslaved men and women retained elements of their original African cultures in the New World. Archaeology was immediately relevant to this debate because of the archaeologists' potential to provide material evidence of African stylistic traits on physical objects made and used outside Africa. The search for such material "Africanisms" also suited the disciplinary needs of historical archaeologists because it presented a way for them to prove that their field of study, always something of a second cousin in American archaeology (Little 1994, p. 30), had a serious contribution to make to anthropological scholarship. Clearly, archaeological excavation at sites associated with participants of the African diaspora could provide clues about cultural survival as no other discipline could. At the same time, the ability of historical archaeologists to offer tangible information about a subject that bridged anthropology, history, folklore, architecture, and several other disciplines proved that the field really was as cross-disciplinary as its proponents claimed.

Thus, when the founder of American plantation archaeology, Charles Fairbanks, began his excavations at Kingsley Plantation in 1968, he sought to support Herskovits by finding Africanisms at the plantation's old slave cabins.

When he was forced to conclude "that no surely African elements in the material culture could be identified" (Fairbanks 1974, p. 90), it was clear that even archaeologists would have difficulty identifying Africanisms. It is important to note, however, that the lack of evidence did not convince archaeologists that Frazier had been correct that the horrors of the Middle Passage had destroyed the slaves' cultural knowledge. On the contrary, most historical archaeologists steadfastly retained their belief in the resilience of African cultures.

The controversy over the presence of Africanisms continues to be a subject of intense interest to scholars in several disciplines (Palmié 1995), and the subject continues to attract the attention of archaeologists. As the number of historical archaeologists has grown since the late 1960s, so too has the intensity of the search for Africanisms in archaeological deposits.

Archaeologists interested in locating evidence of African survivals in archaeological deposits have been perhaps the most optimistic about the potential of research at cemeteries. After conducting years of research at numerous prehistoric cemeteries throughout Native North America, archaeologists had come to rely on the assumption that the temporally static nature of burial would preserve the social elements of life in the material accoutrements of death. Based on reams of comparative information, it seemed reasonable to conclude that a person expressing an African heritage in life would reflect this persona in death. Even in cases where it can be shown that grave accompaniments refer more to the social identity of living mourners than to the deceased, the presence of Africanisms in graves could still indicate a persistence of cultural traditions outside Africa.

One of the most successful examples of mortuary analysis related to the recognition of African identity was undertaken by Jerome Handler at Newton Plantation, a late seventeenth- and eighteenth-century estate in Barbados (Handler & Lange 1978). In two carefully argued studies, Handler demonstrated that African social persona could be discerned in the interment of individuals who in life had been perceived both positively and negatively (Handler 1996, 1997). To make these interpretations, Handler relied on his extensive historical knowledge of Barbadian culture as well as the careful analyses of the artifacts contained within the burials, supplemented with bioanthropological data.

With the growth of historical archaeology and the burgeoning perception that African diasporic studies had the potential to provide insights on a wide range of intellectually significant issues, post-Columbian archaeologists soon merged their interest in Africanisms with their long-standing fascination with ceramics. One of the most important and often-cited studies in this regard is Leland Ferguson's (1978) reconsideration of what had formerly been termed "Colono-Indian ware."

Ferguson argued that many of the morphological elements of this low-fired, unglazed pottery found on sites associated with Africans along the coast of the

American Southeast were consistent with pottery manufactured in the Caribbean and even in Africa. This interpretation placed Africa firmly in the archaeological picture and demonstrated that historical archaeologists could
provide tangible contributions to historical and cultural knowledge about subjects that had hitherto remained undocumented in the historical record.

The decision to link the New World and Africa via Colono ware ceramics
was an important turning point for the archaeology of the African diaspora because it clearly illustrated the global nature of the research. At the same time, it
supported the claims of cultural anthropologists that the identification of African culture outside Africa would be complex and multicultural (Mintz & Price
1976). Thus, when thinking about the cultural implications of this pottery further, Ferguson (1991) later proposed that the ceramics represented more than
just tangible Africanisms. The sherds were also symbolic representations of an
otherness that served both to empower African American slaves in their collective cultural difference and to provide a Pan-African sense of syncretic culture.
From here, it was only a short step to the realization that any African culture
outside Africa would be a creolized mixture of diverse elements and that many
of the cultural elements of Africa would be masked, hidden, or even missing
from archaeological deposits, even in mortuary contexts (Garman 1994, pp.
80–82; Jamieson 1995, pp. 51–54).

Research suggests that time may structure the presence of Africanisms at
archaeological sites, with cemeteries again being instructive. Early interments,
such as those at Newton Plantation in Barbados, tend to exhibit African characteristics, whereas later ones, such as those excavated in New Orleans, dating
to around 1800 (Owsley et al 1987), show no obvious signs of African heritage. By the same token, though, burials salvaged from a cemetery on Montserrat contained no obvious African elements, even though the site was contemporaneous with Newton Plantation (Watters 1987, p. 307). As a result, today's archaeologists have learned to be cautious when making comparisons
between sites (Thomas 1995). In any case, the temporal aspects of the current
evidence have the potential to take archaeologists back to the largely unsatis-
fying acculturation studies of the past (e.g. Wheaton & Garrow 1985). Still, the
end of African burial customs and the demise of the Colono ware industry provide evidence for important issues of cultural accommodation and survival
that archaeologists must address.

The difficulty of discovering Africanisms at archaeological sites has not
caused archaeologists to abandon the project. On the contrary, many historical
archaeologists have simply moved to new kinds of evidence, typically involved with ritual, religion, and symbolism (Brown & Cooper 1990; Franklin
1996; Orser 1994a; Russell 1997; Stine et al 1996; Wilkie 1995; Young 1996,
1997). These studies not only follow current archaeological practice, they also
demonstrate the tenacious character of cultural customs embedded within peo-

ples' beliefs systems and ritual behaviors. At the same time, the symbolic or ritual use of Africanisms by men and women outside Africa may speak to issues of resistance and cultural boundary maintenance that may exist in no other source.

## THE ARCHAEOLOGY OF FREEDOM FROM SLAVERY

Given the importance of examining resistance and cultural survival, many archaeologists are beginning to show great interest in maroon communities as truly fertile ground for anthropological research. This archaeology, though in its true infancy, is inexorably diasporic by nature, and archaeologists have already investigated sites in Brazil (Allen 1995; Funari 1995a,b, 1995/96, 1996a,b; Guimarães 1990; Guimarães & Lanna 1980; Orser 1992, 1993, 1994b, 1996), the Dominican Republic, Cuba (García Arévalo 1986), Jamaica (Agorsah 1990, 1993), and the United States (Deagan & MacMahon 1995; Nichols 1988; Weik 1997). Archaeologists are undoubtedly attracted to the study of maroon settlements for diverse reasons, not the least of which may be the romantic notion of African rebels openly defying the slave regime. In the often-overwhelming abundance of research on slavery, there is something refreshingly bold about examining men and women who threw off the shackles of slavery and demanded freedom on their own terms. At the same time, it is clear that many people of African descent have grown tired of hearing only about slavery and wish to know more about the material conditions of freedom (Leone et al 1995, p. 112).

But in addition to the romantic and often noble character of research on maroon settlements, archaeologists are intrigued by what maroon sites may reveal about African culture. Maroon research may offer important information about power relationships; the creation and maintenance of diverse social connections; and the preservation of economic, political, and spiritual life. In addition, archaeological research on maroons has the potential to provide information about the creation of syncretic cultures. The famous settlement of Palmares in Brazil provides an excellent example.

Slaves of African ancestry who ran away from the sugar plantations of the northeastern coast of Brazil created Palmares sometime around 1605. (Accessible overviews of Palmares can be found in Anderson 1996; Kent 1965; and Orser 1994a,b, 1996.) As the community cemented itself in the Brazilian backlands, the people of Palmares sustained numerous bloody attacks from Dutch and Portuguese militias that, as the shock troops of colonialism, were attempting to control the countryside for their nations' governments. But even in the face of such annual onslaught, the men and women of Palmares continued to prosper, and by the 1670s colonial observers reported that the maroon settlement housed about 20,000 people in 10 major villages. Given its geographic size and sociopolitical complexity, several scholars have referred to Palmares as both a kingdom and a state. Regardless of its sociopolitical designation, there is little doubt that Palmares was one of history's greatest maroon societies.

Current evidence suggests that Palmares retained a vibrant African character throughout its existence, based on the Angolan roots of its rulers and many of its inhabitants. Still, the settlers of Palmares incorporated diverse cultural elements within their towns and constructed strong connections with Native South Americans (who had lived in this part of Brazil for centuries), colonial Portuguese and Dutch government officials (who used alliances with Palmares for expedient political purposes), and Portuguese frontier settlers (who often clashed with a colonial government that represented the needs and desires of wealthy plantation owners, often to the exclusion of all else).

Archaeologists have only recently begun to study Palmares, concentrating their efforts on the Serra da Barriga, a hill in the State of Alagoas that was both the center of the settlement and the location of Palmares's final military defeat in 1694. The next several years' research at Palmares and other maroon sites promises to provide information that may prove central to our understanding of how diverse peoples created and maintained the syncretic cultures of the African diaspora. The men, women, and children of Palmares forged their own freedom through running away, an act that served as a blow to the slave regime on the Brazilian coast. The rigorous efforts of the Portuguese to destroy Palmares amply demonstrated the danger maroon settlements created for their oppressive power, and the people of Palmares tenaciously fought to retain their freedom in the face of enslavement or death if recaptured. Thus, it is the attainment and retention of freedom in an inhuman environment of slavery that characterizes the history of Palmares and all other maroon communities wherever they may be found.

Another site of importance to the archaeology of the African diaspora is Gracia Real de Santa Teresa de Mose, located two miles north of colonial St. Augustine, Florida. In 1738, more than 100 enslaved Africans fled their British captors in the Carolinas and headed south for the safety of Spanish St. Augustine. Serving as a beacon of freedom to the thousands of enslaved men and women living along the Carolina coast, the settlement of Mose and its adjoining fort became a regular part of the Spanish defenses in Florida (Deagan & MacMahon 1995, p. 20). As was true of Palmares, the people of Mose created a new culture, speaking several European and Native American languages, converting to Christianity, and celebrating Catholic feast days with traditional African dress and music (Landers 1990, p. 28).

Palmares and Mose are important places within the cultural history of the African diaspora. As locales where formerly enslaved men and women openly flaunted the slave regime, both sites promise to provide abundant material information about the cultural aspects of African life outside Africa and to present new information about creolization, an emerging topic of importance to historical archaeologists (Ferguson 1992). At the same time, increased research may encourage some anthropologists to move away from creolization studies in favor of studies of cultural maintenance.

Some historians (e.g. Chambers 1996, Thornton 1992) are beginning to question the creolization thesis, arguing that slaves imported into various parts of the world did not create populations as heterogeneous as we might suppose. In some cases, for example, slave importers tended to seek men and women from specific parts of Africa. Historians have learned, for example, that rice-growing plantation owners sought to acquire laborers from areas of Africa already familiar with rice cultivation (Joyner 1984, pp. 13–14). Thus, populations of Africans with long rice-growing traditions appear congregated in various parts of the world. By the same token, we may well suppose that free Africans able to resettle where they pleased would have sought social environments with people of similar cultural backgrounds and traditions. Given this developing understanding, it appears that maroon societies also have the potential to provide information about the efforts of displaced Africans to maintain their traditional cultures in unfamiliar environments.

The archaeology of maroons will surely grow in prominence over the next several years. Before this archaeology can assume its rightful place in scholarship, however, archaeologists must confront several important practical and theoretical problems. In the first place, maroon sites are difficult to locate. Fugitive slaves sited their rebel communities in secluded, often inaccessible places. Archaeological research supports this simple reality, and many maroon sites are still difficult to reach today. As a result, archaeological efforts to examine maroon settlements can be extremely time consuming and expensive. The research at Fort Mose was a success, not only because of the expert collaborative team assembled to complete the study, but also because the State of Florida took a strong interest in the site and passed a bill to provide funds for its investigation (Deagan & MacMahon 1995, p. vii). Similar funds have not been forthcoming for archeological research at Palmares, and at least until 1990, Jamaica had shown no real interest in its maroon history (Agorsah 1990, p. 15).

The discovery of maroon sites presents a practical problem for archaeologists, but once found, these sites offer problems in analysis and interpretation. Many of the most pressing questions are simplistic, beginning with the most basic one: How do archaeologists recognize the material culture of marronage? Research at Gracia Real de Santa Teresa de Mose provides an understanding of the depth of this problem.

The analysis of the almost 29,000 animal bones collected from excavations at Mose suggests a distinctive pattern of subsistence at this free, African American town and fort (Reitz 1994). Its people consumed more domestic animal meat than did the surrounding Native Americans, but less than the Spanish residents of nearby St. Augustine. Nonetheless, it seems clear that the men and women of Mose had a measure of culinary self-sufficiency that was generally unknown on the coastal plantations to the north, where slaves had more access to domestic animal species. Like the surrounding Native Americans, the residents of Mose exploited the locally available wild animal populations, including both terrestrial and aquatic species.

The archaeological understanding that Africans in the New World used wild food species for subsistence is not new. In fact, the zooarchaeologist who studied the Mose remains made this discovery long ago (Reitz et al 1985), and this knowledge has served the archaeologists of the African diaspora exceedingly well ever since. But even though we have a good knowledge of the subsistence patterns of Mose, the faunal information offers little in the way of social clues about the community. Thus, the investigator used Africanisms to explain the sociocultural elements of the people's food usage. In her words, "Daily tasks may have been performed by each ethnic group in accordance with traditional beliefs, values, and customs not readily identified in faunal assemblages" (Reitz 1994, p. 38). We can conclude, then, that the animal bones, though providing an important glimpse of subsistence at Gracia Real de Santa Teresa de Mose, does not provide information that can be used to address questions of cultural formation and maintenance. This observation amply shows how far historical archaeologists are from advancing sophisticated interpretations of maroon culture based on archaeological remains, even from sites that are expertly excavated with adequate funds.

Today's archaeologists simply do not understand enough about how the material culture of resistance correlates with or diverges from the material elements of cultural formation or transformation. The artifact photographs reproduced in the beautifully presented study of Fort Mose (Deagan & MacMahon 1995, pp. 27, 43, 44) depict artifacts that one could find at almost any Spanish colonial site in the world. Included in the collection are gunflints, lead shot, spoon handles, buttons, potsherds, bottle necks, and belt buckles. Comparative archaeological information is woefully inadequate in northeastern Brazil, but the artifacts excavated from the Serra da Barriga are similarly unenlightening. The collection contains sherds that resemble local Native American pottery as well as pieces of majolica that could have been made on the Brazilian coast, in Portugal, or in any unidentified colonial workshop. Thus, it is no exaggeration to state that archaeologists have yet to devise intellectually satisfying ways to interpret the material lives of fugitive men, women, and children living in freedom on their own terms in maroon settlements.

It is perhaps for this reason that archaeologists examining maroon sites have usually turned to the interpretation of single artifacts. One type of artifact to which archaeologists have often turned is the smoking pipe. In my interpretation of Palmares, for example, I used four pipes collected from the Serra da Barriga by a local resident (Orser 1996, pp. 123–29). I could not verify the precise context of these pipes, but they bore strong morphological similarities to pipes collected at the Newton Plantation cemetery (Handler & Lange 1978, p. 130; Handler 1983) and at maroon settlements in the Dominican Republic and Cuba (García Arévalo 1986, p. 50; Deagan & MacMahon 1995, p. 14).

Many pipes from maroon settlements exhibit incised decorations. The pipes found in Cuba and the Dominican Republic were etched with geometrical designs (García Arévalo 1986, p. 50), reminiscent of pipes known both from Africa and from seventeenth-century sites in the Chesapeake region of the United States (Emerson 1988, 1994). In contrast, the artisans who made the Palmares pipes had carved or molded designs into them rather than using an etching technique. I interpreted the decorations on two of the pipes as representing stylized palm tree fronds. I argued that the pipes, rather than being just functional artifacts, were material proclamations about Palmares. As tangible, largely immutable objects, the pipes said to the world that Palmares continued to exist. Historians believe that the people of Palmares called their settlement Angola Janga, or Little Angola, even though the Portuguese knew it as the "place of palm trees." As such, it is possible that these pipes were small but meaningful reminders that the men, women, and children of Palmares continued openly to flaunt the slave regime using a symbol understood outside Palmares. At the same time, it is possible that these smoking pipes served as physical links between Brazil and maroons everywhere, just as they functioned as links of a different kind to the Portuguese and indeed the entire European system of enforced African bondage.

## ARCHAEOLOGY AND RACE

Issues of cultural identity and the interpretation of maroon settlements will continue to challenge historical archaeologists for many years. Obstacles to interpretation and understanding in these two areas have already proven to be formidable. Still, the challenges faced in these areas of research will be equaled by the problems presented when historical archaeologists turn to issues of race (Orser 1998).

We saw above that many historical archaeologists have sought to associate past human populations with specific types or classes of material culture. In relation to peoples of African heritage, this urge has caused many historical archaeologists, following a long-standing anthropological tradition, to refer to these material markers of identity as Africanisms. In other contexts, they often refer to such tangible aspects of identity as ethnic markers.

The use of the term "ethnic" is not accidental. Because historical archaeologists usually have access to textual documentation that supports their archaeological work, they can generally associate certain peoples with particular sites. These identifications sometimes assume stereotypic form, so that Asian immigrants appear at historic Chinatowns, men and women from Wales at mining communities, and people of African heritage on slave plantations. Many historical archaeologists have come to realize that such easy connections between specific kinds of artifacts and past groups of men and women are often too facile to have meaning (e.g. Muller 1994; Paynter 1990). At worst, such linkages often carry racist overtones, such as assuming that only Chinese immigrants used opium pipes when in reality opium use among non-Chinese was widespread in the late nineteenth century (Sando & Felton 1993, p. 169).

Stereotypic interpretations unfortunately have not entirely left historical archaeology, but some archaeologists are pursuing more fruitful lines of research. Some researchers now acknowledge that artifacts, rather than being simply static containers of ethnic self-identity, can serve as symbols of group identity whose meanings can be manipulated at the same time they promote a sense of peoplehood (Praetzellis et al 1987; Praetzellis 1991; Staski 1990, 1993).

Although some historical archaeologists have presented sophisticated ways in which to perceive the material aspects of ethnic self-identification, as a group they have been far less willing to examine race. In fact, many archaeologists have equated race with ethnicity. Race, though a significant element in the history of the African diaspora, has been largely absent from most archaeological research, even though race has never been absent from the sociohistorical realities of the diaspora.

Historical archaeologists have occasionally been willing to tackle the study of race where people of African ancestry are concerned. For example, in 1980, John Otto examined the material culture excavated at Cannon's Point Plantation, Georgia, along several social dimensions, one of which incorporated the concept of race as an imposed condition. Otto (1980) argued that race was a fixed legal status that created a division between "free white" owners and overseers and "unfree black" slaves. Otto used a caste model that was largely unsuccessful (Orser 1988), but he did insert the word "race" into the archaeological lexicon. Years later, David Babson (1990) used spatial patterns at a plantation in South Carolina to argue that racism was a factor in the physical arrangement of large antebellum estates, and more recently, Robert Fitts (1996) showed how racist attitudes were expressed spatially in the early history of Rhode Island. In another plantation study, Terrence Epperson (1990a, p. 36) argued that archaeologists must learn to examine race to aid in the "valorization of the African-American culture of resistance and the denaturalization of essentialist racial categories." This dual perspective permits archaeologists to realize that racism includes "contradictory tendencies to exclusion and incorporation, simultaneously providing a means of oppression and a locus of resistance" (Epperson 1990b, p. 341).

The kinds of studies historical archaeologists have so far undertaken demonstrate the difficulties of investigating a mutable designation like race with immutable physical objects. Clear interpretations are difficult to compose when we conceptualize groups as representing identifiable cultural dyads— e.g. Africans and non-Africans—but the act of interpretation grows considerably more complex when we also introduce the forces of market capitalism. Most archaeologists now examining the post-Columbian world readily acknowledge the role of capitalism in helping to shape the modern world. For many, the conduct of archaeology, particularly an archaeology that deals with the recent past, is impossible without capitalism. In concert with this view, several archaeologists are beginning to conduct extremely sophisticated analyses linking the forces of capitalism with the realities of race and racism. Paul Mullins (1996) has provided one of the most well constructed and potentially significant studies of this sort. Mullins examined a recent period of American history, 1850 to 1930, but his findings have ramifications for the study of the African diaspora everywhere in the world.

Mullins proposed that capitalism posed both an opportunity and a threat to African Americans. While the marketplace provided mechanisms for men and women of African heritage to improve their place in American society, it also presented a way for racists to pass a sentence of material inferiority on them. As we might imagine, this complex process was enacted in numerous historical ways in many material forms, but one example Mullins used was bric-a-brac. Although today we may be inclined to perceive knickknacks as meaningless kitsch without interpretive potential, Mullins viewed them as symbolically charged representations of American abundance, nationalism, and racial purity. In this sense, we may posit that these items had the same structural meaning as the maroon pipes mentioned above, except that the knickknacks were mass produced and sold as commodities. As signifiers of the national ideology, knickknacks were small pieces of the American dream that could assume prominent places in the parlors of non-African Americans, even though the objects themselves were inexpensive. According to Mullins, the meaning of these apparently insignificant pieces of kitsch changed with Emancipation. Understanding such altered meanings, some nineteenth-century social commentators opposed to enfranchisement argued that with freedom, African American men and women would waste their money on cheap objects like knickknacks. The answer to this recontextualization, in the American South at least, was to build plantation commissaries and to pay freed men and women tenant farmers with commissary tickets redeemable only at plantation stores. Even where tenants received wages, widespread racism in the countryside often kept them out of nearby towns where they could spend their money as they wished.

Mullins argued that when knickknacks began to appear in the homes of African Americans in the late nineteenth century, they were especially meaningful because they distanced their owners from the racial and class caricatures that racist America had constructed. When non-African American employers gave knickknacks to their African American domestic servants, this act of giving was charged with meaning. For the givers, the apparently inexpensive and trivial objects provided a mechanism to cement relationships of power and dominance. Those receiving the gifts, however, may have perceived these items as symbolic redefinitions of their material circumstances, in that they now owned and could display objects that had once been completely off limits to them (Mullins 1996, pp. 532–33).

Mullins's research shows that historical archaeologists still have much to learn about the relationship between material culture and racial perception. This line of investigation, if pursued throughout the world, has the potential to provide profound insights into the social dimensions of African life outside Africa. Before this sort of research can occur, historical archaeologists must be willing to confront race and racism, a trend that is just now beginning.

## THE RELEVANCE OF THE ARCHAEOLOGY

One of the points to emerge from research like that conducted by Mullins concerns the relevance of archaeological research to men and women living today. His interpretations have potential meaning for all people seeking to understand how the social inequalities of today were materially expressed in the past, even in fairly recent history.

It can no longer be denied that archaeology is a public pursuit. Recent controversies between archaeologists and traditional peoples around the globe over the repatriation of skeletal remains are a well-known case in point (Biolsi & Zimmerman 1997; Hubert 1988; Swidler et al 1997), and similar controversies have arisen over the excavation of African and African American remains (Harrington 1993; La Roche & Blakey 1997; Orser et al 1986; Powell & Dockall 1995).

The archaeologist's role in society at large has become a major topic of inquiry, particularly where it concerns nationalism and the use of archaeological remains to construct national identity (Díaz-Andreu & Champion 1996; Kohl & Fawcett 1995; Potter 1994). By the same token, the archaeologist's role in telling the story of the African diaspora has also been debated (Belgrave 1990; Blakey 1990; Epperson 1990a; Franklin 1995; Martin et al 1997; McDavid & Babson 1997). In historical archaeology, the debate has been conducted largely by scholars who believe that they carry their biases with them into their research (Leone et al 1995; Potter 1991) and those who believe, contrary to this view, that the strength of archaeology derives from its ability to provide fresh insights about the past (Farnsworth 1993; McKee 1994).

The controversy over the very foundations of archaeological interpretation was precipitated by Parker Potter's (1991) critique of plantation archaeologists who provided interpretations that, though they were not racist, could be used by racists to support their prejudiced way of looking at the world. Potter called attention to the idea that archaeological research could be used outside the profession by people with political agendas inconsistent with the goals of the original, scholarly research effort. The misapplication of research findings is, of course, nothing new in anthropology or archaeology, and Potter argued that archaeologists should learn to question why they make certain interpretations as opposed to others.

One of Potter's most controversial assertions was that African Americans should be the plantation archaeologist's primary audience because they are the people most likely to be affected by the archaeological interpretations (Potter 1991, p. 94). Arguing against this perspective, Farnsworth (1993) and McKee (1994) proposed that the archaeology of the African diaspora, as a scientific pursuit, should interest all people regardless of heritage. They argued that people of African descent have always had the ability to construct their own histories without the help of archaeologists, and any suggestion to the contrary is both condescending and patronizing. Leone and his associates in Annapolis, Maryland, learned this lesson well with their interpretation of a hot, or straightening, comb excavated from the Gott's Court site (Leone et al 1995, pp. 113–14). Whereas Leone et al initially interpreted the comb in terms of assimilation, African Americans countered that the comb provided for social negotiation wherein by straightening their hair they could appear to be assimilating while they in fact were striving for cultural survival.

The presentation of counterinterpretations by nonarchaeologists has caused some archaeologists to wonder ever more seriously about which audiences should be served by their research. The recent publication of a collection of papers about public participation in African American archaeology illustrates not only that archaeologists are cognizant of the issues of inclusion, but also that solutions will be complex and often locally formulated in a global environment (McDavid & Babson 1997).

The problems of inclusion attach to sites located throughout the world of the African diaspora, particularly in cases where the sites may figure into local conceptions of identity. We discovered in our research at Palmares, for example, just how important the idea of this maroon settlement, as a mythology, was to the people of the African Brazilian community. Signs of this importance are easy to identify. In 1994, the Brazilian Ministry of Culture held an international conference entitled "Palmares: 300 Years" to pay homage to the men and women of the maroon, and today the Serra da Barriga is a national monument. Zumbi, the last ruler of Palmares, is widely revered; he is often referred to as the "first great Negro of Brazil" (Souza 1963, p. 15). In Maceió, the largest city near the Serra da Barriga, jets land at Palmares Field, and the main highway to the city runs past a Zumbi Auto Parts store. In the town of União dos Palmares, at the foot of the Serra da Barriga, a huge image of Zumbi adorns the outer wall of the bus depot, and a Foto Zumbi—a film processing store—sits nearby. In 1969, a leftist group took the name Armed Revolutionary Vanguard—Palmares, and movie companies have produced two feature films about Palmares (Orser 1996, p. 202). All archaeological research at the site must be approved by the Brazilian government and receive the endorsement of the local black power movement. Anyone who thinks that the archaeology of Palmares is only about the past is sorely mistaken.

## CONCLUSION

In this brief essay, I have only been able to touch upon four elements in the current archaeology of the African diaspora: the material identification of African identity, the material aspects of maroon culture, the archaeology of race, and the relevance of the archaeological research to nonarchaeologists. These topics will be explored in great detail in the future, and new areas of research will undoubtedly be proposed. At this point in time, much of the archaeology of the African diaspora is an archaeology of the New World. Archaeologists' overwhelming focus on the United States and the Caribbean is more a statement on the current condition of global historical archaeology than any assessment of the importance of certain geographic locales. Even though African men and women, both free and enslaved, have traveled the world for generations, today's archaeologists know little about them and the cultures they helped to construct. Happily, however, a whole cadre of dedicated archaeologists are working diligently to rectify the current paucity of research. Within the next few years, these scholars are sure to develop truly global perspectives on the African diaspora.

Visit the *Annual Reviews home page* at
http://www.AnnualReviews.org.

## Literature Cited

Agorsah EK. 1990. Archaeology of maroon heritage in Jamaica. *Archaeol. Jam.* 2: 14–19

Agorsah EK. 1993. Archaeology and resistance history in the Caribbean. *Afr. Archaeol. Rev.* 11:175–95

Allen SJ. 1995. *Africanisms, mosaics, and creativity: the historical archaeology of Palmares.* MA thesis. Brown Univ., Providence, RI

Anderson RN. 1996. The quilombo of Palmares: a new overview of a maroon state in seventeenth-century Brazil. *J. Lat. Am. Stud.* 28:545–66

Babson DW. 1990. The archaeology of racism and ethnicity on southern plantations. *Hist. Archaeol.* 24(4):20–28

Belgrave R. 1990. Black people and museums: the Caribbean heritage project in Southampton. In *The Politics of the Past*, ed. P Gathercole, D Lowenthal, pp. 63–73. London: Unwin Hyman

Biolsi T, Zimmerman J, eds. 1997. *Indians and Anthropologists: Vine Deloria, Jr. and the Critique of Anthropology.* Tucson: Univ. Ariz. Press

Blakey ML. 1990. American nationality and ethnicity in the depicted past. In *The Politics of the Past*, ed. P Gathercole, D Lowenthal, pp. 38–48. London: Unwin Hyman

Brown K, Cooper D. 1990. Structural continuity in an African-American slave and tenant community. *Hist. Archaeol.* 24(4): 7–19

Bullen AK, Bullen RP. 1945. Black Lucy's garden. *Bull. Mass. Archaeol. Soc.* 6(2): 17–28

Cabak MA, Groover MD, Wagers SJ. 1995. Health care and the Wayman A.M.E. Church. *Hist. Archaeol.* 29(2):55–76

Chambers DB. 1996. "He is an African but speaks plain": historical creolization in eighteenth-century Virginia. In *The African Diaspora*, ed. A Jalloh, SE Maizlish, pp. 100–33. College Station: Texas A&M Univ. Press

Curtin PD. 1990. *The Rise and Fall of the Plantation Complex: Essays in Atlantic History.* Cambridge: Cambridge Univ. Press

Deagan K, MacMahon D. 1995. *Fort Mose: Colonial America's Black Fortress of Freedom.* Gainesville: Univ. Press Fla./ Fla. Mus. Nat. Hist.

Deetz J. 1977. *In Small Things Forgotten: The Archaeology of Early American Life.* Garden City, NY: Anchor/Doubleday

Díaz-Andreu M. 1996. Islamic archaeology and the origin of the Spanish nation. See Díaz-Andreu & Champion 1996, pp. 68–89

Díaz-Andreu M, Champion T, eds. 1996. *Nationalism and Archaeology in Europe.* London: Univ. Coll. London Press

Emerson MC. 1988. *Decorated clay tobacco pipes from the Chesapeake.* PhD thesis. Univ. Calif., Berkeley

Emerson MC. 1994. Decorated clay tobacco pipes from the Chesapeake: an African connection. In *Historical Archaeology of the Chesapeake*, ed. PA Shackel, BJ Little, pp. 35–49. Washington, DC: Smithson. Inst. Press

Epperson TW. 1990a. Race and the disciplines of the plantation. *Hist. Archaeol.* 24(4): 29–36

Epperson TW. 1990b. *"To fix a perpetual brand": the social construction of race in Virginia, 1675–1750.* PhD thesis. Temple Univ., Philadelphia

Fairbanks CH. 1974. The Kingsley slave cabins in Duval County, Florida, 1968. *Conf. Hist. Site Archaeol. Pap.* 7:62–93

Fairbanks CH. 1983. Historical archaeological implications of recent investigations. *Geosci. Man* 23:17–26

Fairbanks CH. 1984. The plantation archaeology of the Southeastern Coast. *Hist. Archaeol.* 18(1):1–14

Farnsworth P. 1993. "What is the use of plantation archaeology?" no use at all, if no one else is listening! *Hist. Archaeol.* 27(1): 114–16

Ferguson L. 1978. Looking for the "Afro-" in Colono-Indian pottery. *Conf. Hist. Site Archaeol. Pap.* 12:68–86

Ferguson L. 1991. Struggling with pots in colonial South Carolina. In *The Archaeology of Inequality*, ed. RH McGuire, R Paynter, pp. 28–39. Oxford: Blackwell

Ferguson L. 1992. *Uncommon Ground: Archaeology and Early African America, 1650–1800.* Washington, DC: Smithson. Inst. Press

Fitts RK. 1996. The landscapes of northern bondage. *Hist. Archaeol.* 30(2):54–73

Franklin M. 1995. Rethinking the Carter's Grove slave quarter reconstruction: a proposal. In *The Written and the Wrought: Complementary Sources in Historical Archaeology*, ed. ME D'Agostino, E Prine, E Casella, M Winer, pp. 147–64. *Kroeber Anthropol. Soc. Pap. 79.* Berkeley, CA: Kroeber Anthropol. Soc.

Franklin M. 1996. *The material expressions of Black American protective symbolism in art and archaeology.* Presented at Mus. Early South. Dec. Arts Conf., Winston-Salem, NC

Funari PPA. 1995a. The archaeology of Palmares and its contribution to the understanding of the history of African-American culture. *Hist. Archaeol. Lat. Am.* 7:1–41

Funari PPA. 1995b. A cultura material de Palmares: o estudo das relações sociais de um quilombo pela arqueologia. In *Idéieas: A Luta Contra o Racismo na Rede Escolar*, pp. 37–42. São Paulo, Brazil: Fundação Desenvolv. Educação

Funari PPA. 1995/96. A "república de Palmares" e a arqueologia da Serra da Barriga. *Revista USP* 28:6–13

Funari PPA. 1996a. A arqueologia de Palmares: sua contribuição para o conhecimento da história da cultura Afro-Americana. In *Liberdade por um Fio: História dos Quilombos no Brasil*, ed. JJ Reis, FdS Gomes, pp. 26–51. São Paulo, Brazil: Companhia das Leitras

Funari PPA. 1996b. Novas perspectivas abertas pela arqueologia na Serra da Barriga. In *Negras Imagens*, ed. LM Schwarcz, LVdS Reis, pp. 139–230. São Paulo, Brazil: Editora Univ. de São Paulo

García Arévalo MA. 1986. El Maniel de Jose Leta: evidencias arqueológicas de un posible asentamiento cimarrón en la región sudoriental de la Isla de Santo Domingo. *Cimarron*, pp. 33–55

Garman JC. 1994. Viewing the color line through the material culture of death. *Hist. Archaeol.* 28(3):74–93

Gilroy P. 1993. *The Black Atlantic: Modernity and Double Consciousness.* Cambridge: Harvard Univ. Press

Guimarães CM. 1990. O quilombo do Ambrósio: lenda, documentos, e arqueologia. *Estud. Ibero-Am.* 16:161–74

Guimarães CM, Lanna ALD. 1980. Arqueologia de quilombos em Minas Gerais. *Pesquisas* 31:146–63

Handler JS. 1983. An African pipe from a slave cemetery in Barbados, West Indies. In *The Archaeology of the Clay Tobacco Pipe, Vol. VIII. America*, ed. P Davey, pp. 245–54. Oxford: BAR

Handler JS. 1996. A prone burial from a plantation slave cemetery in Barbados, West Indies: possible evidence for an African-type witch or other negatively viewed person. *Hist. Archaeol.* 30(3):76–86

Handler JS. 1997. An African-type healer/diviner and his grave goods: a burial from a plantation slave cemetery in Barbados, West Indies. *Int. J. Hist. Archaeol.* 1: 91–130

Handler JS, Lange FW. 1978. *Plantation Slavery in Barbados: An Archaeological and Historical Investigation.* Cambridge: Harvard Univ. Press

Harrington SPM. 1993. Bones and bureaucrats: New York's great cemetery imbroglio. *Archaeology* 46(2):28–38

Harris JE. 1996. The dynamics of the global African diaspora. See Jalloh & Maizlish 1996, pp. 7–21

Harris JE, ed. 1993. *Global Dimensions of the African Diaspora*. Washington, DC: Howard Univ. Press

Hubert J. 1988. The disposition of the dead. *World Archaeol. Bull.* 2:12–39

Jalloh A, Maizlish SE, eds. 1996. *The African Diaspora*. College Station: Texas A&M Univ. Press

Jamieson RW. 1995. Material culture and so-

cial death: African-American burial practices. *Hist. Archaeol.* 29(4):39–58

Joyner C. 1984. *Down by the Riverside: A South Carolina Slave Community*. Urbana: Univ. Ill. Press

Kent RK. 1965. Palmares: an African state in Brazil. *J. Afr. Hist.* 6:161–75

Kohl PL, Fawcett C, eds. 1995. *Nationalism, Politics, and the Practice of Archaeology*. Cambridge: Cambridge Univ. Press

Landers J. 1990. Gracia Real de Santa Teresa de Mose: a free black town in Spanish colonial Florida. *Am. Hist. Rev.* 95:9–30

La Roche CJ, Blakey ML. 1997. Seizing intellectual power: the dialogue at the New York African Burial Ground. *Hist. Archaeol.* 31(3):84–106

Lemelle SJ, Kelley RDG. 1994. *Imagining Home: Class, Culture, and Nationalism in the African Diaspora*, ed. SJ Lemelle, RDG Kelley, pp. 1–16. London: Verso

Leone MP, Mullins PR, Creveling MC, Hurst L, Jackson-Nash B, et al. 1995. Can an African-American historical archaeology be an alternative voice? In *Interpreting Archaeology: Finding Meaning in the Past*, ed. I Hodder, M Shanks, A Alexandri, V Buchli, J Carman, et al, pp. 110–24. London: Routledge

Little BJ. 1994. People with history: an update on historical archaeology in the United States. *J. Archaeol. Method Theory* 1:5–40

Martin E, Parsons M, Shackel P. 1997. Commemorating a rural African-American family at a national battlefield park. *Int. J. Hist. Archaeol.* 1:157–77

McDavid C, Babson DW, eds. 1997. In the realm of politics: prospects for public participation in African-American and plantation archaeology. *Hist. Archaeol.* 31(3): 1–152

McKee L. 1994. Is it futile to try and be useful? historical archaeology and the African-American experience. *Northeast Hist. Archaeol.* 23:1–7

Mintz SW, Price R. 1976. *An Anthropological Approach to the Afro-American Past: A Caribbean Perspective*. Philadelphia: Inst. Study Hum. Issues

Muller NL. 1994. The house of the black Burghardts: an investigation of race, gender, and class at the W. E. B. DuBois boyhood homesite. In *Those of Little Note: Gender, Race, and Class in Historical Archaeology*, ed. EM Scott, pp. 81–94. Tucson: Univ. Ariz. Press

Mullins PR. 1996. *The contradiction of consumption: an archaeology of African America and consumer culture, 1850–1930*. PhD thesis. Univ. Mass., Amherst

Nichols E. 1988. *No Easy Run to Freedom:*

ARCHAEOLOGY OF AFRICAN DIASPORA 81

*Maroons in the Great Dismal Swamp of North Carolina and Virginia, 1677–1850.* MA thesis. Univ. S.C., Columbia

Orser CE. 1984. The past ten years of plantation archaeology in the southeastern United States. *Southeast. Archaeol.* 3: 1–12

Orser CE. 1988. The archaeological analysis of plantation society: replacing status and caste with economics and power. *Am. Antiq.* 53:735–51

Orser CE. 1990. Archaeological approaches to New World plantation slavery. In *Archaeological Method and Theory,* ed. MB Schiffer, 2:111–54. Tucson: Univ. Ariz. Press

Orser CE. 1992. *In Search of Zumbi: Preliminary Archaeological Research at the Serra da Barriga, State of Alagoas, Brazil.* Normal: Midwest. Archaeol. Res. Cent., Ill. State. Univ.

Orser CE. 1993. *In Search of Zumbi: The 1993 Season.* Normal: Midwest. Archaeol. Res. Cent., Ill. State. Univ.

Orser CE. 1994a. The archaeology of African-American slave religion in the antebellum South. *Cambridge Archaeol. J.* 4:33–45

Orser CE. 1994b. Toward a global historical archaeology: an example from Brazil. *Hist. Archaeol.* 28(1):5–22

Orser CE. 1996. *A Historical Archaeology of the Modern World.* New York: Plenum

Orser CE. 1998. The challenge of race to American historical archaeology. *Am. Anthropol.* In press

Orser CE, Owsley DW, Shenkel JR. 1986. Gaining access to New Orleans' first cemetery. *J. Field Archaeol.* 13:342–45

Orser CE, Fagan BM. 1995. *Historical Archaeology.* New York: HarperCollins

Otto JS. 1980. Race and class on antebellum plantations. See Schuyler 1980, pp. 3–13

Owsley DW, Orser CE, Mann RW, Moore-Jansen PH, Montgomery RL. 1987. Demography and pathology of an urban slave population from New Orleans. *Am. J. Phys. Anthropol.* 74:185–97

Palmié S. 1995. Introduction. In *Slave Cultures and the Cultures of Slavery,* ed. S. Palmié, pp. ix-xlvii. Knoxville: Univ. Tenn. Press

Paynter R. 1990. Afro-Americans in the Massachusetts historical landscape. In *The Politics of the Past,* ed. P Gathercole, D Lowenthal, pp. 49–62. London: Unwin Hyman

Potter PB. 1991. What is the use of plantation archaeology? *Hist. Archaeol.* 25(3): 94–107

Potter PB. 1994. *Public Archaeology in Annapolis: A Critical Approach to History in*

*Maryland's Ancient City.* Washington, DC: Smithson. Inst. Press

Powell LC, Dockall HD. 1995. Folk narratives and archaeology: an African-American cemetery in Texas. *J. Field Archaeol.* 22: 349–53

Praetzellis AC. 1991. *The archaeology of a Victorian city: Sacramento.* PhD thesis. Univ. Calif., Berkeley

Praetzellis AC, Praetzellis M, Brown M. 1987. Artifacts as symbols of identity: an example from Sacramento's gold rush era Chinese community. In *Living in Cities: Current Research in Urban Archaeology,* ed. E Staski, pp. 38–47. Tucson, AZ: Soc. Hist. Archaeol.

Proust K. 1993. Public archaeology and the physical legacy of European colonisation in South East Asia. *Australa. Hist. Archaeol.* 11:108–17

Reitz EJ. 1994. Zooarchaeological analysis of a free African community: Gracia Real de Santa Teresa de Mose. *Hist. Archaeol.* 28(1):23–40

Reitz EJ, Gibbs T, Rathbun TA. 1985. Archaeological evidence for subsistence on coastal plantations. In *The Archaeology of Slavery and Plantation Life,* ed. TA Singleton, pp. 163–91. Orlando, FL: Academic

Russell AE. 1997. Material culture and African-American spirituality at the Hermitage. *Hist. Archaeol.* 31(2):63–80

Samford P. 1996. The archaeology of African-American slavery and material culture. *William and Mary Q.* 53:87–114

Sando RA, Felton DL. 1993. Inventory records of ceramics and opium from a nineteenth-century Chinese store in California. In *Hidden Heritage: Historical Archaeology of the Overseas Chinese,* ed. P Wegars, pp. 151–76. Amityville, NY: Baywood

Saunders AC de CM. 1982. *A Social History of Black Slaves and Freedmen in Portugal, 1441–1555.* Cambridge: Cambridge Univ. Press

Schuyler RL. 1974. Sandy ground: archaeological sampling in a Black community in metropolitan New York. *Conf. Hist. Site Archaeol. Pap.* 7:13–51

Schuyler RL, ed. 1980. *Archaeological Perspectives on Ethnicity in America: Afro-American and Asian American Culture History.* Farmingdale, NY: Baywood

Singleton TA. 1991. The archaeology of slave life. In *Before Freedom Came: African-American Life in the Antebellum South,* ed. EDC Campbell, KS Rice, pp. 155–75. Richmond, VA: Mus. Confederacy

Singleton TA. 1995. The archaeology of slavery in North America. *Annu. Rev. Anthropol.* 24:119–40

Solow BL. 1991. *Slavery and the Rise of the Atlantic System.* Cambridge: Cambridge Univ. Press

Souza Y de. 1963. *Grandes Negros do Brasil.* Rio de Janeiro, Brazil: Livraria São José

Staski E. 1990. Studies of ethnicity in North American historical archaeology. *North Am. Archaeol.* 11:121–45

Staski E. 1993. The overseas Chinese in El Paso: changing goals, changing realities. In *Hidden Heritage: Historical Archaeology of the Overseas Chinese*, ed. P Wegars, pp. 125–49. Amityville, NY: Baywood

Stine LF, Cabak MA, Groover MD. 1996. Blue beads as African-American cultural symbols. *Hist. Archaeol.* 30(3):49–75

Swidler N, Dongoske KE, Anyon R, Downer AS, eds. 1997. *Native Americans and Archaeologists: Stepping Stones to Common Ground.* Walnut Creek, CA: AltaMira

Thomas BW. 1995. Source criticism and the interpretation of African-American sites. *Southeast. Archaeol.* 14:149–57

Thornton JK. 1992. *Africa and Africans in the Making of the Atlantic World, 1400-1680.* Cambridge: Cambridge Univ. Press

Watters DR. 1987. Excavations at the Harney Site slave cemetery, Montserrat, West Indies. *Ann. Carnegie Mus.* 56:289–318

Weik T. 1997. The archaeology of maroon societies in the Americas: resistance, cultural continuity, and transformation in the African diaspora. *Hist. Archaeol.* 31(2):81–92

Wheaton TR, Garrow PH. 1985. Acculturation and the archaeological record in the Carolina Lowcountry. In *The Archaeology of Slavery and Plantation Life*, ed. TA Singleton, pp. 239–59. Orlando, FL: Academic

Wilkie LA. 1995. Magic and empowerment on the plantation: an archaeological consideration of African-American world view. *Southeast. Archaeol.* 14:136–48

Young AL. 1996. Archaeological evidence of African-style ritual and healing practices in the Upland South. *Tenn. Anthropol.* 21: 139–55

Young AL. 1997. Risk management strategies among African-American slaves at Locust Grove Plantation. *Int. J. Hist. Archaeol.* 1:5–37

*Annu. Rev. Anthropol. 1998. 27:83–104*
*Copyright © 1998 by Annual Reviews. All rights reserved*

# MULTIPLE MODERNITIES:
# Christianity, Islam, and Hinduism
# in a Globalizing Age

*Robert W. Hefner*

Department of Anthropology, Boston University, 232 Bay State Road, Boston,
Massachusetts 02215; e-mail: rhefner@bu.edu

KEY WORDS: world religions, modernity, globalization, secularization, conversion

---

## ABSTRACT

The late twentieth century has seen far-reaching changes in the translocal
cultural regimes known as world religions. This review examines the politics
and meanings of recent changes in three such religions: Christianity, Islam,
and Hinduism. It highlights the nature of the forces reshaping religious
meanings and authority, the processes promoting conversion and standardization, and the implications of these religious refigurations for our understanding of late modernity itself. Though modernity is multiple and every
tradition unique, this review suggests that all contemporary religions confront a similar structural predicament, related to the globalization of mass societies and the porous pluralism of late modernity.

---

## INTRODUCTION

One does not have to go back too many years to recall a time when anthropologists concerned themselves primarily with tribal, ancestral, or otherwise localized religious traditions. The early editions of Lessa & Vogt's (1979) *Reader
in Comparative Religion*, for example, had only a handful of chapters on world
religions, most of which dealt with syncretized or village traditions. Though
postwar anthropologists of religion might not go as far as Radcliffe-Brown
(1952:2) in defining anthropology as the sociology of so-called primitive societies, their general preference was for the local and particularistic rather than
the world-civilizational (Bowen 1993:5, Stocking 1989).

83

Early in the postwar period, however, some anthropologists began to address the nature of translocal religion. Influenced by Redfield's (1956) studies of peasant societies, anthropologists of Hinduism, Buddhism, folk Christianity, and Islam examined the interaction of localized "little traditions" with translocal "great traditions" (Marriot 1955, Singer 1972). Marxist and historical-evolutionary anthropologists examined the politics and meanings of religious movements over vast tracts of time and space (Wolf 1958, Wolf & Hansen 1972, Worsley 1968). Heir to the tradition that had pioneered the sociological concept of world religions, Weberian anthropologists—particularly those influenced by Parsons' and Shils' American reading of Weber—invoked the triad of tradition, rationality, and modernity to assert that world religions are more rationalized than traditional religions (Geertz 1960, 1973; cf Hefner 1993b, van der Veer 1994).

With the tectonic shifts in politics and culture of the 1960s, the "orthodox consensus" (Giddens 1984:xv) that underlay social theory during the early postwar period collapsed. With it went agreement on the analytic utility of the distinction between traditional and world religions. Most anthropologists rightly rejected the overextended generalizations of modernization theory. Lacking an alternative framework for the analysis of translocal religion, most also limited themselves to careful analyses of religion in local context; a few denied the intellectual validity of cross-cultural comparison at all.

All this changed in the 1980s under the influence of two shifts in the discipline: a renewal of interest in the history and genealogy of culture, and the rediscovery of the problem of power. These theoretical interests were reinforced by a third shift in anthropological practice: the turn of ever larger numbers of anthropologists toward complex societies and translocal culture. As the social reach of the state, markets, mass media, and other macrocosmic agencies grew, anthropologists' interest in translocal religions increased. The resulting expansion of spatial and temporal horizons did not revive the discipline's faith in Weberian categories. Instead it led to a heightened interest in the hybrid nature of translocal religions and the "political economies of meaning" that sustain them (Eickelman 1979, 1983; cf Cohn 1981, Comaroff 1985:6, Hefner 1987, Ortner 1984).

This review examines the new anthropology of religion from the perspective of modern change in Christianity, Islam, and Hinduism. The discussion highlights three central questions: first, the nature of the forces reshaping religious meanings and authority; second, the processes promoting conversion and religious standardization; and, third, the implications of these religious refigurations for our understanding of late modernity itself. These issues illustrate the high-stakes efforts of contemporary anthropologists of religion to position themselves as theorists, not merely of local life-worlds but of the "global ecumene" (Hannerz 1992; see Appadurai 1996, Barth 1992, James 1995). All

three also highlight the daunting challenges still facing this effort at disciplinary redefinition.

## PUBLIC RELIGION AND THE PROBLEM OF MODERNITY

One of the most significant influences on recent research in the anthropology
of religion has been the growing influence of religious institutions in public
politics and culture around the world (Casanova 1994, Hefner 1998). This resurgence ranks as one of the most remarkable events in global politics and culture at the end of the twentieth century, challenging long-held assumptions
about the secular nature of modernization and modernity (Dobbelaere 1981,
Luckmann 1967, Wilson 1966). In policy-oriented circles outside anthropology, this resurgence has led once-optimistic proponents of modernization theory to embrace a Western-centric relativism pessimistic about the prospects
for democracy and social justice in the non-Western world (Cooper 1996,
Huntington 1996).

For more than a century, the vast majority of Western social theorists have
been convinced that religion was a declining historical force. In mainstream
social analysis, this confidence was expressed in either of two narratives on
secularization. The first, a relatively robust version of the secularization thesis,
characterized religion as an instrument of enchanted explanation and control
whose influence declines as the light of reason illuminates what had previously been cloaked in darkness. As in Weber's (1958) account of capitalism's
origins, this modernist prognosis was sometimes linked to a subsidiary thesis
stating that secular disenchantment also occurs when institutions such as the
state and market acquire institutional autonomy, thereby marginalizing the
very religious traditions that had earlier assisted their ascent.

Less robust statements of secularization theory placed more emphasis on
the pluralized nature of the modern world than on science and secular reason.
Proponents of this view argued that the key to modernity is not enlightened
reason but qualities of social organization peculiar to the late modern age, especially its structural differentiation, technical specialization, and pluralization of life-worlds (Luhmann 1984). Long before postmodern theorists spoke
of the collapse of "totalizing narratives" (Lyotard 1992, Bauman 1993), proponents of this version of secularization theory asserted that modern pluralism is
so radical that it frustrates efforts to project overarching ethical values into the
public sphere. Where previously a "sacred canopy" (Berger 1967) stabilized
life experience and provided shared public meanings, it was said, in modern
times the canopy is rent and the collective bases of morality and identity are diminished or destroyed (Beckford 1989:74–107; Bruce 1996:29–52; Wilson
1985).

In the light of retrospective history, it is clear that both versions of classical secularization theory oversimplified modernity and its nonmodern "other." Rather than recognizing that modernity might be multiple, both accounts offered an idealized model of the West as the prototype for modernization in all societies. Furthermore, they failed to do justice to the fate of religion in the West. Anthropologists who rightly challenge the application of secular-modernization narratives to the non-Western world are sometimes less critical of these theories' portrayal of religion in the modern West. In an age in which anthropology aspires to be globally comparative, however, a more nuanced understanding of religion in the modern West is essential.

## RETHINKING WESTERN RELIGION

Though conventional secularization theory is monolithic and teleological, the real-world process of secularization is hardly illusory. The transition from the agrarian worlds of the Middle Ages into the differentiated landscapes of early modern Europe did witness a decline in church authority, a pluralization of high-cultural traditions, and vigorous assaults on church doctrine and leadership. Renaissance Italy, for example, saw a dramatic upsurge of elite interest in Greco-Roman political philosophy, part of a broader assault on received Christian doctrines in European political theory (Skinner 1990, Tuck 1993). By sponsoring state churches, the Protestant Reformation at first seemed to strengthen the linkage between church and state, but it also released the genie of religious dissidence and anti-establishmentarianism. Asserting their duty to interpret scripture for themselves, Protestant nonconformists in England, Germany, and the Netherlands challenged the rights of princes and kings to decide the religion of their subjects (Martin 1978). These dissidents created precedents not just for religious nonconformists but for later advocates of democratic pluralism as well (Walzer 1965).

The decline in Christianity's public influence reached new heights, of course, in the eighteenth-century Enlightenment, a subject that has been the focus of debate in recent commentaries on Western modernity (Asad 1993b, James 1995, Werbner 1996; cf Foucault 1996, Habermas 1996). Hegel observed that Catholic Europe had been spared the earlier Protestant Reformation only to awake in the eighteenth century to a far more ambitious challenge. For some historians of this era, the Enlightenment represented nothing less than the triumph of a "new paganism" over the church in the fields of politics, the arts, and public ethics (Gay 1966, cf Vovelle 1978). Though the French Revolution and Napoleonic wars inspired conservative campaigns to restore church authority, these efforts were undercut by the nationalist movements that subsequently swept Europe. By emphasizing principles of sovereignty and ethnocultural identity unacknowledged in Christian political doctrine, modern nationalism furthered the de-Christianization of popular political discourse.

Examples like these at first lend credence to Anderson's claim that the dawn of nationalism presumed the "dusk of religious modes of thought" (Anderson 1991:11). This observation is correct in the limited sense that most European nationalisms made only perfunctory references to the organic political theories of Medieval Christendom. In Italy, Spain, and France, moreover, anticlerical nationalists directly challenged church authority. Extrapolated to the whole of Western public life, however, Anderson's observation distorts the degree to which religion continued to play a public role in much of the Western world, especially the United States. In the non-Western world, Anderson's secularist argument is even less apposite. As numerous scholars have noted (Antoun & Hegland 1987, Bowen 1993, Hefner 1995, Tambiah 1996, Tonnesson & Antlov 1996:8, van der Veer 1994), Anderson overlooks the far-reaching influence of religious ideals and networks on non-Western nationalisms.

In northwestern Europe, however, conventional measures of public religiosity since the end of the nineteenth century, and especially since the 1960s, confirm that Christianity's public influence has fallen, though at a different pace in different countries (Martin 1978). Post-1960s Europe has seen a steady decline in the numbers of Europeans entering the ministry, attending church, expressing a belief in God, and otherwise conforming to conventional indices of Christian religiosity. Though it was once believed that the Catholic nations of southern Europe might escape this trend, recent research shows that they too are now following the Western European pattern of church decline (Bruce 1996: 29–37, Hervieu-Léger 1990). Developments like these seem to confirm the arguments of Habermas and others that the structural transformation of the Western public sphere requires the privatization of religious conviction (Habermas 1991, but cf Casanova 1994).

Even in the West, however, modernity is not singular, least of all as regards religious matters. It is important to remember that the eighteenth and nineteenth centuries witnessed not merely Enlightenment attacks on religious authority but new and vibrant religious movements. These included Methodism in England, Hassidism in Poland, Pietism in Germany, and in the United States, the Protestant Great Awakening (Halévy 1927, Outram 1995:34, Thompson 1963:350–400). Though their leadership had a complex class profile, most of these movements drew from the ranks not of the aristocratic guardians of the old order—many of whom no longer regarded themselves as particularly Christian—but the newly urbanized working and middle classes. In their class-base and cultural ethos, these movements anticipated the late twentieth century's movements of Islamic reform and non-Western Pentecostalism. Like these latter movements, nineteenth-century Methodism provided opportunities for leadership and social respectability otherwise unavailable to unpedigreed urbanites. Methodism also provided emotive and individualistic forms of religious devotion. Finally, and significantly, it instilled a time sense and social self-control well-suited to the disciplinary demands of the ascendant industrial order (Comaroff 1985: 29–137, Comaroff & Comaroff 1991, Hobsbawm 1957, Thompson 1963: 350–400).

If most models of modernity fail to acknowledge the complexity of religious change in industrializing Europe, the same is true in spades for the United States. Republican America opted against establishing a state church, still the norm in Europe. This decision opened the way, not for religion's decline, but for a marketplace competition that spurred galloping sectarianism and fierce denominational rivalries. The primary beneficiaries of this tumult proved to be not the patrician elders of Episcopalianism and Presbyterianism but populist Methodists and Baptists. Like Islamists and evangelicals in the non-Western world today, these latter groups thrived because they minimized social distance between clergy and laity, allowed a heightened measure of congregational autonomy, and provided easy access to positions of authority for non-elite individuals (Wuthnow 1988:20).

Developments like these pluralized American religion, but—again contrary to conventional secularization narratives—also kept religious ideals very much in the public sphere. Looking back on the American experience, Bellah et al (1985) have suggested that the rise of industrial capitalism in the aftermath of the Civil War undermined a previously hegemonic (and essentially Protestant) "civic" religion by promoting a separation of economic organization from heretofore extensive moral controls. The result in their view was a colonization of the public sphere by the self-interested authorities of market and state (compare Habermas 1984).

Though national capitalism was certainly in ascent, other studies suggest that American religion in the late nineteenth and early twentieth centuries was more heterogeneous in its influences and varied in its outcomes than this account implies. Jewish and Catholic immigration in the last half of the nineteenth century undermined Protestant hegemony, dashing the hopes of ultra-conservative Christians to make Protestantism the religion of state. The efforts of Jews (secular and religious), Catholics, and dissident Baptists encouraged more, not less, religious freedom. The consequence was not the evacuation of religion from public life, but—in a pattern that resembles trends in Hindu and Muslim nations today (see below)—a potent mix of pluralization and heightened competition. At a time when religiosity among the European working classes was already in decline, American society was becoming more "churched." Between 1860 and 1900, membership in churches and temples grew from 20 to 40 percent (Wuthnow 1988:21–22). For the first time in American history, Protestant denominations also established national bureaucracies to coordinate their outreach.

Public religion in the United States at the turn of the century was not a civic religion of unperturbed consensus, therefore, but an element in a broader and agonistic debate over popular identity and morality. Between 1920 and 1950, conservative Protestants warned repeatedly of the growing power of Roman Catholicism, appealing for an end to denominational sectarianism so as to contain the perceived Catholic menace (Wuthnow 1988:78). Despite these appeals, fierce controversies raged between Protestant modernists and fundamentalists, leading some in the fundamentalist camp to call for separation from corrupted modernists (Marsden 1980, Wuthnow 1988:137). As the 1925 Scopes trial indicated, the tension was not at all confined to matters of personal piety but centered on each group's efforts to regulate activities seen as part of the public sphere.

These comparisons between the United States and Western Europe underscore that the history of religion in the modern West varies from country to country in a manner that reflects a broad balance of forces in state and society. Martin (1978) and Casanova (1994) have argued that Western Christianity continued to play a significant public role where it avoided alliances with reactionary ruling classes and opted for a marketplace pattern of denominational competition rather than state-imposed religion. As Casanova (1998) has observed, the countries in Eastern Europe where religion is today most vibrant are those, like the Ukraine, where a similar mass-based denominationalism prevails.

Secularization has occurred in vast portions of Western public life, but not as a result of a systemic teleology, as mainstream secularization theory would hold. In some Western societies, religion continues to exercise a significant influence on civil society and the public sphere (Casanova 1994, cf Smith 1995). Elsewhere, as in much of northwestern Europe, traditional denominations have experienced sharp declines in public influence. In Western countries as a whole, organized religion has done best where its primary social carriers have chosen not to attempt to reimpose an organic union of religion and state on the unsettled modern landscape, and have instead moved down-market to develop organizations closer in ethos and organization to mass society's working and middle classes. Having migrated away from the elite, these denominations expose themselves to less containable social influences, some of which can destabilize religion itself. This embedded and pluralistic understanding of religious change in the West is a sounder ground than classical secularization theory on which to compare Christian, Hindu, and Muslim modernities.

# FRAGMENTATION AND OBJECTIFICATION

With their confidence that modern religion experiences privatization and decline, it is not surprising that proponents of conventional secularization theories have been baffled by the recent resurgence of Islam, Hinduism, and Christianity around the world. Some have reacted to this development with the argument that it is all just a matter of time; as non-Western societies modernize, they too will experience the privatization of religion assumed to have taken place in the West. This line of argument is made, for example, by the German-trained sociologist Tibi, who states that, as Muslim societies modernize, they will follow the path of privatization experienced by Western Christianity. Having once aspired to organize all of society, a modernized Islam must inevitably be "domiciled within the sphere of interiority" (Tibi 1990:139).

Other commentators on the Muslim world take issue with this prognosis even while accepting elements of secularization theory. Agreeing that modernization brings secularization, Gellner has nonetheless argued that Islam has shown a unique ability to survive this secularist juggernaut. This Muslim exceptionalism, Gellner argues, has to do with Islam's ability to take advantage of the mobilizational opportunities of the modern nation-state. In the West, Gellner observes (in an argument that recalls Anderson's), nationalist movements furthered the secularization of political discourse by placing an idealized ethnic culture, rather than Christendom, at the center of the idea of the nation. By contrast, Gellner argues, Muslims have been able to invoke their great tradition of religious scholar jurists (*ulama*) and law (*shariah*) as symbols of nationhood. The national renaissance in Muslim nations has thus been able to promote purified religion as an alternative to the idealized folkways so central to European nationalisms. "Thus in Islam, and only in Islam, purification/modernization on the one hand, and the re-affirmation of a putative old *local* identity on the other, can be done in one and the same language and set of symbols" (Gellner 1981:5, cf Gellner 1992:5–13).

There are problems with this claim of Muslim exceptionalism. First, the model greatly oversimplifies religion's fate in the West. Second, the model ignores the continuing ability of Hindus, Buddhists, and other non-Muslims to project religious influences into the public sphere (Kapferer 1988, Keyes 1987, Tambiah 1992, 1996, Queen 1996). Finally, Gellner's account makes Islamic nationalism look too strong, overlooking the strong appeal of ethnic and secular nationalisms in the Muslim world. The exceptionalism thesis also errs in taking at face value the claims of conservative Islamists that Islam allows no separation of social spheres and thus no differentiation of political and religious authority. This unitarian view of Islam and politics has been bitterly contested by liberal Muslims who insist, with good reason, that there is a long precedent for just such a civil separation of powers in Islam (Eickelman & Piscatori 1996, Goldberg 1993, Hefner 1997a, Munson 1993, Norton 1995).

If a theologically conservative Islamic nationalism has achieved a certain influence in recent years, then, this has less to do with a disposition unique to Islam (and shared by all Muslims) than it does with a battle raging among rival interpreters of Islam. In a manner that recalls battles between American fundamentalists and modernists earlier in this century, the Muslim world is being shaken today by competition over "the interpretation of symbols and control of the institutions, formal and informal, that produce and sustain them" (Eickelman & Piscatori 1996:5). A widely noted feature of this contest has been what Eickelman and Piscatori (p. 38) call the objectification of religious knowledge (cf Bourdieu 1989). In contrast to an age when Islamic knowledge was the monopoly of a small number of jurists, Islamic knowledge and practice today are objects of interest for growing numbers of people. Many Muslims have come to think of their religion as something complete, self-contained, and objective—a system (*minhaj*) that can be distinguished clearly from other ideologies and belief systems. This claim that Islam is a complete social order (*al-nizam al-islami*) remains a contentious issue dividing liberal and conservative Muslims (Eickelman & Piscatori 1996:159; Mitchell 1969:234–45; Moussalli 1995: 69–70, 87).

In a manner that recalls Anderson's remarks on the influence of print capitalism on European nationalism, Eickelman and Piscatori also observe that this process of objectification has been abetted by the expansion of mass higher education, the emergence of vast markets for inexpensive "Islamic books" and newspapers (Atiyeh 1995, Eickelman 1993, Gonzalez-Quijono 1994, Hefner 1997b), and the unsettled pace of urbanization in much of the Muslim world. Traditional social structures have collapsed at the same time that religious scholars have lost their monopoly of discursive power. Today populist preachers (Antoun 1989, Gaffney 1994), neotraditionalist Sufi masters (Launay 1992, Mardin 1989, Villalon 1995), and secularly educated "new Muslim intellectuals" (Meeker 1991, Roy 1993) vie with state-supported scholars to define the practice and meanings of Islam. In some countries, the resulting fragmentation of authority (Eickelman & Piscatori 1996:71) has pluralized social power and been a force for democratization (Hefner 1997a, Villalon 1995). Where the contest of carriers has coincided with civil war, economic collapse, ethnic polarization, or severe state violence, however, the struggle has often abetted the ascent of a "neofundamentalism" hostile to pluralism, women's emancipation, and proponents of an Islamic civil society (Fuller 1996, Roy 1993).

Fragmentation and objectification are not the only influences, however, reshaping public religion in the modern Muslim world. The recent spread of the woman-centered Zar possession cult (Boddy 1989, Lewis 1986) in North Africa and the Middle East indicates that there are subaltern religious experiences within or alongside Islam. Boddy (1989:35) observes that the Zar has gained ground "in virtual tandem with local Islamization" since it began its geographic expansion in the nineteenth century. The continuing diffusion of the cult shows that urbanization and migration have opened avenues for new religious forms, some of which present "an alternative view of the world in response to an elite's implicit domination of discourse" (p. 157). Unlike the hybrid cults Obeyesekere (1981) has explored among Sinhalese ecstatics, efforts to amplify the Zar cult into a fully public ritual form provoke serious challenge from those who insist that there can be only one practice of Islam. At one time, the "eclectic religious practice" promoted by prominent Buddhists in Sri Lanka (Spencer 1995:198) had its counterparts in the Muslim world (see Eaton 1993: 71–81, Geertz 1960, Hefner 1987, Lambek 1993), but religious politics in Muslim countries today often lead to heightened demands for a unitary profession of the faith. For ordinary Muslims who have long believed that Islam can coexist with other systems of knowledge (see Lambek 1993), these demands for a unitary Islam evoke deep ambivalence (Peletz 1997).

Even as homogenizing pressures have grown, the Muslim world has witnessed a counter-resurgence of pluralized expressions of faith. In Indonesia, Iran, Syria, and Turkey, among other nations, there is a growing interest in Islamic poetry, art, and other personalized vehicles of divine wonder. Indeed, some Muslims call openly for a civil Islam that renounces state-enforced standardization of the faith (Eickelman 1993, Hefner 1997a, Ibrahim 1993, Mardin 1995, Mottahedeh 1993, Norton 1995). This struggle between monolithic and pluralistic interpretations of Islam has its counterparts in Hinduism and Christianity. Developments in all three religions underscore that the real "clash of civilizations" in our era is not between the West and some homogeneous "other" (cf Huntington 1996) but between rival carriers of tradition within the same nations and civilizations.

## MODULARIZED HINDUISM

Though Gellner implied that Islam is unique in its ability to respond to the secularist juggernaut, in recent years Hinduism has undergone an equally vibrant pubic reformation, in a manner that reflects somewhat different cultural preoccupations than those of Christianity and Islam. Historically, Hinduism lacked the centralized ecclesiastical structures of Christianity and the legal traditions and scholastic authorities of Islam. Noting the absence of such stabilizing structures, some scholars have wondered whether it is right to speak of Hinduism as a single religion at all (Hawley 1991). As van der Veer (1994:46) has observed, however, Hinduism has long possessed "a not fully integrated family of ideas and practices spread by ascetics and priestly families over an enormous region," and in premodern times it was already marked by "long-term processes of centralization and homogenization." Though the standardization of Hindu culture has reached new heights in this century, the process builds on deep historic precedents.

An interesting parallel between van der Veer's revisionist characterization of Hinduism and ideas on African society and religion is presented by Kopytoff, Ranger, and Vail. Kopytoff (1987) has shown there was an internal frontier on the African subcontinent, across which there was vibrant cultural flow. With Vail (1989), Ranger (1986, 1993) has demonstrated that well before the coming of the Europeans, southern Africa was crisscrossed by large networks of trade and religious pilgrimage. Religious cults and symbols moved rapidly and regularly across tribal borders. These insights take exception with the arguments of Horton (1971) and others (Ikenga-Metuh 1987, Mbiti 1969) who characterize premodern African religion as localized and organic. This tendency to attribute closure to premodern societies has been the object of recent criticism in general anthropology (Barth 1992, Hannerz 1996).

In a similar fashion, Assayag (1995), Babb (1975), and van der Veer (1988, 1994), among others, have demonstrated that precolonial Hinduism was more than a collection of isolated little traditions. Shrines and pilgrimage centers were tied into a vast pilgrimage circuit extending across the South Asian continent. Pilgrimage channels doubled as trading networks (Cohn 1964, van der Veer 1994:44). Rather than the "autarkic villages" of colonial and nationalist discourses, premodern India was a networked civilization of economic and religious exchange.

Specialists of Southeast Asian Hinduism know that a similarly ecumenical movement of people, goods, and ideas underlay the diffusion of Hinduism to Southeast Asia more than 1600 years ago (Hall 1985, Robson 1981). In the less ethnically and class-stratified societies of Southeast Asia, caste was less central to Hinduism's diffusion than it was in South Asia, while the role of kings and monastic orders was correspondingly larger. As in South Asia, kings and clerics often built devotional centers alongside preexisting indigenous cults (Hefner 1985:25, Pigeaud 1963). This cosmological accommodation resembles the relationship between non-Christian cults and saint veneration in European and Latin American Catholicism (Brown 1981, Christian 1989). Over time, however, reform movements in European Christianity tended to attack these pre-Christian inheritances as heretical, especially where doctrinal disputes coincided with cleavages of class, ethnicity, and gender (Schneider 1990; see also Brandes 1990, Merrill 1988). By contrast, in South and Southeast Asia, non-Hindu cults often continued to operate even after elements of the local tradition were drawn up into a Hindu superstructure.

Ritual and cosmological standardization appears to have been more common in South Asia than in Southeast Asia, perhaps because South Asian status groups experienced more pressures to conform to transregional caste ideals (Babb 1975, van der Veer 1994:47). As Geertz (1980) and Wiener (1995) have emphasized, Hindu courts in Bali devoted considerable resources to ritual pronouncements of their own excellence, but popular Balinese Hinduism has preserved strong communitarian and egalitarian elements. Outside of specific ritual contexts, commoner Balinese show much skill at subverting the status pretensions of their high-caste counterparts (Warren 1993; see also Lansing

1991). Parish's (1996) pathbreaking ethnography of caste in Nepal shows that there is an equally deep well of ambivalence toward hierarchy among Newarese. But his study also suggests there are fewer resources there than in Bali with which to challenge caste depredations.

Certainly in the South Asian case this revisionist portrayal of a premodern, translocal Hinduism suggests that, *pace* Anderson and Gellner's modernist models, there were rich historical precedents for modern Hindu nationalism. However, the model does not imply that these precedents were sufficient to engender that movement on their own. Indian nationalisms are not simply derivative of the Western original (Chatterjee 1986), but there is no question that colonialism was central to their formation. Through their censuses and legal reforms, the British in India polarized the distinction between Muslim and Hindu (Cohn 1987, Dirks 1989, van der Veer 1994:20). Colonial policies also popularized the idea of a Hindu majority and Muslim minority, a notion that native political elites later exploited to their advantage. Western orientalists also provided histories of a Hindu Golden Age and standardized versions of religious texts (van der Veer 1994:21), both of which were later used by radical Hindu nationalists to portray Indian Muslims as foreigners.

In the postcolonial era, this process of Hindu regeneration has intensified, as has its political impact. In a manner like that described by Gombrich and Obeyesekere for Sri Lankan Buddhism (1988, but cf Holt 1991), a "Protestant" reformation has occurred in some streams of Indian Hinduism, though its impact seems less pervasive than religious nationalism itself. Recent years have seen campaigns to trim more extravagant flora in the Hindu ritual forest, instill a sense of personal responsibility among laity, and while decrying post-Vedic accretions to Hinduism, modularize ritual and belief (Jaffrelot 1996:201). Much of the effort seems modeled on reformist versions of Islam and Christianity.

A more unusual element in recent Hindu reform has been its elevation of tolerance as a distinctive feature of Hindu tradition. This interpretation also owes a good deal to Western orientalism, overlooking as it does the fact that traditional tolerance was premised on a notably illiberal inequality of divinities and traditions (van der Veer 1994:68). Hindus in modern Bali and Java place a similar emphasis on the unity of all religions and the legacy of Hindu tolerance. A vulnerable minority in a Muslim-majority nation, however, Indonesia's reformist Hindus have used the themes not to promote religious nationalism but to buttress their claims that they are the most faithful supporters of government-imposed Pancasila pluralism (Bakker 1993, Hefner 1985).

As with difference-denying movements among Muslims, some among India's Hindu nationalists have insisted on the need for a religious state based on the presumed authentic culture of the majority. Inevitably this formula imperils nonconformists within the majority religion as well as members of minority religions. In this formula, religious nationalism tends to be internally homogenizing as well as externally antagonistic (van der Veer 1994:105). As with Islam, however, the clash of rival Hinduisms is still in an early phase, and it is by no means clear that Hindu nationalists will succeed in their homogenizing agenda. As in the Muslim world, the drive to make the state an instrument of religious standardization has inspired other believers to look deep into their tradition in search of sacral precedents for pluralism and civility (Hefner 1998).

## THE PROTESTANT ETHIC AND THE SPIRIT OF CONVERSION

These comparisons of recent social change in Islam and Hinduism show that translocal religions confront similar predicaments, but their response varies in a way that illustrates the nature of the resources each religion brings to the encounter with modernity. This modest insight applies all the more forcefully to the Protestant conversion occurring in vast portions of Asia, Africa, and most notably, Latin America.

The social logic of this conversion varies. In one pattern, Protestantism takes hold among long-marginalized populations seeking to maintain an identity apart from the dominant culture even while appropriating the symbols and instruments of modernity. In this case, conversion reproduces the binary logic of ethnic categories even as it transforms their cultural content. Thus Karo Batak outflanked their Malay Muslim neighbors in colonial Sumatra (Kipp 1993), Akha in northern Thailand compete with their Buddhist Thai neighbors (Kammerer 1990, cf Keyes 1993), and Nuer resist state-imposed Islamization in the Sudan (Hutchinson 1996). Untouchable conversion to Christianity, Islam, and Buddhism in India has shown a similar logic (Mujahid 1989), whereby a subordinate people adopt the religion of a distant but high-status outsider to declare their independence from a closer but dominant neighbor.

The regions where Protestant conversion has been more extensive, however, are those where the organic linkage of religion and ethnicity has long since slackened and the differentiating demands of the state, capitalism, and migration have increased. The conversion of large numbers of South Koreans to Christianity in the aftermath of Japanese colonialism and civil war provides one example of this process (Clark 1986, Wells 1990). But the contemporary explosion of Pentecostalism in Asia, Africa, and Latin America also recalls an earlier history, that of Methodism in nineteenth-century Britain. As Thompson (1963) and Halévy (1927) both emphasized (though from different political perspectives), Methodism flourished not in the prosperous English heartland but among the poor and downtrodden of Wales, Scotland, and Ulster. As Martin (1990) has argued, nineteenth-century Methodists looked to their new faith as a "free space" offering opportunities more egalitarian than those available in mainstream church and society. For Martin, the genius of both Methodism and contemporary Pentecostalism is that, though challenging elite monopolies, they do so without expressing that challenge in an explicitly political form. Historians of nineteenth-century Britain, like anthropologists of contemporary Latin America, often remark on the apolitical or conservative bent of these religious movements. But Martin insists that these popular Protestantisms are conservative only in their early phases, and for sound political reasons. They divert political enthusiasm into safe channels so as to keep their antiestablishment challenge "in religious storage to emerge over time when circumstances are propitious to activate them, or when things are safe enough for people to make open political claims" (Martin 1990:44).

Perhaps no topic in the contemporary anthropology of Christianity has been as controversial as this question of the politics of Protestant conversion. Not surprisingly, other studies highlight issues backgrounded in Martin's account. In two important works, for example, David Stoll (1982, 1990) has exposed the web of media, financial, and far-right political interests tying US evangelicals to their well-heeled counterparts in Latin America. Other studies have noted similar linkages between evangelicals and ultra-right politicians in Africa and Asia (Brouwer et al 1996, Nederveen Pieterse 1992).

At the level of the *barrio*, however, the politics of evangelical conversion often takes unexpected forms. Like Martin, Stoll recognizes that Pentecostal evangelicalism is organizationally fissiparous, intensifying sectarian tendencies long latent in popular Protestantism. In Latin America, this divisiveness is exacerbated by elements of African-American spiritualism that draw the Holy Spirit into the work of healing and social empowerment. For most new Pentecostals, this work of the Spirit is of much more interest than the political schemes of North American conservatives. Moreover, the Spirit is hard to contain. Even in the United States, evangelicals span a range of political viewpoints, as their heated debates over capitalism in the Reagan years illustrated (Gay 1991). For many Pentecostal women, the appeal of the Spirit lies not in its directives for masculinist politics but in its sanctions for monogamy, frugality, and abstinence from alcohol. In other words, Pentecostalism provides powerful ammunition against *machismo*.

In their now classical study of Western evangelism in southern Africa, the Comaroffs (1991) have offered a similar reminder on the need to attend to the full life-course of effervescent Christianity. The colonial sponsors of nineteenth-century missions hoped Protestantism would instill the labor and sexual discipline needed for Africans' passage into colonial capitalism. Some natives welcomed this Weberian Protestantism and the habits of literacy, cleanliness, and modesty it promoted. But the church fathers' message was not so easily contained nor was it even consistently conveyed. As Ranger (1993) has shown in Africa and Kipp (1990) in Sumatra, not all Protestant missionaries have been willing apostles of European modernity. Some were romantics who hoped to use the mission to build peasant communitarianism all but destroyed by capitalism and individualism in Europe. In the African case, a first generation of orthodoxy gave rise to a second generation of independent churches, African religious movements, and freelance specialists of fertility, curing, and exorcism. A similar pattern has been seen in other parts of the newly Christian world, whenever control of the faith has slipped into the hands of people less concerned with canons than with bringing the work of the Spirit into their social and spiritual bodies (Barker 1990, Chestnut 1997).

Yet the tie of Christianity to Western modernity rarely slackens entirely. The necktie, Coca-Cola, and calico dresses appear again and again, even where, as in contemporary Sumatra, Java, or Brazil (Kipp 1993, Hefner 1993b, Chestnut 1997), the work of the faithful has long since slipped into native hands. The forces at work in these instances are stronger than missions and evangelicals alone. They are evidence of the cultural hegemony of the United States and Western Europe in global capitalism, consumption, and communications. But this erstwhile ally of a Westernized Christianity can cut the other way. Just as a blossoming consumer culture in nineteenth-century England unleashed an individualistic romanticism hostile to Christianity and capitalist discipline (Cambell 1987, Heelas 1996, Thompson 1993), today's markets and media offer self-idealizations that can undermine Christian ideals.

Converts discover that their religion has ideals and disciplines other than those they expected (Hefner 1993b, Pollock 1993). The work of the Spirit may be put to unlicensed ends, particularly where rather than rebuilding hierarchy, it encourages retreat to islands of personal piety. Even among US evangelicals notorious for their fire-and-brimstone moralism, the past generation has seen a shift away from community fellowship and moralism toward a view of religion as "a service agency for the fulfillment of its individual members" (Wuthnow 1988:55, cf Hunter 1987). Jesus as a nonjudgmental buddy has nudged God-the-Patriarchal-Father.

Other indices of this sea-change in American Protestantism are the heightened incidence of denominational switching (Wuthnow 1988:88) and religious intermarriage. On this evidence, it seems that trace elements of the subjectivized spirituality associated with nineteenth-century spiritualists and today's apostles of the New Age (Heelas 1996, Brown 1997) have seeped even into evangelical wells. In North America and elsewhere, the stabilization of identity and morality offered by proponents of the Word often proves ephemeral indeed.

## CONCLUSION: PUBLIC RELIGION IN A POROUS WORLD

Contemporary refigurations of Islam, Hinduism, and Christianity remind us that, contrary to conventional secularization theories, religion in modern times has not everywhere declined as a public force, nor been domiciled within a sphere of interiority. Not a reaction against but a response to the modern world, the most successful religious refigurations thrive by drawing themselves down into mass society and away from exclusive elites, if and when the latter lose their hold on popular allegiances.

Having moved down-market in this manner, some among the refigured religions tap popular energies only to direct them toward a new leadership's ends. Some replace plural economies of meaning with a homogeneous religious currency. But these standardizations inevitably unleash contestive heterogenizations. Just as the United States saw a struggle for Protestant hearts and minds in the nineteenth century, the broader world today witnesses fierce contests over religion and its sustaining institutions. Corporatist Islamists vie with civic pluralists; conservative nationalists vilify Hindu secularists; and Latin American Pentecostals flee to islands of piety only to discover they cannot quite agree on what should be done there.

A key issue distinguishing rival camps within each tradition is their attitude toward politics and the public sphere. Though each is unique, the religions discussed here share a similar structural predicament on this point. Their refiguration is taking place in a world of nation-states, mass urbanizations, economic specialization, and as Appadurai (1996) and Hannerz (1996) have argued, communications and migrations that render social borders permeable to transcultural flows. In this situation, cultural organizations that lay claim to ultimate meanings (and, whether or not all religions do this, these ones do) face a dilemma: how to maintain a coherent world-view and steadied social engagement while acknowledging the pluralism of the modern world.

An organic and aggressive response to this predicament is to strap on the body armor, ready one's weapons, and launch a holy war for society as a whole. In today's world of bureaucratic states, this option requires a seizure of state and, from there, the imposition of an organic unity on an inorganic social body. This option, a statist one, has its enthusiasts among the three religions considered here. However, this option comes at a high cost: It antagonizes religious minorities, frustrates nonconforming members of the faith, and destroys the freedoms necessary for social pacificity and, at least for societies higher up in the global division of labor, economic dynamism. Nonetheless, as a mobilizing strategy, this option can have its appeal, and some self-promoting elites may be willing to pay its awful price.

A second strategy renounces organic totalism for separatist sectarianism. Like the Essenes of ancient Israel under Roman rule (Kee 1993), proponents of this option take comfort in the uncompromised purity of a small circle of believers. In a complex society rather than in a desolate desert retreat, however, this path brings with it regular reminders of one's marginality. Fleeing the horrors of anti-insurgency violence, some Pentecostals in Latin America in the

1970s were happy to embrace this option, offering as it did (they hoped) a safe haven from a war that would not be won. But when social peace is restored, and where commensuality is not blocked by other walls (such as race and ethnicity), not all believers will still be willing to hold themselves apart from a people otherwise their own.

There is a third option for a refigured religion. Rather than conquest or separation, it accepts the diversity of public voices and visions, acknowledging that, in some sense, this is the nature of modern things. What follows after this varies widely, but the underlying pluralist premise remains. Some religious pluralists will promote a marketplace denominationalism, whereby the hearts and minds of others are fair game. Other believers may accept denominationalism but neutralize its challenge by insisting that the essence of religion lies away from the bustle of the religious market in a wondrous world within. Still others, the civil democrats in Casanova's (1994) appealing synthesis of piety and critical theory, will insist that religion's place in the public world is more important than denominationalism alone. The alternative role is not as a religion of state but as a principled civil voice, whose ethical critique checks the hegemonic aspirations of capital, state, and uncivil society.

These are ideal types; hybrids abound. As with the three traditions discussed in this review, the option elected by the religious mainstream is determined not merely by the cultural resources specific to a religion but by the struggle for influence among its rival carriers. The fate of modern religion, we are reminded once more, is never determined by religion alone.

The predicament of modern religions is not governed by a teleological master plan; the macrocosm created by contemporary globalizations is not one of smooth Weberian affinities; modernity will not know an "end to history" any time soon (Fukuyama 1992). Though the reactions it inspires are heterogeneous, the predicament of modernity is not entirely culturally relative. The rise of mass societies, with their unruly cities, vast migrations, and invasive markets and media, renders local worlds unusually permeable to other cultural ways. Inasmuch as religious solidarities depend upon a public's continuing identification with religious ideals, the easy juxtaposition of alternative realities complicates considerably the task of keeping believers in line. We should not be surprised to see that, as with some players in the Salman Rushdie affair (Asad 1993c, Werbner 1996), religious elites often feel threatened by this too-easy promenade of contrary truths and therefore devote substantial resources to firming up cultural walls. They do so because those walls have become so porous.

Different balances will be struck in the resulting contest of religious creations. Their solutions may vary, but all religions in our age confront common challenges; their message shows the transformative impact of similar structural dilemmas. To weather the onslaught of alternative ways, religions cannot merely invoke the canonical words of the prophets. Even as they profess their unique and unchanging truth, their actions confess they have tasted the forbidden fruit of a pervasive and porous pluralism.

> Visit the *Annual Reviews home page* at
> http://www.AnnualReviews.org.

## Literature Cited

Anderson B. 1991. *Imagined Communities: Reflections on the Origin and Spread of Nationalism.* London: Verso. Revised ed.

Antoun RT. 1989. *Muslim Preacher in the Modern World: A Jordanian Case Study in Comparative Perspective.* Princeton, NJ: Princeton Univ. Press

Antoun RT, Hegland ME, eds. 1987. *Religious Resurgence: Contemporary Cases in Islam, Christianity, and Judaism.* Syracuse, NY: Syracuse Univ. Press

Appadurai A. 1996. *Modernity at Large: Cultural Dimensions of Globalization.* Minneapolis: Univ. Minn. Press

Asad T. 1993a. *Genealogies of Religion: Discipline and Reasons of Power in Christianity and Islam.* Baltimore: Johns Hopkins Univ. Press

Asad T. 1993b. The limits of religious criticism in the Middle East: notes on Islamic public argument. See Asad 1993a, pp. 200–36

Asad T. 1993c. Multiculturalism and British identity in the wake of the Rushdie affair. See Asad 1993a, pp. 239–68

Assayag J. 1995. *Au Confluent de Deux Rivières: Musulmans et Hindous dan le Sud de l'Inde.* Paris: Presses de l'École Française d'Extrême-Orient

Atiyeh GN. 1995. The book in the modern Arab world: the cases of Lebanon and Egypt. In *The Book in the Islamic World: The Written Word and Communication in the Middle East,* ed. GN Atiyeh, pp. 232–53. Albany: State Univ. NY Press

Babb LA. 1975. *The Divine Hierarchy: Popular Hinduism in Central India.* New York: Columbia Univ. Press

Badone E, ed. 1990. *Religious Orthodoxy and Popular Faith in European Society.* Princeton, NJ: Princeton Univ. Press

Bakker FL. 1993. *The Struggle of the Hindu Balinese Intellectuals: Developments in Modern Hindu Thinking in Independent Indonesia.* Amsterdam: VU Univ. Press

Barker J. 1990. Introduction: ethnographic perspectives on Christianity in Oceanic societies. In *Christianity in Oceania: Ethnographic Perspectives,* ed. J Barker, pp. 1–24. Lanham, MD: Univ. Press Am. See Clark 1986

Barth F. 1992. Towards greater naturalism in conceptualizing societies. See Kuper 1992, pp. 17–33

Bauman Z. 1993. *Postmodern Ethics.* Oxford: Blackwell

Beckford JA. 1989. *Religion and Advanced Industrial Society.* London: Unwin Hyman

Bellah R, Madsen R, Sullivan WM, Swidler A, Tipton SM. 1985. *Habits of the Heart: Individualism and Commitment in American Life.* New York: Harper & Row

Berger PL. 1967. *The Sacred Canopy: Elements of a Sociological Theory of Religion.* New York: Doubleday

Boddy J. 1989. *Wombs and Alien Spirits: Women, Men, and the Zar Cult in Northern Sudan.* Madison: Univ. Wis. Press

Bourdieu P. 1989. *La noblesse d'état.* Paris: Édit. Minuit

Bowen JR. 1993. *Muslims Through Discourse: Religion and Ritual in Gayo Society.* Princeton, NJ: Princeton Univ. Press

Brandes S. 1990. Conclusion: reflections on the study of religious orthodoxy and popular faith in Europe. See Badone 1990, pp. 185–99

Brouwer S, Gifford P, Rose SD. 1996. *Exporting the American Gospel: Global Christian Fundamentalism.* New York: Routledge

Brown MF. 1997. *The Channeling Zone: American Spirituality in an Anxious Age.* Cambridge, MA: Harvard Univ. Press

Brown P. 1981. *The Cult of the Saints: Its Rise and Function in Latin Christianity.* Chicago: Univ. Chicago Press

Bruce S. 1996. *Religion in the Modern World: From Cathedrals to Cults.* Oxford: Oxford Univ. Press

Cambell C. 1987. *The Romantic Ethic and the Spirit of Modern Consumerism*. Oxford: Blackwell

Casanova J. 1994. *Public Religions in the Modern World*. Chicago: Univ. Chicago Press

Casanova J. 1998. Between nation and civil society: ethnolinguistic and religious pluralism in independent Ukraine. See Hefner RW 1998. In press

Chatterjee P. 1986. *Nationalist Thought and the Colonial World: A Derivative Discourse?* London: Zed

Chestnut RA. 1997. *Born Again in Brazil: The Pentecostal Boom and the Pathogens of Poverty*. New Brunswick, NJ: Rutgers Univ. Press

Christian WA. 1989. *Person and God in a Spanish Valley*. Princeton, NJ: Princeton Univ. Press. Revised ed.

Clark DN. 1986. *Christianity in Modern Korea*. Lanham, MD: Univ. Press Am.

Cohn BS. 1964. The role of Gosains in the economy of the eighteenth- and nineteenth-century Upper India. *Indian Econ. Soc. Hist. Rev.* 1:175–82

Cohn BS. 1981. Anthropology and history in the 1980s. *J. Interdisc. Hist.* 12:227–52

Cohn BS. 1987. *An Anthropologist Among the Historians and Other Essays*. Delhi: Oxford Univ. Press

Comaroff J. 1985. *Body of Power, Spirit of Resistance: The Culture and History of a South African People*. Chicago: Univ. Chicago Press

Comaroff Jean, Comaroff John. 1991. *Of Revelation and Revolution: Christianity, Colonialism, and Consciousness in South Africa*. Vol. 1. Chicago: Univ. Chicago Press

Cooper R. 1996. *The Post-Modern State and the World Order*. London: Demos

Dirks N. 1989. The invention of caste: civil society in colonial India. *Soc. Anal.* 25:42–51

Dobbelaere K. 1981. *Secularization: A Multi-Dimensional Concept*. Beverly Hills, CA: Sage

Eaton RM. 1993. *The Rise of Islam and the Bengal Frontier: 1204–1760*. Berkeley: Univ. Calif. Press

Eickelman DF. 1979. The political economy of meaning. *Am. Ethnol.* 6:386–93

Eickelman DF. 1983. Changing interpretations of Islamic movements. In *Islam and the Political Economy of Meaning*, ed. WR Roff, pp. 13–30. London: Croom Helm

Eickelman DF. 1993. Islamic liberalism strikes back. *Middle East Stud. Assoc. Bull.* 27:163–68

Eickelman DF, Piscatori J. 1996. *Muslim Politics*. Princeton, NJ: Princeton Univ. Press

Foucault M. 1996. What is critique? See Schmidt 1996, pp. 382–98

Fukuyama F. 1992. *The End of History and the Last Man*. New York: Avon

Fuller GE. 1996. *Algeria: The Next Fundamentalist State?* Santa Monica, CA: RAND

Gaffney PD. 1994. *The Prophet's Pulpit: Islamic Preaching in Contemporary Egypt*. Berkeley: Univ. Calif. Press

Gay CM. 1991. *With Liberty and Justice For Whom? The Recent Evangelical Debate Over Capitalism*. Grand Rapids, MI: Eerdmans

Gay P. 1966. *The Enlightenment: An Interpretation. The Rise of Modern Paganism*. New York: Norton

Geertz C. 1960. *The Religion of Java*. New York: Free

Geertz C. 1973. "Internal conversion" in contemporary Bali. In *The Interpretation of Cultures*, ed. C Geertz, pp. 170–89. New York: Basic Books

Geertz C. 1980. *Negara: The Theatre-State in Nineteenth-Century Bali*. Princeton, NJ: Princeton Univ. Press

Gellner E. 1981. Flux and reflux in the faith of Men. In *Muslim Society*, ed. E Gellner, pp. 1–85. Cambridge: Cambridge Univ. Press

Gellner E. 1992. *Postmodernism, Reason and Religion*. London: Routledge

Giddens A. 1984. *The Constitution of Society: Outline of the Theory of Structuration*. Berkeley: Univ. Calif. Press

Goldberg E. 1993. Private goods, public wrongs, and civil society in some Medieval Arab theory and practice. In *Rules and Rights in the Middle East: Democracy, Law, and Society*, ed E. Goldberg, R. Kasaba, JS Migdal, pp. 248–71. Seattle: Univ. Wash. Press

Gombrich R, Obeyesekere G. 1988. *Buddhism Transformed: Religious Change in Sri Lanka*. Princeton, NJ: Princeton Univ. Press

Gonzalez-Quijono Y. 1994. *Les Gens du livre: Champ intellectuel et édition dans l'Égypte republicaine (1952–1993)*. PhD thesis. Paris: L'Inst. Étud. Pol.

Habermas J. 1984. *The Theory of Communicative Action*. Vol. 1: *Reason and the Rationalization of Society*. Transl. T McCarthy. Boston: Beacon

Habermas J. 1991. *The Structural Transformation of the Public Sphere: An Inquiry into a Category of Bourgeois Society*. Transl. T Burger. Cambridge, MA: MIT Press

Habermas J. 1996. The unity of reason in the diversity of its voices. See Schmidt 1996, pp. 399–425

Halévy E. 1927. *A History of the English People 1830–1841*. London: Fisher Unwin

Hall KR. 1985. *Maritime Trade and State Development in Early Southeast Asia*. Honolulu: Univ. Hawaii Press

Hannerz U. 1992. The global ecumene as a network of networks. See Kuper 1992, pp. 34–56

Hannerz U. 1996. *Cultural Complexity: Studies in the Social Organization of Meaning*. New York: Columbia Univ. Press

Hawley W. 1991. Naming Hinduism. *Wilson Q.* 15:3:20–34

Heelas P. 1996. *The New Age Movement: The Celebration of the Self and the Sacralization of Modernity*. Oxford: Blackwell

Hefner RW. 1985. *Hindu Javanese: Tengger Tradition and Islam*. Princeton, NJ: Princeton Univ. Press

Hefner RW. 1987. The political economy of Islamic conversion in modern East Java. In *Islam and the Political Economy of Meaning*, ed. WR Roff, pp. 53–78. London: Croom Helm

Hefner RW, ed. 1993a. *Conversion to Christianity: Historical and Anthropological Perspectives on a Great Transformation*. Berkeley: Univ. Calif. Press

Hefner RW. 1993b. World building and the rationality of conversion. See Hefner 1993a, pp. 3–44

Hefner RW. 1995. Reimagined community: a social history of Muslim education in Pasuruan, East Java. In *Asian Visions of Authority: Religion and the Modern States of East and Southeast Asia*, ed. CF Keyes, L Kendall, H Hardacre, pp. 75–95. Honolulu: Univ. Hawaii Press

Hefner RW. 1997a. Islamization and democratization in Indonesia. See Hefner & Horvatich 1997, pp. 75–127

Hefner RW. 1997b. Print Islam: mass media and ideological rivalries among Indonesian Muslims. *Indonesia* 64:77–103

Hefner RW, ed. 1998. *Democratic Civility: The History and Cross-Cultural Possibility of a Modern Political Ideal*. New Brunswick, NJ: Transaction Books

Hefner RW, Horvatich P, eds. 1997. *Islam in an Era of Nation States: Politics and Religious Renewal in Muslim Southeast Asia*. Honolulu: Univ. Hawaii Press

Hervieu-Léger D. 1990. Religion and modernity in the French context: for a new approach to secularization. *Sociol. Anal.* 51: S15–25

Hobsbawm EJ. 1957. Methodism and the threat of revolution in Britain. *Hist. Today* 7:115–24

Holt JC. 1991. Protestant Buddhism? *Relig. Stud. Rev.* 17:312–27

Horton R. 1971. African conversion. *Africa* 41:85–108

Hunter JD. 1987. *Evangelicalism: The Coming Generation*. Chicago: Univ. Chicago Press

Huntington SP. 1996. *The Clash of Civilizations and the Remaking of World Order*. New York: Simon & Schuster

Hutchinson SE. 1996. *Nuer Dilemmas: Coping with Money, War, and the State*. Berkeley: Univ. Calif. Press

Ibrahim SE. 1993. Civil society and prospects for democratization in the Arab World. See Norton 1993, pp. 27–54

Ikenga-Metuh E. 1987. The shattered microcosm: a critical survey of explanations of conversion in Africa. In *Religion, Development, and African Identity*, ed. KH Petersen, pp. 11–27. Uppsala, Sweden: Scand. Inst. Afr. Stud.

Jaffrelot C. 1996. *The Hindu Nationalist Movement in India*. New York: Columbia Univ. Press

James W. 1995. Introduction: Whatever happened to the Enlightenment? In *The Pursuit of Certainty: Religious and Cultural Formations*, ed. W James, pp. 1–14. New York: Routledge

Kammerer CA. 1990. Customs and Christian conversion among Akha Highlanders of Burma and Thailand. *Am. Ethnol.* 17: 277–91

Kapferer B. 1988. *Legends of People, Myths of State: Violence, Intolerance, and Political Culture in Sri Lanka and Australia*. Washington, DC: Smithson. Inst. Press

Kee HC. 1993. From the Jesus movement toward institutional church. See Hefner 1993a, pp. 47–63

Keyes CF. 1987. *Thailand: Buddhist Kingdom as Modern Nation-State*. Boulder, CO: Westview

Keyes CF. 1993. Why the Thai are not Christians: Buddhist and Christian conversion in Thailand. See Hefner 1993a, pp. 259–83

Kipp RS. 1990. *The Early Years of a Dutch Colonial Mission: The Karo Field*. Ann Arbor: Univ. Mich. Press

Kipp RS. 1993. *Dissociated Identities: Ethnicity, Religion, and Class in an Indonesian Society*. Ann Arbor: Univ. Mich. Press

Kopytoff I. 1987. *The African Frontier: The Reproduction of Traditional African Societies*. Bloomington: Indiana Univ. Press

Kuper A, ed. 1992. *Conceptualizing Society*. London: Routledge

Lambek M. 1993. *Knowledge and Practice in Mayotte: Local Discourses of Islam, Sorcery, and Spirit Possession*. Toronto: Univ. Toronto Press

Lansing JS. 1991. *Priests and Programmers:*

*Technologies of Power in the Engineered Landscape of Bali*. Princeton, NJ: Princeton Univ. Press

Launay R. 1992. *Beyond the Stream: Islam and Society in a West African Town*. Berkeley: Univ. Calif. Press

Lessa WA, Vogt EZ. 1979. *Reader in Comparative Religion: An Anthropological Approach*. New York: Harper & Row. 4th ed.

Lewis IM. 1986. *Religion in Context: Cults and Charisma*. Cambridge: Cambridge Univ. Press

Luckmann T. 1967. *Invisible Religion*. New York: Macmillan

Luhmann N. 1984. *Religious Dogmatics and the Evolution of Societies*. New York: Mellen

Lyotard JF. 1992. *The Postmodern Explained*. Minneapolis: Univ. Minn. Press

Mardin S. 1989. *Religion and Social Change in Modern Turkey: The Case of Bediuzzaman Said Nursi*. Albany: State Univ. NY Press

Mardin S. 1995. Civil society and Islam. In *Civil Society: Theory, History, Comparison*, ed. JA Hall, pp. 278–300. London: Polity

Marriott M, ed. 1955. *Village India: Studies in the Little Community*. Chicago: Univ. Chicago Press

Marsden GM. 1980. *Fundamentalism and American Culture: The Shaping of Twentieth-Century Evangelicalism, 1870–1925*. Oxford: Oxford Univ. Press

Martin D. 1978. *A General Theory of Secularization*. New York: Harper & Row

Martin D. 1990. *Tongues of Fire: The Explosion of Protestantism in Latin America*. Oxford: Blackwell

Mbiti J. 1969. *African Religions and Philosophy*. London: Heinemann Educ.

Meeker ME. 1991. The new Muslim intellectuals in the Republic of Turkey. In *Islam in Modern Turkey: Religion, Politics and Literature in a Secular State*, ed. R Tapper, pp. 189–219. London: Tauris

Merrill WL. 1988. *Raramuri Souls: Knowledge and Social Process in Northern Mexico*. Washington, DC: Smithson. Inst. Press

Mitchell RP. 1969. *The Society of the Muslim Brothers*. New York: Oxford Univ. Press

Mottahedeh RP. 1993. Toward an Islamic theology of toleration. In *Islamic Law Reform and Human Rights: Challenges and Rejoinders*, ed. T Lindholm, K Vogt, pp. 25–36. Copenhagen: Nordic Hum. Rights

Moussalli AS. 1995. Modern Islamic fundamentalist discourses on civil society, pluralism and democracy. See Norton 1995, pp. 79–119

Mujahid AM. 1989. *Conversion to Islam: Untouchables' Strategy for Protest in India*. Chambersburg, PA: Anima

Munson H Jr. 1993. *Religion and Power in Morocco*. New Haven: Yale Univ. Press

Nederveen Pieterse J, ed. 1992. *Christianity and Hegemony: Religion and Politics on the Frontiers of Social Change*. New York: Berg

Norton AR. 1995. *Civil Society in the Middle East*. Leiden: Brill

Obeyesekere G. 1981. *Medusa's Hair: An Essay on Personal Symbols and Religious Experience*. Chicago: Univ. Chicago Press

Ortner SB. 1984. Theory in anthropology since the sixties. *Comp. Stud. Soc. Hist.* 26:126–66

Outram D. 1995. *The Enlightenment*. Cambridge: Cambridge Univ. Press

Parish SM. 1996. *Hierarchy and Its Discontents: Culture and the Politics of Consciousness in Caste Society*. Philadelphia: Univ. Penn. Press

Peletz MP. 1997. "Ordinary Muslims" and Muslim resurgents in contemporary Malaysia: notes on an ambivalent relationship. See Hefner & Horvatich 1997, pp. 231–73

Pigeaud TGT. 1963. *Java in the 14th Century*. Five volumes. The Hague: Martinus Nijhoff

Pollock DK. 1993. Conversion and "community" in Amazonia. See Hefner 1993a, pp. 165–97

Queen CS. 1996. Introduction: the shapes and sources of engaged Buddhism. In *Engaged Buddhism: Buddhist Liberation Movements in Asia*, ed. CS Queen, SB King, pp. 1–44. Albany: State Univ. NY Press

Radcliffe-Brown AR. 1952. *Structure and Function in Primitive Society*. New York: Free Press

Ranger T. 1986. Religious movements and politics in sub-Saharan Africa. *Afr. Stud. Rev.* 29:2:1–69

Ranger T. 1993. The local and the global in Southern African religious history. See Hefner 1993a, pp. 65–98

Redfield R. 1956. The social organization of tradition. In *Peasant Society and Culture: An Anthropological Approach to Civilization*, pp. 67–104. Chicago: Univ. Chicago Press

Robson SO. 1981. Java at the crossroads. *Bijdr. Taal-, Land-, Volkenk.* 137:259–92

Roy O. 1993. *The Failure of Political Islam*. Cambridge, MA: Harvard Univ. Press

Schmidt J, ed. 1996. *What Is Enlightenment? Eighteenth-Century Answers and Twentieth-Century Questions*. Berkeley: Univ. Calif. Press

## 104   HEFNER

Schneider J. 1990. Spirits and the spirit of capitalism. See Badone 1990, pp. 24–54

Singer M. 1972. When a Great Tradition Modernizes: An Anthropological Approach to Indian Civilization. New York: Praeger

Skinner Q. 1990. Machiavelli's Discorsi and the pre-humanist origins of republican ideas. In Machiavelli and Republicanism, ed. G Bock, Q Skinner, M Viroli, pp. 121–41. Cambridge: Cambridge Univ. Press

Smith C. 1995. The spirit and democracy: base communities, Protestantism, and democratization in Latin America. In Religion and Democracy in Latin America, ed. WH Swatos Jr, pp. 27–44. New Brunswick, NJ: Transaction Books

Spencer J. 1995. The politics of tolerance: Buddhists and Christians, truth and error in Sri Lanka. See James 1995, pp. 195–214

Stocking GW Jr. 1989. Romantic Motives: Essays on Anthropological Sensibility. History of Anthropology, Vol. 6. Madison: Univ. Wis. Press

Stoll D. 1982. Fishers of Men or Founders of Empire? London: Zed

Stoll D. 1990. Is Latin America Turning Protestant? The Politics of Evangelical Growth. Berkeley: Univ. Calif. Press

Tambiah SJ. 1992. Buddhism Betrayed? Religion, Politics, and Violence in Sri Lanka. Chicago: Univ. Chicago Press

Tambiah SJ. 1996. Leveling Crowds: Ethnonationalist Conflicts and Collective Violence in South Asia. Berkeley: Univ. Calif. Press

Thompson EP. 1963. The Making of the English Working Class. New York: Vintage

Thompson EP. 1993. Witness Against the Beast: William Blake and the Moral Law. New York: New Press

Tibi B. 1990. Islam and the Cultural Accommodation of Social Change. Boulder, CO: Westview

Tonnesson S, Antlov H, eds. 1996. Asian Forms of the Nation. Richmond, UK: Curzon

Tuck R. 1993. Philosophy and Government 1572–1651. Cambridge, UK: Cambridge Univ. Press

Vail L. 1989. The Creation of Tribalism in Southern Africa. London: Currey

van der Veer P. 1988. Gods on Earth: The Management of Religious Experience and Identity in a North Indian Pilgrimage Centre. London: Athlone

van der Veer P. 1994. Religious Nationalism: Hindus and Muslims in India. Berkeley: Univ. Calif. Press

Villalon LA. 1995. Islamic Society and State Power in Senegal: Disciples and Citizens in Fatick. Cambridge, UK: Cambridge Univ. Press

Vovelle M. 1978. Piété baroque et déchristianisation en Provence au XVIII siècle. Paris: Seuil

Walzer M. 1965. The Revolution of the Saints: A Study in the Origins of Radical Politics. Cambridge, MA: Harvard Univ. Press

Warren C. 1993. Adat and Dinas: Balinese Communities in the Indonesian State. Kuala Lumpur: Oxford Univ. Press

Weber M. 1958. The Protestant Ethic and the Spirit of Capitalism. New York: Scribner's

Wells KM. 1990. New God, New Nation: Protestants and Self-Reconstruction Nationalism in Korea 1896–1937. Honolulu: Univ. Hawaii Press

Werbner P. 1996. Allegories of sacred imperfection: magic, hermeneutics and passion in The Satanic Verses. Curr. Anthropol. 37(Suppl.):S56–78

Wiener MJ. 1995. Visible and Invisible Realms: Power, Magic, and Colonial Conquest in Bali. Chicago: Univ. Chicago Press

Wilson BR. 1966. Religion in Secular Society. London: Watts

Wilson BR. 1985. Morality in the evolution of the modern social system. Br. J. Sociol. 36:315–32

Wolf ER. 1958. The virgin of Guadalupe: a Mexican national symbol. J. Am. Folkl. 71:34–39

Wolf ER, Hansen EC. 1972. The role of religion. In The Human Condition in Latin America, pp. 100–17. New York: Oxford Univ. Press

Worsley P. 1968. The Trumpet Shall Sound: A Study of "Cargo" Cults in Melanesia. New York: Schocken

Wuthnow R. 1988. The Restructuring of American Religion: Society and Faith Since the Second World War. Princeton, NJ: Princeton Univ. Press

*Annu. Rev. Anthropol. 1998. 27:105–28*
*Copyright © 1998 by Annual Reviews. All rights reserved*

# WHEN ANTHROPOLOGY IS AT HOME: The Different Contexts of a Single Discipline

*Mariza G. S. Peirano*

Departamento de Antropologia, Universidade de Brasília, 70.910-900 Brasília, DF, Brazil; mpeirano@uol.com.br

KEY WORDS: otherness, exoticism, difference, anthropology in context

---

## ABSTRACT

For a long time anthropology was defined by the exoticism of its subject matter and by the distance, conceived as both cultural and geographic, that separated the researcher from the researched group. This situation has changed. In a few years we may assess the twentieth century as characterized by a long and complex movement, with theoretical and political implications, that replaced the ideal of the radical encounter with alterity with research at home. But "home" will, as always, incorporate many meanings, and anthropology will maintain, in its paradigmatic assumption, a socio-genetic aim toward an appreciation for, and an understanding of, difference. In some cases, difference will be the route to theoretical universalism via comparison; in others, it will surface as a denunciation of exoticism or a denial of its appeal. This review examines different moments and contexts in which an attempt at developing anthropology "at home" became an appropriate quest.

---

## INTRODUCTION

Until recently, the idea of an anthropology at home was a paradox and a contradiction of terms. Throughout the twentieth century, however, the distances between ethnologists and those they observed—once seen as "informants"—have constantly decreased: from the Trobrianders to the Azande, from these groups to the Bororo by way of the Kwakiutl, by midcentury the academic community discovered that the approach, not the subject matter, had unwit-

0084-6570/98/1015-0105$08.00

tingly always defined the anthropological endeavor. Lévi-Strauss (1962) played a fundamental role in this change of perspective by imprinting a horizontal sense to social practices and beliefs in any latitude; Firth (1956) and Schneider (1968) provided the necessary test of validity in the realm of kinship studies. The awareness that the search for radical otherness contained a political component allowed "indigenous" anthropologies to enter the scene during the 1970s (Fahim 1982); in the 1980s Geertz (1983) could proclaim that "we are all natives now." But admonitions from the older generation attested that the movement from overseas to across the hall was not smooth; studying at home was seen by many as a difficult task and better entrusted to researchers who had gained experience elsewhere (Dumont 1986).

From the beginning, anthropologists who had their origins in former anthropological sites were exempted from the search for alterity—provided that their training had been undertaken with the proper mentors. Thus Malinowski gave his approval to Hsiao-Tung Fei to publish his monograph on Chinese peasants, remarking that if self-knowledge is the most difficult to gain, then "an anthropology of one's own people is the most arduous, but also the most valuable achievement of a fieldworker" (Malinowski 1939:xix). The approval that Radcliffe-Brown and Evans-Pritchard gave to the study by Srinivas (1952) on the Coorgs of India also suggests that the canon could be developed independent of shared practices. The ideal of overseas research, however, remained the goal to be reached. Decades later, and as part of a tradition that had firmly questioned the need for external fieldwork (Béteille & Madan 1975; Srinivas 1966, 1979; Uberoi 1968), Saberwal (1982) remarked that for many, fieldwork in India could be seen as a soft experience, because it was accomplished mostly within the language, caste, and region of origin of the researcher.

In the case of researchers from metropolitan centers, who recently came to accept that they too are natives, the drive for bringing anthropology home has various motivations. Some explain it as one of the inevitable conditions of the modern world (Jackson 1987a); for others, it emerges from the purpose to transform anthropology into cultural critique (Marcus & Fischer 1986). In the United States particularly, when anthropology comes home it is recast as "studies" (cultural, feminist, science and technology) and seen as part of "anti-disciplinary" arenas (Marcus 1995), thus attesting to an inherent affinity between anthropology and exoticism. Whatever the case, a lineage that justifies the attempt is always traced, be it from Raymond Firth and Max Gluckman (Jackson 1987b), or from Margaret Mead and Ruth Benedict (Marcus & Fischer 1986 for Mead, Geertz 1988 for Benedict).

In places where anthropology was ratified locally via social sciences during the 1940s and 1950s (e.g. Brazil and India), mainly as part of movements toward "modernization," an open dialogue with national political agendas became inevitable, thus reproducing canonical European patterns (E Becker

1971). In these contexts, alterity has rarely been uncommitted and (Weberian) interested aspects of knowledge are oftentimes explicit. This distinct quality has blinded many observers to a timeless quest for theoretical excellence, fundamental in these contexts, which results in a pattern of a threefold dialogue: with peer anthropologists and sociologists, with the metropolitan traditions of knowledge (past and present), and with the subjects of research (Madan 1982b, Peirano 1992, Das 1995).

In this essay I look at some of the indexical components of the term home in the expression "anthropology at home." First, I examine the moment and the context in which the attempt to develop anthropology at home became an appropriate goal. I focus my attention on the socially legitimate centers of scholarly production—that is, as per Gerholm & Hannerz (1982b), the sites of "international anthropology"—where the ideal of a long period of fieldwork and overseas research was first established. This endeavor includes Europe and the United States. (I assume that nowadays the United States plays a role socially equivalent to that of England during the first half of the century or France in the golden moments of structuralism.)

In a second part, I shift to a different perspective. I take a look at otherness in contemporary anthropology in Brazil. Contrary to traditional canons of anthropology, the overall pattern has been to undertake research at home (though the expression "anthropology at home" is not usual). I point to a configuration of different projects that, though not exclusive, may be distinguished as attempts at radical otherness, at the study of "contact" with otherness, at "nearby" otherness, or as a radicalization of "us."

By indicating variances in the notion of otherness, I conclude with an agenda for the examination of anthropology with its dual face: at the same time one and many.

## ANTHROPOLOGY AT HOME

In the context of a new historical awareness at "international" centers of production, personal concerns about the future of anthropology in the 1960s gave way in the 1970s to more sociological analysis, denouncing political relations that had always been a trait of anthropological fieldwork. Soon the idea of an anthropology at home made its debut in Europe, while in the United States it twirled into "studies," at the intersection of several experiments in the humanities.

### Antecedents: Worries in the Center

In the 1960s, two minor papers by prestigious anthropologists expressed paradoxical feelings about the future of anthropology. Exactly at the point in time when the discipline had gathered momentum, its subject matter ran the risk of disappearing. In France, Lévi-Strauss (1961) warned that anthropology might become a science without an object because of the physical disappearance of whole populations following contact or because of the rejection of anthropology by newly independent nations. Would it survive? For Lévi-Strauss, this development was a unique chance for anthropologists to become aware, if they had not been previously, that the discipline had never been defined as the study of primitives in absolute terms but instead had been conceived as a certain relationship between observer and observed. Thus, to the extent that the world became smaller, and Western civilization ever more expansive and complex— reborn everywhere as *creole*—differences would be closer to the observer. There should be no fear: No crisis of anthropology was in sight.

For Goody (1966) the "single-handed community study of uncomplicated societies" (1966:574) was no longer possible as primitives became players in much larger and complex social networks in Third World countries. It was a crossroads for anthropology, which could either become social archaeology, a branch of historical sociology based on "traditional preserve," or accept turning into comparative sociology. Suggesting a "decolonization of the social sciences," Goody stressed that the distinction between sociology and social anthropology in England was basically xenophobic: Sociology was the study of complex societies, social anthropology of simple ones, but in the new nations, their "other culture" was "our sociology" (1966:576).

Lévi-Strauss's optimism and Goody's proposal for disciplinary adjustment in the 1960s must be seen in the context of the undisputed prestige of the discipline. Latour (1996) has characterized the ethnographer of that period as an antithetical King Midas, "cursed with the gift of turning everything to dust" (1996:5). But that decade also witnessed Leach's (1961) rethinking of anthropology, the legitimization of the study of complex societies (Banton 1966), Firth (1956) and Schneider (1968) making incursions into studying their own societies via kinship, and the publication of Malinowski's field diaries. The latter alone led to much dispute (Darnell 1974), and in a rejoinder first published in 1968 in the United States, Stocking (1974) reminded us that anthropological fieldwork was a historical phenomenon, thus implying that it could just as well be transient.

## Relations of Power and Self-Reflection

Of course, in 1965 Hallowell (1974) had already laid the foundations for looking at anthropology as "an anthropological problem," and soon after, Hymes (1974) proposed a reinvention of anthropology. Retrospectively, the idea of centering one's questions on the conditions that produced anthropology in the West proved to be the basis for much in the self-reflection projects that followed. International conferences resembling collective rituals of expiation were a mark of the 1970s. These conferences led to books that became well known to the profession, and the frequent publication of profiles of different national trends of the discipline became usual in prominent journals. In some cases, journals published special issues on these topics.

CONFERENCES OF THE 1970S   Asad (1973a) was the classic publication of the period, the result of a conference under the auspices of the University of Hull in 1972. It was direct in its denunciation that British (functional) anthropology had been based on a power relationship between the West and the Third World. Anthropology had emerged as a distinctive discipline at the beginning of the colonial era, became a flourishing academic profession toward its close, and throughout this period devoted itself to description and analyses "carried out by Europeans, for a European audience—of non-European societies dominated by European power" (Asad 1973b:15). Such an inequitable situation could be transcended only by its inner contradictions.

Diamond (1980a) and Fahim's (1982) papers came out of conferences sponsored by the Wenner-Gren Foundation for Anthropological Research. Openly Marxist, Diamond (1980b) alluded to national traditions only to dismiss them; for him, professional anthropology was an instance of diffusion by domination meaning that "an Indian or African anthropologist, trained in this Western technique, does not behave as an Indian or African when he behaves as an anthropologist. . . . he lives and thinks as an academic European" (1980b:11–12). [In this sense, Diamond was in a position different from the positions of those who, like Crick (1976), at that moment tried to encourage anthropologists of other cultures to develop "traditions of their own—scrutinizing themselves in ways which are not just a pale reflection of our interest in them—but also that they will make us the object of their speculation" (1976:167).]

In this context, when Fahim (1982) brought together a number of anthropologists from different non-Western parts of the world (the organizer was an Egyptian anthropologist), the term indigenous anthropology was proposed as a working concept to refer to the practice of anthropology in one's native country, society, and/or ethnic group.[1] From the organizer's point of view, the symposium accomplished its goal of replacing the Western versus non-Western polemics with a constructive dialogue, in the same process shifting the focus from indigenous "anthropology" to "anthropologists" (Fahim & Helmer 1982). Madan (1982a,b) received special credit from the editor for his forceful defense of the idea that the crucial discussion should not address where anthropology is done or by whom, merely replacing one actor with another, but rather should face up to a much-needed change in anthropology's perspective. Because anthropology is a kind of knowledge, or a form of consciousness, that

[1]Mott (1982) expressed his surprise that in Brazil the term indigenous is used to denote Amerindians; he also wondered why Brazil had been included among non-Western countries.

arises from the encounter of cultures in the mind of the researcher, it enables us to understand ourselves in relation to others, becoming a project of heightened self-awareness.

ANTHROPOLOGY OF ANTHROPOLOGY   A second perspective concerning different contexts for anthropology can be discerned in the challenge some anthropologists felt about looking at the discipline with anthropological eyes, thus following the wise lead given by Hallowell (1974). McGrane (1976) attempted to face the paradoxical situation that the discipline sees everything (everything but itself) as culturally bound by tracking the European cosmographies from the sixteenth to the early twentieth centuries. [See Fabian (1983) for a similar later attempt.] Peirano (1981) contrasted Lévi-Strauss's classical position on the issue of the reversibility of anthropological knowledge with Dumont's (1978) assertion that there is no symmetry between the modern pole where anthropology stands and the nonmodern pole (thus frustrating the idea of a multiplicity of anthropologies). The thesis explored the variability of anthropological questions in different sociocultural contexts, and Brazil was used as its starting point.

Also framed within the concern for an anthropology of anthropology was Gerholm & Hannerz (1982a), whose editors, untroubled by whether traditions were Western or non-Western, invited anthropologists from different backgrounds (which included India, Poland, Sudan, Canada, Brazil, and Sweden) to discuss the shaping of national anthropologies. Distinguishing between a prosperous mainland of British, US, and French disciplines (i.e. "international" anthropology) and "an archipelago of large and small islands" on the periphery (Gerholm & Hannerz 1982b:6), they inquired into the structure of center-periphery relations and its inequalities; confronted the variety of discipline boundaries; looked at the backgrounds, training, and careers of anthropologists; and asked: Could it be that if anthropology is an interpretation of culture, this interpretation itself is shaped by culture? Diamond (1980a) and Bourdieu (1969) were mentioned as stimuli, and, as in Fahim's book, here Saberwal's (1982) far-reaching implications were given special attention by the editors. Stocking (1982) closed the special issue with "a view from the center" in which, taking the lead from O Velho (1982), he highlighted the "privileges of underdevelopment" while distinguishing between anthropologies of "empire-building" and of "nation-building," alluding to the question of the reversibility of anthropological knowledge suggested by Peirano (1981). (See Stocking 1982:178.)

## Doing Anthropology at Home

Displayed in the titles of the books, doing anthropology at home became a legitimate undertaking for Messerschmidt (1981) and Jackson (1987a). But

home, for them, was basically the United States and Europe. That the Mediterranean area, for instance, remained unstudied by insiders—and, if it had been
studied, the literature could be ignored—is shown in Gilmore (1982), where the
author reveals his explicit choice to review only works published in English.

In Messerschmidt (1981), the subjects of research were those nearby the
ethnographers in the United States and Canada: kinspeople, elderly in a large
city, a bureaucratic environment, a mining company. Offering an extensive
bibliography, the editor proposed that the term "insider anthropology" carried
less-negative connotations than, for instance, "indigenous" or "native." (The
same term was also proposed by Madan 1982b.)

Jackson (1987a) went further and brought together anthropologists from
Britain, Sweden, Denmark, Zimbabwe, Israel, and France, under the sponsor-
ship of the Association of Social Anthropologists in England. Once again,
home was Europe (or, suggestively enough, Africa), and non-European research would be a specific category. Jackson (1987b) asked why the close relationship between anthropology, folklore, and archaeology that existed in England no longer obtained, and Jackson suspected—in a comparison to sociology—that the difference between them was a love of (by one) and a distaste for
(by the other) modern society: Anthropologists were the folklorists of the exotic (1987b:8). Although research abroad would continue, it was clear that
fieldwork at home was here to stay. For some of the contributors, home was always transient, but wherever it was (Strathern 1987), there was a need to proceed by a phenomenology of the idea of remoteness (Ardener 1987). Okely
(1987) maintained that home was an increasingly narrow territory in a postcolonial era; Dragadze (1987) commented on the fact that a Soviet anthropologist is a historian, not a sociologist; and Mascarenhas-Keyes (1987) discussed
the process by which a native anthropologist becomes a "multiple native."

IN THE UNITED STATES   The project of bringing anthropology home in the
United States was cast with an enormous measure of social legitimacy and success as "cultural critique." Following Geertz's interpretive proposal, postmodernism caught on as if by powerful magic. In due time, the affinity with the
idea of bringing anthropology home was lost, but it may yet be recalled: "Indeed, we believe that the modern formulation of cultural anthropology depends for its full realization on just such a catching up of its lightly attended to
critical function at home with the present lively transformation of its traditionally emphasized descriptive function abroad" (Marcus & Fischer 1986:4).
"Home" and "abroad" continued to be distinctive sites, but by denouncing exoticism, there was a sense that a metamorphosis was being advanced and ethnographers were moving past anthropology toward experimentation and cultural studies. The term "post anthropology" was hinted in Clifford & Marcus
(1986), with novel intellectual lineages drawn or emphasized, whether from

the Chicago school of urban sociology (Clifford 1986) or from Margaret Mead in the United States and Raymond Williams in England (Marcus & Fischer 1986). In this context, the term "repatriated anthropology" was suggested.

For Clifford (1986), the new experimentation was being developed in works such as Latour & Woolgar (1979) on laboratory biologists, Marcus (1983) on the dynastic rich, Crapanzano (1980) on new ethnographic portraits, all of them opening the way for successors, such as Traweek (1988) on physicists, Fischer & Abedi (1990) on postmodern dialogues across cultures, and the subsequent questionings of classic fields and concepts such as ethnography (Thomas 1991) and culture (Abu-Lughod 1991). For some, repatriated (or at home) anthropology was identified as "American culture" studies: "The boundaries between 'foreign,' 'overseas,' 'exotic,' or even 'primitive' or 'nonliterate' and 'at home' or 'in our culture' are disappearing as the world culture becomes more uniform at one level and more diverse at another" (Spindler & Spindler 1983:73; see also Moffatt 1992, Brown 1994, Traube 1996).

Parallel to these developments, Stocking (1983a,b) launched the successful HOA (History of Anthropology) series, explaining in the first introductory text that the profound issues of disciplinary identity that the discipline was facing in the early 1980s had mobilized anthropologists into looking at the history of anthropology. The diagnosis was familiar: "With the withdrawal of the umbrella of European power that long protected their entry into the colonial field, anthropologists found it increasingly difficult to gain access to (as well as ethically more problematic to study) the non-European 'others' who had traditionally excited the anthropological imagination" (1983b:4).

Conferences and congresses continued to produce publications well received by the profession (e.g. Fox 1991), and the launching of new journals (e.g. *Cultural Anthropology* in 1986 and, a few years later, in 1988, *Public Culture*) signaled new arenas for experimentation and for the remaking of existing disciplines: "One source of transformation is from the sheer power and influence of ideas from the margins toward the putative center or mainstream. Another simultaneous source is from distaff voices situated within the realm of the official" (Marcus 1991:564). [Meanwhile, *Dialectical Anthropology* (1985) dedicated part of an issue to discuss "National Trends," which included the cases of French, British, Soviet, and German anthropology.]

Of course, Said (1978) had been a main reference from the moment it was published, and issues about colonialism continued to be analyzed (e.g. Thomas 1994), with close connections to the literature on gender and feminism (e.g. Dirks et al 1994, Behar & Gordon 1995, Lamphere et al 1997).

## Post-Exotic Anthropology?

A shift from the concerns with writing to attention on sites and audiences has marked the present decade. Strathern (1995) examines the (shifting) contexts within which people make different orders of knowledge for themselves (including anthropologists) as a prelude to questioning assumptions about global and local perspectives. (Meanwhile the European Association of Social Anthropologists was founded in 1990 and two years later launched *Social Anthropology*.)

Almost simultaneously, two books on locations were published: Clifford (1997) examines "routes" as spatial practices of anthropology, noting that fieldwork has been based on a distinction between a home base and an exterior place of discovery. However, notions of "homes and abroads, community insides and outsides, fields and metropoles are increasingly challenged by post-exotic, decolonizing trends" (1997:53). Fields must be negotiated; and because there is no narrative form or way of writing inherently suited to a politics of location, anthropological distance sometimes may be "challenged, blurred, relationally reconstructed" (1997:81). Gupta & Ferguson (1997a,b) also recognize that anthropology has developed as a body of knowledge based on regional specialization. The spatial separation between "the field" and "home" leads the authors to examine the fieldworker as an anthropological subject. Whether "postmodern migrancy" (Ahmad 1992) may be at stake or not, authors feel a need to propose solutions: Clifford (1997) suggests that traditional fieldwork will certainly maintain its prestige, but the discipline may come "to resemble more closely the 'national' anthropologies of many European and non-Western countries, with short, repeated visits the norm and fully supported research years rare" (1997:90). Gupta & Ferguson see possible alternative solutions for fieldwork in strong and long-established "national" traditions as those of Mexico, Brazil, Germany, Russia, or India (1997b:27), and they suggest that from "spatial sites" anthropologists move to "political locations," following feminist scholarship.

Such alternatives were the guiding inspiration for Moore (1996), who looked at local practices and discourses as sets of "situated knowledges" (cf Haraway 1988), all of which are simultaneously local and global. For the editor, the future of anthropological knowledge must be seen as the result of a challenge by Third World, Black, and feminist scholars.

Audiences have become another topic. Almost two decades after the unsuccessful attempt by MMJ Fischer (unpublished data) to include an introduction for Iranians different from one for Americans (see Fischer 1980), the concern with readership finally emerged in Europe (Driessen 1993) and in the United States (Brettell 1993), in the context of queries related to a "politics of ethnography." An awareness of audiences led Marcus (1993a,b), in his introduction to the first issue of *Late Editions*, to propose that the different volumes of the series had "globally-minded U.S. academics" (1993b:3) as their privileged targets, in an attempt to prompt a meeting of anthropology and cultural studies. The purpose was "to evoke a combined sense of familiarity and strangeness in

U.S.-university educated readers," by selecting subjects that share a sort of frame of reference and experience with them "but then differ from them by cultural background and situated fin-de-siècle predicament" (Marcus 1993b:5). Questions of audience, location, politics, and theory were present in the special issue of *Public Culture* devoted to the discussion of Ahmad (1992), but only to reveal the disparity of interpretations about what theory is all about and whether there could be any agreement on the field of "politics of theory" (Appadurai et al 1993, Ahmad 1993). Another attempt at an international discussion was put forward by Borofsky (1994), in a collective publication that came out of a session organized for the 1989 American Anthropological Association's annual meeting. The book included individual statements on authors' "intellectual roots." The project was extended in 1996, with another section at the same meeting, in which the title "How others see us: American cultural anthropology as the observed rather than the observer" indicated an exercise in reversibility (despite the fact that "others," with few exceptions, were located in the United States or Europe).

Among contemporary ethnographies at home, I single out Rabinow (1996), on the invention of the polymerase chain reaction, for a number of reasons: first, for the classic anthropological motivation ["I was often intrigued by, but skeptical of, the claims of miraculous knowledge made possible by new technologies supposedly ushering a new era in the understanding of life and unrivaled prospects for the improvement of health" (Rabinow 1996:2)]. Second, I single out this reference for its canonical structure: The first two chapters present the ecology of the invention, the (ever noble) third chapter focuses on the processes that culminated in the invention, while the last two demonstrate that an idea has little value unless it is put in action. Third, the book is innovative in the process of making both interviewees and readers collaborate in the text; in the style of *Late Editions*, transcripts of conversations with scientists, technicians, and businessmen are presented. Finally, despite protests of antidisciplinarity, the book also reinforces the idea that even at home, the ethnologist needs to learn another language (in this case, molecular biology) during a long period of socialization and, as always, to face the problem of who has the authority and the responsibility to represent experience and knowledge (Rabinow 1996:17). The fact that the book is not found on anthropology shelves in US bookstores, but on science shelves, reinforces by exclusion an enduring ideological association of anthropology with exoticism.[2]

---

[2]See Peirano (1997) for a comparison of four recent books, two of which were published in the United States (Geertz 1995, Rabinow 1996), two of which were published in India (Madan 1994, Das 1995).

# FROM (AN)OTHER POINT OF VIEW

Observing the Greek case from anthropologists' own accounts, Kuper (1994) criticizes what he calls "nativist ethnography"—an extreme case of anthropology at home. Oftentimes taking a lead from Said and postmodern reflexive discourse, nativist ethnography assumes that only natives understand natives and that the native must be the proper judge of ethnography, even its censor. Sensibly, the author shares a skeptical view of this trend. He spares some native and foreign individual ethnographers, while sanctioning different traditions of ethnographic study, and proposes a "cosmopolitan" alternative for anthropology. For Kuper, cosmopolitan ethnographers should write only to other anthropologists (and not for curious foreigners and armchair voyeurs; nor should they write for natives or even the native community of experts, i.e. social scientists, planners, intellectuals). For him, such a cosmopolitan anthropology is a social science closely allied to sociology and social history that cannot be bound in the service of any political program.

Kuper's notion of a cosmopolitan anthropology may be contrasted to the multicentered project of Indian anthropologists (Uberoi 1968, 1983; Madan 1994; Das 1995). Well before the current concerns with anthropology at home, India offered the academic world long discussions on the study of "one's own society" (Srinivas 1955, 1966, 1979; Uberoi 1968; Béteille & Madan 1975; Madan 1982a,b; Das 1995), which directly lead to the question of audiences for anthropological writing. India was also the scene of the unique rebirth of *Contributions to Indian Sociology*, after its founders, Louis Dumont and David Pocock, decided to cease publication of the journal in Europe after 10 years of existence (see Madan 1994). The debates carried on in the section "For a Sociology of India," the title of the first article published by the editors (Dumont & Pocock 1957) and later a regular feature of the journal, revealed it as a forum for theoretical, academic, and political (even pedagogical) discussion, involving scholars from a variety of backgrounds and orientations. If science's life, warmth, and movement may best be perceived in debate (Latour 1989), then this 30-year-old forum has a most thoughtful history to tell.

Indian anthropologists are aware of their multiple readerships. Madan (1982b:266) mentions two types of triangular connections: (*a*) the relationship between insider and outsider anthropologists and the people being studied and (*b*) the relationship between the anthropologist, the sponsor of research, and the people. Das (1995) also points to three kinds of dialogues within sociological writing on India: the dialogue with (*a*) the Western traditions of scholarship in the discipline, (*b*) with the Indian sociologist and anthropologist, and (*c*) with the "informant," whose voice is present either as information obtained in the field or as the written texts of the tradition. In this sense, anthropology in India evaluates and refines, at one and the same time, anthropological discourse and the scholarship about one's own society. In this context, it is worth recalling that outsider anthropologists who have worked in India have also engaged in dialogues with insider scholars; some of these exchanges deeply influenced both sides. Good examples are the unending debate between Dumont and Srinivas, the reactions by Dumont to the Indian philosopher AK Saran (see Srinivas 1955, 1966; Dumont 1970, 1980; Saran 1962), and the subaltern historians' (Guha & Spivak 1988) dissension with Dumont and their reception and influence in Europe and elsewhere.

## ALTERITY IN BRAZIL

A characteristic feature of anthropology in India is that social scientists aim at a mode of social reflection that does not merely duplicate Western questions. Yet Indian social scientists are fully aware that Western questions predirect their efforts, even their contestation. In Brazil, the image of an unavoidable dialogue with the centers of intellectual production is invariably present, but the undertone is different: Brazilian anthropologists feel that they are part and parcel of the West—even if, in important aspects, they are not. As one of the social sciences, anthropology in Brazil finds its usual intellectual niche at the intersection of different streams: first, canonical and/or current trends of Western scholarship; second, a sense of social responsibility toward those observed; and third, the lineage of social thought developed in the country at least from the early 1930s onward (which of course includes previous borrowings and earlier political commitments).

In this complex configuration, theory is the noble route to actual or idealized intellectual dialogues, and social commitment is in fact a powerful component of social scientists' identity (see, e.g., Candido 1958, Peirano 1981, Bomeny et al 1991, Schwartzman 1991, H Becker 1992, Reis 1996). Where theory has such an ideological power, communication is made more intricate by the fact that Portuguese is the language of intellectual discussion (oral and written) and English and French are the languages of scholarly learning. A quick glance into current anthropology in Brazil thus reveals no great surprises in terms of individual production—provided one knows Portuguese well. However, exactly because a dialogue is always taking place with absent interlocutors, alternative answers to existing concerns such as ethnicity, cultural and social pluralism, race, national identity, and so on are routine. [It is in this context that Arantes (1991) has ironically characterized Brazilian intellectual milieu as a "settling tank in the periphery."]

Somewhat of a singularity arises when academic production is depicted collectively. As opposed to the United States or Europe today, the critical point is neither exoticism nor the guilt generally associated with it. Concern over exoticism took a different path in Brazil. A (Durkheimian) notion of "difference" rather than "exoticism" has generally drawn the attention of anthropologists whenever and wherever they encounter "otherness," thus sanctioning the idea that French influence has been stronger than the German heritage. Moreover, because of an overall inclination that is both broadly theoretical and political, and therefore congenial to nation-building values and responsibilities, otherness is recurrently found within the limits of the country (but see exceptions in G Velho 1995) and often related to an urge to track down a possible "Brazilian" singularity (DaMatta 1984; see Fry 1995 for the explicit question).

In this section I look at different conceptions of otherness in Brazil. This endeavor results from an inquiry into possible equivalent notions of exoticism in the Brazilian context (and may eventually help decipher why anthropologists in Brazil do not partake the current sense of crisis as in other contexts).[3] I discern four configurations, presented here for heuristic purposes, which are neither discrete nor mutually exclusive. Cutting across a continuum of concerns about the location of otherness, many authors move from one to another or combine them at different moments in their careers; all of them are socially recognized as legitimate anthropology. I cite publications that I take as representative, but by no means do I touch below the surface of the available literature.

## Radical Otherness

The canonical search for radical otherness may be illustrated in Brazil in terms of ideological and/or geographical remoteness: first, in the study of indigenous or so-called tribal peoples; second, in the recent wave of research beyond Brazilian's frontiers. In both cases, radical otherness is not extreme.

In the first case, as befalls the study of Indian societies, interlocutors for Brazilian specialists are located both inside and outside the local community of social scientists. This is the area where outside debates are more visible. (Is one's difference another's exoticism?) Actual fieldwork, however, has been restricted to the limits of the country, even when the larger ethnological area is perceived as South America. Though funding may be one major constraint, there are crucial political and ideological implications in this fact.

A distinguished body of literature on South American ethnology is available to inform contemporaneous specialists, going back to nineteenth-century German expeditions seeking answers in Brazil to European questions about the state of "naturalness" of the primitives (Baldus 1954) up to more recent generations, such as Nimuendaju's (e.g. 1946) celebrated monographs on the social organization of the Gê tribes and the late 1930s research of Tupi groups

---

[3]A different approach was adopted in Peirano (1981), which examines the process by which, from the 1950s on, a common stock of sociological questions was progressively dismembered and couched as sociology, anthropology, and political science.

(e.g. Baldus 1970, Wagley & Galvão 1949). Soon after, Ribeiro & Ribeiro (1957) carried out research among the Urubu-Kaapor; during the late 1940s and early 1950s Fernandes (1963, 1970) published his classic reconstruction of Tupinambá social organization and warfare based on sixteenth-century chroniclers, and Schaden (1954) studied the different aspects of Guarani culture. Having been the best-studied peoples in Brazil, after Nimuendaju the Gê attracted the attention of Lévi-Strauss (1956) and, following suit, the Harvard Central-Brazil Project (Maybury-Lewis 1967, 1979). In due time, the results of this large-scale research program emerged as the strongest ethnographical cases supporting structural anthropology, having served as fieldwork experience for a generation of ethnologists (among those who developed their careers in Brazil, see DaMatta 1982; Melatti 1970, 1978).

Today, newcomers to the field can thus discern some antinomies: Tupi or Gê; kinship or cosmology; Amazonian and Central Brazil or Xingu; external historical sociology or internal synchronic analysis; ecology or culture; history or ethnography; political economy or descriptive cosmology (see Viveiros de Castro 1995b). As in every antinomy, reality is a step removed. But in this context, Tupi research, having practically disappeared from the ethnological scene during the 1960s and early 1970s (but see Laraia 1986), has recently reemerged with a driving force both within and beyond the limits of the Portuguese language (Viveiros de Castro 1992, T Lima 1995, Fausto 1997; see also Muller 1990, Magalhães 1994). Prompted by that body of research, interest in kinship was also rehabilitated (Viveiros de Castro 1995a,b; Villaça 1992; for a recent debate with French ethnographers, see Viveiros de Castro 1993, 1994; Copet-Rougier & Héritier-Augé 1993). Meanwhile, research on Gê groups continued (e.g. Vidal 1977, Carneiro da Cunha 1978, Seeger 1981, Lopes da Silva 1986).

The second trend of radical otherness is more recent. While it takes the observer away from the geographical limits of the country, it still confirms the idea that some relative link to home is essential. In this context the United States has become a sort of paradigmatic other for comparative studies, from the classic study on racial prejudice by Nogueira (see 1986) to more recent analyses of hierarchy and individualism by DaMatta (1973a, 1981, 1991). This trend has unfolded in the works of L Cardoso de Oliveira (1989), R Lima (1991), and, in this issue, Segato (1998). An emergent topic is the study of Brazilian immigrants (e.g. G Ribeiro 1996). A recent interest in Portuguese anthropology, as indicated by congresses and conferences in Brazil and Portugal, attests again to historical and linguistic links.

## Contact with Otherness

Considered by many the most successful theoretical innovation produced in Brazil, the idea of interethnic friction made its appearance in anthropology as a bricolage of indigenist concerns and sociological theoretical inspiration. Coined by R Cardoso de Oliveira (1963), interethnic friction was proposed as a syncretic totality emerging from the contact of Indian populations with the national society and revealing "a situation in which two groups are dialectically unified through opposing interests" (1963:43). Seen from this perspective, concerns about the integration of Indians into the national society—which have always been a source of distress for ethnologists and indigenists—were shifted onto theoretical grounds. Contact was seen as a dynamic process, and the notion of totality did not rest with one agent or the other (national or Indian) but in the universe of the observed phenomenon. Interethnic friction was proposed in a context in which British and US theories of contact, namely social change (Malinowski) and acculturation (Redfield, Linton, and Herskovitz), had proved inadequate; Balandier's views and Fernandes's (1972) studies on race relations in Brazil were chosen instead as inspiration.

Contact with Indians had been a major social concern in Brazil since the foundation of the Service for the Protection of Indians (SPI) in 1910. In the 1940s and 1950s it proceeded through observations carried out by ethnologists (generally published apart from their major ethnographical work) and set shore in academic anthropology as a legitimate topic in the 1950s, merging academic with public-policy concerns for indigenous populations (see D Ribeiro 1957, 1962). During the 1960s a peculiar academic scene emerged in Brazil: Sharing the same space, and often involving the same individual researchers (Laraia & DaMatta 1967, DaMatta 1982, Melatti 1967), studies were being developed that, on the one hand, focused on specific features of Indian social systems (cf Harvard Central-Brazil Project) and, on the other hand, focused on contact as interethnic friction.

This thematic inspiration survives today in studies that bear the hallmark of interethnic friction but have become a distinct lineage of concern (though theoretical bonds span from postmodern to historical and sociological concerns). Its topics vary from an evaluation of Yanomami ethnography in a context of crisis (Ramos 1995) to analyses of indigenism, Indian lands, and frontiers (Oliveira 1987, 1988; Ramos 1998, Souza Lima 1995) to social conditions of South American Indians (Carneiro da Cunha 1992).

During the 1970s, in due course the concern with contact embraced the theme of frontiers of expansion, making issues related to internal colonialism, peasants, and capitalist development a legitimate anthropological subject (O Velho 1972, 1976). At the same time, studies on peasants gained their own thematic status, as extensive studies were carried out by both anthropologists and sociologists (among the former, see Palmeira 1977, Sigaud 1980, Moura 1978, Seyferth 1985, K Woortmann 1990, E Woortmann 1995). This thematic movement's location eventually reached the fringes of large cities (Leite Lopes 1976).

## Nearby Otherness

As early as the 1970s, anthropologists in Brazil began to do research nearby. Because academic socialization takes place within social science courses, anthropological approaches have become a counterpart to sociology. In the unfolding of political authoritarianism in the 1970s, anthropology was seen by many as a promising counterpart to Marxist challenges coming from sociology—a silent dialogue that has persisted ever since. For some, the qualitative aspects of anthropology were appealing; others were attracted by the microscopic approach to social life; still others were attracted by the challenge of understanding certain aspects of the "national" ethos. The preferred route was via theory.

The Chicago school of sociology was one of G Velho's significant interlocutors (e.g. 1972, 1975, 1981) in his choice of sensitive urban issues, ranging from middle-class and elite lifestyles to psychic cultural habits, drug consumption, and violence. His students enlarged this universe by including popular sectors, aging, gender, prostitution, kinship and family, and politics. One major motivation of the overall project was to uncover urban values and the criteria for defining social identity and difference. Theses and books produced by this line of inquiry are numerous and far-reaching (e.g. Duarte 1986, Gaspar 1985, Lins de Barros 1989, Vianna 1995; Salem 1985 for a review on middle-class family).

In the horizontality bestowed on each society by structuralism, DaMatta (1984, 1991) found a legitimate avenue for his long-standing inquiry into the national ethos through the relationship between individualism and holism in Brazil. Of course, Gilberto Freyre's monumental work (see Segato 1998) is a predecessor in any search for Brazilian identity and DaMatta acknowledges the link. Having participated in the two major Indian research projects in the 1960s (cf above), since the 1980s the author has shifted to national themes. DaMatta (1973a) may be seen as a point of transition, pulling together a canonical structuralist analysis of an Apinajé myth, a story by Edgar Allan Poe, and an examination of *communitas* in Brazilian carnival. By means of a dialogue with Dumont's notion of hierarchy, DaMatta (1991) develops a comparative analysis of carnival in Brazil and the United States, discloses hierarchy in popular sayings and songs, and probes literary works.

In neither of the two approaches above was the relevance or appropriateness of developing anthropology at home ever seriously questioned. After a short exchange on the nature of fieldwork in general, on the disposition of ethnographers toward "anthropological blues," and on the idea of familiarity (DaMatta 1973b, 1981; G Velho 1978), both nearby and far from home, the issue was put to rest. (This debate was contemporaneous to Indian anthropologists' discussion on the study of one's own society.)

Meanwhile, other topics have emerged since the 1950s, first related to the social integration of different populations and later to minority rights. Such topics brought together sociology and anthropology, thereby reaffirming and giving historical validation to authors such as Candido (1995), who had never totally distinguished the social sciences from each other. To mention just a few, on immigrants see Azevedo (1994), Cardoso (1995), Seyferth (1990); on race relations, see Segato (1998), Borges Pereira (1967), Fry (1991); on gender studies, Bruschini & Sorj (1994), Gregori (1993); on religion, messianism, and Afro-Brazilian cults, R Ribeiro (1978), Maggie (1975), O Velho (1995), Birman (1995); and on popular festivities, Magnani (1984), Cavalcanti (1994). More directly focused on politics as a social domain in Brazil are studies in Palmeira (1995) and Palmeira & Goldman (1996).

## Radical Us

As if to confirm that social sciences in Brazil have a profound debt to Durkheim—who proposed that other forms of civilization are sought not for their own sake but to explain what is near to us—from the 1980s on anthropologists have launched a wave of studies on the social sciences themselves, with the overall purpose of understanding science as a manifestation of modernity. Although topics of study vary from local social scientists to classic authors of social theory, interlocutors are often French: See, for example, Castro Faria (1993), Corrêa (1982, 1987), Miceli (1989), Goldman (1994), and Neiburg (1997). Melatti (1984) stands as the richest bibliographical account of contemporary anthropology in Brazil. A comprehensive project to study different styles of anthropology was launched in Cardoso de Oliveira & Ruben (1995), with proposals to focus on different national experiences. This project was preceded by an independent study by Peirano (1981), who later, having chosen social sciences developed in India for interlocution (Peirano 1991), attempted a comparative approach based on the theoretical enigma put forth by Dumont (1978). For a comparison between Brazilian folklorists and sociologists vis-à-vis nation-building ideology, see Vilhena (1997); for a comparison between Brazilian and Hungarian folk musicians and intellectuals in the first half of the century, see Travassos (1997). An examination of the literature on anthropology and psychoanalysis in Brazil is found in Duarte (1997).

In these studies, one striking feature is that the vast majority deal with broad issues related to Western intellectual traditions but, because they are published in Portuguese, have a limited audience. The question of for whom these works are produced thus steps in; these dialogues with major sources of scholarship result in local exercises that (either by design or owing to power relationships) are free from external disputes. Nonetheless they fulfill the performative function of ideologically linking Brazilian social scientists to the larger world.

## *Brazil as Site, or Otherness in Context*

The founding of the social sciences at a moment of thrusts toward nation building is a well-known phenomenon (E Becker 1971 for France and the United States; Saberwal 1982 for India), as is the paradox of a critical social science surviving against the vested interests of the elites that created them. In these contexts, social science is not necessarily specialized; anthropology and sociology separate at times and in places that create a (political and conceptual) need for differentiating approaches, theories, or perspectives.

In Brazil in the 1930s, social science was adopted to provide a scientific approach to designing the new country's future. It was then believed that, in due time, social science would replace the literary social essay, which had been, "more than philosophy or the human sciences, the central phenomenon of spiritual life" (Candido 1976:156). Thus, from the 1930s to the 1950s, while social science was maturing a sociology "feita-no-Brasil" (which actually became hegemonic during the next two decades), canonic anthropological studies of Indian groups were the rule. In the 1960s, these studies began to share the stage with the new wave of studies on contact as interethnic friction and, immediately afterward, in the 1970s, with peasants and urban studies. Throughout these decades the blurring of disciplines has gone hand in hand with the quest for social commitment and ambitions for academic standards of excellence, difference being found nearby or, at most, not far from home.

Some decades ago, Anderson (1968) suggested that a flourishing British anthropology was the result of the export of critical social thought to subject peoples during the first half of the century and that the sociology England failed to develop at home had given rise to a prosperous anthropology abroad. More recently, Fischer (1988) suggested that North American anthropologists do not seem to play the same role enjoyed by Brazilian anthropologists as public intellectuals, not because of the formers' lack of engagement, but because of "the loss of a serious bifocality, able to be trained simultaneously at home and abroad on American culture as it transforms (and is transformed) by global society" (1988:13). My intention here has been to further discussions on the indexical components of the notions of home and abroad, by pointing out some anthropological difficulties that are inherent in intellectual dialogues. Significantly enough, the juxtaposition of an international experience and a Brazilian experience—as if they were distinct—indicates (and this very review is a good example) that, more often than not, authors meet only in our "Literature Cited" section.

## CONCLUSION

There are many meanings to the expression "anthropology at home," the most obvious of which refers to the kind of inquiry developed in the study of one's own society, where "others" are both ourselves and those relatively different from us, whom we see as part of the same collectivity. In this respect, after banning exoticism, anthropology at home was a historical shift for some. For others it has always been the major trend within a long-standing tradition; others still have chosen to develop their anthropological inquiries both at home and abroad. But whenever observers and observed meet, new hybrid representations arise, which are intensified in comparison to the notions from which they proceed (Dumont 1994). The more modern civilization spreads throughout the world, the more it is itself modified by the incorporation of hybrid products, making it more powerful and, at the same time, modifying it through the constant mix of distinct values.

Anthropologists have taken on multiple roles, as members of transnational communities sharing codes, expectations, rituals, and a body of classic literature—all of which allow dialogues to ensue—and, at the same time, as individuals whose socialization and social identity are tied to a specific collectivity, making their political and social responsibilities context-bound. Their prevailing values may vary, be they national, ethnic, or other. In some cases, a civilizational identity (as in South Asia) is superimposed on this configuration; in others it is hegemonic (as in "America," for instance).

Just as in other complex social phenomena, an examination of the different contexts of anthropology should be approached from a comparative perspective. For this purpose, some conditions are necessary: First, we must grant that academic knowledge, however socially produced, is relatively autonomous from its immediate contexts of production and therefore is capable of attaining desirable levels of communication. Second, we must accept that rigorous comparison, rather than uncontrolled relativism, is the best guarantee against superficial homogenization across national and cultural boundaries. And third, we must examine contemporary currents of anthropology at the convergence of the many socially recognized theoretical histories, including their neighboring disciplines (either models or rivals) and local traditions, where these broader relationships are embedded.

ACKNOWLEDGMENTS

I would like to thank Roque de Barros Laraia, Eduardo Viveiros de Castro, Monique Djokic, Elisa Reis, and Gilberto Velho for their very welcome suggestions and criticisms.

> Visit the *Annual Reviews home page* at
> http://www.AnnualReviews.org

# Literature Cited

Abu-Lughod L. 1991. Writing against culture. See Fox 1991, pp. 137–62

Ahmad A. 1992. *In Theory: Classes, Nations, Literatures.* London: Verso

Ahmad A. 1993. A response. *Public Cult.* 6: 143–91

Anderson P. 1968. The components of a national culture. *New Left Rev.* 50:3–57

Appadurai A, Berlant L, Breckenridge C, Gaonkar D. 1993. Editorial comment: on theory's empire. *Public Cult.* 6(1):vii–xi

Arantes P. 1991. Ideologia francesa, opinião brasileira. *Novos Estudos CEBRAP* 30: 149–61

Ardener E. 1987. "Remote areas": some theoretical considerations. See Jackson 1987a, pp. 39–54

Asad T, ed. 1973a. *Anthropology and the Colonial Encounter.* London: Ithaca

Asad T. 1973b. Introduction. See Asad 1973a, pp. 9–19

Azevedo T. 1994. *Os Italianos no Rio Grande do Sul.* Caxias do Sul: Editora Univ. Caxias do Sul

Baldus H. 1954. *Bibliografia Comentada da Etnologia Brasileira.* Rio de Janeiro: Souza

Baldus H. 1970. *Tapirapé: Tribo Tupi no Brasil Central.* São Paulo: Cia. Editora Nacional

Banton M, ed. 1966. *The Social Anthropology of Complex Societies.* London: Tavistock

Becker E. 1971. *The Lost Science of Man.* New York: Braziller

Becker H. 1992. Social theory in Brazil. *Sociol. Theory* 10:1–5

Behar R, Gordon D, eds. 1995. *Women Writing Culture.* Berkeley: Univ. Calif. Press

Béteille A, Madan TN, eds. 1975. *Encounter and Experience: Personal Accounts of Fieldwork.* Delhi: Vikas

Birman P. 1995. *Fazer Estilo Criando Gêneros.* Rio de Janeiro: Relume-Dumará

Bomeny HM, Birman P, Paixão AL, eds. 1991. *As Assim Chamadas Ciências Sociais.* Rio de Janeiro: Relume-Dumará

Borges Pereira JB. 1967. *Cor, Profissão e Mobilidade: o Negro e o Rádio de São Paulo.* São Paulo: Pioneira

Borofsky R, ed. 1994. *Assessing Cultural Anthropology.* New York: McGraw-Hill

Bourdieu P. 1969. Intellectual field and creative project. *Soc. Sci. Inf.* 8(2):89–119

Brettell CB, ed. 1993. *When They Read What We Write: The Politics of Ethnography.* Westport, CT: Bergin & Garvey

Brown BA. 1994. Born in the USA: American anthropologists come home. *Dialec. Anthropol.* 19(4):419–38

Bruschini MC, Sorj B, eds. 1994. *Novos Olha-*

res: *Mulheres e Relações de Gênero no Brasil.* São Paulo: Fundação Carlos Chagas/Marco Zero

Candido A. 1958. Informação sobre sociologia em São Paulo. In *Ensaios Paulistas,* pp. 510–21. São Paulo: Anhambi

Candido A. 1976. *Literatura e Sociedade.* São Paulo: Cia. Editora Nacional

Candido A. 1995. *On Literature and Society* (trans. and intro. by Howard Becker). Princeton: Princeton Univ. Press

Cardoso R. 1995. *Estrutura Familiar e Mobilidade Social: Estudo dos Japoneses no Estado de São Paulo.* São Paulo: Primus

Cardoso de Oliveira LR. 1989. *Fairness and communication in small claims courts.* PhD thesis. Harvard Univ.

Cardoso de Oliveira R. 1963. Aculturação e "fricção" interétnica. *Am. Lat.* 6:33–45

Cardoso de Oliveira R, Ruben GR, eds. 1995. *Estilos de Antropologia.* Campinas: Unicamp

Carneiro da Cunha M. 1978. *Os Mortos e os Outros. Uma Análise do Sistema Funerário e da Noção de Pessoa Entre os Índios Krahó.* São Paulo: Hucitec

Carneiro da Cunha M, ed. 1992. *História dos Índios no Brasil.* São Paulo: Cia. das Letras

Castro Faria L. 1993. *Antropologia. Espetáculo e Excelência.* Rio de Janeiro: UFRJ/ Tempo Brasileiro

Cavalcanti ML. 1994. *Carnaval Carioca: Dos Bastidores ao Desfile.* Rio de Janeiro: Editora UFRJ/MinC/Funarte

Clifford J. 1986. Partial truths. See Clifford & Marcus 1986, pp. 1–26

Clifford J. 1997. *Routes: Travel and Translation in the Late Twentieth Century.* Cambridge, MA: Harvard Univ. Press

Clifford J, Marcus GE, eds. 1986. *Writing Culture: The Poetics and Politics of Ethnography.* Berkeley: Univ. Calif. Press

Copet-Rougier E, Héritier-Augé F. 1993. Commentaires sur commentaire. Réponse à E Viveiros de Castro. *L'Homme* 33:139–48

Corrêa M. 1982. *As ilusões da liberdade. A escola de Nina Rodrigues.* PhD thesis. Univ. de São Paulo

Corrêa M, ed. 1987. *História da Antropologia no Brasil. Testemunhos: Emilio Willems e Donald Pierson.* Campinas: Editora da Unicamp

Crapanzano V. 1980. *Tuhami: Portrait of a Moroccan.* Chicago: Univ. Chicago Press

Crick M. 1976. *Explorations in Language and Meaning.* London: Malaby

DaMatta R. 1973a. *Ensaios de Antropologia Estrutural.* Petrópolis: Vozes

DaMatta R. 1973b. O ofício de etnólogo ou como ter "anthropological blues." *Comunicações do PPGAS* 1. Rio de Janeiro: Museu Nacional

DaMatta R. 1981. *Relativizando: Uma Introdução à Antropologia Social*. Petrópolis: Vozes

DaMatta R. 1982. *A Divided World: Apinaye Social Structure*. Transl. A Campbell. Cambridge, MA: Harvard Univ. Press

DaMatta R. 1984. *O Que Faz o Brasil, Brasil?* Rio de Janeiro: Guanabara

DaMatta R. 1991. *Carnivals, Rogues, and Heroes: An Interpretation of the Brazilian Dilemma*. Transl. J Drury. Notre Dame, IN: Univ. Notre Dame Press

Darnell R, ed. 1974. *Readings in the History of Anthropology*. New York: Harper & Row

Das V. 1995. *Critical Events: An Anthropological Perspective on Contemporary India*. Delhi: Oxford Univ. Press

*Dialec. Anthropol.* 1985. Natl. Trends, pp. 165–348

Diamond S, ed. 1980a. *Anthropology: Ancestors and Heirs*. Paris: Mouton

Diamond S. 1980b. Anthropological traditions: the participants observed. See Diamond 1980a, pp. 2–16

Dirks N, Eley G, Ortner S, eds. 1994. *Culture/Power/History: A Reader in Contemporary Social Theory*. Princeton, NJ: Princeton Univ. Press

Dragadze T. 1987. Fieldwork at home: the USSR. See Jackson 1987a, pp. 155–63

Driessen H, ed. 1993. *The Politics of Ethnographic Reading and Writing: Confrontations of Western and Indigenous Views*. Saarbrücken, Germany/Fort Lauderdale, FL: Breitenbach

Duarte LFD. 1986. *Da Vida Nervosa (nas Classes Trabalhadoras Urbanas)*. Rio de Janeiro: Zahar/CNPq

Duarte LFD. 1997. *Dois regimes históricos das relações da antropologia com a psicanálise no Brasil*. Presented at Seminário Ciências Sociais, Estado e Sociedade, Rio de Janeiro

Dumont L. 1970. *Religion, Politics and History in India*. Paris: Mouton

Dumont L. 1978. La communauté anthropologique et l'ideologie. *L'Homme* 18: 83–110

Dumont L. 1980. *Homo Hierarchicus: The Caste System and Its Implications*. Chicago: Univ. Chicago Press

Dumont L. 1986. *Essays on Individualism: Modern Ideology in Anthropological Perspective*. Chicago: Univ. Chicago Press

Dumont L. 1994. *German Ideology: From France to Germany and Back*. Chicago: Univ. Chicago Press

Dumont L, Pocock D. 1957. For a sociology of India. *Contrib. Indian Sociol.* 1:7–22

Fabian J. 1983. *Time and the Other. How Anthropology Makes Its Object*. New York: Columbia Univ. Press

Fahim H, ed. 1982. *Indigenous Anthropology in Non-Western Countries*. Durham, NC: Carolina Acad. Press

Fahim H, Helmer K. 1982. Themes and counterthemes: the Burg Wartenstein Symposium. See Fahim 1982, pp. xi–xxxiii

Fausto C. 1997. *A dialética da predação e familiarização entre os Parakanã da Amazônia oriental*. PhD thesis. Univ. Fed. Rio de Janeiro

Fernandes F. 1963. *A Organização Social dos Tupinambá*. São Paulo: Difusão Européia do Livro

Fernandes F. 1970. *A Função Social da Guerra na Sociedade Tupinambá*. São Paulo: Pioneira

Fernandes F. 1972. *O Negro no Mundo dos Brancos*. São Paulo: Difusão Européia do Livro

Firth R, ed. 1956. *Two Studies of Kinship in London*. London: Athlone

Fischer MMJ. 1980. *Iran: From Religious Dispute to Revolution*. Cambridge, MA: Harvard Univ. Press

Fischer MMJ. 1988. Scientific theory and critical hermeneutics. *Cult. Anthropol.* 3(1):3–15

Fischer MMJ, Abedi M. 1990. *Debating Muslims: Cultural Dialogues in Postmodernity and Tradition*. Madison: Univ. Wis. Press

Fox R, ed. 1991. *Recapturing Anthropology: Working in the Present*. Santa Fe, NM: Sch. Am. Res. Press

Fry P. 1991. Politicamente correto em um lugar, incorreto em outro. *Estudos Afro-Asiáticos* 21:167–77

Fry P. 1995. Why is Brazil different? *Times Lit. Suppl.*, Dec. 8, no. 4836:6–7

Gaspar MD. 1985. *Garotas de Programa: Prostituição em Copacabana e Identidade Social*. Rio de Janeiro: Zahar

Geertz C. 1983. *Local Knowledge: Further Essays in Interpretive Anthropology*. New York: Basic Books

Geertz C. 1988. *Works and Lives: The Anthropologist as Author*. Stanford, CA: Stanford Univ. Press

Geertz C. 1995. *After the Fact: Two Countries, Four Decades, One Anthropologist*. Cambridge, MA: Harvard Univ. Press

Gerholm T, Hannerz U, eds. 1982a. The shaping of national anthropologies. *Ethnos* 42 (special issue). 186 pp.

Gerholm T, Hannerz U. 1982b. Introduction: the shaping of national anthropologies. See Gerholm & Hannerz 1982a, pp. 5–35

Gilmore DD. 1982. Anthropology of the Mediterranean area. *Annu. Rev. Anthropol.* 11:175–205

Goldman M. 1994. *Razão e Diferença: Afetividade, Racionalidade e Relativismo no Pensamento de Lévy-Bruhl.* Rio de Janeiro: Grypho/UFRJ

Goody JR. 1966. The prospects for social anthropology. *New Soc.*, Oct. 13, pp. 574–76

Gregori MF. 1993. *Cenas e Queixas: Mulheres, Relações Violentas e a Prática Feminista.* Rio de Janeiro: Paz e Terra/AN-POCS

Guha R, Spivak GC, eds. 1988. *Selected Subaltern Studies.* Oxford: Oxford Univ. Press

Gupta A, Ferguson J, eds. 1997a. *Anthropological Locations: Boundaries and Grounds of a Field Science.* Berkeley: Univ. Calif. Press

Gupta A, Ferguson J. 1997b. Discipline and practice: "The Field" as site, method and location in anthropology. See Gupta & Ferguson 1997a, pp. 1–46

Hallowell AI. 1974. The history of anthropology as an anthropological problem. See Darnell 1974, pp. 304–21

Haraway DJ. 1988. Situated knowledges: the science question in feminism and the privilege of partial perspective. *Fem. Stud.* 14(4):575–99

Hymes D, ed. 1974. *Reinventing Anthropology.* New York: Random

Jackson A, ed. 1987a. *Anthropology at Home.* London: Tavistock

Jackson A. 1987b. Reflections on ethnography at home and the ASA. See Jackson 1987a, pp. 1–15

Kuper A. 1994. Culture, identity and the project of a cosmopolitan anthropology. *Man* (NS) 29:537–54

Lamphere L, Ragone H, Zavella P, eds. 1997. *Situated Lives: Gender and Culture in Everyday Life.* New York: Routledge

Laraia RB. 1986. *Tupi: Índios do Brasil Atual.* São Paulo: FFLCH/USP

Laraia RB, DaMatta R. 1967. *Índios e Castanheiros.* São Paulo: Difusão Européia do Livro

Latour B. 1989. Pasteur et Pouchet: hétérogenèse de l'histoire des sciences. In *Éléments d'Histoire des Sciences*, ed. M Serres, pp. 423–45. Paris: Bordas

Latour B. 1996. Not the question. *Anthropol. Newsl.* 37(3):1, 5

Latour B, Woolgar S. 1979. *Laboratory Life: The Social Construction of Scientific Facts.* Beverly Hills, CA: Sage

Leach ER. 1961. *Rethinking Anthropology.* London: Athlone

Leite Lopes JS. 1976. *O Vapor do Diabo.* Rio de Janeiro: Paz e Terra

Lévi-Strauss C. 1956. Les organisations dualistes, existent-elles? *Bijdr. Tot Taal Land Volkenkd.* 112:99–128

Lévi-Strauss C. 1961. La crise moderne de l'anthropologie. *Le Courr.* (UNESCO) 14(11):12–17

Lévi-Strauss C. 1962. *La Pensée Sauvage.* Paris: Plon

Lima RK. 1991. *Ordem pública e pública desordem. Anu. Antropol.* 88:21–44

Lima TS. 1995. *A parte do cauim. Etnografia Juruna.* PhD thesis. Univ. Fed. Rio de Janeiro

Lins de Barros M. 1989. *Autoridade e Afeto: Avós, Filhos e Netos na Família Brasileira.* Rio de Janeiro: Zahar

Lopes da Silva A. 1986. *Nomes e Amigos: Da Prática Xavante a uma Reflexão Sobre os Jê.* São Paulo: FFLCH/USP

Madan TN. 1982a. Anthropology as the mutual interpretation of cultures: Indian perspectives. See Fahim 1982, pp. 4–18

Madan TN. 1982b. Indigenous anthropology in non-western countries: an overview. See Fahim 1982, pp. 263–68

Madan TN. 1994. *Pathways: Approaches to the Study of Society in India.* Delhi: Oxford Univ. Press

Magalhães AC. 1994. *Os Parakanã: espaços de socialização e suas articulações simbólicas.* PhD thesis. Univ. de São Paulo

Maggie Y. 1975. *Guerra de Orixá: Um Estudo de Ritual e Conflito.* Rio de Janeiro: Zahar

Magnani JG. 1984. *Festa no Pedaço: Cultura Popular e Lazer na Cidade.* São Paulo: Braziliense

Malinowski B. 1939. Preface. In *Peasant Life in China: A Field Study of Country Life in the Yangtze Valley*, H-T Fei, pp. xix–xxvi. New York: Dutton

Marcus GE, ed. 1983. *Elites: Ethnographic Issues.* Albuquerque: Univ. NM Press

Marcus GE. 1991. Editorial retrospective. *Cult. Anthropol.* 6(4):553–64

Marcus GE, ed. 1993a. *Perilous States. Conversations on Culture, Politics, and Nation.* Late Editions, Vol. 1. Chicago: Univ. Chicago Press

Marcus GE. 1993b. Introduction to the series and to volume 1. See Marcus 1993a, pp. 1–16

Marcus GE. 1995. Ethnography in/of the world system: the emergence of multisited ethnography. *Annu. Rev. Anthropol.* 24:95–117

Marcus GE, Fischer MMJ. 1986. *Anthropology as Cultural Critique: An Experimental Moment in the Human Sciences.* Chicago: Univ. Chicago Press

Mascarenhas-Keyes S. 1987. The native anthropologist: constraints and strategies in research. See Jackson 1987a, pp. 180–95

Maybury-Lewis D. 1967. *Akwë-Shavante Society*. Oxford: Oxford Univ. Press

Maybury-Lewis D, ed. 1979. *Dialectical Societies: the Gê and Bororo of Central Brazil*. Cambridge, MA: Harvard Univ. Press

McGrane BD. 1976. *Beyond Europe: An archaeology of anthropology from the 16th to the early 20th century*. PhD thesis. NY Univ.

Melatti JC. 1967. *Índios e Criadores: Situação dos Krahó na Área Pastoril do Tocantins*. Rio de Janeiro: Inst. Ciências Soc.

Melatti JC. 1970. *O sistema social Krahó*. PhD thesis. Univ. de São Paulo

Melatti JC. 1978. *Ritos de uma Tribo Timbira*. São Paulo: Ática

Melatti JC. 1984. A antropologia no Brasil: um roteiro. *Bol. Inf. Biblio. Ciênc. Soc.—BIB* 17:3–52

Messerschmidt DA, ed. 1981. *Anthropologists at Home in North America. Methods and Issues in the Study of One's Own Society*. Cambridge: Cambridge Univ. Press

Miceli S, ed. 1989. *As Ciências Sociais no Brasil*. São Paulo: Vértice

Moffatt M. 1992. Ethnographic writing about American culture. *Annu. Rev. Anthropol.* 21:205–29

Moore HL. 1996. *The Future of Anthropological Knowledge*. London: Routledge

Mott LR. 1982. Indigenous anthropology and Brazilian Indians. See Fahim 1982, pp. 112–17

Moura MM. 1978. *Os Herdeiros da Terra*. São Paulo: Hucitec

Muller R. 1990. *Os Assurini do Xingu: História e Arte*. Campinas: Unicamp

Neiburg F. 1997. *Os Intelectuais e a Invenção do Peronismo*. São Paulo: Edusp

Nimuendaju C. 1946. *The Eastern Timbira*. Berkeley: Univ. Calif. Press

Nogueira O. 1986. *Tanto Preto Quanto Branco. Ensaios de Relações Raciais*. São Paulo: Queiroz

Okely J. 1987. Fieldwork up the M1: policy and political aspects. See Jackson 1987a, pp. 55–73

Oliveira JP, ed. 1987. *Sociedades Indígenas e Indigenismo no Brasil*. Rio de Janeiro: Marco Zero/UFRJ

Oliveira JP. 1988. *O Nosso Governo: Os Ticuna e o Regime Tutelar*. São Paulo: MCT/CNPq/Marco Zero

Palmeira M. 1977. Emprego e mudança sócio-econômica no nordeste. *Anu. Antropol.* 76: 201–38

Palmeira M, ed. 1995. *Política e Relações Pessoais. Comunicações do PPGAS* 5. Rio de Janeiro: Museu Nacional

Palmeira M, Goldman M, eds. 1996. *Antropologia, Voto e Representação*. Rio de Janeiro: Contracapa

Peirano MGS. 1981. *The anthropology of anthropology: The Brazilian case*. PhD thesis. Harvard Univ., Cambridge, MA

Peirano MGS. 1991. For a sociology of India: some comments from Brazil. *Contrib. Indian Sociol.* (NS) 25:321–27

Peirano MGS. 1992. *Uma Antropologia no Plural*. Brasília: Editora Univ. Brasília

Peirano MGS. 1997. Onde está a antropologia? *Mana* 3(2):67–102

Rabinow P. 1996. *Making PCR: a Story of Biotechnology*. Chicago: Univ. Chicago Press

Ramos AR. 1995. *Sanumá Memories: Yanomami Ethnography in Times of Crisis*. Madison: Univ. Wis. Press

Ramos AR. 1998. *Indigenism: Ethnic Politics in Brazil*. Madison: Univ. Wis. Press. In press

Reis EP. 1996. Making sense of history: political sociology in Brazil. *Curr. Sociol.* 44: 81–105

Ribeiro D. 1957. Culturas e línguas indígenas do Brasil. *Educação e Ciências Sociais* 2:5–100

Ribeiro D. 1962. *A Política Indigenista Brasileira*. Rio de Janeiro: Ministério da Agricultura

Ribeiro D, Ribeiro B. 1957. *Arte Plumária dos Índios Kaapor*. Rio de Janeiro: Seikel

Ribeiro GL. 1996. *Brazilians are hot, Americans are cold. A non-structuralist approach to San Francisco's carnival*. Presented at Annu. Meet. Am. Anthropol. Assoc., 95th, San Francisco

Ribeiro R. 1978. *Cultos Afro-Brasileiros do Recife*. Recife: MEC/Inst. Joaquim Nabuco

Saberwal S. 1982. Uncertain transplants: anthropology and sociology in India. *Ethnos* 42(1–2):36–49

Said E. 1978. *Orientalism*. New York: Pantheon

Salem T. 1985. Família em camadas médias: uma revisão da literatura. *Boletim do Museu Nacional* (NS) 54. Rio de Janeiro: UFRJ

Saran AK. 1962. Review of contributions to Indian sociology, n. IV. *East. Anthropol.* 15:53–68

Schaden E. 1954. *Aspectos Fundamentais da Cultura Guarani*. São Paulo: Difusão Européia do Livro

Schneider D. 1968. *American Kinship: A Cultural Account*. Englewood Cliffs, NJ: Prentice Hall

Schwartzman S. 1991. *A Space for Science: The Development of the Scientific Commu-*

*nity in Brazil.* University Park, PA: Penn. State Univ. Press

Seeger A. 1981. *Nature and Society in Central Brazil.* Cambridge, MA: Harvard Univ. Press

Segato RL. 1998. The color-blind subject of myth; or, where to find Africa in the nation. *Annu. Rev. Anthropol.* 27:In press

Seyferth G. 1985. Herança e estrutura familiar camponesa. *Boletim do Museu. Nacional* 52. Rio de Janeiro: UFRJ

Seyferth G. 1990. *Imigração e Cultura no Brasil.* Brasília: Editora Univ. Brasília

Sigaud L. 1980. A nação dos homens. *Anu. Antropol.* 78:13–114

Souza Lima AC. 1995. *Um Grande Cerco de Paz.* Petrópolis: Vozes

Spindler GD, Spindler L. 1983. Anthropologists view American culture. *Annu. Rev. Anthropol.* 12:49–78

Srinivas MN. 1952. *Religion and Society Among the Coorgs of South India.* Oxford: Clarendon

Srinivas MN. 1955. Village studies and their significance. *East. Anthropol.* 8:215–58

Srinivas MN. 1966. Some thoughts on the study of one's own society. In *Social Change in Modern India*, pp. 147–63. New Delhi: Allied

Srinivas MN, ed. 1979. *The Fieldworker and the Field.* Oxford: Oxford Univ. Press

Stocking GW Jr. 1974. Empathy and antipathy in the heart of darkness. See Darnell 1974, pp. 281–87

Stocking GW Jr. 1982. Afterword: a view from the center. *Ethnos* 47(1–2):172–86

Stocking GW Jr, ed. 1983a. *Observers Observed. Essays on Ethnographic Fieldwork.* HOA 1. Madison: Univ. Wis. Press

Stocking GW Jr. 1983b. History of anthropology: whence/whither. See Stocking 1983a, pp. 3–12

Strathern M. 1987. The limits of auto-anthropology. See Jackson 1987a, pp. 16–37

Strathern M, ed. 1995. *Shifting Contexts: Transformation in Anthropological Knowledge.* London: Routledge

Thomas N. 1991. Against ethnography. *Cult. Anthropol.* 6(3):306–21

Thomas N. 1994. *Colonialism's Culture: Anthropology, Travel and Government.* Princeton: Princeton Univ. Press

Traube EG. 1996. "The popular" in American culture. *Annu. Rev. Anthropol.* 25:127–51

Travassos E. 1997. *Os Mandarins Milagrosos. Arte e Etnografia em Mário de Andrade e Béla Bartók.* Rio de Janeiro: Zahar

Traweek S. 1988. *Beamtimes and Lifetimes. The World of High Energy Physicists.* Cambridge, MA: Harvard Univ. Press

Uberoi JPS. 1968. Science and swaraj. *Contrib. Indian Sociol.* (NS) 2:119–28

Uberoi JPS. 1983. *The Other Mind of Europe: Goethe as Scientist.* Delhi: Oxford Univ. Press

Velho G. 1972. *A Utopia Urbana: Um Estudo de Antropologia Social.* Rio de Janeiro: Zahar

Velho G. 1975. *Nobres e anjos: um estudo de tóxicos e hierarquia.* PhD thesis. Univ. de São Paulo

Velho G. 1978. Observando o familiar. In *A Aventura Sociológica*, ed. E Nunes, pp. 36–46. Rio de Janeiro: Zahar

Velho G. 1981. *Individualismo e Cultura.* Rio de Janeiro: Zahar

Velho G, ed. 1995. *Quatro Viagens: Antropólogos Brasileiros no Exterior. Comunicações do PPGAS* 6. Rio de Janeiro: Mus. Nac.

Velho O. 1972. *Frentes de Expansão e Estrutura Agrária.* Rio de Janeiro: Zahar

Velho O. 1976. *Capitalismo Autoritário e Campesinato.* São Paulo: Difel

Velho O. 1982. Through Althusserian spectacles: recent social anthropology in Brazil. *Ethnos* 47(1–2): 133–49

Velho O. 1995. *Besta-Fera. Recriação do Mundo.* Rio de Janeiro: Relume-Dumará

Vianna H. 1995. *O Mistério do Samba.* Rio de Janeiro: Zahar/Editora UFRJ

Vidal L. 1977. *Morte e Vida de uma Sociedade Indígena Brasileira: Os Kayapo-Xikrin do Rio Catete.* São Paulo: Hucitec

Vilhena LR. 1997. *Projeto e Missão: O Movimento Folclórico Brasileiro (1947–1964).* Rio de Janeiro: Funarte/Fundação Getúlio Vargas

Villaça A. 1992. *Comendo como Gente: Formas do Canibalismo Wari.* Rio de Janeiro: Anpocs/UFRJ

Viveiros de Castro E. 1992. *From the Enemy's Point of View. Humanity and Divinity in an Amazonian Society.* Transl. C Howard. Chicago: Univ. Chicago Press

Viveiros de Castro E. 1993. Structures, régimes, stratégies. *L'Homme* 33:117–37

Viveiros de Castro E. 1994. Une mauvaise querelle. *L'Homme* 34:181–91

Viveiros de Castro E, ed. 1995a. *Antropologia do Parentesco: Estudos Ameríndios.* Rio de Janeiro: Editora UFRJ

Viveiros de Castro E. 1995b. Pensando o parentesco ameríndio. See Viveiros de Castro 1995a, pp. 7–24

Wagley C, Galvão E. 1949. *The Tenetehara Indians of Brazil: A Culture in Transition.* New York: Columbia Univ. Press

Woortmann E. 1995. *Herdeiros, Parentes e Compadres.* São Paulo/Brasília: Hucitec/EdUnB

Woortmann K. 1990. "Com parente não se neguceia": o campesinato como ordem moral. *Anu. Antropol.* 87:11–76

*Annu. Rev. Anthropol. 1998. 27:129–51*
*Copyright © 1998 by Annual Reviews. All rights reserved*

# THE COLOR-BLIND SUBJECT OF MYTH; Or, Where To Find Africa in the Nation

## R. L. Segato

Department of Anthropology, University of Brasilia, 70910-900 Brasília-DF, Brazil;
e-mail: rsegato@nutecnet.com.br

KEY WORDS: multiculturalism, ethno-racial paradigms, Afro-Brazilians, African-Americans,
Afro-Brazilian religion

### ABSTRACT

African influence in a nation must be examined within the framework of the nation's formation of diversity, ethno-racial paradigm, and particular history. Based on the paradigmatic cases of Brazil and the United States, I contend here that racial attitudes and the position and role of African traditions in a nation are interrelated. Discerning racial conceptions, perceptions, and patterns of discrimination in a nation provides us with strong clues about the place and role assigned to the African presence in that context. Racisms may not differ much in intensity, but they do in the cognitive operations they imply, because they are grounded in encoded ethnic knowledge accumulated through specific historical experiences.

## LOCALIZING INFLUENCE

An examination of Africa in the New World and the influence of its traditions should consider more than just form, content, and diffusion of cultural practices and beliefs. It must also look at location and reception. Where is Africa to be found in the nation? What is its place in the national formation? How was the African element processed in the construction of each national society over time? How have African traditions found their way into history? One cannot speak adequately of Africa in the New World without locating it within the equation of the nation. There is no Africa in the New World without hyphenation signaling its insertion in continental subsections (e.g. Afro–Latin America, African–North America) and specific countries (Afro-Brazil).

129

By the same token, there is no way to speak of the participation of Africa wherever it has flourished after slavery without contemplating the variety of cognitive operations of discrimination and exclusion we blend under the common term racism. African civilization and blackness bear upon each other; the place of Africa and the place of race in New World nations are mutually suffused in a complex articulation extremely difficult to disentangle. However, part of my contention here is that this articulation varies according to national framework. The peculiar feelings that are at the basis of racism in each case are deeply ingrained in the structures of relationships developed through a particular national history. These feelings, when disclosed, have much to say about the insertion of the bearers of African culture in each particular national setting. The idea of a common Africa—i.e. a transnational, hemispheric notion of Africa—is attractive and strategic, and it is truthful in regard to form, content, and diffusion when color is backed with some common content. But this idea is misleading and, above all, inefficient when one is trying to appeal to people still well embedded in their local niches, engaged in their traditional, perhaps premodern or at least "hybrid" (Canclini 1989), processes of production of subjectivity, entrenched in their own borders of alterity.

An updated examination is needed of two emergent discussions in the literature on the influence of African traditions in the New World. I refer here to two issues that have an impact on the way we come to understand the insertion of the African presence in the countries of this continent, presenting us with alternative avenues for that understanding. Depending on what side we place ourselves along the axis of these two questions, we come out strolling along one avenue or the other.

The first of these discussions can be synthetically portrayed as the following: Is the stated ideal of miscegenation in Latin American countries a misleading myth or a legitimate utopia? The second discussion is as follows: Are the transnational political identities that are emerging under the pressures of globalization representative of the shapes of alterity outside the centers commanding the process of their diffusion?

To these two questions, a third encompassing concern must be added. We may reasonably wonder whether it is possible to have radical diversity of cultures in a full market regime or, relevant for us here, to have Africa amid America in a unified regime of economic rules.

These three broad questions constitute the indispensable framework in which one can think of the location of Africa in the nations of the New World today, and they come about as I examine the presence of Africa within the Anglo and Iberian national formations. I use Brazil and the United States as paradigmatic examples in my analysis.

These discussions are relevant because, first, if we decide that the founding myth of Latin American nations is mere deception, then we have to endorse the notion that only after establishing segregation as the point zero of racial truth can we initiate a truly antiracist politics and provide a legitimate stand for the African presence in these countries. Conversely, if we see, from a Latin American perspective, segregation coming from the top or bottom, as a dystopia of conviviality, we are compelled to envisage alternative political roads toward a society free of discrimination on the basis of race. We also have to strive for a new consciousness of the pervading African presence in culture and society instead of a discrete African niche. Whichever choice we make, it urges a discussion of the contemporary trend that counterposes the multicultural matrix of the United States, which anchors minority politics in the field of culture substantively considered, to the now imputed myth of miscegenation and its denounced effacement of pluralism. I contend here that only within a well-understood framework of national formation as idiosyncratic matrix of diversity is it possible to assess the fate of the African contribution in every national context in the New World.

Second, if we believe that all experience of alterity must be translated into identity politics, we are ready to accept that traditional ways of interacting across the boundaries of race may be given up without a cost. However, we may choose not to believe this, to instead remain faithful to the idea that there is more than one modality of production of an African-related subjectivity and more than one strategy to defend the reproduction of Africa in the New World.

Finally, if we take the position that no Africa is possible within a full market regime, with all of its derivations, we have to question our certainties concerning the worth of identity politics in a global world. This latter issue is probably the most decisive with regard to Africa, race, and politics in the New World.

As an anthropologist, I am compelled, ethically and theoretically, to defend variety in human solutions, to disclose these solutions, and to claim recognition and respect for them. However, to put it succinctly, if in other cases the moral dilemma has been how to introduce gender within the framework of race loyalties (see, for example, Pierce & Williams 1996), here my dilemma is how to introduce nation within the African/racial struggle for rights. And I would even say that my difficulties are of greater magnitude, because we live in an age where the framework of the nation is looked upon and declared negligible as a variable in a world euphemistically represented as globalized.

## THE NORTH AMERICAN MYTH OF SEPARATION AND ITS CRITICS

In recent years, a handful of publications by North American researchers have appeared that compare the situation of the African-American population in Brazil with that in the United States. This generation of studies contradicts and rejects the views of a previous generation, for which the Brazilian model, based on the idea of miscegenation, was considered to bring an alternative and, in that sense, to have an original contribution to make (Hellwig 1992). Contemporary authors not only contest the assumptions of economic determinism and the preeminence of class to explain exclusion in Brazil (see, for example, the critiques of Fernandes 1969 in Nogueira 1955, Andrews 1991, and Winant 1994), but they also dismiss the idea of a "mulatto escape hatch" (initially formulated by Degler 1971) to suggest miscegenation as a path to social ascension.

If a group of scholars, especially but not exclusively Brazilian, have contributed to the critique of miscegenation as a myth, in the precise sense of a deceptive representation deployed to preserve the false notion of a Brazilian racial democracy (see, among others, Dzidzienyo 1971; do Nascimento 1978; Hasenbalg 1979, n.d.; Skidmore 1990; do Valle Silva & Hasenbalg 1992; Fontaine 1985), North American students have increasingly tended to focus on a comparison of the Brazilian situation with the US situation or, more precisely, to read the Brazilian scene from the North American perspective and experience using the latter as a model (see, especially, Gilliam 1992, Winant 1994, Hanchard 1994). Particularly revealing in this respect is the review by Anani Dzidzienyo presented on the back cover of Hellwig's book (1992): "If as it is commonly argued, the United States is a standard against which other American polities are judged in the matter of race relations, then what more deeply felt source of insight than the observations of African Americans themselves?"

Besides Howard Winant (1994), with his proposal of a "racial formation," where race is a fact that cuts across contextual boundaries, perhaps the most representative author of this latter group is Michael Hanchard. His views about racial politics in Brazil (1993, 1994) and his proposal of a divided, overtly racialized (instead of unified and disputed) public sphere (1996a) have been forcefully contested in Brazil (Fry 1995a,b, 1996; Bairros 1996). Hanchard has been engaged in this polemic for a while (1996b,c). To make myself clear, I pick up the parts of Hanchard's argument that better reveal my discrepancies with the position he represents. In line with his perspective, for example, Hanchard regrets that no racially divided Christian churches, in the modalities known in South Africa, pre-Zimbabwe Rhodesia, and the United States, have existed in Brazil (Hanchard 1994:83). "Afro-Brazilians," says Hanchard, "did not develop parallel institutions" of the kind African–North Americans did, and the Candomble religious organization should not be considered as such (1994:18). He also suggests that to look at *quilombos* (communities of descendants of runaway slaves) or other traditional African institutions as a source of reference and strength is a "backward glance" (1994:164ff)—a glance toward a kind of already lost Euridice, who decided Orpheus's death in the Greek myth. In considering *quilombos* as facts of the past, the author grossly disregards the contemporary growing struggle of Brazilian maroon populations for their rights to the land (Leite 1991; Carvalho 1996, 1997). Denying Afro-

Brazilian religions the status of African institutions, he demonstrates a complete lack of ethnographic sensitivity for the national scene of his research. And one is, therefore, led to wonder why he should so forcefully deny the idiosyncrasies of Brazilian black history and strategies. Moreover, reducing the whole problem to the development of the public sphere, Hanchard does not take notice of a lineage of social analysts who have repeatedly emphasized the dualities of the Brazilian normative system, which combines modern civil standards with traditional premodern relational principles (da Matta 1988, da Matta & Hess 1995, Soares 1996) and, as opposed to North American practices, puts a premium on solidarity and face-to-face settlements to the detriment of universal, abstract procedures (Cardoso de Oliveira 1997).

While criticizing what he sees as the "culturalist" perspective of the leaders of the Brazilian black movement—to the detriment of a real immersion in a "cultural process"—Hanchard asserts that "many of the working poor do *not* have a 'hidden transcript,' that is to say, a strategic agenda of private, ideological interests that contradict public articulations of either consent or material compliance with dominant actors in a given society" (1994:71, italics added). This belief is well in tune with Hanchard's dismissal of Afro-Brazilian cultural institutions altogether, to which I referred earlier. One is left speculating about what is, in this case, the content of the "cultural process" or the "culture of a deeply political process" he refers to. One is also led to suspect that the main proposition of the thesis is the plain transference of African–North American slogans, strategies, and objectives to Brazil.

Hanchard's view of culture does not differ much from the very culturalism he rejects. The problem with the leaders of the Afro-Brazilian movement is not, as Hanchards suggests, that they value Afro-Brazilian cultural symbols too much but that they value them too little; they are unable to hear the inspirational voices that resound in them. As Hanchard says, culture has been taken in a mere emblematic fashion in an effort to counteract the constant appropriation of African symbols by the whole of the Brazilian nation and their consequent nullification for a political identity (Hanchard 1993:59). The question, however, is not to reappropriate the culture, in a new act of cannibalism, but, after we accept that a sound Afro-Brazilian transcript exists, to become able to learn, through an honest act of ethnographic "hearing" and dialogue, what the voices inscribed in it have being saying all along. In other words, the move should not be to infuse new meaning in the emblems, politizicing them, but to look for what is encoded in them and where one could find a plausible political strategy within them. Symbols do not constitute an ornamental, epiphenomenal secretion; rather, they convey values, choices, and a metaphorically expressed philosophy that all too often contradicts, in its own terms, state hegemony.

In short, a hidden transcript is exactly what the black working poor have in Brazil. This hidden transcript differs from that of North American blacks, though, and I refer to this difference below. However, before moving to that point, I would like to call attention to the weaknesses of the separatist modality of contestation in black politics, which have been pointed out from several points of view. A critique of the essentialist premise in the understanding of ethnicity was laid down by Michael Fischer (1986), and the disputable consequences of the essentialist injunction on the subject were convincingly argued, for example, by Kwame Appiah (1990b, 1992, 1994). In more radical terms, the perils of segregation as defensive political strategy has been described by Gerhard Kubik (1994) as "an assignment" proposed by the white to which the black may be uncritically yielding. The politics of multiculturalism has also been questioned for putting forward canned, marketable identities of ethnics as labeled consumers (Segato 1997a,b), where the social value of the citizen and that of the consumer do not merely converge, but above all become indistinguishable from the social value of ethnicity, which ends up by being reduced to the latter. [When published, ongoing discussions in Brazilian Afro-oriented meetings about the one-year-old fashion magazine *Raça Brasil* (Race Brazil), inspired by its North American twin publication *Ebony,* may come to shed light on this issue.] More recently, some voices have manifested how a new set of representations of transnational, ethnic identities have been induced by the influence of transnational agents (Mato 1997) or through the interpellation of the national state itself, under the pressures of the globalizing process led by those same agents (Gros 1997a:55–56, 1997b).

Other authors have sensed the imposition of "hyperreal" or abstract identities on Indians, African-Americans, and women (Ramos 1994, Mohanty 1995). And in influential texts, authors have pointed out the somewhat empty, artificially enforced regime of ethnicity in the United States. Herbert Gans, in an already classical article (1979), termed "symbolic ethnicity" the reduction of ethnic traits to an almost merely emblematic function in the modern North American scene. And Werner Sollors (1986, 1989) has emphasized how the North American classification of literary lineages in terms of ethnicity not only serves to keep borders in place but also is quite devoid of content (in the United States, "the cultural *content* of ethnicity . . . is largely interchangeable and rarely historically authenticated," Sollors 1986:28). The authors made these statements without even approaching the question of whether "whitening" takes place in the United States, because despite the apparent loyalty to the race struggle on the part of African-Americans classified by descent, one can still question the obvious and exemplary cosmetic "bleaching" of the artists of Black Entertainment Television.

From still a different set of concerns, Homi Bhabha criticized a dead, inert idea of "diversity"—in opposition to a dialogical and, of necessity, "hybrid" and lively production of difference—as being at the basis of "anodyne [sic], liberal multiculturalism" (Bhabha 1994:34). Peter McLaren (1994) tried to break through status quo notions of multiculturalism by suggesting a "critical" practice of it, which would imply a kind of difference in relationship, better propitiated in "border cultures" where a new *mestizo* consciousness or bric-à-brac subjectivity could arise. David Hollinger proposed a "post-ethnic" multiculturalist society where double ethnic loyalties would be possible and a matter of choice (Hollinger 1995:21). Finally, writers like Stuart Hall and Paul Gilroy have stressed hybridity as an often silenced quality of African diasporic culture (Hall 1996a:472, 474; Gilroy 1994:100).

The main point of my argument here, however, is not merely to pinpoint the pitfalls of racial politics in the United States, but rather to emphasize the significance of the specific racial politics and "formation of diversity" (Segato 1997a,b) within national contexts as the outcome of particular national histories. Although, as several authors have argued, it would not be correct to reduce race to ethnicity (see discussion in Goldberg 1993:78), discerning racial conceptions, perceptions, and patterns of discrimination in a national context provides us with strong clues about the place and role assigned to the African presence in that context. If, perhaps, racisms do not differ much in scope or intensity, they do in the cognitive operations they imply. On the one hand, as Kwame Appiah (1990a) has shown, they are grounded on implicit theoretical propositions of various kinds and, on the other, as I contend, on encoded ethnic knowledge accumulated through diverse historical experiences. The paradigmatic cases of Brazil and the United States show that specific modalities of exclusion and ethnic conceptions are deeply related.

## RACISMS AND THE PLACE OF AFRICA IN THE NEW WORLD: THE ETHNO-RACIAL PARADIGM FROM TOP TO BOTTOM AND BACK

### National Constructions of Race

Although today the politics of minorities presents a postnational, globalized trend very much influenced by the historical experience of African-North Americans, the features of racism are, as Stuart Hall has pointed out, "modified and transformed by the historical specificity of the contexts and environments in which they become active" (Hall 1996b:472). So, not only nation cannot be disregarded as a framework for the production of particular forms of racism over time (many authors have already pointed this out, from Harris 1974 and Skidmore 1974 to an updated discussion in Sansone 1996). Even more important today, local politics, strategies, and slogans ought to be shaped out of these specificities. Diversity (ethnic or otherwise) is not a fact of nature but a production of history, where national constructions of diversity played a crucial role. In addition, the tensions and discrimination along the lines of diversity have to be understood and dealt with accordingly.

As far as Brazil and the United States are concerned, their race conceptions and racisms have been repeatedly reported as different in the literature. It is generally accepted today that race in Brazil is associated with phenotypical mark, whereas in the United States race is linked to origin (Nogueira 1985). Also accepted is that race in Brazil depends on consent, whereas in the United States race follows the compulsory rule of descent (Sollors 1986). For that reason, the North American trend is to abolish ambiguity, whereas in Brazil the road to ambiguous, negotiated, and changeable affiliation is permanently left open. In Brazil, color is open to interpretation (Maggie 1991, Sansone 1996, Viveiros de Castro Cavalcanti 1996:19).

Other characteristics place them apart as well. In Brazil, race is not a relevant factor in every situation, whereas in the United States it is an ever-present concern, a visible dimension of interaction, significant and discursively indicated in any social setting. For example, race is not a salient, recorded trait of trade union leaders or of the members of the Movement of Landless Workers, and introducing segmentation by race into those popular fronts would not only be spurious but would also have disastrous consequences. Also, in Brazil, discrimination is never expressed as racism of contingents and enacted as aggression between belligerent groups, as in the United States, but always assumes the form of virulent interpersonal aggression. Finally, while the Anglo-Saxon white is distinctly white in racial and genealogical terms and racial mixture will inescapably signify exclusion from that category, the Brazilian white is "polluted" and insecure as a bearer of such status (Carvalho 1988). For a variety of reasons involving either biological or cultural "contamination," no Brazilian white is ever fully, undoubtedly white.

These differences are understandable only in relation to the ethnic formation in both nations. As Brackette Williams has shown, the nation has a decisive role in shaping its internal diversity and fractures. She has spoken of "the process of nation building as race-making" (Williams 1989:436; see also Allen 1995 for the origin of this structure in the racialization of the Irish by the British). From her observation of countries of Anglo-Saxon colonization (Guyana and the United States), Williams concludes that racial groups have always been constructed as a function of the unity of the nation and have been expected to behave, then, as nothing less and nothing more than an "ethnic" component, the *other* inside, in opposition to the so-believed "non-ethnic," dominant element (Williams 1993:154). Seen this way, and within the histories studied by Williams and Allen, the circuit of nation and minority is circular, closed, self-feeding; a twofold, integrated reality; two sides of the same coin.

However, the articulations and the rhetoric of power within the nation and its internal cleavages in the countries of Iberian colonization are not the same. If we are to analyze, as Paul Gilroy did for England (1991), the ethnic bases for representing the nation in Brazil, we will have to accept that Brazil describes and institutes itself in its official texts as a nation of mixed blood. For example, when Gilroy states that "phrases like 'the Island Race' and 'the Bulldog Breed' vividly convey the manner in which this nation is represented in terms which are simultaneously biological and cultural" where "the distinction between 'race' and nation" is erased (Gilroy 1991:45), he exposes a difference with the Brazilian ethnic paradigm, where the "Brazilian race" is always presented as mixture, a "fable of the three races" (da Matta 1984). The representation of the nation puts a premium on blood mixture and a convergence of civilizations, whatever the practices that grow under that facade. Various authors have called attention to the role of miscegenation in the whole of Latin America as a deceptive racial ideology (see, for an updated discussion, Wade 1995; see also Maggie & Gonçalves 1995 for a sophisticated discussion of the Brazilian "triangle of the three races").

If, from top to bottom, the North American ethnic paradigm is based on separation under the umbrella of a common, color-blind myth of shared effort and meritocratic reward, in Brazil the ethnic paradigm is based on encompassing the other, inclusion is its strong motif, and the myth here is the color-blind myth of an interrelating people. I call the color-blind myth a unified field of belief, a hegemonic ideology or system of values, where everyone in a given society, independent of that person's position, may find expression. If separation is the lingua franca of the whole society in the United States, from top to bottom, relation is the key to access in the Brazilian social environment. To acknowledge this difference is not merely doing comparative ethnography but has important consequences when trying to deploy efficacious strategies for contestation.

## *The North American Ethnic Paradigm: Reciprocating the Gaze*

Analyzing the genesis of the "ethnic pentagon" that today organizes ethnicity in the United States, David Hollinger recounts that the image of the melting pot was initially coined by Israel Zangwill to convey the idea of a social amalgam, that is, a single outcome from a variety of components. Nonetheless, it was later reinterpreted under the light of Horace Kallen's model of cultural pluralism with its analogy of a symphonic orchestra: "Each instrument was a distinctive group transplanted from the Old World, making harmonious music with other groups. He emphasized the integrity and autonomy of each descent-defined group" (Hollinger 1995:92). This model prevailed and today takes the shape of an "ethno-racial pentagon" formed by African-Americans, Euro-Americans, Asian-Americans, indigenous Americans, and Latino-Americans (Hollinger 1995:8). This ethnic paradigm is indeed two-sided: Today it is enforced as a way of controlling fairness in the distribution of jobs and other opportunities, but it originated from the process of "race making" described by Brackette Williams: "If the classical race theory of the nineteenth century is not directly behind the pentagon, this structure's architecture has its unmistakable origins in the most gross and invidious of popular images of what makes human beings different from each other. Yet it was enlightened antiracism that led to the manufacturing of today's ethno-racial pentagon out of old, racist materials" (Hollinger 1995:32). Therefore, contestation is formulated, under that ethnic paradigm, in the same language as discrimination. And, as I show later, it is not as removed from what happens in Brazil as Hanchard and authors of his generation believe. In Brazil, a paradigm of inclusion runs from the top to bottom of society, emanating from the classes that control the state as much as from those oppressed by them.

However, the main problem with the North American ethnic paradigm is not merely the consistency of the code of oppression with the code of contestation but rather that all the conflagrating parts strive under the same myth. This unification of the ideological field has grown steadily over time. So, we have a separated society but a common set of values whereby today the excluded are no longer protected by an alternative myth setting an alternative array of ends for life. Destitute from an alternative world, with its proper forms of solidarity and satisfaction, they are left abandoned to a nihilistic outlook (West 1993: 17ff). At best, the nihilistic attitude can be interpreted as a practice of resistance (De Genova 1995), but always as reactive behavior rather than a positive proposition of withdrawal into a distinctive life-world. Within the ideological frame of the North American nation, no open avenue seems to be left for black dignity within alternative mores. We may be before a case of separation between ethos and worldview, where ethos has been reduced to diacritic, emblematic signs of separation as an interest group no longer related to the density of a specific worldview. With the unification of the ideological field, contestation becomes plain competition for the same ends.

Commenting on a media production paradigmatic for understanding the unification of the ideological field, Herman Gray states that "*The Cosby Show* . . . appealed to the *universal* themes of mobility and individualism" (Gray 1995:89). "It is a separate-but-equal inclusion. In this television world, blacks and whites are just alike save for minor differences of habit and perspective. . . . African Americans face the same experiences, situations, and conflicts as whites except for the fact that they remain separate but equal" (Gray 1995:87). This situation is, evidently, the dominant, all-pervading myth of meritocratic individual achievement in the United States. But, contrary to what the author states, it is not universal. America, as a set of national values stamped by its Anglo-Saxon, white foundation, seems to have definitely taken over. Only blackness is retained as a platform for claiming, but the claims themselves have turned white.

Cornell West (1993:17ff) has described the "nihilism" of excluded blacks in North America and has dated its origins to the post–civil rights era. In this sense, nihilism is coeval with the process of inclusion of African North Americans in the market as producers and consumers of growing importance. His description of the lack of meaning and purpose, as well as of the self-destructive drive that has installed itself among poor, marginalized—newly peripheralized, in my own vocabulary—black North Americans is touching. Unfortunately, he does not analyze the coincidence between the timing of unprecedented access to opportunities by a part of the black North American population and the fall into the nihilist attitude of the ones excluded from this process. It seems reasonable to conclude that the loss of a truly alternative set of mores, that is to say, the decline of an African-American traditional space, speaking in properly ethnic terms, is directly linked to the expansion of market rule. An analysis of this kind would certainly raise painful doubts about the true character of the achievements brought about by the struggle of the 1960s, but it would nevertheless lead to important, unavoidable questions regarding the kind of ideological commitments and compromises that came together with new opportunities. Without a thorough examination of the myth lurking behind the jobs, professions, privileges, responsibilities, and obligations now embraced by blacks, no black North American activist is fully entitled to address Brazilians in the tone adopted by Hanchard and others, lest the self-destructive nihilism described by West reaches to the farthest corners, where alterity still has a place and the negative experience of being at the margins of the rule of the market has not yet fully taken over.

In his classic essay on the relevance of Gramsci for the study of race and ethnicity, Stuart Hall forcefully argues against the view that the economic foundation has a unifying impact on social subjects. In his view, capital does not make the sociocultural field homogeneous; in addition, it can even prevent this uniformization: "What we actually find is the many ways in which capital can preserve, adapt to its fundamental trajectory, harness and exploit these particularistic qualities of labour power, building them into its regimes. The ethnic and racial structuration of the labour force, like its gendered composition, may provide an inhibition to the rationalistically conceived 'global' tendencies of capitalist development. And yet, these distinctions have been maintained, and indeed *developed and refined*, in the global expansion of the capitalist mode" (1996b:436). Hall's view may hold true for Britain, the Caribbean, or even Brazil. In Britain, particularly, a strong labor movement shares the political arena with the political awareness of minorities. However, in conditions of extreme market enshrinement as one can witness in the United States, where the imperatives of productivity and profit scarcely leave room for a residue of gratuity or gift in human social relationships, the full market economy is no longer innocuous for the field of culture. What I mean is that it is no longer clear whether, under the totalizing shadow of the market (which is nearly the present situation in the United States), any kind of sociocultural arrangements can continue flourishing disencumbered. I would say that from the point of view of culture, full market rule is monopolistic. Enshrined and made sacred, ruling above any other set of values, the market does not allow for lesser gods. And other gods are needed to have a plurality of cultures in a radical sense, a multiethnic society. This situation is so because the economic system is not, as it is increasingly seen, outside, above, and exempt from the cultural realm; rather, the economic system is in itself a cultural choice, intertwined with other cultural aspects in society.

Adapting Habermas's expression, the market economy has thoroughly colonized the life-world and, in this condition, one does not see where and how values other than the maximization of productivity and profit can find a legitimate place under the sun. This situation, I think, is new, and it allows for an understanding of globalization as the expansion of the rules of the market to encompass all aspects of social life and overdetermine not only locality but also minority groups. In other words, I cannot envisage how, under this pressure, a group can subsist bearing a different view about the meaning of resources, their mode of production, and their destination in human life. And divergent conceptions about what resources are and to what end they serve are better indicators of ethnic plurality than those who seize resources in society. What Stuart Hall calls "the differentiated terrain" of ideology, with its "different discursive currents, their points of juncture and break and the relations of power between them" (1996b:434), should not refer merely to discrepancies with regard to who accedes to profit but should also refer to what profit is and how it is to be obtained and used. Only this refinement would be able to provide for a radical diversity and multiculturalism in a strong sense.

From my Latin American–situated perspective, my perception is that this terrain of true cultural dissent is being progressively banished from the social field and that the United States leads this process, even when its intellectuals and activists disseminate a racial politics based on the particular experience of blacks in the United States.

Moreover, Hall's insistence on acknowledging heterogeneity (of class, gender, race, and so on) within the capitalist economy does not imply that blacks, just because of the color of their skin, will safely secure a territory of culture. That is, it does not imply that blackness, by itself, guarantees difference and ethnicity. When the "structures of feeling, producing, communicating and remembering" that Paul Gilroy (1994:3) calls the "black Atlantic world" cease to be foundational for the constant reproduction of an alternative (though constantly negotiating and dialogical) niche of culture and become just an ornamental residue of a previous difference in the strong sense, a fashionable tribal diacritic set of signs take over. These signs start behaving as market emblems linking particular ethnically marked merchandise to a population of ethnically marked consumers—in a more constrained and less creative relationship between consumption and citizenship than the one proposed by Nestor García Canclini (1995). This canned ethnicity so characteristic of the United States does not necessarily correspond to an ethnic discourse, and it does not constitute a real alternative to total integration and the thorough eradication of marks of difference.

From the perspective I am taking here, in a context like the North American one, ethnic politics within a unified ideological field must of necessity mean competition for the same resources and not the properly political conflict between diverging views on resources. This is true for a society where hegemony, in Gramsci's terms, is totalizing and where, despite outward appearances, diversity, in the strong sense of diverse conceptions about resources, their production and usufruct has been overridden. Even religion, which usually plays the role of warranting diversity in this strong sense of content, has been largely homogenized behind the facades of ornamental diacritic: "In the United States of America . . . a particular form of Bible interpretation has served as a rationale for the whole country as well as for many ethnic groups" (Sollors 1986:39). Individual dropping out is the only available road to escape.

In strictly anthropological, Geertzian terms, a difference exists not only when a distinctive style or ethos is present under the form of diacritical signs but also when there is some form (even hybrid from the point of view of the cultural materials it incorporates) of alternative conception with regard to the finality and meaning of social life, that is to say, a nonintegrated system of values and worldview. This alternative conception certainly involves priorities other than maximization of profit and productivity and certainly implies a degree of dysfunctionality with the rule of the market (as Hall points out). Continuing with this line of argumentation, when a minority group fights for or expands access to its rights to a larger share in profit and power, what matters is not the amount of wealth or power that becomes available to it but to what extent it imposes a change on the meaning and destination of that profit or power. An example of this is provided by Paul Gilroy (1991:32) when he talks about the "new kinds of solidarity and new patterns of communication" imprinted by the participation of women in the English coal strike of 1984–1985. My point here is that under certain conditions of extreme pressure by the rule of the market, as is the case of social movements in the United States today, it becomes increasingly unattainable for gender and race struggles to preserve such forms of alternative solidarity. The radically diverging values that support them are inevitably receding.

We fall back into the trap of some kind of formulation of a "culture of poverty," where, by means of the action of the overpowering rhetoric of the myth of individual achievement and unlimited profit, poverty is the only thing left as culture to the blacks who do not participate in the white myth. Where is Africa, then, in the United States? Shall we accept once and for all the equation of Af-

rica with poverty? Is there nothing left as African outside of material depriva-
tion? Is there anything at all in between this and its assigned reversal of a
minority-within-a-minority of achievers in white terms? Is politics to be reduced to a mere struggle for a share in the profit, while people forget to reflect
on the very nature of profit and satisfaction? Is this not the shipwreck of Africa, left over by the American myth? To find an alternative, to find a true territory of culture, we have to find alternative mythical spaces, with alternative
sets of values, and produce from it a carefully articulated alternative rhetoric: a
politics of radical difference. This myth will not be an encapsulated, solipsistic
myth, because none of the working myths are, but a living one: a myth in relationship, a negotiating, conversational platform; hybrid by the interlocution-
ary inclusions processed through history; an inscription of ethnic history and
aspirations; and also a commentary on the *other*, an encoded inscription of
white history in ethnic terms. I contend that in Brazil, as in other Latin American countries, radical alterity—in these nonfundamentalist, nonessentialist
terms—still exists, and that the Afro-American world continues to be truly diverse and diverging and continues to speak of a lively Africa.

## The Brazilian Ethnic Paradigm: Repatriating the Gaze

A similar analysis of the Brazilian case will shed light on what I have said so
far. In Brazil, the market has not colonized life to the extent it has in the United
States. Besides the problem that is usually called exclusion or social apartheid,
which alludes to those in the population who live at the margins and under the
shadow of the market economy as a periphery in relation to it, an *other* population exists. This situation does not mean that this *other* population is closed
upon itself, unrelated to the market economy, but that it is not fully engulfed by
its myths—it continues to comply with its own traditional values. By the same
token, it is possible to say that while in some parts of Brazil, those fully engaged in a quest for modernity can be said to be a periphery—economically,
socially, and culturally—of the technologically developed world, there still is
a cultural *other*. This *other* culture becomes interpreted as a culture of poverty,
exclusively defined by lack and default, only when seen from the perspective
of the economic centers. Postcolonial writing also sometimes implies that the
periphery is the only space (geographical, cultural, ideological) available for
otherness. But it is important to recognize the existence of an *other* space,
where material indigence may be the case but also cultural density and symbolic wealth of an *other* kind. Therefore through the process of globalization,
the simultaneous engulfing and peripheralization of the radically *other* world
is a growing reality. It is also true that as long as there remain autonomous enclaves not fully engulfed by the inexorable logic of the market, there will be alternative myths, with incompatible conceptions of resources and exotic no-

tions of what to do with them and how to reach satisfaction. These conceptions are often seen by modernizing agents as simply dysfunctional beliefs.

The Afro-Brazilian religions are one such set of conceptions and constitute a very important niche of culture preservation and creativity. These traditions have inscribed a monumental African codex containing the accumulated ethnic experience and strategies of African descendants as part of a nation. It also holds the record of their perception of that national setting and their place in it. This codex tells us, in its own metaphoric language, not only about religion but also about the relationships between blacks and the white state (Segato 1995a,b). It contains a stable repertoire of images that make up a truly alternative myth, and the forms of conviviality they enforce spread far, affecting the society at large, well beyond the niches of orthodoxy where the work of elaboration and preservation of this codex takes place. In this sense, this codex operates as a stable reservoir of meaning from which flows a capillary, informal, and fragmentary impregnation of the whole of society. At certain corners of society, its presence becomes diffuse and tenuous, but it is there.

Evidence of this impregnation was gathered by Yvonne Maggie (1992) in the courts of Rio de Janeiro, from the trials for witchcraft between 1912 and 1945. This research showed that judges and defendants shared a common set of beliefs. It is always visible and at hand for everyone, under the form of therapeutic services, aesthetic inspiration, as a source of answers about the meaning of the most varied circumstances of life, or even as a symbolic repertoire to locally process the materials of other religions (I refer here particularly to popular Catholicism and the varieties of Pentecostalisms proliferating in Brazil; Segato 1997a). A similar idea is supported by Gilberto Velho (1992), when he sees belief in spirits and the experience of possession as the most extensive and agglutinating practice of the Brazilian social scene as a whole. This loose (in the sense of not really organic, consistent, or rationally articulated) penetration in all levels of Brazilian society depends, in turn, on the existence of enclaves of orthodoxy preserved by the most conservative temple houses. These enclaves do not dominate the cultural scene of the country but are among the references that secure its heterogeneity in the field of culture. Also, these enclaves guarantee the nonperipheral kind of alterity whose space is receding in the United States, after the market economy and its own inexorable precepts took over the black enclaves and made recede positive "dysfunctional" forms of traditional solidarity, gratuity, and gift.

However, as I have contended elsewhere (Segato 1995a,b), the philosophy and politics espoused by this *other* codex cannot be racialized and transformed into a racial politics. This inability should not be understood as an indication of weakness, as Hanchard would have it, but as a consequence of strength. Paradoxical as it may seem, the philosophy contained in this codex resists racialization because it perceives itself as bigger than race and aspires to universality.

Significantly, it perceives itself as encompassing, embracing the white. All whites are seen, sooner or later, knowingly or unknowingly, as subject to its logic. Its recent expansion toward new, white territories in Argentina, Uruguay, Spain, Italy, and Portugal proves this aspiration well founded (Segato 1991, 1996). The introduction of Afro-Brazilian religious lineages into a country like Argentina, where African presence had, as generally accepted by historians, mysteriously faded away (Andrews 1980), shows the strength of an "African ancestry" not based on commonality of blood, in North American terms, but on commonality in belief and on philosophical community. Indeed, the part of Brazil that more forcefully expanded into the so-perceived white countries of the south in the past few years is the black part. African Brazil is seen by many there as a source of religion, art, well-being, philosophy, therapeutic knowledge, and civilizing potential. Black is also an exporting force, through trade with the south, though informally in most cases, in the paraphernalia related to the cults. The expansive potential of Afro-Brazilian culture and the ability of its brokers are evidenced by the highly elaborate altars of the newly formed cult-houses of Montevideo and Buenos Aires, where 20 years ago there were none.

The encompassing, universal element of Afro-Brazilian culture is inscribed in the religious codex as a precept for inclusiveness, preventing, as I said, racialization and hindering the participation of the bearers of the African tradition in Brazil in any politics based on an ethnic divide. As a prestigious priest told me recently, "that would be overtly political. Our *ase* [power] lies somewhere else." This inclusive determination could be read as a text expressing the perception, on the part of Afro-Brazilians, of three historical processes that are characteristic of the Brazilian formation.

The first is the syncretic, pan-African substratum that must have begun constituting itself inside the slave ships during the journey from Africa to America and continued in the New World, structuring an African environment in Brazil along the lines of artificially architected religious nations. In this recreation of Africa in Brazil, openness to individuals of any origin was and continues to be the rule and, also, the clue to understanding the survival and gradual expansion of the whole system. The second historical process speaks of the thoroughly mixed breeding that forms the basis of contemporary Brazilian population, including the elites, with regard to their racial composition; that is to say, the perception of the formation of Brazilian society through massive miscegenation. The third speaks of the deep mingling and interpenetration of the European environment of the landowners by Afro-Brazilian culture—mingling that took place and continues to take place in the intimacy of so-called white households, starting early in life and long ago in history with the socialization of white children by black nurses.

The popular voices that speak in the Afro-Brazilian codex take notice of these three processes and transform to their advantage the ethnic, biological, and cultural mergings that took place in history, turning them into a fundamental piece of their philosophy, as evidence of the strength and scope of the African presence in Brazil. If we are to apply the Gramscian view that there are ethical, moral, and cultural aspects of hegemony, we conclude that in Brazil, the ethical state has failed to raise "the great mass of the population to a particular cultural and moral level (or type) which corresponds to the needs of the productive forces for development, and hence to the interests of the ruling class" (Gramsci 1971:258, quoted by Hall 1996b:429). In this sense, the state was forced to, at least, share this encompassing, ethical function with black enclaves that actively produce and expand African culture through the nation and beyond.

Perhaps we have here a peculiar aspect of what Stuart Hall, in his forceful criticism of essentialisms [including even the "strategic essentialism" proposed by Gayatri Spivak (1990:12)], has described as the inherent dialogy and hybridity of black culture (1996b:472, 474) but has, in this particular case, I believe, transformed into the pillar of its very strength. In its specificity, this codex in no case presents the essentialist "mystical Africentrism"or "anti-assimilationist unintelligibility" that Paul Gilroy (1994:100) criticizes as a trait of some hard-line black music styles but hammers precisely on the opposite key: its universality. This codex is universal not because it denies its Africanness (as in the antiessentialist position also mapped by Gilroy) or because it is hybrid and dialogical as a product (as Hall and Gilroy say of diasporic black culture), but because it intends to talk for all and it represents itself as an all-embracing and agglutinating tradition—its messages are assumed to be as relevant for an African Brazilian as they are for a Chinese person. Because of this characteristic, the codex is capable of survival, growth, and expansion in the most adverse circumstances.

However, at stake here are not these multiple mergings but their perception and transcription into an encoded knowledge. Charles Lemert, in an article investigating the "dark side of self," reports on a North American clinical case that can be considered very close to the Brazilian experience. A white, middle-class, North American male discovered in therapy a black caretaker who played the role of a mother figure in his childhood: "David came to realize that, if he had an emotionally satisfying relation with an adult in his family of origin, it had been with Annie. . . . Annie was, in effect, David's mother. David is white. Annie is black." So, Lemert wonders: "If Annie was David's mother, in whatever sense, in what sense is David white?" To conclude: "This is a question about which our culture does not permit us to talk. For David to consider that in *some* sense he might think of himself as something other than white, perhaps even black, is a thought that contradicts strong-we claims at their foundation" (Lemert 1994:110). And this dilemma is exactly where the divide lies with the Brazilian environment. The African codex in Brazil tells the white of this dark side (literally and metaphorically) of the white's self by appointing it the tutelage of an African deity, by encompassing it within the African tradition, by offering it engagement in an African religious genealogy. The problem is that within the North American cultural climate, the self will have to produce, sooner or later, a "narrative of conversion" (Sollors 1986:31). That is, it will be mandatory to opt for a clear and exclusive identity affiliation, either within a strong-we position (identified with whiteness and universality) or a weak-we position (identified with an ethnic mark). In Brazil this option is not mandatory or even meaningful, and the possibility of a permanent ambiguity will remain open. Precisely, the premium is placed on openness. The "dark," African self will constantly and explicitly aspire to particularity and universality simultaneously. The model is not mechanical; it allows for ambivalence and multiple affiliations and places a premium on transits.

Moreover, even though in Brazil any strong sense of self of the white is impeached by the African codex, blacks do not imitate the movement of the white self into a concretion but simply undermine the pretension of purity in ethnic identity, challenging the blood principle and all racial determinations (Segato 1995b). In this way, the philosophy of the Afro-Brazilian religious codex can be said to avoid the pitfalls of what Kwame Appiah calls "intrinsic racism," with its "moral error" (Appiah 1990a:12) and its fallaciously restrictive "familism." In Brazil, a sense of community and solidarity—available to all, regardless of origin—is created by religious genealogies (open to everyone through a ritual vow) and the universal value attributed to the orixas to speak about human personality and predict behavior. Supported by these two pillars, this philosophy counterposes a true alternative to white racist essentialism, setting itself free from the trap this essentialism poses to a black sense of self—a trap that confines it within a rigid, essentialist, substantive definition of selfhood and identity, typical of the monological dominant style of Western civilization.

At the same time, the cultural materials are hybrid and malleable themselves, as Hall and Gilroy point out, incorporating elements from other religious traditions such as Catholicism, native Indian beliefs, and even, lately, Eastern religions. The universalistic pretension is matched here by a great dynamism in the proliferation and appropriation of materials for the symbolic repertoire. Therefore, with regard to its contents, the codex does not represent an essentialist position either. However, its originality lies in its militant proposition of an idea of a universal Africa, which, though ever changing, Brazilian and diasporic, can be located as a reservoir of meaning for all. Finally, it never slips into an Africentric position because of its radically pluralistic outlook. Of course, the main question remains whether black and white traditions exist or if there are only people of different origins participating in varied traditions. The culture I have dealt with seems to be clear in stating that it represents a corpus of knowledge originally created by Africans and African descendants in the New World but that has been adamant to include in its lineages people from any ancestry.

With regard to the white elites, they are in an extremely fragile position under this flexible, diffuse resistance. Their apprehension of the various mergings with the black component has important consequences, to the extent that it can be maintained that white racism in Brazil is not, as in the United States, the outcome of a barrier that separates and excludes "we" from "them," that is to say, a discrimination of two mutually exclusive cultural, ethnic, and social territories with its political and economic implications. In Brazil, racism denominates a different cognitive operation, whereby a great proximity, intimacy, and even identity with the black "other" has to be exorcised—hence the extreme virulence and passion it sometimes involves—always on an individual, interpersonal basis and never as a confrontation of one community against another, which is so characteristic of US racist behavior. It is the outcome of an I/thou, intimate interracial relationship that was there and continues to be lurking in the background of "white" self-formation; it has to be repelled. In Brazil, racist hatred is the outcome of the horror caused by this very private secret carried by families: the twilight memory of the black great-grandmother, the violently repressed oedipal love for the black wet nurse. Racism in Brazil is a purge that starts from the inside of the white being, a fear (and a certainty) of being contaminated somewhere. It has to do with intimacy and relatedness, not with ethnic distance and fear of aliens. Whiteness in Brazil is impregnated by blackness. "Whiteness," in Brazil, as a sign of safe, uncontested status, is never fully achieved, never certain (Carvalho 1988). These complexities would call for a politics able to touch the Achilles' heel of such a structure, a structure leaning more on a psychological and status-based premodern (patriarchal) organization than on a categorical, modern, contractual one.

My analysis takes us, undoubtedly, close to Gilberto Freyre's classic thesis of 1933, also supporting the idea of a Brazil, in his terms, fully contaminated by the African presence—a white Brazil that hides a black spot, a mark of Africa in the skin, concealed somewhere, a Brazil where black and white do not estrange each other to the extent they do in the United States. The ultimate meaning of this thesis was identified with an attack on modernity and modernizing forces (Needell 1995). Ricardo Benzaquem de Araujo (1994:133) also asserts that in Gilberto Freyre's account, with the modernization of the economic forms of exploitation and the transformation of the traditional slave-owning household (the *casa grande*) into the modern wealthy mansion (the *sobrado*), "the less patriarchal they grew, the more *excluding* they became, turning into a more conventional type of aristocratic domination, founded on difference but also, and mainly, on separation." Therefore, the entrance here into a full modernity becomes related to a particular kind of race relations that follows the apartheid pattern. The premodern, traditional system, as known in Brazil, was and continues to be marked by interpersonal hierarchical relationships. These relationships are based on different assumptions and work according to different systems of rules. Racism, in this sense, is an entirely modern attitude, a correlate of the modern laws that enforce equality and freedom for all.

In the Freyrian model, the Brazilian traditional arrangement for race relations appears opposite the "modern" North American landscape, where two social groups with clear borders compete for resources of various kinds. In the former, power is exerted amid promiscuity and intimacy ("excess" in Benzaquem de Araujo's vocabulary); in the latter, in open confrontation.

However, several substantial differences exist between my contention here and what could be perceived as neo-Freyrism; two differences are the most relevant for the scope of my argument. First, I point out the existence of a virulent racist attitude and feeling in Brazil against people of black color while suggesting the examination of the complexities and ambivalences of the subject of such feelings and attitudes. My focus is on a critique of the kind of mental and affective processes that are at stake, and my contention is that the cognitive, psychological operations at work in Brazil are of a different kind and embedded in a different structure of relationships than those in the United States. But my ultimate goal takes me far from Freyre's in that I intend this whole comparative exercise to contribute to the formulation of an adequate politics to fight racism in Brazil. Any good strategy results only from awareness of this difference and therefore demands an adequate examination of the peculiar processes that lie behind the Brazilian form of racism. The second difference between my thesis and that of Freyre and the neo-Freyrians is that I contend that the people identified with the black enclaves of the Afro-Brazilian religious orthodoxy are themselves claiming that their culture encompasses white culture. The scope and pervasiveness of African culture in Brazil, according to my interpretation, are inscribed in the Afro-Brazilian religious codex. Therefore, although I seem to confirm Freyre's idea of Brazil being thoroughly impregnated by black presence, I do not see this characteristic as a benign, conceding trait on the part of the landowning elite but as a revindication of black discourse by itself and for itself. Accordingly, in my study of Afro-Brazilian religions I found that the agents of black culture themselves raise this point, thus changing the ideological sign of this statement. If an equivalent of the soul food of blacks in the southern United States is absent in Brazil, in the sense that the whole of the population eats from it (Fry 1982), this is not the outcome of a process of expropriation and cannibalization of black symbols by Brazilian society at large but is, much to the contrary, the result of a strong African presence that has invaded and conquered the white cultural space in an irreversible process. Any wise politics for a racially fair society in Brazil has to take advantage of this precedent. If we do not take this piece of popular wisdom and translate it into political discourse, into the stuff of which slogans are made, antiracist politics will either twist and colonize the Brazilian environment or never reach a capacity for interpellation able to mobilize people outside the group of Brazilian black intellectuals who, following the North American agenda, have lost contact with their cultural and social basis.

> Visit the *Annual Reviews home page* at
> http://www.AnnualReviews.org.

## Literature Cited

Allen T. 1995. *The Invention of the White Race. Racial Oppression and Social Control*, Vol. 1. London: Verso

Andrews GR. 1980. *The Afro-Argentines of Buenos Aires, 1800–1900*. Madison: Univ. Wis. Press

Andrews GR. 1991. *Blacks and Whites in Sao Paulo, Brazil. 1888–1988*. Madison: Univ. Wis. Press

Appiah KA. 1990a. Racisms. In *Anatomy of Racism*, ed. D Goldberg, pp. 3–17. Minneapolis: Univ. Minn. Press

Appiah KA. 1990b. But would that still be me? Notes on gender, 'race', ethnicity, as sources of 'identity'. *J. Philos.* 87:493–509

Appiah KA. 1992. *In My Father's House: Africa in the Philosophy Culture*. New York: Oxford Univ. Press

Appiah KA. 1994. Identity, authenticity, survival: multicultural societies and social reproduction. In *Multiculturalism. Examining the Politics of Recognition*, ed. A Gutmann, pp. 149–63. Princeton: Princeton Univ. Press

Bairros L. 1996. Orfeu e Poder: uma perspectiva Afro-Americana sobre a política racial no Brasil. *Afro-Ásia* 17:173–86

Benzaquem de Araujo R. 1994. *Guerra e Paz. Casa-grande e Senzala e a Obra de Gilberto Freyre nos anos 30*. Rio de Janeiro: Editora 34

Bhabha H. 1994. The commitment to theory. In *The Location of Culture*, pp. 19–39. New York: Routledge

Canclini NG. 1989. *Culturas Híbridas. Estrategias para Entrar y Salir de la Modernidad*. México, DF: Grijalbo

Canclini NG. 1995. *Consumidores y Ciudadanos. Conflictos Multiculturales de la Globalización*. México, DF: Grijalbo

Cardoso de Oliveira LR. 1997. Ação afirmativa e equidade. In *Multiculturalismo e Racismo. Uma Comparação Brasil—Estados Unidos*, ed. J Souza, pp. 145–56. Brasília: Paralelo 15

Carvalho JJ. 1988. Mestiçagem e segregação. *Humanidades* 5(17):35–39

Carvalho JJ, ed. 1996. *O Quilombo do Rio das Rãs. Histórias, Tradições, Lutas*. Salvador, Bahia: CEAO/EDUFBA

Carvalho JJ. 1997. Quilombos: símbolos da luta pela terra e pela liberdade. *Cultura VOZES* 5(91):149–60

da Matta R. 1984. *Relativizando*. Petropolis: Vozes

da Matta R. 1988. Introduçao. Brasil & EUA; ou as lições do número três. In *Brasil e EUA. Religião e Identidade Nacional*, RC Fernandes et al, pp. 11–27. Rio de Janeiro: Graal

da Matta R, Hess D. 1995. *The Brazilian Puzzle. Culture on the Borderlands of the Western World*. New York: Columbia Univ. Press

De Genova N. 1995. Gangster rap and nihilism in black America. Some questions of life and death. *Soc. Text*, pp. 89–132

Degler CN. 1971. *Neither Black Nor White: Slavery and Race Relations in Brazil and the United States*. New York: Macmillan do Nascimento A. 1978. *O Genocídio do Negro Brasileiro. Processo de um Racismo Mascarado.* Rio de Janeiro: Paz e Terra

do Valle Silva N, Hasenbalg CA. 1992. *Relações Raciais no Brasil Contemporâneo.* Rio de Janeiro: Rio Fundo

Dzidzienyo A. 1971. *The Position of Blacks in Brazilian Society.* London: Minor. Rights Group

Fernandes F. 1969. *The Negro in Brazilian Society.* New York: Columbia Univ. Press

Fischer MJ. 1986. Ethnicity and the postmodern arts of memory. In *Writing Culture: The Poetics and Politics of Ethnography,* ed. J Clifford, G Marcus, pp. 194–233. Berkeley: Univ. Calif. Press

Fontaine P-M, ed. 1985. *Race, Class and Power in Brazil.* Los Angeles: Cent. Afro-Am. Stud., Univ. Calif.

Fry P. 1982. *Para Inglês Ver. Identidade e Política na Cultura Brasileira.* Rio de Janeiro: Zahar

Fry P. 1995a. O que a Cinderela negra tem a dizer sobre a 'política racial' no Brasil. *Rev. USP* 28:122–35

Fry P. 1995b. Why Brazil is different. *Times Lit. Suppl.,* Dec. 8, pp. 6–7

Fry P. 1996. Resenha: *Orpheus and Power* de Michael Hanchard. *Rev. Bras. Ciên. Soc.* 31:178–82

Gans HJ. 1979. Symbolic ethnicity in America. *Ethn. Racial Stud.* 2:1–20

Gilliam AM. 1992. From Roxbury to Rio—and back in a hurry. In *African-American Reflections on Brazil's Racial Paradise,* ed. DJ Hellwig, pp. 173–81. Philadelphia: Temple Univ. Press

Gilroy P. 1991. *'There Ain't No Black in the Union Jack'. The Cultural Politics of Race and Nation.* Chicago: Univ. Chicago Press

Gilroy P. 1994. *The Black Atlantic. Modernity and Double Consciousness.* Cambridge: Harvard Univ. Press

Goldberg DT. 1993. *Racist Culture. Philosophy and the Politics of Meaning.* Oxford, UK/Cambridge, MA: Blackwell

Gramsci A. 1971. *Selections from the Prison Notebooks.* New York: Int. Publ.

Gray H. 1995. *Watching Race. Television and the Struggle for "Blackness."* Minneapolis: Univ. Minn. Press

Gros C. 1997a. Indigenismo y etnicidad: el desafío neoliberal. In *Antropología en la Modernidad,* ed. MV Uribe, E Restrepo, pp. 15–60. Bogotá: Inst. Colomb. Antropol.

Gros C. 1997b. *Los Grupos Étnicos y el Estado Nacional en Colombia.* Presented at *Cent. Symp. Conf. Anthropol., 7th, Colombia,* Univ. Nac., Bogotá

Hall S. 1996a. What is this 'black' in black popular culture? In *Stuart Hall. Critical Dialogues in Cultural Studies,* ed. D Morley, K-H Chen, pp. 465–75. London/New York: Routledge

Hall S. 1996b. Gramsci's relevance for the study of race and ethnicity. See Hall 1996a, pp. 411–40

Hanchard MG. 1993. Culturalism versus cultural politics: 'movimento negro' in Rio de Janeiro and Sao Paulo, Brazil. In *The Violence Within: Cultural and Political Opposition in Divided Nations,* ed. K Warren, pp. 57–86. Boulder, CO: Westview

Hanchard MG. 1994. *Orpheus and Power. The 'Movimento Negro' of Rio de Janeiro and São Paulo, Brazil, 1945–1988.* Princeton: Princeton Univ. Press

Hanchard MG. 1996a. Cinderela negra? raça e esfera pública no Brasil. *Estud. Afro-Asiát.* 30:41–59

Hanchard MG. 1996b. "Americanos", Brasileiros e a cor da espécie humana: uma resposta a Peter Fry. *Rev. USP* 31:164–75

Hanchard MG. 1996c. Resposta a Luíza Bairros. *Afro-Ásia* 18:227–34

Harris M. 1974. *Patterns of Race in the Americas.* New York: Norton Library

Hasenbalg CA. 1979. *Discriminação e Desigualdades Raciais no Brasil.* Rio de Janeiro: Graal

Hasenbalg CA. n.d. *Race Relations in Modern Brazil.* Albuquerque: Latin Am. Inst., Univ. NM

Hellwig DJ, ed. 1992. *African-American Reflections on Brazil African Paradise.* Philadelphia: Temple Univ. Press

Hollinger DA. 1995. *Postethnic America. Beyond Multiculturalism.* New York: Basic Books

Kubik G. 1994. Ethnicity, cultural identity, and the psychology of culture contact. In *Music and Black Ethnicity: The Caribbean and South America,* ed. G Béhague, pp. 17–46. New Brunswick, NJ/London: Transaction Book

Leite IB, ed. 1991. *Terras e Territórios Negros no Brasil, Textos y Debates.* Florianópolis: Núcleo de Estudos sobre Identidade e Relações Interétnicas, UFSC

Lemert C. 1994. Dark thoughts about the self. In *Social Theory and the Politics of Identity,* ed. C Calhoun, pp. 100–29. Oxford, UK/Cambridge, MA: Blackwell

Maggie Y. 1991. *A ilusão do concreto: análise do sistema de classificação racial no Brasil.* Presented at Annu. Meet. Associação Nacional Pósgraduação Ciências Sociais, 15th, Caxambu

Maggie Y. 1992. *Medo do Feitiço: Relações Entre Magia e Poder no Brasil.* Rio de Janeiro: Arquivo Nac., Minist. Justiça

Maggie Y, Gonçalves MA. 1995. Pessoas fora do lugar: a produção da diferença no Brasil. In *O Brasil na Virada do Século,* ed. G Villas Bôas, MA Gonçalves, pp. 165–76. Rio de Janeiro: Relume Dumará

Mato D. 1997. On global agents, transnational relations, and the social making of transnational identities and associated agendas in "Latin" America. *Identities* 4(2):155–200

McLaren P. 1994. White terror and oppositional agency: towards a critical multiculturalism. In *Multiculturalism. A Critical Reader,* ed. DT Goldberg, pp. 45–74. Cambridge, MA: Basil Blackwell

Mohanty CT. 1995. Under Western eyes: feminist scholarship and colonial discourses. In *The Post-Colonial Studies Reader,* ed. B Ashcroft, G Griffiths, H Tiffin, pp. 196–220. London/New York: Routledge

Needell JD. 1995. Identity, race, gender, and modernity in the origins of Gilberto Freyre's oeuvre. *Am. Hist. Rev.* 100(1): 51–77

Nogueira O. 1955. Relações raciais em itapetininga. In *Relações Raciais Entre Negros e Brancos em São Paulo,* ed. F Fernandes, R Bastide, pp. 40–79. São Paulo: Anhembi

Nogueira O. 1985. *Tanto Preto Quanto Branco: Estudos de Relações Raciais.* São Paulo: Queiroz

Pierce P, Williams BF. 1996. "And your prayers shall be answered through the womb of a woman." Insurgent masculine redemption and the Nation of Islam. In *Women Out of Place,* ed. BF Williams, pp. 186–215. New York/London: Routledge

Ramos A. 1994. The hyperreal Indian. *Crit. Anthropol.* 14(2):153–71

Sansone L. 1996. Nem somente preto ou negro. O sistema de classificação racial no Brasil que muda. *Afro-Ásia* 18:165–87

Segato RL. 1991. Uma vocação de minoria: a expansão dos cultos Afro-Brasileiros na Argentina como processo de re-etnização. *Dados-Rev. Ciênc. Soc.* 34(2):249–78

Segato RL. 1995a. *Santos e Daimones. O Politeísmo Afro-Brasileiro e a Tradicao Arquetipal.* Brasilia: Edit. Univ. Brasilia

Segato RL. 1995b. Cidadania: porque nao? Estado e sociedade no Brasil à luz de um discurso religioso Afro-Brasileiro. *Dados-Rev. Ciênc. Soc.* 38(3):581–602

Segato RL. 1996. Frontiers and margins: the untold story of the Afro-Brazilian religious expansion to Argentina and Uruguay. *Crit. Anthropol.* 16(4):343–59

Segato RL. 1997a. 'Formações de diversidade': um modelo para interpretar a recepção de opções religiosas nos países da América Latina no contexto da globalização. In *Religião e Globalização na America Latina,* ed. AP Oro, pp. 219–48. Petropolis: Vozes

Segato RL. 1997b. *Alteridades históricas/ identidades políticas: una crítica a las certezas del pluralismo global.* Presented at the Cent. Symp. Conf. Anthropol., Colombia, 7th, Univ. Nac., Bogotá

Skidmore TE. 1974. *Black into White: Race and Nationality in Brazilian Thought.* New York: Oxford Univ. Press

Skidmore TE. 1990. Racial ideas and social policy in Brazil, 1870–1940. In *The Idea of Race in Latin America, 1879–1940,* ed. R Graham, pp. 7–36. Austin: Univ. Texas Press

Soares LE. 1996. *The double bind of Brazilian culture.* Presented at Conf. Negotiating Rights in Emerging Democracies: The Case of Brazil. Stanford Univ., Cent. Lat. Am. Stud., Stanford

Sollors W. 1986. *Beyond Ethnicity. Consent and Descent in American Culture.* New York: Oxford Univ. Press

Sollors W, ed. 1989. *The Invention of Ethnicity.* Oxford: Oxford Univ. Press

Spivak GC. 1990. *The Post-Colonial Critic: Interviews, Strategies, Dialogues,* ed. S Harasym. London: Routledge

Velho G. 1992. Unidade e fragmentação em sociedades complexas. In *Duas Conferências,* ed. G Velho, O Velho, pp. 13–46. Rio de Janeiro: Forum Ciênc. Cult./UFRJ

Viveiros de Castro Cavalcanti ML. 1996. Oracy Nogueira e a antropologia no Brasil: o estudo do estigma e do preconceito racial. *Rev. Bras. Ciênc. Soc.* 31:5–28

Wade P. 1995. *Blackness and Race Mixture. The Dynamics of Racial Identity in Colombia.* Baltimore/London: Johns Hopkins Univ. Press

West C. 1993. *Race Matters.* New York: Vintage Books

Williams BF. 1989. A class act: anthropology and the race to nation across ethnic terrain. *Annu. Rev. Anthropol.* 18:401–44

Williams BF. 1993. The impact of the precepts of nationalism on the concepts of culture: making grasshoppers of naked apes. *Cult. Crit.* 24:143–91

Winant H. 1994. *Racial Conditions: Theories, Politics and Comparisons.* Minneapolis: Univ. Minn. Press

*Annu. Rev. Anthropol. 1998. 27:153–69*
*Copyright © 1998 by Annual Reviews. All rights reserved*

# MODELING THE GENETIC ARCHITECTURE OF MODERN POPULATIONS

*S. T. Sherry,*[1] *M. A. Batzer,*[1] *and H. C. Harpending*[2]

[1]Departments of Pathology and Biometry and Genetics, Stanley S. Scott Cancer Center, Neuroscience Center of Excellence, Louisiana State University Medical Center, New Orleans, Louisiana 70112, e-mail: ssherr@lsumc and mbatze@lsumc.edu; [2]Department of Anthropology, University of Utah, Salt Lake City, Utah 84112; e-mail: henry.harpending@anthro.utah.edu

KEY WORDS: population expansion, Paleolithic, human evolution, effective population size, molecular anthropology

---

ABSTRACT

This article summarizes recent genetic evidence about the population history of our species. There is a congruence of evidence from different systems showing that the genetic effective size of humans is about 10,000 reproducing adults. We discuss how the magnitude and fluctuation of this number over time is important for evaluating competing hypotheses about the nature of human evolution during the Pleistocene. The differences in estimates of effective size derived from high mutation rate and low mutation rate genetic systems allow us to trace broad-scale changes in population size. The ultimate goal is to produce a comprehensive history of our own gene pool and its spread and differentiation over the world. The genetic evidence should also complement archaeological evidence of our past by revealing aspects of our history that are not readily visible from the archaeological record, such as whether hominid populations in the Pleistocene were different species.

---

## INTRODUCTION

Our purpose is to write an accessible summary, from a population history perspective, of the current research that addresses questions about Pleistocene population size and geographic structure. This summary extends the discus-

153

0084-6570/98/1015-0153$08.00

sion of ancient human demography presented by Harpending et al (1998) with a consideration of some common models of population growth and their implications for the structure of contemporary human diversity. The interested reader may refer to Harpending et al (1998) for a more complete discussion of the behavior of the coalescent process with expanding and contracting populations and for discussion of techniques that recover the signatures of such dynamic processes with trees and other graphical methods.

Paleontology's story of the evolution of the genus *Homo* is taken from the fossil record, and it indicates that upright, bipedal hominids occupied much of the Old World from maybe 1.5 to 0.5 Mya. During this time there was a succession of forms from *Homo erectus* to *Homo antecessor* to archaic *Homo sapiens* (Gibbons 1997). Neanderthals are a familiar example of the latter (Tattersall 1997). About 40,000 years ago, in the Levant, modern humans replaced archaics after a period of coexistence of perhaps 50 millennia and in just a few millennia (Stringer & Andrews 1988). In Indonesia, archaics may have persisted until as recently as 25,000 years ago (Swisher et al 1996). It is difficult to establish a clear description of the human evolutionary process from these data alone because the limited number of fossils leave gaps in the record. Most important, questions of local continuity are hard to evaluate.

Fortunately, gene differences in modern populations have been shaped and sculpted by ancient demographic events as well as by historical ones. Research into the empirical structure of these differences in human groups, and a theory of the population processes that can produce these changes, have produced an immense set of data. The current data set is sufficiently informative to allow consideration of traditional evolutionary hypotheses in population genetic terms and to make explicit their assumptions about evolutionary processes. We seek to retain and improve the hypotheses that are consistent with empirical data.

## MODELS OF HUMAN ORIGINS

Real population histories are exceedingly complex over long time intervals, and we can only hope to reveal their most general features with the current set of tools and methods. Complex population histories of unknown character must usually be reduced to very simple models.

The two models of modern human origins frequently debated in the literature—the out of Africa (OOA) and multiregional evolution (MRE) models—are contemporary versions of the long-standing debate in anthropology between splitters and lumpers. A generation ago, this division in the interpretation of variation was discussed in terms of models of replacement or catastrophism versus phyletic evolution (Weiss & Maruyama 1976). The relevant point to the discussion that follows is that both models are essentially simple specifications of the population size of our ancestors during the early Upper Pleistocene (ca 125,000 to 75,000 years ago).

The MRE hypothesis (Wolpoff 1989, Wolpoff et al 1994) suggests that modern humans evolved directly from archaic forms in several different locations in the Old World. Gene flow among these populations, combined with natural selection for advantageous genes, spread a new modern human gene complex globally and maintained genetic homogeneity of the species. Under this hypothesis, our species had hundreds of thousands, perhaps millions, of ancestors for most of the past million years. Without a large population, gene flow would have been impossible among populations distributed widely over the temperate and tropical Old World.

In contrast, the OOA hypothesis (Cann et al 1987, Stringer & Andrews 1988), or Garden of Eden (GOE) hypothesis, as it is alternatively known (Harpending et al 1993), posits that modern humans appeared in a subpopulation of *Homo erectus*, perhaps as a new species, and spread continuously over much of the Old World via population growth. The weak version of this hypothesis decouples early population fission events from later episodes of population growth (Harpending et al 1993). In both the strong and the weak versions of the hypothesis, however, the contribution of archaic populations to the modern gene pool was negligible. The number of ancestors just prior to the expansion (origin) of modern humans was small: only several thousand breeding adults. This model has also been presented in the literature as the candelabra (Templeton 1997) or replacement model (Weiss & Maruyama 1976) of recent human evolution. Our use of the term "population expansion" to indicate growth in population size should not be confused with an expansion in a population's geographic range. A recent review of the evidence for the latter in human populations may be found in Templeton (1997), and comments on the technique may be found in Rogers & Jorde (1995).

We describe the familiar positions in the debate about modern human origins in these terms to emphasize that the differences among these models are essentially the result of demographic assertions about the size of the past human population. Casting the positions in this context suggests other interesting aspects of the demography of our ancestors as well. Were these ancestors subdivided into partially isolated demes? Under MRE they must have been because they occupied several continents. Under OOA/GOE they could not have been isolated, at least in the simplest formulation of the hypothesis, because under this model our origins were from a single population. How fast did human populations expand after the origin of the human species? The nature of population growth in ancient human populations is the most important factor determining how we interpret contemporary gene differences among populations as well as genetic diversity within populations. The utility of such a demographic-behavioral perspective on the question of human origins has been argued for some time (Weiss & Maruyama 1976). To address these questions we shall consider in turn some estimates of Middle Pleistocene effective size for *H. sapiens,* the structure of contemporary gene diversity ($F_{ST}$) for systems of differing mutation rates, and the evidence for Late Pleistocene population expansions by continental region.

## POPULATION SIZE DURING THE EARLY AND MIDDLE PLEISTOCENE

Even though anatomically modern humans do not make their appearance in the fossil record until the Late Pleistocene (Stringer & Andrews 1988), the estimated size(s) of parental population(s) during the Early and Middle Pleistocene are also of interest. If the size of the ancestral population that produced modern humans had been large throughout much of its history, extant genetic variation should be substantial. Alternatively, a small human population would result in relatively little genetic variation. Many genetic systems provide reassuringly congruent estimates: All indicate that human genetic variation is relatively low and that the approximate effective size (i.e. the number of breeding adults) of humans is on the order of 10,000 (Nei & Graur 1984, Takahata 1993, Takahata et al 1995, Goldstein et al 1996, Donnelly et al 1996, Takahata & Satta 1997, Sherry et al 1997, Harding et al 1997).

The genetic relationship between modern humanity and the world population of Middle Pleistocene archaics remains an unspecified but important parameter (Harpending et al 1998). If the current small effective size of humans reflects a population history of a transient, but drastic, reduction in size, then the number of our ancestors prior to the reduction was large and a graph of our population history looks like an hourglass. Alternatively, if we are descended from a subpopulation of archaic humans that was effectively a separate species for the past million years or so, then the graph of our population history is a bottleneck, with a short bottle representing the large population size of contemporary populations and a very long neck representing the small populations of our archaic ancestors in the Middle and Late Pleistocene.

The hourglass hypothesis posits a contraction in the number of our ancestors at some time during the Pleistocene, perhaps before the last interglacial. It also specifies that prior to the contraction, this ancestral population was integrated by gene flow with a network of archaic groups that spanned the whole temperate Old World. In other words, if the genes in the small founding population of modern humans were traced backward in time, they would be dispersed over a large part of the Old World in a population of hundreds of thousands to millions, as in the multiregional hypothesis. Humanity's small apparent effective size, in this case, is the result of a loss of genetic diversity during the contraction.

The long-neck hypothesis, however, posits that the ancestral population was small during most of the Pleistocene, for the past million years or so, and that genes in this population traced backward in time were restricted to the range of some particular species of archaic humans that were our ancestors. The essential difference in the two hypotheses is the effective size before the constriction in the Middle or Late Pleistocene. We can contrast the expected topologies of gene genealogies generated under a coalescent process for these hypotheses as well (Hudson 1990). Because the size of the Middle Pleistocene population governs the expected level of ancient allelic diversity, the larger effective size specified by the hourglass hypothesis would serve as a reservoir for a larger number of alleles. Genealogies derived from the coalescent process under the hourglass hypothesis assumptions of effective size would occasionally show very deep differences between alleles. Genealogies derived from the long-neck hypothesis, however, are not expected to show this characteristic. The consequences for the shape of trees of descent of nuclear genes for a range of demographic scenarios are discussed in more detail by Harpending et al (1998). Noting that the pattern of deep allelic differences for nuclear genes are conspicuously absent in humans, they conclude that there is no support in current genetic data for the hourglass hypothesis, while the long-neck hypothesis finds strong support. The one exception to this observation is the HLA system (Takahata 1993, Ayala 1995), which owes its deep allelic lineages to the effects of balancing selection instead of large ancient effective size (Erlich et al 1996, Takahata & Satta 1998).

## RELATING EFFECTIVE SIZE AND CENSUS SIZE

Support for one model or the other comes from estimates of population effective size. Effective size estimates a kind of average of the breeding size of the population over the past; the average is over different time frames for different genetic systems depending on their particular modes of inheritance and rates of mutation. Relating effective size to census size of human populations is complicated. Genetic systems with a high mutation rate, for instance, contain mutations whose global distribution has been structured by population size changes over the past 10 to 20 millennia. Systems with a low mutation rate, in contrast, contain mutational distributions that were established by population processes a million or more years ago. These kinds of differences allow us to trace broad-scale changes over time in population size.

The standard model treats a population as a collection of genes that give birth each generation to a Poisson-distributed number of progeny in such a way that the overall number of genes in the population, $N$, remains constant from one generation to the next. Under this model, the probability that two genes picked at random will have the same parent (i.e. that they coalesce) is just $1/N$, so the expected waiting time until they coalesce is $N$ generations (Hudson 1990). This result can serve as a definition of effective size at a single time or of the long-term effective size if population size and breeding structure do not change. Felsenstein (1971) showed that the effective size of human populations is about one half the census size. This fraction may have been higher before the evolution of our long postreproductive life span.

When effective size changes over time, the long-term effective size is usually closer to the minimum size than to the average size (Hartl & Clark 1989), and in some simple cases long-term effective size is the harmonic mean of the changing instantaneous effective size (Hartl & Clark 1989, Chesser et al 1993).

Population breeding structure can change effective size in significant ways. If a population is subdivided into partially isolated subpopulations, then the effective size is greater than that of an equivalent randomly mating population because the waiting time for two lineages to coalesce is increased by the time that the lineages spend in different subpopulations (Nei & Takahata 1993). At the level of subdivision among human populations today, this effect would be minor, elevating the ratio of effective size to census size by 10% or 15%.

If subpopulations frequently go extinct and are replaced by members of a neighboring subpopulation, then effective size is reduced relative to census size (Whitlock & Barton 1997). In the extreme case where there is almost no gene flow among subpopulations and catastrophic extinction rates for entire subpopulations are high, the descendants of a single subpopulation will ultimately replace all others and effective size over time can be closer to the size of a single subpopulation than to the size of the whole population. If something like this happened in our evolution (Takahata 1994, Takahata & Satta 1998), the effective size of the founding subpopulation is exactly what we want to estimate. If there were substantial gene flow among subpopulations during the extinction/replacement process, the effective size over time would reflect the size of the whole population rather than that of a single population. What, then, is our effective size, and given this size, how is human diversity across continents and populations structured?

## EFFECTIVE SIZE ESTIMATES

There are two standard approaches to estimating effective size. Each does not estimate size per se, but rather a parameter called theta, which is the product of size and mutation rate. These two parameters are almost always confounded in population genetic models because the level of diversity for a gene is intimately related to both its intrinsic mutation rate and the number of copies available to mutate. The effective size may be computed directly from estimates of theta, if knowledge of the mutation rate is available. Human-specific

Alu insertions, described below, illustrate the properties of a genetic system that can be used to estimate effective size without prior knowledge of the mutation rate.

The familiar way to estimate size uses the differences we can observe within a sample of DNA sequences. The mean time to coalescence of pairs of sequences is $N$ generations, so the total path length between them is $2N$ generations. With the infinite sites assumption, according to which every mutation occurs at a new nucleotide position, the expected number of differences between two sequences is $2Nu$, where $u$ is the mutation rate for the whole sequence, that is, the per nucleotide rate multiplied by the sequence length. This method requires knowledge of the mutation rate, which may suffer from its own problems in estimation (Gibbons 1998). When the infinite sites assumption is violated, it is often necessary to correct this mean pairwise difference estimate for repeated mutations (Watterson 1975, Tajima 1983). The effective number of females has been estimated from mtDNA at 500–3000 in this fashion (Rogers & Harpending 1992, Harpending et al 1993, Sherry et al 1994). An important recent extension of the pairwise method simultaneously estimates the effective sizes of two related species and the effective size of their common ancestral population by using maximum likelihood (Takahata & Satta 1997).

An alternative method of estimating $N$ from DNA sequences relies on the overall branch length of the genealogical tree of a sample of $n$ genes and on the infinite sites assumption. The genealogy of a sample of $n$ genes can be divided into $n - 1$ epochs during which there are $n, n - 1, n - 2, \ldots, 2$ ancestors of the sample in the population of $2N$ chromosomes (because humans are diploid). The expected branch length at each epoch, the product of the number of lines present and the duration of the epoch, has a simple form under the constant size hypothesis. The oldest epoch, when there were two genes ancestral to the sample, has expected duration $2N$ generations, as derived above. During a more recent epoch, when there are $j$ genes ancestral to the sample present in the population, the hazard of coalescence between any pair is just $1/2N$ per generation and there are $j(j - 1)/2$ ways that pairs can be formed. The total hazard is $j(j - 1)/4N$ for epoch $j$, so the expected duration of this epoch is $4N/j(j - 1)$ generations. The expected total branch length of the tree is obtained by multiplying the expected length of each epoch by $j$ (because there are $j$ lines present during epoch $j$) and then summing over all $j$ epochs in the tree. Thus, the expected total branch length is

$$\sum_{j=2}^{n} j \frac{4N}{j(j-1)} = 4N \sum_{j=1}^{n-1} \frac{1}{i}$$

1.

generations, a familiar expression because of Watterson (1975).

The expected time back to the most recent common ancestor, in contrast to the total branch length, is the sum of the interval lengths rather than the sum of the branch lengths. This quantity approaches $2N$ generations as the sample size $n$ becomes moderately large. This is called the coalescent of the tree. The expected number of mutations in the whole tree, equivalent to the total number of segregating sites in the sample, is the tree length multiplied by the mutation rate $u$. Although this estimator of $N$ based on equation [1] has better statistical properties, in theory, than the estimator based on pairwise differences, it is more sensitive to violations of the assumption of constant population size in the past.

A third approach uses maximum likelihood (ML) methods to recover information on effective size from the explicit structure of the sample genealogy (Felsenstein 1992). An exciting extension of this approach uses a Metropolis-Hastings Markov chain Monte Carlo method to direct the sampling of the vast universe of potential genealogies toward the sets that are the most likely to be consistent with the data (Kuhner et al 1995). Harding et al (1997) report an ML estimate of 10,000 for human effective size in an analysis of their β-globin gene data that used an ML computational method proposed by Griffiths & Tavaré (1994a,b).

Takahata & Satta (1997) provide another ML estimate of nuclear effective size in their study of orthologous nuclear gene sequences collected in humans, chimpanzees, gorillas, Old World monkeys, and New World monkeys. Their method considers the variation in pairs of sequences from different taxa and then partitions this variation into two sets based on whether the variation was present before or after the two taxa diverged. The authors conclude that $N$ in the lineage leading to modern humans was of the order of 100,000 through the Pliocene and Late Miocene and upward to 1 million during the Oligocene and Paleocene. Effective size during the Pleistocene, however, was estimated to range from roughly 6000 to 17,000 for the past 300,000–400,000 years. The contrast between Takahata and Satta's estimates of ancestral effective size in the Pleistocene and the Miocene also suggests that the speciation events for modern humans and our australopithecine ancestors, for example, were qualitatively different events.

The above methods all require knowledge of the mutation rate to estimate $N$. A different approach is to use the time of separation between the ancestral chimpanzee and human species to calibrate a genetic estimate of human effective size through Alu insertions. Most Alu elements are short (~300 bp) pseudogenes (Deininger & Batzer 1993). They are stable, transcriptionally inactive copies of a few active Alu elements, scattered randomly throughout the entire nuclear genome (Arcot et al 1995). Collectively, there are about 500,000 copies per haploid genome or 5% of the genome by mass (Deininger & Batzer 1993, 1995). Some Alu elements are shared with prosimians, monkeys, and apes, whereas others are so recent that they are polymorphic in humans (Batzer et al 1994, Stoneking et al 1997). Sherry et al (1997) use coalescent theory to compute expected total branch lengths from the numbers of monomorphic and polymorphic Alu elements observed in a sample of 120 individuals. The branch length estimates they derive under conditions of ascertainment bias suggest an effective size of 17,500, with the method giving greater weight to effective size near the top of the coalescent tree, which corresponds roughly to the Lower and Middle Pleistocene. The difference between this value and conventional values of 10,000 might be due to sampling error, or it might indicate a mild contraction in population size sometime during the early Upper Pleistocene.

## POPULATION GROWTH, DIVERSITY, AND $F_{ST}$

If we accept these estimates of a small Middle Pleistocene size for the moment, then we must accept some version of the bottleneck model and consider modern human diversity as the product of some series of population expansions. Discussions of the significance of population expansions can be found in Cavalli-Sforza et al (1994) and Sherry et al (1994). An excellent review of the details of how a population expansion is impressed on the structure of contemporary gene diversity and a presentation of the mitochondrial evidence for Late Pleistocene population expansions can be found in Rogers & Jorde (1995).

Let us begin by considering the possibility that today's races are the descendants of ancestral populations, each numbering a few thousand. These populations separated from each other and grew very slowly in relative isolation. In this case we might consider that the modern genetic differences between races reflects this isolation. However, if these ancestral groups grew rapidly, then genetic differences would have been essentially frozen, because genetic drift among large subdivisions would be so slow that it could hardly change the ancient pattern (Kimura 1955). Differences between groups would be slow to accumulate, and we would be forced to posit that the evolution of differences among populations preceded the expansion of groups and their spread into new areas.

To get a feeling for these differences, we will discuss several possible scenarios about ancient populations with the real numbers involved and then show each scenario's consequences for contemporary gene differences.

Let us suppose that during the Late Pleistocene the population of Africa grew from about 5000 people to about 5 million over a 50,000-year interval. These numbers represent growth by a factor of 1000 in 50,000 years, corresponding to a rate of increase of 0.0035 per generation. A group of 5000 people would contain 5017 people one generation later, 5035 after two generations, and so on. This is an infinitesimal rate of growth, corresponding to nothing that we have ever seen in our species' history. To consider rates at the other plausible end of the spectrum, let us suppose that growth occurred at a rate that doubles the population each generation—slightly greater than the rate of world population growth today and similar to that of the Y nomamö of Brazil and Venezuela, a low-technology group whose demography has been well studied (Neel & Weiss 1975). A population doubling in 25 years expands by a factor of 1000 in only 250 years, that is, in one half of 1% of the 50,000-year interval we are considering. Although this time span is the blink of an eye in archaeological time, it seems a much more feasible model of our history than the scenario of vanishingly slow constant growth.

Now we can think about how these two extreme models of ancient growth would affect the accumulation of differences between separated groups by genetic drift. In population genetics we measure the magnitude of the variance in gene frequencies by a statistic called $F_{ST}$, which is roughly the ratio of differences between groups to the total gene differences or diversity between two random individuals from the whole set of groups in the population. The value of this statistic among major human races, for neutral loci with low mutation rates, is about 12% (Nei & Livshits 1989, Cavalli-Sforza et al 1994, Barbujani et al 1997). We consider these loci first because the "memory" of a genetic system is roughly the reciprocal of the mutation rate, and we want to consider diversity that had its origins in the Early and Middle Pleistocene. Given that diversity is potentially that old, we must ask ourselves, How did we get to be 12% different from people in the next continent?

If ancestral populations diverge and, after the divergence, were genetically isolated from each, then $F_{ST}$ would grow according to a well-known formula of Wright such that at generation $t$ it should be about

$$F_{ST}(t) = 1 - \exp(-t/2N),$$

where $N$ is the long-term effective size of each daughter population (Nei 1987). The use of the value 0.12 for $F_{ST}$ and 2500 generations for $t$ suggests that $N \approx 10,000$. This shows that the modern variance in gene frequencies could have accumulated after 50,000 years if each race had an effective size of 10,000 reproductive people. We know that there are many more than 10,000 people in each major race today, and there have been more than 10,000 people per race for a long time, so this is certainly not a good model.

What if racial populations separated, then grew exponentially? In this case, drift slows as population size increases, and as a result, $F$, the probability of gene identity resulting from shared ancestry, approaches a limit even though the populations continue to grow. Most of the differences thus accumulate early in the process, while daughter populations are small. The divergence produced by exponential growth from initial population size $N$ must satisfy

$$- \ln(1 - F_{ST}) = 1/2Nr,$$

and a calculator shows that if $r$ is as low as 0.0035, then the initial racial population sizes would have been ~1100 breeding adults, while if $r$ is as high as 1, like the Y nomamö, then initial racial population sizes were ~4 breeding adults. Neither of these figures seems feasible; they are presented only to reinforce the point that the model of bifurcating isolated daughter populations, along with the corpus of methods for reconstructing trees and thus reconstructing the sequence of splits, requires assumptions about ancient population size that are unlikely to be even approximately true.

One way to save the model is to posit that the ancestral populations of extant races were very small, on the order of several hundreds of people, and that drift occurred early in the founding phase. Such a process could perhaps be modeled after the expansion of Austronesian speakers into Polynesia (Bellwood 1989, 1991), where the heterogeneity of the region is interpreted to be the result of extreme genetic drift caused by the small size of the islands (Cavalli-Sforza et al 1994). This process fails in the end, however, because the carrying capacities of the settled islands are too low to sustain the levels of final growth we need to consider.

There is also a primate model for the postulated demic structure of the earliest modern humans. Common chimpanzees occupy the forested belt across central Africa, and they are very differentiated (Goldberg & Ruvolo 1997). The western populations are so different from the others that there is some argument that they should be a different species (Morin et al 1994, Gonder et al 1997). Currently, there are few chimpanzees, although their genetics suggests that they have not been such a rare species for very many millennia. Perhaps their fortunes fell as our own species expanded at their expense. At any rate, if chimpanzees were to find a dramatically successful new adaptation and expand from their present base to occupy the world by the millions with some low level of population mixing accompanying the expansion, then differences between chimp races would be something on the same order as differences between human races.

There are several implications of this argument that group differences are too great to reflect a history of bifurcations. First, differences must have preceded the origin and expansion of modern humans, that is to say, we must have expanded from several previously isolated subpopulations. This is exactly the ancestral population structure implied by the model of multiregional evolution, even though it has not been stated explicitly by the model's proponents. This model is frequently dismissed, however, because of the low diversity of our species and the various lines of genetic evidence suggesting that the total effective size of our ancestors was at most several tens of thousands. New models such as the weak version of GOE (Harpending et al 1993) or the multiple dispersals model of Lahr & Foley (1994) should be considered in more detail to address this problem.

A second implication is that the literature reconstructing the tree of human population differentiation may be spurious. This literature regularly finds that the genetic distance between Africans and non-Africans is the largest difference, which is correct. Then the conclusion is drawn that the earliest bifurcation in our history is between African and non-African populations, and this is not appropriate at all. If our ancestors were members of a highly subdivided species, then the implication is that ancestors of Africans were simply more isolated genetically from the rest of the species than were the other founding demes. There is not necessarily any historical bifurcating process at all reflected in the data. Certainly the relative isolation of sub-Saharan Africa has been a feature of the history of our species until the advent of sea travel, and it may have been a feature of the demography of our species during the whole Upper Pleistocene. We examine the issue of excess African diversity in more detail, because the African contribution to the genetic structure of modern populations is substantial.

## THE STRUCTURE OF CONTEMPORARY DIVERSITY

African populations south of the Sahara exhibit higher diversity than other populations in mitochondrial DNA sequences, in craniometric traits, and in short tandem repeat polymorphisms (Harpending et al 1993, Relethford & Harpending 1994, Bowcock et al 1994, Mountain & Cavalli-Sforza 1994, Armour et al 1996, Shriver et al 1997). They do not show increased diversity in dimorphic Alu repeats, in classical genetic markers like blood groups and proteins, or in nuclear DNA polymorphisms (Nei & Roychoudhury 1974, Batzer et al 1994, Cavalli-Sforza et al 1994, Stoneking et al 1997). One possible explanation for the discrepancies between the different kinds of systems is ascertainment bias (Mountain & Cavalli-Sforza 1994). The classical markers and many newer nuclear markers were discovered and defined mostly in European populations, so there is a built-in bias to find systems that are diverse in Europeans. It is not clear, however, that this mechanism can completely explain the differences.

Accepting for the moment that the greater diversity of Africans is real, what does it mean? Some have suggested that it supports the idea of an African origin of our species, that the population of Africans is "older" than non-Africans (Tishkoff et al 1996). It is not clear, however, what this means in demographic terms because we are all descended from the earliest modern humans. The simplest explanation for greater African diversity is that the ancestral population of Africans was larger than the population ancestral to other continental groups. Diversity accumulates at a constant rate, or so our models say, and it is lost at a rate inversely proportional to total population size. Therefore, greater diversity immediately suggests a larger population. A competing explanation for higher African diversity is that the population ancestral to Africans expanded earlier than the populations ancestral to non-African people. In other words, Africans have been a larger group longer.

The simple model, that Africans have always been larger, predicts that African diversity would be greatest in all genetic systems. The model of earlier African expansion, on the other hand, predicts that African diversity would be greatest only in systems with high mutation rates—rates high enough for diversity to accumulate in the time since our ancestors expanded into large populations. The data clearly support the second model.

For mitochondrial DNA control region sequences, divergence rate estimates are around 20% per million years (Stoneking et al 1992). For a sequence of, say, 700 bases of the control regions, this becomes three or four mutations per thousand generations. The generic estimate of the analogue of the mutation rate for quantitative traits (the rate of appearance of new heritability from mutation) is about one in a thousand (Lynch & Hill 1986), and this is also a reasonable estimate of the rate of mutations for many tandem repeat loci (Goldstein et al 1995). These are all comparatively high mutation systems. If the expansion of African ancestors started 100,000 or so years ago, there has been enough time for mutations to accumulate since this expansion in Africans.

Classical nuclear markers, in contrast, mutate at a rate of about one per million generations (Nei 1975), and the rate for small nuclear polymorphisms is even lower (Takahata & Satta 1997). At these low rates, mutations have not had enough time to accumulate in a population that has been large for only 100,000 years. The polymorphisms we observe for those loci must have been the ones that passed through the common bottleneck in our history implied by our small effective size, because they do not show any meaningful race differences in diversity.

The differences in $F_{ST}$ between the high and low mutation rate systems suggest that the ancient expansion of African ancestors predated expansions of the ancestors of other major regional groups by at least several tens of thousands of years (Harpending et al 1996). This conclusion has also been reached by other researchers (Deka et al 1996, Tishkoff et al 1996, Stoneking et al 1997, Relethford 1998). The model of successive bifurcations does not fit the data. Thus today's differences between populations cannot be used to estimate separation times of races because there are no separation times. Population trees do not represent the history of human races, and maps of the world with snakelike arrows repeatedly undergoing mitosis do not portray the history of human differentiation in the right way.

This pattern seems clear enough that it ought to lead to research designs for archaeologists (Gibbons 1995, Gutin 1995, Brooks et al 1995, Yellen et al 1995). The suggestion is that the ancestors of today's sub-Saharan Africans have been a big population, a visible presence in the record, for 100,000 years or so, while the ancestors of other continental groups have been small and perhaps archaeologically invisible or elusive until 40,000 or so years ago. It is interesting that the history of multiple dispersals from Africa suggested by genetic evidence (Harpending et al 1993, Harpending et al 1996, Stoneking et al 1997) is nearly the same as the scenario proposed by Lahr & Foley (1994) from the fossil and archaeological evidence.

## CONCLUSIONS

We have tried to suggest that there are interesting demographic issues involved in the prehistory of our species and that genetic data and properties of genetic systems can be of value in testing model predictions. We have described and reviewed the evidence for several models: models of Middle Pleistocene population size, models of the source of greater African diversity, and models of the genesis of race differences in our species.

We found support for bottleneck history of Pleistocene population size for our species. We conclude that most of the familiar specimens of *Homo erectus* and of archaic humans known from the Pleistocene were not members of the population ancestral to us. Rather, we are descended from a population that was effectively a separate species from the Pleistocene onward. Although the size of this population certainly fluctuated over time, it must have been reduced at times to only a few thousand individuals. A population of this size would not be expected to be distributed over an entire continent, but rather a much smaller range, perhaps the size of Swaziland or Rhode Island. An identification of this population would be of great archaeological interest.

Race differences in genetic marker frequencies could have been generated by successive bifurcations of a single founding population of modern humans under very stringent and unlikely conditions on the sizes of these founding branches. A more feasible model of today's differences is that they reflect ancient differences that were "frozen" by the great expansions of modern humans during the last glaciation. Common chimpanzees furnish a model of what the population structure of our ancestors might have been prior to these expansions.

The pattern of expansion from an ancient set of partially isolated demes is just the pattern predicted by the multiregional model. Most geneticists, however, do not support the model of MRE because the total size of the ancestral human population was no greater than several tens of thousands. Such a small population could not have occupied the whole temperate Old World (Harpending et al 1993, Takahata 1993). New models are needed to incorporate these facts.

Diversity is greater in sub-Saharan Africans in genetic systems with high mutation rates, but it is not greater in low mutation rate systems. The evidence is consistent with an African origin of modern humans, in the sense that the population ancestral to Africans underwent demographic expansion tens of millennia before the ancestors of other major races. These facts are in excellent agreement with the predictions of the multiple dispersals model of Lahr & Foley (1994).

ACKNOWLEDGMENTS

We are grateful to Ken Weiss for valuable comments on this manuscript. This work was supported by a National Institutes of Health National Research Service Award (GM19110-01) to STS and a National Science Foundation grant (SBR-9610147) to MAB.

> **Visit the *Annual Reviews home page* at
> http://www.AnnualReviews.org.**

## *Literature Cited*

Arcot SS, Shaikh TH, Kim J, Bennett L, Alegria-Hartman M, et al. 1995. Sequence diversity and chromosomal distribution of "young" Alu repeats. *Gene* 163:273–78

Armour JA, Anttinen T, May CA, Vega EE, Sajantila A, et al. 1996. Minisatellite diversity supports a recent African origin for modern humans. *Nat. Genet.* 13:154–60

Ayala FJ. 1995. The myth of Eve: molecular biology and human origins. *Science* 270: 1930–36

Barbujani G, Magagni A, Minch E, Cavalli-Sforza LL. 1997. An apportionment of human DNA diversity. *Proc. Natl. Acad. Sci. USA* 94:4516–19

Batzer MA, Stoneking M, Alegria-Hartman M, Bazan H, Kass DH, et al. 1994. African origin of human-specific polymorphic Alu insertions. *Proc. Natl. Acad. Sci. USA* 91: 12288–92

Bellwood PS. 1989. The colonization of the Pacific: some current hypotheses. In *The Colonization of the Pacific: A Genetic Trail*, ed. AVS Hill, SW Serjeantson, pp. 1–59. Oxford: Oxford Univ. Press. 298 pp.

Bellwood PS. 1991. The Austronesian dispersal and the origin of languages. *Sci. Am.* 265:88–93

Bowcock AM, Ruiz-Linares A, Tomfohrde J, Minch E, Kidd JR, Cavalli-Sforza LL.

1994. High resolution of human evolutionary trees with polymorphic microsatellites. *Nature* 368:455–57

Brooks AS, Helgren DM, Cramer JS, Franklin A, Hornyak W, et al. 1995. Dating and context of three Middle Stone Age sites with bone points in the Upper Semliki valley, Zaire. *Science* 268:548–53

Cann RL, Stoneking M, Wilson AC. 1987. Mitochondrial DNA and human evolution. *Nature* 325:31–36

Cavalli-Sforza LL, Menozzi P, Piazza A. 1994. *The History and Geography of Human Genes.* Princeton: Princeton Univ. Press. 518 pp.

Chesser RK, Rhodes OEJ, Sugg DW, Schnabel A. 1993. Effective sizes for subdivided populations. *Genetics* 135:1221–32

Deininger PL, Batzer MA. 1993. Evolution of retroposons. In *Evolutionary Biology*, ed. MK Hecht, RJ MacIntyre, MT Clegg, 27:157–96. New York: Plenum. 458 pp.

Deininger PL, Batzer MA. 1995. SINE master genes and population biology. In *The Impact of Short Interspersed Elements (SINEs) on the Host Genome,* ed. RJ Maraia, pp. 43–60. Austin, TX: Landes. 236 pp.

Deka R, Jin L, Shriver MD, Yu LM, Saha N, et al. 1996. Dispersion of human Y chromosome haplotypes based on five microsatellites in global populations. *Genome Res.* 6:1177–84

Donnelly P, Tavaré S, Balding DJ, Griffiths RC. 1996. Estimating the age of the common ancestor of men from the ZFY intron. *Science* 272:1357–59

Erlich HA, Bergstrom TF, Stoneking M, Gyllensten U. 1996. HLA sequence polymorphism and the origin of humans. *Science* 274:1552–54

Felsenstein J. 1971. Inbreeding and variance effective numbers in populations with overlapping generations. *Genetics* 68: 581–97

Felsenstein J. 1992. Estimating effective population size from samples of sequences: a bootstrap Monte Carlo integration method. *Genet. Res.* 60:209–20

Gibbons A. 1995. Old dates for modern behavior. *Science* 268:495–96

Gibbons A. 1997. A new face for human ancestors. *Science* 276:1331–33

Gibbons A. 1998. Calibrating the mitochondrial clock. *Science* 279:28–29

Goldberg TL, Ruvolo M. 1997. The geographic apportionment of mitochondrial genetic diversity in east African chimpanzees, *Pan troglodytes schweinfurthii*. *Mol. Biol. Evol.* 14:976–84

Goldstein DB, Ruiz LA, Cavalli-Sforza LL, Feldman MW. 1995. Genetic absolute dating based on microsatellites and the origin of modern humans. *Proc. Natl. Acad. Sci. USA* 92:6723–27

Goldstein DB, Zhivotovsky LA, Nayar K, Linares AR, Cavalli-Sforza LL, Feldman MW. 1996. Statistical properties of the variation at linked microsatellite loci: implications for the history of human Y chromosomes. *Mol. Biol. Evol.* 13:1213–18

Gonder MK, Oates JF, Disotell TR, Forstner MR, Morales JC, Melnick DJ. 1997. A new west African chimpanzee subspecies? *Nature* 388:337

Griffiths RC, Tavaré S. 1994a. Ancestral inference in population genetics. *Stat. Sci.* 9:307–19

Griffiths RC, Tavaré S. 1994b. Sampling theory for neutral alleles in a varying environment. *Philos. Trans. R. Soc. London Ser. B* 344:403–10

Gutin J. 1995. Do Kenya tools root birth of modern thought in Africa? *Science* 270: 1118–19

Harding RM, Fullerton SM, Griffiths RC, Bond J, Cox MJ, et al. 1997. Archaic African and Asian lineages in the genetic ancestry of modern humans. *Am. J. Hum. Genet.* 60:772–89

Harpending HC, Batzer MA, Gurven M, Jorde LB, Rogers AR, Sherry ST. 1998. Genetic traces of ancient demography. *Proc. Natl. Acad. Sci. USA* 95:1161–67

Harpending H, Relethford JH, Sherry ST. 1996. Methods and models for understanding human diversity. In *Molecular Biology and Human Diversity*, ed. AJ Boyce, CGN Mascie-Taylor, pp. 283–99. Cambridge: Cambridge Univ. Press. 305 pp.

Harpending HC, Sherry ST, Rogers AR, Stoneking M. 1993. The genetic structure of ancient human populations. *Curr. Anthropol.* 34:483–96

Hartl DL, Clark AG. 1989. *Principles of Population Genetics*. Sunderland, MA: Sinauer. 682 pp.

Hudson RR. 1990. Gene genealogies and the coalescent process. In *Oxford Surveys in Evolutionary Biology*, ed. DJ Futuyma, J Antonovics, 7:1–44. Oxford: Oxford Univ. Press. 307 pp.

Kimura M. 1955. Solution of a process of random genetic drift with a continuous model. *Proc. Natl. Acad. Sci. USA* 41:144–50

Kuhner MK, Yamato J, Felsenstein J. 1995. Estimating effective population size and mutation rate from sequence data using Metropolis-Hastings sampling. *Genetics* 140:1421–30

Lahr MM, Foley R. 1994. Multiple dispersals and modern human origins. *Evol. Anthropol.* 3:48–60

Lynch M, Hill WG. 1986. Phenotypic evolution by neutral mutation. *Evolution* 40: 915–35

Morin PA, Moore JJ, Chakraborty R, Jin L, Goodall J, Woodruff DS. 1994. Kin selection, social structure, gene flow, and the evolution of chimpanzees. *Science* 265: 1193–201

Mountain JL, Cavalli-Sforza LL. 1994. Inference of human evolution through cladistic analysis of nuclear DNA restriction polymorphisms. *Proc. Natl. Acad. Sci. USA* 91:6515–19

Neel JV, Weiss KM. 1975. The genetic structure of a tribal population, the Yanomama Indians. XII. Biodemographic studies. *Am. J. Phys. Anthropol.* 42:25–51

Nei M. 1975. *Molecular Population Genetics and Evolution*. Amsterdam: North Holland. 288 pp.

Nei M. 1987. *Molecular Evolutionary Genetics*. New York: Columbia Univ. Press. 512 pp.

Nei M, Graur D. 1984. Extent of protein polymorphism and the neutral mutation theory. In *Evolutionary Biology*, ed. MK Hecht, B Wallace, GT Prance, pp. 73–118. New York: Plenum. 306 pp.

Nei M, Livshits G. 1989. Genetic relationships of Europeans, Asians and Africans and the origin of modern Homo sapiens. *Hum. Hered.* 39:276–81

Nei M, Roychoudhury AK. 1974. Genic variation within and between the three major races of man, Caucasoids, Negroids, and Mongoloids. *Am. J. Hum. Genet.* 26:421–43

Nei M, Takahata N. 1993. Effective population size, genetic diversity, and coalescence time in subdivided populations. *J. Mol. Evol.* 37:240–44

Relethford JH. 1998. Mitochondrial DNA and ancient population growth. *Am. J. Phys. Anthropol.* 105:1–7

Relethford JH, Harpending HC. 1994. Craniometric variation, genetic theory, and modern human origins. *Am. J. Phys. Anthropol.* 95:249–70

Rogers AR, Harpending H. 1992. Population growth makes waves in the distribution of pairwise genetic differences. *Mol. Biol. Evol.* 9:552–69

Rogers AR, Jorde LB. 1995. Genetic evidence on modern human origins. *Hum. Biol.* 67:1–36

Sherry ST, Harpending HC, Batzer MA, Stoneking M. 1997. Alu evolution in human populations: using the coalescent to estimate effective population size. *Genetics* 147:1977–82

Sherry ST, Rogers AR, Harpending H, Soodyall H, Jenkins T, Stoneking M. 1994. Mismatch distributions of mtDNA reveal recent human population expansions. *Hum. Biol.* 66:761–75

Shriver MD, Jin L, Ferrell RE, Deka R. 1997. Microsatellite data support an early population expansion in Africa. *Genome Res.* 7:586–91

Stoneking M, Fontius JJ, Clifford SL, Soodyall H, Arcot SS, et al. 1997. Alu insertion polymorphisms and human evolution: evidence for a larger population size in Africa. *Genome Res.* 7:1061–71

Stoneking M, Sherry ST, Redd AJ, Vigilant L. 1992. New approaches to dating suggest a recent age for the human mtDNA ancestor. *Philos. Trans. R. Soc. London Ser. B* 337:167–75

Stringer CB, Andrews P. 1988. Genetic and fossil evidence for the origin of modern humans. *Science* 239:1263–68

Swisher CC, Rink WJ, Anton SC, Schwarcz HP, Curtis GH, et al. 1996. Latest *Homo erectus* of Java: potential contemporaneity with Homo sapiens in southeast Asia. *Science* 274:1870–74

Tajima F. 1983. Evolutionary relationship of DNA sequences in finite populations. *Genetics* 105:437–60

Takahata N. 1993. Allelic genealogy and human evolution. *Mol. Biol. Evol.* 10:2–22

Takahata N. 1994. Repeated failures that led to the eventual success in human evolution. *Mol. Biol. Evol.* 11:803–5

Takahata N, Satta Y. 1997. Evolution of the primate lineage leading to modern humans: phylogenetic and demographic inferences from DNA sequences. *Proc. Natl. Acad. Sci. USA* 94:4811–15

Takahata N, Satta Y. 1998. Improbable truth in human MHC diversity? *Nat. Genet.* 18:204–6

Takahata N, Satta Y, Klein J. 1995. Divergence time and population size in the lineage leading to modern humans. *Theor. Popul. Biol.* 48:198–221

Tattersall I. 1997. Out of Africa again . . . and again? *Sci. Am.* 276:60–67

Templeton AR. 1997. Out of Africa? What do genes tell us? *Curr. Opin. Genet. Dev.* 7:841–47

Tishkoff SA, Dietzsch E, Speed W, Pakstis AJ, Kidd JR, et al. 1996. Global patterns of linkage disequilibrium at the CD4 locus and modern human origins. *Science* 271:1380–87

Watterson GA. 1975. On the number of segregating sites in genetical models without recombination. *Theor. Popul. Biol.* 7:256–76

Weiss KM, Maruyama T. 1976. Archeology, population genetics and studies of human racial ancestry. *Am. J. Phys. Anthropol.* 44:31–50

Whitlock MC, Barton NH. 1997. The effective size of a subdivided population. *Genetics* 146:427–41

Wolpoff MH. 1989. Multiregional evolution: the fossil alternative to Eden. In *The Human Revolution: Behavioral and Biological Perspectives on the Origins of Modern Humans*, ed. PA Mellars, CB Stringer, pp. 62–108. Edinburgh: Edinburgh Univ. Press. 800 pp.

Wolpoff MH, Thorne AG, Smith FH, Frayer DW, Pope GG. 1994. Multiregional evolution: a world-wide source for modern human populations. In *Origins of Anatomically Modern Humans*, ed. MH Nitecki, DV Nitecki, pp. 175–200. New York: Plenum. 341 pp.

Yellen JE, Brooks AS, Cornelissen E, Mehlman MJ, Stewart K. 1995. A Middle Stone Age worked bone industry from Katanda, Upper Semliki valley, Zaire. *Science* 268:553–56

*Annu. Rev. Anthropol. 1998. 27:171–95*
*Copyright © 1998 by Annual Reviews. All rights reserved*

# WITTGENSTEIN AND ANTHROPOLOGY

## *Veena Das*

Department of Anthropology, Graduate Faculty, New School for Social Research, New York, New York 10003, and Department of Sociology, University of Delhi, Delhi 110007, India; e-mail cdedse@del2.vsnl.net.in

KEY WORDS: culture, language, rules, skepticism, everyday life

## ABSTRACT

This essay explores the theme of Wittgenstein as a philosopher of culture. The primary text on which the essay is based is *Philosophical Investigations*; it treats Stanley Cavell's work as a major guide for the understanding and reception of Wittgenstein into anthropology. Some Wittgensteinian themes explored in the essay are the idea of culture as capability, horizontal and vertical limits to forms of life, concepts of everyday life in the face of skepticism, and the complexity of the inner in relation to questions of belief and pain. While an attempt has been made to relate these ideas to ethnographic descriptions, the emphasis in this essay is on the question of how anthropology may receive Wittgenstein.

## INTRODUCTION

I wish to invite reflection in this paper on a certain kinship in the questions that Wittgenstein asks of his philosophy and the puzzles of anthropology. Consider his formulation—"A philosophical problem has the form: 'I don't know my way about'" (Wittgenstein 1953:para. 123). For Wittgenstein, then, philosophical problems have their beginnings in the feeling of being lost and in an unfamiliar place, and philosophical answers are in the nature of finding one's way back. This image of turning back, of finding not as moving forward as toward a goal but as being led back, is pervasive in the later writings of Wittgenstein. How can anthropology receive this way of philosophizing? Is there

171

something familiar in the feeling of being lost in anthropological experience? Wittgenstein's fear, "the seed I am likely to sow is a certain jargon" (Diamond 1976:293), is to be respected so that the translation of his ideas into anthropology should not be taken as the opportunity for merely a new set of terms. Instead of rendering a systematic account of any one aspect of his philosophy, I shall try to follow a few lines of thought that might interest anthropologists, hoping to convey the tones and sounds of Wittgenstein's words. My thought is not that this will help us reach new goals but that it might help us stop for a moment: to introduce a hesitancy in the way in which we habitually dwell among our concepts of culture, of everyday life, or of the inner. In this effort I am indebted to the work of Stanley Cavell, whose thoughts on several of these questions have acted like signposts in my own efforts to move within *Philosophical Investigations.*

## THE PICTURE OF CULTURE

### Definitions

In his recent, passionate work on the "anthropography" of violence, Daniel (1997) is moved to say, "Anthropology has had an answer to the question, What is a human being? An answer that has, on the whole, served us well, with or without borrowings from philosophers. The answer keeps returning to one form or another of the concept of culture: humans have it; other living beings do not" (p. 194). He goes on to discuss how Tylor's (1974) founding definition of culture helped to move it away from the "clutches of literature, philosophy, classical music, and the fine arts—in other words, from the conceit of the Humanities" (Daniel 1997:194). Let us consider for a moment the actual definition proposed by Tylor: "Culture or civilization taken in its widest ethnographic sense, is that complex whole which includes knowledge, belief, art, morals, law, custom, and any other capabilities and habits acquired by man as a member of society" (Tylor 1974:1). What is interesting in this definition is not only the all-inclusive nature of culture but also the reference to it as capability and habit acquired by man as a member of society. As Asad (1990) has noted, this notion of culture with its enumeration of capabilities and habits, as well as the focus on learning, gave way in time to the idea of culture as *text* "that is as something resembling an inscribed text" (p. 171). Within this dominant notion of culture as text, the process of learning came to be seen as shaping the individual body as a picture of this text, inscribing memory often through painful rituals so that the society and culture of which the individual is a member is made present, so to say, on the surface of the body (Clasteres 1974, Das 1995a, Durkheim 1976). The scene of instruction in Wittgenstein (1953) is entirely different.

## Scenes of Instruction

*Philosophical Investigations* begins with an evocation of the words of Augustine in *Confessions*. This opening scene has been the object of varying interpretations. The passage reads as follows:

> When they (my elders) named some object, and accordingly moved towards something, I saw this and grasped that the thing they called was the sound they uttered when they meant to point it out. Their intention was shewn by their bodily movements, as it were the natural language of all peoples: the expression of the face, the play of the eyes, the movement of other parts of the body, and the tone of voice which expresses our state of mind in seeking, having, or avoiding something. Thus as I heard words repeatedly used in their proper places in various sentences, I gradually learnt to understand what objects they signified; and after I had trained my mouth to form these signs, I used them to express my own desires. (Wittgenstein 1953:para. 1)

Stanley Cavell (1982, 1990), who has given the most sustained reading of this passage, senses here the presence of the child who moves invisible among his or her elders and who must divine speech for himself or herself, training the mouth to form signs so that he or she may use these signs to express his or her own desires. Now contrast this scene of instruction with the famous builders' scene, which follows soon after in Wittgenstein (1953:para. 2):

> Let us imagine a language for which the description given by Augustine is right. The language is meant to serve for communication between a builder A and an assistant B. A is building with building stones: there are blocks, pillars, slabs, and beams. B has to pass the stones, and that in order in which A needs them. For this purpose they use a language consisting of the words "block", "pillar", "slab", "beam". A calls them out; B brings the stone which he has learnt to bring at such-and-such a call.—Conceive this as a complete primitive language.

If we transpose the scene of instruction in which the child moves among the adults with that of the builders, we might see that even if the child were to use only four words, these may be uttered with charm, curiosity, a sense of achievement. The child has a future in language. The builders' language is, in a way, closed. Wittgenstein wills us to conceive of this as a "complete primitive language." Yet as Cavell (1995) points out, there is no standing language game for imagining what Wittgenstein asks us to imagine here. It has been noted often enough that Wittgenstein does not call upon any of the natural languages from which he could have taken his examples: Thus his game in this section—whether with reference to the child or the dreamlike sequence by which one might arrive at an "understanding" of what the words five red apples mean or with reference to the builders' language—is in the nature of a fiction through which his thoughts may be maintained in the region of the primitive. But the "primitive" here is conceived as the builders' tribe, which seems bereft of the possession of its culture or of an undoubted shared language—the language the tribe uses is invented language, not to be confused either with the natural languages found among people who maintain full forms of sociality or with the language of the child.

Wittgenstein's sense of the child who moves about in his or her culture unseen by the elders and who has to inherit his or her culture as if by theft appears to find resonance in the anthropological literature in the register of the mythological [for instance, in the bird nester myths analyzed by Lévi-Strauss (1969)]. Despite the studies on socialization, rarely has the question of how one comes to a sense of a shared culture as well as one's own voice in that culture in the context of everyday life been addressed anthropologically. If asked at all, this question has been formulated as a question of socialization as obedience to a set of normative rules and procedures. But juxtaposing the child with the builders seems to suggest that whatever else it may be, the inheritance of culture is not about inheriting a certain set of rules or a certain capacity to obey orders. As Wittgenstein (1953:para. 3) says, "Augustine does describe a system of communication: only not everything we call language is this system." And then, as if the surest route to understand this concept is to understand it through the eyes of the child, he points out that the words in a gamelike ring-a-ring-a-roses are to be understood as *both the words and the actions in which they are woven* (Wittgenstein 1953:para. 7).

Concern with childhood in early anthropological literature has not been absent but has been expressed through the intricacies of age ranking, rites of passage, attitudes toward someone called "the average child," and the construction of "childhood" in a given society. Both Nieuwenhuys (1996) and Reynolds (1995) have recently shown how sparse the ethnographic descriptions of children and their agency have been. Reynolds's (1995) work on political activism of children and youth in the volatile and traumatic context of South Africa is special because she shows how tales of folk heroes might have provided a perspective to young people with which to view their defiance of the regime of apartheid even as they had to negotiate questions of obedience, authority, and kinship solidarity within the domains of family and kinship. I would also draw attention to the remarkable account by Gilsenan (1996) and to Das (1990b,c) and Chatterji & Mehta (1995) on the complicated question of what it is for children to inherit the obligation to exact vengeance, to settle for peace, or to bear witness in a feud or in the aftermath of a riot. Claims over inheritance are not straightforward in these contexts, but even in relatively stable societies, anthropological descriptions of culture as either shared or contested have excluded the voice of the child. As in Augustine's passage, the child seems to move about unseen by its elders.

Let me go on to the question that the figure of the child raises here: What is it to say that the child has a future in language?

There are several scenes of instruction in *Philosophical Investigations*—those pertaining to completing a mathematical series, those pertaining to reading, those pertaining to obeying an order. All raise the issue of what it is to be able to project a concept or a word or a procedure into new situations. "A" writes down a series of numbers; "B" watches him and tries to find a law for the sequence of numbers. If he succeeds, he exclaims, "Now I can go on." What has happened here?

One powerful way of understanding what gives a child the confidence to say "I can go on" is provided by Kripke (1982) with the example of what it is to follow a mathematical procedure or a rule. He points out that Wittgenstein shows convincingly that we cannot speak of an inner understanding having occurred; nor can we say that there are some basic rules that can tell us how to interpret the other rules. Here is how the problem appears to Kripke (1982:17):

> Here of course I am expounding Wittgenstein's well known remarks about a "rule for interpreting a rule". It is tempting to answer the skeptic from appealing from one rule to another more 'basic' rule. But the skeptical move can be repeated at the more basic level also. Eventually the process must stop—"justifications come to an end somewhere"—and I am left with a rule which is completely unreduced to any other. How can I justify my present application of such a rule, when a skeptic could easily interpret it so as to yield any of an indefinite number of other results? It seems my application of it is an unjustified stab in the dark. I apply the rule *blindly*.

Without going into this argument in any detail, I want to comment on one formulation that is proposed by Kripke (1982):, that our justification for saying that a child has learned how to follow a rule comes from the confidence that being a member of a community allows the individual person to act "unhesitatingly but blindly." Kripke (1982) gives the example of a small child learning addition and says that it is obvious that his teacher will not accept just any response from the child. So what does one mean when one says that the teacher judges that, for certain cases, the pupil must give the "right" answer? "I mean that the teacher judges that the child has given the same answer that he himself would have given. . . . I mean that he judges that the child is applying the same procedure he himself would have applied" (Kripke 1982:90).

For Kripke (1982) this appeal to community and to criteria of agreement is presented in Wittgenstein as a solution to the "skeptical paradox"—that if everything can be made out to be in accord with a rule, then it can also be made to conflict with it. But this skepticism with regard to justification, says Kripke (1982), applies to the isolated individual: It does not hold for one who can apply unhesitatingly but blindly a rule that the community *licenses* him or her to apply. As with application of a word in future contexts, there is no "inner state" called "understanding" that has occurred. Instead, as he says, there are language games in our lives that license under certain conditions assertions that someone means such and such and that his present application accords with what was said in the past.

My discomfort with this description arises from the centrality that Kripke (1982) places on the notion of rule as well as from the processes he privileges for bringing the child in agreement with a particular form of life that would license such blind and unhesitating obedience to the rule.

If we take the teacher in Kripke (1982) to be the representative of the community within which the child is being initiated, then I am compelled to ask whether the "agreement" in a form of life that makes the community a community of consent can be purely a matter of making the child arrive at the same conclusion or the same procedure that the adult would have applied. Rather, it appears to me that as suggested by Cavell (1990), this agreement is a much more complicated affair in which there is an entanglement of rules, customs, habits, examples, and practices and that we cannot attach salvational importance to any one of these in questions pertaining to the inheritance of culture. Wittgenstein (1953) speaks about orders or commands in several ways: There is the gulf between the order and its execution or the translation of an order one time into a proposition and another time into a demonstration and still another time into action. I do not have the sense that the agreement in forms of life requires the child to produce the same response that the teacher does. To have a future in language, the child should have been enabled to say "and after I had trained my mouth to form these signs, I used them to express my own desires." There is of course the reference in Wittgenstein (1953:para. 219) to following a rule blindly.

> "All the steps are already taken" means: I no longer have any choice. The rule, once stamped with a particular meaning, traces the line along which it is to be followed through the whole of space,—But if something of this sort really were the case, how would it help?
> No; my description only made sense of it was to be understood symbolically.—I should have said: *This is how it strikes me* [emphasis in the original].
> When I obey a rule, I do not chose.
> I obey the rule *blindly* [emphasis in the original].

And then in paragraph 221, he explains, "My symbolical expression was really a mythological description of the rule." I cannot take up fully the question here of what it is to speak mythologically or symbolically, but from the aura that surrounds the discussion of these issues, speaking of obeying a rule blindly seems to be similar to the way one speaks of wishes, plans, suspicions, or expectations as, by definition, unsatisfied or the way one speaks of propositions as necessarily true or false, that is, that they are grammatical statements. When Wittgenstein (1953) talks about rules and agreement being cousins, the kinship between them seems more complicated than Kripke's (1982) rendering of either of these two concepts allows.

I want to take an ethnographic vignette now to show the entanglement of the ideas of rule, custom, habit, practice, and example in what might be seen as constituting agreement within a particular form of life. Gilsenan (1996) has given us a stunning ethnography of violence and narrative in Akkar, a northern province of Lebanon, in the 1970s. From the several narratives in this text, one can infer the rules by which issues of vengeance and honor are articulated in the exchange of violence. Indeed, if one reads Evans-Pritchard (1940) on the feud among the Nuer, it all seems like a matter of kinship obligations that can be stated in terms of clear genealogical principles through which feuds are organized. One could imagine that a male child being socialized into such a society could be taught his place in the community in terms of *rules* that he learns, much as Kripke's child learns to follow the same procedures as the adults who are initiating him if he is to learn how to add. But here are sketches from a story from Gilsenan (1996:165–66) of how a boy becomes a man even as he is being initiated into the rules of vengeance.

> . . . the chosen young man walked, alone and in broad daylight, up the steep hill separating the quarters of the fellahins and the aghas. . . . Everyone could see him, a fact much insisted upon in accounts. At the top of the hill, he approached the small ill provisioned shop owned by Ali Bashir who was standing at the entrance looking on to the saha (public space) before him . . . the boy simply said to him: "Do you want it here in the shop or outside?" Ali ran back inside, grabbed the gun, and was shot in the wrist, his weapon falling to the ground. The killer then emptied his revolver into Ali's chest. He died instantly.
>
> Turning his back on those fellahin who had witnessed his deed, the killer—and now hero—walked back down the hill. . . . All agreed that he presented his back to the enemies in a grand disregard for his own safety. No one dared retaliate.
>
> This archetypal *geste* of agnostic indifference filled every requirement of the heroic act. He was superb in exit as he had been on entry. The aesthetics of violence were in all respects harmoniously achieved.
>
> My informants all remembered that the senior of their number, a renowned hunter, companion of the lords, and also a paternal half-brother of the wounded man, hailed the young hero when he came down to the lower mosque at the entrance of the village exclaiming: "Ya `aish! Reja`it shabb!" (Long may you live! You have returned a man!). He saluted one who had gone up the hill a boy and come down a true, arms bearing young man.

Some may argue that the scene of the instruction in Kripke (1982) bears little resemblance to the scene in which this young man is chosen by the elders as the appropriate instrument of revenge. (But then is the example of learning a procedure for solving a mathematical problem a good analogy for what it is to obey rules—a particularly clarifying one, as Kripke claims?) As for the young boy, it is his display of the aesthetics of violence that makes him a man. No one can say that he acted exactly as the elder would have acted in his place, for such scenes are also marked by contingencies of all kinds in which one might end up not a hero but a buffoon. Yet it is through the entanglement of rule, custom, habit, and example that the child has not only been initiated in the community of men but has also found his own style of being a man. In fact, the aftermath of the story of this young hero converts him into a source of danger, always looking for some replication of the originating moment of his public biography, and who finally dies in a quarrel as if he were predestined to have such a death. A consideration of that event would take us into a different region of Wittgenstein's thought: the region of the dangers that the otherness of this hero posed for the rest of the community.

Anthropological accounts have suggested that attention to Wittgenstein's discussion on rules and especially the distinction between regulative rules and constitutive rules, as suggested by Searle (1969), may give new direction to questions of how to distinguish the nature of prescriptions in ritual actions and other kind of actions. Humphrey & Laidlaw (1994) have not only written a fascinating account of the Jain ritual of *puja* (worship), they have also argued that what is distinctive about ritual prescriptions in general is the constitutive nature of rules that go to define rituals.

> Constitutive rituals create a form of activity, by defining the actions of which it is composed. We pointed out that ritualized action is composed of discrete acts which are disconnected from agents' intentions and we said that this feature of ritualization depends upon stipulation. It is this stipulation, as distinct from mere regulation which is constitutive of ritual. Only ritual acts (like valid moves in chess) count as having happened, so the celebrant moves from act to act, completing each in turn and then moving on to the next. This is unaffected by delays, false moves, extraneous happenings, or mishaps. (Humphrey & Laidlaw 1994:117)

They use this distinction then to show the wide variation in the ways of performing the ritual act of *puja*, which are nevertheless considered right by the participants because they may be said to accord with the constitutive rules. The importance of this formulation is not only that it breaks away from the distinctions between instrumental action and expressive action, or from the overdetermined view of ritual as a form of communication, but also that it addresses some puzzling features of ritual observations that are often ironed out of final ethnographic texts. I refer to the kinds of mundane activities that may be carried on during a ritual but are nevertheless not seen as constitutive of the ritual and hence can be ignored in judgments about "rightness" of a ritual act.

There is an explicit analogy in Humphrey & Laidlaw's (1994) discussion of the constitutive rules of ritual and of chess. Wittgenstein's (1953) observations on chess may be pertinent here. He has talked not only about the *rules* that constitute the game but also *customs*—for example, the use of the king to decide by lots which player gets white in drawing lots (para. 563) or not stamping and yelling while making the moves (para. 200). But Wittgenstein leads us to a different direction, one in which the entanglement of rules with customs, practices, and examples comes to the fore: "Where is the connection effected between the sense of the expression 'Lets play a game of chess' and all the rules of the game?—Well, in the list of rules of the game, in the teaching of it, in the day-to-day practice of playing" (para. 197). Wittgenstein used the analogy of a chess game to illuminate what it means for language to be governed by rules. In both language and chess there are rules that have no foundation, that is, the rules cannot be justified by reference to reality: They are autonomous, and they could be different. But there are limits to this analogy. The most important difference, as pointed out by Baker & Hacker (1980), is that the rules of chess are devised to cover every possible situation whereas our language cannot lay down the rules that will cover every conceivable circumstance. Hence there is always a gap between the rule and its execution. Could we say that the constitutive rules of ritual can cover every conceivable circumstance? I suggest that while this is sometimes the ambition of the theoreticians of ritual, as the *mimamsa* school of Indian philosophy claimed (see Das 1983), the embedding of ritual in the forms of life do not allow for this. In fact a situation of completeness would make ritual like the invented languages of Wittgenstein rather than the natural languages, which are never complete (Wittgenstein 1953:para. 18).

Baker & Hacker (1980) suggest that natural language games may be distinguished from invented ones by the fact that the former are mastered only in fragments while the latter are presented as complete languages. The feeling in reading about the builders' language is that they seemed particularly bereft of culture. I suggest it comes precisely from thinking of their language as if it were complete.

An anthropological text, we know, is marked by a certain kind of excess or a certain surplus. Call it thick ethnography, call it fascination with detail. Most ethnographies provide more than the theoretical scaffolding requires. It has been argued by some that this excess is embedded in the emplotment of ethnography as a performance (Clifford 1990). Others have spoken of the difficulty of portraying ways of life that are "experience distant" to their readers (Scheper-Hughes 1992). I suggest that this excess or this surplus expresses equally the distrust of formal rules and obligations as sources of social order or moral judgment. If culture is a matter of shared ways of life as well as of bequeathing and inheriting capabilities and habits as members of society, then clearly it is participation in forms of sociality (Wittgenstein's forms of life) that define simultaneously the inner and the outer, that allow a person to speak both within language and outside it. Agreement in forms of life, in Wittgenstein, is never a matter of shared opinions. It thus requires an excess of description to capture the entanglements of customs, habits, rules, and examples. It provides the context in which we could see how we are to trace words back to their original homes when we do not know our way about: The anthropological quest takes us to the point at which Wittgenstein takes up his grammatical investigation. It seems a natural point to break here and inquire into what are "forms of life," "criteria," and "grammatical investigation" in Wittgenstein.

## LANGUAGE AND SOCIALITY

### Forms of Life

The idea of forms of life is what has often been taken to signal the availability of Wittgenstein's thought for sociology and anthropology. Wittgenstein takes language to be the mark of human sociality: Hence human forms of life are defined by the fact that they are forms created by and for those who are in possession of language. As it is commonly understood, Wittgenstein's notion of language is to see it in the context of a lived life, its use within human institutions rather than its systematic aspects. But is this enough? Cavell (1989) has expressed anguish at the conventional views of this text, which in his understanding eclipse its spiritual struggle.

> The idea [of forms of life] is, I believe, typically taken to emphasize the social nature of human language and conduct, as if Wittgenstein's mission is to rebuke philosophy for concentrating too much on isolated individuals, or for emphasizing the inner at the expense of the outer, in accounting for such matters as meaning, or states of consciousness, or following a rule etc. . . . A conventionalized sense of form of life will support a conventionalized, or contractual sense of agreement. But there is another sense of form of life that will contest this. (Cavell 1989:41)

What Cavell finds wanting in this conventional view of forms of life is that it is not able to convey the mutual absorption of the natural and the social—it emphasizes *form* but not *life*. A hasty reading of Cavell on this point may lead readers (especially anthropologists) to the conclusion that the idea of natural is taken as unproblematic in this interpretation. Let me dwell for a moment on this point. Cavell suggests a distinction between what he calls the ethnological or horizontal sense of form of life and its vertical or "biological" sense. The first captures the notion of human diversity—the fact that social institutions, such as marriage and property, vary across societies. The second refers to the distinctions captured in language itself between "so-called 'lower' or 'higher' forms of life, between say poking at your food, perhaps with a fork, and pawing at it or pecking at it" (Cavell 1989:42). It is the vertical sense of the form of life that he suggests marks the limit of what is considered human in a society and provides the conditions of the use of criteria as applied to others. Thus the criteria of pain does not apply to that which does not exhibit signs of being a form of life—we do not ask whether a tape recorder that can be turned on to play a shriek is feeling the pain. Cavell suggests that the forms of life have to be accepted but that it is in the sensibility of *Investigations* to call not so much for change as for transfiguration. I am going to leave aside, for the moment, the relevance of this question for or against skepticism. Instead I want to point to a direction in which this distinction between the horizontal and the vertical may also show what happens at the limit of each. What is it that human societies can represent as the limit? Here I draw from some of my own work to show how such an idea may strike a chord on the keys of anthropological imagination.

For some years now I have been engaged in trying to understand the relation between violence (especially sexual violence) in everyday domestic contexts and violence in the extraordinary context of riots during political events, such as the Partition of India or the violence against Sikhs following the assassination of then prime minister Indira Gandhi. In one of my recent papers (Das 1996) I have tried to conceptualize the violence that occurs within the weave of life as lived in the kinship universe, as having the sense of a *past continuous*, while the sudden and traumatic violence that was part of the Partition experience seems to have a quality of frozen time to it. In discussing the life of a woman, Manjit, who had been abducted and raped during the Partition and subsequently married to an elderly relative, I argued that while the violence she was submitted to by her husband was something sayable in her life, the other violence was not (could not be?) articulated. The horizontal and vertical limits seemed to me to be particularly important in formulating this difference.

> It is this notion of form of life, i.e. its vertical sense of testing the criteria of what it is to be human, that I think is implicated in the understanding of Manjit's relation to the non-narrative of her experience of abduction and rape. Men beat up their wives, commit sexual aggression, shame them in their own self creations of masculinity—but such aggression is still "sayable" in Punjabi life through various kinds of performative gestures and through story telling (I do not mean to say that it is therefore passively accepted—indeed the whole story of Manjit shows that it is deeply resented). Contrast this with the fantastic violence in which women were stripped and marched naked in the streets; or the magnitudes involved; or the fantasy of writing political slogans on the private parts of women. This production of bodies through a violence that was seen to tear apart the very fabric of life, was such that claims over culture through disputation became impossible. If words now appear, they are like broken shadows of the motion of everyday words. . . . Such words were indeed uttered and have been recorded by other researchers, but it was as if one's touch with these words and hence with life itself had been burnt or numbed. The hyperbolic in Manjit's narration of the Partition recalls Wittgenstein's sense of the conjunction of the hyperbolic with the groundless. (Das 1996:23)

I have taken this example in some detail because it suggests, through means of an ethnography, that while the range and scale of the human is tested and defined and extended in the disputations proper to everyday life, it may move through the unimaginable violence of the Partition (but similar examples are to be found in many contemporary ethnographies of violence) into forms of life that are seen as not belonging to life proper. Was it a man or a machine that plunged a knife into the private parts of a woman after raping her? Were those men or animals who went around killing and collecting penises as signs of their prowess? There is a deep moral energy in the refusal to represent some violations of the human body, for these violations are seen as being against nature, as defining the limits of life itself. The precise range and scale of the human form of life is not knowable in advance, any more than the precise range of the meaning of a word is knowable in advance. But the intuition that some violations cannot be verbalized in everyday life is to recognize that work cannot be performed on these within the burned and numbed everyday. We reach through a different route the question of what it is to have a future in language. I believe that the limits of the forms of life—the limits at which the differences cease to be criterial differences—are encountered in the context of life as it is lived and not only in the philosopher's reflections on it. These are the times in which one may be so engulfed by doubts of the other's humanity that the whole world may appear to be lost.

In his work on violence, Daniel (1997) calls this point the counterpoint of culture: "The counterpoint I speak of is something that resists incorporation into the harmony of a still higher order of sound, sense, or society" (p. 202). Other accounts of violence similarly suggest that certain kinds of violence cannot be incorporated into the everyday (Langer 1991, 1997; Lawrence 1995): But then how is everyday life to be recovered?

## Everyday Life and the Problem of Skepticism

In describing what he calls the counterpoint to culture, Daniel (1997) interviewed several young men in Sri Lanka who were members of various militant movements and who had killed with ropes, knives, pistols, automatic fire, and grenades. But it is clear from his powerful descriptions that what was traumatic for Daniel in hearing these accounts of killings was the manner in which the styles of killing and the wielding of words was interwoven. Here are some extracts.

> He was hiding in the temple when we got there. . . . This boy was hiding behind some god. We caught him. Pulled him out. . . The boy was in the middle of the road. We were all going round and round him. For a long time. No one said anything. Then someone flung at him with a sword. Blood started gushing out. . . . We thought he was finished. So they piled him on the tyre and then set it aflame. (Daniel 1997:209)

Daniel finds the shifting between the we and the they to be noteworthy, but what stuns him is the next thing that happened.

> This was the early days of my horror story collecting and I did not know what to say. So I asked him a question of absolute irrelevance to the issue at hand.

Heaven knows why I asked it; I must have desperately wanted to change the subject or pretend that we had been talking about something else all along. "What is your goal in life?" I asked. The reply shot right back: "I want a video (VCR)." (Daniel 1997:209)

Wittgenstein's sense of exile of words is what comes to mind here. It is not that one cannot understand the utterance but that in this context when these words are spoken, they seem not to belong—they seem not to have a home. Daniel's (1997) turning away from this event is a desperate one. He lurches toward a hope (p. 211)—the rustle of a hope—wherever it may be found and whenever it may be found. And it is found in a scene of almost quiet domesticity. He recounts an event in the 1977 anti-Tamil riots in which a Sinhala woman is journeying on a train; she is in one part of the compartment, and on another seat is a retired Tamil schoolteacher. A mob began to drag out Tamils and to beat them. The Sinhala woman, recognizable easily as a Kandyan Sinhalese because of the way she wore her *sari,* moved over to his side and quietly held his hand. Some members of the mob entered the compartment, but the gesture of conjugal familiarity persuaded them that the gentleman was a Sinhala, so they proceeded elsewhere. Daniel (1997) thinks of the gesture of the woman as a sign, gravid with possibilities. But what are these possibilities? From a Wittgensteinian perspective, these seem to be only possibilities of recovery through a descent into the ordinariness of everyday life, of domesticity, through which alone the words that have been exiled may be brought back. This everydayness is then in the nature of a return—one that has been recovered in the face of madness.

The intuition of everydayness in Wittgenstein appears therefore quite different from, say, that of Schutz (1970), who emphasizes the attention to the "paramount reality" of the everyday and conceptualizes transcendence as momentary escapes from these attentions. It is also different from the many attempts made in recent years to capture the idea of the everyday as a site of resistance (Jeffery & Jeffery 1996; Scott 1985, 1990). My sense of these approaches is that there is a search in these attempts for what Hans Joas (1996) calls the creativity of social action. Rather than searching for agency in great and transgressive moments of history, it is in the everyday scripts of resistance that it is thought to be located. There is nothing wrong with this way of conceptualizing the everyday, for it has the advantage of showing society to be constantly made rather than given. The problem is that the notion of the everyday is too easily secured in these ethnographies because they hardly ever consider the temptations and threats of skepticism as part of the lived reality and hence do not tell us what is the stake in the everyday that they discovered.

In Cavell's (1984, 1988, 1990) rendering of Wittgenstein's appeal to the everyday, it is found to be a pervasive scene of illusion and trance and artificiality of need. This, to my understanding and experience, is because both the temptations and threats of skepticism are taken out from the study of the philosopher and reformulated as questions about what it is to live in the face of the unknowability of the world (for my purposes especially the social world). Let me depart for the moment from the kinds of scenes of violence that have been described by Das (1990b, 1995a,b, 1997), Daniel (1997), Langer (1991, 1997), Lawrence (1995), and many others. These scenes may appear exceptional to many. Instead, I ask, is the sense of the unknowability of the social world also encountered in other contexts, in the context of normal suffering, so to speak? Some scholars suggest that this unknowability of the social world has been made more acute by the processes of modernity or globalization (see Appadurai 1996:158–78), whereas my sense is that uncertainty of relations is part of human sociality as it is embedded within certain weaves of social life (Das & Bajwa 1994). But let me take my example from an anthropological classic.

Evans-Pritchard's (1937) account of witchcraft among the Azande has often been seen as that society's way of dealing with misfortune rather than with the essential unknowability of other minds. For instance, Taussig (1992) has written,

> To cite the common phraseology, science like medical science, can explain the "how" and not the "why" of disease; it can point to chains of physical cause and effect, but as to why I am struck down now rather than at some other time, or as to why it is me rather than someone else, medical science can only respond with some variety of probability theory which is unsatisfactory to the mind which is searching for certainty and for significance. In Azande practice, the issue of "how" and "why" are folded into one another; etiology is simultaneously physical, social, and moral. . . . My disease is a social relation, and therapy has to address that synthesis of moral, social, and physical presentation. (p. 85)

It is true that Evans-Pritchard (1937) veered in several directions in accounting for the Azande beliefs in witchcraft, including questions about the rationality of the Azande. If we pay some attention to the descriptions that he provides, however, we find not so much a search for certainty and significance, but rather a shadow of skepticism regarding other minds (Chaturvedi 1998). Moreover, this skepticism seems to have something to do with the manner in which language is deployed.

Evans-Pritchard (1937) reports that those who speak in a roundabout manner and are not straightforward in their conversation are suspected of witchcraft: "Azande are very sensitive and usually in the lookout for unpleasant allusions to themselves in apparently harmless conversation" (p. 111). Very often they find double meaning in a conversation (p. 116) and assume that harm would be done to them, as in the following instance recounted by Evans-Pritchard shows:

> An old friend of mine, Badobo of the Akowe clan, remarked to his companions who were cleaning up the government road around the settlement that he

had a found a stump of wood over which Tupoi had stumbled and cut himself a few days previously when he had been returning late at night from a beer feast. Badobo added to his friends that they must clear the road well, as it would never do for so important a man as Tupoi to stumble and fall if they could help it. One of Tupoi's friends heard this remark and repeated it to his father who professed to see a double meaning in it and to find a sarcastic nuance in Badobo's whole behaviour. (pp. 115–16)

A pervasive uncertainty of relations is indicated by many factors: the Azande aphorism "One cannot see into a man as into an open woven basket"; the Azande belief that one cannot be certain that anyone is free from witchcraft; and the care that a Zande man takes not to anger his wives gratuitously because one of them may be a witch and by offending her he may bring misfortune on his head. And although a Zande would not state that he is a witch, Evans-Pritchard (1937) reports that one may know nothing about the fact of one's own witchcraft (p. 123). Uncertainty about other minds here is linked to a certain alienation from the language that one speaks, as if the language always revealed either more or less than the words spoken. Indeed it is the intimate knowledge of how Azande converse and interpret one another's meanings that Evans-Pritchard (1937) considers important to an understanding of how attributions of witchcraft are made: "Once a person has been dubbed a witch anything he says may be twisted to yield a secret meaning. Even when there is no question of witchcraft Azande are always on the look-out for double meaning in their conversations" (p. 131). Here we have the intuition of the humans as if one of the aspects under which they could be seen is as victims of language that could reveal things about them of which they were themselves unaware.

This idea touches upon the Wittgensteinian theme of language as experience (and not simply as message). He takes examples of punning, or of a feel for spelling: If you did not experience the meaning of words (as distinct from only using them), then how could you laugh at a pun? The sense is of being controlled by the words one speaks or hears or sees rather than of controlling them. There is some similarity to Austin's (1975) concerns with performatives especially with perlocutionary force.

A context that I consider decisive for understanding these themes is that of panic rumor. I shall take the example of anthropological studies of rumor to show how the theme of the unknowability of the social world and the theme of humans becoming victims to words come to be connected. Although rumor is not an example that figures in Wittgenstein, I propose that one may find connections in the way in which there is a withdrawal of trust from words and a special vulnerability to the signifier in the working of rumor and the exile of words under skepticism.

Several historians and anthropologists have emphasized the role of rumor in mobilizing crowds (Rudé 1959, 1964; Thompson 1971). Historians of the subaltern school have seen it as a special form of subaltern communication, "a necessary instrument of rebel transmission" (Guha 1983:256). Other characteristics of rumor identified by Guha (1983) are the anonymity of the source of rumor, its capacity to build solidarity, and the overwhelming urge it prompts in listeners to pass it on to others. The excessive emphasis on communication, however, obscures the particular feature of language that is often brought to the fore when we consider the susceptibility to rumor during times of collective violence (Das 1990a,b, 1998; Tambiah 1996). Bhabha (1995) has posed the question in an incisive manner: What is special to rumor as distinct from other forms of communication? He goes on to isolate two of its aspects. The first is rumor's enunciative aspect, and the second its performative aspect. "The indeterminacy of rumour," he says, "constitutes its importance as a social discourse. Its intersubjective, communal adhesiveness lies in its enunciative aspect. Its performative power of circulation results in its contiguous spreading, an almost uncontrollable impulse to pass it on to another person" (p. 201). He concludes that psychic affect and social fantasy are potent forms of potential identification and agency for guerrilla warfare and hence rumors play a major role in mobilization for such warfare.

Other views of rumor, especially those derived from mass psychology, have emphasized the emotional, capricious, temperamental, and flighty nature of crowds (Le Bon 1960). Something common in these situations is an essential grammatical feature (in Wittgenstein's sense) of what we call rumor: that it is conceived to spread. Thus while images of contagion and infection are used to represent rumor in elite discourse, the use of these images is not simply a matter of the elite's noncomprehension of subaltern forms of communication. It also speaks to the transformation of language; namely, that instead of being a medium of communication, language becomes communicable, infectious, causing things to happen almost as if they had occurred by nature. In my own work on rumor in a situation of mounting panic of communal riots, I have identified the presence of an incomplete or interrupted social story that comes back in the form of rumor and an altered modality of communication (Das 1998). The most striking feature of what I identify as panic rumors (in which it is difficult to locate any innocent bystanders) is that suddenly the access to context seems to disappear. In addition, there is an absence of signature in panic rumors so that rumor works to destroy both the source of speech and the trustworthiness of convention. (This characteristic seems to distinguish perlocutionary force from illocutionary force. In the latter, trust in convention and law allows promises to be made and marriages to be contracted.) Cavell (1982) has invoked *Othello* as the working out of a skeptical problematic. The mounting panic in which the medium of rumor leads to the dismantling of relations of trust at times of communal riots seems to share the tempo of skepticism. Once a thought of a certain vulnerability is lost, as Cavell shows (1982, 1994), the world is engulfed without limit.

Unlike Cavell, Williams (1996) considers skeptical doubts to be unnatural doubts. He holds that the experience that we know nothing about the real world has to arise from a particularly striking experience of error. Yet no experience of error, he argues, can give us a feel of a total loss of the world. The threat of skepticism for Cavell lies in our feeling that our sensations may not be of this world: But for Williams this threat arises in the philosophizing of Cavell because he has internalized a contentious theoretical view. Cavell, on the other hand, suggests in all his work that skeptical doubt arises in the experience of living. Skepticism is for him a site on which we abdicate our responsibility toward words—unleashing them from our criteria. Hence his theme of disappointment with language as a human institution (Cavell 1994). The site of panic rumor suggests similarly a subjection to voice (comparable to Schreber's subjection to the voices he heard). There seems a transformation from social exchange to communal trance, and if this trance is to be resisted, one has to lead works back to the everyday, much as one might lead a horse gone suddenly wild to its stables.

## COMPLEXITY OF THE INNER

It might be tempting to suppose that the unknowability of the social world essentially relates to the unknowability of the other. But the question of skepticism in Wittgenstein does not posit an essential asymmetry between what I know about myself and what I know about the other. His famous arguments against the possibility of a private language is not that we need shared experience of language to be communicable to one another but that without such a sharing I will become incommunicable to myself. The inner for Wittgenstein is thus not an externalized outer—there is no such thing as a private inner object to which a private language may be found to give expression. This view is not to be construed as Wittgenstein's denial of the inner but rather that inner states are, as he says, in need of outward criteria (Johnston 1993, Schulte 1993). Thus what appear often in our language as intrinsic differences between different kinds of inner states are basically grammatical differences in disguise. Part II of *Philosophical Investigations* begins with the following:

> One can imagine an animal angry, frightened, unhappy, happy, startled, but hopeful? And why not?
> A dog believes his master is at the door. But can he also believe his master will come day after to-morrow? And *what* can he not do here?—How do I do it?—How am I supposed to answer this?
> Can only those hope who can talk? Only those who have mastered the use of a language? That is to say, the phenomena of hope are modes of this complicated form of life. (Wittgenstein 1953:174)

The reference to language here is obviously not to suggest that those who have mastered the use of a language have acquired the logical skills necessary to express hope but rather that grammar tells us what kinds of objects hope and grief are. Thus the inner states are not distinguished by some reference to content but by the way we imagine something like an inner state for creatures complicated enough to possess language (and hence culture). I would like to illustrate this idea with reference to the discussion of belief and then follow the illustration with a discussion on pain.

## Belief

The question of belief in *Philosophical Investigations* appears as the asymmetry between the use of first-person indicative and third-person indicative. Two observations in the second part of this text are crucial. The first is "If there were a verb meaning to believe falsely it would not have a first person indicative" (Wittgenstein 1953:190). The second, closely related to that observation, is "I say of someone else 'He seems to believe. . . .' And other people say it of me. Now, why do I never say it of myself, not even when others *rightly* say it of me?—Do I not myself see or hear myself, then?" (Wittgenstein 1953:191).

Wittgenstein is asking, What does a belief look like from the inside? When he says that it is possible to misinterpret one's own sense impressions but not one's beliefs, he is not referring to the content of an inner experience but rather to the grammatical impossibility of inferring one's belief (or one's pain) introspectively. That is why he says that if there were a verb that meant "to believe falsely," it would lack a first-person present indicative. Wittgenstein is not stating a metaphysical truth about belief here, but a grammatical one. Even when it is possible to make such statements as "It is raining and I do not believe it," the grammar of the term belief does not allow us to make these statements, for we cannot imagine a context for such statements—they violate the picture of the inner in the grammar of the word belief.

Anthropologists have wrestled with the problem of belief in the context of translation of cultures. The problem has been persistent: When anthropologists attribute belief statements to members of other cultures (i.e. non-Western cultures), are they making a presumption that a common psychological category of most Western languages and cultures is to be treated as a common human capacity that can be ascribed to all men and women? Such questions have been asked of several categories of emotion (see Lutz & Abu- Lughod 1990, Lutz & White 1986), but the case of belief is special because it has been anchored to questions of universal human rationality on the one hand (Gellner 1970, Lukes 1977) and common human condition of corporeality on the other (Needham 1972).

As far as the side of universal rationality is concerned, the puzzle for many scholars seems to be to account for the apparent irrationality of beliefs like that of witchcraft or of other scandalous statements: for example, that the Nuer believe that twins are birds (Evans-Pritchard 1956). In his polemic against the anthropological tendency to find coherence in such statements, Gellner (1970) states that only through an excessive charity of translation can such beliefs be rendered intelligible. He seems to suggest that they are either to be taken as evidence of prelogical thought or as ideological devices to hide the power exercised by privileged classes in society (the latter point is made with regard to the category of *barak* among Moroccan Berbers). Gellner warns that "[t]o make sense of the concept is to make non-sense of the society" (1970:42). Asad (1990) has given a devastating critique of Gellner's method, especially of the manner in which in his haste to pronounce on the irrationality of such concepts he actually manages to evade all questions on their use in everyday life of the society under consideration. Wittgenstein's general view seems to be that there are many empirical assertions that we affirm without specially testing them and that their role is to establish the frame within which genuine empirical questions can be raised and answered (Cavell 1969, Williams 1996). If this scaffolding is questioned, then we are not in the realm of mere differences of opinion. Thus to someone who is offering an explanation of the French Revolution I will probably not ask whether she has any proof that the world is not an illusion. If such a question is asked, we shall have to say that our differences are noncriterial differences that cannot be resolved by adducing more evidence.

Thus, for the Azande there are genuine empirical questions about how one is to know whether one's illness is to be attributed to the witchcraft of a neighbor or a wife. The final empirical proof of the cause is provided by the postmortem of a body to show whether witchcraft substance is found in the body. Obviously if one shifts this kind of question to the kind of question in which we ask a Zande if he or she believes witches to exist, one is shifting the frame completely. In this revised frame (in which we are certain that witches do not exist), one can ask questions only about witchcraft beliefs, or witchcraft craze, but not about superiority of one kind of witchcraft medicine over another or whether unknowing to oneself one may be a witch—a source of danger to one's neighbors and friends. What does this mean for the practice of ethnography? One strategy is that adopted by Fevret-Saada (1977), who felt that to open her mouth on issues of witchcraft in Bocage was to become implicated in utterances that constitute the practices of witchcraft. Thus her ethnography becomes an account of the complicated relation that the ethnographer comes to have with the "bewitched" and the "unwitchers." It does not raise questions about the rationality or truth of witchcraft beliefs because there is no way in which such questions may be asked from within the language games of the Bocage. The other strategy is to think of ethnography as a persuasive fiction (Strathern 1988). I shall return to the question of translation. For the moment let me say only that the disappointment in the indeterminate place of anthropological knowledge is perhaps like the disappointment with language itself, as somehow natural to the human. This disappointment is a great Wittgensteinian theme and should perhaps lead us to think that the reason why so-called contradictions in belief do not paralyze one in any society is that one's relation to the world is not on the whole that which would be based on knowing (Cavell 1969, 1982, 1994, 1995).

## Belief and Corporeality

Needham's (1972) enquiry on the status of belief statements and the problem of translation is on entirely different lines. He states,

> If they [beliefs] are assertions about the inner states of individuals, as by common usage they would normally be taken to be, then, so far as my acquaintance with the literature goes, no evidence of such states, as distinct from the collective representations that are thus recorded, is ever presented. In this case we have no empirical occasion to accept such belief-statements as exact and substantiated reports about other people. (p. 5)

Needham goes on to address this problem through Wittgenstein's idea of grammatical investigation and particularly that an inner process stands in need of outward criteria. However, his notion of grammatical does not appear to be that of Wittgenstein's—it is hasty and confuses philosophical grammar with the notion of grammar in linguistics (perhaps it is comparable to a case of surface grammar in Wittgenstein, but I am not on sure ground here). The burden of Needham's argument is that even when we are convinced that a person genuinely believes what he says he believes, our conviction is not based on objective evidence of a distinct inner state: "We can thus be masters, as we are, of the practical grammar of belief statements yet remain wholly unconvinced that these rest on an objective foundation of psychic experience" (Needham 1972:126).

Now if I am correct that the inner is not like a distinct state that can be projected to the outer world through language in Wittgenstein but rather like something that lines the outer, then language and the world (including the inner world) are learned simultaneously. Neeedham is right in suspecting that a grammar of belief in the English language and in forms of life in which beliefs are held, confessed, defended, solicited, guarded, and watched over may be different from the way in which similar concepts through which the world and the word are connected in the woof and weft of some other society's life. However, the solution Needham (1972) offers to the problem of translation—that some inner states are accompanied by bodily expressions (such as body resemblance, natural posture, gesture, facial expression) whereas other inner states (such as belief) have no specific behavioral physiognomy—is to misread grammatical differences as intrinsic differences in the content of experience. Wittgenstein's way of describing this idea was to say that the body is a picture of the soul or that the soul stands next to the body as meaning stands next to the word.

We are thus not going to get out of the problem of translation by an appeal to certain human capacities that are real and universal, as contrasted with others that are artificial constructs of various cultural traditions, as proposed by Needham (1972). That is not to say that we do not *read* the body but rather that we depend on grammar to tell us what kind of an object something is. Inserting the centrality of the body in human society is important not in inferring internal states of mind but in the intuition of language as a bodying forth, as in Wittgenstein saying, "Sometimes a cry is wrenched out of me." Let us now consider this question with regard to pain.

## Pain and Private Objects

Wittgenstein on pain is a major philosophical and anthropological issue, yet there is no highway of thought available to traverse. It would have to be from the side roads and the meandering in uncharted territories that one would find the relation between Wittgenstein's thoughts on pain and the anthropological task of studying forms of sociality. Consider Cavell (1997), who says,

> *Philosophical Investigations* is the great work of philosophy of this century whose central topic may be said to be pain, and one of its principal discoveries is that we will never become clear about the relation of attributions of the concept of pain, nor about any of the concepts of consciousness, nor of any unconsciousness—neither of my attribution of pain to myself nor of my attribution of pain to others—without bringing into question the endless pictures we have in store that prejudicially distinguish what is internal or private to creatures (especially ones with language, humans) from what is external or public to them. (p. 95)

In some of the most creative anthropological writing on this issue, we find the disappointment with language to somehow be integral to the experience of pain (Good et al 1992). Wittgenstein emphatically denies the possibility of a private language in this case, as in other cases, that refers to what is internal or private to creatures. But what this means is that for Wittgenstein the statement "I am in pain" is not (or not only) a statement of fact but is also an expression of that fact (Cavell 1997). The internal, as I have stated, is not an internalized picture of the outer—nor is the external only a projection of the internal. In this context, what is unique about pain is the absence of any standing languages either in society or in the social sciences that could communicate pain, yet it would be a mistake to think of pain as essentially incommunicable (Das 1997). At stake here is not the asymmetry between the first person ("I am never in doubt about my pain") and the third person ("you can never be certain about another person's pain"), but rather that to locate pain I have to take the absence of standing languages as part of the grammar of pain. To say "I am in pain" is to ask for acknowledgment from the other, just as denial of another's pain is not an intellectual failure but a spiritual failure, one that puts our future at stake: "One might even say that my acknowledgement is my presentation, or handling of pain. You are accordingly not at liberty to believe or disbelieve what it says—that is the one who says it—our future is at stake" (Cavell 1997:94). Some passages from *The Blue and Brown Books* (Wittgenstein 1958) are remarkable in the notion of language as embodied or bodying forth.

> In order to see that it is conceivable that one person should have pain in another person's body, one must examine what sorts of facts we call criterial for a pain being in a certain place. . . . Suppose I feel that a pain which on the evidence of the pain alone, e.g. with closed eyes, I should call a pain in my left hand. Someone asks me to touch the painful spot with my right hand. I do so and looking around perceive that I am touching my neighbour's hand. . . . This would be pain felt in another's body. (p. 49)

I have interpreted this passage (see Das 1995a,b, 1997) to propose that Wittgenstein's fantasy of *my pain* being located in *your body* suggests either the intuition that the representation of shared pain exists in imagination but is not experienced, in which case I would say that language is hooked rather inadequately to the world of pain or that the experience of pain cries out for this response to the possibility that my pain could reside in your body and that the philosophical grammar of pain is about allowing this to happen. As in the case of belief, I cannot locate your pain in the same way as I locate mine. The best I can do is to let it happen to me. Now it seems to me that anthropological knowledge is precisely about letting the knowledge of the other happen to me. This is how we see Evans-Pritchard finding out about himself that he was "thinking black" or "feeling black" though he resisted the tendency to slip into idioms of witchcraft. In the Introduction to this paper, I talked of Wittgenstein's idea of a philosophical problem as having the form "I do not know my way about." In his remarks on pain, to find my way is similar to letting the pain of the other happen to me. My own fantasy of anthropology as a body of writing is that which is able to receive this pain. Thus while I may never claim the pain of the other, nor appropriate it for some other purpose (nation building, revolution, scientific experiment), that I can lend my body (of writing) to this pain is what a grammatical investigation reveals.

## THE DARKNESS OF THIS TIME

In the preface to *Philosophical Investigations*, Wittgenstein (1953) wrote, "It is not impossible that it should fall to the lot of this work, in its poverty and darkness of this time, to bring light into one brain or another—but, of course, it is not likely" (p. vi). Bearn (1998) writes that the destructive moment of the *Investigations* threatens the fabric of our daily lives, so it is more destructive than textbook skepticism of the philosopher or the café skeptic. If in life, said Wittgenstein, we are surrounded by death, so too in the health of our understanding we are surrounded by madness (Wittgenstein 1980:44). Rather than forcefully excluding this voice of madness, Wittgenstein (1953) returns us to the everyday by a gesture of waiting. "If I have exhausted the justifications, I have reached bedrock, and my spade is turned. Then I am inclined to say: 'This is simply what I do (handle)' " (para. 217). In this picture of the turned spade, we have the picture of what the act of writing may be in the darkness of this time. The love of anthropology may yet turn out to be an affair in which when I reach bedrock I do not break through the resistance of the other. But in this gesture of waiting, I allow the knowledge of the other to mark me. Wittgenstein is thus a philosopher of both culture and the counterpoint of culture.

**Visit the *Annual Reviews home page* at http://www.AnnualReviews.org.**

## Literature Cited

Appadurai A. 1996. *Modernity at Large: Cultural Dimensions of Globalization*, pp. 48–66, 158–78. Minneapolis: Univ. Minn. Press

Asad T. 1990. The concept of cultural translation in British social anthropology. In *Genealogies of Religion: Discipline and Reasons of Power in Christianity and Islam*, pp. 171–200. Baltimore/London: Johns Hopkins Univ. Press

Austin JL. 1975. *How to Do Things with Words*. Cambridge, MA: Harvard Univ. Press

Baker JP, Hacker PMS. 1980. *Wittgenstein: Meaning and Understanding*, Vol. 1. Oxford: Blackwell

Bearn GCF. 1977. *Waking to Wonder: Wittgenstein's Existential Investigations*. New York: State Univ. NY Press

Bhabha HK. 1995. By bread alone: signs of violence in the mid-nineteenth century. In *Location of Culture*, pp. 198–212. London: Routledge

Cavell S. 1969. *Must We Mean What We Say?* Cambridge, UK: Cambridge Univ. Press

Cavell S. 1982. *The Claim of Reason: Wittgenstein, Skepticism, Morality, and Tragedy*. Oxford: Clarendon

Cavell S. 1984. Existentialism and analytical philosophy. In *Themes Out of School: Effects and Causes*, pp. 195–234. San Francisco: North Point

Cavell S. 1988. The uncanniness of the ordinary. In *In Quest of the Ordinary: Lines of Skepticism and Romanticism*, pp. 153–78. Chicago: Univ. Chicago Press

Cavell S. 1989. Declining decline: Wittgenstein as a philosopher of culture. In *This New Yet Unapproachable America: Lectures After Emerson After Wittgenstein*, pp. 29–77. Chicago: Univ. Chicago Press

Cavell S. 1990. The argument of the ordinary: scenes of instruction in Wittgenstein and in Kripke. In *Conditions Handsome and Unhandsome: The Constitution of Emersonian Perfectionism*, pp. 64–101. Chicago: Univ. Chicago Press

Cavell S. 1994. A *Pitch of Philosophy*. Cambridge, MA: Harvard Univ. Press

Cavell S. 1995. Notes and afterthoughts on the opening of Wittgenstein's *Investigations*. In *Philosophical Passages: Wittgenstein, Emerson, Austin, Derrida*, pp. 125–87. Oxford: Blackwell

Cavell S. 1997. Comments on Veena Das's essay "Language and body: transactions in the construction of pain." See Kleinman et al 1997, pp. 93–99

194    DAS

Chatterji R, Mehta D. 1995. A case study of a communal riot in Dharavi, Bombay. *Relig. Soc.* 42(4):5–26

Chaturvedi R. 1998. *Witchcraft and other minds.* M.Phil. diss. Univ. Delhi, Delhi, India. 120 pp.

Clasteres P. 1974. *Société contre l'état.* Paris: Les Editions Minuit

Clifford J. 1990. On ethnographic allegory. In *Writing Culture: The Poetics and Politics of Ethnography,* ed. J Clifford, GE Marcus, pp. 98–122. Delhi, India: Oxford Univ. Press

Daniel EV. 1997. *Charred Lullabies: Chapters in an Anthropography of Violence.* Princeton: Princeton Univ. Press

Das V. 1983. The language of sacrifice. *Man* 18:445–62

Das V, ed. 1990a. *Mirrors of Violence: Communities, Riots and Survivors in South Asia.* Delhi, India: Oxford Univ. Press

Das V. 1990b. Our work to cry: your work to listen. See Das 1990a, pp. 345–99

Das V. 1990c. Voices of children. *Daedalus.* Special issue on *Another India,* pp. 48–65

Das V. 1995a. *Critical Events: An Anthropological Perspective on Contemporary India,* pp. 175–97. Delhi, India: Oxford Univ. Press

Das V. 1995b. Voice as birth of culture. *Ethnos* 60(3–4):159–81

Das V. 1996. *Violence and the work of time.* Presented at Plenary Sess. Violence. Univ. Edinburgh, Edinburgh, Scotland

Das V. 1997. Language and body: transactions in the construction of pain. See Kleinman et al 1997, pp. 67–93

Das V. 1998. Official narratives, rumour, and the social production of hate. *Soc. Ident.* 4(1):1–23

Das V, Bajwa RS. 1994. Community and violence in contemporary Punjab. In *Purushartha* (Special issue on *Violences et Non-Violences en Inde),* ed. D Vidal, G Tarabout, E Mayer, 16:245–59

Diamond C, ed. 1976. *Wittgenstein's Lectures on the Foundations of Mathematics, Cambridge 1939.* Ithaca, NY: Cornell Univ. Press

Durkheim E. 1976. (1915). *The Elementary Forms of the Religious Life.* London: Allen & Unwin

Evans-Pritchard EE. 1937. *Witchcraft, Oracles and Magic Among the Azande.* Oxford: Clarendon

Evans-Pritchard EE. 1940. *The Nuer: A Description of the Modes of Livelihood and Political Institutions of a Nilotic People.* Oxford: Clarendon

Evans-Pritchard EE. 1956. *Nuer Religion.* Oxford: Clarendon

Fevret-Saada J. 1977. *Les mots, la mort, les sorts.* Paris: Gallimard

Gellner E. 1970. Concepts and society. In *Rationality,* ed. BR Wilson, pp. 18–49. Oxford: Blackwell

Gilsenan M. 1996. *Lords of the Lebanese Marches: Violence and Narrative in an Arab Society.* Berkeley: Univ. Calif. Press

Good MJD, Brodwin PE, Good B, Kleinman A, eds. 1992. *Pain as Human Experience: An Anthropological Perspective.* Berkeley: Univ. Calif. Press

Guha R. 1983. *Elementary Aspects of Peasant Insurgency in Colonial India.* Delhi, India: Oxford Univ. Press

Humphrey C, Laidlaw J. 1994. *The Archetypal Actions of Ritual. A Theory of Ritual Illustrated by the Jain Act of Worship.* Oxford: Clarendon

Jeffery P, Jeffery R. 1996. *Don't Marry Me to a Plowman! Women's Everyday Lives in Rural North India.* Boulder/Oxford: Westview

Joas H. 1996. *The Creativity of Action.* Transl. J Gaines, P Keast. Chicago: Univ. Chicago Press

Johnston P. 1993. *Wittgenstein: Rethinking the Inner.* London/New York: Routledge

Kleinman A, Das V, Lock M, eds. 1997. *Social Suffering.* Berkeley: Univ. Calif. Press

Kripke S. 1982. *Wittgenstein on Rules and Private Language.* London: Oxford Univ. Press

Langer L. 1991. *Holocaust Testimonies: The Ruins of Memory.* New Haven: Yale Univ. Press

Langer L. 1997. The alarmed vision: social suffering and holocaust atrocity. See Kleinman et al 1997, pp. 47–67

Lawrence P. 1995. *Work of oracles: overcoming political silences in Mattakalapu.* Presented at Srilankan Conf., 5th, Indiana

Le Bon G. 1960. (1895). *The Crowd: A Study of the Popular Mind.* New York: Viking

Lévi-Strauss C. 1969. (1964). *The Raw and the Cooked: Introduction to a Science of Mythology,* Vol. 1. New York: Harper & Row

Lukes S. 1977. Some problems about rationality. In *Essays in Social Theory,* pp. 122–74. London: Macmillan

Lutz C, White GM. 1986. The anthropology of emotions. *Annu. Rev. Anthropol.* 15:405–36

Lutz CA, Abu-Lughod L, eds. 1990. *Language and the Politics of Emotion,* pp. 1–24. Cambridge, UK: Cambridge Univ. Press

Needham R. 1972. *Belief Language and Experience.* Oxford: Blackwell

Nieuwenhuys O. 1996. The paradox of child labor and anthropology. *Annu. Rev. Anthropol.* 25:237–51

Reynolds P. 1995. 'Not known because not looked for': ethnographers listening to the young in Southern Africa. *Ethnos* 60(3–4): 159–81

Rudé G. 1959. *The Crowd in the French Revolution.* Oxford: Clarendon

Rudé G. 1964. *The Crowd in History, 1730–1848.* New York: Wiley

Scheper-Hughes N. 1992. *Death Without Weeping: The Violence of Everyday Life in Brazil.* Berkeley: Univ. Calif. Press

Schulte J. 1993. *Experience and Expression: Wittgenstein's Philosophy of Psychology.* Oxford: Clarendon

Schutz A. 1970. *On Phenomenology and Social Relations: Selected Writings*, ed. HR Wagner. Chicago: Univ. Chicago Press

Scott JC. 1985. *Weapons of the Weak.* New Haven: Yale Univ. Press

Scott JC. 1990. *Domination and the Arts of Resistance: Hidden Transcripts.* New Haven: Yale Univ. Press

Searle JR. 1969. *Speech Acts.* Cambridge, UK: Cambridge Univ. Press

Strathern M. 1988. *The Gender of the Gift: Problems with Women and the Problems with Societies in Melanesia.* Berkeley: Univ. Calif. Press

Tambiah SJ. 1996. *Leveling Crowds: Ethnonationalist Conflicts and Collective Violence in South Asia.* Berkeley: Univ. Calif. Press

Taussig M. 1992. Reification and the consciousness of the patient. In *The Nervous System*, pp. 83–111. New York: Routledge

Thompson EP. 1971. The moral economy of the English crowd in the eighteenth century. *Past Present* 50:76–126

Tylor EB. 1974. (1878). *Primitive Culture.* New York: Gordon

Williams M. 1996. *Unnatural Doubts.* Princeton: Princeton Univ. Press

Wittgenstein L. 1953. *Philosophical Investigations.* New York: Macmillan

Wittgenstein L. 1958. *The Blue and Brown Books.* Oxford: Blackwell

Wittgenstein L. 1980. *Culture and Value*, ed. GH von Wright. Transl. P Winch. Oxford: Blackwell

*Annu. Rev. Anthropol. 1998. 27:197–221*
*Copyright © 1998 by Annual Reviews. All rights reserved*

# THE COMPARATIVE DEMOGRAPHY OF PRIMATES: With Some Comments on the Evolution of Life Histories

*Timothy B. Gage*

Anthropology Department, University at Albany, State University of New York, Albany, New York 12222; e-mail: tbg97@albany.edu

KEY WORDS: mortality, fertility, population dynamics, modeling, stability

### ABSTRACT

This chapter reviews the current state of knowledge concerning the demography of primates. It compiles demographic systems (mortality and fertility estimates) for four broad grades of primates: New World monkeys, Old World monkeys, chimpanzees, and humans. The characteristics of each system, including its demographic stability, are presented and discussed. The environmentally induced variation in human and nonhuman primate vital rates are explored whenever possible. Findings include (*a*) that more data are needed particularly with respect to nonhuman primate fertility, (*b*) that human demographic systems are the least stable, and (*c*) that *Pan troglodytes* demography is probably evolutionarily derived from the general primate pattern.

## INTRODUCTION

The literature on the evolution of life history characteristics can be divided into two basic categories. One is empirically based and proceeds by examining the associations among various life history characteristics; for example, the correlation of age at maturity, body weight, and brain size (Harvey & Clutton-Brock 1985). The second body of literature is theoretical and examines the demo-

0084-6570/98/1015-0197$08.00

graphic conditions necessary for the evolution of characteristics such as age at maturity, length of the reproductive span, and senescence (Stearns 1992). In general, however, there are only a few of what might be called "midlevel" studies in which good empirical demographic data are available to operationalize the theoretical models and examine the evolution of life histories in detail. The purpose of this review is to draw together the available empirical data on the demography of the primates to identify the needs for additional empirical work and to begin the development of midlevel models of the evolution of primate life histories.

The approach taken here is borrowed largely from human demography. Over the past 30 years, human demographers have found that model demographic systems are particularly useful for advancing the study of human demographic systems, especially where data are difficult to obtain, incomplete, or biased. The result has been the development of a number of "systems of model life tables" (Coale et al 1983) and "model fertility schedules" (Coale & Trussell 1974). These models have proved their worth for (*a*) estimating vital rates when demographic data are inadequate or biased and (*b*) operationalizing theoretical or simulation models of human population dynamics. For example, data on a population may be sufficient to estimate the level of mortality, but not the age patterns of mortality. In such a case, a Coale and Demeny model life table can be selected from those at the appropriate level of mortality (Howell 1979, Gage et al 1984). Alternatively, model life tables have proved useful in simulation studies and/or other testing procedures where generic human life tables are required (Gage et al 1986). Overall, these models have led to a clearer understanding of human demographic patterns and their variability by providing a standard to which new data can be compared and a point of departure for developing more accurate models.

The basic assumption that underlies the application of model demographic systems is that vital rates are similar across populations of the same species (Howell 1976) and perhaps across families or even orders. For example, the Coale and Demeny model life tables are based almost entirely on the observed mortality of European populations (Coale et al 1983). These data were chosen because they are considered to be the most accurate demographic data available. However, the models have been regularly applied to non-European populations where accurate data are lacking. The assumption is that the patterns of mortality characteristic of Europeans are also characteristic of other human groups. If all human groups shared the same genes and environments, this assumption would clearly be reasonable. While there is currently little evidence that human groups differ with respect to the genetics influencing demographic characteristics, it is clear that all human populations do not share similar environments. As a consequence, the uniformitarian view is overly simplistic and clearly incorrect at some level of specificity. The question is, What level of specificity? Consequently, several models are described here that include more than one species. These models should also prove useful if only as a point of departure for new, better, and more specific models.

In this paper, model demographic systems for several broad grades of primates are developed and compared. In most cases, the primary sources of data are captive and/or closely observed (provisioned) populations. Most, but not all, of the reliable demographic data on these species come from populations of this type. The assumption, as in the human case, is that demographic patterns are a result of the interaction of endogenous factors (genetic or epigenetic) and environmental factors. The demography of primates living in captivity must therefore represent the interaction of the captive environment (ad lib feeding, modern veterinary care) with the endogenous substrate, while primates living in the wild are a product of the interaction of the natural environment (natural feeding systems, no veterinary care) with the endogenous substrate. These differences are not completely dissimilar to the variation in human demographic patterns observed between (a) the human populations of developed nations (overfed, modern medical care) and (b) prehistoric populations and contemporary developing nations (more traditional feeding systems, little or no modern medical care). Consequently, careful development and cautious use of model primate demographic systems, even on captive animals, should provide better estimates of the characteristics and range of variation of demographic patterns among the primates.

The specific aims are (a) to review the model life table systems available for primate populations, (b) to begin to develop model fertility schedules for primate populations, (c) to combine the mortality and fertility models into demographic systems for primate populations, (d) to examine the dynamics of these systems, and (e) to briefly discuss their evolutionary implications. Systems are presented for four grades of primates: New World monkeys (NWMs), Old World monkeys (OWMs), chimpanzees (*Pan*), and prehistoric human populations. Comparative models for contemporary human populations are included. When models are available for both sexes, only the female data are presented. This presentation is consistent with simple models of population dynamics, which are all female dominant.

## REVIEW OF PRIMATE MODEL LIFE TABLE SYSTEMS

This section documents the similarities and differences in mortality among the four primate grades. In general there appears to be a single mammalian mortality pattern that is relatively consistent across species. Mortality is high at birth and declines rapidly with age, typically reaching a minimum prior to reproductive maturity. The risk of mortality then begins to increase at an ever-increasing rate into the older ages (Caughly 1977). Two controversial features of the mammalian mortality curve are (*a*) an accident hump in mortality just prior to the reproductive age and (*b*) the trajectory of mortality among the oldest individuals. The accident hump occurs in some human life tables and may occur in nonhuman primate life tables as well. In human affairs it is not a particularly important risk factor (Gage & Mode 1993). The accident hump is most common in low-mortality populations of European extraction (notably Australia, the United States, and Canada) and is most pronounced in males. It is curious that in humans this hump occurs not at the age of biological sexual maturity but at an older age, just prior to marriage, the age of social sexual maturity. Good data on the accident hump in the nonhuman primates are lacking. Luder (1993) argues for the existence of this feature in *Macaca fascicularis*, but his evidence is based on a single death. Additional research is necessary to determine the importance of this feature on the mortality curve in nonhuman primates. In any event, mortality at these ages is generally low. With respect to the second feature, that the general mammalian mortality pattern increases at older ages suggests that senescence is a universal feature of mammalian populations. However, it is possible that mammalian mortality does not increase at an ever-increasing rate at the oldest ages, as is implied by the definition of senescence. This deceleration in the rate of increase affects only the extreme oldest ages, for which little data are available even on humans. Consequently this characteristic need not concern us here.

Because of the general similarity of mammalian age patterns of mortality, most (if not all) mammalian life tables can be described through use of a single mathematical model, the Siler model (Siler 1979). This model is the sum of the three types of mortality originally defined by Pearl & Miner (1935). It has been applied successfully to many human populations (Siler 1983, Gage & Dyke 1986, Gage 1990, Gage & Mode 1993, O'Connor 1995), a number of primate populations (Dyke et al 1986; Gage & Dyke 1988, 1993; Dyke et al 1993, 1995), and several nonprimate species (Siler 1983). It is thus ideal for the development of model life table systems and the comparative study of mortality patterns, both within and across mammalian species. Furthermore, it decomposes mortality into components that are theoretically appropriate for studies of the evolution of life histories (Finch et al 1990, Kirkwood 1985, Promislow 1991). The mathematical function describing this model is

$$h_t = a_1 e^{-b_1 t} + a_2 + a_3 e^{b_3 t},$$

1.

where ht is the risk of mortality at age t, a1 is the risk of immature mortality at the moment of birth, b1 is the rate of decline with age of this risk, a2 is a simple constant risk, a3 is the risk of senescent mortality at the moment of birth, and b3 is the rate of increase in senescent mortality with age.

The immature component of this model represents the decline in mortality with age during early life. This component of mortality is assumed to result from biological adjustments to the environment (outside the womb) that are eventually outgrown. It is a negative Gompertz function that has the corresponding property that survivorship at age infinity is greater than 0 (Siler 1979, Gage & Dyke 1986). The proportion of individuals surviving the immature component is

$$l'_\infty = e^{-\frac{a_1}{b_1}}$$

2.

It is sometimes difficult to estimate a1 and b1 precisely because in some populations mortality declines very rapidly with age and an insufficient number of ages are reported to accurately estimate two parameters. However, the ratio of these parameters can be estimated precisely, and thus the overall risk of immature mortality can be estimated.

The second component of mortality was originally proposed by Makeham as an addition to the Gompertz mortality model (Makeham 1860). This component is age independent and is often considered to represent extrinsic and accidental causes of death (Finch et al 1990, Kirkwood 1985).

The third and final component of the Siler model is the well-known Gompertz mortality model, which accounts for the increase in mortality at the older ages. It represents the intrinsic process of senescence. In particular, $b_3$ is the rate of aging. A value of $b_3$ greater than 0.0 is considered to be definitive evidence for senescence (Strehler 1977, Economos 1982, Finch et al 1990, Kirkwood 1985, Promislow 1991).

Model life tables have been developed for a variety of nonhuman and human primate populations through the Siler model. The basic strategy is to collect as many observed life tables as possible for each primate grade, fit them to the Siler model, and obtain an average across all of the observed life tables. For human populations, where many observed life tables at various levels of mortality are available, averages have been obtained by ordinary least squares regression while controlling for expectation of life.

## New World Monkeys

The model life table for the smaller New World monkeys (NWMs) (Dyke et al 1993) is based on four life tables, each representing a different species: *Callithrix jaccus* (common marmoset), *Leontopithecus rosalia* (golden lion tamarin), *Saguinus fuscicollis* (saddleback tamarin), and *Saguinus oedipus* (cottontop tamarin). All populations represent captive populations either at the Oak Ridge Associated Universities Marmoset Research Center or reported in the International Golden Lion Tamarin Studbook (Smithsonian Institution, National Zoological Park). Mortality estimates are based on natural deaths only.

Deaths resulting from nonnatural causes, research procedures, and so on are controlled through standard censoring procedures. Sex-specific models have not been developed.

## Old World Monkeys

The model life table for the larger Old World monkeys (OWMs) (Gage & Dyke 1988, 1993) is also based on life tables from several populations. These populations include four *Macaca mulatta* (rhesus macaque) populations, two *Macaca fuscata* (Japanese macaque) populations, and two populations of mixed *Papio* ssp (mostly yellow baboons). One of the *M. fuscata* populations is wild, one *M. fuscata* and one *M. mulatta* population were provisioned, and the remaining populations are captive. For captive and provisioned animals, research-related deaths are censored and not incorporated into the model life table estimates. Sex-specific tables have not been developed.

## Chimpanzees

The model life table for chimpanzees (Dyke et al 1995) is based on three captive populations of *Pan troglodytes* (common chimpanzee). The data were pooled and a single life table developed, one for each sex. These colonies are primarily breeding facilities, and no deaths are known to have resulted from research or experimental procedures. Consequently, censored techniques were not employed. Sex-specific tables are available, but only the female model is presented here.

## Prehistoric Humans

The model life table for prehistoric humans (from O'Connor 1995) is included here because the observed age pattern of mortality of these populations differs significantly from that of contemporary human populations. It is not yet clear whether these differences are due to environmental differences between the two types of population or result simply from biased data (Gage 1998). The prehistoric life table is based on 12 reconstructed life tables. Each of these life tables is derived through the use of standard methods, with the assumption that the population is stationary. An advantage of using several life tables to develop this model is that while the assumption of stationariness is unlikely for any particular population, it is more likely to be correct when several populations, some of which may be declining while others are increasing, are combined. Because of difficulties in sexing the skeletal remains of infants and children, sex-specific tables are not available.

## Contemporary Humans

There are many model life table systems for contemporary human populations. However, for comparative purposes it is simplest to use the Coale and Demeny

"West model" life tables, which represent the approximate human average age pattern of mortality from expectations of life of 20 years to about 80 years. These model tables have been studied through the Siler model by Gage & Dyke (1986). Two additional contemporary life tables are included here. These represent mortality in the national populations of Costa Rica (Arriaga 1968) and Sweden (Keyfitz & Fleiger 1971) in the mid-1960s. Sex-specific tables are available, but only the female models are employed here.

The Siler parameter values of all of these model life tables are presented in Table 1.

Comparisons of the model life tables for captive populations of NWMs, OWMs, and *Pan* and developed populations of humans (Swedish data) are shown in Figure 1. In general, infant mortality declines from NWMs to OWMs and *Pan* and finally to humans of a developed nation. OWMs and *Pan* have approximately similar infant mortality rates, although the mortality in *Pan* appears to be slightly higher (Table 1). Adult survivorship becomes progressively more rectangular (Figure 1*a*) from NWM to OWM to *Pan* and finally to the Swedish life table. Expectation of life increases in the same order.

In all cases the minimum risk of mortality appears to occur immediately after the first year of life. This result is an unrealistic characteristic of the Siler model. According to accurate data, in low-mortality human populations, mortality typically declines until the age of 10 or so. Perhaps the negative Gompertz is not the ideal function to describe the decline in infant mortality. Comparisons among the model life tables should thus be limited to the overall size of immature mortality and not its age pattern. On the other hand, mammalian mortality is universally low at these ages. As a result, cross-grade variation in risk of mortality is also low compared to mortality during other periods of the life span.

**Table 1**  Parameter estimates for primate model life tables[a]

| Model | $a_1$ | $b_1$ | Proportion | $a_2$ | $a_3$ | $b_3$ | $e_0$ |
|---|---|---|---|---|---|---|---|
| New World monkey | 19.242 | 25.468 | 0.4698 | 0.0000 | 0.1027 | 0.0798 | 2.98 |
| Old World monkey | 0.936 | 8.330 | 0.8937 | 0.0000 | 0.0190 | 0.0682 | 15.83 |
| *Pan* | 2.864 | 21.311 | 0.8742 | 0.1669e-1 | 0.5260e-4 | 0.1469 | 29.44 |
| Prehistoric | 0.270 | 0.723 | 0.6887 | 0.0093 | 0.0041 | 0.0767 | 19.65 |
| Costa Rica | 0.116 | 1.237 | 0.9096 | 0.1110e-2 | 0.3353e-4 | 0.0997 | 65.08 |
| Sweden | 0.287 | 28.595 | 0.9900 | 0.4679e-3 | 0.7419e-5 | 0.1160 | 76.07 |
| West 1 | 0.692 | 1.042 | 0.5146 | 0.1448e-1 | 0.7707e-3 | 0.0687 | 20.00 |
| West 23 | 0.814 | 54.759 | 0.9852 | 0.3774e-3 | 0.10632e-4 | 0.1125 | 75.00 |

[a] $a_1$, the risk of immature mortality at the moment of birth; $b_1$, the rate of decline with age of immature mortality; *proportion*, the proportion surviving the immature component of mortality; $a_2$, age-independent risk of mortality; $a_3$, risk of senescent mortality at the moment of birth; $b_3$, rate of increase in senescent mortality with age (the rate of aging).

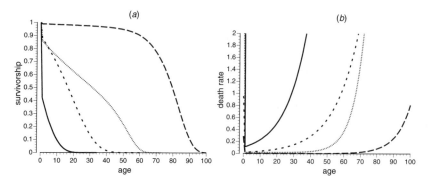

*Figure 1*   Comparison of model life tables for the various grades of primates: New World monkey (*solid line*), Old World monkey (*medium dashed line*), *Pan* (*short dashed line*), and human (*long dashed line*). Panel *a* presents the survivorships, while panel *b* shows the death rates.

Of greater interest are the age trends in senescence, that is, mortality at the older ages. In particular, the $a_3$ parameter decreases and the rate of aging ($b_3$) increases from NWM, OWM, to humans (Table 1). The death rate curves nest nicely within each other (Figure 1*b*). This trend appears to be general across the primates. The *Pan* model, however, differs in that it has a relatively low $a_3$ parameter but the highest rate of aging. The result is that senescent mortality does not increase until the end of life, at which point it increases rapidly. In fact, the death rate for *Pan* eventually crosses that for OWMs. Whether the evolution of senescence in *Pan* differs from that in the remaining primates or is simply an artifact of current data and/or analytic methods will require additional research. Further discussion of the evolutionary implications of this issue is presented later.

Comparison of environmental effects suggest that wild (and developing-nation) populations display higher mortality than captive (and developed-nation) populations. Comparison between the model OWM survivorship (primarily captive and provisioned) and the observed survivorship of wild *M. fuscata* (Sugiyama & Ohsawa 1982) are presented in Figure 2*a*. A similar comparison of the model *Pan* survivorship and a life table for Gombe chimpanzees (Mode 1988) is shown in Figure 2*b*. Figure 2*c* presents a comparison of prehistoric, Coale and Demeny West Level 1, Costa Rican, and Swedish survivorship. No data on wild NWMs are available. NWMs may be the exception to the rule that wild populations experience higher mortality than captive populations. NWMs do not appear to have adapted well to the captive environment. In all cases for which there are data, however, the wild (developing) populations have higher mortality (lower survivorship) than their captive (developed) counterparts. This finding is particularly true for infants. There is less consis-

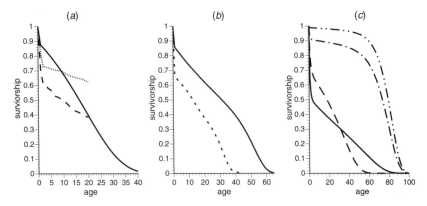

*Figure 2*   Comparison of model life tables based on captive, provisioned, and developed populations with wild, prehistoric, and developing populations. Panel *a* presents a comparison of wild (*long dashed line*) and provisioned (*short dashed line*) OWM survivorships with the Old World monkey model (*solid line*). Panel *b* is a comparison of wild chimpanzee survivorship (*dashed line*) with the *Pan* model (*solid line*). Panel *c* is a comparison of the prehistoric model (*dashed line*), Coale and Demeny West Level 1 (*solid line*), Costa Rican (*long-short dashed line*), and Swedish (*long-short-short dashed line*) survivorship.

tency among adult mortality. In two cases, wild OWM and the West Level 1 life table, adult survivorship tends to converge at older ages with lower-mortality, captive OWM and the Swedish life tables, respectively. This finding indicates that lower age-specific mortality occurs at some point during the adult ages in the wild OWM and West Level 1 life table. On the other hand, in wild *Pan* and the prehistoric model life tables, survivorship appears to parallel that of captive *Pan* and Sweden. In these cases the length of the life span actually appears to be shorter in wild *Pan* and the prehistoric model tables.

This lack of convergence has caused human demographers to question the validity of the prehistoric mortality pattern. It is generally assumed that high-mortality human populations have high infant mortality, but once infancy is outgrown, longevity is similar in both high- and low-mortality populations. This pattern is indicated by the West Level 1 and the Swedish model life tables. This view is derived from the European mortality experience, where mortality this high is associated with high-density urban areas in the early 1800s. It has been argued that mortality in low-density populations may not follow this pattern (Gage 1998, Lovejoy et al 1977). Consequently, it is not clear whether the prehistoric pattern is a result of biased data resulting from problems with aging skeletal data or whether the differences between West Level 1 and the prehistoric pattern are due to different environmental conditions. That *Pan* provides a second example increases the likelihood that these differences are at least in part due to environmental conditions. On the other hand, the wild *Pan* life table may also be in error. The sample size on which this life table is based is small, so longevity may be underestimated. Additional data, particularly on wild populations, will be necessary to more fully document the range of variation for the various grades of primates.

## REVIEW OF PRIMATE FERTILITY PATTERNS

Less work has been done to model consistently the age patterns of fertility of primates than to model consistently the mortality of primates. This situation may be because fertility is thought to be easier to estimate from data and hence models are not needed. In any event, no models of fertility are available for nonhuman primates, and only a few models are available for humans (Coale & Trussell 1974, Brass 1975). To begin to rectify this situation, several preliminary models are developed here. The data presented in the above model life tables have been screened as carefully as possible, but the fertility data below have not been verified as carefully. Consequently, these fertility models should be considered preliminary.

Human demographers and biologists do not agree on the definitions of several terms regarding fertility. Because this paper spans both literatures, some explanations of the conventions used here are in order. In human demography, fertility refers to realized births, while fecundity indicates the capability of giving birth. In biology, fecundity is generally defined as realized births, and fertility indicates the capability of giving birth. In the discussion below, fertility will be used to indicate realized births, while the capability of giving birth is not discussed at all.

Unlike mortality, which displays a single mammalian pattern, fertility appears to have two patterns. In the first case, fertility increases rapidly with age, reaches a peak, and then declines at the older ages. The alternative pattern resembles the first except that fertility does not decline at the older ages. The decline in fertility at the older ages in the first pattern is sometimes called reproductive senescence. Fertility patterns without senescence have been observed in sheep (Caughly 1977) and mysticete whales (Promislow 1991). Promislow argues that species that lack reproductive senescence may engage in little parental investment. In general, however, primates appear to display reproductive senescence [NWM (Tardif & Ziegler 1992), OWM (Dyke et al 1986), *Pan* (Sugiyama 1994), and humans (Coale & Trussell 1974, Brass 1975)]. Based on the assumption that all primates follow the senescent fertility pattern, the Brass polynomial method of graduating fertility was selected for use here. This method has been used successfully to graduate (or smooth) the fertility of Przewalski's horse (Gage 1995). However, additional applications are necessary to determine its general applicability to the analysis of fertility in nonhuman species and primates in particular.

Brass's polynomial, modified here for use on populations with varying life spans and life histories (Gage 1995), is

$$m_t = c(t-s)(s+w-t)^2 \qquad \qquad 3.$$

where $t$ is age, $s$ is the age at first reproduction, $w$ is the length of the reproductive period, $c$ is a coefficient describing the level of fertility, and $m_t = 0.0$ when $t < s$ or $t > s + w$. The constraints on $m_t$ are necessary to avoid negative values of fertility outside the fecund ages, which are biologically meaningless. This function, like the Siler model, can be fitted through the use of nonlinear least squares regression. Although largely untested, this model is convenient because it directly estimates several parameters of particular interest in life history analysis—the initial age of reproduction ($s$) and the length of the reproductive period ($w$)—independently of the level of fertility. The fertility data used to develop model schedules are as follows.

## New World Monkeys

The data on New World monkeys are unpublished data on the fertility of captive NWMs from the Oak Ridge Associated Universities Marmoset Research Center. (I am grateful to S Tardif for permission to use these results.)They include data on *Callithrix jaccus* (common marmoset), *Saguinus fuscicollis* (saddleback tamarin), and *Saguinus oedipus* (cotton-top tamarin). These data are not corrected for exposure to risk of fertility; that is, caging arrangements and colony management decisions may have influenced fertility rates. However, the primary emphasis of this colony was breeding, so it is unlikely that fertility was intentionally limited. In any event, problems with exposure to risk are likely to influence the overall level of fertility, although they might also affect the age patterns of fertility if caging or management decisions are made on an age-specific basis.

## Old World Monkeys

The data on Old World monkeys are based on *M. mulatta* (rhesus macaque) births at the Wisconsin Regional Primate Center from 1972 to 1982 (Dyke et al 1986). The period 1962–1971 was excluded because the dam of a number of births was unknown. However, overall fertility declined 25% to 30% from the 1962–1972 decade. Consequently, the potential maximum level of fertility is considerably higher.

## Chimpanzees

The data on chimpanzees consist of observations on wild *Pan troglodytes* (common chimpanzee) (Sugiyama 1994). Consequently this model represents a natural fertility rate for this species.

## Contemporary Humans

Two schedules on contemporary humans are examined, including the fertility of the national populations of Costa Rica (1966) and Sweden (1967) (Keyfitz & Fleiger 1971). These schedules were chosen to match the Costa Rican and Swedish life tables, presented above. The Costa Rican example represents a high, but not extremely high, natural fertility rate (Campbell & Wood 1988), characteristic of developing populations. Sweden, on the other hand, displays the low (controlled) fertility rate characteristic of developed populations.

All five of these data sets have been graduated through the Brass polynomial method and a standard nonlinear fitting routine. Because this method has not been well tested on primates, several examples of the fitted model against the raw data are presented in Figure 3. A comparison of all five fitted models is shown in Figure 4.

The prereproductive span increases from 1 year to 15 years across NWM to OWM to *Pan* and finally to human (Table 2). There is, of course, evidence for a large secular trend in human age at menarche; that is, a historical decline in menarche from about 17 to perhaps 12 years of age with modernization (Short 1976). A similar phenomenon is known to occur in *Pan*. Among captive *Pan,* first birth occurs at about 7 years of age (Fragaszy & Bard 1997), while estimates for first parturition in wild *Pan* are closer to 12 years (Sugiyama 1994, Tutin 1994). The fitted *Pan* model predicts an age at first birth of about 9 years, although the first birth in this particular wild population occurred at age 12.

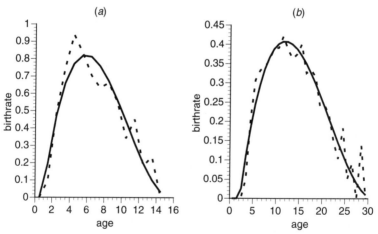

*Figure 3*   Raw (*dashed line*) and fitted (*solid line*) fertility data. Panel *a* shows the results for New World monkeys, while panel *b* indicates the results for Old World monkeys. The parameter estimates for all five models are presented in Table 2, and a comparison of all five fitted models is shown in Figure 4.

Consequently, two *Pan* fertility schedules are studied below. The model has been used "as is" for captive *Pan,* but the age-specific fertilities prior to age 12 have been set to 0 for wild *Pan.* Similar environmental effects probably occur in the rate of maturation of NWMs and OWMs as well and need to be explored. However, the exact differences between *Pan* and humans become important with respect to population dynamics.

The length of the reproductive period generally increases from NWM to OWM to human (Table 2). However, the reproductive span of *Pan* is 6 to 8 years longer than that of humans. On the other hand, the end of the reproductive career as estimated by the Brass polynomial is similar for *Pan* and humans (Table 2). Given the small sample of *Pan* births, the predicted end of *Pan's reproductive career appears reasonable. Eight births were observed in the age category 40 to 44 (Sugiyama 1994). It is likely that births occasionally occur at even older ages in Pan.*

Little significance should be placed on the level of fertility indicated by these models. Those models based on captive animals may reflect colony management issues more than the biological or social limits. Of course, the fertility of humans varies widely as well, from natural fertility levels almost twice that of the Costa Rican example presented here to controlled fertility illustrated by the Swedish example (Campbell & Wood 1988). The fertility of nonhuman primates needs to be studied in a variety of environments, wild and captive,

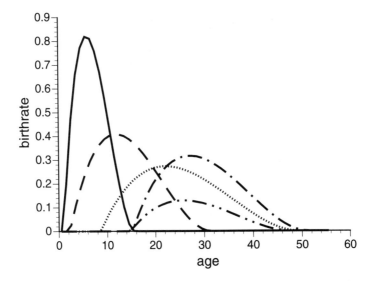

*Figure 4*  Comparison of model fertility schedules for the various grades of primates: New World monkeys (*solid line*), Old World monkeys (*long dashed line*), *Pan* (*short dashed line*), Costa Rican (*long-short dashed line*), and Swedish (*long-short-short dashed line*).

**Table 2**  Parameter estimates for primate model fertility tables[a]

| Model | s | w | c | TFR |
|---|---|---|---|---|
| New World monkey | 0.938 | 14.690 | 0.17494e-02 | 6.803 |
| Old World monkey | 2.220 | 29.044 | 0.11252e-03 | 6.647 |
| *Pan* | 8.629 | 40.516 | 0.27690e-04 | 6.217[b] |
| Costa Rica | 15.181 | 35.947 | 0.45970e-04 | 6.398 |
| Sweden | 14.810 | 32.829 | 0.24572e-04 | 2.379 |

[a]$s$, Age at first reproduction; $w$, length of the reproduction period; $c$, level of fertility; TFR, total fertility rate.

[b]5.871 if ages prior to 12 in *Pan* (wild) are ignored.

too. Nevertheless, it is interesting to note that the total fertility rates (TFRs), that is, the number of offspring born to an individual that lives throughout its reproductive career, are remarkably similar, about six (Table 2).

## THE COMPARATIVE DYNAMICS OF PRIMATE DEMOGRAPHIC SYSTEMS

The dynamics of a population depends on the specifics of the combined mortality and fertility regimes. Population dynamics can be divided into three issues: (*a*) the growth rate of the population, (*b*) the stability of the population, and (*c*) density dependence. Only the first two issues are considered here. The growth rate of a population is dependent largely on the levels of mortality and fertility. Consequently, estimates of growth rate are subject to the combined limitations of the levels of mortality and fertility. The stability, or ergoticity, of the population is defined here as the rate at which the age structure of a population returns to the stable age structure after a perturbation. This stability varies among human populations, and it depends on the rate of growth of the population and the age patterns of mortality and fertility. However, the standard procedure in demography is to examine the stability of populations while holding the intrinsic rate of increase constant at 0.0. When examined in this manner, the differences in stability among populations are due only to the characteristic age patterns of mortality and fertility. Because our models of mortality and fertility capture the characteristic age patterns for the different species to a better extent than the levels of mortality and fertility, the analyses of stability are more reliable than the estimated growth rates. This section briefly presents the relationship between mortality and fertility schedules, reviews the growth rates characteristic of the grades of primates, and explores the variation in stability properties among the grades. The demographic systems examined are as follows:

1. New World Monkeys. This system is based on the mortality and fertility models for NWMs presented above.

2. Old World Monkeys. This system consists of the mortality and fertility models for OWMs presented above.

3. *Pan* (captive). This system includes the mortality and fertility models for *Pan* presented above. Age at first parturition is assumed to be 9 years.

4. *Pan* (wild). This system combines estimates of Gombe mortality (Mode 1988) with the *Pan* fertility model. Age at first parturition is set to 12 years.

5. Prehistoric. This system is based on the prehistoric mortality model combined, for want of more appropriate data, with the Costa Rican fertility schedule.

6. West Level 1. This system consists of West Level 1 mortality and Costa Rican fertility.

7. Costa Rica (mid-1960s). This system includes the modeled Costa Rican mortality and fertility patterns.

8. Sweden (mid-1960s). This system incorporates the modeled Swedish mortality and fertility patterns.

The dynamics of populations can be studied mathematically by solving for the roots of the net maternity function (NMF), which is

$$NMF = l_t m_t \hspace{4cm} 4.$$

where $l_t$ is female survivorship, $m_t$ is fertility based on female births only, and $t$ is age. The analyses were carried out through the use of two programs originally designed for the analysis of human demographic data in 5-year age categories, LOTKA and ZEROES (Keyfitz & Fleiger 1971). These programs were modified by the author to analyze data by single year of age. The sex ratio at birth is assumed to be 50:50 in all cases.

In most mammals, the end of the reproductive life span is thought to be closely associated with the end of the life span. Humans are considered to be one of a few species with a significant postreproductive life span. However, in most of the captive examples, the models display significant levels of postreproductive survival; that is, survivorship at the end of the reproductive life span is 0.15 or greater. NWMs are the exception here, with survival to age 16 about 0.02. The proportion surviving is much higher in the contemporary human systems (0.81 in Costa Rica and 0.95 in Sweden). On the other hand, these rates of postreproductive life span are likely to be a recent phenomenon among humans. The prehistoric system indicates that survival at the end of the reproductive span, about age 50, is only 0.03. Even if West Level 1 is used instead, only 0.16 of individuals survive to postreproductive ages. In wild *Pan,* survivorship is essentially 0.0 a few years before the estimated end of the reproductive span.

The reproductive characteristics and growth rates for the various model demographic systems are presented in Table 3. The net reproductive rate

(NRR) is the number of same-sex children a woman contributes to the next generation. The NRR is simply the integral or sum of the NMF. Thus an NRR of 1 indicates that a female has replaced herself and the population is stationary; that is, growth is 0.0. Larger and smaller NRRs indicate population growth and decline, respectively. The intrinsic rate of increase ($r$) is the rate of growth of the population provided that the age structure is in its stable state. Also shown are the mean age of reproduction, the variance in age at reproduction, and the generation length. By LOTKA's definition the mean age of reproduction and the generation length are equivalent in a stationary population (Keyfitz & Fleiger 1971).

The vital rates for captive NWM and wild *Pan* models are clearly not sufficient to maintain population growth. In NWMs, the rate of decline is almost 7% per year ($r = -0.068$). The rate of decline for wild *Pan* is 1% per year. In either case, these populations would rapidly go extinct. Apparently the level of mortality is lower or the level of fertility is higher under the conditions in which these organisms normally survive. The OWM and captive *Pan* models, on the other hand, indicate healthy 6% and 3% rates of population growth, respectively. Interestingly, the prehistoric demographic system indicates a small positive rate of growth, while the growth rate of the West Level 1 system is slightly negative despite that the levels of mortality (expectations of life) and fertility are identical. Thus, slightly lower levels of fertility are necessary to maintain growth in human populations having the prehistoric age pattern of mortality compared to the extrapolated West pattern of mortality. The Costa Rican and Swedish models reflect the growth characteristics of contemporary high- and low-fertility populations, respectively. The generation lengths range from about 6 years for NWMs to 29 years for humans, as is expected.

Table 3    Reproductivity of the primate model demographic systems

| Model | Net reproductive rate | Mean age of reproduction[a] | Variance in age at childbearing | $r$[b] | Generation length |
|---|---|---|---|---|---|
| New World monkey | 0.679 | 5.447 | 6.476 | −.068 | 5.668 |
| Old World monkey | 1.902 | 12.214 | 28.062 | 0.056 | 11.424 |
| *Pan* (captive) | 1.770 | 23.542 | 60.661 | 0.025 | 22.782 |
| *Pan* (wild) | 0.824 | 21.344 | 32.637 | −.009 | 21.491 |
| Prehistoric | 1.043 | 27.097 | 40.293 | 0.002 | 27.066 |
| West Level 1 | 0.996 | 28.493 | 48.420 | 0.000 | 28.499 |
| Costa Rica | 2.796 | 29.455 | 51.385 | 0.036 | 28.530 |
| Sweden | 1.160 | 27.907 | 43.041 | 0.005 | 27.792 |

[a]Based on the assumption that the net maternity function is normally distributed. It is the generation length of the stationary population.

[b]Intrinsic rate of increase.

The age structure of mammalian populations (or any population that has a nontrivial prereproductive span) is ultimately dependent only on the age patterns of mortality and fertility. If these patterns remain constant, the age structure will approach a stable age structure regardless of the initial age structure. Consequently, a population that is perturbed from its stable age structure will tend to return to this age structure. An example is the baby boom that followed World War II. In this case fertility increased, possibly a reaction to the war itself, and created a perturbation in the age structure of many contemporary nations. This increase in fertility can be viewed as a wave that runs up the age structure (from the youngest age classes) until it reaches the fertile years, at which point it begins to reappear in the youngest age classes once again. The amplitude of this wave declines over time, and the age structure eventually returns to its stable age distribution. This stable distribution is completely defined by the mortality and fertility patterns. However, the rate at which a population approaches this stable state following a perturbation also depends on the details of the age-specific fertility and mortality patterns, in addition to the size of the perturbation. This rate of return, called stability or ergoticity, is known to vary among contemporary human populations (Coale 1972, Keyfitz & Fleiger 1971), and thus it can be expected to vary among the grades of primates.

Among human populations, the predominant wavelength of a perturbation in the age structure is about the length of a generation, and the rate of decline in the amplitude of the wave depends on the variance in age at childbearing (Table 3). In general, the greater the variance in age at childbearing, the greater the stability. However, these rules need not apply to nonhuman populations (Coale 1972). For example, in theory, the wavelength of disturbances in the age structure can be up to twice as long as the generation time, if the prereproductive span is less than some particular limit (Coale 1972, Wachter 1991). This has never been observed in human populations, suggesting that the prereproductive span among humans is always greater than this limit.

To extend these generalizations to include the grades of primates considered here, estimates of the characteristic wavelengths and half-lives of waves in the age distribution are presented in Table 4. In each example, the NMF was normalized on the integral of the NMF. Thus the intrinsic rate of increase, which is represented by the first root, is 0.0 and the remaining roots are uninfluenced by the growth rate of the demographic system. To save space, only the next four pairs of complex roots (in order of their importance, i.e. their absolute value) are presented here.

Comparisons suggest that in general, nonhuman primate demographic systems tend to be more stable than human demographic systems. First, the periodicity of the dominant wave produced by a perturbation in the age structure is about one generation in human demographic systems (Tables 3 and 4). However, in most of the model nonhuman primate systems presented, the periodic-

**Table 4**   Stability of the primate model demographic systems

| | Root | | | | |
| | Real part | Imaginary part | Wavelength | Half-life | Relative decline[a] |
|---|---|---|---|---|---|
| New World monkeys | | | | | |
| 2–3 | .5395 | ±.4307 | 9.3209 | 1.8702 | 0.03 |
| 4–5 | .3073 | ±.5567 | 5.8890 | 1.5313 | 0.07 |
| 6–7 | .0627 | ±.6065 | 4.2788 | 1.4008 | 0.12 |
| 8–9 | −.1806 | ±.5677 | 3.3427 | 1.3384 | 0.18 |
| Old World monkeys | | | | | |
| 2–3 | .8073 | ±.2799 | 18.8160 | 4.4069 | 0.05 |
| 4–5 | .6984 | ±.4145 | 11.7258 | 3.3314 | 0.09 |
| 6–7 | .5825 | ±5274 | 8.5348 | 2.8744 | 0.13 |
| 8–9 | .4550 | ±6174 | 6.7123 | 2.6122 | 0.17 |
| *Pan* (captive) | | | | | |
| 2–3 | .9051 | ±.1954 | 29.5380 | 9.0140 | 0.10 |
| 4–5 | .8511 | ±.2976 | 18.6682 | 6.6964 | 0.18 |
| 6–7 | .7863 | ±.3934 | 13.5384 | 5.3849 | 0.18 |
| 8–9 | .7150 | ±.4833 | 10.5649 | 4.7047 | 0.21 |
| *Pan* (wild) | | | | | |
| 2–3 | .8973 | ±.2457 | 23.4900 | 9.5966 | 0.20 |
| 4–5 | .8146 | ±.3573 | 15.1933 | 5.9192 | 0.17 |
| 6–7 | .5803 | ±.6025 | 7.8092 | 3.8841 | 0.25 |
| 8–9 | .6875 | ±.4703 | 10.4679 | 3.7926 | 0.15 |
| Prehistoric | | | | | |
| 2–3 | .9311 | ±.2127 | 27.9557 | 15.0699 | 0.28 |
| 4–5 | .8395 | ±.2863 | 19.1094 | 5.7810 | 0.10 |
| 6–7 | .7702 | ±.3916 | 13.3510 | 4.7411 | 0.14 |
| 8–9 | .7173 | ±.4787 | 10.6721 | 4.6810 | 0.21 |
| Costa Rica | | | | | |
| 2–3 | .9393 | ±.1901 | 31.4572 | 16.2986 | 0.26 |
| 4–5 | .8735 | ±.2811 | 20.1729 | 8.0655 | 0.18 |
| 6–7 | .8100 | ±.3877 | 14.0692 | 6.4429 | 0.22 |
| 8–9 | .7495 | ±.4816 | 10.9966 | 5.9989 | 0.28 |
| Sweden | | | | | |
| 2–3 | .9370 | ±.2025 | 29.5076 | 16.4150 | 0.29 |
| 4–5 | .8620 | ±.2991 | 18.8055 | 7.5620 | 0.18 |
| 6–7 | .7929 | ±.4127 | 13.0869 | 6.1806 | 0.23 |
| 8–9 | .7266 | ±.5089 | 10.2782 | 5.7855 | 0.29 |

[a]The proportion of the original perturbation remaining one wavelength later.

ity of the dominant wave is significantly longer than the generation length. For example, in the case of NWMs the periodicity of this wave is 9.3 years, while the generation length is 5.7 years. In the case of Sweden, the periodicity is 29.5 years, while the generation length is 27.8 years. Second, the rate at which this wave declines is higher in most of the nonhuman primate systems. For example, the half-life of this wave is 1.87 years in NWMs and about 16.42 years in the Swedish demographic system. Therefore, about nine years after a perturbation in an NWM age structure (the time at which the wave returns to the same point of the age structure), the wave has diminished to 3% of its original size. However, by the time this wave returns to the same point of the Swedish age structure (29.5 years), the wave is still 29% of its original size. Thus, the decline in this wave is both absolutely (in years) and relatively (in relation to the periodicity of the wave) faster in NWMs compared to humans. This is also true for OWMs and for captive *Pan*, although the differences tend to decline, e.g. for captive *Pan* the size of the wave has declined to only 10% of its original size.

The remaining roots have periodicities shorter than, and half-lives less than, those of the dominant pair of roots. Cross-grade comparisons again indicate consistent differences between most of the nonhuman and human primates. In each case, the nonhuman primates have faster absolute but slower relative rates of decline in the secondary waves in the age structure, compared to the primary wave in the age structure. In human demographic systems, the secondary waves (at least the first few) decline absolutely and relatively faster than the primary wave. As a generality, therefore, the return to stability in human demographic systems is characterized by a single dominant wave that declines relatively slowly, while nonhuman primate demographic systems are characterized by a number of waves that decline comparatively rapidly. Further, because the multiple waves of the nonhuman primate demographic systems have different wavelengths, their impacts on the age structure tend to cancel each other out. These empirical analyses suggest that baby booms are a human and not a general primate trait.

The exception is the wild *Pan* demographic system, which appears to be intermediate between the nonhuman and human primate patterns. Wild *Pan* has a dominant wave with a wavelength close to the generation length, similar to the human primate system; however, the relationships of the rates of decline in these waves are similar to the nonhuman primate system.

Current theory of the dynamics of populations indicates that wavelengths of the second and third roots of the NMF are controlled by a threshold value in the prereproductive span (Coale 1972, Wachter 1991). If the prereproductive period exceeds this threshold, the wavelength of the second and third roots is about the generation length. If the prereproductive period is shorter than this threshold, then the wavelength of the second and third roots can be up to twice the generation length. The examples above suggest that this threshold occurs at about the prereproductive period of wild *Pan* (12 years). However, the empirical results presented here suggest that survivorship also plays a role in this threshold. Analysis of a *Pan* demographic system composed of wild *Pan* fertility (first birth at age 12) coupled with captive *Pan* mortality (as opposed to wild *Pan* mortality) provides a stability profile similar to that of nonhuman primate systems. Additional demographic data on *Pan* will be necessary to determine which side of the threshold *Pan* falls on. It is possible that this is a function of environmental conditions, because the prereproductive span displays large phenotypic plasticity. Further theoretical work is also necessary to determine the role that variation in mortality patterns plays in the dynamics of demographic systems.

## SOME COMMENTS ON THE EVOLUTION OF PRIMATE LIFE HISTORIES

Three aspects of the evolution of primate life histories are discussed further here: (*a*) the evolution of delayed maturation, (*b*) the evolution of the reproductive life span, and (*c*) the evolution of senescence or the rate of aging. Interestingly, delayed maturation appears to have progressed furthest in humans, but the extension of the reproductive period and the rate of aging are greatest in *Pan troglodytes*. If these findings are correct, then the demography of *P. troglodytes* may not be a good model for the common ancestor of chimpanzees and humans. The contemporary *Pan* demographic system may be derived.

The conditions necessary for the evolution of delayed maturation are that the offspring of younger mothers be at some additional risk or that the survival and/or future fertility of younger mothers be at some additional risk compared to older mothers. If not, fitness will always increase with shorter maturation times because the generation length will be shorter even if survival to reproductive age remains the same. Stearns (1992) has developed models of this process that incorporate age and size at maturation as well as phenotypic plasticity. Stearns shows that based on some simple assumptions, the historical trends in human sexual maturation are consistent with this theory. The model could be refined through the use of demographically more realistic assumptions. The major shortcoming of this model from an empirical demographic perspective is quantitatively associating age (and/or size) of mother with the increased risk to the offspring and/or the mother's future reproduction. Stern bases his model on general reports that infant mortality is higher in teenage mothers (Stearns 1992). A more detailed study of this association needs to be conducted. There appears to be no association between early reproduction and infant survival in the chimpanzee. Sugiyama (1994) in his study of *Pan troglodytes* fertility provides evidence that the offspring of younger mothers may have better survival than births at the older ages, although this study is based on a small sample of births. It would be useful to develop more realistic models of age and size at maturation for both human and nonhuman primates.

One implication of the evolution of delayed maturation is decreased demographic stability. In particular, human and possibly wild *Pan* demographic systems return to the stable age structure more slowly following a perturbation. This pattern is likely to have influenced evolution in two ways. First, there is the direct problem of adapting to variations in the age structure and its impact on social organization. The impact of the baby boom of the 1950s and 1960s on the Social Security System of the United States in the early twenty-first century is a well-known example. Most likely, similar problems have occurred in earlier human societies and might have had implications for the evolution of culture. Second, evolution in nonstable or nonequilibrium populations may differ in very complex ways from evolution in stable populations (Cohen 1977, Orzack & Tuljapurkar 1989). Fitness cannot necessarily be equated with the intrinsic rate of increase in nonequilibrium populations, as is the case when evolution occurs in stable populations. In particular, available life history theory suggests that the evolution of the reproductive life span may differ between equilibrium and nonequilibrium populations. Based on equilibrium conditions, selection for a lengthened reproductive span is strong if adult levels of mortality are low and constant relative to infant and juvenile mortality (Stearns 1992). If, on the other hand, adult mortality is more variable than infant mortality, then selection for further survival and reproduction is weak. The conditions for evolution of longer reproductive spans in nonequilibrium populations are considerably more complex and are beyond the scope of this paper. On the other hand, the evolution of senescence is not known to be affected by equilibrium issues and is thought to be due to "antagonistic pleiotrophic" effects (Williams 1957). The latter refers to the accumulation of mutations favoring survival and reproduction early in life that interfere with survival later in life, when the force of selection is lower.

Provided that equilibrium theories can be applied to the characteristics of *Pan* demography (*P. troglodytes*), it appears that the unique characteristics of this grade represent an adaptation to high infant mortality. *Pan* displays relatively high infant mortality even in captivity, an extended reproductive span, and a high rate of aging. The general life history strategy appears to include long birth intervals, extended breastfeeding, and concomitant parental investment. Adult mortality is relatively constant until the end of the reproductive period at about age 50, at which point the death rate begins to increase dramatically (Figure 1*b*). Based on the fertility data available for *Pan*, few infants die when born to young mothers (Sugiyama 1994). Thus selection for delayed maturity is not present. However, a large proportion of infants born to older mothers die (100% in the 40- to 44-year age range), possibly as a result of the deaths of their parents and subsequent loss of further parental investment. This finding suggests that there is continued selection pressure to lengthen the life span further. Curiously, overall longevity does not appear to have increased. The antagonistic pleiotrophic effects appear to be compressed into the last few years of life (Figure 1*b*). All of these findings are consistent with the equilibrium theories of the evolution of the reproductive life span.

In comparison to *Pan* demographic strategies, human demographic strategies follow the general primate pattern, with the exception of delayed maturation and increased longevity. Humans have a shorter reproductive period than *Pan*, so the end of the reproductive career is similar in both organisms. Delayed maturation is presumably due to poor reproductive outcomes of young mothers. As noted above, whether this effect is the case in humans needs to be clarified further. However, Stearns's models, which support this contention, predict human phenotypic plasticity in age at maturation remarkably well (Stearns 1992). Long interbirth intervals do not appear to be as necessary for human infant survival and hence the reproductive period has not been extended. While longevity is greatest in humans, the age pattern of mortality follows the general primate pattern rather than the *Pan* pattern.

Given these patterns, the common ancestor of *Pan* and humans probably had a prereproductive span shorter than or similar to that of *Pan*, a reproductive span similar to or shorter than that of humans, and mortality following the general primate pattern. The expectation of life of the common ancestor may have been in the lower range of both *Pan* and humans, perhaps 20 years or slightly shorter. Perhaps *Pan paniscus* (pygmy chimpanzee) displays these life history characteristics. However, few demographic data are available for the species. The unique characteristics of *P. troglodytes* demography, driven by environmental factors causing highly variable infant mortality, and the unique characteristics of humans, driven by forces favoring delayed maturation, must have developed since the common ancestor. Bogen & Smith (1996), in their review of the evolution of human life cycle based on growth patterns, place the evolution of delayed maturation rather late in hominid evolution, probably post *Homo erectus*.

## SUMMARY

This review is an attempt to assemble a series of model demographic systems for several grades of primates. Models of this sort have proved useful for human demographic estimation and for simulation and experimentation for more than 30 years. Their applicability to life history analysis has been demonstrated briefly here. However, the models presented here are not intended to be an end in themselves, simply a place to begin.

Additional demographic data on primates living in a variety of environments—wild, provisioned, and captive—are needed to verify and extend the models presented above. Data on age-specific fertility, in particular, are not well developed in the literature, even though these data are easier to collect than mortality data. Statistical methods for controlling exposure to risk of fertility are available but have not been used to study primate demography. Data on additional species will help refine the general primate trends in demography and make possible the exploration of species variation within primate grades. Further evidence of environmentally induced variation can also provide important information on the evolution of primate life histories. Only when good data are available will midlevel models of the evolution of primate life histories become a reality.

Nevertheless, several tentative characteristics of primate demography can be listed. Not all are new. Some may be due to flaws in the current database.

First, there is a general increase in longevity from NWM to OWM to *Pan* and to human. In general, infant mortality declines and adult mortality becomes more rectangular. *Pan* breaks with the usual primate pattern because it displays relatively high infant mortality and extreme rectangularization.

Second, age at first birth generally increases from NWM to OWM to *Pan* and to human, as does the length of the reproductive span, except that *Pan*'s reproductive span is longer than the human reproductive span.

Third, human demographic systems display more general primate characteristics than do *Pan* demographic systems. *Pan* systems, at least *P. troglodytes,* appear to be evolutionarily specialized.

Fourth, the demographic stability of human demographic systems and possibly wild *Pan* demographic systems is lower than the stability of the other primates studied here. Humans may be the only primates, with the possible exception of wild *Pan*, to have baby booms. This finding may have implications for the evolution of culture, and it may have theoretical implications for the evolution of some life history characteristics.

Fifth, the unusual characteristics of *Pan* demographic rates may be an adaptation to high rates of prereproductive mortality, while the human pattern of delaying sexual maturity can evolve only if prereproductive mortality rates are low. This divergence is likely to have evolved since a common ancestor. In the case of humans, evolution of delayed maturation may be recent.

> **Visit the *Annual Reviews home page* at**
> **http://www.AnnualReviews.org.**

# Literature Cited

Arriaga EE. 1968. *New Life Tables for Latin American Populations.* Berkeley: Univ. Calif. Press

Bogen B, Smith BH. 1996. Evolution of the human life cycle. *Am. J. Hum. Biol.* 8: 703–16

Brass W. 1975. *Methods for Estimating Fertility and Mortality from Limited and Defective Data.* Chapel Hill, NC: The Carolina Popul. Cent.

Campbell KL, Wood JW. 1988. Fertility in traditional societies. In *Natural Human Fertility: Social and Biological Determinants,* ed. P Diggory, M Potts, S Teper. pp. 39–69. London: Macmillan

Caughly G. 1977. *Analysis of Vertebrate Population.* London: Wiley

Coale A, Trussell JT. 1974. Model fertility schedules: variations in the age structure of childbearing in human populations. *Popul. Index* 40:185–258

Coale AJ. 1972. *The Growth and Structure of Human Populations.* Princeton, NJ: Princeton Univ. Press

Coale AJ, Demeny P, Vaughan B. 1983. *Regional Model Life Tables and Stable Populations.* New York: Academic

Cohen JE. 1977. Ergodicity of age structure in populations with Markovian vital rates. III. Finitestate moments and growth rate; an illustration. *Adv. Appl. Probab.* 9: 462–75

Dyke B, Gage TB, Alford PL, Senson B, Williams-Blangero S. 1995. A model life table for captive Chimpanzees. *Am. J. Primatol.* 37:25–37

Dyke B, Gage TB, Ballou JD, Petto AJ, Tardif SD, Williams LJ. 1993. Model life tables for the smaller new world monkeys. *Am. J. Primatol.* 29:269–85

Dyke B, Gage TB, Mamelka PM, Goy RW, Stone WH. 1986. A demographic analysis of the Wisconsin Regional Primate Center Rhesus Colony 1962–1982. *Am. J. Primatol.* 10:257–69

Economos AC. 1982. Rate of aging, rate of dying and the mechanisms of mortality. *Arch. Gerontol. Geriatr.* 1:3–27

Finch CE, Pike MC, Witten M. 1990. Slow mortality rate in some animals approximates that of humans. *Science* 249:902–6

Fragaszy DM, Bard K. 1997. Comparison of development and life history in *Pan* and *Cebus. Int. J. Primatol.* 18:683–701

Gage TB. 1990. Variation and classification of human age patterns of mortality: analysis using competing hazards models. *Hum. Biol.* 62:589–617

Gage TB. 1995. Robust estimator of the intrinsic rate of increase and generation length. In *Population Management for Survival and Recovery,* ed. J Ballou, M Gilpin, TJ Foose, pp. 9–24. New York: Columbia Univ. Press

Gage TB. 1998. Demography. In *Human Biology: An Evolutionary and Biocultural Approach,* ed. S Stinson, B Bogin, R Huss-Ashmore, D O'Rourke. New York: Wiley. In press

Gage TB, Dyke B. 1986. Parameterizing abridged mortality tables: the Siler three-component hazard model. *Hum. Biol.* 58: 275–91

Gage TB, Dyke B. 1988. Model life tables for the larger old world monkeys. *Am. J. Primatol.* 16:305–20

Gage TB, Dyke B. 1993. Model life tables for the larger old world monkeys: a revision. *Am. J. Primatol.* 29:287–90

Gage TB, Dyke B, MacCluer JW. 1986. Estimating mortality rates for small populations: a test of the non-stable two-census methods. *Popul. Stud.* 40:263–73

Gage TB, Dyke B, Riviere PG. 1984. Estimating mortality from two censuses: an application to the Trio of Surinam. *Hum. Biol.* 56:489–502

Gage TB, Mode CJ. 1993. Some laws of mortality: how well do they fit? *Hum. Biol.* 65:445–61

Harvey PH, Clutton-Brock TH. 1985. Life history variation in primates. *Evolution* 39: 559–81

Howell N. 1976. Toward a uniformitarian theory of human paleo-demography. In *The Demographic Evolution of Human Populations,* ed. RH Ward, KM Weiss, pp. 25–40. London: Academic

Howell N. 1979. *Demography of the Dobe !Kung.* New York: Academic

Keyfitz N, Fleiger W. 1971. *Population.* San Francisco: Freeman

Kirkwood TBL. 1985. Comparative and evolutionary aspects of longevity. In *Handbook of the Biology of Aging,* ed. CE Finch, EL Schneider, pp. 27–43. New York: Van Nostrand Reinhold

Lovejoy CO, Meindl RS, Pryzbeck TR, Barton TS, Heiple KG, Knotting D. 1977. Paleodemography of the Libben Site, Ottawa County, Ohio. *Science* 198: 329–52

Luder HU. 1993. Hazard rates and causes of death in captive group of crab-eating monkeys *(Macaca fascicularis). Am. J. Primatol.* 39:40–50

Makeham WM. 1860. On the law of mortality. *J. Inst. Actuaries* 13:325–58

Mode C. 1988. On statistically assessing critical population size of an endangered species in a random environment. *IMA J. Math. Appl. Med. Biol.* 5:147–66

O'Connor KA. 1995. *The age pattern of mortality: a micro-analysis of Tipu and a meta-analysis of twenty-nine paleodemographic samples.* PhD diss., Univ. Albany, State Univ. NY

Orzack SH, Tuljapurkar S. 1989. Population dynamics in variable environments. VII. The demography and evolution of iteroparity. *Am. Nat.* 133:901–23

Pearl R, Miner JR. 1935. Experimental studies on the duration of life. XIV. The comparative mortality of certain lower organisms. *Q. Rev. Biol.* 10:60–79

Promislow DEL. 1991. Senescence in natural populations of mammals: a comparative study. *Evolution* 45:1869–87

Short RV. 1976. The evolution of human reproduction. *Proc. R. Soc. London Ser. B* 195:3–24

Siler W. 1979. A competing-risk model for animal mortality. *Ecology* 60:750–57

Siler W. 1983. Parameters of mortality in human populations with widely varying life spans. *Stat. Med.* 2:373–80

Stearns SC. 1992. *The Evolution of Life Histories.* Oxford: Oxford Univ. Press

Strehler BL. 1977. *Time, Cells and Aging.* New York: Academic. 2nd ed.

Sugiyama Y. 1994. Age-specific birth rate and life time reproductive success of chimpanzees at Bossou, Guinea. *Am. J. Primatol.* 32:311–18

Sugiyama Y, Ohsawa H. 1982. Population dynamics of Japanese monkeys with special reference to the effect of artificial feeding. *Folia Primatol.* 39:238–63

Tardif SD, Ziegler TE. 1992. Features of female reproductive senescence in tamarins (Saguinus spp.), a New World primate. *J. Reprod. Fertil.* 94:411–21

Tutin C. 1994. Reproductive success story: variability among chimpanzees and comparison with gorillas. In *Chimpanzee Cultures,* ed. R Wrangham, WC McGrew, F de Waal, P Heltne, pp. 181–93. Cambridge, MA: Harvard Univ. Press

Wachter KW. 1991. Pre-procreative ages in population stability and cyclicity. *Math. Popul. Stud.* 3:79–103

Williams GC. 1957. Pleiotrophy, natural selection, and the evolution of senescence. *Evolution* 11:398–411

*Annu. Rev. Anthropol. 1998. 27:223–46*
*Copyright © 1998 by Annual Reviews. All rights reserved*

# NATIONALISM AND ARCHAEOLOGY: On the Constructions of Nations and the Reconstructions of the Remote Past

*Philip L. Kohl*

Department of Anthropology, Wellesley College, Wellesley, Massachusetts 02181;
e-mail: pkohl@wellesley.edu

KEY WORDS: history of archaeology, ethnic and national identities, archaeological cultures, ethnogenesis, nationalism and state formation

---

## ABSTRACT

Nationalism requires the elaboration of a real or invented remote past. This review considers how archaeological data are manipulated for nationalist purposes, and it discusses the development of archaeology during the nineteenth and early twentieth centuries and the relationship of archaeology to nation-building, particularly in Europe. Contrastive conceptions of nationality and ethnicity are presented, and it is argued that adoption of modern constructivist perspectives is incompatible with attempting to identify ethnic/national groups solely on the basis of archaeological evidence. The political uses of archaeology are also reviewed for the construction of national identities in immigrant and postcolonial states. The problematic nature of nationalistic interpretations of the archaeological record is discussed, and the essay concludes with a consideration of the professional and ethical responsibilities of archaeologists confronted with such interpretations.

---

L'oubli, et je dirai même l'erreur historique, sont un facteur essentiel de la création d'une nation, et c'est ainsi que le progrès des études historiques est souvent pour la nationalité un danger. . . . Peut-être, après bien des tâtonnements infructueux, reviendra-t-on à nos modestes solutions empiriques. Le moyen d'avoir raison dans l'avenir est, à certaines heures, de savoir se résigner à être démodé...

Renan 1947–1961:891, 906

0084-6570/98/1015-0223$08.00

# INTRODUCTION

Numerous recent publications attest to considerable interest in the relationship between archaeology and nationalism (e.g. Atkinson et al 1996, Diaz-Andreu & Champion 1996, Kohl & Fawcett 1995). The current popularity of this topic seems relatively easy to explain for reasons related both to the recent upsurge in nationalist movements and conflicts throughout the world and to the practice of archaeology. The dissolution of the Soviet Union and the concomitant restructurings of states in eastern Europe have led to the outbreak of numerous ethnic/national conflicts, many of which, as in the Balkans and in the Caucasus, involve contentious territorial and proprietary claims based on the ancient past and the archaeological record. Archaeological remains frequently are the sites of violent demonstrations or targets of attacks, as recently demonstrated by the Palestinian response to the opening of a new entrance to a tunnel through the old center of Jerusalem. Even more violent consequences ensued from the destruction of the Babri Masjid at the site of Ayodhya in northern India in December 1992, an event in which fabricated archaeological evidence (Mandal 1993, Bernbeck & Pollock 1996) played a critical role. In short, archaeology figures prominently in current national events, and this visibility naturally raises questions as to the political uses of and significance accorded to archaeological remains. The innocence of the discipline, sometimes cloaked behind a facade of empirical objectivity, cannot be maintained in the light of such graphic, well-covered current events.

The present interest in exploring the relationship between archaeology and nationalism, however, is not exclusively explained by reference to these events. Equally important have been developments internal to the practice of archaeology and advances in the broader historical study of nationalism. Recent histories of archaeology (e.g. Trigger 1989, Patterson 1995) have stressed the social and political settings in which the discipline functions—its social dimension. This concern inevitably leads to a consideration of archaeology's relationship to the political unit or state in which it functions. Similarly, there has been an increasing awareness of the differences among various "regional traditions" of conducting archaeological research (e.g. Trigger & Glover 1981; Politis 1992, 1995), and these traditions characteristically coincide with specific nation-states. That is, there are distinctive Russian (Shnirelman 1995; Dolukhanov 1995, 1996; Guliaev 1995), French (Audouze & Leroi-Gourhan 1981, Dietler 1994, Schnapp 1996), German (Härke 1995, Arnold & Hassman 1995, Marchand 1996a,b), and Spanish (Diaz-Andreu 1995, 1996a,b) archaeological traditions, for example, and these can be profitably compared and contrasted (e.g. the comparision of Spanish and Russian archaeological traditions in Martínez-Navarrete 1993). Certain international archaeological organizations, such as the World Archaeological Congress (Ucko 1987, Rao 1995) and the

European Association of Archaeology (Kristiansen 1993, 1996; Shore 1996) have been established in the wake of political controversy and/or with explicit political agendas; such organizations highlight the political dimensions of the discipline, including inevitably the ways in which archaeological research is structured by the policies of specific nation-states. Finally, a central tenet of the entire postmodern critique of science, which in the most visible Anglophone archaeological literature takes the form of postprocessual archaeology (e.g. Hodder 1986, 1991; Shanks & Tilley 1992), is its rejection of total objectivity and of the possibility of conducting neutral, value-free research. Rather, this critique emphasizes the subjective interests/perpectives of scholars and the political contexts in which archaeological research is conducted.

For similar external and internal reasons, historians and social theorists have increasingly addressed the phenomenon of nationalism, and it can be argued that they are doing so with increasing sophistication and insight (see Hobsbawm 1992:2–5). There is considerable debate in this literature on the following issues: the degree to which nationalism represents a radically modern form of consciousness, a novel collective identity linked to processes of modernization and tied exclusively to the basic unit of contemporary political organization, i.e. the nation-state (e.g. contrast Gellner 1983 and Anderson 1991 with Duara 1995); the extent to which the nineteenth-century European experience of nation-building is emulated throughout the postcolonial world; whether the new nations that have emerged in Asia and Africa in this century have followed a fundamentally different, less secular, and more spiritual path to join the recognized league of nations (e.g. van der Veer 1994, Chatterjee 1993); and whether in the process of nation-making the past is "invented" or "rediscovered" through the selective use of inherited symbols, myths, and material remains (contrast Hobsbawm & Ranger 1983 with Smith 1986). Nevertheless, these theorists concur in emphasizing the socially constructed character of nationalism and in rejecting "essentialist" or "primordialist" accounts that view nations as objective, durable phenomena, the origins of which typically can be traced back to remote antiquity (for an intelligent anthropological review of this literature and the distinction between essentialist/primordialist and instrumentalist/constructivist accounts, see Eriksen 1993).

The relationship of archaeology to nationalism is changing. Historically, archaeologists have helped underwrite many nationalist programs, according historical significance to visible material remains within a national territory (Anderson 1991:163–85). They are still playing this role throughout many areas of the world (Kohl & Tsetskhladze 1995; Kaiser 1995; Chernykh 1995; Ligi 1993, 1994). Today, however, some are critically examining how archaeological data are manipulated for nationalist purposes (Kohl & Fawcett 1995, Ben-Yehuda 1995, Diaz-Andreu & Champion 1996, Silberman 1989, Gathercole & Lowenthal 1990), while others are celebrating the inevitable political nature of the discipline and promoting alternative indigenous reconstructions of the remote past (Ucko 1995a,b; Graves-Brown et al 1996).

This article reviews the historical relationship between the emergence of modern nation-states and the development of archaeology. It briefly examines examples of nationalist archaeology that emerged throughout the world in both the nineteenth and twentieth centuries, and it analyzes the evolutionary archaeology that developed particularly in imperial and colonial settings (Trigger 1984). This paper also considers why archaeological data are peculiarly susceptible to political manipulations and why this evidence is often accorded great significance in nationalist constructions. Finally, the essay addresses the professional and ethical responsibilities of archaeologists when they confront problematic nationalist interpretations of the material culture record.

## NATIONAL AND NATIONALIST ARCHAEOLOGIES: DEFINING THE SUBJECT

After a long discussion of the relative merits and problems with defining a nation according to objective or subjective criteria, Hobsbawm (1992:8) opted for the working definition of "a sufficiently large body of people whose members regard themselves as members of a 'nation.'" From an anthropological perspective, such a definition does not sufficiently distinguish a nation from an ethnic group or *ethnos*, so additional criteria must be postulated in which a nation is equated with a certain kind of modern territorial state so that there is a congruence—either achieved or desired—between the national and political unit. The important point is that national*ism* is the program for creating nations and exists prior to the formation of the nation (Hobsbawm 1992:9–13): Nations are constructed by nationalist politicians and intellectuals, and these processes are supported by social classes that benefit economically and politically from their construction (cf Karakasidou 1997 for an extremely well documented example).

The emphasis on the eminently political character of nation-formation is important and can be applied to our treatment of archaeology's relationship to nationalism. That is, it is important to distinguish national from national*ist* archaeology. The former refers to the archaeological record compiled within given states. The latter refers more inclusively not only to that record but also to policies adopted by the state that make use of archaeologists and their data for nation-building purposes, and such policies may extend beyond the borders of the state. Nationalist archaeology is frequently involved in the creation and elaboration of national identities, processes that occur not only within states but also as states expand and interact with other states. This perspective makes it impossible to maintain Trigger's (1984) seminal but too sharply divided typology of nationalist, colonialist, and imperialist archaeologies.

A great unscrupulous scramble for Egyptian antiquities followed in the wake of Napoleon's invasion of Egypt at the end of the eighteenth century. Monumental works of ancient art were hauled home and redefined the changing Parisian landscape—most famously with the placement of an obelisk from Luxor in the Place de la Concorde in 1836, an event attended by the French king and over 200,000 spectators (Fagan 1975:261). Colossal artifacts from ancient civilizations now became peculiarly transformed into national symbols, and the subsequent French and British competition for such loot served the useful national function of filling up both the Louvre and the British Museum. Archaeologists, employed as colonial officers in imperialist settings, were engaged in a form of nationalist archaeology in the sense that their work was used to puff up the glory and sense of self of their employer; Layard, wanting to dig at Nimrod in northern Mesopotamia in 1846, provided a classic example of this form of nationalist archaeology when he wrote the British Ambassador to Constantinople, Sir Stratford Canning: "The national honour is also concerned in competing with the French in deciphering the cuneiform inscriptions. To accomplish this task materials are necessary. . . . If the excavation keeps its promise to the end there is much reason to hope that Montagu House [the British Museum] will beat the Louvre hollow" (Larsen 1996:95–96).

Britain had to outpace France in the quest to exhume and send home texts and colossal works of ancient art. The British Museum was then and remains now an eminently nationalist institution, even though many of its finest acquisitions were pilfered from abroad, having been excavated by archaeologists in its employ. The study of the past promoted by Napoleon or the archaeology practiced by Layard can be described as simultaneously imperialist, colonialist, and nationalist.

## NATIONALISM AND THE EARLY DEVELOPMENT OF EUROPEAN ARCHAEOLOGY

Archaeology's origins can be traced back to the Renaissance, if not earlier, and the antiquarians' descriptions of material monuments, such as William Camden's *Britannia* (1586), predate the American and French revolutions, which ushered in the age of modern nation-making, by as much as two centuries. Nevertheless, archaeology became a legitimate scientific pursuit and an academic discipline during the nineteenth century, the heyday of nation-building in Europe. These processes were chronologically coincident and causally interrelated.

The establishment of the Musée des Monuments Français and the transformation of the Louvre into a museum occurred in the wake of the French Revolution and became models for other "national" museums that, in turn, became characteristic institutions of the nascent states of post-Napoleonic Europe.

Probably the most famous example of this process was the establishment of the Museum of Northern Antiquities, which opened in Copenhagen in 1819 under the direction of CJ Thomsen, who had organized its materials under his newly devised Three Age system of successive Stone, Bronze, and Iron periods. Denmark had suffered setbacks in the Napoleonic Wars, and the precocious development of Danish prehistory during the early and mid-nineteenth century must be understood against this backdrop of territorial loss and cultural retrenchment (Sorensen 1996). Each emergent nation-state had to construct its own national identity, which required the active forgetting or misremembering (cf the opening quote of Renan) and the rediscovery or inventing of one's past. Myths of national origin had to be elaborated from a variety of sources, including, notably, the material remains found within the state's demarcated territorial borders.

The association between the development of archaeology and nation-building was so obvious as to remain largely unquestioned throughout the nineteenth century and most of the twentieth century; the roots of countries were extended back into the mists of the prehistoric past. The practice of archaeology and the institutional forms it acquired differed from state to state in part because each state had its own specific history and time of national consolidation; the nationalist significance accorded to archaeological data also varied according to the availability of historical records, the relative weighting of historical to archaeological sources, and the empirical contents of those records. Schnapp (1996), for example, argues that archaeologists have always been handmaidens to historians in France and that "archaeology's contribution [to the construction of French national identity throughout most of the nineteenth century] was minimal" (Schnapp 1996:54). Others (e.g. Dietler 1994) perceive a greater role for archaeology in the process of turning "peasants into Frenchmen." The Romans may have defeated the Gauls, but different aspects of this defeat could be celebrated, and national monuments to the Gallic ancestors were built on the sites of the battles, such as at Alésia, and the state supported their excavations. Later French prehistory (or protohistory) may have remained relatively undeveloped throughout the nineteenth century, but France was the center of Palaeolithic archaeology, and Boucher de Perthes was conceived as the father of archaeology not only in France but elsewhere throughout continental Europe, which was a source of considerable national pride. Nationalist archaeology in France—in the sense discussed above—was also embroiled in the establishment of French schools throughout the Classical and Near Eastern worlds, first in Athens and Rome, then later in Iran, Egypt, Afghanistan, and Algiers.

Following the brilliant study of Marchand (1996a), the development of archaeology in Germany has to be explained not principally by reference to German Romanticism or the reaction against the universalist ideals of the Enlightenment. It must also be associated with the development of ancient art history and Germany's pronounced "cultural obsession" with philhellenism, the glories of ancient Greece, and their subsequent establishment of exacting standards of scholarship in allied disciplines, such as comparative philology and *Altertumskunde*. Wilhelm von Humboldt's promotion and institutionalization of a neohumanist *Bildung,* based on a rigorous Classical education, also, of course, served many eminently practical purposes, such as the training of dedicated, apolitical civil servants (cf Marchand 1996a:27–31; BG Trigger, personal communication). As in France, German nationalist archaeology found its purest expression in the excavation of Classical sites (e.g. at Olympia in Greece and Pergamum in Anatolia) and in the establishment of German institutes throughout the Mediterranean and later the Near East. The Institut für Archäologische Korrespondenz was established in 1829 by private individuals interested in Classical antiquities, though it received occasional state support throughout the middle decades of the nineteenth century; in 1872 this institute was transformed into a *Reichsinstitut* and became the Deutsches Archäologisches Institut, a heavily state-subsidized organization meant to showcase the achievements of German scholarship. *Kulturpolitik* was a state policy intended to enhance German national prestige through the support of "disinterested" German philanthropy and scholarship abroad, particularly throughout the lands of the Ottoman Empire; in reality, it disguised imperialist aspirations that occasionally were made explicit. Baron von Wangenheim, the second-in-command at the German embassy in Constantinople, stated the policy unequivocally: "The interim intellectual goals already pursued, or to be pursued by our schools, our doctors, and our archaeologists could very well become, in the course of time, the crystallization point onto which German economic and colonizing undertakings are grafted. The economic will follow the intellectual conquest . . . and then these two . . . will naturally be followed by political exploitation" (cited in Marchand 1996b:318).

*Kulturpolitik* engaged the energies of German archaeologists working throughout Classical lands and the ancient Near East. Nationalist archaeology in Germany thus developed largely beyond the borders of Germany, resulting in a corresponding lack of attention to German prehistory, a neglect first addressed by G Kossinna at the turn of the century. This situation was later "rectified" by the Nazis, particularly under the programs extolling the German past that were headed by H Himmler and A Rosenberg. The state attention that the Nazis lavished on German prehistory proved, of course, catastrophic, leaving behind a "Faustian legacy" from which the discipline has yet to recover fully (Arnold 1990, Arnold & Hassman 1995).

The ways in which nationalism and archaeology intersected in Greece and Italy have to be explained internally in terms of the specific making of those modern nation-states and the constructing of modern Greek and Italian national identities as well as in terms of the international prestige accorded to their Classical antiquities and to their consequent plunder (cf McConnell 1989). Archaeology in Spain, on the other hand, represents a different case. Spanish archaeology did not develop during a time of imperial expansion, as in France and Britain, or imperial aspiration, as in Germany; rather, it emerged and its national identity was refashioned in the wake of the losses of its Latin American empire in the early nineteenth century and most of its other possessions at the end of the century (cf Diaz-Andreu 1995:43). Focus on the medieval origin of the Spanish nation involved the partial denial or begrudging recognition of its Islamic heritage (Diaz-Andreu 1996b), a factor that was specific to the Iberian peninsula. An overtly nationalist Spanish archaeology, associated with sites such as Numantia—also a scene of defeat—was relatively weak and developed late. The florescence or curtailment of regional nationalist traditions in Spanish archaeology (among the Galicians, Catalans, and Basques, in particular) reflects restructurings of the Spanish state during this century; in post-Franco times, however, Spanish archaeology has been decentralized, encouraging the development of regional archaeologies within the country's 17 autonomous provinces (Ruiz Zapatero 1993).

Archaeology's relationship to the state varied from country to country. It could take the relatively innocuous and necessary form of the detailed compilation of the prehistoric and early historic sequence for a region or an entire nation. Nationalist archaeology in this sense can be equated with the cultural-historical approach and evaluated positively in the sense of the more systematic and complete tracing of temporal and spatial variations in the archaeological record than was often achieved, for example, by the more schematic unilinear evolutionary approaches of the late nineteenth and early twentieth centuries. Trigger (1995:277) even suggests that archaeologists establishing their regional or national prehistoric sequences could provide a justifiable collective pride in the past and help resist colonial and imperial domination.

## PEOPLING THE PAST: THE ADVENT OF THE ARCHAEOLOGICAL CULTURE CONCEPT, THE SOVIET *ETHNOS,* AND ETHNOGENESIS

The introduction of the archaeological culture concept, developed by Kossinna and popularized by Childe, entailed certain dangers for the nationalist-inspired archaeology that became obvious during the 1930s and 1940s. It is, however, useful to recall that the urge to people the past that culminated with the proliferation of archaeological cultures was itself a healthy reaction against the epochal and homotaxial evolutionary approaches championed by de Mortillet and Morgan (Daniel 1962:82–84, 1975:236–51). Unfortunately, the advance in interpretation achieved by the use of the archaeological culture concept came at a considerable price, a sum that is still being calculated today

(Shennan 1989, Graves-Brown et al 1996, Diaz-Andreu 1996a). It also paved the way for nationalist interpretations, where specific archaeological cultures were unproblematically seen as ancestral to contemporary ethnic or national groups. This procedure, which implied a a static, durable, or essentialist conception of ethnicity/nationality, could even be promulgated by explicit state policies. The case of Soviet archaeology and its use of ethnogenesis, the formation of *ethnoi*, is instructive.

The officially sanctioned Soviet conception of an *ethnos*, long championed by Yu V. Bromlei (1973, 1983) among others, can be characterized as primordialist or essentialist; i.e, attachment to an ethnic group was based on objective, relatively durable, and fixed criteria, such as language, racial group, dress, house forms, cuisine, and other cultural traditions or time-honored ways of doing things (cf also Gellner 1980, Shnirelman 1996:8–9, and Tishkov 1997:1–12). This view contrasts sharply with the more situational and relational conception of ethnic identity favored by most Western anthropologists (Eriksen 1993:10–12). From this latter perspective, a group is a distinct *ethnos* that considers itself such and is considered such by other groups. This attribute of categorization is most important, a feature for which there is no necessary material culture correlate.

The Soviet *ethnos* and the classic concept of an archaeological culture resemble each other, and both contrast sharply with more modern views of ethnicity. These modern views insist that ethnic groups are malleable and constantly changing as the historical situation in which they exist unfolds; ethnicity, like culture, is never made but is always "in the making" or, perhaps, if times are tough, "in the unmaking" or "disappearing." Ethnicity and nationality are conceived similarly in that they are socially constructed phenomena in which traditions are invented and consciously manipulated for political, economic, and social reasons. Ethnicity is a more universal form of group identity with a past that may extend back to earlier historic times, indeed, perhaps, into the mists of prehistory, but it can never be securely traced. An archaeology of ethnicity, in short, is an impossible undertaking if one accepts this constructivist perspective on ethnic and national identity (*contra* Jones 1997; cf also Trigger 1994:103), while it is a relatively straightforward exercise if one adopts the Soviet concept of *ethnos* or if one uncritically equates archaeological cultures with living or past ethnic groups.

A related concept that became central to the practice of Soviet ethnology, archaeology, and physical anthropology from the mid-1930s on is ethnogenesis, or the formation, of peoples (cf the seminal studies of VA Shnirelman 1993, 1995). The determination of ethnogenesis became one of the central tasks of Soviet archaeology when the discipline switched from a Marxist-inspired internationalism (or, perhaps, politically motivated universalism) to one concerned principally with the ethnogenetic history of the early Slavs, i.e.

when Great Russian chauvinism and the buildup to the Great Patriotic War replaced internationalism. Ironically, the effect of this transformation was to have every ethnicity/nationality alike, Russian and non-Russian, engaged in this ethnogenetic mandate or search for its origins. Competition over the remote past was intimately tied to the very structure of the Soviet multiethnic federal state (Suny 1993, Zaslavsky 1993, Tishkov 1997). Administrative units (republics and autonomous republics, provinces, and regions) were named for specific ethnic groups, although they always contained more than a single *ethnos* and in many there was no ethnic majority. It was an easy and logical step to transform the precisely defined borders of these units into the national territory or homeland of the eponymous *ethnos*. This process, in turn, could be legitimized through the selective ethnic interpretation of the archaeological record (for an example, see Lordkipanidze 1989), reifying the political unit by according it great antiquity. In Ronald Suny's striking phrase (1993:87), the Soviet Union became the great "incubator of new nations," a source for many of the conflicts that have arisen since the state self-destructed.

The concept of ethnogenesis is linked directly to the concept of the *ethnos*: durable and well-nigh permanent in the Soviet perspective or constantly changing in the opinion of most Western scholars. For the former, the determination of origins is the critical question. When did the ethnic group, conceived as a little, preformed homunculus already possessing all the essentially defined characteristics of the given *ethnos*, come into being: during the Bronze Age, during the Iron Age, with the collapse of Classical Antiquity and the ensuing Great Migrations, or after the conquests of Timur or Genghis Khan? It is perceived as a straightforward historical question with an ascertainable answer to be provided by the archaeologist's spade or by some long-overlooked or recently discovered historical document.

For the Western scholar, the problem is much more complex, indeed essentially unsolvable. Ethnogenesis is only a relatively minor matter associated with the beginnings or initial formation of a given ethnic group; more significant and more complex are the changes that group will experience over time—its ethnomorphosis (Kohl 1992:172, Wolf 1984). These changes may—though not necessarily will—lead to the appearance of new ethnic groups through processes of assimilation and/or fundamental change or disappearance through various natural or human-induced processes, such as ethnocide. Even an ethnic group that exhibits considerable continuity and stability over long periods of historical time will nevertheless change in fundamental ways; thus, for example, pre-Christian Armenia of the Iron Age differs from Christian Armenia of the Middle Ages and from the newly formed Republic of Armenia today (cf Kohl 1996).

Obviously, both perspectives have some degree of merit: Continuities, as well as changes, can be documented for the Armenian experience or for many relatively long-lived ethnic groups. Cultural traditions cannot be fabricated out of whole cloth; there are real limits to the inventions of tradition. As Hobsbawm (1992) argues, states or nationalist politicians may, in fact, make nations, but they cannot totally make them up. It should be obvious that one could not have constructed mid- to late nineteenth-century Italians out of the Chinese or New Guinean cultural traditions. Here it is useful to distinguish between strict and contextual constructionism (Ben-Yehuda 1995:20–22 and personal-communication). The former denies any constraints imposed by past or current realities and quickly devolves into the hopelessly relativist morass of some postmodern criticisms. Contextual constructivism, the theory advocated here, on the other hand, accepts that social phenomena are continuously constructed and manipulated for historically ascertainable reasons, but it does not deny an external world, a partially apprehensible objective reality, that cannot totally be reduced to invention or social construction. Representations or constructed cultural perceptions are real, but reality encompasses more than representations and exists independently from them.

## ARCHAEOLOGY AND THE CONSTRUCTION OF NATIONAL IDENTITIES IN IMMIGRANT AND POSTCOLONIAL NATION-STATES

The relationship of nationalism to archaeology is not limited to Europe; it can be traced throughout the world. Different areas exhibit different forms of nationalism, not all of which emulate perfectly, or even closely, the European pattern. This essay cannot be totally inclusive, but it will briefly discuss the relationship of archaeology to two alternative nationalisms: (*a*) modern states that are composed principally of immigrants to the country, such as the United States, Argentina, and Israel, or that are relatively new, composite constructions formed by the mixture of peoples of diverse origins, such as Mexico and Peru; and (*b*) states that have freed themselves from colonial rule and/or emerged particularly during the second half of this century, such as Zimbabwe and India.

The construction of a national identity for a nation of immigrants is a different task from that for a nation whose citizens believe has been theirs since time immemorial. The role of archaeology in the construction of the former correspondingly differs and typically has been associated with the adoption of a universal evolutionary/natural historical perspective on its prehistoric past and on its still-surviving indigenous peoples. Prehistory becomes part of nature, and its makers may at first go unrecognized—as in the Moundbuilder controversy—romanticized as noble or denigrated as savages. In any event, they are conceptualized as different and less than the civilized European immigrants, who have a real history forged in the Western tradition that can be traced back to Classical and biblical sources and beyond to the Bronze Age civilizations of the ancient Near East. Trigger's well-known critical assessment of the static, uncreative image of the American Indian in archaeology (1980) can be more generally extended to other treatments of indigenous peoples in other immigrant lands, such as Australia. It also closely resembles the perspective of natives promulgated by imperialist archaeologies elsewhere, such as in Africa or Asia (Trigger 1984).

In terms of archaeology's role in the construction of national identities, three additional points should be made. First, the task of constructing identities differs greatly depending on how many indigenous peoples survived contact or conquest and the nature of the cultural remains they left behind. Thus, obviously, the continuously changing, increasingly inclusive character of Mexican identity differs profoundly from what it means to be Argentinian. For these reasons, Mexican and Argentinian elements of identity differ in terms of their symbols of state (e.g. the Mexican flag with its Aztec eagle and snake on a cactus); the contents of their national museums; their efforts to include the various peoples who once lived in their country or their efforts to effectively deny their very existence [as celebrated in Argentina's "la conquista del desierto" of the 1870s and museum collection of dead and live natives; cf Podgorny & Politis 1990–1992)]; and the general scale and significance of archaeological research in these countries. As in Europe, the relationship of archaeology to nationalism must be traced state by state; generalizations are either hazardous or trite.

The case of Mexico demonstrates that Trigger's static image of the American Indian cannot be applied uniformly throughout the Americas (or at least uniformly south of the Rio Grande). The Mexican Revolution of 1910 assured the victory of *indigenismo*, a movement that consciously incorporated the indigenous pre-Hispanic peoples of Mexico into a redefined and more inclusive national identity (Lorenzo 1981:199). The state controls archaeological research in Mexico and has promoted the recovery of its pre-Hispanic past, even at the expense of its colonial heritage. Thus, for example, the state-sponsored excavations of the Aztec Templo Mayor destroyed part of the colonial center of Mexico City. It may be fair to query whether all the indigenous peoples of Mexico have been equally incorporated in this process or whether some—the Aztec/Mexicans, in particular—have received preferential treatment. Nevertheless, the perceptions of Mexican archaeologists about their pre-Hispanic past may differ profoundly from those of foreign, particularly US, archaeologists working in Mexico whose activities may be viewed with suspicion and mistrust (Lorenzo 1981). Is questioning the concept of a pre-Hispanic Mesoamerica value free or is it peculiarly divisive for Mexico, particularly its ethnically distinctive regions, such as Chiapas? Are US archaeologists who interpret the prehistoric cultures of the US Southwest as evolving separately from those of northwest Mexico most plausibly interpreting the archaeological record or are they effectively naturalizing the border defined by the 1848 Treaty of Guadalupe that ended La Guerra de Agresíon Norte Americana (Weigand 1991)? Nationalism and archaeology are intricately interwoven into the very fabric of the Mexican state for internal and external reasons. An external reason is its relations with its very large, powerful, and expansionary northern neighbor.

Second, the process of national identity formation is continuous and ongoing; what it means to be Mexican, Argentinian, Native American, and so on today differs from what it did during the last century or earlier this century. Many changes may be considered progressive in that more peoples' pasts are incorporated into increasingly inclusive national identities, although it is unclear whether such processes reflect anything more than a specific state's security and stability. Legislation has been passed by different countries to protect the cultural heritage of indigenous peoples, including the repatriation of culturally significant objects. Even long-extinct peoples lacking obvious heirs can be resurrected through archaeological research and incorporated into the national identity. Thus, for example, 10,000- to 12,000-year-old Palaeo-Indian remains from southern Patagonia are seen today as the first Argentinians, *los primeros Argentinos*, who initiated the national adventure (see the cover to Wroclavsky 1997), and their excavations are appropriately celebrated by the state (L Miotti, personal communication).

The cultural patrimonies of immigrant and newly independent states are being redefined and extended in part as a result of ongoing archaeological investigations. This too can be viewed as progressive and desirable, although other, fundamentally economic, factors undoubtedly also are at work, including the growth in tourism and the remarkably high prices currently being paid for antiquities on the art market. Thus, for example, the government of Guatemala recently protested the opening of an exhibit of pre-Columbian antiquities at the Boston Museum of Fine Arts, claiming that the materials on display were illegally excavated and stolen from the country. The Guatemalan Vice Minister of Culture bitterly complained that the objects were "pages ripped out of the history book of the nation"—a striking metaphor of national identity (Yemma & Robinson 1997:A28). Regardless of the sincerity and justice of the complaint, it is not irrevelant or irreverent to note that looted Mayan artifacts are fetching astronomical prices at auction houses, such as Sotheby's, where a gold object recently sold for more than half a million dollars, and that tourism, which in Guatemala often includes visiting famous pre-Hispanic sites, currently ranks as the country's second most important industry—after coffee (Delle & Smith 1997).

The third and final consideration concerns the political uses of evolutionary theory. While it is undoubtedly true that the universal evolutionary/natural history perspective initially adopted by most immigrant states served the then-useful function of relegating the indigenes to a lower rung on the evolutionary ladder, it must be emphasized that there was no reason inherent in the theory of cultural evolution that it function in this manner. The same point can be made for diffusionism, a perspective contrasted to the doctrine of evolution from the late nineteenth century onward and which easily devolved into emphasizing the unique contributions of a gifted people/master race. That is, both explanatory approaches were and still can be used for racist purposes, but such use has to be explained historically and not seen as intrinsic to the doctines themselves. Indeed, both can have the opposite result: evolution stressing the unity of humankind and diffusion documenting how all peoples contribute to a shared history.

Nation-states that have arisen out of the ruins of empire face their own peculiar problems of constructing their national identities. One common difficulty is that the borders they inherit frequently correspond to colonial administrative units and contain multiple ethnic groups, none of which could function unproblematically as the new nationality. Archaeology can be implicated in these processes (Schmidt & Patterson 1995). Zimbabwe, of course, is not only a nation named after an archaeological site, it is also a site that became an exceptionally powerful symbol of colonial misrepresentations and native accomplishments (Hall 1990, 1995). It maintains that function today, but it also has become a site of ethnic tensions within the new state. Are the ruins to be identifed exclusively with the majority Shona people or interpreted more broadly as also ancestral to the Ndebele (cf Schmidt 1995:126–27)? As elsewhere, control of the past provides a source of legitimization for control of the present. Archaeology can be an expensive undertaking, and many new nation-states in Africa and elsewhere simply cannot afford to support adequately a state archaeological service or national museum; this problem is compounded when foreign archaeologists still dominate the ongoing research conducted in the country and when the discipline is perceived by state officials—fairly or unfairly—as a relic of colonial rule (Schmidt 1995). The future relationship between archaeology and nationalism in such cases is unclear, though a type of development may be envisaged that is associated with the seemingly ineluctable growth of tourism. Archaeologists can expect to receive state support when officials recognize the profits to be made from affluent tourists eager to visit archaeological sites. Whether such development is a blessing or a curse remains to be seen.

Another difficulty faced by many postcolonial nation-states concerns the inheritance of the ethnic/national identities that were formed or refashioned during colonial rule. For example, castes in India—their functions and degree of segregation/separation—were transformed during the time of British rule. Similarly, recognition that there was an Indo-European family of languages suggested historical relations between speakers of this family of languages, connections that stretched westward from South Asia across the Eurasian land mass to northwestern Europe; this discovery led to new ways of classifying peoples (Aryans versus non-Aryans, for example) both by the British and by the South Asians themselves. New questions then could be asked of the historical and accumulating archaeological evidence: Did the archaeological record support an Aryan invasion of the subcontinent? If so, when and who was defeated and displaced? In this instance, the British also established an enormously large and complex archaeological service that the Indians inherited and the Pakistanis imitated after independence. Scholars differ sharply on their assessment of this inherited legacy of colonial rule and the manner and degree to which it continues to structure an understanding of the past and its relevance for the present (contrast Paddayya 1995 with Chakrabarti 1997; cf also Lamberg-Karlovsky 1998).

The case of Chinese archaeology and its relationship to nationalism presents a special case. The millennia-long continuity of Chinese civilization sets it apart, as does the traditional respect accorded its antiquities and the humiliation—perceived and real—it suffered at the hands of Western powers during the nineteenth century. The development of Chinese archaeology during this century cannot be understood apart from the early Western-initiated excavations (e.g. JG Andersson at Yangshao, Davidson Black at Zhoukoudian) and the anti-imperialist sentiments they fueled, particularly in terms of what were perceived to be their denigration of Chinese civilization and assessment of its derivative character (Tong 1995:184–88). The consequent backlash still profoundly affects the practice of archaeology in China today. Whether the cradle or nuclear center of Chinese civilization is restricted to the middle reaches of the Yellow River or extended to encompass essentially all the Han-dominated regions of contemporary China, its origins are pure and unsullied by any diffusionary processes, especially those emanating from the West (Falkenhausen 1993, 1995). After the revolution and the founding of the People's Republic of China in 1949, the infrastructural state support of archaeology and its guiding theoretical model—Marxism—were initially patterned on the Soviet model, but expanded or contracted for internal reasons, such as the Great Cultural Revolution (1966–1976), during which time archaeologists were persecuted and antiquities destroyed on a massive scale (Tong 1995). Archaeology and nationalism in China remain closely interrelated today.

An article on archaeology and nationalism cannot fail to mention the unique role archaeology has played in the construction of Israel and Israeli national identity. Arguably, archaeology has contributed more to this case of state formation than to any other (Elon 1994, Shavit 1986). In terms of the above discussion, how do we even classify Israel? It certainly is not an immigrant state, in the sense of the United States, Argentina, or Australia, for the century-old migration to Palestine has been perceived by most as a return to an ancestral homeland, a view that is tangibly reinforced through the continuous excavation of antiquites dated to biblical times. Certainly, it is impossible to characterize Israeli archaeology as dominated by a universal evolutionary or natural history perspective in the sense of American archaeology. Is its practice, then, better considered a specific form of colonialist archaeology, as defined by Trigger (1984)? The question itself is charged with political significance. Three features of Israeli archaeology are particularly distinctive: (*a*) The state significance accorded to and popular interest in certain archaeological remains are extraordinary, as perhaps best exemplified by the former swearing-in ceremony of the Israeli army (IDF) at Masada (Ben-Yehuda 1995:147–62); (*b*) the excavation and presentation of past remains is highly selective and directed to the reconstruction of Iron Age through early Roman times or to the First and Second Temple periods (cf Abu el-Haj 1998); and (*c*) the form of nationalism that both inspires and sometimes impedes the practice of Israeli archaeology is explicitly religous, not secular, which means that archaeology fulfills a certain sacred or, for some, sacrilegious function. The combination of archaeology and religious nationalism can prove extremely volatile, as the recent destruction of the Babri Masjid in India so poignantly demonstrated.

## MANIPULATING ARCHAEOLOGICAL REMAINS FOR NATIONALIST PURPOSES: WHEN THE MAKING OF ALTERNATIVE HISTORIES BECOMES PROBLEMATIC

The interpretation of the archaeological record is hardly ever straightforward, resulting in unambiguous, certain reconstructions of the past. This well-recognized fact, however, does not mean that archaeological data are capable of an infinite number of possible interpretations or that there are no canons of evidence and criteria that would allow most professional archaeologists in many, if not most, cases to arrive at the same most plausible "reading" of that record. There are or should be limits to one's embrace of hearing alternative, multiple voices on the archaeologically reconstructed past. Basic historiographic principles still apply. Certain facts are capable of being documented. For example, archaeological research can establish unequivocally that some Classic Mayan polities not only practiced extensive slash-and-burn cultivation but also constructed raised fields and engaged in a more intensive and productive form of agricultural production. It is an altogether more problematic exercise to assess the historical significance of the fact that the Mayans had raised fields. Were these fields a contributing factor to the decline of Classic Mayan civilization? If so, how and to what extent? Even with the continuous accumulation of evidence, there is always room for disagreement on answering these second types of questions, and archaeologists are not known for shunning controversies; scholarly disagreements, indeed, may reflect a healthy, robust discipline trying to advance itself.

How then does one evaluate patently nationalist interpretations of the archaeological record? Are legitimate, long-neglected, and overlooked voices on the past now finally being articulated? Is such a development something to welcome or to query, and, if the latter, why and on what basis: scientific or ethical? Are nationalist interpretations inherently different and more problematic than other readings of archaeological evidence? A common nationalist reading of the past is to identify the entities archaeologists define, particularly archaeological cultures, in terms of an ethnic group ancestral to the nationality or aspirant nationality of interest. Such identifications provide the nationality in question with a respectable pedigree extending back into the remote past, firmly rooted in the national territory; land and people are united. Once made, such identifications then can be extended to interpret progressive changes, cultural developments in the archaeological record, as due to the activities of this ancestral ethnic group. If other evidence, such as that provided by linguistics and historical comparative philology, contradicts the model of autochthonous development, it typically can be accommodated. Now the gifted group in question moves into the national territory—it migrates, finding either empty space or benighted indigenes whom it civilizes or eradicates (for examples, see Shnirelman 1996 and Ligi 1993, 1994). Such nationalist interpretations seem able to accommodate flatly contradictory evidence. For example, today's Macedonians, the dominant ethnic group in the former Yugoslav Republic of Macedonia, are linguistically and culturally related to other southern Slavic peoples who migrated into the Balkans roughly during the middle of the first millennium AD; like the Serbs, they profess a form of Christian Orthodoxy. Nevertheless, they consider themselves heirs of the ancient Macedonians of Classical times and claim Alexander the Great as an ancestor, a view that is patently untenable.

Even when such reconstructions seem perfectly consistent with the archaeological record, the consistency is deceptive. The principal problem lies in the purported ethnic identification; as discussed above, archaeological cultures and ethnic groups are not synonymous, and modern constructivist perspectives on ethnicity and nationality preclude the possibility of a perfect correlation between material remains and ethnicity. Peoples' sense of themselves—who they are and what they have done—continuously changes and cannot be held constant over centuries, much less millennia. Ethnicities are not little perfectly formed homunculi or crystallized essences containing within them all the characteristics of their future development; rather, they are caught up in, even buffeted by, larger historical processes capable of altering and destroying them. The identification of some archaeological culture as ancestral to a given ethnic group represents a hopeless will-o'-the-wisp, a chimera incapable of satisfactory determination. Moreover, the quest for such identifications is not only misleading, it is also dangerous, as a consideration of both the past and current practice of archaeology abundantly makes clear. Changes in the archaeological record cannot be explained exclusively by the activities of efficient causal agents, the gifted ethnic actors; numerous other factors, such as environmental and climatic changes, must also always be considered. If prehistory teaches us anything, it is that cultures borrow from one another, that technological developments are shared and diffuse rapidly, and that specific cultures and areas have not only advanced and developed but have also declined, often catastropically. In short, for many reasons, nationalist interpretations of the past are, at best, problematic and should be so recognized.

Archaeological evidence may be peculiarly susceptible to manipulation for nationalist purposes because it is physical and visible to a nation's citizens who interact with it, consciously or not, on a daily basis. Archaeological sites become national monuments, which are increasingly being transformed into lucrative tourist attractions. Their artifacts are stored and displayed in national museums and constitute an invaluable part of the national patrimony, a heritage that becomes more and more broadly defined; both sites and artifacts frequently are incorporated into state regalia as symbols appearing on national flags, currency, and stamps or memorialized in patriotic songs and national anthems. Maps are compiled showing the distribution of sites identifed ethnically and considered to be part of the state's cultural patrimony; not infrequently, such sites are located beyond the state borders, their represenation then constituting an implicit ancestral claim on a neighboring state's territories. Even objects of mass consumption, such as postcards and cigarette brands, may depict or be named after ancient sites. All such uses demonstrate forcefully how national identity is continuously constructed through the commemoration of the remote, archaeologically ascertainable past.

Nationalism and archaeology are also inextricably related at the level of state support for research and employment. Archaeologists often work directly for state institutions, such as museums, research institutes, and antiquities services; even in the unusually decentralized context of the United States, most US archaeologists, whether employed by private or state institutions, must still solicit federally financed foundations for funds to support their research. Is archaeology then peculiarly vulnerable to state pressures and manipulation for current political purposes? Should archaeologists function as agents of the state, and is it inevitable that the discipline in some critical respects, such as funding, is necessarily at the service of the state? Most of the time the connection between the state and archaeology may be mutually beneficial—a source of strength, not difficulty. A state needs an educated elite citizenry, and the instillment of national pride in past accomplishments may be appropriate and laudatory. But what happens when the state's agenda or the popular movements driving that agenda appear more questionable on moral grounds or when the archaeologist is asked to verify some implausible, nationalist-inspired reading of the past? What are the professional and ethical responsibilities of archaeologists who function in the shadow of such states? This essay concludes by considering these issues.

## PROFESSIONAL RESPONSIBILITIES AND ETHICAL CONSIDERATIONS: ATTEMPTING TO MANAGE NATIONALIST INTERPRETATIONS OF THE PAST

During the past two centuries, modern nation-states have become the basic unit of political organization recognized throughout the world; during that same period, our knowledge of the remote past has continuously advanced largely because of the ever-increasing corpus of evidence unearthed by archaeologists. Many questions remain unanswered; some indeed may be unanswerable. It is also true that alternative interpretations of archaeological evidence are not only possible but also common and characteristic. Mute material remains are inherently ambiguous—at least to some extent. Nevertheless, certain facts of prehistory and early history can be considered established; many other reconstructions of archaeological evidence constitute plausible working hypotheses that can be confirmed by additional research. Archaeology has developed—and this also is an ongoing continuous process—standards of recording *and* interpreting material culture remains. Thus, fantastic science-fiction interpretations of archaeological materials can be dismissed for violating the principle of uniformitarianism, which remains a basic tenet of archaeology, geology, and other natural sciences despite the recognition of past unique events and catastrophes.

Archaeologists, thus, can distinguish between what is well established, plausibly known, a matter of problematic conjecture, or sheer fantasy. Nationalist interpretations fall within this range of certainty to impossibility, depending on the arguments being made and the evidence used to support them. Ethnic identifications extending back over millennia, which are a favorite form of nationalist interpretation, are problematic and hazardous for reasons already discussed. The professional responsibility of the archaeologist confronted with such interpretations is straightforward: Emphasize that the identification is uncertain and tenuous and stress the real epistemological limits that circumscribe our ability to people the remote prehistoric past.

Archaeology benefits from the critically reflexive recognition that its data are inherently political: They are excavated and interpreted in a political context and are capable of being used for a variety of political purposes, including legitimizing nationalist programs. Nevertheless, archaeologists' recognition may come at the high price of superficial analyses and facile generalizations.

Archaeologists are not only citizens of nation-states and necessarily political animals, like their fellow humans; they are also scholars interested in reconstructing the past as best and objectively as they can. Knowledge of an archaeologist's politics does not provide a foolproof guide to his/her activities as an archaeologist. The Marxist VG Childe corresponded with the fascist O Menghin and interacted more intensely and productively over a much longer period with the elitist G Clark; all were great prehistorians in terms of contributing to our knowledge of the past, regardless of their wildly divergent political philosophies and how these philosophies helped shape their work. The discipline advances cumulatively for reasons that are both internal and external to the discipline and which may be only imperfectly correlated with larger political processes. Major Spanish prehistorians, such as P Bosch-Gimpera and H Obermaier, lost their jobs and were replaced by Nazi sympathizers and Falangists following Franco's victory in the Spanish Civil War, but these obviously politically mandated changes had little practical or immediate effect on the practice of Spanish prehistory (Gilman 1995:2). State politics at the highest level were involved in the establishment of the Délégation archéologique française en Afghanistan, yet a review of the activities of that institute over the 60-year period of its existence (1922–1982) reveals that it concerned itself mostly with addressing specific archaeological problems (searching, in particular, for the easternmost traces of Alexander the Great). The institute's archaeological work, of course, was not value free and had numerous political dimensions; nevertheless, its primary activities were concerned with the reconstructions of the region's remote past, and this work overshadowed its contemporary political functions (Olivier-Utard 1997:311).

Politics and archaeology are unquestionably interrelated phenomena; indeed, this entire essay has attempted to document how archaeology may be implicated in a potentially dangerous form of politics, nationalism. Nevertheless, a caveat is necessary: Archaeology is not to be equated with politics or nationalism. They are related, yes—even inevitably so—but they are still distinct and separate phenomena that must be understood on their own terms as well as through interaction with each other.

Acceptance of the political dimension of archaeology also entails moral and ethical consequences, and it is useful to distinguish these from the professional responsibilities, though these considerations, of course, may overlap. That is, an archaeologist who questions a specific prehistoric ethnic identification may be behaving in a way that is both professionally and ethically responsible. Archaeologists should be capable of distinguishing between what they can responsibly say as professional archaeologists or as prehistorians attempting to reconstruct the past and their own political views and the ways in which their knowledge can be used for political purposes. Archaeologists then may be able to support a particular reconstruction of the past as plausible or as the most reasonable interpretation of the data and still condemn the political uses to which it may be put (Kohl & Tsetskhladze 1995:161). For example, even if the foundation of a Hindu temple had been uncovered by archaeologists beneath the Babri Masjid in Ayodhya, India (which it had not; cf Mandal 1993), responsible archaeologists still could and should have decried the destruction of the mosque; similarly, whether today's Slavic-speaking Macedonians deserve an internationally recognized nation-state is a different question from whether they can trace their ancestry back to Alexander. The archaeological evidence can be decoupled from the political movement or state policy.

Ethical standards for accepting or rejecting nationalist uses of archaeology may vary in specific cases, but they should ideally satisfy the following three criteria: (a) the construction of one group's national past should not be made at the expense of others'; (b) all cultural traditions should be recognized as worthy of study and respect; and (c) the construction of a national past should not be made at the expense of abandoning the universal anthropological perspective of our common humanity and shared past and future, the positive lessons to be learnt from evolutionary and diffusionary prehistory. It may be unfashionable to suggest that some views of the past are problematic and dangerous and that certain universal standards be met. Although many people today question such views and impositions, it is useful to recall Renan's (1947–1961) sage counsel: To be right in the long run at times requires accepting the burden of knowing how to resign oneself to being démodé.

ACKNOWLEDGMENTS

This essay benefitted from the close readings of many individuals. Among others, I would like to thank N Ben-Yehuda, A Karakasidou, and B Trigger for their helpful suggestions and criticisms. I remain, of course, fully responsible for this final version and for any problematic facts or interpretations that it contains.

> **Visit the *Annual Reviews* home page** at
> **http://www.AnnualReviews.org.**

## Literature Cited

Abu el-Haj N. 1998. Translating truths: nationalism, the practice of archaeology, and the remaking of past and present in contemporary Jerusalem. *Am. Ethnol.* In press

Anderson B. 1991. *Imagined Communities.* London: Verso. Revised ed.

Arnold B. 1990. The past as propaganda: totalitarian archaeology in Nazi Germany. *Antiquity* 64(244):464–78

Arnold B, Hassman H. 1995. See Kohl & Fawcett 1995, pp. 70–81

Atkinson JA, Banks I, O'Sullivan J, eds. 1996. *Nationalism and Archaeology: Scottish Archaeological Forum.* Glasgow: Cruithne

Audouze F, Leroi-Gourhan A. 1981. France: a continental insularity. *World Archaeol.* 13(2):170–89

Ben-Yehuda N. 1995. *The Masada Myth: Collective Memory and Mythmaking in Israel.* Madison: Univ. Wis. Press

Bernbeck R, Pollock S. 1996. Ayodhya, archaeology and identity. *Curr. Anthropol.* 37(Suppl.):138–42

Bromlei YuV. 1973. *Etnos i Etnografiia.* Moscow: Nauka

Bromlei YuV. 1983. *Ocherki Teorii Etnosa.* Moscow: Nauka

Chakrabarti D. 1997. *Colonial Indology Sociopolitics of the Ancient Indian Past.* New Delhi: Munshiram Manoharlal

Chatterjee P. 1993. *The Nation and Its Fragments.* Princeton: Princeton Univ. Press

Chernykh EN. 1995. Postscript: Russian archaeology after the collapse of the USSR - infrastructural crisis and the resurgence of old and new nationalisms. See Kohl & Fawcett 1995, pp. 139–48

Daniel G. 1962. *The Idea of Prehistory.* Harmondsworth, UK: Penguin

Daniel G. 1975. *A Hundred and Fifty Years of Archaeology.* Cambridge, MA: Harvard Univ. Press

Delle J, Smith M. 1997. Archaeology, the tourist industry, and the state. Presented at Annu. Meet. Am. Anthropol. Assoc., 97th, Washington, DC

Diaz-Andreu M. 1995. Archaeology and nationalism in Spain. See Kohl & Fawcett 1995, pp. 39–56

Diaz-Andreu M. 1996a. Constructing identities through culture: the past in the forging of Europe. See Graves-Brown et al 1966, pp. 48–61

Diaz-Andreu M. 1996b. Islamic archaeology and the origin of the Spanish nation. See Diaz-Andreu & Champion 1996, pp. 68–89

Diaz-Andreu M, Champion T. 1996. *Nationalism and Archaeology in Europe.* Boulder, CO: Westview

Dietler M. 1994. "Our ancestors the Gauls": archaeology, ethnic nationalism, and the manipulation of Celtic identity in modern Europe. *Am. Anthropol.* 96(3):584–605

Dolukhanov PM. 1995. Archaeology in Russia and its impact on archaeological theory. See Ucko 1995a, pp. 327–42

Dolukhanov PM. 1996. Archaeology and nationalism in totalitarian and post- totalitarian Russia. See Atkinson et al 1996, pp. 200–13

Duara P. 1995. *Rescuing History from the Nation: Questioning Narratives of Modern China.* Chicago: Univ. Chicago Press

Elon A. 1994. Politics and archaeology. *NY Rev. Books* Sept. 22, pp. 14–18

Eriksen TH. 1993. *Ethnicity and Nationalism: Anthropological Perspectives.* New York\ London: Pluto

Fagan B. 1975. *The Rape of the Nile: Tomb Robbers, Tourists and Archaeologists in Egypt.* New York: Scribner's

Falkenhausen Lv. 1993. On the historiographical orientation of Chinese archaeology. *Antiquity* 67: 839–49

Falkenhausen Lv. 1995. The regionalist paradigm in Chinese archaeology. See Kohl & Fawcett 1995, pp. 198–217

Gathercole P, Lowenthal D, eds. 1990. *The Politics of the Past.* London: Unwin Hyman

Gellner E, ed. 1980. *Soviet and Western Anthropology.* New York: Columbia Univ. Press

Gellner E. 1983. *Nations and Nationalism.* Oxford: Blackwell

Gilman A. 1995. Recent trends in the archaeology of Spain. In *The Origins of Complex Socieites in Late Prehistoric Iberia,* ed. KT Lillios. Ann Arbor, MI: Int. Monogr. Prehist.

Graves-Brown P, Jones S, Gamble C, eds. 1996. *Cultural Identity and Archaeology: The Construction of European Communities.* London: Routledge

Guliaev VI. 1995. *Antologiya Sovetskoi Arkheologii,* ed. VI Gulaiev, Vols. 1–3. Moscow: State Hist. Mus.

Hall M. 1990. "Hidden history": Iron Age archaeology in southern Africa. In *A History of African Archaeology,* ed. P Robertshaw, pp. 59–77. London: Currey

Hall M. 1995. Great Zimbabwe and the lost city: the cultural colonization of the South African past. See Ucko 1995a, pp. 28–45

Härke H. 1995. "The Hun is a methodical chap": reflections on the German tradition of pre- and proto-history. See Ucko 1995a, pp. 46–60

Hobsbawm E. 1992. *Nations and Nationalism Since 1780: Programme, Myth, Reality.* Cambridge, UK: Cambridge Univ. Press. 2nd ed.

Hobsbawm E, Ranger T. 1983. *The Invention of Tradition.* Cambridge, UK: Cambridge Univ. Press

Hodder I. 1986. *Reading the Past: Current Approaches to Interpretation in Archaeology.* Cambridge, UK: Cambridge Univ. Press

Hodder I. 1991. *Archaeological Theory in Europe: The Last Three Decades.* London: Routledge

Jones S. 1997. *The Archaeology of Identity: Constructing Identities in the Past and Present.* London: Routledge

Kaiser T. 1995. Archaeology and ideology in southeast Europe. See Kohl & Fawcett 1995, pp. 99–119

Karakasidou A. 1997. *Fields of Wheat, Hills of Blood: Passages to Nationhood in Greek Macedonia 1870–1990*. Chicago: Univ. Chicago Press

Kohl PL. 1992. Ethnic strife: a necessary amendment to a consideration of class struggles in antiquity. In *Civilization in Crisis: Anthropological Perspectives (Essays in Honor of Stanley Diamond)*, ed. CW Gailey, 1:167–79. Gainesville: Univ. Fla. Press

Kohl PL. 1996. L'Arménie avant le christianisme: son émergence et son évolution jusqu'au d ébut du IVᵉ siècle après J.-C. In *Arménie: Trésors de l'Arménie Ancienne*, ed. J Santrot, pp. 18–25. Paris: Somogy Editions d'Art

Kohl PL, Fawcett C, eds. 1995. *Nationalism, Politics, and the Practice of Archaeology*. Cambridge, UK: Cambridge Univ. Press

Kohl PL, Tsetskhladze GR. 1995. Nationalism, politics, and the practice of archaeology in the Caucasus. See Kohl & Fawcett 1995, pp. 149–74

Kristiansen K. 1993. The strength of the past and its great might, an essay on the use of the past. *J. Eur. Archaeol.* 1(1):3–33

Kristiansen K. 1996. European origins - "civilisation" and "barbarism." See Graves-Brown et al 1996, pp. 138–44

Lamberg-Karlovsky CC. 1998. Colonialism, nationalism, ethnicity and archaeology. *Rev. Archaeol.* In press

Larsen MT. 1996. *The Conquest of Assyria: Excavations in an Antique Land*. London: Routledge

Ligi P. 1993. National romanticism in archaeology: the paradigm of Slavonic colonization in north-west Russia. *Fennoscand. Archaeol.* 10:31–39

Ligi P. 1994. "Active Slavs" and "passive Finns": a reply. *Fennoscand. Archaeol.* 11:104–12

Lordkipanidze O. 1989. *Nasledie Drevnei Gruzii*. Tbilisi: Metsniereba

Lorenzo JL. 1981. Archaeology south of the Rio Grande. *World Archaeol.* 13(2):190–208

Mandal D. 1993. *Ayodhya: Archaeology after Demolition - A Critique of the "New" and "Fresh Discoveries."* New Delhi: Orient Longman

Marchand S. 1996a. *Down from Olympus: Archaeology and Philhellenism in Germany, 1750–1970*. Princeton: Princeton Univ. Press

Marchand S. 1996b. Orientalism as Kulturpolitik: German archaeology and cultural imperialism in Asia minor. In *Volksgeist as Method and Ethic: Essays on Boasian Ethnography and the German Anthropological Tradition*, ed. GW Stocking Jr, pp. 298–336. Madison: Univ. Wis. Press

Martínez-Navarrete MI, ed. 1993. *Teoría y Práctica de las Prehistoria: Perspectivas desde los Extremos de Europa (Theory and Practice of Prehistory: Views from the Edges of Europe)*. Santander: Univ. Cantabria

McConnell BE. 1989. Mediterranean archaeology and modern nationalism: a preface. *Rev. Archéol. Hist. d'Art Louvain* 22:107–13

Olivier-Utard F. 1997. *Politique et Archéologie: Histoire de la Délégation archéologique française en Afghanistan (1922–1982)*. Paris: Éditions Rech. Civilis.

Paddayya K. 1995. Theoretical perspectives in Indian archaeology: an historical review. See Ucko 1995a, pp. 110–49

Patterson TC. 1995. *Toward a Social History of Archaeology in the United States*. Orlando, FL: Harcourt Brace

Podgorny I, Politis G. 1990–1992. ¿Que sucedió en la historia? Los esqueletos Araucanos del Museo de La Plata y la Conquista del desierto. *Arqueol. Contemp.* 3:73–78

Politis G. 1992. *Arqueología en América Latina Hoy*. Bogotá: Banco Popular

Politis G. 1995. The socio-politics of the development of archaeology in Hispanic South America. See Ucko 1995a, pp. 197–235

Rao N. 1995. *Archaeology of empire and multinational archaeological organizations: the case of Ayodhya and WAC*. Presented at Annu. Meet. Eur. Assoc. Archaeol., 1st, Santiago de Compostela, Spain

Renan E. 1947–1961. Qu'est-ce qu'une nation? In *Oeuvres Complètes*, 1:887–907. Paris: Calmann-Lévy

Ruiz Zapatero G. 1993. La organizacíon de la arqueología en España (the organization of the archaeology in Spain). See Martínez-Navarrete 1993, pp. 45–73

Schmidt PR. 1995. Using archaeology to remake history in Africa. See Schmidt & Patterson 1995, pp. 119–47

Schmidt PR, Patterson TC, eds. 1995. *Making Alternative Histories: The Practice of Archaeology and History in Non-Western Settings*. Santa Fe, NM: Sch. Am. Res.

Schnapp A. 1996. French archaeology: between national identity and cultural identity. See Diaz-Andreu & Champion 1996, pp. 48–67

Shanks M, Tilley C. 1992. *Re-constructing Archaeology: Theory and Practice*. London: Routledge

Shavit Y. 1986. Truth will rise from the land: points to the development of public Jewish interest in archaeology (till the 1930s). *Katedra* (Hebrew) 44:27–54

Shennan S. 1989. Introduction. In *Archaeological Approaches to Cultural Identity*, ed. S Shennan, pp. 1–32. London: Unwin & Hyman

Shnirelman VA. 1993. Archaeology and ethnopolitics: why Soviet archaeologists were so involved in ethnogenetic studies. In *Interpreting the Past: Presenting Archaeological Sites to the Public*, ed. A Killebrew. Haifa, Isr: Univ. Haifa Publ.

Shnirelman VA. 1995. From internationalism to nationalism: forgotten pages of Soviet archaeology in the 1930s and 1940s. See Kohl & Fawcett 1995, pp. 120–38

Shnirelman VA. 1996. *Who Gets the Past? Competition for Ancestors among Non-Russian Intellectuals in Russia*. Baltimore, MD: The Johns Hopkins Univ. Press

Shore C. 1996. Imagining the new Europe: identity and heritage in European community discourse. See Graves-Brown et al 1996, pp. 96–115

Silberman NA. 1989. *Between Past and Present: Archaeology, Ideology, Nationalism in the Modern Middle East*. New York: Doubleday

Smith AD. 1986. *The Ethnic Origins of Nations*. Oxford: Blackwell

Sorensen MLS. 1996. The fall of a nation, the birth of a subject: the national use of archaeology in nineteenth-century Denmark. See Diaz-Andreu & Champion 1996, pp. 24–47

Suny RG. 1993. *The Revenge of the Past: Nationalism, Revolution and the Collapse of the Soviet Union*. Stanford, CA: Stanford Univ. Press

Tishkov V. 1997. *Ethnicity, Nationalism and Conflict In and After the Soviet Union: The Mind Aflame*. London: Sage

Tong E. 1995. Thirty years of Chinese archaeology (1949–1979). See Kohl & Fawcett 1995, pp. 177–97

Trigger BG. 1980. Archaeology and the image of the American Indian. *Am. Antiq.* 45: 662–76

Trigger BG. 1984. Alternative archaeologies: nationalist, colonialist, imperialist. *Man* 19:355–70

Trigger BG. 1989. *A History of Archaeological Thought*. Cambridge, UK: Cambridge Univ. Press

Trigger BG. 1994. Ethnicity: an appropriate concept for archaeology? *Fennoscand. Archaeol.* 11:101–3

Trigger BG. 1995. Romanticism, nationalism, and archaeology. See Kohl & Fawcett 1995, pp. 263–79

Trigger BG, Glover I, eds. 1981. *World Archaeol.* 13(2):133–37

Ucko PJ. 1987. *Academic Freedom and Apartheid: The Story of the World Archaeological Congress*. London: Duckworth

Ucko PJ. 1995a. *Theory in Archaeology: A World Perspective*. London: Routledge

Ucko PJ. 1995b. "Introduction: archaeological interpretation in a world context." See Ucko 1995a, pp. 1–27

van der Veer P. 1994. *Religious Nationalism: Hindus and Muslims in India*. Berkeley: Univ. Calif. Press

Weigand P. 1991. *Idées Fixes: Attitudes about disengagement, ownership, and the 1848 Treaty of Guadalupe*. Presented at Annu. Meet. Am. Anthropol. Assoc., 91st, Chicago

Wolf E. 1984. Culture: panacea or problem? *Am. Antiq.* 49(2):393–400

Wroclavsky D. 1997. Tras las huellas de los primeros hombres de América. *La Revista de Clarin VIVA*, pp. 36–49

Yemma J, Robinson WV. 1997. Questionable collection: MFA pre-Columbian exhibit faces acquisition queries. *Boston Globe*, Dec. 4, pp. A1, A28–29

Zaslavsky V. 1993. Success and collapse: traditional Soviet nationality policy. In *Nations and Politics in the Soviet Successor States*, ed. I Bremmer, R Taras, pp. 29–42. Cambridge, UK: Cambridge Univ. Press

*Annu. Rev. Anthropol. 1998. 27:247–71*
*Copyright 1998 by Annual Reviews. All rights reserved*

# EMERGING AND RE-EMERGING INFECTIOUS DISEASES: The Third Epidemiologic Transition

*Ronald Barrett, Christopher W. Kuzawa, Thomas McDade, and George J. Armelagos*

Department of Anthropology, Emory University, Atlanta, Georgia 30322; e-mail:
rbarret@learnlink.emory.edu; antga@learnlink.emory.edu; ckuzawa@emory.edu;
tmcdade@emory.edu

KEY WORDS: health transition, history of disease, political ecology, paleopathology,
medical anthropology

---

### ABSTRACT

We use an expanded framework of multiple epidemiologic transitions to review the issues of re/emerging infection. The first epidemiologic transition
was associated with a rise in infectious diseases that accompanied the Neolithic Revolution. The second epidemiologic transition involved the shift
from infectious to chronic disease mortality associated with industrialization. The recent resurgence of infectious disease mortality marks a third epidemiologic transition characterized by newly emerging, re-emerging, and
antibiotic resistant pathogens in the context of an accelerated globalization
of human disease ecologies. These transitions illustrate recurring sociohistorical and ecological themes in human–disease relationships from the Paleolithic Age to the present day.

---

## INTRODUCTION

The problem of emerging infectious disease has recently captured the public's
imagination and the attention of the scientific community. Popular books (e.g.
Preston 1994) and movies (e.g. *Outbreak*, released in 1995) tell grisly tales of
hapless victims bleeding from all orifices, prey to mutating microbes that chal-

0084-6570/98/1015-0247$08.00

lenge the supremacy of Western biomedical progress. A number of books aimed at an educated general audience chronicle the scientific research effort to understand these deadly pathogens (Garrett 1994; Rhodes 1997; Ryan 1993; Ryan 1997). Recent academic conferences (Lederberg et al 1992; Morse 1994) have brought together researchers in microbiology, public health, and bio-medicine to survey the seriousness of the problem; they report an ominous re-surgence of morbidity and mortality from new and old infectious diseases. These reports warn of the eroding efficacy of antimicrobial therapies in the face of growing multidrug resistance (Lewis 1994; Swartz 1994; Vareldzis et al 1994). They note the first rise in infectious disease deaths in affluent post-industrial nations since the Industrial Revolution: In the US, age-adjusted mor-tality from infectious disease has increased by 40% from 1980 to 1992 (Pinner et al 1996). For its part, the US Centers for Disease Control and Prevention (CDC) has compiled a list of 29 pathogens that have emerged since 1973 (Satcher 1995), and has initiated an online journal—*Emerging Infectious Dis-eases*—to address this growing problem.[1]

The current spate of attention belies the fact that emerging infections are not a recent phenomenon but have always played a major role throughout human history (Armelagos & McArdle 1975; Boyden 1970; Cockburn 1971; Fenner 1970; Lambrecht 1985; Polgar 1964). We seek to contextualize these recent emerging infectious disease trends within an evolutionary and historical per-spective, using an expanded framework of epidemiologic transition theory. By tracing the emergence of disease in the Paleolithic Age, the Neolithic Age, the Industrial Revolution, and contemporary global society, we argue for the exis-tence of three distinct epidemiologic transitions, each defined by a unique pat-tern of disease that is intimately related to modes of subsistence and social structure. We suggest that current trends—the re/emergence of infectious dis-ease in the industrialized world and an increasingly globalized disease ecology (Colwell 1996; Elliot 1993; Gubler 1996; Patz et al 1996)—herald the arrival of a qualitatively distinct third epidemiologic transition in human health.

Recognizing the complexity of the diverse sociocultural processes involved in the re/emergence of infectious disease, many researchers in biology, medi-cine, and public health are calling for input from the social and behavioral sci-ences (Sommerfeld 1995). With its integrative approach to complex biocul-tural issues, anthropology is well positioned to make significant theoretical and practical contributions.

In the sections that follow, we provide a brief overview of epidemiologic transition theory and propose an expanded framework to consider the recur-ring social, political, and ecological factors implicated in emerging disease patterns from the late Paleolithic era to the Industrial Revolution. We apply this broader framework to explain the most recent pattern of emerging disease as part of a third, qualitatively distinct, epidemiologic transition.

## AN OVERVIEW OF EPIDEMIOLOGIC TRANSITIONS

The concept of the epidemiologic transition was first formulated by Omran as a model for integrating epidemiology with demographic changes in human populations (Omran 1971). Omran stated that this model "focuses on the complex change in patterns of health and disease and on the interactions between these patterns and the demographic, economic, and sociological determinants and consequences." Omran described the epidemiologic transition as occurring in three successive stages, or "ages": 1. of pestilence and famine; 2. of receding pandemics; and 3. of degenerative and man-made diseases. The third age described the shift in age-specific disease mortality from infectious diseases to chronic degenerative diseases in England and Wales following the Industrial Revolution. Classically associated with the concept of the epidemiologic transition as a whole, this particular sequence of events represented an important tradeoff between mortality and morbidity as a result of the interaction between epidemiological and demographic processes. On one hand, decreased child and maternal mortality resulting from declining infectious diseases resulted in an overall increase in population size. On the other hand, a subsequent increase in life expectancy entailed an aging population with increasing mortality because of chronic degenerative diseases associated with the latter years of life.

Important criticisms have been made concerning this initial framing of the epidemiologic transition. Akin to assumptions of unilinear evolutionary progress in early models of cultural evolution, this framework implies that each stage of the transition is more advanced and desirable than previous stages. Because epidemiologic transition theory focuses solely upon trends in mortality, debates surrounding the ramifications of increased longevity for quality of life and well-being are not addressed by the model. It has been argued that the increase in life expectancy associated with the shift from acute infectious to chronic disease may be gained at the expense of increased total suffering and ill-health (Johansson 1992; Riley 1992; Riley & Alter 1989). However, others contend that populations undergoing the epidemiologic transition may eventually experience a delay in the age of onset of chronic disabilities and disease (Fries 1980; Olshansky & Ault 1986).

Second, although this framework emphasizes socioeconomic and ecological factors as chief determinants in disease mortality transition, the use of whole nations as units of analysis has been criticized for burying the differential experience of these events according to race, gender, and class within population statistics (Gaylin & Kates 1997). A parallel criticism has been made of "emerging infectious diseases," a classification which may not signify the emergence of new pathogens as much as a re-emerging awareness among affluent societies of old problems that never went away (Farmer 1996). These critiques underscore the need to expand this model to account for the heterogeneity of disease experience within populations undergoing epidemiologic transitions.

While Omran accounted for accelerated, delayed, and transitional variants of his "classical" model of epidemiologic transition in Europe and North America (Omran 1971, 1983), more recent modifications have improved its applicability to a broader array of contexts and issues. Bobadilla and colleagues adapted the model to fit observations in "middle income" nations such as Mexico, where trends in chronic disease have increased despite a persistence of infectious disease morbidity and mortality, resulting in what they describe as an overlap of eras (Bobadilla et al 1993). Popkin suggests that some chronic conditions have entered a refractory stage in populations such as in the United States, where individuals have changed their diet and lifestyle in an effort to prolong a healthy lifespan (Popkin 1994). This is akin to an additional stage of the epidemiologic transition proposed to explain the delayed onset of the symptoms and ill-health associated with chronic conditions in some industrial nations (Olshansky & Ault 1986).

Even with these modifications, however, the epidemiologic transition is restricted to a particular set of historical circumstances in the recent shift from infectious to chronic disease mortality. Yet, by further expanding this framework to include multiple transitions from the Paleolithic Age to the present day, we are able to illustrate how recurring sociohistorical and ecological themes have had an important influence on shifting disease patterns throughout modern human evolution. In this manner, we have reset the baseline for three distinct epidemiologic transitions to the conditions that existed just prior to the widespread changes that occurred with the adoption of agriculture in human populations.

## EPIDEMIOLOGIC TRANSITIONS: FROM THE LATE PALEOLITHIC AGE TO THE INDUSTRIAL REVOLUTION

### Paleolithic Age Baseline

During much of our evolutionary history, hominid ancestors of modern humans roamed the African savanna as small, nomadic bands of foragers. Early hominid populations likely were too small and dispersed to support many of the acute communicable pathogens common in densely populated sedentary communities (Burnet 1962), especially those for which human populations are the only disease pool (Cockburn 1971; Polgar 1964). Acute upper respiratory infections decline soon after being introduced to isolated communities, suggesting that they would have been absent from the dispersed populations of the Paleolithic era (Popkin 1994). Similarly, pathogens such as smallpox, measles, and mumps were unlikely to afflict early hominid groups (Cockburn 1967a).

Hominid social organization and demographics would have presented less of a barrier to the transmission and perpetuation of pathogens with long periods of latency or low virulence. Viruses such as chickenpox and herpes simplex may survive in isolated family units, suggesting that they could have been sustained in early dispersed and nomadic population. The current distribution of parasite species common to human and nonhuman primates provides evidence for longstanding hominid-parasite relationships that predate the divergence of the hominid lineage (Cockburn 1967b; Kliks 1983). Sprent (1969b) coined the apt term "heirloom species" to describe such parasites, which he distinguished from the "souvenir" parasites contracted through chance encounters with infected nonhuman hosts or vectors.

Long-term coevolutionary relationships between hominids and a heirloom parasite imply a good match between the parasite's mode of transmission, virulence, and lifecycle, and the lifestyle and demographics of early foraging bands (Sprent 1962, 1969a). As one example, the gregarious behavior, nesting habits, and frequency of hand-to-mouth contact typical of hominoid primates likely favored the persistence of the pinworm *Enterobius vermicularis* in hominid evolution, which continues to inflict contemporary human populations (Kliks 1983). Similarly, ectoparasites such as head and body lice (*Pediculus humanus*) and enteric pathogens such as *Salmonella* would likely have infested early hominids (Cockburn 1971; Polgar 1964).

Hominids would have contracted novel, or souvenir, parasites in their daily rounds of collecting, preparing, and eating raw plants, insects, meat, and fish (Audy 1958; Bennett & Begon 1997). The distribution and characteristics of these pathogens would have placed constraints on the ecosystems open to hominid exploitation. Lambrecht contends that the trypanosomiasis parasite carried by the tsetse fly opened ecological niches for hominid exploitation by eliminating trypanosome-susceptible fauna (Lambrecht 1980). Because modern humans are trypanosome-susceptible and thus have not developed genetic resistance to the disease, Lambrecht argues that early hominids must have adapted culturally and behaviorally to tsetse by residing in fly-free areas, and perhaps through the advent and use of fire. Similarly, Kliks argues that particularly problematic and ubiquitous helminths, such as those associated with schistosomiasis and onchocerciasis, may have limited access to productive niches, much as they do throughout large tracts of Africa today (Kliks 1983).

The distinction between the heirloom and souvenir parasites afflicting early hominid bands underscores the antiquity of disease "emergence" in human populations, which is as old as the hominid lineage itself (Sprent 1969a,b).

Then as today, the environment provided the pool of potential emerging infections or parasites, and the social, demographic, and behavioral characteristics of hominid adaptation provided the opportunity for disease emergence. The rate of emergence may have increased as tool use allowed exploitation of novel ecological niches (Kliks 1983), and as ecological zones shifted with climate change during glacial and interglacial periods (Lambrecht 1980). The eventual movement of hominid populations out of Africa into Europe, Asia, and beyond would have exposed migrating bands to novel ecologies and parasites, increasing the rate of emergence at least temporarily in such groups. However, it is likely that disease ecologies in these new habitats would have remained qualitatively similar, owing to the continuation of a nomadic foraging adaptation and low population densities.

## The First Epidemiologic Transition

Beginning about 10,000 years ago, a major shift occurred in most human populations, from a nomadic hunting and gathering lifestyle to sedentism and primary food production. This shift involved major changes in human social organization, diet, demographics, and behavior that created conditions favorable for zoonotic infections to make the transition to human hosts, and for preexisting human pathogens to evolve to more virulent forms. We describe the subsequent increase in infectious disease mortality that arose in the context of these changes as the first epidemiologic transition.

The shift to permanent settlements created larger aggregates of potential human hosts while increasing the frequency of interpersonal contact within and between communities, likely fostering the spread and evolution of more acute infections (Ewald 1994). In addition, accumulation of human waste would have created optimal conditions for dispersal of macroparasites and gastrointestinal infections. Skeletal remains from archaeological sequences spanning this cultural transition generally show an increase in the prevalence of infectious lesions as populations shifted from foraging to sedentism and food production (Cohen & Armelagos 1984), adding empirical support to these expectations.

The appearance of domesticated animals such as goats, sheep, cattle, pigs, and fowl provided a novel reservoir for zoonoses (Cockburn 1971). Tuberculosis, anthrax, Q fever, and brucellosis could have been readily transmitted through the products of domesticated animals such as milk, hair, and skin, as well as increased ambient dust (Polgar 1964). In these contexts, it should not be surprising that many contemporary human infections have their origins in the zoonoses of domesticated animals (Bennett & Begon 1997).

Agricultural practices increased contact with nonvector parasites such as schistosomal cercariae, contracted in irrigation work, and intestinal flukes, which were acquired through use of feces as fertilizer (Cockburn 1971). With the advent of food storage, the threat of contamination and wide-scale outbreaks of food poisoning increased (Brothwell 1972). Breaking the sod during cultivation may expose workers to insect bites and diseases such as scrub typhus (Audy 1961). Other vectors developed dependent relationships with human habitats, as in the case of the yellow and dengue fever-carrying mosquito, *Aedes aegypti*, which breeds preferentially in artificial containers (Thompson & O'Leary 1997; Whiteford 1997).

Reliance upon staple crops and a decline in dietary diversity may have predisposed Neolithic populations to nutritional problems similar to those experienced by subsistence-level agrarian communities in developing nations today (Harrison & Waterlow 1990). Most staple crops are efficient producers of calories capable of supporting more dense populations yet often lack critical micro- or macronutrients. Nutrient deficiencies are thus common in agrarian societies and are often exacerbated during periods of seasonal hunger or periodic droughts (Chambers et al 1981). Skeletal evidence suggests that such nutritional problems were typical in early agrarian communities and increased with agricultural intensification in some areas (Cohen & Armelagos 1984), and may have contributed to a more vulnerable host population.

Skeletal analyses demonstrate that women, children, and—with development of stratified societies—the lower classes suffered disproportionately from the first epidemiologic transition. Female remains among Neolithic populations indicate higher frequencies of bone loss and nutritional anemia (Martin & Armelagos 1979). Comparisons between agricultural populations and their foraging predecessors show greater mortality, dental defects, and impaired bone growth among infants and young children for populations in transition (Cohen & Armelagos 1984). Artifacts indicating social status differences correlate positively with nutrition and bone-growth among Lower Illinois Valley males during the Middle Woodland Period, emphasizing the role of early social stratification in the differential experience of disease (Buikstra 1984). Related issues of political organization also had health implications, as in the case of Nubian populations during the Neolithic period, in which life expectancies were inversely related to the degree of political centralization (Van-Gerven et al 1990).

The severity of disease outbreaks during the first epidemiologic transition intensified as regional populations increased and aggregated into urban centers. The crowded, unsanitary living conditions and poor nutrition characteristic of life in these early cities fostered rapid and devastating regional epidemics (Flinn 1974; McNeill 1976; McNeill 1978). The establishment of large cities increased problems of supplying clean water and removing human waste, while facilitating spread of more virulent pathogens in enclosed and densely crowded habitations (McNeill 1976; Risse 1988). Cholera contaminated water supplies, epidemics of vector-borne disease such as plague and typhus devastated populations, and outbreaks of measles, mumps, smallpox, and other viral infections were increasingly common (Knapp 1989). Unlike the infectious disease mortality common in early Neolithic populations, adults were frequently the target of epidemic outbreaks, paralyzing societies economically in their wake. As a dramatic example, tuberculosis routinely killed one third of all adults in many European communities, and by the end of the nineteenth century had claimed an estimated 350 million lives (Knapp 1989). Similarly, the Black Death of the 1300s is estimated to have eliminated at least a quarter of the European population in a decade (Laird 1989).

McNeill (1976) also discusses two important historical trends that initiated the global spread of pathogens across previously intractable geographic boundaries. First, increasing migration and trade between state-level societies in Eurasia led to the convergence of regional infectious disease pools beginning in the fifth century CE. Second, expansion of these networks into the New World through exploration and conquest brought European populations with acquired immunity to childhood infections into contact with Native Americans with no history of exposure to these pathogens (Black 1990). This contact resulted in massive pandemics of smallpox and typhoid that killed millions of people and facilitated the colonial domination of two continents (McNeill 1976, Dobyns 1993). It also probably resulted in the introduction of treponemal infections to Europe (Baker & Armelagos 1988), where sexual promiscuity in crowded urban centers may have favored a venereal mode of transmission in the form of syphilis (Hudson 1965). These historical events illustrate how the globalization of state-level societies has provided opportunities for pathogens to cross considerable social and geographic boundaries.

## The Second Epidemiologic Transition

The second epidemiologic transition roughly coincided with the Industrial Revolution in mid-nineteenth century Europe and North America. It is distinguished by a marked decline in infectious disease mortality within developed countries. This decline is the major focus of the second proposition in Omran's model of epidemiologic transition: "a long-term shift in mortality and disease patterns whereby pandemics of infection are gradually displaced by degenerative and manmade disease as the chief form of morbidity and primary cause of death"(Omran 1971:516).

The decline of infectious diseases in the nineteenth and twentieth centuries has often been cited as an objective landmark in the progress of modern civilization—a product of developments in medical science and technology in the industrialized world that would eventually diffuse to less-developed societies. Garrett shows how early successes in the eradication of polio and smallpox influenced western medical establishments in their confident forecast for the eminent demise of infectious diseases before the end of this century (Garrett 1994). However, these projections did not consider that the larger secular trend of declining infectious disease mortality was already well under way before the advent and application of antimicrobial technologies (McKeown 1976).

Based largely upon data from Scandinavia, Germany, France, Italy, and England, Schofield & Reher roughly estimated the decline in European infectious disease mortality to have occurred in three major phases beginning in the late seventeenth century (Schofield & Reher 1991). The first phase, lasting from the late seventeenth century to the beginning of the nineteenth century, is characterized by a flattening of crisis mortality peaks owing to sporadic epidemics of diseases such as plague, smallpox, and typhus. Beginning in the mid-nineteenth century, the second phase was characterized by an overall secular decline in mortality that, although subject to significant regional variation, contributed to an increased life expectancy by more than three decades, resulting in a major overall population increase despite concurrent fertility declines. The third phase began with the advent of antimicrobial therapies in the 1940s, representing a more modest decline in infectious disease mortality in more affluent nations that continued until the early 1980s.

McKeown argued for the primacy of nutritional factors in declining European mortality (McKeown 1976). However, McKeown has been criticized for weighing nutritional inferences beyond the resolution of available data (Schofield & Reher 1991; Johansson 1992). While evidence suggests that the creation of an international grain market may have spurred improved agricultural yields and distribution networks, the relative importance of other factors such as pasteurization, public hygiene, and home-based primary health care deserve further evaluation (Kunitz 1991; Woods 1991). Moreover, there is little disagreement that certain biomedical innovations such as the worldwide vaccination campaigns against smallpox played a significant role in mortality decline.

The decrease in infectious disease in industrialized nations and the subsequent reduction in infant mortality has had unforeseen consequences for human health. Namely, the subsequent extension of life expectancy has also brought increased morbidity from chronic diseases (Riley & Alter 1989). These so-called "diseases of civilization" include cancer, diabetes, coronary artery disease, and the chronic obstructive pulmonary diseases (Kaplan & Keil 1993). Other health tradeoffs of the second transition concern the role of industrial technology in the creation of artificial environments that have influenced the appearance of chronic diseases. Particularly in urban environments, increasing water and air pollution subsequent to industrialization has been linked to significantly higher rates of cancer (Anwar 1994; Dietz et al 1995), allergies (Barnes et al 1998), birth defects (Palmer 1994), and impeded mental development (Perrera 1993). These issues are compounded by the psychosomatic effects of urbanization, which is correlated with increased levels and incidences of hypertension (Grossman & Rosenthal 1993), as well as depression and anxiety (Harpham 1994).

As in the cases of the Paleolithic-era baseline and the first epidemiologic transition, social inequalities account for many of the differences in the way the second transition has been experienced within and between populations. Within more industrialized societies, socioeconomic, ethnic, and gender differences are strongly associated with differences in morbidity and mortality for both chronic and infectious diseases (Arriaga 1989; Blair 1993; Dressler 1993). Buried within national statistics, and temporarily masked by antibiotics, the conditions selected for the first transition persisted among the poorest people of the richest nations in the second.

Following the Second World War, the second epidemiologic transition made a more modest appearance in many less-developed nations and was marked by improvements in child survival and life expectancy at birth (World Bank 1993). Unlike the epidemiologic transitions experienced in the United States and Europe, which largely proceeded the advent of modern biomedical innovation, biomedical fixes such as oral rehydration therapy, immunizations, and antibiotics played a pivotal role in the initial successes in mortality reduction in these societies (Gwatkin 1980; Hill & Pebley 1989; Ruzicka & Kane 1990). While variability of these declines between countries and their possible deceleration since the 1960s has been a source of controversy (Gwatkin 1980; United Nations 1982), there is little doubt that the second transition has fallen short of optimistic projections for the developing world (Gobalet 1989). Rapid urbanization combined with marked social inequalities and a continued lack of public health infrastructure have led to communicable diseases among the urban poor, with chronic degenerative diseases among the affluent and slowly emerging middle classes (Muktatkar 1995). In middle-income countries such as Mexico and Brazil, socioeconomic status now relates inversely to important chronic disease risk markers like obesity and hypertension (Popkin 1994), akin to similar associations in the United States, the United Kingdom, and other affluent nations (Kaplan & Keil 1993).

## THE THIRD EPIDEMIOLOGIC TRANSITION

The current phenomenon of emerging infectious diseases indicates a third epidemiologic transition characterized by three major trends. First, an unprecedented number of new diseases have been detected over the last 25 years that are becoming significant contributors to adult mortality. Second, there is an increased incidence and prevalence of preexisting infectious diseases that were previously thought to have been under better control. Third, many of these reemerging pathogens are generating antimicrobial-resistant strains at a faster rate than safe new drugs can be developed. These three trends are occurring within the broader context of an increasing globalization, involving not only international trade, migration, and information networks, but also the convergence of human disease ecologies.

## Recently Emerging Infections

The Centers for Disease Control and Prevention (CDC) has compiled a list of 29 newly emerging pathogens since 1973 (Satcher 1995). It is possible that the overall size of this list is more a function of increased detection than the actual emergence of new pathogens in human populations. Such is the case of the *Legionella* bacterium responsible for the high-mortality pneumonia known as Legionnaire's Disease. Following its initial detection during a 1976 outbreak in a convention of American World War II veterans (Fraser et al 1977), environmental and retrospective patient cultures subsequently indicated that *Legionellae* had long been responsible for 2000 to 6000 deaths previously diagnosed as pneumonias of unknown etiology (McDade et al 1977), many of which were attributed to the exposure of susceptible elderly hosts to contaminated large-scale air conditioning units (Miller 1979; Morris et al 1979; Saravolatz et al 1979).

Despite possible increases in detection rates, it cannot be denied that at least some of these new diseases are making unprecedented contributions to adult mortality. The most dramatic example of this is the Human Immunodeficiency Virus (HIV). Although retrospective studies have detected cases in Europe and Africa going back as far as 1959 (Huminer et al 1987; Nahmias et al 1986), HIV has more recently become the second leading cause of death among adult males aged 25–40 years of age in the United States, and the chief contributor to a 40% increase in infectious disease mortality over the past 15 years (Pinner et al 1996). With the exception of the flu pandemic of 1918, this trend marks the first of such increases in affluent societies since the Industrial Revolution.

Phylogenetic analyses of HIV and related retroviruses indicate a recent evolution from a simian virus of Central African origin (Essex & Kanki 1988). Yet biological evolution alone does not account for the rampant spread of this disease, nor its unequal distribution within and between populations (Ewald 1994; Feldman 1990; MacQueen 1994). Throughout Asia, Africa, and the Americas, high HIV and sexually transmitted disease (STD) prevalence rates have been indices of deeper sociohistorical issues such as neocolonialism (Alubo 1990), the disintegration of poor families because of seasonal labor migrations (Hunt 1995), sexual decision-making strategies (Bolton 1992; Waddell 1996), and the gendered experience of poverty (Connors 1996; Daily et al 1996; Farmer et al 1993; MacQueen et al 1996; McCoy et al 1996). Yet, neither is this simply a case of the poor transmitting their problems to the affluent. For example, contrary to the myth of Haitian origin following the initial discovery of AIDS, evidence suggests an earlier transmission to urban Haiti by more affluent Westerners engaging in sex tourism (Farmer 1992).

The social history of AIDS provides a prototype for similar issues surrounding the transmission of other infectious diseases. Outbreaks of Ebola hemorrhagic fever have received much attention in the popular press, which has mainly focused on the gory aspects of its clinical manifestations, high mortality rates, and fears of airborne transmission accentuated with images of "virus hunters" running around in spacesuits (Preston 1994). Contrary to these dramatized accounts, however, the instances of possible airborne transmission was restricted to very close contact between unprotected healthcare workers and patients in the late stages of this disease (Garrett 1994). The Ebola outbreaks along Kinshasa Highway of Central and Eastern Africa in the 1970s mainly involved transmission via the commercial sex trade and the reuse of dirty syringes by untrained Western missionaries and underequipped healthcare workers (Garrett 1994). Regarding fears of transmission across national borders, the appearance of the closely related filoviruses detected in Reston, Virginia, and Marburg, Germany, were caused by the importation of primates for drug research, which ironically included the development of vaccines for other viruses (Bonin 1971; Morse 1993, 1995).

Ebola and Marburg are but two examples of a much larger set of recently discovered hemorrhagic diseases. Recent outbreaks of these diseases in the New World have been linked to climatic fluctuations and ecological disruption. In 1993, a sudden outbreak of a virulent hemorrhagic fever in the Four Corners region of the American Southwest was quickly identified as a novel strain of hantavirus spread through the excreta of the deer mouse, *Peromyscus maniculatus*, but not before infecting 98 individuals in 21 states and claiming 51 lives (Weigler 1995). The 1993 outbreak was associated with abnormal weather patterns (Epstein 1995), and oral histories of local American Indian healers describe three clusters of similar outbreaks that coincide with identifiable ecological markers (Chapman & Khabbaz 1994), supporting the idea that this disease has long coexisted with and periodically afflicted human populations across the United States without detection by the medical community (Weigler 1995). The initial outbreaks of Argentinian hemorrhagic fever, or Junin, were traced to ecological disruption associated with the spread of maize agriculture and increasing rodent vector habitats (Benenson 1995).

First identified in the mid 1970s, tick-borne Lyme disease has since surfaced in all 50 states as well as overseas (Jaenson 1991), and has rapidly become the most often reported anthropod-born disease in the United States (Oliver 1996). Regrowth of Eastern forests felled in the eighteenth and nineteenth centuries to make way for agricultural fields has greatly expanded the habitat of deer, mice, and their *Ixodes* tick parasites, which carry the disease-causing *Borrelia* spirochete (Walker et al 1996). Residential housing has expanded into forested areas, bringing populations into contact with the ticks and their wild-animal reservoirs. As exemplified by diseases as distinct as HIV, Ebola virus, and Lyme disease, pathogens are often provided the opportunity to jump the "species barrier" (Lappe 1994) by a combination of ecological disruption or change, and increased contact between humans and wild reservoir species. The size and mobility of human populations increases the potential for the pathogen to escape its geographic barrier (Armelagos 1998).

RE-EMERGING INFECTIONS    Ecological disruption has also been cited as a major factor in re-emerging infectious diseases as well. Warmer climates have led to increased coastal blooms of algae, creating favorable environments for the proliferation of *Vibrio cholerae*, and inland changes in temperature and humidity are increasing the reproduction of malaria vectors (Martens et al 1995; Patz et al 1996). In addition, climactic fluctuations such as El Niño are thought to have significant effects on pathogen and disease vector environments (Bouma & Dye 1997; Colwell 1996).

While acts of nature may account for changing disease patterns, most of these ecological changes have anthropogenic origins (Brown 1996; Coluzzi 1994; de Zulueta 1994). In the last 15 years, dengue fever has shown a dramatic resurgence in Asia and Latin America, where poorly developed urban environments have led to the proliferation of the *Aedes egypti* mosquito vectors in open water pools (Chinery 1995; Whiteford 1997), contributing as well to sporadic outbreaks in the Southwestern United States (Gubler & Clark 1995). The practice of combined swine-duck agriculture in Southern China as well as commercial swine and turkey farming in the United States is thought to contribute to the genetic adaptability of flu viruses (Shortridge 1992; Shu et al 1994; Wright et al 1992). Bradley critically reviewed the practice of "third-world dumping" by multinational corporations, in which industrial production facilities are "outsourced" into developing countries with cheap labor pools and greatly relaxed environmental regulations, resulting in localized climate changes (Bradley 1993a,b). Increases in mosquito populations have compounded the problem of malaria and dengue in places where poor living conditions and the unequal distribution of health resources have already contributed to higher levels of preventable mortality (Brown et al 1996; Gubler & Clark 1995).

Among the re-emerging infectious diseases, tuberculosis (TB) is the greatest contributor to human mortality, and it is estimated that nearly a third of the world's population has been latently infected with the mycobacterium (Malin et al 1995). After more than a century of steady decline, the incidence of reported TB cases in the United States increased by more than 20% from 1985 to 1992. This trend is particularly unsettling given that the previous decline of TB was the single largest contributor to North American and European declines in infectious disease mortality during the middle stages of the second epidemiologic transition (Caselli 1991; Puranen 1991).

The resurgence of tuberculosis in affluent nations was preceded by decreased public health expenditures, becoming a forgotten disease in the context of overly optimistic predictions for its continued decline (Ryan 1993). Yet TB has remained the leading cause of infectious disease mortality in developing countries, where 95% of all cases occur (Raviglione et al 1995). Notoriously endemic to populations living under conditions of malnutrition, poor sanitation, and inadequate housing, tuberculosis has long been considered to be the classic disease of poverty (Darbyshire 1996). While HIV comorbidity is implicated in the most recent first world resurgence of TB, especially among young adults, higher rates of both diseases among the urban homeless indicate that socioeconomic issues play much the same etiological role in the re/emergence of infectious diseases today as they have in centuries past (Barclay et al 1995; Barnes et al 1996; Farmer 1997; Zolopa 1994).

ANTIMICROBIAL RESISTANCE    The history of antimicrobial resistance is almost as long—or rather, as short—as the widespread use of the drugs themselves. The first recorded instance of drug resistance occurred in 1917 during the initial trials of Optochine in the treatment of pneumococcal pneumonia (Moellering 1995; Moore 1917). Three years after the 1941 introduction of penicillin for clinical use against gram-positive "staph" infections,[2] new strains of *Staphylococcus aureus* began to emerge with penicillin-destroying beta lactamase enzymes (Neu 1992). The lessons of emerging resistance were well known even before the DDT fumigation campaigns to eradicate malaria-carrying *Anopheles* mosquitoes, in which warnings of impending insecticide susceptibility accompanied strong recommendations for a single major international campaign (Brown 1996; Olliaro et al 1996; Roberts & Andre 1994). These unheeded warnings would prove correct, not only for the vectors, but for the quinine and chloroquine-resistant plasmodium parasite itself (de Zulueta 1994; Longworth 1995; Roberts & Andre 1994).

At present, more than 95% of *S. aureus* strains are resistant to most forms of penicillin, and strains resistant to methycilline (MRSA) have become endemic to US nursing homes and acute-care settings around the world (Jacoby 1996). Last year, the first strains of *S. aureus* possessing intermediate resistance to vancomycin were identified in Japan and the United States (Centers for Disease Control 1997), joining the ranks of already emerging *Enteroccoci* with full resistance to this antibiotic (Nicoletti & Stefani 1995; Rice & Shlaes 1995;

---

[2]Although Alexander Fleming first identified a staphylocidal substance in *Penicillium notatum* molds in 1928, the actual development and distribution of penicillin for clinical use took another 13 years.

Swartz 1994). In many cases, vancomycin represents the last in the line of "magic bullet" defenses against these kinds of pathogens (Gruneberg & Wilson 1994; Nicoletti & Stefani 1995; Rice & Shlaes 1995). As such, the emergence of vancomycin-resistant pathogens hails the beginning of what has been called "The Post-Antimicrobial Era" (Cohen 1992).

In many ways, biological evolution provides the ultimate critique of biomedicine by demonstrating the inevitability of genetic adaptations of microorganisms to the selective conditions posed by human technology and behaviors (Lederberg 1997). Beyond this, however, predictions of specific resistance patterns have been problematic. *Streptococcus pneumoniae* provides a good example of this problem. Long since ranked among the pneumonias known as "the old man's friend" in affluent nations (Garrett 1994), *S. pneumoniae* has also been the microbial source of more than 1,000,000 annual deaths of children under five years of age (Obaro et al 1996). In the last five years, drug-resistant strains of this bacteria have emerged worldwide (Gerber 1995; Goldstein & Garau 1994; Jernigan et al 1996), with reported frequencies as high as 50% among clinical isolates (Obaro et al 1996). Yet there is no theoretical explanation for why it took more than 40 years for this organism to develop antibiotic resistance, while other drug-resistant species emerged in less than a decade (Bartlett & Froggatt 1995).

Bartlett & Froggatt outline three general themes in the emergence of antimicrobial resistance: 1. that high-grade resistant organisms are typically foreshadowed by low-grade resistant intermediates; 2. that resistant strains are typically resistant to more than one antibiotic; and not surprisingly, 3. that resistance develops under conditions of extensive antibiotic use (Bartlett & Froggatt 1995). The overuse of antibiotics by both trained and untrained health providers throughout the world is a major factor in the evolution of antimicrobial-resistant pathogens (Kollef 1994; Kunin 1993; Kunin et al 1987).

Besides the practices of health providers, the patients themselves have created selective conditions for antimicrobial resistance by early termination of prescribed courses of antibiotics, providing additional generation time for partly reduced organism populations within the host (Appelbaum 1994). This is especially problematic for diseases such as tuberculosis, which requires up to a year of medication adherence in the absence of detectable symptoms to completely eliminate the mycobacterium (Barnes & Barrows 1993). Acquired resistance owing to incomplete adherence to TB regimens is partly responsible for the emergence of multi-drug–resistant tuberculosis (MDRTB) (Jacobs 1994; Nunn & Felten 1994)—a situation compounded by issues of access and conflicting explanatory models between patients and healthcare providers (Dedeoglu 1990; Menegoni 1996; Rubel & Garro 1992; Sumartojo 1993; Vecchiato 1997).

Host susceptibility is another major factor in the evolution of antimicrobial-resistant pathogens (Morris & Potter 1997). The large majority of MDRTB outbreaks in the United States occurred in the context of comorbidity among HIV-infected patients (Crawford 1994; Zolopa 1994). Multi-drug resistant nosocomial infections are predominantly found among elderly and immunocompromised patients in long-term and acute-care hospital settings (Hayden & Hay 1992; Koll & Brown 1993; Kollef 1994; Rho & Yoshikawa 1995; Schentag 1995; Toltzis & Blumer 1995). The emergence of the eighth cholera pandemic, involving the drug-resistant 0139 Bengal strain, has been found among populations of refugees and the poorest inhabitants of the fourth world already susceptible to the effects of unsanitary water sources (Martin et al 1994; Siddique et al 1995; Islam et al 1995; Toole 1995; Weber et al 1994).

The overuse of antiobiotics in industrial animal husbandry also contributes to the rise of multi-drug resistant strains of food-borne pathogens (Tauxe 1997). Nontyphoid strains of *Salmonella* have been on the rise in the United States since the Second World War, where it is currently the most common food-borne infection. Overuse of antibiotics in chickens has contributed to the emergence of *Salmonella* strains resistant to all known drug therapies. These were recently identified in British travelers returning from the Indian subcontinent (Rowe et al 1997). In Europe, the emergence of strains of *Campylobacter* resistant to enrofloxacin increased in parallel to the use of this antibiotic among poultry (Endtz et al 1991). Similarly, the use of avoparicin as a growth-promoter in European livestock is believed to have created selective conditions for the emergence of vancomycin-resistant enterococci (VRE), which are transmitted to human hosts through fecal-contaminated animal products (McDonald et al 1997).

While antibiotics have played a relatively minor role in the latter stage of the second epidemiologic transition, the erosion of these human cultural adaptations in the face of more rapid genetic adaptations of microorganisms forces us to confront major issues without the aid of technological crutches. We will discover to what degree these magic bullets may have subsequently obscured the relative efficacy of primary prevention in both affluent and underdeveloped societies.

INFLUENZA AND THE GLOBALIZATION OF HUMAN DISEASE ECOLOGIES   Had the historical precedents of influenza been given closer consideration, previous projections for the continued decline in infectious diseases might not have been so optimistic. With an estimated worldwide mortality of over 20,000,000, the Spanish influenza pandemic of 1918–1919 killed more human beings than any previous war or epidemic in recorded history (Crosby 1989). This was followed by the less-virulent pandemics of 1957, 1968, and 1977

(Wiselka 1994), each bringing the millenialist promise of another major outbreak at some unknown year to come (Glezen 1996; Webster et al 1993).

Noting the rapidity with which the Spanish Flu spread throughout the world in the days of steamships and isolationism, Garrett grimly suggested how such an outbreak could spread in the present age of international economics and jet travel (Garrett 1994), a timely subject given the recent appearance of a potentially lethal influenza strain in Hong Kong poultry markets with H5 antigens, to which humans have no known history of previous exposure (Cohen 1997; Shortridge 1995). With revolutionary changes in transportation technology (Reid & Cossar 1993; Wilson 1996), worldwide urbanization (Muktatkar 1995; Phillips 1993), and the increasing permeability of geopolitical boundaries (Farmer 1996), human populations are rapidly converging into a single global disease ecology (McNeill 1976).

McNeill (1976) cites the early effects of transnationalism on the transmission of infectious diseases with the establishment of extensive Eurasian trade networks in the fifth century CE. Intercontinental shipping routes provided for the transport of pathogens as well as trade goods and organized violence. The European conquests of the new World presented a dramatic example of this trend, in which adult carriers of childhood diseases endemic to post-first transition populations suddenly infected unexposed Native American populations, resulting in massive pandemics of smallpox and typhus. Neither was this a one-way trade, as returning sailors brought syphilis and tobacco back to the European continent with them.

The current trend of accelerated globalization challenges us to consider the health implications not just of converging microbial ecologies, but also of the international flow of ideologies, behavior patterns, and commodities that underlie human disease patterns. This broader picture of globalization, involving the international exchange of *memes* (units of cultural information) as well as microbes, entails a convergence of both chronic and infectious disease patterns. This is evidenced in the many developing societies that are suffering what has been called the "worst of both worlds"—the postwar rise in chronic degenerative diseases among the poor without significant declines in infectious disease mortality (Bradley 1993a), while these infections re-emerge in post-second transition societies (Armelagos et al 1996).

## CONCLUSION

Buoyed by early successes in the control of scourges such as polio and smallpox in the 1950s and 1960s, the Western medical establishment claimed that it was time to close the book on infectious diseases and focus research attention on the growing problem of chronic degenerative disease (Garrett 1993). Unfortunately, the book on infectious disease remains very much open, and new chapters continue to be added at an alarming pace. We address this issue from an evolutionary perspective, using the concept of epidemiologic transition theory as an organizing framework. Our discussion of epidemiologic transitions during the course of human evolution reveals that disease "emergence" is not new but has been a dynamic feature of the interrelationships between humans and their sociocultural and ecological environments since the Paleolithic period.

The initial formulations of the epidemiologic transition provided a useful interdisciplinary framework for macrolevel analyses of demographic changes associated with major declines in infectious disease mortality in Europe and North America in the wake of the Industrial Revolution (Omran 1971). Despite later modifications, however, interpretations of this framework still remained largely restricted to a single set of events at a particular period of human history (Omran 1983). The subsequent particularism of this transition fueled notions of unilinear progress, resulting in falsely optimistic projections for the continued decline and eventual elimination of infectious disease in human populations (Garrett 1994). Our expanded framework of multiple epidemiological transitions avoids these pitfalls by providing a broader historical and evolutionary perspective that highlights common themes that pervade changing human-disease relationships throughout modern human evolution.

In our review of epidemiologic transitions, we have highlighted the socioecological, technological, and political factors involved in human disease dynamics. The US Institute of Medicine has identified six principal factors contributing to the current problem of re/emerging infectious diseases: 1. ecological changes; 2. human demographics and behavior; 3. international travel and commerce; 4. technology and industry; 5. microbial adaptation and change; and 6. breakdown in public health measures (Lederberg et al 1992; Morse 1995). The degree to which these factors are fundamentally anthropogenic cannot be overstated, nor can the influence of socioeconomic inequalities across these factors.

Recognizing the complexity of these sociobehavioral dynamics, many researchers in biology, medicine, and public health are calling for greater involvement of social and behavioral scientists in addressing infectious disease issues (Morse 1995; Satcher 1995; Sommerfeld 1995). By taking a holistic approach to these important human issues, anthropologists are well positioned to make significant theoretical and practical contributions within interdisciplinary research settings. For example, 40 years ago, Livingstone described the emergence of malaria following the introduction of agriculture in sub-Saharan Africa in what has become a classic example of the ability of humans to shape their physical environments—with unforeseen health consequences (Livingstone 1958).

Anthropologists have explored the health implications of (*a*) sexual behaviors (Lindenbaum 1991; MacQueen et al 1996; Waddell 1996); (*b*) funerary practices (Lindenbaum 1990); (*c*) ethnic conflict and genocide (Tambiah 1989); and (*d*) population displacement (Bisharat 1995; Malkki 1995; Toole 1995). Recent work in transnationalism identifies the political, economic, and social trends that are increasingly integrating the world's diverse populations (Kearney 1995). The emerging paradigm of evolutionary medicine demonstrates the applicability of evolutionary principles to contemporary health issues (Armelagos 1997), and emphasizes the ability of humans to shape their environment through pathogen selection (Lederberg 1997). Finally, anthropologists have critiqued the political-economic constraints that limit access to health care and basic public-health needs (Farmer 1996; Inhorn & Brown 1990; Risse 1988). Given this range of issues impacting human-disease relationships, even anthropologists not directly concerned with infection can make significant contributions to an improved understanding of disease emergence.

> **Visit the *Annual Reviews* home page** at
> **http://www.AnnualReviews.org.**

## Literature Cited

Alubo SO. 1990. Debt, crisis, health and health services in Africa. *Soc. Sci. Med.* 31:639–48

Anwar WA. 1994. Monitoring of different populations at risk by different cytogenetic points. *Environ. Health Perspect.* 4:131–34

Appelbaum PC. 1994. Antibiotic-resistant pneumococci—facts and fiction. *J. Chemother.* 6(S4):7–15

Armelagos GJ. 1997. Disease, Darwin and medicine in the third epidemiological transition. *Evol. Anthropol.* 5(6):212–20

Armelagos GJ. 1998. The viral superhighway. *Sciences* 38:24–30

Armelagos GJ, Barnes KC, Lin J. 1996. Disease in human evolution: the re-emergence of infectious disease in the third epidemiological transition. *AnthroNotes* 18(3):1–7

Armelagos GJ, McArdle A. 1975. Population, disease, and evolution. In *Population Studies in Archaeology and Biological Anthropology: A Symposium,* ed. AC Swedlund, pp. 57–70. Soc. Am. Archaeol. *Am. Antiq.* 40 (2) Part 2, Mem. 30

Arriaga EE. 1989. Changing trends in mortality decline during the last decades. In *Differential Mortality: Methodological Issues*

*and Biosocial Factors*, ed. L Ruzicka, G Wunsch, P Kane, 1:105–29. Oxford: Clarendon

Audy JR. 1958. The localization of diseases with special reference to the zoonoses. *Trans. R. Soc. Trop. Med. Hyg.* 52:308–34

Audy JR. 1961. The ecology of scrub typhus. In *Studies in Disease Ecology: Studies in Medical Geography*, ed. JM May, pp. 389–432. New York: Hafner

Baker B, Armelagos GJ. 1988. Origin and antiquity of syphilis: a dilemma in paleopathological diagnosis and interpretation. *Curr. Anthropol.* 29(5):703–37

Barclay DM III, Richardson JP, Fredman L. 1995. Tuberculosis in the homeless. *Arch. Fam. Med.* 4(6):541–46

Barnes KC, Armelagos GJ, Morreale SC. 1998. Darwinian medicine and the emergence of allergy. In *Evolutionary Medicine*, ed. W Trevethan, J McKenna, EO Smith. New York: Oxford Univ. Press.

Barnes PF, Barrows SA. 1993. Tuberculosis in the 1990s. *Ann. Intern. Med.* 119(5): 400–10

Barnes PF, Elhajj H, Preston-Martin S, Cave MD, Jones BE, et al. 1996. Transmission of tuberculosis among the urban homeless. *J. Am. Med. Assoc.* 275(4):305–7

Bartlett JG, Froggatt JW III. 1995. Antibiotic resistance. *Arch. Otolaryngol. Head Neck Surg.* 121(4):392–96

Benenson A. 1995. *Control of Communicable Disease Manual.* Washington, DC: Am. Public Health Assoc.

Bennett M, Begon ME. 1997. Virus zoonoses—a long-term overview. *Comp. Immunol. Microbiol. Infect. Dis.* 20(2):101–9

Bisharat G, ed. 1995. *Mistrusting Refugees.* Berkeley: Univ. Calif. Press

Black FL. 1990. Infectious disease and the evolution of human populations: the examples of South American forest tribes. See Swedlund & Armelagos 1990, pp. 55–74

Blair A. 1993. Social class and the contextualization of illness experience. In *Worlds of Illness: Biographical and Cultural Perspectives on Health and Disease,* ed. A Radley, pp. 114–47. New York: Routledge

Bobadilla JL, Frenk J, Lozano R, Frejka T, Stern C, et al. 1993. Cardiovascular disease. In *Disease Control Priorities in Developing Countries,* ed. DT Jamison, WH Mosley, AR Measham, JL Bobadilla, pp. 51–63. Oxford, UK: Oxford Univ. Press

Bolton R. 1992. AIDS and promiscuity: muddles in the models of HIV prevention. *Med. Anthropol.* 14(2–4):145–223

Bonin O. 1971. *Marburg Virus: Consequences for the Manufacture and Control of Virus Vacine,* ed. GA Martini, R Siegert. New York: Springer-Verlag

Bouma MJ, Dye C. 1997. Cycles of malaria associated with El Niño in Venezuela. *J. Am. Med. Assoc.* 278(21):1772–74

Boyden SV, ed. 1970. *The Impact of Civilization on the Biology of Man.* Toronto: Univ. Toronto Press

Bradley DJ. 1993a. Environmental and health problems of developing countries. In *Environmental Change and Human Health. Ciba Found. Symp.* 175:234–46. Chichester, UK: CIBA Found.

Bradley DJ. 1993b. Human tropical diseases in a changing environment. See Bradley 1993a, pp. 147–70

Brothwell D. 1972. The question of pollution in earlier and less developed societies. In *Population and Pollution,* ed. PR Cox, J Peel, pp. 15–27. London: Academic

Brown PJ. 1996. Culture and the global resurgence of malaria. In *The Anthropology of Infectious Disease: International Health Perspective,* ed. MC Inhorn, PJ Brown, pp. 119–44. Amsterdam: Gordon & Breach

Brown PJ, Inhorn M, Smith D. 1996. Disease, ecology and human behavior. In *Medical Anthropology: Contemporary Theory and Methods,* ed. CF Sargent, TM Johnson, pp. 183–218. Westport, CT: Praeger

Buikstra JE. 1984. The lower Illinois river region: a prehistoric context for the study of ancient diet and health. See Cohen & Armelagos 1984, pp. 217–36

Burnet FM. 1962. *Natural History of Infectious Disease.* Cambridge, UK: Cambridge Univ. Press

Caselli G. 1991. Health transition and cause-specific mortality. See Schofield et al 1991, pp. 68–96

Centers for Disease Control. 1997. *Staphylococcus aureus* with reduced susceptibility to vancomycin—United States, 1997. *Morbid. Mortal. Wkly. Rep.* (46):765–66

Chambers R, Longhurst R, Pacey A. 1981. *Seasonal Dimensions to Rural Poverty.* London: Osmun

Chapman LE, Khabbaz RF. 1994. Etiology and epidemiology of the Four Corners hantavirus outbreak. *Infect. Agents Dis.* 3(5):234–44

Chinery WA. 1995. Impact of rapid urbanization on mosquitoes and their disease transmission potential in Accra and Tema, Ghana. *Afr. J. Med. Med. Sci.* 24(2):179–88

Cockburn TA. 1967a. The evolution of human infectious diseases. See Cockburn 1967b, pp. 84–107

Cockburn TA. 1967b. Infections of the order primates. In *Infectious Diseases: Their Evolution and Eradication,* ed. TA Cockburn. Springfield, IL: Thomas

Cockburn TA. 1971. Infectious disease in ancient populations. *Curr. Anthropol.* 12(1):45–62

Cohen J. 1997. The flu pandemic that might have been. *Science* 277(5332):1600–1

Cohen ML. 1992. Epidemiology of drug resistance: implications for a post-antimicrobial era. *Science* 257(5073):1050–55

Cohen MN, Armelagos GJ, eds. 1984. *Paleopathology at the Origins of Agriculture.* New York: Academic

Coluzzi M. 1994. Malaria and the afrotropical ecosystems: impact of man-made environmental changes. *Parassitologia* 36(1–2):223–27

Colwell RR. 1996. Global climate and infectious disease: the cholera paradigm. *Science* 274(5295):2025–31

Connors M. 1996. Sex, drugs, and structural violence: unraveling the epidemic among poor women in the United States. See Farmer et al 1996, pp. 91–123

Crawford JT. 1994. The epidemiology of tuberculosis: the impact of HIV and multidrug-resistant strains. *Immunobiology* 191:337–43

Crosby AW. 1989. *The Forgotten Pandemic: The Influenza Pandemic of 1918.* Cambridge, UK: Cambridge Univ. Press

Daily J, Farmer P, Rhatigan J, Katz J, Furin J, et al. 1996. Women and HIV infection. See Farmer et al 1996, pp. 125–45

Darbyshire J. 1996. Tuberculosis—out of control? The Mitchell Lecture 1995. *J. R. Coll. Physicians London* 30(4):352–59

Dedeoglu N. 1990. Health and social inequities in Turkey. *Soc. Sci. Med.* 31(3): 387–92

de Zulueta J. 1994. Malaria and ecosystems: from prehistory to posteradication. *Parassitologia* 36(1–2):7–15

Dietz A, Senneweld E, Maier H. 1995. Indoor air pollution by emissions of fossil fuel single stoves. *J. Otolaryngol. Head Neck Surg.* 112(2):308–15

Dobyns HF. 1993. Disease transfer at contact. *Annu. Rev. Anthropol.* 22:273–91

Dressler W. 1993. Health in the African American community: accounting for health inequalities. *Med. Anthropol. Q.* 7(4):325–35

Elliot P. 1993. Global epidemiology. In *Environmental Change and Human Health, Ciba Found. Symp.* 175, pp. 219–33. Chichester, UK: Wiley

Endtz HP, Ruijs GJ, Vankling B, Jansen WH, Vanderreijden T, Mouton RP. 1991. Quinolone resistance in campylobacter isolated from may and poultry following the introduction of fluoroquinolones in veterinary medicine. *J. Antimicrob. Chem.* 27(2):199–208

Epstein P. 1995. Emerging diseases and ecosystem instability: new threats to public health. *Am. J. Public Health* 85(2):168–72

Essex M, Kanki PJ. 1988. The origin of the AIDS virus. *Sci. Am.* 259(4):64–71

Ewald PW. 1994. *Evolution of Infectious Disease.* New York: Oxford Univ. Press

Farmer P. 1992. *AIDS and Accusation: Haiti and the Geography of Blame.* Berkeley: Univ. Calif. Press

Farmer P. 1996. Social inequalities and emerging infectious diseases. *Emerg. Infect. Dis.* 2(4):259–69

Farmer P. 1997. Social scientists and the new tuberculosis. *Soc. Sci. Med.* 44(3):347–58

Farmer P, Connors M, Simmons J, eds. 1996. *Women, Poverty, and AIDS: Sex, Drugs, and Structural Violence.* Monroe, ME: Common Courage

Farmer P, Lindenbaum S, Good MJ. 1993. Women, poverty and AIDS: an introduction. *Cult. Med. Psychiatry* 17(4):387–97

Feldman DA. 1990. *Assessing Viral, Parasitic, and Socioeconomic Cofactors Affecting HIV-1 Transmission in Rwanda*, ed. DA Feldman, pp. 45–54. New York: Praeger

Fenner F. 1970. The effects of changing social organization on the infectious diseases of man. In *The Impact of Civilization on the Biology of Man*, ed. SV Boyden. Canberra: Aust. Natl. Univ. Press

Flinn MW. 1974. The stabilization of mortality in preindustrial Western Europe. *J. Eur. Econ. Hist.* 3:285–318

Fraser DW, Tsai TR, Orenstein W, Parkin WE, Beecham HJ, et al. 1977. Legionnaires' disease: description of an epidemic of pneumonia. *N. Engl. J. Med.* 297(22):1189–97

Fries JF. 1980. Aging, natural death, and the compression of morbidity. *N. Engl. J. Med.* 303(3):130–35

Garrett L. 1994a. *The Coming Plague: Newly Emerging Diseases in a World Out of Balance.* New York: Farrar Straus & Giroux

Garrett L. 1994b. Human movements and behavioral factors in the emergence of diseases. *Ann. NY Acad. Sci.* 740:312–18

Gaylin DS, Kates J. 1997. Refocusing the lens: epidemiologic transition theory, mortality differentials, and the AIDS pandemic. *Soc. Sci. Med.* 44(5):609–21

Gerber MA. 1995. Antibiotic resistance in group *A* streptococci. *Pediatr. Clin. North Am.* 42(3):539–51

Glezen WP. 1996. Emerging infections: pandemic influenza. *Epidemiol. Rev.* 18(1): 64–76

Gobalet JG. 1989. *World Mortality Trends Since 1870.* New York: Garland

Goldstein FW, Garau J. 1994. Resistant pneumococci: a renewed threat in respiratory infections. *Scand. J. Infect. Dis. Suppl.* 93: 55–62

Grossman E, Rosenthal T. 1993. Effect of urbanization on blood pressure in Ethiopian immigrants. *J. Hum. Hypertens.* 7(6): 559–61

Gruneberg RN, Wilson APR. 1994. Antiinfective treatment in intensive care: the role of glycopeptides. *Intensive Care Med.* 20(S4):S17–22

Gubler DJ. 1996. The global resurgence of arboviral diseases. *Trans. R. Soc. Trop. Med. Hyg.* 90(5):449–51

Gubler DJ, Clark GG. 1995. Dengue/dengue hemorrhagic fever: the emergence of a global health problem. *Emerg. Infect. Dis.* 1(2):55–57

Gwatkin DR. 1980. Indications of change in developing country mortality trends: the end of an era? *Popul. Dev. Rev.* 33(2): 615–44

Harpham T. 1994. Urbanization and mental health in developing countries: a research role for social scientists, public health professionals, and social psychiatrists. *Soc. Sci. Med.* 39(2):233–45

Harrison G, Waterlow J, eds. 1990. *Diet and Disease in Transitional and Developing Societies.* Cambridge, UK: Cambridge Univ. Press

Hayden FG, Hay AJ. 1992. Emergence and transmission of influenza *A* viruses resistant to amantadine and rimantadine. *Curr. Top. Microbiol. Immunol.* 176:119–30

Hill K, Pebley LR. 1989. Child mortality in the developing world. *Popul. Dev. Rev.* 15(4): 657–87

Hudson EH. 1965. Treponematosis and man's social evolution. *Am. Anthropol.* 67: 885–901

Huminer D, Rosenfeld JB, Pitlik SD. 1987. AIDS in the pre-AIDS era. *Rev. Infect. Dis.* 9:1102–8

Hunt CW. 1995. *Migrant Labor and Sexually Transmitted Disease: AIDS in Africa,* ed. ER Bethel, pp. 137–56. Boston: Allyn & Bacon

Inhorn MC, Brown PJ. 1990. The anthropology of infectious disease. *Annu. Rev. Anthropol.* 19:89–117

Islam MS, Siddique AK, Salam A, Akram K, Majumdar RN, et al. 1995. Microbiological investigations of diarrhoea epidemics among Rwandan Refugees in Zaire. *Trans. R. Soc. Trop. Med. Hyg.* 89:506

Jacobs RF. 1994. Multiple-drug-resistant tuberculosis. *Clin. Infect. Dis.* 19(1):1–8

Jacoby GA. 1996. Antimicrobial-resistant pathogens in the 1990s. *Annu. Rev. Med.* 47:169–79

Jaenson TGT. 1991. The epidemiology of Lyme borreliosis. *Parasit. Today* 7:39–45

Jernigan DB, Cetron MS, Breiman RF. 1996. Minimizing the impact of drug-resistant *Streptococcus pneumoniae* (DRSP): a strategy from the DRSP working group. *J. Am. Med. Assoc.* 275(3):206–9

Johansson SR. 1992. Measuring the cultural inflation of morbidity during the decline in mortality. *Health Transit. Rev.* 2(1):78–89

Kaplan G, Keil J. 1993. Socioeconomic factors and cardiovascular disease: a review of the literature. *Circulation* 88:1973–98

Kearney M. 1995. Local and the global: the anthropology of globalization and transnationalism. *Annu. Rev. Anthropol.* 24: 547–65

Kliks MM. 1983. Paleoparisitology: on the origins and impact of human-helminth relationships. In *Human Ecology and Infectious Disease,* ed. NA Croll, JH Cross, pp. 291–313. New York: Academic

Knapp VJ. 1989. *Disease and its Impact on Modern European History,* Vol. 10. Lewiston, NY: Mellen

Koll BS, Brown AE. 1993. The changing epidemiology of infections at cancer hospitals. *Clin. Infect. Dis.* 17(Suppl. 2):S322–28

Kollef MH. 1994. Antibiotic use and antibiotic resistance in the intensive care unit: are we curing or creating disease? *Heart Lung* 23(5):363–67

Kunin CM. 1993. Resistance to antimicrobial drugs—a worldwide calamity. *Ann. Intern. Med.* 118(7):557–61

Kunin CM, Lipton HL, Tupasi T, Sachs T, Schekler WE, et al. 1987. Social, behavioral, and practical factors affecting antibiotic use worldwide: report of Task Force 4. *Rev. Infect. Dis.* 9(3):270–84

Kunitz SJ. 1991. The personal physician and the decline of mortality. See Schofield et al 1991, pp. 248–62

Laird M. 1989. Vector-borne disease introduced into new areas due to human movements: a historical perspective. In *Demography and Vector-Borne Diseases,* ed. MW Service, pp. 17–33. Boca Raton, FL: CRC

Lambrecht FL. 1980. Paleoecology of tsetse flies and sleeping sickness in Africa. *Proc. Am. Philos. Soc.* 124(5):367–85

Lambrecht FL. 1985. Trypanosomes and hominid evolution. *BioScience* 35(10): 640–46

Lappe M. 1994. *Evolutionary Medicine: Rethinking the Origins of Disease.* San Francisco: Sierra Club Books

Lederberg J. 1997. Infectious disease as an evolutionary paradigm. *Emerg. Infect. Dis.* 3(4):417–23

Lederberg J, Shope RE, Oaks SC Jr, eds. 1992. *Emerging Infection: Microbal Threats to Health in the United States.* Washington, DC: Inst. Med., Natl. Acad. Press

Lewis K. 1994. Multidrug resistance pumps in bacteria: variations on a theme. *Trends Biochem. Sci.* 19(3):119–23

Lindenbaum S. 1990. The ecology of kuru. See Swedlund & Armelagos 1990

Lindenbaum S. 1991. Anthropology rediscovers sex. Introduction. *Soc. Sci. Med.* 33(8): 865–66

Livingstone FB. 1958. Anthropological implications of sickle-cell distribution in West Africa. *Am. Anthropol.* 60:533–62

Longworth DL. 1995. Drug-resistant malaria in children and in travelers. *Pediatr. Clin. North Am.* 42(3):649–64

MacQueen KM. 1994. The epidemiology of HIV transmission: trends, structure, and dynamics. *Annu. Rev. Anthropol.* 23: 509–26

MacQueen KM, Nopkesorn T, Sweat MD. 1996. Alcohol consumption, brothel attendance, and condom use: normative expectations among Thai military conscripts. *Med. Anthropol. Q.* 10(3):402–23

Malin AS, McAdam KP, Keith PW. 1995. Escalating threat from tuberculosis: the third epidemic. *Thorax* 50:S37–42

Malkki LH. 1995. Refugees and exile: from "refugee studies" to the national order of things. *Annu. Rev. Anthropol.* 24:495–523

Martens WJM, Niessen LW, Rotman J, Jetten TH, McMichael AJ. 1995. Potential impact of global climate change on malaria risk. *Environ. Health Perspect.* 103(5): 458–64

Martin AA, Moore J, Collins C, Biellik R, Kattel U, et al. 1994. Infectious disease surveillance during emergency relief to Bhutanese refugees in Nepal. *J. Am. Med. Assoc.* 272(5):377–81

Martin DL, Armelagos GJ. 1979. Morphometrics of compact bone: an example from Sudanese Nubia. *Am. J. Phys. Anthropol.* 51: 571–78

McCoy CB, Metsch LR, Inciardi JA, et al. 1996. Sex, drugs, and the spread of HIV/AIDS in Belle Glade, Florida. *Med. Anthropol. Q.* 10(1):83–93

McDade JE, Shepard CC, Fraser DW, Tsai TR, Redus MA, et al. 1977. Legionnaires' disease: isolation of a bacterium and demonstration of its role in other respiratory disease. *N. Engl. J. Med.* 297(22): 1197–203

McDonald LC, Kuehnert MJ, Tenover FC, Jarvis WR. 1997. Vancomycin-resistant enterococci outside the health care setting; prevalence, sources and public health implications. *Emerg. Infect. Dis.* 3:311–17

McKeown T. 1976. *The Modern Rise of Population.* New York: Academic

McNeill WH. 1976. *Plagues and People.* Garden City, NY: Anchor/Doubleday

McNeill WH. 1978. Disease in history. *Soc. Sci. Med.* 12:79–81

Menegoni L. 1996. Conceptions of tuberculosis and therapeutic choices in Highland Chiapas, Mexico. *Med. Anthropol. Q.* 10(3):381–401

Miller RP. 1979. Cooling towers and evaporative condensers. *Ann. Intern. Med.* 90(4): 667–70

Moellering RC Jr. 1995. Past, present, and future of antimicrobial agents. *Am. J. Med.* 99(6A):29

Moore HF. 1917. A study of ethylhydrocupreine (optochin) in the treatment of acute lobar pneumonia. *Arch. Intern. Med.* (19): 611

Morris GK, Patton CM, Feeley JC, Johnson SE, Gorman G, et al. 1979. Isolation of the Legionnaires' disease bacterium from environmental samples. *Ann. Intern. Med.* 90(4):664–66

Morris JG, Potter M. 1997. Emergence of new pathogens as a function of chnages in host susceptibility. *Emerg. Infect. Dis.* 3(4): 435–41

Morse SS. 1994. Prediction and biological evolution. Concept paper. *Ann. NY Acad. Sci.* 740:436–38

Morse SS. 1995. Factors in the emergence of infectious diseases. *Emerg. Infect. Dis.* 1(1):7–15

Muktatkar R. 1995. Public health problems of urbanization. *Soc. Sci. Med.* 41(7):977–81

Nahmias AJ, Weiss J, Yao X, Lee F, Kodsi R, et al. 1986. Evidence for human infection with an HTLV-III-LAV-like virus in central Africa, 1959. *Lancet* 1:1279–80

Neu HC. 1992. The crisis in antibiotic resistance. *Science* 257(5073):1064–73

Nicoletti G, Stefani S. 1995. Enterococci: susceptibility patterns and therapeutic options. *Eur. J. Clin. Microbiol. Infect. Dis.* 14(1):S33–37

Nunn P, Felten M. 1994. Surveillance of resistance to antituberculosis drugs in developing countries. *Tuberc. Lung Dis.* 75(3): 163–67

Obaro SK, Monteil MA, Henderson DC. 1996. The pneumococcal problem. *Br. Med. J.* 312(7045):1521–25

Oliver JH. 1996. Lyme borreliosis in the southern United States: a review. *J. Parasitol.* 82(6):926–35

Olliaro P, Cattani J, Wirth D. 1996. Malaria, the submerged disease. *J. Am. Med. Assoc.* 275(3):230–33

Olshansky SJ, Ault AB. 1986. The fourth stage of the epidemiologic transition: the age of delayed degenerative diseases. *Milbank Mem. Fund Q.* 64(3):355–91

Omran AR. 1971. The epidemiologic transition: a theory of the epidemiology of population change. *Millbank Mem. Fund Q.* 49(4):509–37

Omran AR. 1983. The epidemiologic transition theory: a preliminary update. *J. Trop. Pediatr.* 29(6):305–16

Palmer JR. 1994. Advances in the epidemiology of gestational trophoblastic disease. *J. Reprod. Med.* 39(3):155–62

Patz JA, Epstein PR, Burke TA, Balbus JM. 1996. Global climate change and emerging infectious diseases. *J. Am. Med. Assoc.* 275(3):217–23

Perrera F. 1993. Prevention of environmental pollution: good for our health. *Environ. Health Perspect.* 101(7):562–63

Phillips DR. 1993. Urbanization and human health. *Parasitology* 106(107):S93–107

Pinner R, Teutsch SM, Simonsen L, Klug LA, Graber JM, et al. 1996. Trends in infectious diseases mortality in the United States. *J. Am. Med. Assoc.* 275(3):189–93

Polgar S. 1964. Evolution and the ills of mankind. In *Horizons of Anthropology*, ed. S Tax, pp. 200–11. Chicago: Aldine

Popkin BM. 1994. The nutrition transition in low-income countries: an emerging crisis. *Nutr. Rev.* 52(9):285–98

Preston R. 1994. *The Hot Zone*. New York: Random House

Puranen B. 1991. Tuberculosis and the decline of mortality in Sweden. In *The Decline of Mortality in Europe*, ed. R Schofield, D Reher, A Bideau, pp. 68–96. Oxford, UK: Clarendon

Raviglione MC, Snider DE, Kochi A. 1995. Global epidemiology of tuberculosis: morbidity and mortality of a worldwide epidemic. *J. Am. Med. Assoc.* 273: 220–26

Reid D, Cossar JH. 1993. Epidemiology of travel. *Br. Med. Bull.* 49(2):257–68

Rho JP, Yoshikawa TT. 1995. The cost of inappropriate use of anti-infective agents in older patients. *Drugs Aging* 6(4):263–67

Rhodes R. 1997. *Deadly Feasts: Tracking the Secrets of a Terrifying New Plague*. New York: Simon & Schuster

Rice LB, Shlaes DM. 1995. Vancomycin resistance in the enterococcus. Relevance in pediatrics. *Pediatr. Clin. N. Am.* 42(3): 601–18

Riley JC. 1992. From a high mortality regime to a high morbidity regime: is culture everything in sickness? *Health Transit. Rev.* 2(1):71–78

Riley JC, Alter G. 1989. The epidemiologic transition and morbidity. *Ann. Demogr. Histor.* 1989:199–213

Risse GB. 1988. Epidemics and history: ecological perspectives and social responses. In *AIDS: The Burdens of History*, ed. E Fee, DM Fox, pp. 33–66. Berkeley: Univ. Calif. Press

Roberts DR, Andre RG. 1994. Insecticide resistance issues in vector-borne disease control. *Am. J. Trop. Med. Hyg.* 50(6): 21–34 (Suppl.)

Rowe B, Ward LR, Threlfall EJ. 1997. Multidrug-resistant *Salmonella typhi*: a worldwide epidemic. *Clin. Infect. Dis.* 24(Suppl. 1):S106–9

Rubel AJ, Garro LC. 1992. Social and cultural factors in the successful control of tuberculosis. *Public Health Rep.* 107(6): 626–35

Ruzicka L, Kane P. 1990. Health transition: the course of morbidity and mortality. In *What We Know About Health Transition: The Cultural, Social, and Behavioral Determinants of Health*, ed. J Caldwell, S Findley, P Cadwell, G Santow, W Cosford, J Braid, D Broers Freeman, pp. 1–24. Proc.

Int. Workshop. Canberra: Health Transit. Cent.

Ryan F. 1993. *The Forgotten Plague: How the Battle against Tuberculosis Was Won—and Lost*. Boston: Little Brown

Ryan F. 1997. *Virus X: Tracking the New Killer Plagues: Out of the Present into the Future*. Boston: Little Brown

Saravolatz LD, Burch KH, Fisher E, Madhavan T, Kiani D, et al. 1979. The compromised host and Legionnaires' disease. *Ann. Intern. Med.* 90(4):533–37

Satcher D. 1995. Emerging infections: getting ahead of the curve. *Emerg. Infect. Dis.* 1(1):1–6

Schentag JJ. 1995. Understanding and managing microbial resistance in institutional settings. *Am. J. Health Syst. Pharm.* 52 (Suppl. 2):S9-14

Schofield R, Reher D. 1991. The decline of mortality in Europe. See Schofield et al 1991, pp. 1–17

Schofield R, Reher D, Bideau D, eds. 1991. *The Decline of Mortality in Europe*. Oxford, UK: Clarendon

Shortridge KF. 1992. Pandemic influenza: a zoonosis? *Semin. Respir. Infect.* 7(1):11–25

Shortridge KF. 1995. The next pandemic influenza virus?. *Lancet* 346(8984):1210–12

Shu LL, Lin YP, Wright SM, Shortridge KF, Webster RG. 1994. Evidence for interspecies transmission and reassortment of influenza *A* viruses in pigs in southern China. *Virology* 202(2):825–33

Siddique AK, Salam A, Islam MS, Akram K, Majumdar RN, et al. 1995. Why treatment centres failed to prevent cholera deaths among Rwandan refugees in Goma, Zaire. *Lancet* 345(8946):359–61

Sommerfeld J. 1995. Emerging and resurgent infectious diseases: a challenge for anthropological research. *Proc. Annu. Meet. Am. Anthropol. Assoc., 94th, Washington, DC*

Sprent JFA. 1962. Parasitism, immunity and evolution. In *The Evolution of Living Organisms*, ed. GS Leeper, pp. 149–65. Melbourne: Melbourne Univ. Press

Sprent JFA. 1969a. Evolutionary aspects of immunity of zooparasitic infections. In *Immunity to Parasitic Animals*, ed. GJ Jackson, 1:3–64. New York: Appleton

Sprent JFA. 1969b. Helminth "zoonoses": an analysis. *Helminthol. Abstr.* 38:333–51

Sumartojo E. 1993. When tuberculosis treatment fails: a social behavioral account of patient adherence. *Am. Rev. Respir. Dis.* 147:1311–20

Swartz MN. 1994. Hospital-acquired infections: diseases with increasingly limited therapies. *Proc. Natl. Acad. Sci. USA* 91(7):2420–27

Swedlund AC, Armelagos GJ, eds. 1990. *Diseases in Population in Transition: Anthropological and Epidemiological Perspectives.* New York: Bergin & Garvey

Tambiah S. 1989. Ethnic conflicts in the world today. *Am. Ethnol.* 16:335–49

Tauxe RV. 1997. Emerging foodborne diseases: an evolving public health challenge. *Emerg. Infect. Dis.* 3(4):425–34

Thompson CS, O'Leary JP. 1997. The discovery of the vector for "yellow jack." *Am. Surg.* 63(5):462–63

Toltzis P, Blumer JL. 1995. Antibiotic-resistant gram-negative bacteria in the critical care setting. *Pediatr. Clin. N. Am.* 42(3):687–702

Toole MJ. 1995. Mass population displacement. A global public health challenge. *Infect. Dis. Clin. N. Am.* 9(2):353–66

United Nations. 1982. *Levels and Trends in Mortality Since 1950: A Joint Study by the United Nations and the World Health Organization.* New York: UN

VanGerven DP, Hummert J, Pendergast Moore K, Sanford MK. 1990. Nutrition, disease and the human life cycle: a bioethnography of a medieval Nubian community. In *Primate Life History and Evolution,* ed. CJ deRousseau, pp. 297–324. New York: Wiley-Liss

Vareldzis BP, Grosset J, Dekantori I, Crofton J, Laszlo A, et al. 1994. Drug-resistant tuberculosis: laboratory issues. World Health Organization recommendations. *Tuber. Lung Dis.* 75(1):1–7

Vecchiato NL. 1997. Sociocultural aspects of tuberculosis control in Ethiopia. *Med. Anthropol. Q.* 11(2):183–201

Waddell C. 1996. HIV and the social world of female commercial sex workers. *Med. Anthropol. Q.* 10(1):75–82

Walker DH, Barbour AG, Oliver JH, Lane RS, Dumler JS, et al. 1996. Emerging bacterial zoonotic and vector-borne diseases: ecological and epidemiological factors. *J. Am. Med. Assoc.* 275(6):463–69

Weber JT, Mintz ED, Canizares R, Semiglia A, Gomez I, et al. 1994. Epidemic cholera in Ecuador: multidrug-resistance and transmission by water and seafood. *Epidemiol. Infect.* 112(1):1–11

Webster RG, Wright SM, Castrucci MR, Bean WJ, Kawaoka Y. 1993. Influenza—a model of an emerging virus disease. *Intervirology* 35(1–4):16–25

Weigler BJ. 1995. Zoonotic hantavirus; new concerns for the United States. *J. Am. Veterin. Med. Assoc.* 206(7):979–86

Whiteford LM. 1997. The ethnoecology of dengue fever. *Med. Anthropol. Q.* 11(2): 202–23

Wilson ME. 1996. Travel and the emergence of infectious diseases. *Emerg. Infect. Dis.* 1(2):39–46

Wiselka M. 1994. Influenza: diagnosis, management, and prophylaxis. *Br. Med. J.* 308(6940):1341–45

Woods R. 1991. Public health and public hygiene: the urban environment in the late nineteenth and early twentieth centuries. See Schofield et al 1991, pp. 233–47

World Bank. 1993. *World Development Report 1993: Investing in Health.* Oxford, UK: Oxford Univ. Press

Wright SM, Kawaoka Y, Sharp GB, Senne DA, Webster RG. 1992. Interspecies transmission and reassortment of influenza A viruses in pigs and turkeys in the United States. *Am. J. Epidemiol.* 136(4):488–97

Zolopa AR. 1994. HIV and tuberculosis infection in San Francisco's homeless adults. *J. Am. Med. Assoc.* 272(6):455–61

*Annu. Rev. Anthropol. 1998. 27:273–300*
*Copyright 1998 by Annual Reviews. All rights reserved*

# COMING TO TERMS WITH HUMAN VARIATION

## Kenneth M. Weiss

Department of Anthropology, Pennsylvania State University, University Park,
Pennsylvania 16802; e-mail: kmw4@psu.edu

KEY WORDS: human genetics

ABSTRACT

Genetics has become the major tool of the life sciences. This is driven partly
by technology, and partly by the belief that genes are the ultimate units of
biomedical or evolutionary information. The search for variation associated
with disease has motivated the Human Genome Project to construct a detailed road map of the entire set of human genetic material, and some additional form of globally representative human genome diversity resource has
been proposed for the anthropological purposes of reconstructing human
population history. Any such resource raises complex societal and ethical issues as well as scientific ones. However, the amount and complexity of genetic variation has frustrated hopes for simple genetic answers to important
biomedical or anthropological questions, and a consequent converging of
these differing interests suggests that developing a genetic variation resource
will be important in many disciplines.

## INTRODUCTION

We are in the genetic era. An explosion of technological advances has enabled
hundreds of scientists around the world to collect more, and better, data on genetic variation than has ever before been possible. Journals of many kinds are
filled with these data, indeed are rapidly being founded for the purpose, and
online data bases are becoming accessible to almost anyone who wants to look
at them. A new science, called bioinformatics, has formed to deal with the con-

273

sequent deluge of data, which many investigators characterize as an information implosion.

New methods for identifying genetic variation are used by the biomedical community to study disease and other physical traits, and genetics has taken a prominent place in biological anthropology. There is no end in sight to the new questions, and improved answers to long-standing questions, that will be provided by these new data. The questions include those about human origins, relationships among primates, original settlement patterns, and local biodemography (marriage, migration, social subdivision, paternity, lineage).

In spite of the stimulation that these new data provide, there are important scientific problems that need to be addressed. Many pronouncements about human settlement history are being made from genetic data that are essentially stripped of a reasonable understanding of the origin of the sample, or the cultural processes that have been responsible for the distribution of variation—that is, from the *anthropology* of the samples. In addition to a knowledge gap between most geneticists and anthropologists, there is often a cavernous communication gap between nonbiological and biological anthropologists. If a naïve view of human ethnic or 'racial' variation exists among geneticists, a comparably uninformed view of the biology of human variation is held by most anthropologists, even by many biological anthropologists. Added to this, genetics is under suspicion in many quarters of our society.

The data documenting human genetic variation have always been rather haphazard. The world's populations have not been sampled in a systematic, anthropologically informed way. Efforts have been made to synthesize the data available at various times, but these have been based on aggregations of heterogeneous data from different laboratories, data that have been collected and analyzed according to different methods, standards, sampling approaches, and sample sizes.

Samples available to one investigator are not generally available to other investigators, so that laboratories with differing viewpoints on the same question must work out those differences using different data. Yet a basic criterion of good science is to be able to repeat the same experiment or to reanalyze the same data to prove or disprove a point of view. This situation is something like two linguists arguing about the origin of French but each using a dictionary, inaccessible to the other, that contains only half the words in the language. Or Dickens scholars arguing about that author but each only having access to half his books. Not even post-modernists would stand for such a situation.

Fortunately, there is action afoot for a remedy. This paper reviews the state of human genetic variation in the context of current efforts to build systematic studies of that variation that would solve these problems.

# THE BIOMEDICAL POINT OF VIEW OF HUMAN VARIATION

Throughout its history, the study of human genetics has been concerned mostly with inherited disease (see Vogel & Motulsky 1997), largely the afflictions of childhood, like cystic fibrosis, that follow Mendel's classical rules of inheritance in families. It has also been possible to study aspects of the genetics of the immune system, first empirically via blood types and transfusion compatibility, then maternal-fetal compatibility at the Rh system, and more recently the human leukocyte antigen (HLA) system and tissue transplantation autoimmune disorders. These problems have often been approached by studying populations rather than, or in addition to, families. Recently, there has been progress in finding variation associated with more complex traits such as cancer or cardiovascular disease; risk for these traits aggregates in families, but the traits do not segregate in unambiguous Mendelian fashion.

Until modern technology was developed for directly manipulating and sequencing DNA, most genetics studies depended on the pattern of appearance of disease in family members as evidence for a genetic etiology. That information could be used in genetic counseling (risk estimation in families), but rarely in treatment. Only a few causal genes were identified, usually from biochemical approaches. The classic examples are the hemoglobinopathies, such as sickle cell anemia, the understanding of which were advanced by the identification and characterization of hemoglobin, the protein product coded by the genes involved.

An explosion of knowledge resulted from methods that were developed largely in the 1970s and 1980s to clone (isolate and copy) specific segments of DNA, to identify the sequence of its string of component nucleotides (conventionally denoted A,C,G,T), and to identify the location of genes (protein coding sequences) on specific chromosomes. A few landmark studies showed that the available methods were capable in principle of identifying genes responsible for the familial occurrence of disease, and it became clear that a systematic study of the human genome itself (the entire complement of DNA) could be immensely helpful in this regard.

## The Human Genome Project

The Human Genome Project (HGP) was initiated to characterize the normal set of human genes (Collins 1991, Collins & Galas 1993, www.nhgri.nih. gov.hgp/hgp_goals/5yrplan.html, Cook-Deegan 1994, Olson 1993, Watson 1990). In this context, 'normal' means as found in persons without known genetic disease. This daunting task was made possible by the promise of new technological advances; indeed, not all the requisite technology was, or even is, available, and technology development is part of the HGP. The HGP is probably the most extensive and expensive single, systematic biological research program ever undertaken. Other mega-ventures in biology have been less systematic, like the US 'war on cancer,', or of less broad applicability, like the half-century of genetic studies of the radiation effects done in Hiroshima and Nagasaki. A description of the HGP, its rationale, and its implementation is given for general readers in books such as Cook-Deegan (1994), which explains the political as well as scientific issues. Recent perspectives on the HGP and where we should go next can be found in various places (Lander & Schork 1995, Lander 1996). (Because high material stakes may be involved in strategic decisions that are made, there is often unstated advocacy by authors of prospectus papers in this field.) *Science* publishes annual issues devoted entirely to progress in genomics.

The purpose of the HGP was to produce a kind of 'consensus' road map of the structure of the human genome. This includes identification of the identity and arrangement of all genes in the set of 23 human chromosomes and a plan to obtain the basic sequence of the entire genome, that is, of all gene-coding regions as well as intervening DNA with other or unknown function. The work would be done on DNA samples from a small collection of families and individuals. The idea is that all humans are similar in respect of the chromosomal location of their genes, and that a reference sequence, while not representing any individual, will approximate the sequence in every human. Much of the work has been done on a set of three-generation, European-derived families with large sibships, collected in Utah and in France and maintained in consortium with the Centre pour L'Etude de Polymorphism Humain (CEPH). A large number of organized, collaborating investigators in many countries have parceled out the work, which is ongoing. In the United States, the HGP is part of the activities of the National Institutes of Health National Human Genome Research Institute (NHGRI), the Department of Energy, and others, and in France by an organization called Généthon, and so on.

The HGP is in a sense a grand exercise in Platonic essentialism, even to the extent that its stereotype of the human genome will be a collage of elements from one or a few individuals, so the sequence being obtained will not be possessed by any individual. This is unimportant relative to the location of genes and to a reference sequence, because almost every normal person has the same gene arrangement and approximately the same sequence (see below). Exceptions would be persons with unusual, often pathogenic, chromosomal rearrangements.

The stereotype of the HGP serves as a reference from which applied studies can examine the variation in special samples, such as people affected with a given disease, or for anthropological purposes. The reference also provides directly usable resources. For example, the landmark sequence can be used to identify and amplify (copy) a given gene from any investigator's human DNA samples. The knowledge of the locations of all genes will greatly enhance the ability to find specific genes that contribute materially to a given disease (e.g. Lander & Schork 1995, Weiss 1995a).

Enormous progress has been made in a short time. One can now navigate various web sites to see just how much is available. (Two places to start are www.genethon.fr, and www.ncbi.nlm.nih.gov; *Trends in Genetics* regularly publishes web and internet addresses for genetics.) A substantial fraction of all functional genes has been identified, the chromosomal location of these genes has been determined, and sizeable segments (though still a small overall percent) of the entire genome of 3 billion nucleotide units have been sequenced. Victory ahead of schedule is being proclaimed, although important unsolved technical problems impede the progress of the sequencing effort. In addition, there is some skepticism about the value of sequencing through the many thousands of difficult and extensive regions of stretches of tandemly repeated sequence with little apparent function.

One of the major initial objectives of the HGP has been to develop what is called a genetic map of the human genome, meaning the identification of genetic markers, or short sequences of known chromosomal location, spaced more or less evenly across all chromosomes at a density such that any two adjacent pairs of markers would be co-inherited 99% of the time. The other 1% of the time, recombination during meiosis (the process of egg and sperm formation) exchanges the two copies of one of the markers that the individual carries (humans, being diploid, have two copies of each chromosome). This recombination, or genetic, distance corresponds to about one marker for every million base pairs, the latter distance referred to as the physical map; relationships between the physical and genetic maps vary along the chromosomes and between males and females, in complex ways, and another HGP objective was to work out that relationship.

These short genetic marker sequences need have no function; they are identified strictly to serve as locators for specific chromosome regions that any investigator could find in any individual's DNA. The attribute of a desired marker, besides a baseline bit of unique sequence to identify it, and a known chromosomal location is that the sequence at the marker location itself be highly variable from person to person, again, regardless of any function this variation may have (e.g. Olson 1993). Hundreds of markers closely spaced across the entire human genome have been identified, and relatively inexpensive ways to genotype individuals for the variants they carry at such markers have been developed as part of the HGP effort.

The most useful markers are called microsatellites (for historical reasons), or tandem repeat loci, because they are characterized by numerous contiguous repeats of the same short sequence of 2, 3, or 4 base pairs. At these sites, the number of repeated copies of this short motif mutates rapidly compared to other types of mutation, to the extent that each person may have different alleles (sequence variants) on their two homologous chromosomes.

Microsatellites occur at thousands of places across the human genome and are very useful for finding genes associated with disease. Except for serendipitous discoveries, the main *systematic* way to find disease genes has been to study families in which the disease was segregating (being passed down from parent to offspring), to type all family members for a set of 200–400 microsatellite markers distributed evenly across the genome, and to search for chromosomal regions in which a specific set of marker alleles are found more often in affected than unaffected family members, which will happen if the markers are very close to the disease gene. This is called linkage mapping (see Olson 1993, Lander & Schork 1995, Ott 1991, Weiss 1995a). The strength of association between a marker and a trait is a function of the degree to which possession of a particular variant at a locus causally involved in the disease actually produces the disease in persons who carry that variant, and the closeness, in terms of distance along the chromosome (called the genetic or linkage distance), of marker sites and the causally associated gene. Importantly, the estimated strength of association is also a product of the assumptions made in the analysis, such as relationship between genetic and physical distance, which is why it is so important to have a very good genomic data infrastructure.

Chromosomal regions in which markers that seem to be co-transmitted with disease in families are considered to be likely locations for the genes involved (that is, the variable site 'marks' the region but need not itself be directly related to a causal gene or the disease). Laboratory methods have been developed to identify, or clone, the functional genes in the region of the markers in question. Unless the signal strength is very good, or there are other ancillary data, however, linkage mapping methods often cannot unambiguously identify a small enough region for such positional cloning to be done quickly or easily, and we seem to be reaching the limits of resolution of linkage mapping methods (discussed later). Nonetheless, this general approach has led to the mapping of a great number of human diseases, and for some of these, the causal genes have been identified (see gene maps in the web sites cited above).

An outpouring of studies reporting genes or chromosomal regions associated with disease has resulted from the widespread, systematic use of these tools; examples are far too numerous to cite here but can easily be found by perusal of disease-specific web sites, or by looking at *Nature, Science, American Journal of Human Genetics, Human Mutation, Nature Genetics, Genetic Testing, Nature Medicine, Human Genetics,* and other journals. The success of searches for genes related to relatively simple diseases has led to hopes that genes for complex chronic diseases like cancer and heart disease might be found, and indeed, that has occurred. The diseases themselves are typically too complex to be understood by single gene effects, but there is at least progress.

Similarly, complex behavioral traits ranging from disorders like Alzheimer's disease to addictive behavior have been studied. Generally, evidence is found for the involvement of multiple genes, and studies vary and are often inconsistent among populations, families, or samples. The degree of success varies and is open to interpretation (e.g. Chadwick & Cardew 1996), but the enthusiastic belief that such methods can find genes for any trait that is meaningfully definable is very high. Anthropologists wanting to understand modern human genetics or the degree to which behavioral traits really can be understood in terms of causal components, should take the trouble to get a sense of this literature.

## Patterns of Genetic Variation

There is no doubt that the HGP has been one of the most successful planned projects in the history of science, in terms of rapidly achieving specified objectives, the number and diversity of its users, and the way it has helped transform our understanding of basic as well as human genetics. Of course, predictable success usually indicates engineering rather than new basic science, which is to some extent a fair characterization of the HGP to date, and the project was designed to provide the material with which subsequent specific research would make new discoveries. Even so, the process of developing the resource has already led to new technological methods and advances in our understanding of the genome.

The intended ultimate scientific advances of the HGP have to do with understanding disease causation. Finding genes potentially associated with disease is only the first step. Once such a candidate gene is identified, the next step is to identify variation within that gene or its regulatory regions that is causally responsible for some trait, such as susceptibility to disease. Initially, 'responsible' means statistically associated with the trait in family or population data, but direct biological tests are then required to demonstrate the causal effects of the variations. Recent work has shown clearly that there is a much greater amount and more complex structure in human genetic variation than was anticipated (Weiss 1996a, Chadwick & Cardew 1996), and this has led to the development of a more 'anthropological' perspective on disease (for example, an understanding of why prevalence and causal-association differences exist among populations). The pattern of complexity is such that, except for traits that are quite severe but generally rare, causal inference has not been easy and in some ways may not be tractable even when candidate genes have been found.

Based on nearly a century of work with cruder resolution, human geneticists came to think of a typical gene as having a normal (sometimes called wild type) and one or a small number of abnormal (or disease) alleles. Such dichotomous thinking derives directly from Mendel, who set up a two-state experimental system designed to improve agricultural plant breeding rather than to consider natural variation. Genetic causal models, and some of the available data, had shown that such expectations could be an oversimplification, but for most purposes a two-state Mendelian model suited well for those few genes or traits for which we had reasonably specific information (e.g. simply inherited pediatric diseases like cystic fibrosis).

Evolutionary theory of the time had suggested that natural selection kept harmful mutations down to a small number and low frequency, preserving the normal allele, the presumed product of long adaptive natural selection, at high frequency. Recurrent mutations were assumed to occur, back and forth between the normal and abnormal states, at some small frequency. Terms like 'dominant' and 'recessive' for the effects of the alleles involved have been very useful in biomedical genetics and are built into our thinking, based on two-state notions of genetic variation.

Even as recently as the 1980s, the discovery of a multiplicity of alleles at a human gene was a publishable finding, because most practicable methods were too crude to identify more than two or three alleles at a locus. Despite this empirical fact, theoretical evolutionary population geneticists had even by the 1960s developed the theoretical understanding, based on the nature of DNA as a long concatenation of nucleotides, that for many purposes we could consider each new mutant allele to be unique (the chance a mutation would affect the same nucleotide in the same way as an earlier mutation was small compared to the chance it would affect some different nucleotide). This was called the unique mutation model, and its implication was that there was, for practical purposes, an essentially unlimited number of alleles that could be generated by mutation at a locus. A locus is expected to have many alleles in a population of any substantial size. As DNA sequencing and other new types of tests for variation were developed, it became clear that this was a good approximation to the truth, and in a 180-degree turn from earlier times, the convincing demonstration of a truly recurrent mutation became a publishable finding.

We now know that classical two-allele thinking is inaccurate. Human genes typically have hundreds of alleles (often referred to as mutations or mutant alleles, because all variants arise as new mutations) at any locus that has been looked at in sufficient detail. The reader can browse the web, by name, for known diseases such as cystic fibrosis and phenylketonuria, or for cancer-related genes, where catalogs of known mutations are being maintained (www.uwcm.ac.uk/uwcm/mg/hmgdø.htm)

In population terms, the unique mutation model had a couple of other interesting consequences. Not only would our species have many mutations at each gene, but if each arose only once then each geographic population would have its own 'private' mutations. A new allele begins as a single copy of the mutant sequence in the population in which the causal mutation occurred, but if it survived extinction because of natural selection or the chance elements of reproduction, the allele might grow in frequency and could increase in relative frequency over time. Simultaneously, because of the natural movement of bearers of the mutation during their lifetimes (from their own birth to the birth of their children), due to demographic exogamy, migration, etc, the allele would diffuse from its source. The older a mutation is, the more likely it is to be common and geographically widespread, strictly as a function of population history, whether or not aided by natural selection favoring that allele.

The upshot is that we have come to understand several things (Weiss 1996a): (*a*) a locus has many alleles, (*b*) the many genotypes—combinations of these alleles—have their own effects on disease risk factors or severity, leading to a much more complex genotype-phenotype relationship than, for example, simple Mendelian dominance or recessiveness, (*c*) alleles found in different populations differ for the population-historic reasons just mentioned. Awareness of these characteristics of human genes has grown gradually in biomedical genetics, a field that in many ways has not yet fully awakened from a two-allele classical Mendelian world view.

The existence of a much greater and more complex pattern of variation means that diagnosis and screening have to be more population-specific, and struggles to understand prevention and therapy have to face a complexity of causal effects that may necessitate a comparable complexity of therapeutic approaches. Continued progress requires that we learn to accept and expect, rather than resist, these facts of life.

## THE ANTHROPOLOGICAL POINT OF VIEW

Anthropologists have a rather different view of human genetics. Variation is usually used not as a tool for identifying their functional effect; rather, the variation per se is of interest. The traditional anthropological questions concern human and primate evolution and systematics, ethnohistory, geographic distribution, or population history and pre-history. From this perspective, it is obvious that the stereotypic nature of the HGP leaves out a major aspect of the human genome that is as basic as its nominal structure. An evolutionary perspective makes it clear that variation is not an incidental aspect but has always been intrinsic to the human genome. Evolution works by selecting from available biological variation; this is the process by which genes, DNA sequences, and chromosomes have come to be in their current configuration, and there has never been a time when any species had an invariant genome.

In this sense, the HGP probably never should have been conceived without a consideration of variation (beyond that needed as a mapping tool). In part, the decision was an active one not to have a mapping/sequencing effort slowed by uncontrolled variation. Variation was also not taken very seriously a decade ago but is an important, perhaps the most important, fact of life. For example, in work we have done (Nickerson et al, submitted), we find that even in 9734 base pairs of a single gene (for lipoprotein lipase, a protein involved in lipid metabolism), studied in only 72 people, the average person differs at 22 of these positions from a reference sequence for this gene. As this is only about 1/300,000 of the entire genome, humans on average would differ from the HGP's sequence of 'the' human genome in nearly 8 million ways (not considering variation in the thousands of tandem repeat elements), hardly our usual notion of a reference.

## A Brief History of Anthropological Genetics

Studies of human variation date back to about 1919, when the Hirzfelds demonstrated that there was variation in the ABO blood group system among human races as then conceived (Weiss & Chakraborty 1982). Over the subsequent decades this, the Rh system, and then numerous additional blood-borne proteins, along with other clearly segregating (mendelian) traits, like PTC tasting, attached earlobes, and so on, were studied in human populations (see the history and references in Boyd 1950; Cavalli-Sforza et al 1994; Mourant et al 1978a,b; Roychoudhury & Nei 1988; Vogel & Motulsky 1997; Weiss & Chakraborty 1982). Genotypes were determined from blood samples (or trait-counting for the latter type of variation). These were functional genes, but were selected as markers, not for mapping, but for differences in frequency among human populations that could be related to evolutionary history. Functional genes were used because variation in their coded protein products could be detected; there were no generally available methods for typing DNA directly. However, it was not known whether the observed variation in these proteins was of functional importance, although a number of studies suggested disease susceptibility effects (e.g. see Weiss 1995a, Vogel & Motulsky 1997) or climatic correlations (see Cavalli-Sforza et al 1994).

Whether one should attempt to study relations among peoples for genes that had been affected by natural selection or variation that had no effect on natural selection and hence was strictly the product of demographic history was debated. Traits affected by selection could be helpful—or confusing. For example, if skin color reflects solar exposure, peoples with similar skin color may have had common ancestry in a given environment, or they may be historically unrelated but were independently exposed to the same selective factor. Selectively 'neutral' variation should behave in a more clock-like, strictly probabilistic way over time and space and be more useful for purely historical questions; at the least, such variation is easier to model mathematically. Most anthropologists have sought neutral variation to study, although we now know that selection does not remove traces of population history at the DNA level (e.g. because of the unique nature of mutations), although selection can obscure time estimates. But there are still inconsistencies that are too often not considered; for example, there is evidence that regions such as are often used are differentially affected by selection, which will affect conclusions that are drawn from these regions (Hey 1997).

Over the decades, studies of genetic variation became a standard part of anthropology. Numerous investigators have addressed questions of human relationships to other primates, studies of racial variation and population relationships, and detailed documentation of regional variation in tribal populations (e.g. see Weiss 1989, Weiss & Chakraborty 1982 for references and examples). Among the studies in the classic era when this field was maturing were those of Frank Livingstone on the origins of sickle cell and other hemoglobin variants (Livingstone 1958), by JV Neel's group on the Yanomama and other South American populations (e.g. Neel 1978), by Henry Harpending and others in the indigenous groups of the Kalahari (Harpending 1974), by Jonathan Friedlaender (1975) in the Pacific, and others (Weiss 1989). Unlike most other work, Livingstone's helped bring to human and anthropological genetics what for many years was the only good example of the impact of natural selection on the function of a human gene.

Part of this work was driven by a 'salvage' view of the aboriginal world that was common up through the 1970s at least. It was widely felt that studies should be done before the imminent disappearance of indigenous cultures occurred around the world, permanently removing from our understanding a kind of cross-sectional museum of how humans used to live. Although done in an era of civil rights awareness, with eugenics and Naziism fresh memories, there was little, if any, protest about the probity of this activity, to my knowledge, and the view of tribes as mirrors on human nature was accepted by honorably liberal anthropologists. A major idea in anthropology was that we had something to learn from these other peoples about ourselves, about human life. The motive may have been selfish, but it was not imperialistic. Attitudes about this have changed, as is discussed later, at least as reflected in the more virulent public debate.

The early 1970s were a golden era for anthropological genetics, even though the markers that could be studied at the time were not powerfully informative. Several authors used gene frequency data to estimate times since the separation of major 'racial' (continental) populations (e.g. Cavalli-Sforza & Bodmer 1971), treating groups at extremities of the human species distribution as if they had been in complete isolation and estimating how long the current differences between them would have taken to accumulate. These time estimates consistently suggested that all human populations shared a common ancestor about 150,000 years ago, much shorter than the fossil record indicated that human ancestors emerged from Africa, and Weiss & Maruyama (1976) suggested that perhaps migration, via exchange of mates between adjacent demes, may not have been a negligible modifier of those time estimates.

Although most attention was paid to the use of genetic variation to work out geographic relationships through models of microevolutionary processes, an important addition contributed to macroevolution as well. Sarich & Wilson

(1967) used immunological measures of genetic divergence between species, calibrated by known phylogenetic relationships from the fossil record, to challenge the accepted wisdom about the age of human origins from a common ancestor with chimpanzees. Again, the time estimates were much shorter than had been thought. After much vigorous argument, the genetic estimates have generally prevailed, showing the power of genetics to provide convincing data on the subject of speciation and phylogeny, in a way less ambiguous than might even be inferred from the fossils themselves (or, since based on differences among living species, even in the absence of fossils). Again, this is because genetic differences accumulate in a reasonably clock-like way that can be modeled in terms of population parameters (population size, mutation rates, etc).

Allan Wilson's lab stirred the pot again with the innovative development of a new kind of direct DNA-based study of human variation—-that is, one that looked at DNA itself, rather than relying on the relative insensitivity of methods for typing variation in coded proteins present in blood. Wilson perceptively took advantage of the observation that mtDNA is a short DNA molecule in the cytoplasm rather than in the nucleus of the cell, and is inherited through the maternal line. Nuclear genes exist in two copies and can exchange pieces, as a result evolving sequence differences more slowly, and have mutation-repair mechanisms not enjoyed by mtDNA. mtDNA evolves more simply and rapidly. Its variation can be used as a molecular clock for evolutionary events at subspecies time ranges, calibrated by known historical or paleontological events, that are useful for studying modern human origins (as well as continental population history).

These ideas led to a paper in 1987 in which Cann, Stoneking, and Wilson transformed anthropological genetics by asserting the authority of genetics as a definitive method relative to paleontology for many purposes. Their paper and much work that has followed have appeared to show from this new kind of data that modern humans had originated from Africa about 100,000 years ago, displacing in some way the previous hominid populations well represented in the fossil record (Stoneking 1996). The recent sequencing of a small part of the mtDNA extracted from a Neanderthal fossil shows only deep (old) relationship to any known human mtDNA sequence, that is, modern humans are all more like each other than they are to the Neanderthal sequence, suggesting that Neanderthals may not have left any descendants today and that the ancestors of modern humans may have replaced Neanderthals in Europe (Krings et al 1997). Of course, so far this is just a single sample.

The Y-chromosome is the complement to the mtDNA in that it is possessed as a single copy by males and transmitted only through the male lineage. Y-based variation would provide an effective test of the mtDNA-based story on human origins. After many years of trying to find typable variation on the Y-chromosome, this was accomplished, and the new data support the basic picture found in the mitochondrial data (e.g. Deka et al 1996, Hammer & Zegura 1997, Underhill et al 1997). Evidence has also been provided by recent studies of various aspects of nuclear gene variation (Deka et al 1995, Harding et al 1997, Tishkoff et al 1996, Bowcock et al 1994). Besides a recent settlement date, most data show more variation in Africans than in other continental populations, and the patterns outside of Africa can be interpreted as cladistic subsamples of common African ancestral genotypes. However, not all loci show this (Jorde et al 1997), and the finding of deep (old) lineages in the beta-globin genes, contained strictly within Asia, have been used to raise doubt about a simple replacement-from-Africa model (Harding et al 1997). The Y data to date show less variation in Africans. There is also indication in the data of gene flow back into Africa after an original expansion from there.

Variation in the pattern from locus to locus is expected, and it is not yet possible to make definitive statements about settlement patterns from the amount of data now available, if that will indeed ever be possible. Good recent reviews of this subject are in Harpending et al (1998), von Haeseler et al (1995), Templeton (1997), and the papers by Sherry and Relethford in this volume. These authors stress the way that contemporary genetic variation is molded by major characteristics of population history; that is, evolution is largely a demographic phenomenon. There is an element of nonidentifiability in the data: Different population histories can generate the same genetic outcome. The upshot is that even the fundamental issues remain unresolved, and this field is as lively as ever. The reason is essentially that both times to coalescence at a gene and relative genetic diversity among and between populations are affected by population size, growth rates, and structure. Large, long-standing populations with intermixture (gene flow) can yield results similar to a recent expansion. Different population sizes or growth rates can yield greater or lesser diversity in any part of a species.

## Methods for the Anthropological Analysis of Human Genetic Variation

How were these conclusions reached? There are a few basic ways in which such data can be analyzed, each related to different questions, but all directly reflecting the population history of alleles under consideration. The original methods relied on the frequency of the variant alleles present among individuals in a sampled population, for a gene or genes (or DNA regions) of interest (Nei 1987, Hartl & Clark 1997, Cavalli-Sforza et al 1994). Frequency is inherently a population-based measure (i.e. has meaning only in regard to populations treated as discrete sampling units). Statistical models have been developed for the rate at which two genetically identical populations that become isolated will accumulate differences in their allele frequencies over time. This is how the 100,000-year estimate of human origins, referred to above, was first made based on frequency differences among the most disparate 'major' racial groups of our species.

The frequency differences between pairs of populations can be portrayed by dendograms, or tree-like diagrams, in which the branch lengths between the populations are proportional to those differences. Populations with similar frequencies will be neighboring 'twigs' on the diagram. This can be misread as being derived from an assumption that the populations are distinct, species-like entities, a very categorical way to approach human beings (Moore 1996a,b). In fact, it is simply a way of portraying relative similarities among sampling units (populations), however they were defined. Some authors prefer such presentations, but we know that local populations are almost as variable as our entire species (Barbujani et al 1997), and that the variation that exists is more or less continuously distributed over space. An alternative presentation of the frequency data, to reflect these facts, treats populations as spot samples of a continuous reality and plots frequency variation as continuous gradients on a map, filling in unsampled regions by interpolating frequencies between sampled populations, visualized on maps by, for example, gradations of color. Such an approach was developed by Cavalli-Sforza and others (Cavalli-Sforza et al 1994, Suarez et al 1985, O'Rourke & Suarez 1985, O'Rourke et al 1985), integrating data over many genes simultaneously. This is an analog approach that is a more accurate depiction of the dispersion of human variation and that demonstrates the considerable extent to which people or populations differ from each other as a result of a basically continuous process of geographic isolation by distance rather than categorically. A nice presentation of methods is in Sherry & Batzer (1997).

An alternative approach is to look at DNA sequence variation rather than variation in the frequency of the same alleles across space. Recent technology has made it possible to identify all the sequence variation in a gene. Because mutation is a discrete and relatively rare event, and because most of the time a new mutation will affect a different part of the gene's DNA sequence, a sequence develops a naturally bifurcating or hierarchical set of variants whose history can be portrayed on tree-like diagrams relating contemporary variation to descent from a common ancestral sequence. Models of this process in terms of population and mutation parameters can be constructed and calibrated by known geologic or phylogenetic events, to estimate the time since that common ancestor (often known as the *coalescent*). This type of analysis has become common, beginning with the mtDNA studies (Cann et al 1987).

Unlike a population or frequency tree, the elements on a gene tree are individual sequences; branch lengths between sequences are proportional to the number of mutations by which they differ (and hence, time since they shared an ancestor). Such a tree presents the history of the gene, not populations; the two are usually statistically related, but they are not identical, and much misunderstanding persists about this, especially because gene coalescents have often been assumed to be identical to population separation events, which they are not (Stoneking 1996, Nei 1987, Harpending et al 1998, von Haeseler et al 1995). But sequences can provide some information about population history. For example, each individual sequence comes from some population. If all sequences on a given branch of the tree were from people native to the New World, the evolution of the differences among those sequences might reflect the time since New World settlement. Debates about settlement 'waves' center around how widely dispersed a set of lineages is within the New World and whether these lineages are also found in Asia (Merriwether & Ferrell 1996, Torroni & Wallace 1995, Torroni et al 1993, Stone & Stoneking 1998). Asian globin sequence lineages that coalesce strictly within Asia have similarly been used to infer that human ancestry is very ancient there (Harding et al 1997). Inferences have sometimes been made on very small sample sizes; these samples miss much variation and are used to infer demographically implausible settlement scenarios in which too few people are said to found a continent, for example. Larger samples usually correct this problem. When recombination occurs (as it does in nuclear genes), gene trees do not have nice cladistic structure, but trees of their quantitative sequence similarity can be constructed and used in similar ways, although the inferences one can draw are perhaps even more problematic.

Most genetic systems studied show higher levels of diversity in Africa. This has so often been taken to imply an African origin for humans that such a view has become dogma. However, the argument is largely a plausibility one, because such a pattern could also arise if Africa simply has had a larger ancestral population size, for which there is some evidence (Harpending et al 1998, Jorde et al 1997). That modern humans have origins in Africa still seems likely, but only because archeological and biogeographic evidence also suggests that. Likewise, the other current dogma, a recent origin for modern humans, can be debated because population and gene trees are not identical. Again, various types of data, including fossil evidence (at least according to many paleontologists), support recent origins. For example, the distribution of pairwise differences in sequence similarity, which take into account sequence differences as well as frequencies, indicates a recent common origin for the human species, probably characterized by a series of regional population expansions occurring well within the last 100,000 years (Harpending et al 1993, 1998).

Much of the discussion in anthropological genetics relates to the nature of the assumptions that must be made to draw inferences from each type of data. In particular, not everyone agrees that studies of human history should be based on the rather arbitrary way in which populations are often defined, as noted earlier. An example may illustrate the issues. One of the most potentially interesting uses of genetic data is to help reconstruct ethnohistory. Cultural traits such as language, and genes, share at least some aspects of population processes, and the results of those processes are important for anthropology. Like genes, cultural traits arise in a local area and either subsequently disappear or become diffuse. As such traits spread over space and time, they modify by some process analogous to genetic mutation. Treating populations defined by language (or culture, etc) as historical units, one might expect genetic differences to reflect temporal relationships among the populations. These groups might be expected to evolve cladistically, in a branching fashion, by periodically branching (separating) and then diverging over time. Many interesting cultural and biological traits might co-evolve in such a way (e.g. Durham 1991). If so, genetic variation could tell us about the history of the other traits. Using language as a marker of population separation, Cavalli-Sforza and colleagues have demonstrated a good correspondence among linguistic, geographic, and genetic differences (e.g. see Cavalli-Sforza et al 1994). They draw population-historical conclusions accordingly.

However, many persons hold very different views on language, or think the definition of the populations sampled for such study (which were defined by classical anthropological or linguistic labels) is arbitrary or anthropologically naïve. For example, Moore (1994, 1995) considers the degree to which cultures, language groups, etc, really are units that evolve cladistically. Instead, human populations may be more fluid, temporary constructs, joining and separating in a reticulated or 'rhizotic' fashion. One might score populations today for some trait like language or some cultural attribute, and one may be able to draw cladistic diagrams for each trait. But the traits need not have corresponding trees, or histories.

The fact that one can classify and draw cladistic relationships among populations found today may falsely reinforce stereotypical notions of populations (languages, races, etc) as historically stable and meaningful units. For example, no one would accept a sample of the United States labeled by language (for instance, I live in North America, speak English, but have no ancestors from the British Isles; other English speakers, who live nearby, have African but not British origin). Cavalli-Sforza et al (1994) endeavored to sample people and assign them to their aboriginal language in situ; but this depends on a classic kind of labeling by tribe or language designators that has long been under fire even within anthropology for being unduly classificatory and often an impress of inapt Western concepts onto subordinate peoples. Even if the definitions of language families that they used were accepted (they are hotly debated), this analytic, in situ approach may simply be finding that language is a surrogate for geographic location; that is, we may be learning little about language as a cultural barrier per se. To use an image provided to me by Paul Durrenberger, we should be careful about trying to use digital sampling to represent an analog world (Weiss 1998).

## RECENT ACTIVITY AND PROSPECTS

The deficiency inherent in the stereotypical nature of the HGP was quickly recognized and raised as an issue by Cavalli-Sforza (1990). He asked how we might obtain a satisfactory understanding of variation in the human genome. He and a number of other human population geneticists proposed that a Human Genome Diversity Project (HGDP) be established to fill this information gap (e.g. Cavalli-Sforza 1990, Cavalli-Sforza et al 1991, Kidd et al 1993, Weiss et al 1992). Such a project would be designed to remedy several specific problems historically afflicting the genetic study of human variation. These included that (*a*) data collected in the past were typically opportunistic, and not systematic in terms of the nature and sizes of the samples collected, (*b*) samples were not collected with uniformly high quality data about the nature of the population being samples (e.g. its culture, history, language, the relationships among individuals sampled, etc), (*c*) different genes were typed by different investigators from different samples, preventing a complete set of worldwide typings on the same set of chosen genes, (*d*) actual genotype data were not always made available to all interested investigators, and (*e*) physical samples were collected as part of individual investigators' projects and were not available to others who might wish to study them. Some of these limitations were technical in nature; for example, really accessible data bases have become easily available only with the advent of the worldwide web, and physical samples can be distributed without practical limit because new genotyping methods do not use very much DNA and because cell transformation can provide an essentially endless supply of DNA from a single sample.

In the eight or so years since the idea for an HGDP was conceived, there has been intense activity to organize, structure, and fund some version of it. Many potential problems such a project might raise have had to be discussed and worked out. These problems include statistical sampling issues to obtain representative data, sample size and preservation issues, ethical issues, and numerous issues about the definition of the questions that could be asked or answered. Discussions of the proposed project has engaged many anthropologists. A brief interpretive history of this activity, from the viewpoint of the author, is given as an Appendix for anthropologists wanting to know more about that history. Many of the ethical and legal issues that were raised are discussed by Henry Greely in this volume, from a Western point of view. Most anthropologists will be familiar with the emotional reaction that indigenous populations could have to a genetic study that could be perceived as but one more exploitation—economic or political—by the outside (e.g. see Greely 1996). Meanwhile, research on human genetic variation has been accelerated, if anything, by individual investigators the world over, collecting and analyzing samples in their respective geographic regions.

## On the Biomedical Front

This anthropological genetic activity reflects and is made possible by the expanding capability of DNA technology and the growing interest in questions that can be addressed with DNA data. There has also been a concurrent, growing recognition of the importance of understanding human genetic variation among the biomedical community. The anthropological reasons for a global study of human variation largely concern reconstructing the history and evolution of human populations and the human genome itself. In the absence of phenotype data, genetic variation alone can say less about what those genes are *doing*. This is a major omission, but complete studies of the contribution of genes to human phenotypes would massively exceed what could be contemplated in a single project. What traits should be measured?

Several ideas have begun to circulate. One involves the possible ways in which gene function could be studied from cell lines representing individuals from our species, by inducing gene expression and interaction in cell culture. Another proposes collecting specific tissues and seeing what genes are expressed, at what levels, and by what specific forms (mRNA sequences) in different individuals or environments. Even without the new technological developments such approaches would require, there is a growing recognition of the value of data on human genetic variation itself as a resource platform from which biomedical studies might be launched, and indeed such studies are currently being proposed (Collins et al 1997), just as the HGP basically serves a resource function.

The HGP recognizes the potential importance of a shift from family-based identification of disease-associated genes to one that is population based. The reason has to do with the technology of searches for such genes. The success of gene mapping in families by linkage methods has run into barriers that seem insurmountable by that approach. Finding marker sites associated with causal genes with standard linkage methods provides only a crude chromosomal location. Following that, the molecular biological work required to clone and identify genes from the implicated region is long, expensive, and often problematic. What is needed is a practicable way to move closer to the location of the causal gene at the association-study stage of the investigation. The kinds of markers that have been used, and their behavior in families, do not provide the required statistical power to do this.

The problem is that there is not enough information about the cotransmission of marker and causal gene variation within families to yield the statistical power required to locate a chromosomal region on a sufficiently fine scale. Over the last few years, another approach has been suggested that is based in populations. The idea is that population rather than family samples essentially integrate the transmission events that have occurred within the population's history so that, with a suitably dense set of markers, fine-scale mapping can be done (Collins et al 1997, Kruglyak 1997, Risch & Merikangas 1996, Terwilliger et al 1998). In a large, stable population, recombination breaks down association, known as linkage disequilibrium, between sites along a chromosome (e.g. between marker locations and causal genes). But if a population is small enough or isolated enough, or if it can be subdivided in a suitable way, then there may be significant linkage disequilibrium to map disease genes. In isolated populations, there may be generally enough disequilibrium that chromosomes with disease alleles in a region may have a different distribution of marker alleles than chromosomes without disease alleles. For example, if a disease is rare, the rate of genetic drift (evolution of allele frequencies) at markers near those causal alleles will be faster than in the more numerous, 'normal' chromosomes (e.g. Terwilliger et al 1998). To detect the difference, a marker map would be required that is much denser (markers more closely spaced) than what exists today.

Developing this type of marker map is a part of current planning for the next 5-year plan of the HGP, which recognizes the importance of variation for biomedical genetics (Collins et al 1997). One suggested type of marker is the simplest type of variation, alternative nucleotides or 'single nucleotide polymorphisms' (SNPs) densely spaced along the entire genome. SNPs evolve more slowly and are more suitable for population studies, because their variant alleles do not often recur, than the copy-number alleles of microsatellites that constitute the current marker map designed for family studies. There is an effort to develop a dense SNP map that would represent allelic variation in our entire species (Collins et al 1997); the idea is to draw stratified (similar size) samples of genomes from every major continental region, based on geographic history rather than the more arbitrary ethnic categories (e.g. Weiss 1998). Indeed, in a salubrious development, anthropologists have been included in the planning of this next stage in human genomics.

Paired with the expected next stage in scaled-up genotyping technology, a map of thousands of markers typed on all individuals could, under ideal causal circumstances with perfectly known physical and genetic maps, be useful for disease gene identification (Kruglyak 1997). Molecular methods for finding an SNP map (i.e. identifying thousands of variable sites), which would have been difficult earlier, are now available.

We have to view the excitement about this new possibility with at least some circumspection. Many technical issues affect such mapping. The arrangement of variation may be too complex, or recombination may have had too large a disorganizing effect (Clark et al, in preparation), and the frequency and recombination distance of SNP alleles may be too difficult to estimate accurately in target populations, to provide close, consistent chromosomal locations for putative disease genes. Older variation may not be as useful for mapping younger causal alleles (or vice versa), and the causal pattern may have to be relatively homogeneous for this to work well. In some situations, a denser microsatellite map in which more individuals had unique alleles might be preferable. Time will tell. At least, it seems likely that clear-cut diseases that have by chance become relatively common in small, relatively isolated populations may be mappable, a modern version of the old idea that small, isolated, inbred populations were ideal places to study recessive disease.

Such a new mapping initiative reflects a de facto convergence of biomedical and anthropological interests in several ways (e.g. Harding & Sajantila 1998). Interestingly, if older, more common variation is not as useful as is being hoped, and special populations must be studied for each disease of interest, this may require the detailed identification of genetic variation in numerous local groups around the world—essentially, the HGDP done for biomedical purposes. Determining the optimal samples will require knowledgeable anthropological participation.

The initiative will produce a DNA bank and statistical data base very similar in nature to that proposed for the anthropologically motivated idea of an HGDP (though using only US-based sampling). *All the same, subject protection and commercial use issues exist and must be faced* (Greely, this volume). The design of the sample must consider the same population choice and definition issues, even if only on a geographically much coarser scale. That is, the effort is designed to identify all major geographic regions of the world and to identify variation present at reasonable frequency in all branches of our species. But what constitutes a satisfactory geographic sample? It is recognized that many local populations experience unique disease risks and/or that local populations may be optimal units in which to search for genes affecting risk of globally important genes. Variants found at restricted frequency, perhaps occurring uniquely in some local population, may be the critical variants to include in a genetic marker map.

How these issues are to be resolved is currently being worked out (Weiss, in press). In any case, one salubrious concomitant of the new initiatives is that studies of the human genome and its variation will become more inclusive, and hence representative, of more of the world's peoples.

## CONCLUSION

Nature and nurture are the yin and yang of human biology. The current genetic era will pass. There are already signs that genetics has been oversold. The HGP and a huge global institution of biomedical geneticists has been built upon the premise that the genome—a DNA sequence—is the blueprint of life and that essentially any important trait can be understood in terms of that sequence. Because of the dreams of intellectual and material riches to come from the assumed discoveries, we are in a gold-rush atmosphere. However, this entails a bit of hubris and a degree of excess reliance on molecular determinism. The relationship of DNA sequences to phenotypes is turning out to be less predictive than has been advertised. Genetic variation is a more ambiguous reflection of history than has been thought. Even some of the most basic anthropological questions, such as the time and location of human origins, remain debatable, so that the sharpness of resolution of historical events rendered by genetic data is more problematic than proponents like to acknowledge.

Nonetheless, the power of genetics is not nearly played out as yet. One way or another, studies of human genetic variation will continue, and such work seems to have attracted much excited interest and activity around the globe. There is a convergence of interest between the needs of anthropological and biomedical geneticists, each group needing refined, detailed information on the nature and geographic distribution of human genetic variation. Biomedical science has discovered that variation cannot be ignored. Variation is becoming, properly, a matter of national policy, and anthropologists are at the policy table.

This should result in a corresponding unification of efforts by the HGP and some form of HGDP, in the form of a coordinated data resource, similar in nature and comparable in scale to many resources that exist in other aspects of modern genetics. This seems to be the best way to obtain the maximum information, accessible to the maximum number of investigators and points of view. Such a resource will be efficient and will be able to provide at least some inhibitory pressure against abuse of subjects and encouragement pressure to agencies and individuals to undertake further studies of human variation as part of the consortium effort. A concerted program will encourage international participation and will make public the data and the DNA so that analyses that an investigator does not like can be 'deconstructed' by reanalysis of the same or additional data.

The new kinds of data that are becoming available have greatly energized biological anthropology and have the potential to add interesting and important activities to all areas of anthropology. Indeed, without the direct involvement of the anthropologically knowledgeable, there is little to constrain geneticists to insure that the provenience of the samples upon which their analysis is based is well known. Geneticists tend to think of populations they choose to sample as discrete biological units, much as one thinks of species. Anthropology deals with cultures, often taken as units, but is often more sensitive to the fluidity of the human condition, and while providing far from perfect knowledge about human populations, it at least provides knowledge that greatly exceeds that of geneticists.

The history and complexity of human biodemography—migration, mating patterns, group definition, etc—is such that it is not easy to reconstruct scenarios by which we can specify which populations should be sampled for which purposes, or just what aspect of variation will be most informative. Different types of data are required for different questions. We know there is a relationship between the location of present diversity and population history. We can collect samples that adequately represent major continental ancestry before the past few centuries of migration. We can use such data to reconstruct aspects of regional and species history. Data of more detail can be used to understand very recent marriage and exogamy/endogamy patterns, lineage structures, and the like. Most problematic is the intermediate range of events and geographic distances, in which a rich history of population interaction—characteristic of nearly every geographic region—suggests that population-specific markers are hard to come by and that we need to think carefully about the demographic question being asked and how to answer it. In fact, more sophisticated thinking about human demography is important to all stages of studies of human diversity—from planning a sample to analyzing it.

The study of human variation is fascinating and important. Our species is better than most for many population-genetics and genome-evolution purposes because of our linguistic, cultural, historical, and archeological records. This is an active area of work. However, a number of ethical issues are raised that must be considered, having to do with how to sample human populations and interpret their variation. These issues are not new, but there is a new consciousness about them, and the occasion should be seized to build them properly into research strategies before the mood passes. Biomedical and other applied geneticists often operate with a naïve, folk-historic idea of human ethnic variation, yet important public policy decisions are made by that same community.

This is a realm in which anthropology should contribute actively, by being directly involved at all levels. But anthropologists who wish to be heard on such subjects as race must be willing to become informed about genetics and directly involved in the research itself; failure to do this effectively cedes authority on these subjects to technical scientists who may know or care little about the anthropologically subtle aspects of these issues. The facts of genetic variation are more subtle and complex than had been anticipated by either anthropologists or biomedical geneticists. Biomedical geneticists will have to accept and expect the uncertainties, but anthropologists should not fear a hidden determinism in these facts. Instead, we should come to terms with the realities of human variation.

Visit the *Annual Reviews home page* at
http://www.AnnualReviews.org.

APPENDIX: THE HUMAN GENOME DIVERSITY PROJECT

*GENERAL HISTORY*

After the idea of an HGDP was proposed, the group of organizers held a series of meetings to formulate a structure for the project (Weiss et al 1992, Kidd et al 1993, Evans 1995, HGDP Committee 1994). A DNA bank of samples would be collected in a systematic way from around the world, chosen to represent human genetic diversity. DNA would be openly available to qualified investigators. Genotypes determined from the samples would be deposited in an on-line statistical data base. The samples would be collected by investigators knowledgeable as to the provenience of the samples so that, to the extent possible, samples from anthropologically well-understood populations would be collected and documented. The supporting documentation would be made available in the online data base (including such things as references to published literature on the populations). Ethical issues would be agreed on by groups wishing to participate in this effort, and a global organization would be established to monitor conditions, select samples, organize and maintain a DNA bank and data base, ensure open communication at all stages of the project, protect against exploitation and private gain, and obtain appropriate informed consent. Individual subjects would, of course, remain anonymous.

Discussion was held on several technical points. First, it was found that a sample of about 25 individuals would include most alleles that have at least modest frequency in the sampled population. Larger samples, in the hundreds, would allow the ascertainment of correspondingly rarer alleles. For some geographically larger-scale questions, only the common alleles need be considered, but for more local or regional questions, rarer variants would be particularly informative. The best way to preserve DNA for open-ended analysis and distribution is to make permanent cell lines from the sample. Technological limitations on the ability to preserve and transform cells could provide practical constraints on the sample sizes that could be achieved for a global project, especially in terms of collections from areas distantly removed from the nearest laboratory capable of making cell lines. However, a meeting was organized by the author on behalf of the NSF, at which it became clear that advances in technology will probably be much more forgiving both for the ability to make cell lines, and for alternative technology (Weiss 1995b), so that samples in the order of 100 should be routinely possible (not all would have to undergo cell line production, a costly procedure, right away, but only as needed and scientifically justified).

Another issue that has been given substantial attention is the number and choice of populations that would be desirable to study in such a project. This issue is discussed at length in the project description developed by the organizers (HGDP Committee 1994, Evans 1995). Essentially, it was thought desirable that at least 25–100 populations should be sampled in each major continental region for a good representation of cultural, spatial, ethnic, and language groups, for addressing many interesting questions. The optimum number of samples is a function of the amount of resources that would be available. Fewer populations would allow only more coarse-grained analysis, while dense sampling would be needed to address microdemographic questions such as lineage relationships among villages or tribal populations as in the Amazon basin, the effect of geographic features on variation, the effect of language and dialect as population barriers in places such as Papua New Guinea, or the effect of historical migrations and movements as in the study of the distribution of African variation in African Americans.

These issues have not been totally settled, but are roughly described in the references cited above, and the major working documents are available on the worldwide web (http://www-leland.stanford.edu/group/morrinst/HGDP.html). As a formal global entity, the HGDP is still an idea more than a reality, for which planning and lobbying work continue. Numerous investigators around the globe are actively collecting and analyzing DNA samples, accelerating activity that has been going on for most of this century. But in the absence of a single, formal HGDP of some form, the difficulties of nonstandard collections and inaccessible samples persist, and while ethical issues are openly discussed more than they may have been otherwise, there is still no satisfactory, much less global, standard for subject and patent protection, nor uniform high standards for sample choice and collection. Ethical issues are reviewed by Greely (this volume) (see also Friedlaender 1996; HGDP Committee 1994; Moore 1995; 1996a,b; Weiss 1996b).

## THE NATIONAL RESEARCH COUNCIL REPORT

The idea of an HGDP has been around for nearly 7 years, and planning meetings and documents have been discussed and rediscussed, as indicated above. It has been difficult for consensus to be obtained as to how such a study should be done, how to handle its international complexities, and how to address the ethical issues that have been raised. No single US federal agency has been willing or able to fund the project in the contemporary competitive funding environment. The National Institutes of Health are generally uninterested in the nonmedical aspects of the proposed project, while the National Science Foundation could not afford its cost.

The potential importance of the project, and the many questions that were raised about the appropriate scientific objectives, structure, and legal/ethical issues, led to the appointment by the National Research Council of the National Academy of Sciences (hereafter, NRC) of a committee to assess the whole idea. In the 1980s, the NRC had constituted a committee that, amidst similar levels of controversy and discussion of goals and objectives, established the programmatic direction of the Human Genome Project itself (Olson

1993, Cook-Degan 1994). The NRC report on human variation was released late in 1997 (NRC 1997), and its basic conclusions can be described. The document should be consulted directly for its supporting references, although the latter are rather haphazard and incomplete. Not unexpectedly, the report is a cautious committee document that notes the potential value of some form of global assessment of human genetic variation, accepts many of the premises of the original HGDP design (like accessible DNA samples), mirrors the ethical concerns, and asks for more precise specification of a design.

Because of the manifest problems one might expect to be involved in any international project of this type, the report recommends a tentative beginning in the form of studies in which US funding agencies could be in control of the various issues, especially ethical ones. That is, a study initially based in the United States, or that involves US investigators in which US-standard IRB approvals could clearly apply, would enable this type of project to begin. International arrangements could be worked out later (one likely outcome is that a consortium of regionally based collections would form in some way).

The NRC report identifies various sampling strategies from a purely random sampling of individuals from around the world, to population- or geography-based sampling, to formal sampling of family structures. The strengths and weaknesses and relative costs are briefly identified. Essentially, family studies are too intensive and costly, and unnecessary. Pure random sampling is free of some of the tangles involved in choosing populations to sample, but is impractical in many ways. Local microdemographic processes, relationships between culture, language, and biological patterns of variation, could not be assessed. But population, culture, or language-based ascertainment involves the controversial and somewhat arbitrary decisions involved in choosing the populations to include or exclude.

The NRC recognized the importance of not designing a study based on 'outmoded social categories,' but of course what is outmoded is in the mind of the person making the judgment, and social politics should not override a sound strategy in this regard. For example, sampling on standard categories (e.g. by language or self-assigned cultural label, tribal name, religion, caste, etc) could be done as a matter of collection practicality as well as to test the degree to which such categories fit the biological facts. The NRC recommend that a population-based sample design in which ethnic identity is recorded be used. Based on an ability to identify most individual variant alleles that exist in a population, and a reasonable power to detect statistically different allele frequencies between populations, sample sizes in the hundreds were recommended, wherever possible, to avoid various artifacts and problems associated with smaller samples.

There had been discussion not only about sample size but about the form of material that should be saved (living cell lines, more expensive and difficult to obtain, or DNA extracted from a blood sample). The report recommended the latter. Similarly, there has been discussion about the value of obtaining a specified set of genotypes from all sampled individuals, but the NRC committee recommended no such action, on the grounds that there is insufficient consensus about which genotypes should be obtained and that the rapid changes in technology might quickly change what people thought on that score. However, the need for standard genotype data from all populations (a statistically balanced data set) was clearly acknowledged.

The NRC report mirrors the kinds of ethical concerns expressed in the model protocol, in the context of current views on the importance of understanding biodiversity as well as contemporary concerns about the misuse of genetic data. The difficulties of informed consent were considered, but the report is rather noncommittal with regard to recommendations beyond the need for awareness of the issues. *But we must be ever vigilant against abuse.*

## CURRENT ACTIVITIES, PROSPECTS, AND INITIATIVES

In addition to a world of individual studies of human variation, and active publishing of data on the subject in many journals, there also has been considerable coordinated activity related to the subject. The National Science Foundation has funded a number of investigators to study aspects of human variation, sample collection and preservation, the use of archival (already collected) samples for an HGDP, and ethical issues related to the formal HGDP proposal. The worldwide HLA community continues to collect and analyze samples to understand variation at this immunologically important set of genes; their efforts should be incorporated into some common plan, if possible. The CEPH organization has expressed an interest to the HGDP organizers in housing a sample of representative DNAs if it is collected. Major meetings occur regularly at which human genetic variation and evolution are the core subject matter. Numerous regions of the world are beginning various systematic, centralized, or at least nationally coordinated collections or analyses of genetic data from their various populations. These include India, China, and Europe.

## Literature Cited

Barbujani G, Magagni A, Minch E, Cavalli-Sforza LL. 1997. An apportionment of human DNA diversity. *Proc. Natl. Acad. Sci. USA* 94:4516–19

Bowcock AM, Ruiz-Linares A, Tomfohrde EJ, Minch E, Kidd JR, Cavalli-Sforza LL. 1994. High resolution of human evolutionary trees with polymorphic microsatellites. *Nature* 368:455–57

Boyd W. 1950. *Genetics and the Races of Man*. Boston, MA: Heath

Cann RL, Stoneking M, Wilson AC. 1987. Mitochondrial DNA and human evolution. *Nature* 325:31–36

Cavalli-Sforza LL. 1990. Opinion: How can one study individual variation for 3 billion nucleotides of the human genome? *Am. J. Hum. Genet.* 46:649–51

Cavalli-Sforza LL, Bodmer W. 1971. *The Genetics of Human Populations.* San Francisco: Freeman

Cavalli-Sforza LL, Menozzi P, Piazza A. 1994. *History and Geography of Human Genes.* Princeton, NJ: Princeton Univ. Press

Cavalli-Sforza LL, Wilson AC, Cantor CR, Cook-Deegan RM, King M-C. 1991. Call for a worldwide survey of human genetic diversity: a vanishing opportunity for the Human Genome Project. *Genomics* 11: 490–91

Chadwick D, Cardew G, eds. 1996. *Variation in the Human Genome. Ciba Found. Symp.* 197. Chichester, UK: Wiley & Sons

Collins F. 1991. The genome project and human health. *FASEB J.* 5:77

Collins F, Galas D. 1993. A new five-year plan for the US Human Genome Project. *Science* 262:43–46

Collins F, Guyer M, Chakravarti A. 1997. Variations on a theme: cataloging human DNA sequence variation. *Science* 278: 1580–81

Cook-Deegan R. 1994. *The Gene Wars: Science, Politics, and the Human Genome.* New York: Norton

Deka R, Jin L, Shriver MD, Yu LM, DeCroo S, et al. 1995. Population genetics of dinucleotide (dC-dA. n·(dG-dT. n polymorphisms in world populations. *Am. J. Hum. Genet.* 56:461–74

Deka R, Jin L, Shriver M, Yu L, Saha N, et al. 1996. Dispersion of human Y chromosome haplotypes based on five microsatellites in global populations. *Genome Res.* 6: 1177–84

Durham W. 1991. *Coevolution: Genes, Culture and Human Diversity.* Stanford, CA: Stanford Univ. Press

Evans E. 1995. The Human Genome Diversity (HGD) Project. *Genome Dig.* 2:12–14

Friedlaender J. 1975. *Patterns of Human Variation: The Demography, Genetics, and Phenetics of Bougainville Islanders.* Cambridge, MA: Harv. Univ. Press

Friedlaender J. 1996. Genes, people, and property: furor erupts of genetic research on indigenous groups. *Cult Surviv. Q.* 20:22–25

Greely H. 1996. Genes, patents and indigenous peoples. *Cult. Surviv. Q.* 20:54–57

Hammer M, Zegura S. 1997. The role of the Y chromosome in human evolutionary studies. *Evol. Anthropol.* 116–34

Harding RM, Fullerton SM, Griffiths RC, Bond J, Cox MJ, et al. 1997. Archaic Afri-can and Asian lineages in the genetic ancestry of modern humans. *Am. J. Hum. Genet.* 60:772–89

Harding RM, Sajantila A. 1998. Human genome diversity—a project? *Nat. Genet.* 18: 307–8

Harpending H. 1974. Genetic structure of small populations. *Annu. Rev. Anthropol.* 3:229–43

Harpending H, Batzer M, Gurven M, Jorde L, Rogers A, Sherry S. 1998. Genetic traces of ancient demography. *Proc. Natl. Acad. Sci. USA:* 95:1961–67

Harpending HC, Sherry ST, Rogers AR, Stoneking M. 1993. The genetic structure of ancient human populations. *Curr. Anthropol.* 34: 486–96

Hartl D, Clark A. 1997. *Principles of Population Genetics.* Sunderland, MA: Sinauer. 3rd ed.

Hey J. 1997. Mitochondrial and nuclear genes present conflicting portraits of human origins. *Mol. Biol. Evol.* 14:166–72

HGDP Committee. 1994. The Human Genome Diversity (HGD) Project: summary document. London: Hum. Genome Organ. (HUGO)

Jorde LB, Rogers AR, Bamshad M, Watkins WS, Krakowiak P, et al. 1997. Microsatellite diversity and the demographic history of modern humans. *Proc. Natl. Acad. Sci. USA* 94:3100–3

Kidd JR, Kidd KK, Weiss KM. 1993. Human Genome Diversity initiative. *Hum. Biol.* 65: 1–6

Krings M, Stone A, Schmitz RW, Krainitzki H, Stoneking M, Paabo S. 1997. Neanderthal DNA sequences and the origin of modern humans. *Cell* 90:19–30

Kruglyak L. 1997. The use of a genetic map of biallelic markers in linkage studies. *Nat. Genet.* 17:21–24

Lander E. 1996. The new genomics: global views of biology. *Science* 274:536–39

Lander E, Schork N. 1995. Genetic dissection of complex traits. *Science* 265:2037–48

Livingstone FB. 1958. Anthropological implications of sickle cell gene distribution in West Africa. *Am. Anthropol.* 60:533–62

Merriwether DA, Ferrell RE. 1996. The four founding lineage hypothesis: a critical reevaluation. *Mol. Phylogenet. Evol.* 5: 241–46

Moore J. 1994. Ethnogenetic theory. *Res. Explor.* 10:10–23

Moore J. 1995. Putting anthropology back together again: the ethnogenetic critique of cladistic theory. *Am. Anthropol.* 96: 925–48

Moore J. 1996a. Native Americans, scientists, and the HGDP. *Cult. Surviv. Q.* 20:60–62

Moore J. 1996b. Is the Human Genome Diversity Project a racist enterprise? In *Race and Other Misadventures*, ed. L Reynolds, L Lieberman, pp. 217–229. Dix Hills, NY: General Hall

Mourant A, Kopec A, Domaniewska-Sobczak K. 1978a. *The Distribution of the Human Blood Groups and Other Polymorphisms.* Oxford, UK: Oxford Univ. Press

Mourant A, Kopec A, Domaniewska-Sobczak K. 1978b. *Blood Groups and Disease.* Oxford, UK: Oxford Univ. Press

National Research Council. 1997. *Evaluating Human Genetic Diversity.* Washington, DC: Natl. Acad. Press

Neel J. 1978. The population structure of an Amerindian tribe, the Yanomama. *Annu. Rev. Genet.* 12:365–413

Nei M. 1987. *Molecular Evolutionary Genetics.* New York: Columbia Univ. Press

Olson M. 1993. The human genome project. *Proc. Natl. Acad. Sci. USA* 90:4338–44

O'Rourke D, Suarez B. 1985. Patterns and correlates of genetic variation in South Amerindians. *Ann. Hum. Biol.* 12:13

O'Rourke D, Suarez B, Course J. 1985. Genetic variation in North Amerindian populations: covariance with climate. *Am. J. Phys. Anthropol.* 67:241

Ott J. 1991. *Analysis of Human Genetic Linkage.* Baltimore, MD: Johns Hopkins Univ. Press. 2nd ed.

Risch N, Merikangas K. 1996. The future of genetic studies of complex human diseases. *Science* 273:1516–17

Roychoudhury A, Nei M. 1988. *Human Polymorphic Genes: World Distribution.* New York: Oxford Univ. Press

Sarich V, Wilson A. 1967. Immunological time scale for hominid evolution. *Science* 158:1200–3

Sherry ST, Batzer MA. 1997. Modeling human evolution: To tree or not to tree? *Genome Res.* 7:947–49

Stone A, Stoneking M. 1998. mtDNA analysis of a prehistoric Oneota population: implications for the peopling of The New World. *Am. J. Hum. Genet.* 62:1153–70

Stoneking M. 1996. Mitochondrial DNA variation and human evolution. In *Human Genome Evolution,* ed. M Jackson, T Strachan, G Dover. Oxford, UK: Bios Sci.

Suarez B, Crouse J, O'Rourke D. 1985. Genetic variation in North Amerindian populations: the geography of gene frequencies. *Am. J. Phys. Anthropol.* 67:271

Templeton A. 1997. Out of Africa? What do genes tell us? *Curr. Opin. Genet. Dev.* 7: 841–47

Terwilliger J, Zollner S, Laan M, Paabo S. 1998. Mapping genes through the use of linkage disequilibrium generated by genetic drift. *Hum. Hered.* In press

Tishkoff SA, Dietzcsh E, Speed W, Pakstis AJ, Kidd JR, et al. 1996. Global patterns of linkage disequilibrium at the CD4 locus and modern human origins. *Science* 271: 1380–87

Torroni A, Sukernik RI, Schurr TG, Starikovskaya YB, Cabell MF, et al. 1993. Mitochondrial DNA variation of aboriginal Siberians reveals distinct affinities with Native Americans. *Am. J. Hum. Genet.* 53: 591–608

Torroni A, Wallace D. 1995. mtDNA Haplogroups in Native Americans. *Am. J. Hum. Genet.* 56:1234–36

Underhill PA, Jin L, Lin AA, Mehdi SQ, Jenkins T, et al. 1997. Detection of numerous Y chromosome biallelic polymorphisms by denaturing high-performance liquid chromatography. *Genome Res.* 7 :996–1005

Vogel F, Motulsky A. 1997. *Human Genetics: Problems and Approaches.* New York: Springer-Verlag. 3rd ed.

von Haeseler A, Sajantila A, Paabo S. 1995. The genetic archaeology of the human genome. *Nat. Genet.* 14:135–40

Watson JD. 1990. The human genome project: past, present and future. *Science* 248: 44–49

Weiss K. 1989. A survey of human biodemography. *J. Quant. Anthropol.* 1:79–151

Weiss K. 1995a. *Genetic Variation and Human Disease: Principles and Evolutionary Approaches.* Cambridge, UK: Cambridge Univ. Press

Weiss K. 1995b. *Biotechnology for Genome Diversity Archiving.* Rep. symp. (Public doc. available) Natl. Sci. Found.

Weiss K. 1996a. Is there a 'paradigm' shift in genetics? Lessons from the study of human diseases. *Mol. Phylogenet. Evol.* 5:259–65

Weiss K. 1996b. Biological diversity is inherent in humanity. *Cult. Surviv. Q.* 20:26–28

Weiss K. 1998. In search of human variation. *Genome Res.* In press

Weiss K, Chakraborty R. 1982. Genes, populations, and disease: a problem-oriented review, 1930–1980. In *Physical Anthropology: 50 Years of Progress,* ed. F Spencer, pp. 371–404. New York: Academic

Weiss K, Kidd K, Kidd J. 1992. Human Genome Diversity Project. *Evol. Anthropol.* 1:80–82

Weiss KM, Maruyama T. 1976. Archeology, population genetics, and studies of human racial ancestry. *Am. J. Phys. Anthropol.* 44:31–49

*Annu. Rev. Anthropol. 1998. 27:301–28*
*Copyright © 1998 by Annual Reviews. All rights reserved*

# CULTURE IN NONHUMAN PRIMATES?

## W. C. McGrew

Department of Sociology, Gerontology and Anthropology and Department of
Zoology, Miami University, Oxford, Ohio 45056

KEY WORDS: tradition, social learning, intergroup differences, cultural evolution, behavioral
ecology

## ABSTRACT

Cultural primatology is hypothesized on the basis of social learning of
group-specific behavior by nonhuman primates, especially in nature. Scholars ask different questions in testing this idea: what? (anthropologists), how?
(psychologists), and why? (zoologists). Most evidence comes from five genera: *Cebus* (capuchin monkeys), *Macaca* (macaque monkeys), *Gorilla* (gorilla), *Pongo* (orangutan), and *Pan* (chimpanzees). Two species especially,
Japanese monkey (*Macaca fuscata*) and chimpanzee (*Pan troglodytes*),
show innovation, dissemination, standardization, durability, diffusion, and
tradition in both subsistence and nonsubsistence activities, as revealed by
decades of longitudinal study.

## INTRODUCTION

In the 1990s, a host of books have appeared, with titles like *Chimpanzee Cultures* (Wrangham et al 1994b); *Chimpanzee Material Culture: Implications
for Human Evolution* (McGrew 1992); *Great Ape Societies* (McGrew et al
1996); *Hominid Culture in Primate Perspective* (Quiatt & Itani 1994); *The Information Continuum: Evolution of Social Information Transfer in Monkeys,
Apes, and Hominids* (King 1994); and *Primate Behavior: Information, Social
Knowledge, and the Evolution of Culture* (Quiatt & Reynolds 1993). Clearly,
the wording is deliberate, and some scholars now feel comfortable describing
the existence of culture in primates other than humans. The aim of this chapter
is to scrutinize these efforts at cultural primatology in trying to answer the
question posed in the title.

301

The answers offered to the question by various interested parties run the full gamut from "Of course!" to "Nonsense!" The former see a gradation of quantitative (not qualitative) differences in sociocognitive abilities across phyla, so that natural and cultural phenomena are inextricable. An extreme example of this viewpoint was Bonner's *The Evolution of Culture in Animals* (1980), in which the microbiologist traced the roots of culture as far back as the slime molds (Myxomycetes). In contrast, the latter see a yawning gap between *Homo sapiens* and even the largest-brained species of living mammal, no matter how closely we and they are genetically related. For the skeptics, if culture is a uniquely and essentially human phenomenon, then the general question is just as pointless as a specific one, like "Are humans the only species to build spaceships?" In between these polar positions are degrees of skepticism or inclination, the variation in which needs to be explained (Premack & Premack 1994, Tomasello et al 1993a).

Asking the question is not new: Kroeber (1928) contemplated it 70 years ago. Although coming to a negative conclusion, he was willing to frame a set of testable criteria, based on what he knew of Köhler's (1927) pioneering studies of captive chimpanzees:

> If one ape devised or learnt a new dance step, or a particular posture, or an attitude toward the object about which the dance revolved; and if these new acts were taken up by other chimpanzees, and became more or less standardized; especially if they survived beyond the influence of the inventor, were taken up by other communities, or passed on to generations after him—in that case, we would legitimately feel that we were on solid ground of an ape culture. (Kroeber 1928:331)

The extent to which the titular question has been explicitly addressed has varied across decades (e.g. Hart & Panzer 1925, Menzel 1973, Nishida 1987, Thierry 1994), but here the emphasis is on new findings and insights, with historical aspects kept to a minimum.

The question posed does not read: Is culture found only in *living* humans? That would entail a much different critique about the origins of culture in prehistory: Has culture existed since literacy emerged in the Holocene? Since the advent of depiction in the Upper Paleolithic? Since the appearance of anatomically modern humans? (But what about Neanderthals?) Since the global dispersal of large-brained *Homo erectus*? Since the onset of lithic technology in earliest African *Homo*? Since the origin of bipedal Pliocene hominids? At some point our antecedents *were* nonhuman primates, but were they culture-bearers? To tackle these questions requires a paleoarcheological approach (e.g. Joulian 1996), with one huge constraint: All the subjects of study are extinct (Foley 1991).

This chapter is also not about theories of the evolution of culture, in particular, models that explore parallels between organic or genetic evolution and cultural evolution (Durham 1990, Boyd & Richerson 1985). These theories vary from the speculative to the formulaic, from the heuristic to the pontifical, from the empirical to the notional, but few concern themselves with the ethnography of other species.

## What Is Culture?

The simplest reason for disagreement over whether or not nonhuman primates have culture is definitional. Like all complex processes—consciousness, intelligence, language, and so on—culture has been defined from the broadest, loosest, and most inclusive ways to the narrowest, most precise, and most specific. Examples of the former may border on the epigrammatic: "Culture is the human ecological niche." "Culture is what human beings do." Examples of the latter approximate to checklists of features to be ticked off, inviting challenges, such as what to do with a hypothetical creature that has language, property rights, and taboos but lacks kinship terms, religious rites, and aesthetics. Tylor's (1871) classic definition spans the range: "Culture . . . is that complex whole which includes knowledge, belief, art, law, morals, custom, and any other capabilities and habits acquired by man as a member of society." (1871:1).

There is plenty of room for honest disagreement over the uniqueness of any one of these items, even before tackling the catch-all ending phrase. Depending on how one operationally defines a habit, which could range from a conditioned reflex to a ritual prayer, any number of species could be credited with the feature, or not.

Further bedeviling the exercise is the a priori assumption made by Tylor and many others (Kroeber & Kluckhohn 1963) that culture is by definition human. Logically, this preempts debate, so the answer to the titular question must be no, but resorting to this weasel-out merely passes the buck on to the question of what is humanness. Would we deny humanity to *Homo* (*sapiens*) *neanderthalensis*? To anatomically modern but apparently non-symbol-using *Homo sapiens* before about 40,000 years ago? To fire-using earlier hominids? The further we go into the past, the fuzzier things get, until we reach the Last Common Ancestor of living chimpanzees and living humans, at about 5 million years ago. To define culture as uniquely human may be logically tidy, but it is epistemologically suspect.

As if this were not enough, the presence or absence of culture in either the present or the past in nonhuman creatures could be a result of phyletic conservatism or of derived convergence (McGrew 1992). If the ancestral hominoid had culture, then its absence in living great apes could have been a secondary loss, just as overall body hair, grasping feet, and slashing canine teeth are absent in living humans. If the ancestral hominoid lacked culture, it could later have evolved independently more than once, in nonancestral forms that went extinct, or more recently in extant apes. When we find wild chimpanzees using stone hammers and anvils to crack nuts, it could have been invented once 10 million years ago and retained ever since, or several times only a few decades ago in scattered populations. Arguments about the origins of culture that rely only on homology fail to consider the analogical alternatives.

Another way to avoid confronting the titular question is to relabel the problem. For various reasons, pre-1990s investigators often dichotomized human culture and nonhuman "culture," proto-culture, pre-culture, sub-culture, quasi-culture, etc. (e.g. Kawai 1965). These may be valid distinctions, because each species' cultural heritage is likely to be as unique as its genetic inheritance of DNA. Bonobo culture should not be identical to chimpanzee culture any more than to human culture or to honey bee culture. However, the fact that, for example, human digestion differs from gorillas' does not stop us from considering it to be a largely comparable process, so why should culture be different? Missing from such relative labels are clear, testable criteria for distinguishing the ersatz from the real thing.

Everything said so far about the possibility of nonhuman culture relies on cultural acts (= behavior) in the present or on the products of those acts (= artifacts) in the past. If either is a necessary but not sufficient condition for culture, then methodological problems arise. If culture is knowledge (= information stored in brains) or meaning (= attributions assigned to such knowledge by minds), but neither of these is directly accessible, then what is to be done? Ethnologists infer knowledge and meaning from observation and communication with their human subjects, and students of nonhuman societies do the same. Each faces obstacles. Human informants are adept deceivers, by omission or commission, while nonhumans are far more spontaneous. Humans can be induced to engage in two-way, linguistic communication, while nonhumans cannot, at least in nature. Investigators of other species must constantly walk the line between anthropomorphism and anthropocentrism. Anthropomorphism brings with it the temptation to overly extend the principle of uniformitarianism. Anthropocentrism must remain mindful of the old adage "absence of evidence is not evidence of absence."

One way to ascertain culture is to focus on process. Following Kroeber (1928:331), if one saw:

1. a new pattern of behavior being invented, or an existing one being modified;
2. transmission of this pattern from the innovator to another;
3. the form of the pattern being consistent within and across performers, perhaps even recognizably stylized;
4. the pattern persisting in the repertoire of the acquirer long after the demonstrator was absent;

5. the pattern spreading across social units, be those families or clans, or across troops or bands, in a population;
6. the pattern enduring across generations;

then one might feel able to accord cultural status to that pattern.

Insisting on all six criteria may be overly strict, as few ethnographers of human culture have ever been lucky enough to witness innovation or lived long enough to follow it prospectively through to established tradition. On the other hand, when animals behave in the presence of humans, their performances are always potentially distorted by human influence, e.g. circus tricks. Whether manipulated genetically (by domestication) or ontogenetically (by foster rearing, especially in human homes), humanized nonhumans are uneasy composite creatures, unlikely to be informative about the results of natural selection.

Few of the primary reports cited below are both precise and explicit in their definition of culture. Of those that are, even fewer agree. On pragmatic grounds, the definition adopted here casts the net widely, to be as inclusive as possible: Culture is considered to be group-specific behavior that is acquired, at least in part, from social influences. Here, group is considered to be the species-typical unit, whether it be a troop, lineage, subgroup, or so on. Prima facie evidence of culture comes from within-species but across-group variation in behavior, as when a pattern is present in one community of chimpanzees but is absent in another, or when communities perform different versions of the same pattern. The suggestion of culture in action is stronger when the difference across the groups cannot be explained solely by ecological factors acting independently but simultaneously on individuals; e.g. presence or absence of resources may dictate across-group differences in foraging without any social learning being involved. Thus, diversity in social relations is easier to disentangle from such environment constraints than are subsistence activities. However, the interaction of nature and nurture is always tricky, even for humans: Variation can be innate, and similarity can be acquired.

## Who Studies Culture?

Culture is no longer the exclusive domain of anthropology, at least when other species are involved. This recent expansion of interest has caused confusion, if only because different academic disciplines ask different questions, even when they think these questions look the same. For putative culture in nonhuman primates, there are at least three distinct points of view: anthropology, psychology, and zoology, and primatologists may come from all of these disciplines.

Anthropologists tend to ask *what* questions about the constitution of culture in other primates. Ethnologists question whether a nonlinguistic creature could ever be cultural or how one might be able to study culture adequately without interrogating informants (Washburn & Benedict 1979). Archaeologists ask what might constitute an artifact for another species or how one might recover the past material culture of chimpanzees (Joulian 1996, Wynn & McGrew 1989). The emphasis is on culture as phenomenon.

Psychologists tend to ask *how* questions that concern mechanisms of cultural dissemination, that is, the cognitive processes by which socially acquired information is transmitted, individual to individual (Cheney & Seyfarth 1990, Fragaszy & Visalberghi 1990, Lefebvre 1995). Thus, there is a fascination with the details of means, as opposed to ends. (Figure 1 diagrams an array of mimetic processes that may be implicated in cultural transmission, Whiten & Ham 1993). Comparative psychologists working in laboratories or zoological parks design experiments to distinguish higher-order cognitive capacities such as imitation from lower-order capacities such as stimulus enhancement plus trial-and-error learning (Tomasello 1996, Visalberghi & Fragaszy 1990, Whiten et al 1996). Developmental psychologists compare the ontogenies of mother-reared individuals, nursery-reared individuals, and human-reared individuals, in an effort to disentangle the key variables that contribute to successful or unsuccessful performances (Boinski & Fragaszy 1989, Hauser 1993, Nagell et al 1993, Tomasello et al 1994, Call & Tomasello 1996). The emphasis is on culture as learning process.

Zoologists tend to ask *why* questions that concern the function or survival value of culture, using the theory and concepts of Darwinian evolutionary ecology. Ethologists focus on the motor patterns of spontaneous performances, especially in nature, with a view to being able to calculate the cost-benefit trade-offs of a cultural act. Why do some primates hunt more cooperatively and others less so, for the same species of prey (Boesch 1994b)? Behavioral ecologists apply optimal foraging theory to social aspects of subsistence. Why would any organism ever voluntarily give away food, much less a resource like knowledge (de Waal 1989b)? The emphasis is on culture as adaptation.

To answer the questions posed at the outset, all three disciplines are needed (King 1994, McGrew 1992, de Waal 1994, Parker 1996, Parker & Russon 1996). If human culture is embedded in primate culture, then primate culture may be embedded in mammalian culture, which may be embedded in vertebrate culture. But anthropologists tend to stick to primates, just as psychologists focus on domesticated, laboratory species, leaving only zoologists to range widely across phyla. The vast literature on song learning by passerine birds, which is easily the most elegant and extensive on any aspect of social learning, has been done almost entirely by behavioral biologists (Marler 1996). Laboratory primatologists are the only ones who can do controlled experiments; field primatologists can systematically intervene in natural settings (Matsuzawa 1994, 1996), but only carefully and to a limited extent, lest they

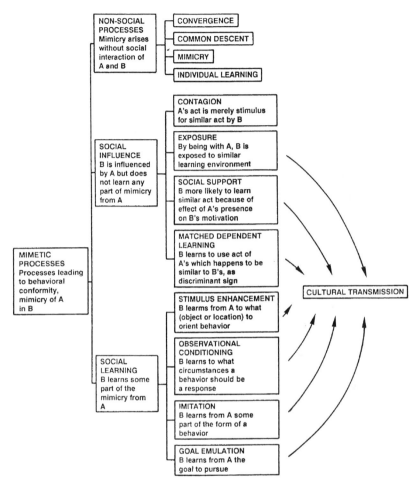

*Figure 1*   Mimetic processes that may be involved in cultural transmission (from Whiten & Ham 1993).

transform the process that they seek to understand. All can capitalize on naturalistic settings, such as wildlife parks, to manipulate variables such as socioecological contexts, but only in nature can primates be studied in their environment of evolutionary adaptedness, with the corresponding ecological validity that is crucial to keeping the whole enterprise on course. In light of this, and given the burgeoning literature on the subject, this synthesis stresses primary, ethnographic data rather than parroting secondary commentary, of which there is plenty (Boesch 1996, Byrne 1995, Parker 1996, Parker & Russon 1996).

## OTHER CULTURES?

*Both communities live along the Pacific Coast of British Columbia and south-eastern Alaska. One subsists largely on marine mammals, such as seals and dolphins; they hunt in small, silent parties, roving widely. The other focuses on fish, especially schools of salmon; they hunt in big, noisy groups and stay close to home. Both societies speak the same language, but with distinct dialects that differ even from group to group.*

*Extended families work together to collect and store a staple plant food upon which all individuals depend. Division of labor is central: While some family members maintain the granary, others seek animal prey that are brought home for sharing. All combine efforts to rear communally the family's youngsters, with some siblings postponing their reproduction in order to care for younger kin. If a parent dies, a replacement mate is sought from outside, rather than commit incest. Family life is a tricky compromise of cooperation and competition over generations.*

Is the first example reminiscent of the seagoing peoples of the Pacific Northwest, with their great canoes, soaring lodge poles, and exuberant pot-latches? In fact, the paragraph describes orcas (or killer whales), *Orcinus orca* (Barrett-Lennard et al 1996).

Is the second example an intriguing combination of a Great Basin foraging society like the Paiute and a utopian colony of Hutterites or Kibbutzniks? In fact, the paragraph encapsulates the life of acorn woodpeckers, *Melanerpes formicivorous* (Stacey & Koenig 1984).

The natural history of group-living vertebrates is full of candidates for culture among species other than primates, and there is a long-standing tradition of such referential modeling that dates back at least as far as Morgan's (1868) celebration of the beaver (*Castor pollux*). Among mammals, other well-known examples are sea otters (*Lutra enhydra*), in which Californian populations use stone anvils to smash open molluscs but their Alaskan counterparts do not (Hall & Schaller 1964).

Among birds, male bower birds (Ptilonorhynchidae) of New Guinea erect gaudily decorated structures that incorporate everything from moss to butter-flies' wings, to attract a mate (Diamond 1987). Styles, including color prefer-ences, vary across populations, but so do individual "signatures": One male may decorate his bower with shiny beetle heads, while another prefers acorns.

Primate longevity and long generation times make the prospective study of cultural processes prohibitive: To follow vertical transmission in long-lived apes takes decades (see below). Thus, one is forced to turn to nonprimates for comprehensive alternatives.

Cowbirds (*Molothrus ater*) are brood-parasites; they lay their eggs in the nests of other species, who rear the interlopers. Yet, male cowbirds must later sing the species- and population-specific song of their genetic parents (whom they never meet) and ignore the song of their foster parents if they are to attract a cowbird mate. How they learn to do so has taken years of integrated study between field and lab, with the conclusion that local dialects in male cowbirds depend ultimately on developmental shaping by female cowbirds (who do not sing!). Female responsiveness reinforces male song learning, resulting in locally preferred patterns of behavior (West & King 1996).

Black rats (*Rattus rattus*) in Israeli pine plantations have opportunistically become "ecological squirrels," to the extent of adopting arboreality and depending on pine seeds for food. Such enterprising exploitation entailed the invention of novel ways to disarticulate a pine cone; this occurred far too quickly for genetic adaptation. Terkel (1996) and his students have methodically dissected the transmission of the food harvesting and processing patterns from mother to offspring by a combination of field and lab studies that includes even the relative metabolic efficiencies of the "stripping" versus "shaving" techniques. It is a sobering thought that no study of comparable phenomena in human beings by ecological anthropologists, or anyone else, matches this research on rodents in terms of rigor or elegance.

## NONHUMAN PRIMATES

The Order Primates contains about 200 species, ranging from tiny, solitary, nocturnal mouse lemurs (*Microcebus* spp.) to the huge, polygynous, diurnal gorilla (*Gorilla gorilla*). However, for the vast majority of these species, the possibility of culture has been ignored. A 12-year (1986–1997) bibliography from the Primate Information Center (1997) showed that for references that specified their subjects to genus, only five genera (*Cebus, Gorilla, Macaca, Pan, Pongo*) accounted for 80% of entries. Of these, 52% came from one species alone, the chimpanzee, *Pan troglodytes*.

What explains this skew? Three of the five genera cover the four species of great apes (bonobo, chimpanzee, gorilla, orangutan), and another, *Cebus*, comprises the capuchin monkeys, a genus often likened to being the monkey equivalent to the great apes (Anderson 1996, Fragaszy et al 1990, Westergaard 1994). All have relatively large brains and are noted for their opportunistic style of extractive foraging in nature and for their superior abilities at problem solving in captivity. The fifth genus, *Macaca*, is a large, widespread radiation of Old World monkeys known for their adaptability; over half of the macaque references come from one species, *Macaca fuscata*, the Japanese monkey. Notably near-absent are two other well-studied genera of Old World monkeys, *Papio* (baboons) and *Cercopithecus* (guenons); had the bibliographic search extended earlier than 1986, their numbers would likely have been greater (see Nishida 1987 for earlier material).

More telling than phylogeny, however, may be methodology. Four of the five genera represent taxa that have been subject to decades of long-term behavioral research in the wild. (The exception is *Cebus*; although *Cebus apella* is well studied in captivity at various sites, it is little studied in nature.) Field sites such as Bossou, Gombe, Kibale, Mahale, and Tai (chimpanzee); Arashiyama, Koshima, Takasakiyama, Yakushima (Japanese monkey); Karisoke (mountain gorilla); and Tanjung Puting (Bornean orangutan) have each yielded thousands of hours of close-range observations over multiple generations of subjects. This point has simple but crucial implications, e.g. we cannot spot what is novel unless we know what is usual, and we cannot know what is usual until we have seen enough, especially for rare but important events. Notably, most of these studies have used *provisioning*, the offering of artificial foods by observers to tame wild primates to human presence. However, enough of the sites (Karisoke, Kibale, Tai, Tanjung Puting, Yakushima) have not used provisioning that one need not directly attribute cultural phenomena in nonhuman primates to such human influence.

This critical review concentrates on the primate taxa about which the most is known but always keeps in mind that ongoing research may yield new findings: Wild orangutans have been studied since the late 1960s, but the discovery that they regularly use tools came only in the mid-1990s (Fox et al 1998, van Schaik et al 1996). This review concentrates on behavioral patterns that occur habitually (repeatedly by several individuals in a group) or customarily (normally by all individuals of appropriate age, sex, and status in a group). Therefore anecdotal or idiosyncratic events are omitted, but it is always recognized that these events could later prove to be important. Earlier reviews of culture in nonhuman primates provide useful background information to the newer material presented here (Menzel 1973, Nishida 1987, Lethmate 1987, Thierry 1994).

## Capuchin *(*Cebus *spp.)*

The four species of capuchin monkey have been studied in nature since the 1960s, over the genus's wide range from Central to South America (Fragaszy et al 1990). Long-term behavioral data from identified individuals are available for two of these, *Cebus olivaceus*, the wedge-capped capuchin, in Venezuela (Robinson & Janson 1987) and *Cebus capucinus*, the white-throated or white-faced capuchin, in Costa Rica (Fedigan 1990). In captivity, almost all research focuses on *Cebus apella*, the brown or tufted capuchin, from laboratories in Europe or the United States (Westergaard 1994, Visalberghi 1997, Anderson 1996). *Cebus albifrons*, the white-fronted capuchin of Amazonian rainforests, is least known in any setting.

The best-known population of wild *Cebus* is that of the dry forests of Santa Rosa in northwestern Costa Rica (Fedigan 1990). Three neighboring groups of white-throated capuchin show differing diets in terms of ratios of fruit to insects to meat. Chapman & Fedigan (1990) tested three hypotheses to explain this: (*a*) relative abundance of prey, (*b*) relative profitability (costs and benefits in terms of nutrients, energetics), and (*c*) local traditions. The first and most ecologically deterministic was disproven, but the second and third could not be distinguished. Individual monkeys may choose the best balance of dietary items in terms of optimal foraging principles, or groups may develop local traditions that transcend environmental constraints. The basis for such across-group variation is present in within-group variation across sexes and age groups (Fragaszy & Boinski 1995) and in across-species variation in finding and processing such food as social insects (Janson & Boinski 1992).

Capuchin monkeys sometimes show uncanny parallels to their distantly related chimpanzee counterparts, e.g. in hunting, sharing, and eating the flesh of mammals (Fedigan 1990). The best data come from Santa Rosa (Rose 1997), where *C. capucinus* preys regularly on squirrels (*Sciurus varigatoides*) and coatis (*Nasua nasica*). Males pursue adult squirrels, usually in groups, while females rob coatis of their nestling young. This behavior mirrors that of chimpanzees: Male chimpanzees specialize in hunting arboreal monkeys, while female chimpanzees more often take the cached young of ungulates (Goodall 1986). Both chimpanzees and capuchins share the meat, mostly from mother to offspring, but rates of sharing vary across seasons and across groups for capuchins, being most frequent in the lean times of the dry season (Rose 1997).

The single best corpus of knowledge on material culture in nonhuman primates in captivity comes from *C. apella* (Westergaard 1994). However, almost all the data have been enabled (goals and raw materials supplied) or induced (programmed in experimental protocols) by human collaborators rather than shown spontaneously by the monkeys. Capuchin can do everything that chimpanzees can do, and more, with regard to making and using tools from wood, bone, bamboo, and metal (e.g. Anderson 1990). Many of the tasks performed model those inferred for early hominids, e.g. flaking stone, throwing missiles, digging up food items, using containers, and cracking open bones (e.g. Westergaard & Suomi 1995; see listing in McGrew & Marchant 1997). However, none of these activities has yet been seen to be even habitual, much less customary in nature.

In summary, capuchin monkeys are highly intelligent and manipulative primates whose extractive, generalist foraging style supplies the potential for cultural variation. However, the only behavioral variation across groups seen so far in the wild has been closely tied to environmental factors, and no social traditions have yet been identified. That the genus has the cognitive capacity for cultural acts is clear from laboratory studies, but fieldwork of the depth and extent of that on other primates is needed, especially on *C. apella* (Visalberghi & McGrew 1997).

## Macaques (Macaca spp.)

The adaptive radiation of Old World macaques is the most widely distributed of any primate genus; macaques are found primarily in Asia, but they are also found in Africa and Europe. More important for this discussion, macaques are perhaps the most ecologically diverse of nonhuman primates. They are found naturally from tropical mangrove swamps to temperate montane conifer forests. Introduced populations thrive on islands in the Outer Banks of the Carolinas and in the cactus scrubland of West Texas (Clark 1979). It is not surprising that such eclecticism is sometimes expressed in cultural diversity (Hauser 1996).

One species of macaque, the Japanese monkey, is familiar to anthropologists because their inclusion in introductory textbooks is almost obligatory (Itani & Nishimura 1973). These are the sweet-potato-washing and wheat-sluicing beach monkeys of Koshima Island, in the south of Japan (Kawamura 1959). This population may be the longest-studied of any wild primates; 1998 marks the fiftieth year of research. The story is well known: In 1953, a juvenile female, Imo, spontaneously washed a muddy sweet potato in a stream. This food-processing technique first spread horizontally to peers and then vertically upward to older kin; in less than 10 years it became the norm for the group, and over generations, it assumed predominance, being shown by 46 of 57 monkeys by 1983 (Watanabe 1994).

In 1956, Imo invented wheat-sluicing, in which handfuls of mixed sand and wheat grains were cast upon the sea, so that the floating cereal could be skimmed from the surface (Kawai 1965). This habit spread more slowly, but by 1974–1975, it had become the norm, shown by 43 of 77 individuals above the age of dependent infants, and by 1983–1984, the technique was used by 93% of the group (Kawai et al 1992).

A third, striking example of newly acquired behavior by Japanese monkeys comes from much further north, in the snowy forests of Honshu: hot-spring bathing (Suzuki 1965). In the Shiga Heights, monkeys learned to spend their leisure time on cold days immersed in natural hot springs, when they were not otherwise engaged in literally scraping a living from eating bark.

When presented in secondary literature, these patterns tend to be seen as static (Galef 1992, Tomasello et al 1993a), but longitudinal studies show them to be dynamic. Early on, Koshima monkeys changed from washing potatoes in freshwater to washing them in seawater, apparently adding seasoning to hygiene. By 1983–1984, the most common form of washing was repeated dipping for saltiness, even when the tuber was clean (Watanabe 1994). In wheat sluicing, dominant individuals learned to parasitize the labor of subordinates, by waiting until the latter had thrown their sand-grain mix into the water and then usurping it. Subordinates adopted a range of countermeasures, such as keeping the mix loosely gripped in the fist while sluicing, thus never losing control of the food. By 1983–1984, some individuals were digging their own small pools near the shore to practice solitary flotation, which provides more security from plunder (Kawai et al 1992). In the beginning, mothers entering hot springs left their young infants at the edge (Suzuki 1965), but now youngsters swim underwater in the pools.

All of these long-standing patterns of behavior satisfy Kroeber's (1928) criteria for culture given above, but two caveats arise: They are restricted to basic subsistence activities, that is, feeding or thermoregulation, and all result directly from human influence. The monkeys were drawn to Koshima's beaches by provisioning with cultivars by investigators seeking to facilitate their observations. At Shiga Heights, apples were thrown into the hot springs by researchers. Green (1975) suggested that the preferential distribution of sweet potatoes effectively shaped the vocal behavior of Koshima's monkeys, amounting to differential operant conditioning that might explain across-group differences in their calls. Does this mean that Japanese monkey culture is only an artificial phenomenon?

No, patterns of culture also exist for *non*subsistence behavior: Sakura (1989) showed that contact calls in grooming varied across troops and that such grooming was divorced from the provisioning process. Tanaka (1995) found that four techniques for removing louse eggs in grooming differed across matrilines in a wild but provisioned group at Jigokudani. The same sort of differences emerged in the courtship gestures and postures of both males and females in three widely separated groups (Stephenson 1973). At Koshima, the dominant male began to masturbate regularly during the breeding season; within three years all the leader and subleader males were doing it (Stephenson 1973). In captive groups, other nonsubsistence patterns have emerged spontaneously and become established: making snowballs big enough to sit on (Eaton 1972), propping up heavy branches against barriers as ladders (Machida 1990), using stones in social grooming (Weinberg & Candland 1981).

However, the best-documented case of nonsubsistence cultural activity is the enigmatic habit of stone handling (Huffman 1984, 1996; Huffman & Quiatt 1986). Japanese monkeys pile, pick up, scatter, roll, rub, clack, carry, cuddle, drop, toss, push pebbles collected from the ground. None of the acts accomplishes any goal; the stones are not used as tools. Since its first observation in 1979, stone handling has spread to the majority of the Arashiyama troop, and by the late 1980s, all infants had acquired it within six months of birth (Huffman 1996). The custom has now been seen in five other geographically isolated populations. It is a widespread, daily occurrence of no known function.

Examples of new subsistence activities that are unrelated to provisioning are also known: Since becoming denizens of the beach, Koshima's monkeys have learned to eat dead fish washed ashore and to go into the water to capture small octopus (Watanabe 1989). A replication of the invention of food-washing has occurred in a Dutch zoo: Before 1981, the monkeys washed their food only in a pool, but in that year, a female started to use a watering spout elsewhere; by 1985, 12 of the 26 monkeys were following suit (Scheurer & Thierry 1985). Monkeys living far from the sea wash dirty roots in a stream; these are natural foodstuffs, not provisioned ones (Nakamichi et al 1998). An adult female at Jigokudani invented a stone-throwing technique to solve a tool-use problem presented by researchers; it was later adopted by three other group members (Tokida et al 1994). However, the most compelling evidence comes from populations that have never been provisioned: Monkeys on Yakushima Island specialize in preying on frogs and lizards, unlike any other Japanese monkeys (Suzuki et al 1990).

Overall, various populations of Japanese monkeys, both captive and wild, have shown a variety of behavioral patterns that fulfill the criteria for culture. These customs range from subsistence to social to recreational, with the richest data coming from studies in which generations of researchers have studied generations of monkeys.

For other *Macaca* spp., surprisingly little is known about cultural phenomena, except for studies of social learning by offspring from their mothers. For example, differences are well known in maternal behavior across groups and across matrilines within groups of rhesus monkeys, *Macaca mulatta* (Simpson & Howe 1986). Often such variation is linked to matrilineal rank, but de Waal (1996) showed that even after kinship had been factored out, the social relations of mothers predicted those of their daughters with other females but not with males, suggesting the transmission of maternal style. Moreover, Berman (1990) found that for free-ranging rhesus macaques, the weaning techniques of adult females more closely resembled those demonstrated by their mothers to their younger siblings than those received by themselves. Thus, what they saw was more influential than what they experienced. Sometimes, rhesus macaque mothers could be inventive: In two captive groups, mothers displayed the "double hold," that is, simultaneously embracing their offspring and that of another female (de Waal 1990). The other offspring held did not appear to be chosen because of their sex or kinship, but they were much more likely to be of higher rank, suggesting that mothers were acting so as to encourage "social climbing" for their young.

Such questions of social development always raise issues of nature versus nurture, given that many factors may co-vary. One way to tease apart these influences is cross-fostering, such as swapping at birth the offspring of high- and low-ranking mothers, all other things being equal, and following the life histories of the offspring. No such studies seem to have been done. However, some cross-fostering across closely related species has been done on a small-scale: The vocalizations of cross-fostered Japanese and rhesus monkeys have been compared, but with little effect (Owren et al 1993). Most of the time, the youngsters exhibited the species-typical calls of their genetic parents. On the other hand, rhesus and stump-tailed macaque (*Macaca arctoides*) juveniles were co-housed for 22.5 weeks and then returned to their same-species groups. The rhesus juveniles persisted in their acquired style of frequent reconciliation after quarrels, à la stump-tails, but the other four measures of social relations were unchanged (de Waal & Johanowicz 1993).

In summary, it is hard to know if the cultural behavior of Japanese monkeys is somehow intrinsic to the species or if it is a reflection of the extent, depth, and type of research done on *M. fuscata*. Until comparable studies, especially of other wild macaques, are done, this remains an open question.

## Great Apes (Pongidae-Hominidae)

Five living species make up the Hominoidea clade: human (*Homo sapiens*); orangutan (*Pongo pygmaeus*, two subspecies); gorilla (*Gorilla gorilla*, three subspecies); bonobo or pygmy chimpanzee (*Pan paniscus*); and chimpanzee (*P. troglodytes*, four subspecies). As our nearest living relations, all great apes are automatically candidates for culture, but as stated above, most research has been on chimpanzees.

The other chimpanzee, *P. paniscus*, is the least known of all apes. Fewer than a hundred are in captivity; wild bonobos inhabit only one country, Congo (formerly Zaire), and there are only two ongoing field sites, Lomako and Wamba (de Waal & Lanting 1997). The captive bonobos outside Africa are scattered in small groups, and species management plans for captivity lead to frequent migrations, so their cultural life is constrained. However, customs can occasionally be seen: The bonobos of San Diego Zoo habitually clap their hands to gain one another's attention, and as their offspring have dispersed to other zoos, the behavior pattern has diffused with them (de Waal 1989a).

The obvious starting point in seeking bonobo culture is to draw comparisons with their close relative, *P. troglodytes*. Comparing material culture is handicapped by the bonobos' virtual lack of tool use in the wild; they habitually use no tools in subsistence or conflict, the two main categories for chimpanzees (Ingmanson 1996). When material culture can be compared, as with nest-building, the similarities stand out, with few exceptions, suggesting nest-building to be a deep-seated, ancestral trait (Fruth & Hohmann 1994, 1996). When differences do emerge between Lomako and Wamba, such as in the size of foraging parties, these can be attributed to greater habituation or provisioning at Wamba and lesser habituation and no provisioning at Lomako (White 1996). Thus, ecological or methodological variables can explain the differences found so far, without having to invoke cultural ones.

For orangutans, only one long-term study, of the Bornean subspecies at Tanjung Puting (Galdikas 1988), has garnered enough behavioral data to look for evidence of culture. It is lacking, perhaps because of the scarcity of comparable information from other populations or, more likely, because it is difficult to speak of group-specific effects in a solitary species, for which any clear-cut social unit has yet to be verified (van Schaik & van Hooff 1996). However, some within-species differences exist: Sumatran orangutans at Suaq Balimbing habitually use probes to get insect prey and scrapers to process fruit (van Schaik et al 1996). These resources are present at other study sites, but even studies of much longer duration (Fox et al 1998, Galdikas 1982) have never recorded any such regular use of tools.

This contrasts notably with results from formerly captive orangutans being rehabilitated back to the wild (Russon & Galdikas 1993, 1995) and from captive-born cage-living individuals (Lethmate 1982, Tomasello 1996). Rehabilitants initiated an astonishing range of activities, e.g. starting outboard motors, applying insect repellent, and hammering nails. However, all but 5 of the 32 actions reproduced were human activities, and no single pattern of imitation occurred more often than 4 times or was done by more than 3 of the 30 orangutans. In a follow-up analysis, the targets of these 56 cases of imitative learning were almost always humans, mostly primary caregivers. Thus, orangutans are superb imitators as individuals, but no evidence of a collective culture has emerged.

Experimental studies of social learning by captive orangutans rarely show positive results of transfer regardless of whether the models are humans or apes (Tomasello 1996), perhaps because the subjects are not motivated to mimic conspecifics to whom they are not attached (Russon & Galdikas 1995). Captive orangutans are superior problem-solvers and can devise technological solutions (Lethmate 1982), but there seem to be no studies of spontaneous social learning from other orangutans, even when living artificially in groups.

Gorillas present a unique challenge for cultural primatology (Byrne 1996): Only one field study has been able to record individual, long-term data, and it is of the most aberrant population of the species. The mountain gorillas of the Virunga Volcanoes of Rwanda, as studied by Fossey and her colleagues at the Karisoke Research Centre, are a tiny, relict population isolated at high elevation (Watts 1984). Their alpine existence is as ecologically representative of the 99% of other gorillas who live in lowland forests, as Tibetans are of *Homo sapiens*. Thus, western lowland gorillas are primarily fruit-eaters, while mountain gorillas are foliage-eaters, and eastern lowland gorillas (who are intermediate both geographically and altitudinally) fall in between (Watts 1996). This inverse correlation between extent of frugivory and altitude is further exemplified on a smaller scale by comparison of two populations of eastern lowland gorillas in the same national park (Yamagiwa et al 1996). The Itebero gorillas at 600–1300 m ate more fruit and less bark than did their Kahuzi counterparts at 1800–3300 m. However striking the differences in diet across or within populations, all could be explained by ecological factors, such as differential abundance or relative value of prey species. Within the Virungas population, but across groups, minor differences in diet exist, but all of these can be accounted for by differential abundance of vegetation (Watts 1984). Social learning need not be implicated if individual learning will suffice.

The best evidence for cultural differences in western lowland gorillas comes from two wild populations, Lop and Belinga, which are 250 km apart in Gabon (Tutin & Fernandez 1992). Weaver ants (*Oecophylla* spp.) and small, fungus-farming termites (*Cubitermes* spp.) are common at both sites, yet Lop gorillas eat the latter but not the former, and Belinga gorillas vice versa. The best data on the details of behavioral ontogeny come from the Virungas: Patterns of diversity in the components of processing plant foods suggest that all individual variation can be accounted for by trial-and-error exploration (Byrne & Byrne 1993).

There are no mountain gorillas in captivity, and few gorillas of any kind in laboratories, so research on cultural processes must depend on uncontrolled observations in zoos. Most zoo groups of gorillas are small by wild standards, but when larger groups are allowed to form and persist, spontaneous group norms may emerge if the context is helpful: Wood (1984) reported that gorillas at Howletts typically used sticks to rake in food from outside their enclosure.

In summary, the relatively impoverished ethnography of great apes is probably less a matter of their limitations and more a matter of data as yet uncollected, except for the solitary orangutan. Close-up behavioral data from multiple groups of identified individuals over generations are eagerly awaited from bonobos and lowland gorillas.

## Chimpanzee (Pan troglodytes)

The ethnography of chimpanzees is voluminous: In addition to published data from over 35 wild populations across sub-Saharan Africa, from Senegal to Uganda (e.g. Tutin et al 1995), there are long-term studies from zoos (e.g. Takeshita & van Hooff 1996) and laboratories (e.g. Tomasello et al 1987). However, apart from material culture, which leaves behind artifacts, the number of wild populations for which behavioral data are suitable for testing Kroeber's criteria are few: Bossou in Guinea (Sugiyama 1997, Matsuzawa 1994), Gombe in Tanzania (Goodall 1986), Kibale in Uganda (Wrangham et al 1994a), Mahale in Tanzania (Nishida 1990), and Tai in Ivory Coast (Boesch & Boesch 1989). This is a function of sustained research and longevity; wild chimpanzee birth intervals and maturation rates are as comparably prolonged as in humans.

The material culture of chimpanzees is ubiquitous and diverse. All populations subject to long-term study have proven to be tool makers and users (McGrew 1992). Each chimpanzee population has its own customary tool kit, made mostly from vegetation, that functions in subsistence, defense, self-maintenance, and social relations (Boesch & Boesch 1990, 1993; Sugiyama 1993). Many have tool sets, in which two or more different tools are used as composites to solve a problem (Brewer & McGrew 1990, Sugiyama 1997). The same raw material serves multiple functions: A leaf may be a drinking vessel, napkin, fishing probe, grooming stimulator, courtship signaler, or medication (Huffman 1997). Conversely, a termite fishing probe may be made of bark, stem, twig, vine, or the midrib of a leaf. An archaeologist would have no difficulty classifying the cross-cultural data in typological terms, based on artifacts alone; for example, only the far western subspecies, *P. troglodytes verus,* uses stone hammers and anvils to crack nuts (Boesch et al 1994, Kortlandt 1986, McGrew et al 1997). Given this ethnographic record, it is difficult to differentiate, based on material culture, living chimpanzees from earliest *Homo* (Wynn & McGrew 1989) or even from the simplest living human foragers (McGrew 1987).

Behavioral data add flesh to the skeleton of artifacts. For example, army ants (*Dorylus* spp.) co-occur with chimpanzees at all five major sites. At Gombe, the apes use a two-handed technique involving a long, straight, smooth stick: One hand holds the tool in a power grip while the other hand skillfully sweeps its length in a precision grip, collecting the ants (McGrew 1974). At Bossou and Tai, the chimpanzees also use tools, but in a one-handed technique in which a short probe is put directly to the mouth and the ants removed with the teeth (Boesch & Boesch 1990, Sugiyama 1995, Sugiyama et al 1988). At Kibale and Mahale, the ants are ignored by the chimpanzees and never eaten, although at Mahale the apes daily use another type of tool to obtain another type of ant (*Camponotus* spp.) (Nishida 1973, Nishida & Hiraiwa 1982). How to account for these interpopulational differences, when both prey and raw materials are plentiful? It may be, in optimal foraging theory terms, that the chimpanzees of Kibale and Mahale have better things to do with their time and so have no need to eat army ants. Thus, the difference can be explained in an ecologically deterministic way. But when techniques differ across groups, it is hard to avoid a cultural interpretation, all other relevant things being equal.

Sometimes the clues to culture are in the nuances of a universal habit (Uehara 1997). Whenever *P. troglodytes* is sympatric with *Colobus badius,* the red colobus monkey, the latter is the preferred prey for the chimpanzee predator (Boesch 1994a). At all studied sites, the meat is avidly sought and shared (Stanford 1998). Differences across sites in the degree to which the hunt is cooperative, or even just social as opposed to solitary, may lie in habitat variables, such as forest structure (Boesch 1994b), but other differences may have social causes. Why else do Gombe chimpanzees prefer to eat red colobus infants, while Tai's apes take all age-classes? Why else do Tai's chimpanzees consume the brain first, while Gombe's chimpanzees prefer to start with the limbs (Boesch & Boesch 1989)? Such habits appear to be conventional, not just coincidental uniformity over a set of individuals.

Materialists may be satisfied with such ecologically grounded evidence, but social behavior that transcends subsistence factors is more convincing: Grooming is the glue of primate societies, however humbly based in hygiene (Dunbar 1996). Monkeys and apes groom selectively, even politically, in that its patterning is explicable in terms of social variables such as status, alliance, and kinship. Given its intimacy and reciprocity, social grooming has been likened to conversation, and chimpanzees devote hours per day to this normative activity (Goodall 1986). The chimpanzee lives to groom, as well as grooms to live.

Because the functional morphology (e.g. thumb and forefinger opposition) of removing parasites or detritus from another's hairy body surface is straightforward, any standardized but apparently nonfunctional variations on the basic theme are likely to be social customs. Both Gombe and Mahale chimpanzees live in similar habitats, i.e. the mosaic forests along the eastern shore of Lake Tanganyika, and the motor patterns of their functional grooming look indistinguishable. However, the Mahale apes have added two striking elaborations on the species-typical activity: the grooming hand clasp and the social scratch.

The hand clasp is a symmetrical postural configuration in which two participants sit facing one another and engage in mutual grooming (McGrew & Tutin 1978; Figure 2). Each extends one arm (either both right or both left) overhead, and they clasp hands; meanwhile the other hand grooms the exposed torso of the other. The hand clasp occurs daily at Mahale but has never been seen in more than 35 years of observation at Gombe. It also is customary at Kibale and Tai but not at Bossou (Boesch & Tomasello 1998). At Kibale, it is common both in the Kanyawara community and in the Ngogo community (Watts, personal communication). Interestingly, the pattern has now emerged in a captive group at Yerkes, where it is spreading from its first performance by a captive-born adult female (de Waal & Seres 1997).

The social scratch is a self-maintenance pattern redeployed to social grooming (Nakamura et al 1998). Chimpanzees rake the tips of their partly flexed fingers in to-and-fro strokes over their own limbs and trunk in a stereotyped way that is common in all populations. Thus, all individuals are adept at the motor pattern, but only at Mahale has it been seen to be directed to others, interspersed with normal grooming components. If we see such differences in body language between groups in *Homo sapiens*, they are assumed to be cultural.

Most mammals, including primates, are thought to be poor relations to birds when it comes to vocal learning, but new findings question this (Janik & Slater 1997, Snowdon & Hausberger 1997, Mitani 1996). For wild chimpanzees, dialect differences exist in the long calls (pant-hoots) of the Gombe and Mahale populations; these are quantifiable acoustic features that distinguish the two sets of males (Mitani et al 1992). The means by which communities come to sound alike is joint participation in choruses (Mitani & Brandt 1994). Analysis

*Figure 2*   Two wild chimpanzees at Mahale engage in the grooming hand clasp (from McGrew & Tutin 1978).

of phrase structure in the calls of the Kanyawara community at Kibale shows these to be additionally distinguishable from the apes of Gombe and Mahale (Arcadi 1996). If French is spoken differently by Parisians, Belgians, French Canadians, and Cajuns, it is deemed cultural. What are we to do with similar diversity in chimpanzees?

All of Kroeber's criteria are met many times over by the ethnographic database on wild chimpanzees, especially at Gombe, where four generations of chimpanzees have been studied. The most challenging to establish are innovation and diffusion. Innovation is rare because chimpanzee society is conservative; few fads or fashions become established as social customs (Kummer & Goodall 1985, Takahata et al 1986, Boesch 1995). Diffusion is hard to study because communities are xenophobic and territorial; only females transfer groups, while males are philopatric (Goodall 1986). Thus to follow the diffusion of a habit means being able to monitor the emigration of known females into strange groups or the immigration of strange females into known groups (Boesch 1993). Both are difficult but yield valuable data (Hannah & McGrew 1987, Matsuzawa & Yamakoshi 1996). The virtues of patience are reinforced when an entirely new habit is discovered: leafy twigs used as sandals and cushions (Alp 1997); "brushsticks" to extract ants (Sugiyama 1985); pestles to pulverize the hearts of palms (Yamakoshi & Sugiyama 1995). The extent and volume of ethnographic data on *P. troglodytes* that continue to accumulate call for the serious consideration of establishing a CRAF (Chimpanzee Relations Area File) (Wrangham et al 1994a).

## HUMAN VERSUS NONHUMAN CULTURE

Some skeptics of the existence of nonhuman culture pose explicit, testable hypotheses about features missing in other species: Tomasello et al (1993a) postulated that only human culture shows (*a*) traditions learned by all group members, (*b*) skillful techniques similarly acquired by adults and youngsters, and (*c*) accumulation of modifications over generations. Thus, they recognized habits, but not customs. All hypotheses are readily falsified. All weaned individuals of the Kasakela community of chimpanzees at Gombe use tools to fish for termites (McGrew 1992). Byrne (1995) has shown in elegant detail how young mountain gorillas learn the plant food–processing skills of their elders. As cited above, Japanese monkeys at Koshima have elaborated over decades their subsistence techniques in a ratcheted way (Kawai et al 1992, Watanabe 1994).

A less direct form of query is to link culture to another phenomenon or premise. Washburn & Benedict (1979) ruled out nonhuman culture a priori on the grounds that nonhumans lacked language and language was essential to culture. Both premises are debatable propositions, but more exasperatingly, their acceptance precludes any further discussion. Relethford (1997) asserts that while nonhumans use tools, only humans depend on tools. All human cultures use tools, but so do all chimpanzee cultures; ipso facto, both are equally dependent, and so not distinguishable on this criteria.

More substantial is the debate, especially among psychologists, on whether certain cognitive capacities with cultural implications are uniquely human (Galef 1992; Heyes 1993; Tomasello 1990, 1994). If such capacities, e.g. imitation, are taken as necessary conditions for culture, and if these are absent in nonhuman species, then the debate is over (see Figure 1). If performances that were previously interpreted as imitative can be more parsimoniously explained by lower-order mimetic processes, such as stimulus enhancement, or even mere mimicry, then (goes the argument) culture can be denied (Galef 1992; Tomasello 1994, 1996). Things get especially sticky if in practice the controlled conditions for proving the existence of imitation can never be met outside the laboratory. And if the impoverished and artificial conditions of captivity (e.g. Call & Tomasello 1995) handicap the subjects so as to produce false-negative results, then culture is effectively precluded. However, more recent findings show chimpanzees to be capable of imitation even in the unnatural conditions of confinement (Custance et al 1995, Whiten et al 1996). More fundamental are the objections that neither imitation nor even social learning is a necessary or sufficient condition for culture (Heyes 1993). The crux with regard to mechanisms is that information transmission among individuals is accomplished, however that occurs (King 1994).

A more beguiling candidate for human uniqueness in cultural transmission is teaching, that is, intentional and directed transmission of information from a knowledgeable individual to a naive one (see Caro & Hauser 1992 for a lengthy but comprehensive operational definition). The evidence for teaching in nonhuman primates ranges from the anecdotal, e.g. Boesch's (1991) observations of Tai chimpanzee mothers and infants with nut cracking, to the systematic, e.g. Maestripieri's (1996) study of pigtail macaque (*Macaca nemestrina*) mothers tutoring their infants' locomotion. Whatever the vexing issues of proving intentionality (Maestripieri 1995) or not (Caro & Hauser 1992), the fact remains that much of human cultural transmission does not involve tuition; for example, of 50 skills of daily life acquired by Aka pygmies, most were learned by watching or by doing, not be being taught (Hewlett & Cavalli-Sforza 1986). Therefore, teaching is not a necessary condition for culture, although it may be a sufficient one.

In conclusion, primate culture in the broad sense seems likely to be a stem trait dating back at least to the last common anthropoid ancestor. As such, it predates all the derived traits of hominization, that is, bipedalism, enlarged and lateralized cerebral cortex, lithic technology, symbol use, and so on. To paraphrase Gertrude Stein, culture is culture is culture, in a variety of species, if culture is taken to be group-specific behavior that is at least partly acquired from social influences (see above). At the same time, human culture does not equal chimpanzee culture does not equal Japanese monkey culture. Each species is unique, but as more and more data accumulate, cross-species differences look more to be ones of degree, not kind.

In a stricter sense, the uniqueness of human culture depends on what is human. Even if, for example, externally stored knowledge in the form of symbolic depiction, whether as cave art or cuneiforms, is unique to modern *Homo sapiens*, we still must explain enculturated apes (Toth et al 1993, Tomasello et al 1993b, Tomasello 1996). That is, we must account for the admittedly unnatural and contrived acts of other species in labs using joysticks to move cursors or to tap out messages on keyboards. Whether or not these are performing beasts or fellow culture-bearers requires further study and so justifies the existence of such a field as cultural primatology. But a discipline requires subjects, and most species of nonhuman primate are endangered by their human cousins. Ultimately, whatever its merit, cultural primatology must be committed to cultural survival.

ACKNOWLEDGMENTS

I thank Jane Goodall and David Hamburg for my first chance to study chimpanzees in situ; Jim Hamill, Linda Marchant, Rob O'Malley, Homayun Sidky, and Andy Whiten for critical comments on the manuscript; Jackie Pritchard of the Primate Information Center for information retrieval; Rebecca Ham and Andy Whiten for Figure 1; and Carol Kist and Christie Smith for manuscript preparation. The paper is dedicated to two social anthropologists, Alison Bowes and Tim Ingold, who caused me to think about nonhuman culture even when they often disagreed with what I thought.

> Visit the *Annual Reviews home page* at
> http://www.AnnualReviews.org

## *Literature Cited*

Alp R. 1997. "Stepping-sticks" and "seat-sticks": new types of tools used by wild chimpanzees (*Pan troglodytes*) in Sierra Leone. *Am. J. Primatol.* 41:45–52

Anderson JR. 1990. Use of objects as hammers to open nuts by capuchin monkeys (*Cebus apella*). *Folia Primatol.* 54:138–45

Anderson JR. 1996. Chimpanzees and capuchin monkeys: comparative cognition. See Russon et al 1996, pp. 23–56

Arcadi AC. 1996. Phrase structure of wild chimpanzee pant hoots: patterns of production and interpopulation variability. *Am. J. Primatol.* 39:159–78

Barrett-Lennard LG, Ford JKB, Heise KA. 1996. The mixed blessing of echolocation: differences in sonar use by fish-eating and mammal-eating killer whales. *Anim. Behav.* 51:553–68

Berman CM. 1990. Intergenerational transmission of maternal rejection rates among free-ranging rhesus monkeys. *Anim. Behav.* 39:329–37

Boesch C. 1991. Teaching among wild chimpanzees. *Anim. Behav.* 41:830–32

Boesch C. 1993. Aspects of transmission of tool-use in wild chimpanzees. In *Tools, Language and Cognition in Human Evolution*, ed. KR Gibson, T Ingold, pp. 171–83. Cambridge: Cambridge Univ. Press

Boesch C. 1994a. Chimpanzees-red colobus monkeys: a predator-prey system. *Anim. Behav.* 47:1135–48

Boesch C. 1994b. Hunting strategies of Gombe and Tai chimpanzees. See Wrangham et al 1994b, pp. 77–91

Boesch C. 1995. Innovation in wild chimpanzees. *Int. J. Primatol.* 16:1–16

Boesch C. 1996. Three approaches for assessing chimpanzee culture. See Russon et al 1996, pp. 404–29

Boesch C, Boesch H. 1989. Hunting behavior of wild chimpanzees in the Tai National Park. *Am. J. Phys. Anthropol.* 78:547–73

Boesch C, Boesch H. 1990. Tool use and tool making in wild chimpanzees. *Folia Primatol.* 54:86–99

Boesch C, Boesch H. 1993. Diversity of tool use and tool-making in wild chimpanzees. In *The Use of Tools by Human and Non-*

Human Primates, ed. A Berthelet, J Chavaillon, pp. 158–68. Oxford: Clarendon

Boesch C, Marchesi P, Marchesi N, Fruth B, Joulian F. 1994. Is nut cracking in wild chimpanzees a cultural behaviour? *J. Hum. Evol.* 26:325–38

Boesch C, Tomasello M. 1998. Chimpanzee and human cultures. *Curr. Anthropol.* 39: In press

Boinski S, Fragaszy DM. 1989. The ontogeny of foraging in squirrel monkeys, *Saimiri oerstedi. Anim. Behav.* 37:415–28

Bonner JT. 1980. *The Evolution of Culture in Animals.* Princeton, NJ: Princeton Univ. Press

Boyd R, Richerson PJ. 1985. *Culture and Evolutionary Process.* Chicago: Univ. Chicago Press

Brewer SM, McGrew WC. 1990. Chimpanzee use of a tool-set to get honey. *Folia Primatol.* 54:100–4

Byrne R. 1995. *The Thinking Ape: Evolutionary Origins of Intelligence.* Oxford: Oxford Univ. Press

Byrne RW. 1996. The misunderstood ape: cognitive skills of the gorilla. See Russon et al 1996, pp. 111–30

Byrne RW, Byrne JME. 1993. Complex leaf-gathering skills of mountain gorillas (*Gorilla g. berengei*): variability and standardization. *Am. J. Primatol.* 31: 241–61

Call J, Tomasello M. 1995. Use of social information in the problem solving of orangutans (*Pongo pygmaeus*) and human children (*Homo sapiens*). *J. Comp. Psychol.* 109:308–20

Call J, Tomasello M. 1996. The effect of humans on the cognitive development of apes. See Russon et al 1996, pp. 371–403

Caro TM, Hauser MD. 1992. Is there teaching in nonhuman animals? *Q. Rev. Biol.* 67: 151–74

Chapman CA, Fedigan LM. 1990. Dietary differences between neighboring *Cebus capucinus* groups: local traditions, food availability or responses to food profitability? *Folia Primatol.* 54:177–86

Cheney DL, Seyfarth RM. 1990. *How Monkeys See the World. Inside the Mind of Another Species.* Chicago: Univ. Chicago Press

Clark TW. 1979. Food adaptations of a transplanted Japanese macaque troop (Arashiyama West). *Primates* 20:399–410

Custance D, Whiten A, Bard KA. 1995. Can young chimpanzees (*Pan troglodytes*) imitate arbitrary actions? Hayes & Hayes (1952) revisited. *Behaviour* 132:837–59

de Waal FBM. 1989a. Behavioral contrasts between bonobo and chimpanzee. In *Under-standing Chimpanzees*, ed. PG Heltne, LA Marquardt, pp. 154–75. Cambridge, MA: Harvard Univ. Press

de Waal FBM. 1989b. Food sharing and reciprocal obligations among chimpanzees. *J. Hum. Evol.* 18:433–59

de Waal FBM. 1990. Do rhesus mothers suggest friends to their offspring? *Primates* 31:597–600

de Waal FBM. 1994. Chimpanzee's adaptive potential: a comparison of social life under captive and wild conditions. See Wrangham et al 1994b, pp. 243–60

de Waal FBM. 1996. Macaque social culture: development and perpetuation of affiliative networks. *J. Comp. Psychol.* 110: 141–54

de Waal FBM, Johanowicz DL. 1993. Modification of reconciliation behavior through social experience: an experiment with two macaque species. *Child Dev.* 64: 897–908

de Waal FBM, Lanting F. 1997. *The Bonobo.* Berkeley: Univ. Calif. Press

de Waal FBM, Seres M. 1997. Propagation of handclasp grooming among captive chimpanzees. *Am. J. Primatol.* 43:339–46

Diamond J. 1987. Bower building and decoration by the bowerbird *Amblyornis inornatus. Ethology* 74:177–204

Dunbar R. 1996. *Grooming, Gossip and the Evolution of Language.* London: Faber & Faber

Durham WH. 1990. Advances in evolutionary culture theory. *Annu. Rev. Anthropol.* 19: 181–210

Eaton G. 1972. Snowball construction by a feral troop of Japanese macaques (*Macaca fuscata*) living under seminatural conditions. *Primates* 13:411–14

Fedigan LM. 1990. Vertebrate predation in *Cebus capucinus:* meat eating in a neotropical monkey. *Folia Primatol.* 54: 196–205

Foley RA. 1991. How useful is the culture concept in early hominid studies? In *The Origins of Human Behaviour*, ed. RA Foley, pp. 25–38. London: Unwin Hyman

Fox EA, Sitompul AF, van Schaik CP. 1998. Intelligent tool use in wild Sumatran orangutans. In *The Mentality of Gorillas and Orangutans*, ed. ST Parker, HL Miles, RW Mitchell. Cambridge, UK: Cambridge Univ. Press. In press

Fragaszy DM, Boinski S. 1995. Patterns of individual diet choice and efficiency of foraging in wedge-capped capuchin monkeys (*Cebus olivaceus*). *J. Comp. Psychol.* 109: 339–48

Fragaszy DM, Robinson JG, Visalberghi E, eds. 1990. Adaption and adaptability of capuchin monkeys. *Folia Primatol. 54*: 113–228

Fragaszy DM, Visalberghi E. 1990. Social processes affecting the appearance of innovative behaviors in capuchin monkeys. *Folia Primatol.* 54:155–65

Fruth B, Hohmann G. 1994. Comparative analyses of nest building behavior in bonobos and chimpanzees. See Wrangham et al 1994b, pp. 109–28

Fruth B, Hohmann G. 1996. Nest building behavior in the great apes: the great leap forward? See McGrew et al 1996, pp. 225–40

Galdikas BMF. 1982. Orangutan tool-use at Tanjung Puting Reserve, central Indonesian Borneo (Kalimantan Tengah). *J. Hum. Evol.* 10:19–33

Galdikas BMF. 1988. Orangutan diet, range, and activity at Tanjung Puting, Central Borneo. *Int. J. Primatol.* 9:1–35

Galef BG. 1992. The question of animal culture. *Hum. Nat.* 3:157–78

Goodall J. 1986. *The Chimpanzees of Gombe: Patterns of Behavior*. Cambridge, MA: Harvard Univ. Press

Green S. 1975. Dialects in Japanese monkeys: vocal learning and cultural transmission of locale-specific vocal behavior? *Z. Tierpsychol.* 38:304–14

Hall KRL, Schaller GB. 1964. Tool-using behavior of the Californian sea otter. *J. Mammal.* 45:287–98

Hannah AC, McGrew WC. 1987. Chimpanzees using stones to crack open oil palm nuts in Liberia. *Primates* 28:31–46

Hart H, Panzer A. 1925. Have subhuman animals culture? *Am. J. Sociol.* 30:703–9

Hauser MD. 1993. Ontogeny of foraging behavior in wild vervet monkeys (*Cercopithecus aethiops*): social interactions and survival. *J. Comp. Psychol.* 107: 276–82

Hauser MD. 1996. Vocal communication in macaques: causes of variation. In *Evolution and Ecology of Macaque Societies*, ed. JE Fa, DG Lindburg, pp. 551–77. Cambridge, UK: Cambridge Univ. Press

Hewlett BS, Cavalli-Sforza LL. 1986. Cultural transmission among Aka pygmies. *Am. Anthropol.* 88:922–34

Heyes CM. 1993. Imitation, culture and cognition. *Anim. Behav.* 46:999–1010

Heyes CM, Galef BG Jr, eds. 1996. *Social Learning in Animals: The Roots of Culture.* San Diego: Academic

Huffman MA. 1984. Stone play of *Macaca fuscata* in Arashiyama B troop: transmission of a non-adaptive behavior. *J. Hum. Evol.* 13:725–35

Huffman MA. 1996. Acquisition of innovative cultural behaviors in nonhuman primates: a case study of stone handling, a socially

transmitted behavior in Japanese macaques. See Heyes & Galef 1996, pp. 267–89

Huffman MA. 1997. Current evidence for self-medication in primates: a multidisciplinary perspective. *Yearb. Phys. Anthropol.* 40:171–200

Huffman MA, Quiatt D. 1986. Stone handling by Japanese macaques (*Macaca fuscata*): implications for tool use of stone. *Primates* 27:413–23

Ingmanson EJ. 1996. Tool-using behavior in wild *Pan paniscus:* social and ecological considerations. See Russon et al 1996, pp. 190–210

Itani J, Nishimura A. 1973. The study of infrahuman culture in Japan. See Menzel 1973, pp. 26–50

Janik VM, Slater PJB. 1997. Vocal learning in mammals. *Adv. Stud. Behav.* 26:59–99

Janson CH, Boinski S. 1992. Morphological and behavioral adaptations for foraging in generalist primates: the case of the Cebines. *Am. J. Phys. Anthropol.* 88:483–98

Joulian F. 1996. Comparing chimpanzee and early hominid techniques: some contributions to cultural and cognitive questions. In *Modelling the Early Human Mind,* ed. P Mellars, K Gibson, pp. 173–89. Exeter: Short Run

Kawai M. 1965. Newly-acquired pre-cultural behavior of the natural troop of Japanese monkeys on Koshima Islet. *Primates* 6: 1–30

Kawai M, Watanabe K, Mori A. 1992. Precultural behaviors observed in free-ranging Japanese monkeys on Koshima Islet over the past 25 years. *Prim. Rep.* 32: 143–53

Kawamura S. 1959. The process of subculture propagation among Japanese macaques. *Primates* 2:43–60

King BJ. 1994. *The Information Continuum: Evolution of Social Information Transfer in Monkeys, Apes, and Hominids.* Santa Fe, NM: Sch. Am. Res. Press

Köhler W. 1927. *The Mentality of Apes.* London: Kegan Paul, Trench, Trubner. 2nd ed.

Kortlandt A. 1986. The use of stone tools by wild-living chimpanzees and earliest hominids. *J. Hum. Evol.* 15:77–132

Kroeber AL. 1928. Sub-human culture beginnings. *Q. Rev. Biol.* 3:325–42

Kroeber AL, Kluckhohn C. 1963. *Culture: A Critical Review of Concepts and Definitions.* New York: Random House

Kummer H, Goodall J. 1985. Conditions of innovative behaviour in primates. *Philos. Trans. R. Soc. London Ser.* B 308:203–14

Lefebvre L. 1995. Culturally-transmitted feeding behaviour in primates: evidence for accelerating learning rates. *Primates* 36:227–39

Lethmate J. 1982. Tool-using skills of orangutans. *J. Hum. Evol.* 11:49–64

Lethmate J. 1987. Tradition bei primaten. *Unterr. Biol.* 121:37–42

Machida S. 1990. Standing and climbing a pole by members of a captive group of Japanese monkeys. *Primates* 31:291–98

Maestripieri D. 1995. Maternal encouragement in nonhuman primates and the question of animal teaching. *Hum. Nat.* 6: 361–78

Maestripieri D. 1996. Maternal encouragement of infant locomotion in pigtail macaques, *Macaca nemestrina. Anim. Behav.* 51:603–10

Marler P. 1996. Are primates smarter than birds? In *Current Ornithology,* ed. V Nolan, ED Ketterson, 13:1–32. New York: Plenum

Matsuzawa T. 1994. Field experiments on use of stone tools by chimpanzees in the wild. See Wrangham et al 1994b, pp. 351–70

Matsuzawa T. 1996. Chimpanzee intelligence in nature and in captivity: isomorphism of symbol use and tool use. See McGrew et al 1996, pp. 196–209

Matsuzawa T, Yamakoshi G. 1996. Comparison of chimpanzee material culture between Bossou and Nimba, West Africa. See Russon et al 1996, pp. 211–32

McGrew WC. 1974. Tool use by wild chimpanzees in feeding upon driver ants. *J. Hum. Evol.* 3:501–8

McGrew WC. 1987. Tools to get food: the subsistence of Tasmanian aborigines and Tanzanian chimpanzees compared. *J. Anthropol. Res.* 43:247–58

McGrew WC. 1992. *Chimpanzee Material Culture: Implications for Human Evolution.* Cambridge, UK: Cambridge Univ. Press

McGrew WC, Ham RM, White LJT, Tutin CEG, Fernandez M. 1997. Why don't chimpanzees in Gabon crack nuts? *Int. J. Primatol.* 18:353–74

McGrew WC, Marchant LF. 1997. Using the tools at hand: manual laterality and elementary technology in *Cebus* spp. and *Pan* spp. *Int. J. Primatol.* 18:787–810

McGrew WC, Marchant LF, Nishida T, eds. 1996. *Great Ape Societies.* Cambridge, UK: Cambridge Univ. Press

McGrew WC, Tutin CEG. 1978. Evidence for a social custom in wild chimpanzees. *Man* 13:234–51

Menzel EW, ed. 1973. *Precultural Primate Behavior.* Basel: Karger

Mitani JC. 1994. Ethological studies of chimpanzee vocal behavior. See Wrangham et al 1994b, pp. 195–210

Mitani JC. 1996. Comparative studies of African ape vocal behavior. See McGrew et al 1996, pp. 241–54

Mitani JC, Brandt KL. 1994. Social factors influence the acoustic variability in the long-distance calls of male chimpanzees. *Ethology* 96:233–52

Mitani JC, Hasegawa T, Gros-Louis J, Marler P, Byrne RW. 1992. Dialects in wild chimpanzees? *Am. J. Primatol.* 27:233–43

Morgan LH. 1868. *The American Beaver and His Works.* Philadelphia: Lippincott

Nagell K, Olguin RS, Tomasello M. 1993. Processes of social learning in the tool use of chimpanzees (*Pan troglodytes*) and human children (*Homo sapiens*). *J. Comp. Psychol.* 107:174–86

Nakamichi M, Kato E, Kojima Y, Itoigawa N. 1998. Carrying and washing of grass roots by free-ranging Japanese macaques at Katsuyama. *Folia Primatol.* 69:35–40

Nakamura M, Marchant LF, McGrew WC, Nishida T. 1998. The social scratch: another grooming custom of wild chimpanzees of the Mahale Mountains. In press

Nishida T. 1973. The ant-gathering behaviour by the use of tools among wild chimpanzees of the Mahale Mountains. *J. Hum. Evol.* 2:357–70

Nishida T. 1987. Local traditions and cultural transmission. See Smuts et al 1987, pp. 462–74

Nishida T, ed. 1990. *The Chimpanzees of the Mahale Mountains. Sexual and Life History Strategies.* Tokyo: Univ. Tokyo Press

Nishida T, Hiraiwa M. 1982. Natural history of a tool-using behaviour by wild chimpanzees in feeding upon wood-boring ants. *J. Hum. Evol.* 11:73–99

Owren MJ, Dieter JA, Seyfarth RM, Cheney DL. 1993. Vocalizations of rhesus (*Macaca mulatta*) and Japanese (*M. fuscata*) macaques cross-fostered between species show evidence of only limited modification. *Dev. Psychobiol.* 26:389–406

Parker ST. 1996. Apprenticeship in tool-mediated extractive foraging: the origins of imitation, teaching, and self-awareness in great apes. See Russon et al 1996, pp. 348–70

Parker ST, Gibson KR, eds. 1990. *"Language" and Intelligence in Monkeys and Apes. Comparative Developmental Perspectives.* Cambridge, UK: Cambridge Univ. Press

Parker ST, Russon AE. 1996. On the wild side of culture and cognition in the great apes. See Russon et al 1996, pp. 430–50

Premack D, Premack A. 1994. Why animals have neither culture nor history. In *Companion Encyclopedia of Anthropology,* ed. T Ingold. London: Routledge

Primate Information Center. 1997. *Topic Bibliography on Social Learning/Culture/Pre-Culture/Social Transmission, 1986–1997.* Seattle: Washington Regional Primate Research Center

Quiatt D, Itani J, eds. 1994. *Hominid Culture in Primate Perspective.* Niwot: Univ. Press Colo.

Quiatt D, Reynolds V. 1993. *Primate Behavior: Information, Social Knowledge, and the Evolution of Culture.* Cambridge, UK: Cambridge Univ. Press

Relethford JH. 1997. *The Human Species: An Introduction to Biological Anthropology.* Mountain View, CA: Mayfield

Robinson JG, Janson CH. 1987. Capuchins, squirrel monkeys, and atelines: socioecological convergence with old world primates. See Smuts et al 1987, pp. 69–82

Rose LM. 1997. Vertebrate predation and food-sharing in *Cebus* and *Pan. Int. J. Primatol.* 18:727–65

Russon AE, Bard KA, Parker ST, eds. 1996. *Reaching into Thought: The Minds of the Great Apes.* Cambridge, UK: Cambridge Univ. Press

Russon AE, Galdikas BMF. 1993. Imitation in free-ranging rehabilitant orangutans (*Pongo pygmaeus*). *J. Comp. Psychol.* 101: 147–61

Russon AE, Galdikas BMF. 1995. Constraints on great apes' imitation: model and action selectivity in rehabilitant orangutan (*Pongo pygmaeus*) imitation. *J. Comp. Psychol.* 109:5–17

Sakura O. 1989. Variability in contact calls between troops of Japanese macaques: a possible case of neutral evolution of animal culture. *Anim. Behav.* 38:900–2

Scheurer J, Thierry B. 1985. A further food-washing tradition in Japanese macaques (*Macaca fuscata*). *Primates* 26:491–94

Simpson MJA, Howe S. 1986. Group and matriline differences in the behaviour of rhesus monkey infants. *Anim. Behav.* 34:444–59

Smuts BB, Cheney DL, Seyfarth RM, Wrangham RW, Struhsaker TT, eds. 1987. *Primate Societies.* Chicago: Univ. Chicago Press

Snowdon CT, Hausberger M, eds. 1997. *Social Influences on Vocal Development.* Cambridge, UK: Cambridge Univ. Press

Stacey PB, Koenig WD. 1984. Cooperative breeding in the acorn woodpecker. *Sci. Am.* 251(2):114–21

Stanford C. 1998. *The Hunting Apes: Meat Eating and the Origins of Human Behavior.* Princeton, NJ: Princeton Univ. Press

Stephenson GR. 1973. Testing for group specific communication patterns in Japanese macaques. See Menzel 1973, pp. 51–85

Sugiyama Y. 1985. The brush-stick of chimpanzees found in south-west Cameroon and their cultural characteristics. *Primates* 26:361–74

Sugiyama Y. 1993. Local variation of tools and tool use among wild chimpanzee populations. In *The Use of Tools by Human and Non-Human Primates*, ed. A Berthelet, J Chavaillon, pp. 175–87. Oxford: Clarendon

Sugiyama Y. 1995. Tool-use for catching ants by chimpanzees at Bossou and Monts Nimba, West Africa. *Primates* 36:193–205

Sugiyama Y. 1997. Social tradition and the use of tool-composites by wild chimpanzees. *Evol. Anthropol.* 6:23–27

Sugiyama Y, Koman J, Bhoye Sow M. 1988. Ant-catching wands of wild chimpanzees at Bossou, Guinea. *Folia Primatol.* 51: 56–60

Suzuki A. 1965. An ecological study of wild Japanese monkeys in snowy areas focused on their food habits. *Primates* 6:31–72

Suzuki S, Hill DA, Maruhashi T, Tsukahara T. 1990. Frog- and lizard-eating behaviour of wild Japanese macaques in Yakushima, Japan. *Primates* 31:421–26

Takahata Y, Hiraiwa-Hasegawa M, Takasaki H, Nyundo R. 1986. Newly acquired feeding habits among the chimpanzees of the Mahale Mountains National Park, Tanzania. *Hum. Evol.* 1:277–84

Takeshita H, van Hooff JARAM. 1996. Tool use by chimpanzees (*Pan troglodytes*) of the Arnhem Zoo community. *Jpn. Psychol. Res.* 38:163–73

Tanaka I. 1995. Matrilineal distribution of louse egg-handling techniques during grooming in free-ranging Japanese macaques. *Am. J. Phys. Anthropol.* 98: 197–201

Terkel J. 1996. Cultural transmission of feeding behavior in the black rat (*Rattus rattus*). See Heyes & Galef 1996, pp. 17–47

Thierry B. 1994. Social transmission, tradition and culture in primates: from the epiphenomenon to the phenomenon. *Tech. Cult.* 23–24:91–119

Tokida E, Tanaka I, Takefushi H, Hagiwara T. 1994. Tool-using in Japanese macaques: use of stones to obtain fruit from a pipe. *Anim. Behav.* 47:1023–30

Tomasello M. 1990. Cultural transmission in the tool use and communicatory signaling of chimpanzees? See Parker & Gibson 1990, pp. 274–311

Tomasello M. 1994. The question of chimpanzee culture. See Wrangham et al 1994b, pp. 301–17

Tomasello M. 1996. Do apes ape? See Heyes & Galef 1996, pp. 319–46

Tomasello M, Call J, Nagell K, Olguin R, Carpenter M. 1994. The learning and use of gestural signals by young chimpanzees: a trans-generational study. *Primates* 35: 137–54

Tomasello M, Davis-Dasilva M, Camak L, Bard K. 1987. Observational learning of tool-use by young chimpanzees. *Hum. Evol.* 2:175–83

Tomasello M, Kruger AC, Ratner HH. 1993a. Cultural learning. *Behav. Brain Sci.* 16: 450–88

Tomasello M, Savage-Rumbaugh S, Kruger AC. 1993b. Imitation of object related actions by chimpanzees and human infants. *Child Dev.* 64:1688–705

Toth N, Schick KD, Savage-Rumbaugh ES, Sevcik RA, Rumbaugh DM. 1993. Pan the tool-maker: investigations into the stone tool-making and tool-using capabilities of a bonobo (*Pan paniscus*). *J. Archeol. Sci.* 20:81–91

Tutin CEG, Fernandez M. 1992. Insect-eating by sympatric lowland gorillas (*Gorilla g. gorilla*) and chimpanzees (*Pan t. troglodytes*) in the Lopé Reserve, Gabon. *Am. J. Primatol.* 28:29–40

Tutin CEG, Ham R, Wrogemann D. 1995. Tool-use by chimpanzees (*Pan t. troglodytes*) in the Lopé Reserve, Gabon. *Primates* 36:181–92

Tylor EB. 1871. *Primitive Culture*. London: Murray

Uehara S. 1997. Predation on mammals by the chimpanzee (*Pan troglodytes*). *Primates* 38:193–214

van Schaik CP, Fox EA, Sitompul AF. 1996. Manufacture and use of tools in wild Sumatran orangutans: implications for human evolution. *Naturwissenschaften* 83: 186–88

van Schaik CP, van Hooff JARAM. 1996. Toward an understanding of the orangutan's social system. See McGrew et al 1996, pp. 3–15

Visalberghi E. 1997. Success and understanding in cognitive tasks: a comparison between *Cebus apella* and *Pan troglodytes*. *Int. J. Primatol.* 18:811–30

Visalberghi E, Fragaszy DM. 1990. Do monkeys ape? See Parker & Gibson 1990, pp. 247–73

Visalberghi E, McGrew WC. 1997. *Cebus* meets *Pan*. *Int. J. Primatol.* 18:677–81

Washburn SL, Benedict B. 1979. Non-human primate culture. *Man* 14:163–64

Watanabe K. 1989. Fish: a new addition to the diet of Japanese macaques on Koshima Island. *Folia Primatol.* 52:124–31

Watanabe K. 1994. Precultural behavior of Japanese macaques: longitudinal studies of the Koshima troops. In *The Ethological Roots of Culture*, ed. RA Gardner, BT Gardner, B Chiarelli, FX Plooij, pp. 81–94. Dordrecht: Kluwer

Watts DP. 1984. Composition and variability of mountain gorilla diets in the Central Virungas. *Am. J. Primatol.* 7:323–56

Watts DP. 1996. Comparative socio-ecology of gorillas. See McGrew et al 1996, pp. 16–28

Weinberg SM, Candland DK. 1981. Brief report: "stone-grooming" in *Macaca fuscata*. *Am. J. Primatol.* 1:465–68

West MJ, King AP. 1996. Social learning: synergy and songbirds. See Heyes & Galef 1996, pp. 155–78

Westergaard GC. 1994. The subsistence technology of capuchins. *Int. J. Primatol.* 15: 899–906

Westergaard GC, Suomi SJ. 1995. The manufacture and use of bamboo tools by monkeys: possible implications for the development of material culture among east Asian hominids. *J. Archeol. Sci.* 22: 677–81

White FJ. 1996. Comparative socio-ecology of *Pan paniscus*. See McGrew et al 1996, pp. 29–41

Whiten A, Custance DM, Gomez J-C, Teixidor P, Bard KA. 1996. Imitative learning of artificial fruit processing in children (*Homo sapiens*) and chimpanzees (*Pan troglodytes*). *J. Comp. Psychol.* 110:3–14

Whiten A, Ham R. 1993. On the nature and evolution of imitation in the animal kingdom: reappraisal of a century of research. *Adv. Stud. Behav.* 21:239–83

Wood RJ. 1984. Spontaneous use of sticks as tools by gorillas at Howletts Zoo Park, England. *Int. Zoo. News.* 31:13–18

Wrangham RW, de Waal FBM, McGrew WC. 1994a. The challenge of behavioral diversity. See Wrangham et al 1994b, pp. 1–18

Wrangham RW, McGrew WC, de Waal FBM, Heltne PG, eds. 1994b. *Chimpanzee Cultures*. Cambridge, MA: Harvard Univ. Press

Wynn T, McGrew WC. 1989. An ape's view of the Oldowan. *Man* 24:383–98

Yamagiwa J, Maruhashi T, Yumoto T, Mwanza N. 1996. Dietary and ranging overlap in sympatric gorillas and chimpanzees in Kahuzi-Biega National Park, Zaire. See McGrew et al 1996, pp. 82–98

Yamakoshi G, Sugiyama Y. 1995. Pestle-pounding behavior of wild chimpanzees at Bossou, Guinea: a newly observed tool-using behavior. *Primates* 36:489–500

*Annu. Rev. Anthropol. 1998. 27:329–46*
*Copyright © 1998 by Annual Reviews. All rights reserved*

# THE ARCHAEOLOGY OF SYMBOLS

*John E. Robb*

Department of Archaeology, University of Southampton, Southampton SO17 1BJ, United Kingdom; e-mail: jer@soton.ac.uk

KEY WORDS: agency, social theory, prehistory, semantics, knowledge

## ABSTRACT

Why should archaeologists deal with symbols and how can they do so? This article outlines three major traditions archaeologists have followed in conceptualizing symbols, each with its own preferred topics of study, understanding of power and social relations, and epistemology. These include the processual view of symbols as tokens that represent reality, the structuralist view of symbols as mental girders framing a cultural reality, and the postmodern view of symbols as arbitrary fragments incorporated into phenomenological experience. The primary conclusions are that (*a*) any serious consideration of ancient society requires us to deal with its symbols; (*b*) human symbolism is so diverse (it includes cognitive structures; ritual icons; identities such as gender, prestige, and ethnicity; technological knowledge; and political ideologies) that multiple approaches are needed to deal adequately with it; and (*c*) a major problem in the archaeology of symbols is understanding how varied kinds of symbols relate to each other.

## THEORIZING SYMBOLS IN ARCHAEOLOGY

Archaeologists probably disagree about symbols more than anything else they dig up. Many believe that however important symbols are, we are wasting our time trying to recover mental phenomena archaeologically. Others believe that symbols are irrelevant to the larger systems that have structured human life over the centuries. In recent years, many other views have emerged beyond these two traditional viewpoints. The relationship of symbols to power and prestige has become an important theme. Both gender archaeology and agency-centered interpretations have forced us to confront ancient identities

329

0084-6570/98/1015-0329$08.00

and motivations. Even under the agency theory umbrella, however, there is diversity. Some theorists deal with "Symbols with a capital S"—pyramids, chiefly insignia, and the obtrusive icons of rank and ritual. Others see every human intervention in material things as a symbolically constructive act.

The archaeology of symbols has been parochialized into gender studies, political studies, cosmological reconstructions, and so on. But symbolic systems work because of the coherent ties between different kinds of meanings, which make political participation compelling, identity meaningful, and ritual effective. Moreover, archaeologists have often studied obvious, iconic symbols but have little sense of the broad range of meanings with which humans invest the material world. In keeping with this, many believe that symbolic archaeology is exceptionally difficult and that few archaeologists study it—a puzzling belief, because a complete archaeological bibliography on symbols could include several thousand works.

The archaeology of symbols is fragmented and contentious but also rich, diverse, and creative. By bringing together archaeological sources on symbols, I hope to demonstrate how much we already know and to provide grounds for optimism for the future.

## Is Symbolic Archaeology Possible? Dismantling Hawkes's Ladder

In 1954 Hawkes pronounced his famous "ladder of inference": Without written texts, archaeologists can investigate economy readily, and political and social systems to a lesser extent, but for the most part, prehistoric symbols and ideas must remain a closed book (Hawkes 1954). Hawkes's dictum was essentially a formalization of common sense, and its intuitive appeal has helped to enshrine it in archaeological theory. Forty years later, the idea remains widespread that symbols are remote, subjective, and archaeologically inaccessible, in contrast to the "hard" realities of environment, economy, and politics.

Hawkes was wrong, and it is worth considering why he was. It is true, as he presumed, that archaeologists are necessarily methodological materialists: With only material remains to deal with, our inferences must be anchored with artifacts. However, this idea is easily conflated with others less sound. In contrast to a long scholarly tradition in which the symbol consists of the unity of referent and meaning (de Saussure 1972), our folk model regards symbols as material "containers" that convey tidy "packages" of information (Lakoff & Johnson 1980). The material/meaning dichotomy is further conflated with folk distinctions between a visible, tangible material world and invisible ideas and feelings, between "hard" scientific approaches and "soft" humanistic approaches, and between "objective" knowledge and "subjective" opinion. The effect is a theoretical sleight of hand transmuting methodological materialism into a theoretical materialism in which signs speak for themselves to the degree that we think they are purely material. The best demonstration of this effect is the double standard we use for judging an archaeological interpretation, based on our prior opinion about its materiality. If we understand how a prehistoric rock carving was made technologically without knowing why it was made culturally, the effort is considered a failure and symbolic archaeology is pronounced impossible. But if we understand how prehistoric people produced their food technologically without knowing the cultural reasons why they produced what and how much they did in the way they did, the effort is considered a successful demonstration of economic archaeology; never mind that we have reduced a complex, value-laden set of social relations to a simple faunal inference. The archaeological world is a cultural world, and by dividing it into a priori categories of material and symbolic, we deny the degree to which things like economy are fundamentally cultural and things like ideas are embodied in material practices.

In many ways, the question is not whether we can find symbols archaeologically, but whether we can find anything cultural that is not symbolic. Many powerful symbols in any culture are the commonest things: bread, water, houses, the river, and the hills beyond. Powerful symbols are not irrational and ethereal but are often highly rationalized and concrete: Money is a symbol rather than mere gold, paper, or numbers in an account. Nor can the symbolic aspect of these things be magically separated from a logically prior economic or material use; indeed, much of our modern, supposedly rational economy is structured by massive efforts to protect symbolically important things—the environment, the small farm, the family home. But, having inextricably entangled the material and the mental, once we get beyond the superficial level, all fields of archaeological inquiry converge in similar epistemological constraints: We must replace the ladder of inference with a level playing field.

## Is Symbolic Archaeology Necessary? Coming to Grips with Culture

Current archaeological studies of symbols descend from many sources: the earliest New Archaeology (Binford 1962), stylistic studies (cf Carr & Neitzel 1995), evolutionary studies (Lindly & Clark 1990), structuralist archaeologies (Conkey 1982, Deetz 1977, Friedrich 1970), structural Marxist and Marxist research (Leone 1984, McGuire 1992, Shanks & Tilley 1988), and diverse postprocessual works (Barrett 1994, Hodder et al 1995, Thomas 1991, Tilley 1993). Recently, several of these lines of research have begun to converge within a general framework involving cultural actors and symbols. Archaeologists interested in social evolution have begun to explain transitions to agriculture (Gebauer & Price 1991, Hayden 1990) and to inequality (Hayden & Gargett 1990, Price & Feinman 1995) in terms of ambitious, strategizing human agents. Marxist and structuralist archaeologies have turned from monolithic constructions of high-level structures to more nuanced accounts of how institutions, individuals, and symbols interact (e.g. McGuire & Saitta 1996, Pauketat & Emerson 1991). Gender archaeology is based on the concept of culturally defined genders, directing attention to the symbolic construction of identities (Conkey & Spector 1984). The broad shift to people-centered approaches coincides with a postmodern view of culture as fragmented and contested rather than integrated and normative. These agency-centered approaches derived from Bourdieu (1977), Giddens (1979), Ortner (1984), and ultimately Marx provide a missing theoretical foundation for the study of symbols. The logical necessities of a practice theory view imply an archaeology dealing with people as people, that is, as actors behaving in culturally specific ways. This approach in turn commits us to taking symbols seriously as a pervasive aspect of the archaeological record.

## ARCHAEOLOGICAL SYMBOLS OF SYMBOLS

While it is no longer the case (if it ever was) that postprocessualists study symbols and processualists do not, there remain deep gulfs among archaeologists dealing with symbols. At the risk of oversimplification, perhaps the best capsule description is that archaeologists in processual traditions tend to view symbols as representing social realities, while postprocessualists and other structuralism-influenced archaeologists generally view symbols as constituting social realities. Root metaphors are central to academic theorizing (Turner 1974), and we might characterize these points of view as "symbols as tokens" versus "symbols as girders." To these may be added a third, recent view, the poststructuralist view of "symbols as tesserae." Each of these traditions has its own conceptualization of social relations and power, epistemology, and canonical case studies. Because the traditions correspond to deep divisions in the field, it is worth reviewing them at some length.

### "Symbols as Tokens": The Information Transmission View

According to many archaeologists, symbols serve primarily as instruments of communication (Wobst 1977). As one recent discussion puts it, "Symbols, including icons, rituals, monuments, and written texts, all convey and transmit information and meaning to their viewers" (DeMarrais et al 1996:16). Thus a sumptuous headdress signals a special status, an exotic artifact boasts about long-range connections, a monument represents a capacity to command labor. As tokens representing meanings, symbols have a material life: They can be produced, exchanged, monopolized, subverted, and destroyed. Much of this material life is governed by human intentions and strategies, and, as Binford (1962) and Wobst (1977) argued, when symbols are put into material form, there may be predictable economies of representation.

This approach has long since proved its value in archaeological interpretation, particularly in the study of strategies of political leadership (Blitz 1993, Clark & Blake 1994, DeMarrais et al 1996, Hayden 1995), prestige goods exchange (Brumfiel & Earle 1987, Ericsson & Earle 1977), and the interpretation of grave goods and burial procedures in terms of the social standing of the deceased (Beck 1995, Binford 1972, Brown 1981, Chapman et al 1981, O'Shea 1984, Saxe 1970). A recent exchange in *Current Anthropology* illustrates both the uses of this approach for analyzing political symbols and some criticisms of it. In three original analyses, Blanton et al (1996) discussed the use of cosmological legitimation in "corporate" and "network" strategies of organization; DeMarrais et al (1996) developed hypotheses about when and how ideology will be deployed in material items; Joyce & Winter (1996) argued that ideology is one tool of many by which elites maintain their position. All three treated power as the self-evident ability to control others (cf Wolf 1990) and ideology as the pragmatic use of symbols to accomplish this power; this point of view contrasts with arguments that the mental reality of symbolic meanings can make them a potent causal factor in politics (e.g. Conrad & Demarest 1984). The strongest reaction to these papers came from Marxists and interpretive archaeologists, who argued that symbols do not merely represent and disguise power relations but actually constitute them; however, many reactions crosscut theoretical approaches. Criado (1996) argued that the autonomous, freely acting individual is an idea peculiar to modernity and that culture cannot be reduced to instrumental ideology. Hodder (1996) argued that the authors did not consider preexisting systems of meaning, the varied experiences of ideology within a society, and ambiguities and disagreements over what symbols mean. Like Hodder, Clark (1996) and Cowgill (1996) demanded greater examination of how ideologies relate to semiotic and phenomenological systems. Clark (1996; cf Miller & Tilley 1984) posed the problem of relating the ambitions of elites and the actions of groups, and Brumfiel (1996a), D'Altroy (1996), and Schortman et al (1996; cf Brumfiel 1992) argued against unitary, "top-down" interpretations of symbols and for consideration of resistance. A key point here may be the dramatic aspect of political ritual (Geertz 1980, Kertzer 1988, Turner 1974), because it is often the public performance of symbols rather than real consensus on their meaning that unites groups. A final problem is how to relate meaning systems and other aspects of social life in a long-term history (Sahlins 1985; e.g. Marcus & Flannery 1996).

The "symbols as tokens" view merits critical discussion because it has been almost unquestioned. Its most problematic assumption is simply that artifacts, actions, and social relations have a meaning or existence logically prior to their translation into symbols, which serve primarily to represent this precultural reality. The concept of prestige is a good example. With few exceptions (Helms 1993, Shennan 1982), there has been little examination of cultural reasons why a particular material, action, or item might have been regarded as prestigious rather than of the strategic mechanics of the pursuit of prestige. Thus, paradoxically, this argument views people as acting politically and economically but not culturally, because it implies that the identities and values signaled and sought after are not themselves symbolic constructions (a view made explicit in models assuming a universal pursuit of power or prestige). There is little investigation of multiple forms of prestige integrated into cosmological schemes, gender, and alternative modes of classifying people and prescribing behavior (Bourdieu 1977, Hatch 1989) or of variations in the symbolic organization of prestige and authority (Godelier 1982). Nor has the interaction of prestige with other supporting or cross-cutting components of identity such as gender, language, and ethnicity (Farr 1993, Hendon 1999) been examined. Artifacts are regarded as self-evident and defined by their function; unless their explicit function was to signal, they were nonsymbolic. The use of symbols, rather than being an inescapable characteristic of human existence, thus becomes a specific realm of cultural life, like ceramic production or mollusk collecting. Not coincidentally, this view of symbols is usually implicit in theorizations of power in which ideological power is understood as an elite tactic comparable to the use of armies, political resources, or economic funds (Mann 1986).

By severing the use of symbols from their context of meanings, the informational view makes belief irrational and hence merely disadvantageous in followers and cynically optional in elites. It replaces meaning with a disenchanted interconvertible value like that of money in a capitalist economy. Without symbolic context, many questions become unanswerable. Why are some exotic goods prestigious and others not? Which specific kinds of status does control of prestige goods confer in a particular society? Why is supplying someone with food understood as largesse in one setting and as tribute or duty in another? Why is prestige competition more important in some societies than in others? What relation do grave goods have to the circumstances of death, social relations among survivors, ideologies of death and burial, and other factors (Bloch & Parry 1982, Brown 1995, Gnoli & Vernant 1982, Huntington & Metcalf 1991, Parker Pearson 1982, Ucko 1969). Long-term changes in the meaning of artifacts become problematic, as does disagreement or misinterpretation over meanings, and it is not obvious that controlling a symbolic artifact always gives one control of the idea it represented and the reactions of others. As recent feminist critiques (Gero 1997) have pointed out, the cross-culturally rational, genderless individual portrayed as manipulating political symbols draws strongly on modern gender and class values.

### "Symbols as Girders": The Mental Reality Approach

In contrast to the information transmission view, many archaeologists have explored how symbols constituted and structured the mental and social world of ancient people. Leroi-Gourhan's (1982) analysis of French Paleolithic cave art is the best-known example of structuralist analysis in archaeology. Other forays into structuralism have treated design rules in ceramics, bone artifacts, art, and vernacular architecture (Conkey 1982, Friedrich 1970, Glassie 1975, Washburn 1983) as well as generative grammars of artifacts (Chippindale 1992). A less purely cognitive approach was developed in the early 1980s (Hodder 1982b), culminating in Hodder's (1990) sweeping analysis of European Neolithic cultural structures, *The Domestication of Europe*. But interest in symbols as components of mental reality resists easy alignment with theoretical schools. Technological studies have investigated the structure of knowledge (see below). Recent "cognitive archaeology" (Flannery & Marcus 1993, Renfrew & Zubrow 1994) has focused on knowledge, religion, mental maps, and the material tools of thinking, using structural analysis, the direct historical approach, technological studies, studies of iconography, and computer modeling.

What this Noah's Ark of theorists have in common is a focus on symbols as mental structures, as girders framing an essentially cultural world and structuring thought processes. Treating symbols as mental building blocks captures a number of important insights. The most important is simply that humans orient themselves in the world, think, and act through learned, culturally specific structures that recur wherever they organize themselves and their material productions. Hence structural symbols such as gender oppositions, principles of spatial and temporal orientation, and cosmological qualities (Rappaport 1979) are embedded deeply in the individual's being. The individual cannot choose not to think and act through them, and their purpose is less to represent specific referential meanings than to organize other symbols. One implication of this is that even rational strategies are governed by generic rules of behavior, prescriptive rituals, symbolic limits, cultural tone, and inappropriate forms of maneuvering.

Proponents of the "symbols as girders" approach have been active in analyzing art and ritual, space and cosmology, and technological knowledge. Upper Paleolithic art has become iconic of human symbolic capacities in evolutionary narratives. Interpretations show a complex historical layering. Pre-1960s interpretations of cave art as representing hunting magic, fertility magic, and clan totems have generally been discredited (Ucko & Rosenfeld 1967). Leroi-Gourhan's (1982) structuralist approach decoded spatial binary oppositions between "male" animals such as bison and "female" animals such as horses. Other analysts focused on small portable items. Marshack (1972) argued that lines and dots on carved bones indicated calendrical uses. Conkey (1982), studying compositional rules in carved bone artifacts, related mobiliary art to information exchange at seasonal aggregation places and suggested (Conkey 1985) that art may have been produced for rituals legitimating social hierarchies. Mithen (1990) argued that Paleolithic images depict animal behavior and would have served to educate young hunters. These approaches have focused on the meaningful aspects of Upper Paleolithic symbolism. In contrast, analyses of art as information exchange include White's (1989) account of Aurignacian ornaments as a medium for creating social identities, and Gamble's (1982) interpretation of figurines from France to Russia as part of a common ritual system that helped to circulate information and mates among low-density foragers (cf Jochim 1983). In other approaches, Clottes (1996) used Lewis-Williams & Dowson's (1993) neurophysiological model to construe cave art images as products of shamanistic trances. Surprisingly, there has been little gender interpretation (though see Leroi-Gourhan 1982 and Rice 1981). Nor has Paleolithic art been dealt with in the postmodern approach (e.g. Tilley 1991), as an ecological system (Rappaport 1979), or as a medium of political history (Dowson 1994).

Probably the most effective archaeological work on cosmology has come through analysis of space. Categories of space relate to gender, personal identity, and cosmological systems (Bourdieu 1977); architectural studies have used this insight to relate space to social action (Wallace-Hadrill 1988, Yates 1989). Other analyses have discussed the experience of being within spaces defined in particular ways (Parker Pearson & Richards 1994). Sophisticated Marxist analyses include Leone's (1984) analysis of the early colonial garden and Kus's (1982) analysis of sacred space in Madagascar. The meaning of space has also been explored formally through network analysis (Broodbank 1993) and Geographical Information Systems (Zubrow 1994).

Technological knowledge is an integral part of the symbolic world (Dobres & Hoffman 1994, Lemonnier 1992, and articles in *World Archaeology*, Volume 27, 1995). That making things always incorporates cosmological beliefs about tools, materials, qualities, and processes has been well documented by studies of metal production in Africa (Herbert 1994), Mesoamerica (Hosler 1994), and South America (Lechtman 1984). The skills, knowledge, and social decisions involved in making things can be investigated through reconstruction of the operational sequence (*chaîne operatoire*) followed (Lemonnier 1992, Schlanger 1994). Because technological processes involve the practice of skills and knowledge associated with particular identities and values, they are a central way in which social agency is created and exercised (Dobres 1995, Dobres & Hoffman 1994, Sinclair 1995). As this argument implies, the archaeology of knowledge is more complex than simply reconstructing a prehistoric road map or recipe. Knowledge may be conscious or unconscious, general principles or specific data, agreed-upon or disputed, and it is often nondiscursive, as with ingrained bodily skills or practices.

Treating symbols as cultural structures, especially in structural analysis, has been criticized on a number of grounds. Reactions to *The Domestication of*

*Europe* are typical: Processualists have questioned the epistemological status of the cultural structures Hodder reconstructs (O'Shea 1992), while later post-processualists criticize Hodder for the coherent nature of his cultural structures, an unchanging script inaccessible to actors (e.g. Thomas 1996:97). Within this framework, it can be difficult to model both geographic variation and temporal change and to account for discrepancies, disbelief, and cynical manipulation. Structuralism also assumes a coherent underlying belief system rather than the fertile chaos cosmologies may appear "on the ground" (Barth 1987). Moreover, symbolic structures must be viewed as products of a specific social order. The archaeology of technology provides a good example: Impersonal knowledge may be a product of the information age, and in the past, the act of possessing and using knowledge may have been as socially important as the actual thing known. Without strong Durkheimian assumptions about elementary social structures, Lévi-Straussian assumptions about elementary mental structures, or Marxist assumptions about hegemony, identifying cultural structures alone usually does not satisfy social-minded archaeologists. For these reasons, already by 1982 a number of studies (in Hodder 1982b) combined structural analysis with other analyses. Hodder (1982a), for instance, explored structural parallels between Neolithic houses and tombs in the context of gender relations, and Shanks & Tilley (1982) discussed the opposition between individual and collective burials with reference to relations of production. Structuralism has lost its identity as a distinctive approach while continuing to contribute to the definition of symbolic structures, particularly cosmological oppositions, within structural Marxist, postmodern, processual, or other approaches (e.g. Roe 1995).

## Symbols as Tesserae: The Poststructuralist Critique

It would be deceptively facile to resolve views of symbolism as strategic manipulation and as cultural structure within the structure-and-action dualism of a practice theory model [for instance, via the "duality of structure" (Giddens 1979; e.g. Marcus & Flannery 1996:31)]. But a trenchant critique of both approaches has recently come from Hodder et al (1995), Tilley (1993), Barrett (1994), Gosden (1994), and Thomas (1996). These analysts begin by rejecting the dichotomy between material signifiers and ideal meanings: "Material culture may be physically embedded but it is at the same time culturally emergent. . . . precisely because material culture has this property of being culturally emergent, there can be no simple or formal demarcation between what is internal to, or is in, and that which is external to, or outside, the object" (Tilley 1993:5). Meaning does not reside in artifacts or in people but in the moment of interaction between the two (Thomas 1996:97); symbols' meanings do not exist outside of the moment in which people apprehend them and assemble them into meaningful formations. Symbols thus resemble mosaic tesserae, or per-haps Legos: fragments with qualities such as color, shape, and size, inherently arbitrary, that are temporarily assembled and experienced as meaningful by people playing with them.

Treating symbols as tesserae has broad implications. Because symbols' meaning is not fixed but contestable, social life involves continual struggle over alternative interpretations of important symbols. Power in this view is the ability to formulate a genuine experience of the world and to resist others' at-tempts to impose their views: a Foucauldian view that relates power to cultural structures more than to personalized political hierarchies and which sees power as enabling as much as restrictive. Proponents of such analyses often dismiss structuralist-inspired interpretations of symbolic structures as essenti-alizing or totalizing simply because they do not believe that cultures have an uncontested essence or totality. Hegemony, counterhegemony, and discord pervade this view of the past. Methodologically, the approach diverts attention from the formal or economic qualities of artifacts toward understanding how they were incorporated into experiences—how they appeared, sounded, chan-neled bodily movement and attitudes, recalled other artifacts, and were fit into collages of images. Because how symbols were used was as important to their meaning as any pre-fixed referent, archaeologists have to carry out close con-textual analysis. Because the emphasis is on the immediate moment of experi-ence, analysis tends to be strictly on the microscale. Epistemologically, ar-chaeology is couched in language appropriate to a socially situated discourse: formulation rather than discovery, interpretation of a text rather than analysis of a corpus, plausibility rather than proof.

Collective burials and megaliths have furnished the paradigmatic case study for postmodern theorists of kinship, time, and landscape. Culture-historical interpretations treated these monuments essentially as religious sites analogous to churches, and New Archaeological interpretation turned toward social structure (e.g. Fleming 1973) and ecology. The Maltese temples were seen as the centers of chiefdoms (Renfrew 1979), and communal tombs were interpreted as territorial markers erected as Neolithic farmers came under population pressure (Chapman 1981, Renfrew 1976). Since the 1980s, Sher-ratt (1990) has argued that monumental tombs were built as organizational sur-rogates for villages as native Mesolithic populations adopted farming. Carv-ings on chambered tombs have been interpreted as "entoptic" designs repre-senting visions during shamanistic trances (Bradley 1989, Lewis-Williams & Dowson 1993).

One common theme in postprocessual approaches, drawing largely on Bloch & Parry (1982) and Meillassoux (1981), has been kinship and cosmo-logical knowledge in the service of social processes. Monuments such as Stonehenge (Bradley 1991) were remodeled and reused over very long periods, showing that ancestral places furnished potent symbols throughout prehistory. Many tombs have inner chambers that may have allowed only restricted elites access to burials, and access to the past may have legitimated an elite of ritual leaders (Bradley 1989) or elders (Patton 1993); collective burials may also have mediated gender relations (Hodder 1982a) and effaced individual identities to mask relations of production (Shanks & Tilley 1982).

But how did people experience the creation and use of monuments? Recent interpretations have focused on local experiences of space, movement, landscape, and the body (Tilley 1993). Whittle (1996) has argued that Neolithic architecture involved the symbolic creation of defined places, and Thomas (1991) interprets Neolithic monuments as part of a new mode of engagement with the land. Tilley's (1994) study focuses on the monuments' landscape settings. As Barrett (1994) points out, space both within the monument and in the surrounding landscape must be understood in terms of patterns of movement imposed by the monument. Megalithic structures thus form part of a "monumental choreography" (Richards 1993). Thomas & Tilley (1993) interpret the iconography of cosmological processes of transformation from life to death.

The limits of the "tesserae" approach mirror those of the other two approaches. In denying the fixity of symbols' meanings, we risk seeing ancient peoples' ongoing reinterpretation of symbols as a quasi-voluntaristic act of will or self-empowerment, and we shortchange the effect of inherited and unquestioned terms of thought. All of symbolic life thus becomes superficial, without historical or psychological roots—a transitory juxtaposition of images on a screen. The insistence that interpretation of symbols is always conflictual owes as much to a particular understanding of modern politics as does the converse view, and it may underestimate the conservativism of ancient societies whose local culture formed a more total environment than ours does. Power tends to become equated too broadly with identity or the ability to experience, making it difficult to analyze its varied uses in hierarchical societies. Rather paradoxically for such a locally oriented approach, interpretations frequently produce generic portraits applicable to virtually any past society.

## DISCUSSION

It would be ingenuous to invoke the fable of the blind men and the elephant and argue that these three ways of looking at symbols are entirely complementary or can be made so by a "definitive" approach. While the case studies reviewed above have been investigated primarily within one tradition, issues such as gender and identity show both how far the three approaches to symbols presuppose one another and how they are sometimes incompatible.

Conkey & Spector (1984) originally argued that gender systems are cultural constructs related in complex ways to economy, society, and politics. The following decade witnessed a profusion of archaeological gender studies in all theoretical traditions (see Bacus et al 1992, Claassen 1992, Claassen & Joyce 1997, Cohen & Bennett 1993, Conkey & Gero 1997, Ehrenberg 1989, Gero & Conkey 1991, Moore & Scott 1997, Nelson 1997, Walde & Willows 1991). In general, archaeologists working in processual and structuralist traditions have focused on the meaning of gender within a system of cognitive categories and on how gender as a preexisting role or identity structures activity regimes and division of labor. Critique of both approaches has concentrated on two points, social context and the nature of gender categories. Studies that treat gender in terms of static economic roles and identities and supplement existing interpretations of the past have been criticized (Spencer-Wood 1991). Gender is central to power relations, including inequality (Kelly 1993), hegemony (Ortner 1990), and resistance (Brumfiel 1992, 1996b). Poststructural feminists have argued that gender does not form a system of static, agreed-upon dualities but must be understood as a process of relational difference (Baker 1997), and the biological basis of male and female sexual categories has been questioned (Nordbladh & Yates 1990). The point is that while much gender archaeology can be accommodated within a range of theoretical points of view, there are real divisions in theoretical approach that cannot be reconciled (for instance, as to the reality of enduring, conventional gender categories and identities). Nor is it clear how desirable a highly abstract and anodyne theoretical umbrella for all gender archaeology would be. The same is true for analysis of other aspects of identity such as prestige, ethnicity (Emberling 1997, Jones 1997, Shennan 1989), kinship, and language as well as for topics generally associated with a single theoretical approach.

Nevertheless, some general points emerge to guide an archaeology of symbols. The "symbols as tokens" view really deals primarily with how symbols are used in specific political contexts, and it works best with iconic badge-like symbols and personal identities. It necessarily presupposes a far broader and, ideally, explicit analysis dealing with how the symbols were constituted meaningfully in the first place and how their meanings affected their usage. But treating symbols as self-imposing cultural deep structures (as in the "symbols as girders" approach) requires a stratified model of the actor as constituted by both broad, abstract, and unconscious "generative structures" (Bourdieu 1977) and concrete, often conscious, and situation-specific symbols and meanings. This model requires us to think about contested alternative meanings and struggles over interpretation rather than assuming that important symbols had unanimous, unproblematic meanings. Finally, we should distinguish the study of cultural structures from that of meaning as an active experience and tackle them separately.

## Beyond "Codebreaking": Getting at Archaeological Meanings

What methods can we use to investigate symbols archaeologically? We must throw out the most popular image, that of codebreaking, of "making mute stones speak" to suddenly render the archaeological record completely transparent. In this Rosetta Stone view, interpreting a symbol involves merely identifying its literal referent; if this were true, there would be no differences of opinion over ethnographic interpretation, because all ethnographers have access to the same dictionaries. Pursuing the linguistic analogy, there are many equally important aspects of symbolism beyond simple reference and grammar: context, medium, intention, genre, register, style, attitude.

There is, then, no specific methodology unique to the archaeology of symbols. Instead, the key starting point for investigation is realizing what are the right questions to ask. Some basic points of study are as follows: (*a*) iconic or representational meaning of symbols; (*b*) structural or relational meaning of symbols; (*c*) phenomenological or experiential meaning of symbols; (*d*) grammars and variations of form, technique, and decoration; (*e*) perceptual aspects of symbolic artifacts (visual, auditory, tactile features); (*f*) cross-artifact styles and semantic associations; (*g*) social connotations and associations of artifacts, representations, and styles; (*h*) technical analysis of techniques of manufacture and use wear; (*i*) economic aspects of artifact manufacture and circulation; (*j*) knowledge and execution of artifact manufacture as cultural process; (*k*) artifact life histories from manufacture through deposition; (*l*) context of usage and interpretation; (*m*) knowledge differentials and layers of interpretation among users of artifacts; and (*n*) ambiguity, multiplicity of interpretations, misunderstanding, and irony. The significance of an artifact may involve a complex combination or juxtaposition of many of these codes, contexts, and circumstances. With such an array of questions to ask, our interpretations can never be final or lawlike. Instead, we will find ourselves crafting (Shanks & McGuire 1996) good ethnographies, which are always controversial.

## Some Future Directions

Formulating the archaeology of symbols as an object of study raises interesting lines of research. If archaeologists can investigate greatly varied kinds of symbols, then the internal organization of symbols of different kinds, at different levels of embeddedness, habituation, exegesis, or maneuver, becomes itself a key focus of theorizing. Can we identify key symbols (Ortner 1972) that structure other symbols and identities? How do knowledge, technological practice, rite, cosmology, and gender relate to one other?

One direction such questions lead us in concerns cross-artifact analyses. Archaeologists typically deal with specific artifacts, but symbolism that crosses boundaries may be a key to understanding how objects are understood and used. Why did a 1930s toaster become streamlined like an automobile? Why did dark green suddenly become popular in 1990s consumer goods? Symbolism of colors, textures, forms, and compositional styles may be the link between social relations, semantics, and artifact variation. Related problems include the question of economy of meanings among media—for instance, why did pottery design simplify rapidly in much of Europe when metals were introduced?—and the importance of artifact life histories. A third problem is that of regionality—the gap between representation and experience, between widespread material culture similarities and local beliefs, habits, and interpretations. To what extent can culture horizons be seen as regional habitus (Bourdieu 1977), zones of similar cultural response containing within them the seeds of rapid differentiation?

Socially, we need to incorporate symbols more fully into our understanding of social relations. One route to this is via the differentiation of prestige into bounded and related spheres of semantic values. Given the importance of the body as a nexus of identity, interpretation, and classification, gender is an obvious axis of differentiation but far from the only one. Methodologically, this problem might involve contextual analysis of artifact use, structural analysis of cultural principles, and iconographies of bodily gestures depicted in figurines and art. We must also confront the paradox that social orders emerge from situations in which participants often have very different interpretations of one another. Material things are central to our understanding of one another's roles, purposes, and values and thus furnish the focal points of ambiguity and of multiple interpretation. But ambiguity is not anarchy, and material culture may productively be viewed as systematic miscommunication.

ACKNOWLEDGMENTS

I am grateful to Liz Brumfiel, Marcia-Anne Dobres, Clive Gamble, Tim Pauketat, and Julian Thomas for their very helpful comments on the manuscript; to Sarah Tomasek for copyediting; and to Starr Farr, Richard Lesure, and the students in my "Archaeology of Symbols" graduate seminar at Southern Illinois University for enlightening discussions. All errors remain mine.

Visit the *Annual Reviews home page* at
http://www.AnnualReviews.org.

# Literature Cited

Bacus EA, Barker AW, Bonevich JD, Dunavan SL, Fitzhugh JB, et al, eds. 1992. *A Gendered Past: A Critical Bibliography of Gender in Archaeology.* Ann Arbor: Mus. Anthropol., Univ. Mich.

Baker M. 1997. Invisibility as a symptom of gender categories in archaeology. See Moore & Scott 1997, pp. 183–91

Barrett J. 1994. *Fragments from Antiquity: An Archaeology of Social Life in Britain, 2900–1200 BC.* Oxford, UK: Blackwell

Barth F. 1987. *Cosmologies in the Making: A Generative Approach to Cultural Variation in Inner New Guinea.* Cambridge, UK: Cambridge Univ. Press

Beck LA, ed. 1995. *Regional Perspectives in Mortuary Analysis.* New York: Plenum

Binford L. 1962. Archaeology as anthropology. *Am. Antiq.* 28:217–25

Binford L. 1972. Mortuary practices: their study and their potential. *Am. Antiq.* 36: 6–29

Blanton RE, Feinman GM, Kowalewski SA, Peregrine PN. 1996. A dual-processual theory for the evolution of Mesoamerican civilization. *Curr. Anthropol.* 37:1–14

Blitz JH. 1993. Big pot for bit shots: feasting and storage in a Mississippian community. *Am. Antiq.* 58:–96

Bloch M, Parry J, eds. 1982. *Death and the Regeneration of Life.* New York: Cambridge Univ. Press

Bourdieu P. 1977. *Outline of a Theory of Practice.* New York: Cambridge Univ. Press

Bradley R. 1989. Deaths and entrances: a contextual analysis of megalithic art. *Curr. Anthropol.* 30:68–75

Bradley R. 1991. Ritual, time and history. *World Archaeol.* 23:209–19

Broodbank C. 1993. Ulysses without sails: trade, distance, power, and knowledge in the early Cyclades. *World Archaeol.* 24: 315–31

Brown JA. 1981. The search for rank in prehistoric burials. See Chapman et al 1981, pp. 25–38

Brown JA. 1995. On mortuary analysis—with special reference to the Saxe-Binford research program. See Beck 1995, pp. 3–26

Brumfiel EM. 1992. Distinguished lecture in archaeology: breaking and entering the ecosystem—gender, class and faction steal the show. *Am. Anthropol.* 94:551–67

Brumfiel EM. 1996a. Commentary. *Curr. Anthropol.* 37:48–50

Brumfiel EM. 1996b. Figurines and the Aztec state: testing the effectiveness of ideological domination. In *Gender and Archaeology,* ed. R Wright, pp. 143–66. Pittsburgh, PA: Univ. Pittsburgh Press

Brumfiel EM, Earle T, eds. 1987. *Specialization, Exchange and Complex Societies.* Cambridge, UK: Cambridge Univ. Press

Carr C, Neitzel J, eds. 1995. *Style, Society, and Person.* New York: Plenum

Chapman RW. 1981. The emergence of formal disposal areas and the 'problem' of megalithic tombs in prehistoric Europe. See Chapman et al 1981, pp. 71–81

Chapman RW, Kinnes I, Randsborg K, eds. 1981. *The Archaeology of Death.* Cambridge, UK: Cambridge Univ. Press

Chippindale C. 1992. Grammars of archaeological design: a generative and geometrical approach to the form of artifacts. In *Representations in Archaeology,* ed. J-C Gardin, C Peebles, pp. 251–75. Bloomington: Indiana Univ. Press

Claassen C, ed. 1992. *Exploring Gender Through Archaeology: Selected Papers from the 1991 Boone Conference.* Madison, WI: Prehistory Press

Claassen C, Joyce RA, eds. 1997. *Women in Prehistory.* Philadelphia: Univ. Penn. Press

Clark J. 1996. Commentary. *Curr. Anthropol.* 37:51–52

Clark J, Blake M. 1994. The power of prestige: competitive generosity and the emergence of rank societies in lowland Mesoamerica. In *Factional Competition and Political Development in the New World,* ed. E Brumfiel, J Fox, pp. 17–30. New York: Cambridge Univ. Press

Clottes J. 1996. Thematic changes in Upper Palaeolithic art: a view from the Grotte Chauvet. *Antiquity* 70:276–88

Cohen M, Bennett S. 1993. Skeletal evidence for sex roles and gender hierarchies in prehistory. In *Sex and Gender Hierarchies,* ed. B Miller, pp. 273–94. Cambridge, UK: Cambridge Univ. Press

Conkey M. 1982. Boundedness in art and society. See Hodder 1982b, pp. 115–28

Conkey M. 1985. Ritual communication, social elaboration, and the variable trajectories of Paleolithic material culture. In *Prehistoric Hunter-Gatherers: The Emergence of Cultural Complexity,* ed. TD Price, J Brown, pp. 299–323. New York: Academic

Conkey M, Gero J. 1997. Programme to practice: gender and feminism in archaeology. *Annu. Rev. Anthropol.* 26:411–37

Conkey M, Spector J. 1984. The archaeology of gender. *Adv. Archaeol. Methods Theory* 7:1–38

Conrad G, Demarest AA. 1984. *Religion and Empire: The Dynamics of Aztec and Inca Expansionism.* Cambridge, UK: Cambridge Univ. Press

Cowgill G. 1996. Commentary. *Curr. Anthropol.* 37:52–53

Criado F. 1996. Commentary. *Curr. Anthropol.* 37:53–55

D'Altroy T. 1996. Commentary. *Curr. Anthropol.* 37:55–56

Deetz J. 1977. *In Small Things Forgotten: The Archaeology of Early American Life.* Garden City, NY: Doubleday

DeMarrais E, Castillo LJ, Earle TK. 1996. Ideology, materialization, and power strategies. *Curr. Anthropol.* 37:15–31

de Saussure F. 1972. *Course in General Linguistics.* London: Gerald Duckworth

Dobres M-A. 1995. Gender and prehistoric technology: on the social agency of technical strategies. *World Archaeol.* 27:25–49

Dobres M-A, Hoffman C. 1994. Social agency and the dynamics of prehistoric technology. *J. Archaeol. Methods Theory* 1: 211–58

Dowson TA. 1994. Reading art, writing history: rock art and social change in southern Africa. *World Archaeol.* 25:332–44

Ehrenberg M. 1989. *Women in Prehistory.* Norman: Univ. Okla. Press

Emberling G. 1997. Ethnicity in complex societies: archaeological perspectives. *J. Archaeol. Res.* 5:295–344

Ericsson J, Earle T, eds. 1977. *Exchange Systems in Prehistory.* New York: Academic

Farr SE. 1993. *Gender and ethnogenesis in the early colonial Lesser Antilles.* Presented at Congr. Int. Assoc. Caribbean Archaeol., 15th, San Juan, Puerto Rico

Flannery K, Marcus J. 1993. Cognitive archaeology. *Cambridge Archaeol. J.* 3:260–70

Fleming A. 1973. Tombs for the living. *Man* 8:177–93

Friedrich MH. 1970. Design structure and social interaction: archaeological implications of an ethnographic analysis. *Am. Antiq.* 35:332–43

Gamble C. 1982. Interaction and alliance in Palaeolithic society. *Man* 17:92–107

Gebauer A, Price TD. 1991. *Transitions to Agriculture in Prehistory.* Madison, WI: Prehistory Press

Geertz C. 1980. *Negara: The Theatre State in Nineteenth-Century Bali.* Princeton, NJ: Princeton Univ. Press

Gero J. 1997. *Agency and gender—a tension.* Presented at Annu. Meet. Soc. Am. Archaeol., 62nd, Nashville, Tenn.

Gero J, Conkey M, eds. 1991. *Engendering Archaeology: Women and Prehistory.* London: Blackwell

Giddens A. 1979. *Central Problems in Social Theory: Action, Structure and Contradiction in Social Analysis.* Berkeley: Univ. Calif. Press

Glassie H. 1975. *Folk Housing in Middle Virginia: A Structural Analysis of Historic Artifacts.* Knoxville: Univ. Tenn. Press

Gnoli G, Vernant J-P, eds. 1982. *La mort, les morts dans les sociétés anciennes.* Cambridge/Paris: Cambridge Univ. Press/Editions Maison Sci. l'Homme

Godelier M. 1982. Social hierarchies among the Baruya of New Guinea. In *Inequality in New Guinea Highlands Societies,* ed. A Strathern, pp. 3–34. New York: Cambridge Univ. Press

Gosden C. 1994. *Social Being and Time.* London: Blackwell

Hatch E. 1989. Theories of social honor. *Am. Anthropol.* 91:341–53

Hawkes C. 1954. Archaeological method and theory: some suggestions from the Old World. *Am. Anthropol.* 56:155–68

Hayden B. 1990. Nimrods, piscatores, pluckers, and planters: the emergence of food production. *J. Anthropol. Archaeol.* 9: 31–69

Hayden B. 1995. Pathways to power: principles for creating socioeconomic inequalities. See Price & Feinman 1995, pp. 15–86

Hayden B, Gargett R. 1990. Big man, big heart? A Mesoamerican view of the emergence of complex society. *Anc. Mesoam.* 1:3–20

Helms MW. 1993. *Craft and the Kingly Ideal.* Austin: Univ. Texas Press

Hendon J. 1999. Multiple sources of prestige and the social evaluation of women in prehispanic Mesoamerica. In *Material Symbols: Culture and Economy in Prehistory,* ed. J Robb. Carbondale: Cent. Archaeol. Invest., South. Ill. Univ. In press

Herbert EW. 1994. *Iron, Gender, and Power: Rituals of Transformation in African Societies.* Bloomington: Indiana Univ. Press

Hodder I. 1982a. Sequences of structural change in the Dutch Neolithic. See Hodder 1982b, pp. 162–77

Hodder I, ed. 1982b. *Symbolic and Structural Archaeology.* Cambridge, UK: Cambridge Univ. Press

Hodder I. 1990. *The Domestication of Europe.* London: Blackwell

Hodder I. 1996. Commentary. *Curr. Anthropol.* 37:57–59

Hodder I, Shanks M, Alexandri A, Buchli V, Carman J, et al, eds. 1995. *Interpreting Archaeology: Finding Meaning in the Past.* London: Routledge

Hosler D. 1994. *The Sounds and Colors of Power: The Sacred Metallurgical Tradi-*

*tion of Ancient West Mexico.* Cambridge, MA: MIT Press

Huntington R, Metcalf P. 1991. *Celebrations of Death: The Anthropology of Mortuary Ritual.* Cambridge, UK: Cambridge Univ. Press. 2nd ed.

Jochim M. 1983. Paleolithic cave art in ecological perspective. In *Hunter-Gatherer Economy in Perspective,* ed. GN Bailey, pp. 212–19. Cambridge, UK: Cambridge Univ. Press

Jones S. 1997. *The Archaeology of Ethnicity: Constructing Identities in the Past and Present.* London: Routledge

Joyce A, Winter M. 1996. Ideology, power and urban society in prehispanic Oaxaca. *Curr. Anthropol.* 37:33–47

Kelly R. 1993. *Constructing Inequality: The Fabrication of a Hierarchy of Virtue Among the Etoro.* Ann Arbor: Univ. Mich. Press

Kertzer D. 1988. *Ritual, Politics, and Power.* New Haven, CT: Yale Univ. Press

Kus S. 1982. Matters material and ideal. See Hodder 1982b, pp. 47–62

Lakoff G, Johnson M. 1980. *Metaphors We Live By.* Chicago: Univ. Chicago Press

Lechtman H. 1984. Andean value systems and the development of prehistoric metallurgy. *Technol. Culture* 25:1–36

Lemonnier P. 1992. *Elements for An Anthropology of Technology.* Ann Arbor: Mus. Anthropol., Univ. Mich.

Leone M. 1984. Interpreting ideology in historical archaeology: using the rules of perspective in the William Paca Garden in Annapolis, Maryland. See Miller & Tilley 1984, pp. 25–35

Leroi-Gourhan A. 1982. *The Dawn of European Art.* Cambridge, UK: Cambridge Univ. Press

Lewis-Williams JD, Dowson TA. 1993. On vision and power in the Neolithic: evidence from the decorated monuments. *Curr. Anthropol.* 34:55–65

Lindly J, Clark G. 1990. Symbolism and modern human origins. *Curr. Anthropol.* 31: 233–61

Mann M. 1986. *The Sources of Social Power.* Cambridge, UK: Cambridge Univ. Press

Marcus J, Flannery KV. 1996. *Zapotec Civilization: How Urban Society Evolved in Mexico's Oaxaca Valley.* London: Thames & Hudson

Marshack A. 1972. Cognitive aspects of Upper Paleolithic engraving. *Curr. Anthropol.* 13:455–77

McGuire RH. 1992. *A Marxist Archaeology.* San Diego, CA: Academic

McGuire RH, Saitta DJ. 1996. Although they have petty captains, they obey them badly:

the dialectics of prehispanic Western Pueblo social organization. *Am. Antiq.* 61: 197–216

Meillassoux C. 1981. *Maidens, Meal and Money.* New York: Cambridge Univ. Press

Miller D, Tilley C, eds. 1984. *Ideology, Power and Prehistory.* Cambridge, UK: Cambridge Univ. Press

Mithen SJ. 1990. *Thoughtful Foragers: A Study of Prehistoric Decision Making.* Cambridge, UK: Cambridge Univ. Press

Moore J, Scott E, eds. 1997. *Invisible People and Processes: Writing Gender and Childhood into European Prehistory.* Leicester, UK: Leicester Univ. Press

Nelson SM. 1997. *Gender in Archaeology: Analyzing Power and Prestige.* Walnut Creek, CA: Altamira

Nordbladh J, Yates T. 1990. This perfect body, this virgin text: between sex and gender in archaeology. In *Archaeology After Structuralism: Post-Structuralism and the Practice of Archaeology,* ed. I Bapty, T Yates, pp. 222–37. London: Routledge

Ortner S. 1972. On key symbols. *Am. Anthropol.* 75:1338–46

Ortner S. 1984. Theory in anthropology since the sixties. *Comp. Stud. Soc. Hist.* 1: 126–66

Ortner S. 1990. Gender hegemonies. *Cult. Crit.* 14:35–80

O'Shea JM. 1984. *Mortuary Variability.* New York: Academic

O'Shea JM. 1992. Review of "The Domestication of Europe." *Am. Anthropol.* 94: 752–53

Parker Pearson M. 1982. Mortuary practices, society and ideology: an ethnoarchaeological study. See Hodder 1982b, pp. 99–113

Parker Pearson M, Richards C, eds. 1994. *Architecture and Order: Approaches to Social Space.* London: Routledge

Patton M. 1993. *Statements in Stone: Monuments and Society in Neolithic Brittany.* London: Routledge

Pauketat TR, Emerson TE. 1991. The ideology of authority and the power of the pot. *Am. Anthropol.* 93:919–41

Price TD, Feinman G. 1995. *Foundations of Social Inequality.* New York: Plenum

Rappaport R. 1979. *Ecology, Meaning and Religion.* Berkeley, CA: North Atlantic

Renfrew C. 1976. Megaliths, territories and populations. In *Acculturation and Continuity in Atlantic Europe,* ed. S De Laet, pp. 198–220. Brugge: De Tempel

Renfrew C. 1979. *Before Civilization.* New York: Cambridge Univ. Press

Renfrew C, Zubrow E. 1994. *The Ancient Mind: Elements of Cognitive Archaeology.* Cambridge, UK: Cambridge Univ. Press

Rice PC. 1981. Prehistoric Venuses: symbols of motherhood or womanhood? *J. Anthropol. Res.* 37:402–14

Richards C. 1993. Monumental choreography: architecture and spatial representation in Late Neolithic Orkney. See Tilley 1993, pp. 143–80

Roe PG. 1995. Style, society, myth, and structure. See Carr & Neitzel 1995, pp. 27–76

Sahlins M. 1985. *Islands of History.* Chicago: Univ. of Chicago Press

Saxe AA. 1970. *Social dimensions of mortuary practices.* PhD thesis, Univ. Mich., Ann Arbor

Schlanger N. 1994. Mindful technology: unleashing the *chaine operatoire* of the mind. See Renfrew & Zubrow 1994, pp. 143–51

Schortman E, Urban P, Ausec M. 1996. Commentary. *Curr. Anthropol.* 37:61–63

Shanks M, McGuire RH. 1996. The craft of archaeology. *Am. Antiq.* 61:75–88

Shanks M, Tilley C. 1982. Ideology, symbolic power and ritual communication: a reinterpretation of neolithic mortuary practices. See Hodder 1982b, pp. 129–54

Shanks M, Tilley C. 1988. *Social Theory and Archaeology.* Albuquerque: Univ. NM Press

Shennan S. 1982. Ideology, change and the European Bronze Age. See Hodder 1982b, pp. 155–61

Shennan S, ed. 1989. *Archaeological Approaches to Cultural Identity.* London: Routledge

Sherratt A. 1990. The genesis of megaliths: monumentality, ethnicity and social complexity in Neolithic north-west Europe. *World Archaeol.* 22:147–67

Sinclair A. 1995. The technique as symbol in Late Glacial Europe. *World Archaeol.* 27: 50–62

Spencer-Wood SM. 1991. Toward a feminist historical archaeology of the construction of gender. See Walde & Willows 1991, pp. 234–44

Thomas J. 1991. *Rethinking the Neolithic.* Cambridge: Cambridge Univ. Press

Thomas J. 1996. *Time, Culture and Identity.* London: Routledge

Thomas J, Tilley C. 1993. The axe and the torso: symbolic structures in the Neolithic of Brittany. See Tilley 1993, pp. 225–325

Tilley C. 1991. *Material Culture and Text: The Art of Ambiguity.* New York: Routledge

Tilley C, ed. 1993. *Interpretative Archaeology.* Oxford: Berg

Tilley C. 1994. *A Phenomenonology of Landscape: Places, Paths and Monuments.* Oxford: Berg

Turner V. 1974. *Dramas, Fields, and Metaphors: Symbolic Action in Human Society.* Ithaca, NY: Cornell Univ. Press

Ucko P. 1969. Ethnography and archaeological interpretation of funerary remains. *World Archaeol.* 1:262–80

Ucko P, Rosenfeld A. 1967. *Palaeolithic Cave Art.* New York: McGraw-Hill

Walde D, Willows ND, eds. 1991. The Archaeology of Gender. *Proc. 22nd Annu. Conf. Archaeol. Assoc. Univ. Calgary.* Calgary, Can: Archaeol. Assoc., Univ. Calgary

Wallace-Hadrill A. 1988. The social structure of the Roman house. *Pap. Br. Sch. Rome* 56:43–97

Washburn DK, ed. 1983. *Structure and Cognition in Art.* Cambridge, UK: Cambridge Univ. Press

White R. 1989. Toward a contextual understanding of the earliest body ornaments. In *The Emergence of Modern Humans*, ed. E Trinkaus, pp. 211–31. Cambridge, UK: Cambridge Univ. Press

Whittle A. 1996. *Europe in the Neolithic: The Creation of New Worlds.* Cambridge, UK: Cambridge Univ. Press

Wobst H. 1977. Stylistic behavior and information exchange. In *For the Director: Research Essays in Honor of James B. Griffin*, ed. C Cleland, pp. 317–42. Ann Arbor: Mus. Anthropol., Univ. Mich.

Wolf E. 1990. Facing power: old insights, new questions. *Am. Anthropol.* 92:586–96

Yates T. 1989. Habitus and social space: some suggestions about meaning in the Saami (Lapp) tent ca. 1700–1900. In *The Meanings of Things: Material Culture and Symbolic Expression*, ed. I Hodder, pp. 249–62. London: Unwin Hyman

Zubrow E. 1994. Knowledge representation and GIS: a cognitive example using GIS. See Renfrew & Zubrow 1994, pp. 107–19

*Annu. Rev. Anthropol. 1998. 27:347–74*
*Copyright © 1998 by Annual Reviews. All rights reserved*

# EVOLUTIONARY ECOLOGY OF HUMAN REPRODUCTION

## Eckart Voland

Zentrum für Philosophie und Grundlagen der Wissenschaft, Universität Giessen,
D-35394 Giessen, Germany; e-mail: eckart.voland@phil.uni-giessen.de

KEY WORDS:  reproductive strategies, fecundity, fertility, differential parental investment,
demography

### ABSTRACT

Evolutionary ecology of human reproduction is defined as the application of
natural selection theory to the study of human reproductive strategies and
decision-making in an ecological context. The basic Darwinian assumption
is that humans—like all other organisms—are designed to maximize their inclusive fitness within the ecological constraints to which they are exposed.
Life history theory, which identifies trade-off problems in reproductive investment, and evolutionary physiology and psychology, which analyzes the
adaptive mechanisms regulating reproduction, are two crucial tools of evolutionary reproductive ecology. Advanced empirical insights have been obtained mainly with respect to the ecology of fecundity, fertility, child-care
strategies, and differential parental investment. Much less is known about
the ecology of nepotism and the postgenerative life span. The following three
theoretical aspects, which are not well understood, belong to the desiderata
of future improvement in evolutionary human reproductive ecology: (*a*) the
significance of and the interactions between different levels of adaptability
(genetic, ontogenetic, and contextual) for the adaptive solution of reproductive problems; (*b*) the dialectics of constraints and adaptive choices in reproductive decisions; and (*c*) the dynamics of demographic change.

## THE EVOLUTIONARY ECOLOGICAL APPROACH TO HUMAN REPRODUCTION

Reproduction takes place in an ecological context. Thanks to a remarkable
growth of knowledge in recent years, we know how external factors exert an

347

0084-6570/98/1015-0347$08.00

impact on the endocrinological mechanisms of both animal and human reproduction. Moreover, reproduction takes place in a behavioral ecological context, because the reproductive preferences and decisions of individuals are influenced to a considerable degree and in numerous ways by their personal life
circumstances. The idea that social and ecological variation affects human reproductive conduct is, of course, not new. In their work, cultural ecologists and
social anthropologists have always paid particular attention to the influence
exerted by prevailing social structures, by technologies, and by the exploitation of resources on the reproductive patterns prevailing in a particular society.
The concept that these types of influences are conveyed by adaptive, i.e. phy-
logenetically shaped, regulatory mechanisms is relatively new, however. To
the more conventional approaches of studying interactions between environment and reproduction, evolutionary ecology adds a Darwinian perspective
and thus has much in common with those adaptationist approaches that run under the label of behavioral ecology, sociobiology, or socioecology. The basic
assumption derived from Darwinian theory is that humans—like all other organisms—can be expected on average to maximize their inclusive fitness
given the socioecological constraints to which they are exposed.

Evolutionary ecology has been defined as "the application of natural selection theory to the study of adaptation and biological design in an ecological
setting" (Winterhalder & Smith 1992, p. 5). When the features under study involve reproduction, then the subset of evolutionary ecology can be termed
evolutionary reproductive ecology. Accordingly, evolutionary reproductive
ecology deals with the issue of the biological evolution of diversity and variability in reproduction. It focuses on the adaptive function of reproductive differences in different biographical, social, cultural, historical, and ecological
contexts.

## REPRODUCTIVE EFFORT, REPRODUCTIVE INVESTMENT, AND THE EVOLUTION OF REPRODUCTIVE STRATEGIES

Life histories evolve so as to maximize the contribution of genetic material to
the following generations. They can be understood as the effort of the "selfish
gene," and depending on the life functions in which investments are being
made, i.e. the target of such effort, various forms of effort can be differentiated. Somatic effort comprises all investments by an organism in its growth,
development, differentiation, and maintenance; in this manner, it accumulates
reproductive potential, thus increasing its residual reproductive value. In contrast, reproductive effort is aimed directly at reproduction; in other words, it
exploits the existing reproductive potential of an individual, therefore decreas-

ing that individual's residual reproductive value (Alexander 1987, Williams 1966).

Reproductive effort can be divided into three segments. Mating effort comprises the stakes of an organism in intra- and intersexual competition; parenting effort designates the efforts directly linked to producing and raising offspring; and finally, nepotistic effort pertains to the investment made in the reproduction of genealogical sidelines. While mating and parenting contribute directly to fitness, nepotistic effort contributes indirectly. The sum of both—inclusive fitness—is the common currency of the various selection processes (natural, sexual, and kin), and all organisms are designed by evolution toward maximizing precisely this parameter.

Reproductive effort may assume very different forms. It may require time, energy, and risks to life, social reputation, or material resources, and it can occur in connection with sexual competition, the formation of gametes, embryonic development, and postnatal care given to one's offspring. Reproductive effort entails costs (Williams 1966), which is why natural selection cannot favor unrestricted reproduction. Instead it optimizes the nature and manner in which reproductive effort is allocated, favoring those measures that lead to the greatest net yield in inclusive fitness over the course of an organism's life. Trade-off problems occur when two or more traits are limited by the shortage of the same resources (Borgerhoff Mulder 1992, Hill 1993, Stearns 1992). Because any "unit of effort" can be invested only once, evolution has shaped humans (and all other organisms) into reproductive strategists, who constantly have to make "decisions" about the best possible allocation of their limited investment possibilities. Some of these allocation decisions have been genetically fixed in the organisms' phylogenesis, but others require spontaneous adjustments to prevailing life circumstances.

To the degree that reproductive effort reduces remaining reproductive value, it is considered an investment (Trivers 1972). Under stable living conditions, there is frequently a monotonic relationship between effort and investment. The more effort that is expended, the more residual reproductive value is reduced, i.e. the more costs there are and, consequentially, the higher the reproductive investment. However, in some situations this simple relation does not apply. If, for example, in an ecological crisis, parents reduce their parental effort (e.g. give their child less food), this reduced effort could very well mean an increase in investment. Giving children food during emergencies can be more costly than transferring a lot of food in times of plenty.

A whole series of allocation conflicts have been described so far, but the following four basic problems have come to the fore time and again. First is the trade-off between somatic effort and reproductive effort. Should an organism continue to invest in itself—reinforce its physical or social quality and competitiveness, repair itself and accumulate resources somatically or extrasomatically (e.g. as education or wealth)—or should it instead begin to reproduce? This situation is the conflict between current and future reproduction. Second is the issue of direct versus indirect reproduction. Should an organism reproduce itself or instead support its relatives in their reproduction and temporarily or permanently assume the role of "helper-at-the-nest"? Third is how to balance mating and parental effort. The male's trade-off is often between what have been called the "cad versus dad" strategies (that is, between maximizing fertilization and maximizing paternal investment). The female's trade-off is often between continuing to search for a better mate versus stopping the search for a mate and starting to reproduce. Fourth is a trade-off between investment in the quantity or the quality of the offspring. With an increasing number of descendants, only a correspondingly reduced share of the total parental effort can be invested into every single offspring. This situation results in an optimization problem with respect to lifetime fitness. Should one aim for a few, but well-endowed, offspring capable of surviving and competing or for many, who are less able to cope with life?

Constraints on personal reproduction can vary greatly among individuals for many reasons (genetic, ecological, social, and also random reasons). Consequently, the individuals of a population will differ in their solutions of the allocation problems, and natural selection will, therefore, not promote the best of all theoretically conceivable allocation strategies, but the best of those actually available in concrete circumstances (McNamara & Houston 1996). This is a strong argument in favor of studying reproductive processes not only on the level of whole populations but also with an eye to the reproductive decisions of individuals.

## THE EVOLUTIONARY ECOLOGY OF PARENTAL EFFORT

### The Evolutionary Ecology of Female Reproductive Physiology and Behavior

BEGINNING WITH REPRODUCTION: AGE AT MENARCHE, AGE AT FIRST INTERCOURSE, AGE AT MARRIAGE, AGE AT FIRST BIRTH   With values between 12.3 years (see Pentzos-Daporte & Grefen-Peters 1984 on Greek girls) and 18.6 years (Wood 1994 on Gainj girls of New Guinea), the mean age at menarche is extremely variable. In addition to a genetic component (Danker-Hopfe 1986), the socioecological and psychosocial environments of adolescent girls contribute to this variability. Generally, nutritionally and socioculturally disadvantaged girls enter puberty later than girls who are favored in these respects (see Khan et al 1996 for a study on Guatemalan girls). The better the development chances are in childhood and youth, the earlier menarche occurs, even if the physiological limit to early sexual development has probably been reached with the current situation in modern industrial nations.

What is the adaptive value of these differences? Why do not all girls begin to ovulate at the same age, namely, as early as possible, especially since one should expect that an early sexual maturity and the early commencement of reproduction would bring an initial advantage in terms of Darwinian selection? The reason why this is not so lies in the costs associated with premature reproduction. Among the Aché, fertility depends on body weight (Hill & Hurtado 1996). Sexual maturity, which would be advanced at the expense of continued growth, would therefore lead to reduced fertility. Moreover, pregnant precocious women run a higher risk of spontaneous abortion or preterm birth (Becker 1993, Riley et al 1993), and the physical growth of undernourished women is impeded by pregnancy (Fleming et al 1985, Garn et al 1984). On the other hand, mothers who experience a burst of growth during pregnancy have a higher probability of having underweight children (Frisancho et al 1984). There is obviously an intraindividual conflict concerning the allocation of physiological nutrients, with the unavoidable consequence that either the pregnant woman or the fetus will be at a disadvantage. However, both solutions are damaging to fitness under most living conditions.

Premature sexual maturity and premature commencement of reproduction involve costs. Therefore, delayed menarche can be advantageous for women, in the interests of maximizing lifetime fitness, even if other types of costs then arise. These costs are as follows: (a) Depending on the prevailing mortality, the risk of total reproductive failure increases; (b) the generation span increases, which leads to disadvantages under conditions of expansionist competition; and (c) the generative life span is reduced. The age at menopause is independent of the age at menarche (Wood 1994), so a later sexual maturity cannot—quasi-automatically—be compensated for by a later menopause. If the living conditions and especially the nutritional situation allow mothers and their offspring to thrive, then early sexual maturity and early commencement of reproduction will be an advantage. Therefore, one should expect that women who mature early will transfer their developmental lead into increased reproduction, and this is precisely the case. The age at menarche correlates positively with the protogenetic interval, the interbirth intervals, the probability of sterility, and the frequency of stillbirths. It correlates negatively with fecundity, fertility, and lifetime reproductive success, which is measured in the number of surviving children (Borgerhoff Mulder 1989, Critescu 1975, Cutler et al 1979, Sandler et al 1984, Udry & Cliquet 1982, Varea et al 1993). In other words, late sexual maturity reduces lifetime fitness in favorable milieus.

Nowadays, the aforementioned rule of thumb of a correlation between stress and age at menarche has been called into question because at least one form of psychosocial stress appears to advance the age at menarche, namely, turbulent relationships between the parents, with the consequence of familial instability. Daughters from broken homes or conflict-laden relationships reach puberty earlier on average (reviewed in Kim et al 1997) and commence sexual activity earlier (Kiernan & Hobcraft 1997) than those from intact or more harmonious families. The evolved background of this correlation is assumed in an adaptive adjustment of one's own reproductive preferences to the existing socioecological conditions. According to the theory of evolutionary socialization (Belsky et al 1991, Chasiotis & Keller 1994, Chisholm 1993), familial relationships experienced during childhood serve as the best possible predictors for one's own probable living conditions later. Girls can, therefore, assess their reproductive opportunities very early by observing their familial environment and then setting the course for their reproductive strategies. Psychosocial stress in childhood and youth, brought on by a difficult situation regarding resources and by parental pair-bond instability, signals for girls an incalculable, fluctuating life perspective, under which continued somatic expense is worth less than an advance of sexual maturity and activity. Variance in the age at menarche thus reflects early childhood variance in the security and stability of life.

Marriage legalizes heterosexual relationships and reproduction. It could be supposed that in the interest of a rapid "harvest" of one's own personal fitness, men and women would strive to marry as soon as possible, to allow as little as possible of their fecund life spans to be lost. This practice is not always observed, however. Instead, mean age at marriage in an ethnohistorical comparison varies greatly. The span of time between sexual maturity and marriage can be considerable. What prevents humans from entering into marriage as early as possible? What are the costs of reproduction at the lowest possible physiological age?

In the traditional and historical populations investigated so far, a correlation between socioeconomic and reproductive success is observed (reviews in Cronk 1991a, Pérusse 1993). Through diverse mechanisms, socioeconomic success secures reproductive success, so that fitness increases when humans try to improve the economic basis of their existence and reproduction. To what extent this also applies to modern industrial societies is contested, however (Kaplan et al 1995, Pérusse 1993, Vining 1986).

Productive and reproductive interests compete with each other, and all humans are faced with the problem of the optimal distribution of their energy and time for coping with life. Age at marriage or age at first birth is an important hinge in this balancing act, and its ethnohistorical variability therefore lies mainly in the trade-off between production and reproduction. In a first approach, and depending on the type of economy, two different directions of influence on age at marriage can be distinguished. In resource- or capital-oriented economic systems, young people frequently require some time to accumulate enough resources or skills to establish an independent household. This delaying effect is well known in the population history of Western Europe. In preindustrial times, the average age at marriage for both men and women was comparatively high, which can be linked regularly to the necessity of economic independence for the young married couple. Only if land or a business is purchased, leased, or inherited can the economic barriers to marriage be overcome in a resource-limited world. Therefore, in peasant societies, the younger (and more frequently) that people married, the more favorable the economic situation was (e.g. Fitzpatrick 1985, Landale 1989, Schellekens 1990). It is plausible that in preindustrial societies the "age at first reproduction" turns out to be the single best predictor for female lifetime reproductive success (Käär et al 1996). Corresponding to the core of the same functional logic, in industrial nations, the time between the age at sexual maturity and the age at first birth is drawn out when investing in education (or other aspects of human capital) is worthwhile for accumulating social opportunities in a competitive labor market. Hence, human reproductive decisions with respect to age at first birth are contingent on both current opportunities and past familial experience (see above). What remains to be done is to estimate the relative importance of both sources of reproductive decision-making.

In economic systems that are less resource- or capital-oriented and are increasingly dependent on labor instead, as in many Third World countries, economic constraints postpone the age at marriage to an unequal degree, because here resource accumulation prior to the wedding does not occur. The dependence of familial living and reproduction opportunities on labor productivity (especially also by women and children) almost forces couples into early marriage. In Western European demographic history, the average age at marriage dropped dramatically when innovative labor-based economic niches opened up during the course of urbanization, industrialization, and protoindustrialization (Anderson 1988, Kriedte et al 1992, Schellekens 1997).

Within these two scenarios, a series of culture-specific peculiarities affect the age at marriage. These peculiarities can be influenced by many socioecological factors. These include the following:

1. The prevalence of polygyny. The greater the frequency of polygynous marriage in a society, the stronger the competition for women and therefore the younger the brides, on average.

2. The valuation of virginity. Especially in patriarchal societies, in which a few men succeed in monopolizing overlarge shares of the "resource pie" for themselves, and in which fathers therefore have much to pass to their offspring, the certainty of paternity appears to be a powerful regulator of the relationships between the sexes (Dickemann 1981). Here virginity (as an indicator of female virtue and loyalty) plays a decisive role in mate se-

lection, which in turn reduces the average age at marriage—partly to include arranged marriages between children.

3. Dowry competition. Societies that tend to exhibit extensive dowry competition also tend to show a relatively young average age at marriage (see Spiess 1993 for the German high nobility in the late Middle Ages).

4. Dynastic interests. A marriage can make an important contribution to the formation or maintenance of cooperative alliances between two lineages. In pursuit of such family-policy goals, the average age at marriage, especially of women, is reduced (e.g. Rheubottom 1988, Spiess 1993).

5. Parent-child conflicts. It can be in the reproductive interests of the mother to delay the marriage of her eldest daughter for as long as possible to have her labor and input into the parents' own family economy and child care (Flinn 1989).

6. Mortality. On average, the higher the prevailing mortality is, the younger and more frequently humans marry (Schellekens 1997).

7. Intrafamilial resource competition. The greater the number of elder brothers a man has (i.e. the greater the number of his competitors for parental investment), the longer his marriage can be delayed (see Mace 1996a on Gabbra pastoralists of Kenya).

FECUNDITY   The expression "natural fertility," which is customary in demography, is highly misleading in terms of evolutionary ecology because in view of the various socioecological influences on fecundity and fertility, no uniformly "natural" pattern of fertility can exist, as is falsely suggested by the term. Even if human populations—and even subgroups within populations—allegedly do not engage in intramarital contraception and thus satisfy Henry's definition of natural fertility, they differ with respect to their "natural fertility" (Wood 1994). Campbell & Wood (1988) compared the fertility patterns of 70 population groups that are considered "naturally" fertile or "controlled" fertile. The overlapping of the fertility rates was extremely large. One of several sources for this "natural variability of fertility" lies in ecologically caused differences in fecundity (i.e. in the ecological impact on one's reproductive potential).

Contrary to earlier opinions, it is becoming increasingly clear that the physiology of reproduction does not follow an "on or off" law but reacts sensitively (though how sensitively is contested: Wood 1994) to changing living conditions when these conditions are reflected in psychogenic stress (Wasser 1994) or in the net energy balance (Cumming et al 1994; Ellison 1990, 1994; Hill & Hurtado 1996; Rosetta 1995). Energetic stress can result from two ecological impacts, namely, the variability of food availability (i.e. energy intake) and the variability of workload (i.e. energy expenditure). Under the conditions of a subsistence economy, both impacts are subject to more or less pronounced seasonal fluctuations.

Evolutionary reproductive ecologists consider the environmental sensitivity of ovarian function to be an adaptive product of natural selection, although this assumption remains to be shown empirically. Interestingly enough, sensitivity to stress is itself subject to ecological impact (Vitzthum 1997). For example, energetic stress in women who live under good conditions leads much more quickly to an impairment of their reproductive function than comparable stresses do in women who are subject to living conditions that have always been much worse. Obviously, baseline experience is taken into consideration when making an adaptive adjustment of one's fecundity to changed circumstances. This finding could explain why in certain ecologies women in relatively bad conditions are more fecund than women in different ecological settings in relatively good conditions. Even the ovulation-inhibiting effect of breastfeeding is made relative by the maternal condition. Poorly fed mothers—who have the same nursing behavior as well-fed mothers—experience a longer postpartum amenorrhea (Ellison 1994, Lunn 1996). If changes in ovarian function can best be understood as biologically functional responses to socioecological conditions, it becomes clear that the terminological equivalence of "adaptive" and "healthy" or "maladaptive" and "pathological" is factually incorrect. Ovarian "dysfunctioning" as a result of physical or mental stress (with anorexia nervosa as its most spectacular manifestation) requires clinical treatment but is also part of normal biological function under certain circumstances (Anderson & Crawford 1992, Surbey 1987, Voland & Voland 1989, Wasser 1994). The uncoupling of the concepts of "healthy" and "adaptive" has a far-reaching impact on our understanding of ourselves, such as is increasingly being pondered in connection with the project of Darwinian medicine (Nesse & Williams 1994).

FERTILITY    A naive interpretation of the Darwinian principle could lead to the erroneous assumption that natural selection has designed human beings to maximum fertility. This theory does not apply, however, because reproduction incurs costs. The biological evolutionary process cannot favor both maximum fertility and maximum offspring fitness. The consequence is a trade-off between the quantity and the quality of offspring. This observation is well known in the theories of evolutionary ecology and life history and has been much discussed and modeled (Beauchamp 1994; Borgerhoff Mulder 1992; Rogers 1990, 1995), but it has only rarely been studied empirically with respect to humans (Hill & Hurtado 1996, Kaplan et al 1995, Mace 1996b). In the end, the successful raising and social placement of one's offspring decides lifetime reproductive success. Therefore, fertility and genetic fitness correlate highly to each other only in certain ecological situations, whereas in other situations they can be linked only very loosely. Birth control—which is frequently achieved by breastfeeding strategies under traditional and historical conditions—therefore definitely belongs to the tactical options of fitness maximization. If the response to precarious ecological situations is slowed-down fertility, presumably this is to increase the number of surviving, competitive children under the given conditions, not to reduce it (Blurton Jones 1986 on the !Kung).

The optimal quantity/quality balance is influenced by a series of factors that affect both the costs and benefits of parental investment. The following factors have the effect of increasing fertility:

1. Low economic costs of parental investment (a low net price of a child). Children are cheapest when they yield economic returns (e.g. in labor-intensive economies). This idea has been elaborated in numerous ways through economic fertility theories (a recent review is Robinson 1997) and is increasingly being adopted by evolutionary ecology (Blurton Jones et al 1992). In contrast to representatives of economic fertility theories, evolutionary ecologists assume that despite considerable contributions (under certain circumstances) by children to family economy, the net intergenerational wealth flow is from parents to offspring. Humans, like all other organisms, usually invest in, rather than exploit, their offspring (Kaplan 1994, Turke 1989).

2. Low efficiency of parental investment. The more advantageous the per capita investment is for the survivorship or competitiveness of children, the more likely parents will aim for quality instead of quantity (Borger-hoff Mulder 1992, Kaplan et al 1995). If, on the other hand, parents have little influence on the fate of their offspring, such as in fluctuating and unpredictable milieus with high mortality rates, then bet-hedging is the pattern: High fertility is probable (Bereczkei 1993).

3. Low opportunity costs, which are typically incurred by the investing mothers who do without income (Borg 1989, Rogers 1995).

4. Relative resource richness (e.g. Clay & Johnson 1992, Klindworth & Voland 1995).

5. Demographic competition for expansion. Typically in growing societies with pronounced expansive competition—such as founder populations—rapid and numerous reproduction can lead to fitness advantages. A high number of children is then the reproductive strategy of choice (e.g. Bouchard 1987).

6. Promising dispersal opportunities. Even in less quickly growing societies, relatively high fertility rates can be observed when the valve of emigration for the "surplus" children becomes a promising option (Brittain 1991, Anderson & Morse 1993).

7. Reproductive returns of children, i.e. children are able to support their parents in their reproductive efforts as "helpers-at-the-nest" (Turke 1988).

8. Delegated mothering. The delegation of maternal care to others (e.g. to wet nurses) can lead to an increase in the fertility of those socially privileged women who are able to pay for professional care (Hrdy 1992).

9. "Replacement behavior." An attempt by parents to compensate for the death of an older child with the birth of another child necessarily leads to increased fertility (e.g. Straka-Geiersbach & Voland 1988).

10. Gender preferences. In the pursuit of gender preferences (i.e. typically a preference for sons), there can also be an increase in fertility when only children of the less desirable sex are born (e.g. Chowdhury et al 1993 for Bangladesh, Krishnan 1993 for Canada, Niraula & Morgan 1995 for Nepal).

The magnitude of the impact of these factors depends on numerous conditions. Age, sex, wealth, vitality, previous reproductive history, kin support, partner support, demographic context, subsistence regime, and resource predictability can play a role and lead to numerous interactive effects between intrinsic and extrinsic determinants of fertility. Fertility decisions, therefore, go back to an extremely complex net of conditions and, for a number of theoretical and methodical reasons, do not allow a simple analysis. This complexity is most likely the reason that despite a long tradition of research in several academic disciplines, with considerable time and money invested, there still has not been a completely satisfactory (i.e. consolidated) fertility theory (cf Kaplan 1994).

The effects of individual reproductive decisions accumulate and can be presented by the familiar figures and rates used in demography. Soon after its beginnings, demography was already more than just a descriptive science. Attempts were made to analyze the causes of its findings and to understand demographic changes. Malthus grasped demographic changes as the expression of regulatory mechanisms. Homeostasis and self-regulation are typical concepts in use in population history, and whenever dramatic changes are observed in demographic patterns, such as in connection with the "demographic transition," self-regulatory mechanisms are suspected of having gone off course (e.g. Lee 1994). From the point of view of evolutionary ecology, there are two reasons for justifiable doubts about such ideas. First, no one has been successful in reliably identifying an institution of demographic self-regulation. There is no obvious mechanism that takes control of demographic change as a kind of switching station. Second, the commonweal, the group benefit, the preservation of the species, the ecological balance, and so on cannot be biologically evolved motives of animal or human behavior in view of the "selfish gene" (Hawkes & Charnov 1988). The necessary target (a "set value") of a possible population regulation is simply missing. From an evolutionary ecology perspective, population effects—the traditional focus of demographic research—are the consequences of numerous adaptive individual decisions and not the target of biological self-regulation. There is neither a proximate mechanism nor an ultimate cause for population self-regulation.

THE POSTGENERATIVE LIFE SPAN   The evolution of a postgenerative life span still puzzles evolutionary biologists because fecundity to the end of life would have to be expected in view of the fact that natural selection rewards reproductive success. Williams (1957) has provided a theory that has had a lasting impact and is frequently referred to in the literature as the so-called grandmother hypothesis. He argues that a postgenerative phase of life is advantageous to the degree that personal fitness can be increased by prolonged parental care after birth. Continued investment in already existing children (or grandchildren) can be more profitable than another birth, which is increasingly risky as the mother gets older. The costs of later reproduction are well known. The probability of spontaneous abortions, underweight and genetically handicapped children, and perinatal mortality rises with the age of the mother (Alberman 1987). Moreover, the fact that the mother's mortality increases with age creates another disadvantage: Previously born children become orphans upon the death of their mother, thus drastically reducing their physical and social chances of life, at least under premodern living conditions (Hill & Hurtado 1996, Voland 1988). Therefore, it would be misleading to speak of the postmenopausal phase of life as a postreproductive phase. The expression "postgenerative life phase" is without a doubt more fitting because even though no more children will be born, personal reproductive success can be increased by parental or grandparental effort during this phase of life.

As plausible and appealing as Williams's reflections may be, the empirical support to date has been weak. Turke (1988) was able to demonstrate that in Ifaluk families, reproductive success correlates with the number of surviving grandparents, thus supporting the hypothesis that in this society old people are beneficial to the reproduction of their children. However, conceivable confounded variables (such as wealth) were not controlled in this study, so causality cannot automatically be concluded from the correlation that was found. Postmenopausal Hadza women engage in the acquisition of food with greater effort than the younger, reproductive women. The increased effort on the part of the grandmothers frees the adult daughters (or other kin) a little from these subsistence tasks, permitting them to provide more parental care and possibly allowing an increase in fertility (Hawkes et al 1989). Whether this effect is big enough to compensate for the costs of menopause remains unclear, however. Hill & Hurtado's (1996) Aché study is also ambiguous in terms of its results. Even if some points favor the idea that older women are able to increase their fitness on average by discontinuing their own reproduction and supporting the reproduction of their children instead, the authors tend to remain skeptical and presume other, to date unknown, reasons for the evolution and maintenance of menopause. Rogers's (1993) model also feeds doubts about the grandmother hypothesis. At any rate, the effect of older women on the fitness of their offspring would have to be considerable, and possibly unrealistically high, before menopause would be worthwhile. In contrast, Peccei (1995) gives the Williams hypothesis good chances, with the restriction, however, that the cessation of one's own reproduction would primarily have to promote the survival of one's own children and not so much that of one's grandchildren.

Recently, Turke (1997) added an interesting twist to the menopause debate. Under conditions of Pleistocene mating systems, he argues, there could regularly have been a considerable age span between the spouses, with the consequence that the men died much earlier than the women on average. Without menopause, these women would have had a number of remaining years of fecundity. They would therefore attract other men, thus exposing their children (especially the younger ones) to the risk of infanticide and, moreover, jeopardizing nepotistic relationships with the families of their first mates. Menopause could thus have evolved as a strategy for avoiding infanticide.

From the point of view of reproductive ecology, questions about the age at last birth, the commencement of secondary sterility and menopause, i.e. the end of the generative phase, are questions about the optimal biographical switchpoint from investment in additional, future offspring versus continued investment in already existing offspring (or other kin). To what extent this trade-off problem is influenced socioecologically has practically not been studied. An evolutionary ecology understanding of menopause is countered particularly by its obligatory character. The age of women at the onset of menopause appears to be rather insensitive to personal reproductive history, to social factors, and perhaps even to the ecological context. Why is this so?

## The Ecology of Male Reproductive Physiology

The study of adaptive variation of male reproductive function in response to socioecological constraints has been overshadowed by studies of female reproductive function. This is due to the fact that population-dynamic processes have only rarely been set in relation to male fecundity. Demographers have therefore had only little interest in intra- and intermale variation in reproductive physiology—a surely painful omission, in case it should prove to be true (contrary to previous opinions) that 50% of the clinically presented sterility problems that couples have are caused by male factors (Campbell & Leslie 1995, but see Wood 1994). Evolutionary ecologists also tended to neglect male variation because the evolved sex-specific reproductive strategies with their sex-specific costs of reproduction make environmental factors more likely to exert an impact on female fecundity than on male fecundity. The trade-off between producing offspring now or later is much weaker in males than in females. Nevertheless, there is remarkable variation in male reproductive function: (*a*) seasonal variation in sperm counts and quality (which might contribute to birth seasonality); (*b*) secular trends in sperm counts (purportedly related to environmental estrogens); and (*c*) impairment of hypothalamic and testicular function by psychosocial and nutritional stress, workloads, and disease (for details see Campbell & Leslie 1995). We simply do not know, however, whether this variation is adaptive. Although there are no reasonable grounds for doubting the adaptive effect of male reproductive mechanisms, no conclusive evidence is available. The findings of Baker & Bellis (1993) are among the best of the references. They were able to demonstrate that coital ejaculate volumes vary with respect to duration of separation from the partner. The rationale for this comes from the selection pressure that sperm competition generates. The longer a couple has been separated, the greater the probability that the female could have mated with another male. The evolved ability to increase the number of sperm after separation can thus be understood as an adaptive measure to increase one's chances in the fertilization lottery.

Age at sexual maturation is known to vary for girls with respect to childhood experience of parental pair-bond stability and resource fluctuation (see above). Something similar appears to apply for boys' age at sexual maturation, because Kim et al (1997) were able to show for their sample of southern Italian boys that spermarche began earlier when the parents' marriage was perceived as being very conflictual. Because earlier spermarche correlates with earlier age at first dating, earlier age at first intercourse, and a greater number of intercourse partners, childhood experiences seem to prepare the way for the adoption of one's own personal reproductive strategy. In this respect, variation in male reproductive physiology does reflect, in all probability, adaptive, environment-sensitive regulatory mechanisms.

## Child-Care Strategies

Parental styles differ widely with regard to the place value that every individual child assumes in the reproductive efforts of his or her parents. On the one hand, one finds more fatalistic attitudes, based on the conviction that the fate of the offspring can practically not be influenced because of the various risks to life. On the other hand, parents may feel extremely responsible for what happens to their children. Depending on the personal attitude in this question, which is frequently rationalized by worldviews colored by religion, parents differ in their efforts to provide the best possible nutritional, medical and psychohygienic care of their offspring and in their attempts to protect them from general risks to life. Evolutionary ecology holds that parental attitudes on one's responsibility for the life and death of one's children in some way reflect the experience of actual survival chances—i.e. they are nurtured ecologically. Indeed, social-historical research shows how everyday experiences with regard to the fragility of life can bury themselves deep in the mentality of a population and in the long run affect attitudes toward children. The more persistently that a population has suffered from Malthusian checks—wars, hunger, epidemics—the more fatalistic the predominant attitudes toward life will be and the more indifferent parents will become toward each of their offspring (Imhof 1984). Life history theory sees parental effort as dependent on adult mortality, which seems to be the key factor affecting parental investment inclinations (Chisholm 1993). The stronger the threat from extrinsic mortality risks (parasites, predators, resource instability, aggressive encounters), the lower the per capita investment in children should be in favor of increased fertility, which in turn contributes to an increase in infant mortality. Infant mortality rates, therefore, also have an intrinsic component, constituting that which can be described as "avoidable deaths." The application of life history theory is accordingly aggravated by the circumstance that infant mortality rates do not represent an independent measure of the extrinsic risk of mortality.

Parental styles vary adaptively not only in response to differences in extrinsic mortality but also in response to other factors, such as subsistence strategies and workload (Blurton Jones 1993, Hurtado et al 1992, Panter-Brick 1995) or the availability of alternative caretakers (Hewlett 1991, Panter-Brick 1995, Turke 1989). What remains unclear in many case studies, however, is the degree to which the child-care strategies found represent adaptive choices or environmental constraints. To clarify this, detailed knowledge of the costs and benefits of various child-care options would be necessary, to enable a precise determination of the parents' trade-off problems. This is what we would have to know in order to recognize the outcomes of parenting favored by natural selection: maximization of production of offspring, maximization of their survivorship, or maximization of their social and material endowment (Blurton Jones 1993).

## Channels and Functions of Differential Parental Investment

In many cases, individual children within families have very different status in parental reproductive strategies, which can been seen, for example, in the fact that there are preferred and less preferred children within the same families or that children are assigned completely different roles within the family. The range of parental possibilities for treating their offspring differently is very broad. It comprises, for example:

1. Intrauterine care of the fetuses and embryos (e.g. Peacock 1991).
2. Abortion and infanticide (Daly & Wilson 1988, Hill & Low 1992).
3. Postnatal parental care—e.g. the duration of breastfeeding (Bereczkei & Dunbar 1997, Gaulin & Robbins 1991), medical care (Cronk 1991b).
4. Upbringing and education (e.g. Bereczkei & Dunbar 1997, Low 1989).
5. Endowment with social opportunities, which can have consequences for the reproductive possibilities during adulthood (e.g. Hager 1992, Spiess 1993).
6. Material endowment through dowry or inheritance payments, with effects particularly on the probability of marriage and other aspects of cultural and biological reproduction (e.g. Gaulin & Boster 1990, Hrdy & Judge 1993, Mace 1996a).

From the perspective of reproductive ecology, it is to be expected that differences in the psychological desirability, care, and endowment of one's offspring have a biologically functional background. The question of in which offspring to invest more and in which less depends on two factors: (*a*) the costs that the parents assume if they invest in a child and (*b*) the benefits promised by an investment in a specific child (Clutton-Brock 1991). The net balance of these two accounts decides the adaptive value of a possible investment. Accordingly, parents should be more willing to assume costs, i.e. be more willing to waive part of their remaining reproductive potential to the benefit of their current offspring, the greater their fitness outcome from this reproductive effort promises to be (Trivers's principle). It is self-evident that a certain degree of investment is going to pay off, the more effective it is in favoring the future reproductive success of one's offspring, whether because it increases their chances of survival or their social or sexual competitiveness or otherwise improves the reproductive chances of their offspring. The benefits side of parental "calculations" is especially determined by the following factors:

1. Their genetic relationship to the offspring (Daly & Wilson 1988, 1994).
2. The age of the offspring (Daly & Wilson 1994).
3. The vitality of the offspring (Daly & Wilson 1988, 1994; Mann 1992).
4. The sex-specific potential for reproduction (Bereczkei & Dunbar 1997, Sieff 1990).
5. Number and sex of previously born offspring (Mace 1996b, Mace & Sear 1997).
6. The extent to which the offspring are able to contribute to the family's economy, be it through involvement in the accumulation of resources (Hewlett 1991, Irwin 1989, Smith & Smith 1994) or by assisting in their parents' reproductive efforts ("helper-at-the-nest" behavior) (Margulis et al 1993).

On the other hand, parents should hesitate more in making investments—under the same expectations of benefits—the more expensive their parental effort will be (Lack's principle). The costs of bringing up a child vary, particularly for the following reasons:

1. Economic-ecological fluctuations, biographical catastrophes, and other factors having an impact on one's personal life history (Daly & Wilson 1988, 1994; Hill & Low 1992; Peyronnet 1976).
2. Economic opportunity costs (Hewlett 1992).
3. Reproductive opportunity costs with respect to future fertility (Hrdy 1992), female remarriage (Bhuiya & Chowdhury 1997, Voland 1988), or male extramarital fertilizations (Hill & Hurtado 1996).
4. Parental age (Voland & Gabler 1994).
5. Economic constraints—e.g. in the form of inheritance and dowry payments in "local resource competition" settings (Hager 1992, Voland & Dunbar 1995).

In reality, numerous interaction effects between these influences make the analysis of differential parental investment a difficult enterprise in terms of research strategy. An aggravating factor is the context-sensitivity of parental cost-benefit ratios, so explanations of the adaptivity of differential parental investment gain plausibility against the background of demo-ecological constraints, such as population growth (Voland et al 1997) or the operational sex ratio (Hill & Hurtado 1996).

## NEPOTISM: A NEGLECTED TOPIC IN EVOLUTIONARY REPRODUCTIVE ECOLOGY

Hamilton's discovery of inclusive fitness is considered to be a decisive detonator for the development of sociobiology and behavioral ecology. Previously not understood phenomena of nepotistic altruism became comprehensible in terms of evolutionary theory. What opened up completely new perspectives in animal research and stimulated innovative research designs, and in the end a much-praised change of paradigm within ethology, has not remained without impact on anthropology. Kinship and nepotism—traditionally one of the very big topics in anthropology—were able to be successfully reanalyzed after discovery of kin selection under recourse to Darwinian theory, especially with regard to the following:

1. Solidarity in catastrophic situations (Grayson 1993, McCullough & Barton 1991).

2. Emotional, material, and social support in social networks (Barber 1994, Berté 1988, Betzig & Turke 1986, Dunbar & Spoors 1995, Essock-Vitale & McGuire 1985, Hames 1987, Hill & Hurtado 1996).

3. Coalition formation in social disputes (Chagnon & Bugos 1979, Dunbar et al 1995, Hill & Hurtado 1996, Johnson & Johnson 1997).

4. Protection against infanticide (Hill & Hurtado 1996).

5. Adoptions and fosterage (Pennington & Harpending 1993, Silk 1990).

6. Differential grandparental investment (Hawkes et al 1989).

7. Differential investment inclinations by grandparents and more distant kin (Euler & Weitzel 1996, Gaulin et al 1997, Hill & Hurtado 1996).

8. "Helpers-at-the-nest" behavior (Flinn 1989, Margulis et al 1993, Turke 1988).

9. The adoption of specific sociocultural roles in connection with familial reproduction strategies (Hager 1992).

The aforementioned studies on the ecology of indirect reproduction are illuminating and promising, but they unfortunately run into barriers that most likely will not be easy to overcome. First, a comprehensive test of kin selection requires a perfect knowledge of the benefits and costs (including the opportunity costs) of nepotism that enter into the inclusive fitness balances, for both the nepotists and the recipients. A quantification of these parameters is, however, not easy to achieve. After all, in a socially complex world, human longevity aggravates the compilation of lifetime reproductive successes; in addition, longevity aggravates a reliable explanation of the variances in lifetime reproductive success resulting from individual components, e.g. the share that could go back to kin support. Even if in very rare exceptions, such as in the Aché study (Hill & Hurtado 1996), reproductive consequences of kin support are able to be counted, the costs side of nepotism remains in the dark. Statements on the current adaptivity of kin support, therefore, continue to have a certain degree of uncertainty adhering to them as a matter of principle. It could also be that although aunts and uncles, for example, have helped their siblings to have more offspring, they have had to pay a high price in direct fitness. On the basis of human data sets, moreover, we can at best ascertain phenotypical correlations that may mask confounded effects, thus distorting the view for the causality (Hill & Hurtado 1996, Reznick 1985). If, for example, in a certain population the probability of survival increases with the number of collateral kin, then this could have occurred either as a result of the effect of kin support or as an expression of the fact that in this society larger kin groups generally enjoy better life chances without indirect reproductive effort by kin having played a role here.

Second, nepotism may be costly, because one's own reproduction increases one's own fitness more than helping does. Helping will, of course, increase the fitness of others, which creates an arena of deep social conflicts. We must ask, therefore, whose interests are being served when we observe nepotistic behavior—those of the nepotist or those of the recipient. In other words, what causes nepotistic altruism: an adaptive choice of the nepotist or social manipulation by the recipient? Trivers (1974) was the first to recognize that parent-offspring conflicts can arise, especially about different expectations concerning altruistic services within families. "Helpers-at-the-nest" may, therefore, by no means increase their inclusive fitness but submit to parental manipulation. Possibly this structural conflict between parents and their offspring explains the evolution of the conscience as an extended phenotype (Dawkins 1982) of the parents' "selfish gene" to exploit their offsprings' reproductive effort (Voland & Voland 1995).

## HOW TO PROCEED?

### Three Levels of Adaptability

Human reproduction takes places under the control of more or less sensitive regulatory mechanisms. Whenever the data permit a link to life history theory, everything appears to indicate that this socioecological sensitivity is biologically functional and leads to adaptive results on average. Flexible responses are, therefore, typical for human reproduction. Adaptive variance can, however, occur on three different levels. Accordingly, differences in the adaptive solutions for a certain reproductive problem can have three different causes:

1. Genetic differences. It is conceivable that different reproductive strategies are directly due to different genotypes. Differential reproduction would then be a reflection of natural selection and would lead to a genetic restructuring of the population.
2. Phenotypic plasticity. Even with a genetic equipotence of all humans (as is the implicit assumption in most of the relevant studies), differences in reproductive tactics can occur. For example, evolutionary socialization theory (Belsky et al 1991) attempts to find a causal link between the perception of early childhood living conditions and later reproductive choices. Variance in reproductive behavior (e.g. in the aspects of mate selection, mate loyalty, and sexual and parental styles) would then be due primarily to ontogenetically different developmental contexts (Bereczkei & Csanaky 1996, Chasiotis & Keller 1994, Chasiotis et al 1997, Chisholm 1993, Hill et al 1994).
3. Situative context. Human strategies are conditional. Our regulatory machinery can lead to situatively different solutions to the same adaptive problem. The change from one option to another would then be understood as accommodation or as adjustment within an adaptive strategy. Most sociobiologists and behavior ecologists probably work from this perspective.

Depending on their academic roots, evolutionary reproductive ecologists have preferred to work on their respective levels without adequately taking the results of adjacent levels into account. To fully understand the evolutionary ecology of human reproduction, we first must achieve a closer integration of the empirical results from the three research strategies, and second, we must try to improve our ideas of the evolution of human reproductive strategies by improved model developments, which take all three levels of adaptability into account.

## Constraints, Opportunities, and Adaptive Choices in Human Reproduction

One's striving for fitness maximization is constrained by numerous features of the socioecological setting. Therefore, people cannot but try to make the best of a bad job. Usually, constraints offer a spectrum of options. The opportunity structure of these options, however, may vary for various reasons between individuals, so the same constraints can lead to different reproductive results and the same reproductive results may be due to different constraints. To give a simple example: In a high-fertility population, the reason that a couple will reduce its number of children can be understood as a shift in the quantity/quality preferences. The couple would have been able to have more children, but they waived this opportunity because they behaved as if considering an increase in the quality of their offspring through increased per capita investment to be more profitable in some way than an increase in quantity. Another couple in the same population with the same number of children did not have this quality-versus-quantity choice. Because of insufficient resources, this couple's fecundity was limited, and the number of children attained was therefore the maximum number possible. The same number of children can therefore be perceived once as an adaptive choice and once as constrained. Strictly speaking, the reduced number of children of the resource-poor couple is also the outcome of an adaptive "decision," because reduction in fecundity, as a reaction to a temporary shortage of resources, can increase lifetime reproductive success under certain circumstances. An attribution of reproductive output to an adaptive choice makes sense only with respect to the decision-making instance involved. The reduced number of children is an adaptive choice for the first couple in the example with regard to the psychological preferences involved, while for the second couple, it is with regard to ovarian function. Without this specification, the attribute "adaptive choice" remains unclear. An unjustified, inflationary use of this term allows critics of the Darwinian approach to discount evolutionary explanations as "Just So Stories." To counter this effect, it is necessary to attempt to cleanly unravel the intertwined links between constraints, opportunities, and adaptive choices.

When the goal is not simply to accept the constraints of human reproduction as a given but to study their reasons and history, an extension of reproductive ecology research into genuine sociobiological fields of research becomes necessary (Borgerhoff Mulder 1992), because constraints, such as the mating system, inheritance patterns, and sex roles, are of a cultural nature. As human culture can be perceived as the cumulative effects of the attempts of earlier generations to maximize their fitness (Alexander 1987), i.e. as the outcome of past adaptive choices, an interesting dialectic arises. In a social world, the personal strategy of one individual can become a constraint for another individual, and in a historical world, the adaptive choice of one forefather can become the constraint of his offspring. The urgently needed study of these types of phenomena necessarily binds evolutionary reproductive ecology to the spheres of interest of sociobiology and evolutionary anthropology.

## Understanding Demographic Change

Population scientists use the term "demographic transition" to describe the complex historic transformation from traditional populations with high fertility and mortality rates to modern populations with low fertility and mortality rates. With considerable regional variation, the beginning of the decline in fertility in Europe dates approximately to the turn of the century. Third World populations are only starting to show signs of a comparable development. Experts do not agree on what changes in which independent variables have ultimately introduced this transformation. The original point of view was an initial decline in infant and child mortality as a crucial impulse for the reduction of marital fertility. One assumed that the improved survival rates of their offspring released parents from the pressure to bring more children into the world than they could even successfully care for. More precise analyses have disclosed, however, that not always and not everywhere did a decline in mortality introduce the demographic transition. Regardless of how this demographic modernization occurred in detail, it was accompanied by a drastic psychological change in needs. The demand for children declined. Evolutionary ecology theorists must provide the causes for this change, and this is all the more urgent as their critics argue that it is precisely this limited fertility in surplus situations that jeopardizes a Darwinian interpretation of modern reproduction (e.g. Vining 1986).

Two very different lines of argumentation have been developed in evolutionary ecology to explain the demographic transition and the reduced fertility in the modern industrial state. The first argument is based on the necessity, induced by the modernization of society in the nineteenth century, to invest more in the competitiveness of one's offspring (e.g. in their education or their wealth). Under conditions of increasing competition, such as the industrial revolution created with its new economic opportunities, it could have been advantageous for parents to limit the number of their offspring but to increase their reproductive value through concentrated investment. An intensification of the per capita investment can occur only at the expense of the number of offspring, of course. The crucial, but as yet unanswered, question is whether parents have increased their genetic fitness by reducing the number of offspring under the conditions of the industrial society that have developed. Should this have been the case, then the flexibility of human reproduction turns out to be functionally rational in a biological sense, even under rapidly changing conditions.

The second argument takes up the observation that on the proximate level, humans obviously frequently value economic opportunities higher than reproductive opportunities. Of primary importance then is the question of how the psychological preferences that rate economic benefits higher than generative ones could even have evolved (see Rogers 1995). It does not appear to be wrong to say that during the Pleistocene, genetic fitness was not necessarily limited by the number of conceptions—it was limited by the availability of resources, which were always a bit in short supply. This is perhaps why those psychological mechanisms were selected that attributed a higher priority to the accumulation of resources than to repeatedly bearing children. The latter was probably not jeopardized, as a rule, but one's own survival and that of one's offspring was, unless the harshness of life was able to be buffered ecologically, at least to some degree. Possibly the pursuit of economic opportunities at the expense of generative activity is a psychological preference that—although adapted to the Pleistocene conditions of latent shortage of resources—is also expressed in modern societies but does not contribute to a maximization of genetic fitness as a result of the changed socioecological conditions. From this point of view, the mechanisms of human reproduction must be distinctly conservative. Because they arose in the environment of evolutionary adaptedness, they are no longer able to adapt to new conditions and therefore can lead to definitely dysfunctional results.

The basic question, therefore, is to what degree—in view of the rapidly changing sociocultural milieu—humans are able to update their knowledge of the costs and benefits associated with different reproductive options. With regard to some aspects of reproductive behavior, they are obviously capable of doing so with amazing speed (Borgerhoff Mulder 1995, Voland et al 1997). To what degree this competence for innovation can be generalized remains subject to a careful study, because it cannot be assumed a priori from every demographic change that it obeys the functional logic of maximization models. Even though potentially instructive "natural experiments" have taken place and are empirically accessible (e.g. the demographic turbulences in Eastern Germany after reunification: Conrad et al 1996, Eberstadt 1994), the elaboration of rapid changes on reproductive preferences in terms of evolutionary ecology is still lacking.

## CONCLUSION

To understand demographic phenomena, one must study which evolved preferences guide us and which opportunity structures characterize our different historical, cultural, ecological, and familial milieus. This means, however, that demographic analyses become more meaningful the more disaggregated their data sets are. Highly aggregated data sets may provide good descriptions and even make those problems visible, the elaboration of which would be worthwhile from the point of view of reproductive ecology. The analysis itself must, however, keep the individual in mind with his or her evolved preferences, strategies, and reproductive mechanisms. What we urgently need is an increased importation of Darwinian theory—especially life history theory and evolutionary psychology—into demographic research.

> **Visit the *Annual Reviews* home page** at
> **http://www.AnnualReviews.org.**

## *Literature Cited*

Alberman E. 1987. Maternal age and spontaneous abortion. In *Spontaneous and Recurrent Abortion,* ed. MJ Bennett, DK Edmonds, pp. 77–89. Oxford: Blackwell

Alexander RD. 1987. *The Biology of Moral Systems.* Hawthorne, NY: Aldine de Gruyter

Anderson JL, Crawford CB. 1992. Modeling costs and benefits of adolescent weight control as a mechanism for reproductive suppression. *Hum. Nat.* 3:299–334

Anderson M. 1988. *Population Change in North-Western Europe, 1750–1850.* Hoioundmills/London: Macmillan

Anderson M, Morse DJ. 1993. High fertility, high emigration, low nuptiality: adjustment process in Scotland′s demographic experience, 1861–1914, part II. *Popul. Stud.* 47:319–43

Baker RR, Bellis MA. 1993. Human sperm competition: ejaculate adjustment by males and the function of masturbation. *Anim. Behav.* 46:861–85

Barber N. 1994. Machiavellianism and altruism: effects of relatedness of target person on machiavellian and helping attitudes. *Psychol. Rep.* 75:403–22

Beauchamp G. 1994. The functional analysis of human fertility decisions. *Ethol. Sociobiol.* 15:31–53

Becker S. 1993. The determinants of adolescent fertility with special reference to biological variables. See Gray 1993, pp. 21–49

Belsky J, Steinberg L, Draper P. 1991. Childhood experience, interpersonal development, and reproductive strategy: an evolutionary theory of socialization. *Child Dev.* 62:647–70

Bereczkei T. 1993. r-Selected reproductive strategies among Hungarian gipsies: a preliminary analysis. *Ethol. Sociobiol.* 14: 71–88

Bereczkei T, Csanaky A. 1996. Evolutionary pathway of child development—lifestyles of adolescents and adults from father-absent families. *Hum. Nat.* 7:257–80

Bereczkei T, Dunbar RIM. 1997. Female-biased reproductive strategies in a Hungarian Gypsy population. *Proc. R. Soc. London Ser. B* 264:17–22

Berté NA. 1988. K'ekchi' horticultural labor exchange: productive and reproductive implications. See Betzig et al 1988, pp. 83–96

Betzig L, Borgerhoff Mulder M, Turke P, eds. 1988. *Human Reproductive Behaviour—A Darwinian Perspective.* Cambridge, UK: Cambridge Univ. Press

Betzig LL, Turke PW. 1986. Food sharing on Ifaluk. *Curr. Anthropol.* 27:397–400

Bhuiya A, Chowdhury M. 1997. The effect of divorce on child survival in a rural area of Bangladesh. *Popul. Stud.* 51:57–61

Blurton Jones N. 1986. Bushman birth spacing: a test for optimal interbirth intervals. *Ethol. Sociobiol.* 7:91–105

Blurton Jones N. 1993. The lives of hunter-gatherer children: effects of parental behavior and parental reproductive strategy. In *Juvenile Primates—Life History, Development, and Behavior,* ed. ME Pereira, LA Fairbanks. pp. 309–26. New York/Oxford: Oxford Univ. Press

Blurton Jones N, Smith LC, O'Connell JF, Hawkes K, Kamuzora CL. 1992. Demography of the Hadza, an increasing and high density population of savanna foragers. *Am. J. Phys. Anthropol.* 89:159–81

Borg MO'M. 1989. The income-fertility relationship: effect of the net price of a child. *Demography* 26:301–10

Borgerhoff Mulder M. 1989. Early maturing Kipsigis women have higher reproductive success than late maturing women and cost more to marry. *Behav. Ecol. Sociobiol.* 24: 145–53

Borgerhoff Mulder M. 1992. Reproductive decisions. See Smith & Winterhalder 1992, pp. 339–74

Borgerhoff Mulder M. 1995. Bridewealth and its correlates. *Curr. Anthropol.* 36: 573–603

Bouchard G. 1987. Sur la reproduction familiale en milieu rural: systèmes ouverts et systèmes clos. *Rech. Sociograph.* 28: 229–51

Brittain AW. 1991. Anticipated child loss to migration and sustained high fertility in an East Caribbean population. *Soc. Biol.* 38: 94–112

Campbell BC, Leslie PW. 1995. Reproductive ecology of human males. *Yearb. Phys. Anthropol.* 38:1–26

Campbell KL, Wood JW. 1988. Fertility in traditional societies. In *Natural Human Fertility: Social and Biological Determinants,* ed. P Diggory, M Potts, S Teper, pp. 39–69. London: Macmillan

Campbell KL, Wood JW, eds. 1994. *Human Reproductive Ecology—Interactions of Environment, Fertility, and Behavior.* New York: NY Acad. Sci.

Chagnon NA, Bugos P. 1979. Kin selection and conflict: an analysis of a Yanomamö ax fight. In *Evolutionary Biology and Human Social Behavior: An Anthropological Perspective,* ed. NA Chagnon, W Irons, pp. 213–38. North Scituate, MA: Duxbury

Chasiotis A, Keller H. 1994. Evolutionary psychology and developmental cross-cultural psychology. In *Journeys into Cross-Cultural Psychology,* ed. A-M Bouvy, FJR Van De Vijver, P Boski, P Schmitz, pp. 68–82. Amsterdam: Swets & Zeitlinger

Chasiotis A, Riemenschneider U, Restemeier R, Cappenberg M, Völker S, et al. 1997. Early infancy and the evolutionary theory of socialization. In *Development of Interaction and Attachment: Traditional and Non-Traditional Approaches,* ed. W Koops, JB Hoeksma, DC Van den Boom, pp. 305–12. Amsterdam: North Holland

Chisholm JS. 1993. Death, hope, and sex—life history and the development of reproductive strategies. *Curr. Anthropol.* 34:1–24

Chowdhury AI, Bairagi R, Koenig MA. 1993. Effects of family sex composition on fertility preference and behaviour in rural Bangladesh. *J. Biosoc. Sci.* 25:455–64

Clay DC, Johnson NE. 1992. Size of farm or size of family: which comes first? *Popul. Stud.* 46:491–505

Clutton-Brock TH. 1991. *The Evolution of Parental Care.* Princeton, NJ: Princeton Univ. Press

Conrad C, Lechner M, Werner W. 1996. East German fertility after unification: crisis or adaptation? *Popul. Dev. Rev.* 22:331–58

Critescu M. 1975. Differential fertility depending on the age of puberty. *J. Hum. Evol.* 4:521–24

Cronk L. 1991a. Human behavioral ecology. *Annu. Rev. Anthropol.* 20:25–53

Cronk L. 1991b. Preferential parental investment in daughters over sons. *Hum. Nat.* 2:387–417

Cumming DC, Wheeler GD, Harber VJ. 1994. Physical activity, nutrition, and reproduction. See Campbell & Wood 1994, pp. 55–76

Cutler WB, Garcia C-R, Krieger AM. 1979. Infertility and age at first coitus: a possible relationship. *J. Biosoc. Sci.* 11:425–32

Daly M, Wilson M. 1988. The Darwinian psychology of discriminative parental solicitude. In *Comparative Perspectives in Modern Psychology,* ed. DW Leger, pp. 91–143. Lincoln/London: Univ. Nebr. Press

Daly M, Wilson M. 1994. Stepparenthood and the evolved psychology of discriminative parental solicitude. In *Infanticide and Parental Care,* ed. S Parmigiani, FS Vom Saal, pp. 121–34. Chur, Switz.: Harwood

Danker-Hopfe H. 1986. Menarchal age in

Europe. *Yearb. Phys. Anthropol.* 29: 81–112

Dawkins R. 1982. *The Extended Phenotype—The Gene as the Unit of Selection.* Oxford/San Francisco: Freeman

Dickemann M. 1981. Paternal confidence and dowry competition: a biocultural analysis of Purdah. In *Natural Selection and Social Behavior—Recent Research and New Theory*, ed. RD Alexander, DW Tinkle, pp. 417–38. New York/Concord: Chiron

Dunbar RIM, ed. 1995. *Human Reproductive Decisions—Biological and Social Perspectives.* Houndsmills/London: Macmillan/New York: St. Martin's

Dunbar RIM, Clark A, Hurst NL. 1995. Conflict and cooperation among the Vikings: contingent behavioral decisions. *Ethol. Sociobiol.* 16:233–46

Dunbar RIM, Spoors M. 1995. Social networks, support cliques, and kinship. *Hum. Nat.* 6:273–90

Eberstadt N. 1994. Demographic shocks after communism: Eastern Germany, 1989–93. *Popul. Dev. Rev.* 20:137–52

Ellison PT. 1990. Human ovarian function and reproductive ecology: new hypotheses. *Am. Anthropol.* 92:933–52

Ellison PT. 1994. Advances in human reproductive ecology. *Annu. Rev. Anthropol.* 23:255–75

Essock-Vitale SM, McGuire MT. 1985. Women's lives viewed from an evolutionary perspective. II. Patterns of helping. *Ethol. Sociobiol.* 6:155–73

Euler HA, Weitzel B. 1996. Discriminative grandparental solicitude as reproductive strategy. *Hum. Nat.* 7:39–59

Fitzpatrick D. 1985. Marriage in post-famine Ireland. In *Marriage in Ireland*, ed. A Cosgrove, pp. 116–31. Dublin: College

Fleming AF, Briggs ND, Rossiter CE. 1985. Growth during pregnancy in Nigerian teenage primigravidae. *Br. J. Obstet. Gynaecol. Suppl.* 5:32–39

Flinn MV. 1989. Household composition and female reproductive strategies in a Trinidadian village. See Rasa et al 1989, pp. 206–33

Frisancho AR, Matos J, Bollettino LA. 1984. Role of gynecological age and growth maturity status in fetal maturation and prenatal growth of infants born to young stillgrowing adolescent mothers. *Hum. Biol.* 56:583–93

Garn SM, LaVelle M, Pesick SD, Ridella SA. 1984. Are pregnant teenagers still in rapid growth? *Am. J. Dis. Child.* 138:32–34

Gaulin SJC, Boster JS. 1990. Dowry as female competition. *Am. Anthropol.* 92:994–1005

Gaulin SJC, McBurney DH, Brakeman-

Wartell SL. 1997. Matrilateral biases in the investment of aunts and uncles: a consequence and measure of paternity uncertainty. *Hum. Nat.* 8:139–51

Gaulin SJC, Robbins CJ. 1991. Trivers-Willard effect in contemporary North American society. *Am. J. Phys. Anthropol.* 85:61–69

Gray R, ed. 1993. *Biomedical and Demographic Determinants of Reproduction.* Oxford: Clarendon

Grayson DK. 1993. Differential mortality and the Donner Party disaster. *Evol. Anthropol.* 2:151–59

Hager BJ. 1992. Get thee to a nunnery: female religious claustration in medieval Europe. *Ethol. Sociobiol.* 13:385–407

Hames R. 1987. Garden labor exchange among the Ye'kwana. *Ethol. Sociobiol.* 8: 259–84

Hawkes K, Charnov EL. 1988. On human fertility: individual or group benefit? *Curr. Anthropol.* 29:469–71

Hawkes K, O'Connell JF, Blurton Jones NG. 1989. Hardworking Hadza grandmothers. In *Comparative Socioecology—The Behavioural Ecology of Humans and Other Mammals*, ed. V Standen, RA Foley, pp. 341–66. Oxford: Blackwell

Hewlett BS. 1991. Demography and childcare in preindustrial societies. *J. Anthropol. Res.* 47:1–37

Hewlett BS. 1992. Husband-wife reciprocity and the father-infant relationship among Aka pygmies. In *Father-Child Relations—Cultural and Biosocial Contexts*, ed. BS Hewlett, pp. 153–76. Hawthorne, NY: Aldine de Gruyter

Hill EM, Low BS. 1992. Contemporary abortion patterns: a life history approach. *Ethol. Sociobiol.* 13:35–48

Hill EM, Young JP, Nord JL. 1994. Childhood adversity, attachment security, and adult relationships: a preliminary study. *Ethol. Sociobiol.* 15:323–38

Hill K. 1993. Life history theory and evolutionary anthropology. *Evol. Anthropol.* 2: 78–88

Hill K, Hurtado M. 1996. *Aché Life History—The Ecology and Demography of a Foraging People.* Hawthorne, NY: Aldine de Gruyter

Hrdy SB. 1992. Fitness tradeoffs in the history and evolution of delegated mothering with special reference to wet-nursing, abandonment, and infanticide. *Ethol. Sociobiol.* 13: 409–42

Hrdy SB, Judge DS. 1993. Darwin and the puzzle of primogeniture: an essay on biases in parental investment after death. *Hum. Nat.* 4:1–45

Hurtado AM, Hill K, Kaplan H, Hurtado I. 1992. Trade-offs between female food acquisition and child care among Hiwi and Ache foragers. *Hum. Nat.* 3:185–216

Imhof AE. 1984. The amazing simultaneousness of the big differences and the boom in the 19th century—some facts and hypotheses about infant and maternal mortality in Germany, 18th to 20th century. In *Preindustrial Population Change—The Mortality Decline and Short-Term Population Movements*, ed. T Bengtsson, G Fridlizius, R Ohlsson, pp. 191–222. Stockholm: Almqvist & Wiksell

Irwin C. 1989. The sociocultural biology of Netsilingmiut female infanticide. See Rasa et al 1989, pp. 234–64

Johnson RC, Johnson SB. 1997. Kinship and the quest for wealth and power as influences on conflict in the Punjab, 1839–1845. *Evol. Hum. Behav.* 18:341–48

Käär P, Jokela J, Helle T, Kojola I. 1996. Direct and correlative phenotypic selection on life-history traits in three pre-industrial human populations. *Proc. R. Soc. London Ser. B* 263:1475–80

Kaplan HS. 1994. Evolutionary and wealth flows theories of fertility: empirical tests and new models. *Popul. Dev. Rev.* 20:753–91

Kaplan HS, Lancaster JB, Bock JA, Johnson SE. 1995. Fertility and fitness among Albuquerque men: a competitive labour market theory. See Dunbar 1995, pp. 96–136

Khan AD, Schroeder DG, Martorell R, Haas JD, Rivera J. 1996. Early childhood determinants of age at menarche in rural Guatemala. *Am. J. Hum. Biol.* 8:717–23

Kiernan KE, Hobcraft J. 1997. Parental divorce during childhood: age at first intercourse, partnership and parenthood. *Popul. Stud.* 51:41–55

Kim K, Smith PK, Palermiti A-L. 1997. Conflict in childhood and reproductive development. *Evol. Hum. Behav.* 18:109–42

Klindworth H, Voland E. 1995. How did the Krummhörn elite males achieve above-average reproductive success? *Hum. Nat.* 6:221–40

Kriedte P, Medick H, Schlumbohm J. 1992. Sozialgeschichte in der Erweiterung— Proto-Industrialisierung in der Verengung?—Demographie, Sozialstruktur, moderne Hausindustrie: eine Zwischenbilanz der Proto-Industrialisierungsforschung (Teil I). *Gesch. Gesell.* 18:70–87

Krishnan V. 1993. Gender of children and contraceptive use. *J. Biosoc. Sci.* 25:213–21

Landale NS. 1989. Agricultural opportunity and marriage: the United States at the turn of the century. *Demography* 26:203–18

Lee R. 1994. Human fertility and population equilibrium. See Campbell & Wood 1994, pp. 396–407

Low BS. 1989. Cross-cultural patterns in the training of children: an evolutionary perspective. *J. Comp. Psychol.* 103:311–19

Lunn PG. 1996. Breast-feeding practices and other metabolic loads affecting human reproduction. In *Variability in Human Fertility*, ed. L Rosetta, CGN Mascie-Taylor, pp. 195–216. Cambridge, UK: Cambridge Univ. Press

Mace R. 1996a. Biased parental investment and reproductive success in Gabra pastoralists. *Behav. Ecol. Sociobiol.* 38:75–81

Mace R. 1996b. When to have another baby: a dynamic model of reproductive decision-making and evidence from Gabbra pastoralists. *Ethol. Sociobiol.* 17:263–73

Mace R, Sear R. 1997. Birth interval and the sex of children in a traditional African population: an evolutionary analysis. *J. Biosoc. Sci.* 29:499–507

Mann J. 1992. Nurturance or negligence: maternal psychology and behavioral preference among preterm twins. In *The Adapted Mind—Evolutionary Psychology and the Generation of Culture*, ed. JH Barkow, L Cosmides, J Tooby, pp. 367–90. New York/Oxford: Oxford Univ. Press

Margulis SW, Altmann J, Ober C. 1993. Sex-biased lactational duration in a human population and its reproductive costs. *Behav. Ecol. Sociobiol.* 32:41–45

McCullough JM, Barton EY. 1991. Relatedness and mortality risk during a crisis year: Plymouth colony, 1620–1621. *Ethol. Sociobiol.* 12:195–209

McNamara JM, Houston AI. 1996. State-dependent life histories. *Nature* 380:215–21

Nesse RM, Williams GC. 1994. *Why We Get Sick—The New Science of Darwinian Medicine.* New York/Toronto: Random House

Niraula BB, Morgan SP. 1995. Son and daughter preferences in Benighat, Nepal: implications for fertility transition. *Soc. Biol.* 42:256–73

Panter-Brick C. 1995. Child-care strategies in Nepal: responses to ecology, demography, and society. In *Human Populations—Diversity and Adaptation*, ed. AJ Boyce, V Reynolds, pp. 174–88. Oxford: Oxford Univ. Press

Peacock NR. 1991. An evolutionary perspective on the patterning of maternal investment in pregnancy. *Hum. Nat.* 2:351–85

Peccei JS. 1995. The origin and evolution of menopause: the altriciality-lifespan hypothesis. *Ethol. Sociobiol.* 16:425–49

Pennington R, Harpending H. 1993. *The Structure of an African Pastoralist Community: Demography, History and Ecology of the Ngamiland Herero.* New York: Oxford Univ. Press

Pentzos-Daponte A, Grefen-Peters S. 1984. Das Menarchealter der Mädchen aus Thessaloniki, Griechenland. *Anthropol. Anz.* 42:219–25

Pérusse D. 1993. Cultural and reproductive success in industrial societies: testing the relationship at the proximate and ultimate levels. *Behav. Brain Sci.* 16:267–322

Peyronnet J-C. 1976. Les enfants abandonnés et leurs nourrices à Limoges au XVIII siècle. *Rev. Hist. Mod. Contemp.* 23: 418–41

Rasa AE, Vogel C, Voland E, eds. 1989. *The Sociobiology of Sexual and Reproductive Strategies.* London/New York: Chapman & Hall

Reznick D. 1985. Costs of reproduction: an evaluation of the empirical evidence. *Oikos* 44:257–67

Rheubottom DB. 1988. "Sisters first": betrothal order and age at marriage in fifteenth-century Ragusa. *J. Fam. Hist.* 13:359–76

Riley AP, Samuelson JL, Huffman SL. 1993. The relationship of age at menarche and fertility in undernourished adolescents. See Gray 1993, pp. 50–64

Robinson WC. 1997. The economic theory of fertility over three decades. *Popul. Stud.* 51:63–74

Rogers AR. 1990. Evolutionary economics of human reproduction. *Ethol. Sociobiol.* 11: 479–95

Rogers AR. 1993. Why menopause? *Evol. Ecol.* 7:406–20

Rogers AR. 1995. For love or money: the evolution of reproductive and material motivations. See Dunbar 1995, pp. 76–95

Rosetta L. 1995. Nutrition, physical workloads and fertility regulation. See Dunbar 1995, pp. 52–75

Sandler DP, Wilcox AJ, Horney LF. 1984. Age at menarche and subsequent reproductive events. *Am. J. Epidemiol.* 19: 765–74

Schellekens J. 1990. Determinants of marriage patterns among farmers and agricultural laborers in two eighteenth-century Dutch villages. *J. Fam. Hist.* 16:139–55

Schellekens J. 1997. Nuptiality during the first industrial revolution in England: explanations. *J. Interdis. Hist.* 27:637–54

Sieff DF. 1990. Exploring biased sex ratios in human populations—a critique of recent studies. *Curr. Anthropol.* 31:25–48

Silk JB. 1990. Human adoption in evolutionary perspective. *Hum. Nat.* 1:25–52

Smith EA, Smith SA. 1994. Inuit sex ratio variation: population control, ethnographic error, or parental manipulation? *Curr. Anthropol.* 35:595–624

Smith EA, Winterhalder B, eds. 1992. *Evolutionary Ecology and Human Behavior.* Hawthorne, NY: Aldine de Gruyter

Spiess K-H. 1993. *Familie und Verwandtschaft im Deutschen Hochadel des Spätmittelalters.* Stuttgart: Steiner

Stearns SC. 1992. *The Evolution of Life Histories.* Oxford: Oxford Univ. Press

Straka-Geiersbach S, Voland E. 1988. Zum Einfluß der Säuglingssterblichkeit auf die eheliche Fruchtbarkeit am Beispiel der Krummhörn, 18. und 19. Jahrhundert. *Homo* 39:171–85

Surbey MK. 1987. Anorexia nervosa, amenorrhea, and adaptation. *Ethol. Sociobiol.* 8(Suppl.):S47–61

Trivers RL. 1972. Parental investment and sexual selection. In *Sexual Selection and the Descent of Man, 1871–1971,* ed. B Campbell, pp. 136–79. Chicago: Aldine

Trivers RL. 1974. Parent-offspring conflict. *Am. Zool.* 14:249–64

Turke PW. 1988. Helpers at the nest: childcare networks on Ifaluk. See Betzig et al 1988, pp. 173–88

Turke PW. 1989. Evolution and the demand for children. *Popul. Dev. Rev.* 15:60–90

Turke PW. 1997. Hypothesis: menopause discourages infanticide and encourages continued investment by agnates. *Evol. Hum. Behav.* 18:3–13

Udry JR, Cliquet RL. 1982. A cross-cultural examination of the relationship between ages at menarche, marriage, and first birth. *Demography* 19:53–63

Varea C, Bernis C, Elizondo S. 1993. Physiological maturation, reproductive patterns, and female fecundability in a traditional Moroccan population (Amizmiz, Marrakech). *Am. J. Hum. Biol.* 5:297–304

Vining DR Jr. 1986. Social versus reproductive success: the central theoretical problem of human sociobiology. *Behav. Brain Sci.* 9:167–216

Vitzthum VJ. 1997. Flexibility and paradox: the nature of adaptation in human reproduction. In *The Evolving Female—A Life History Perspective,* ed. ME Morbeck, A Galloway, A Zihlman, pp. 242–58. Princeton, NJ: Princeton Univ. Press

Voland E. 1988. Differential infant and child mortality in evolutionary perspective: data from late 17th to 19th century Ostfriesland (Germany). See Betzig et al 1988, pp. 253–61

Voland E, Dunbar RIM. 1995. Resource competition and reproduction—the relationship between economic and parental strategies in the Krummhörn population (1720–1874). *Hum. Nat.* 6:33–49

Voland E, Dunbar RIM, Engel C, Stephan P. 1997. Population increase and sex-biased parental investment: evidence from 18th and 19th-century Germany. *Curr. Anthropol.* 38:129–35

Voland E, Gabler S. 1994. Differential twin mortality indicates a correlation between age and parental effort in humans. *Naturwissenschaften* 81:224–25

Voland E, Voland R. 1989. Evolutionary biology and psychiatry: the case of anorexia nervosa. *Ethol. Sociobiol.* 10:223–40

Voland E, Voland R. 1995. Parent-offspring conflict, the extended phenotype, and the evolution of conscience. *J. Soc. Evol. Syst.* 18:397–412

Wasser SK. 1994. Psychosocial stress and infertility—cause or effect? *Hum. Nat.* 5: 293–306

Williams GC. 1957. Pleiotropy, natural selection, and the evolution of senescence. *Evolution* 11:398–411

Williams GC. 1966. Natural selection, the costs of reproduction, and a refinement of Lack's principle. *Am. Nat.* 100:687–90

Winterhalder B, Smith EA. 1992. Evolutionary ecology and the social sciences. See Smith & Winterhalder 1992, pp. 3–23

Wood JW. 1994. *Dynamics of Human Reproduction—Biology, Biometry, Demography.* Hawthorne, NY: Aldine de Gruyter

*Annu. Rev. Anthropol. 1998. 27:375–99*
*Copyright 1998 by Annual Reviews. All rights reserved*

# RECENT ADVANCES IN METHOD AND THEORY IN PALEODEMOGRAPHY

## Richard S. Meindl

Department of Anthropology, Kent State University, Kent, Ohio 44242-0001;
e-mail: rmeindl@kent.edu

## Katherine F. Russell

Department of Biology, University of Massachusetts, Dartmouth, Massachusetts
02747-2300; e-mail: krussell@umassd.edu

KEY WORDS:  archaeological demography, skeletal biology, sex and age estimation,
            model life tables, intrinsic growth rate

### ABSTRACT

Current methods in skeletal biology have improved significantly our ability
to estimate the demographic parameters of extinct populations. Gross morphological and histological age indicators have been developed and tested in
a variety of contexts, revealing great variation in the levels of accuracy of age
prediction of each indicator. Primary attention is given here to the best-
performing hard-tissue indicators of age and to composite methods of recov-
ering the age and sex distribution of a cemetery. It is becoming increasingly
apparent that some cemeteries should not be used for demographic reconstruction. Such collections have no bearing on the feasibility of paleodemographic research. Our review concludes with discussions about the role of
comparing modern mortality patterns to those of paleodemography, and the
issue and impact of departures from stationary demographic conditions during prehistoric times.

## INTRODUCTION

More than 15 years ago Bocquet-Appel & Masset (1982) raised a number of
questions concerning the analysis of vital rates from skeleton-based demogra-

375

0084-6570/98/1015-0375$08.00

phies. Since that time the once-tranquil field of paleodemography has become almost as disputatious as some other areas of anthropology. However, this shift has resulted in constructive debates and timely reexaminations of models and assumptions. Further critical review and new research efforts in this area have increased dramatically, moving paleodemography from the periphery to the forefront of prehistoric studies (Roth 1992).

Paleodemography is more than the study of mortality and fertility of archaeological populations. It also includes the estimation of the distribution, density, and age composition of prehistoric peoples. It considers intrinsic rates of growth or decline, and it may include migration and the age and sex structure of migration as well. The field attracts anthropologists for different reasons. Like Goodman et al (1984), Weiss (1989), and Buikstra (1997), our primary interests in cemeteries have always been the health, life-history, and evolutionary aspects of human biodemography. We limit our comments here to recent methodological advances in estimating the vital structure of an extinct population from the cemetery on which it was based. We discuss some of the sampling problems in paleodemography, methods for estimating the distribution of ages by sex in skeletal series, and life-table mortality schedules and fertility in the context of stable population theory. We also discuss the role of mortality models external to paleodemography and an approach to the problem of unknown intrinsic rates of growth in prehistory.

Space also precludes discussion of recent views concerning morbidity patterns in skeletal populations (Wood et al 1992) or the health status surrounding the adoption of agricultural systems (Cohen 1997). Limits remain to the inferences we can draw from paleodemography; however, studies of living, so-called "demographically inconvenient" populations have their own unique challenges (Leslie & Gage 1989:20). We maintain that archaeological populations offer a special and important view of the biology, cultural evolution, and basic demography of extinct peoples that is not available from other fields of anthropology.

## SAMPLING PROBLEMS IN PALEODEMOGRAPHY

The demographic reconstruction of an extinct society is a sampling process that may involve several potential sources of error. Aboriginal inhumation practices, soil and other conditions of interment including subsequent disturbances of the burials, and the care and skill of the excavators may all affect how well a cemetery represents the population on which it was based. It bears repeating that if "an unbiased, representative sample . . . cannot be assumed, further demographic analysis is not likely to be productive" (Weiss 1973:58).

Certainly, burial customs associated with infanticide have skewed the findings from many cemeteries (Scrimshaw 1984, Saunders 1992). Yet if the practice of infanticide was restricted to such uncommon situations as genetic defects, the birth of twins, and breach births there is little impact on mortality profiles. Conditions that predispose cultures toward (typically female) infanticide for less immediate reasons include very short interbirth intervals, high costs of transporting infants over large distances, perceptions of the need to limit family size, and the greater value of males as economic providers or combatants (Divale & Harris 1976, Scrimshaw 1984). While it might be widely accepted that infanticides were usually not buried with the rest of the population (Saunders 1992), it is important to note that skewed sex ratios resulting from frequent female infanticide would be archaeologically detectable.

In any case, such perinatal deaths may not be recovered, usually took place within a matter of minutes of birth, and would suggest that paleodemographers should alter their definition of the radix by approximately that amount of time. Infanticide in human populations, both living and extinct, is a difficult demographic parameter to estimate. Although a condition of mortality by definition, it should be regarded by anthropological demographers as a deliberate control over fertility. That is, removing infanticide altogether from the calculation of life expectancy at birth would make the metric more reflective of the actual biological conditions of mortality and, therefore, more utilitarian to population scientists across the spectrum of human ecologies and cultures.

Ethnographic evidence indicates that, in many societies, the old and the infirm are killed occasionally, but their remains are rarely treated differently from those of other adult decedents. Any graves containing crippled, injured, or malformed elderly would imply that efforts had been made to return all of that society's members to a common place of burial. Young adults, particularly males, may have died violently or otherwise some distance from the habitation/cemetery. A mixture of bundle burials (i.e. only crania and assorted longbones) with articulated ones further suggest such a general effort, since it indicates return of the kinsmen's essential remains to the cemetery.

It is not the purpose of our review to present and evaluate paleodemographic methods for sites with scattered or poorly preserved remains. Nor is it possible to usefully estimate the levels of bias in preservation by age or sex for any given site, when it is clear that some differential loss of skeletons has occurred (Gordon & Buikstra 1981). If a portion of a cemetery cannot be aged or sexed owing to dissolution of calcified tissues, or if evidence exists for carelessness in excavation and recovery, the value of that site to the study of human demography is diminished by an unknown extent.

Our experience with skeletal sites in the eastern United States leads us to conclude that the general claims about the effect of differential preservation by age or sex of bone remains on the field of paleodemography (Masset 1973, Walker et al 1988, Jackes 1992) are overstated. Any potential for this kind of bias is obvious at once by simple inspection of the integrity of the burial pits, articulations, and periosteal bone layers. Bone and tooth survival is a function of mechanical displacement, soil drainage, and especially pH (Gordon & Buikstra 1981). Unfavorable conditions cause the destruction or agitation of hard-tissue remains with such speed that sites of moderate antiquity fall primarily into two groups—those with demographically useful bone assemblages and those without. An intermediate site in which the human remains are actually in the process of disappearing would probably have such fragile contents that even the adult sample would be in poor condition.

Both Sundick (1978) and Saunders (1992) argued that in such sites the hard evidence required to recognize and age a subadult (i.e. primarily teeth) is preserved at least as well as the bones of a robust adult skeleton. Nevertheless, some added provision may be needed in the wake of moderate mechanical disturbances, such as tree roots and rodents, to estimate accurately the proportion of infants and very young children (Lovejoy et al 1977). The issue of differential preservation of bone microstructure is no different. Although histomorphological data contain instances of age-related preservation bias (Garland 1987, Hanson & Buikstra 1987), the potential for bias should be recognizable, and therefore, any impact on the feasibility of paleodemographic inference is minor.

In nearly all instances the archaeological data themselves should demonstrate clearly which sites are useful to paleodemographers (contra Jackes 1992:199). A case in point is the inappropriate use of the late-eighteenth century Newton Plantation skeletons to question a method of fertility estimation. The divergence of skeletal- and historical-based inferences failed to "promote demographic optimism" despite a meager sample and the fact that "preservation is poor" (Corruccini et al 1989:610). A more widely cited example is the Purisma Mission cemetery in California, again admittedly a "poorly preserved" skeletal collection (Walker et al 1988:184). An argument was made from the field notes and the curated materials that biases in preservation as well as selective archaeological recovery were sizable sources of census error. However, it has always been clear that no demographic analysis should be undertaken with culled skeletons. A companion survey of the Franciscan priests' written burial records for La Purisma only verified the obvious archaeological inferences.

## ESTIMATION OF SEX OF ADULT SKELETONS

Sex, the most important demographic variable, is recoverable directly through the osteology of primary and secondary sexual characteristics. These result principally from differential growth rates during adolescence. Males exhibit a prenatal slowing of maturation beginning early in gestation, protracted prepubescent growth, a greater intensity of the growth spurt (which, because of its delay, acts upon an absolutely larger musculoskeletal frame), and additional changes that occur in late and post-adolescence (Stini 1985).

A remarkable aspect of human development is its degree of canalization: Growth trajectories tend to be self-stabilizing. In longitudinal studies, ultimate growth is found to be largely genetic. In instances in which growth is inhibited temporarily (e.g. hypothyroidism later corrected, or a cortisol-producing tumor later removed), subsequent catch-up rates may be as high as three times the normal (Harrison et al 1977). However, some studies on contemporary populations tend to underestimate and obscure the potential magnitude of environmental effects. The great recuperative powers of children can be overwhelmed when poor conditions are too prolonged, especially malnutrition and illness. Since girls are more resistant than boys to intensive growth-inhibiting stress, the effect is a decrease in dimorphism. [See Hamilton (1982) for an informative survey of the causes of skeletal dimorphism].

Thus, most adult somatic dimensions are environmentally labile, and since the environment most probably played a more powerful role in growth during prehistoric times, any use of pure size measures to determine the sex of a skeleton is problematic. This applies to all methods not based on primary sexual characteristics, including those of the upper limb (Holman & Bennett 1991), radial head (Berrizbeitia 1989), tibia (Holland 1991, Kieser et al 1992), femur and humerus (Dittrick & Suchey 1986), proximal components of the appendicular skeleton (Richman et al 1979), femoral circumference (Black 1978), talus and calcaneous (Steele 1976), sternal rib (İşcan & Loth 1986), first cervical vertebra (Marino 1995), metacarpals (Scheuer & Elkington 1993, Falsetti 1995), metacarpal asymmetry (Lazenby 1994), iliac crest of the pelvis (Fernández Camacho et al 1993), and tooth crowns (Owsley & Webb 1983), just to sample this ongoing industry. [See Buikstra & Mielke (1985) for a comparison of techniques for adult sex determination. For each technique the authors listed the method's accuracy as well as whether it is based on a series of known sex.] Sex determination in paleodemography depends on the true magnitude of sexual dimorphism, the amount of within-sex variation, and the direction of sexing error as well.

As has been recognized for some time (Hrdlička 1952, Krogman 1962, Acsádi & Nemeskéri 1970, Hamilton 1982, White 1991), the *os coxae,* or innominate bone of the pelvis, is the most reliable osteological indicator of sex in the adult owing to the central role this structure plays in parturition. In hominids a critical disproportion between the dimensions of the female inner pelvis and the term fetal head and shoulders developed progressively over the past few million years (Tague & Lovejoy 1986). The dimorphism of the modern bony pelvis is an adaptation to this disproportion. In fact, in nonhominoid primates the *ischiopubic index* is greater in females, and—except for a few lorises and a species of howler monkey—strongly so (Leutenegger 1982). The index is a correlate of the proximity of neonatal cranial dimensions to those of the female adult true pelvis [African apes are too large to be subject to such selection pressures (Tague 1991)] and has its basis in local estrogen receptor sites in the pubis. Evidence indicates antecedent systems for this basis and for the posterior portion of the ilium as well in more generalized mammals such as mice (Uesugi et al 1992). For human females these selection pressures have resulted in (a) altered growth trajectories that position the sacrum more posterior in the birth canal and (b) continued elongation of the iliopubic ramus even into the third decade of life (Budinoff & Tague 1990).

The repositioning of the female sacrum produced a wider sciatic notch (i.e. the large indentation superior to the ischial spine) in the female. The latter adaptation forms the basis of a popular and very accurate method for sex determination based on the morphology of the pubis (Phenice 1969). Covariation of the width of the sciatic notch and the ischiopubic index can be best appreciated in a well-known bivariate plot of Eskimo pelvises (Hanna & Washburn 1953:24). Three variables (ratio of the ischium to the pubis, sciatic notch, and medioventral aspects of the pubis) are the primary bases of the objective methods that paleodemographers and forensic scientists have used traditionally. They are also the basis of the discriminatory power of conventional multivariate approaches to the problem (Schulter-Ellis et al 1983) as well as size-corrected algorithms (Arsuaga & Carretero 1994). Using pelvises from skeletons of known sex, we and others (Richman et al 1979, Meindl et al 1985a, Sutherland & Suchey 1991, Luo 1995) have approximated closely the high accuracies first predicted by the developers of both observational and statistical methods of sexing. Some workers have reported less satisfactory results (Lovell 1989, Rogers & Saunders 1994). Efficacy of the methods appears to depend on the aspects of the innominate bone that are evaluated.

Meindl et al (1985a) suggested that the opposing selection pressures of efficiency in locomotion and success in parturition may have limited female pelvic variability relative to that of the male. However, Tague (1989) found no such sex-specific difference in terms of absolute metric variability. The issue is important in demographic reconstruction because it has some bearing on the likely direction of error in sexing adult skeletons. While Meindl et al (1985a) predicted that the most common error should be "male-called-female," Weiss (1972) has pointed to the high adult sex ratios of many archaeological populations. However, a prehistoric tendency toward heavy female subadult mortality (which may have included infanticide) would explain these observations.

Sex identification using the skull has traditionally been based on differences in the prominence of muscle attachments, the curvature of the frontal profile, the dimensions of the cranial base, and absolute tooth and jaw size and morphology. Although male skulls tend to be larger and more robust, the degree of dimorphism can vary greatly among populations. Giles & Elliot (1963) derived batteries of discriminant functions based on the metrics of crania (i.e. skulls minus mandibles) from cadaver skeletons of known sex. They predicted error rates not much better than some of the longbone methods (see above). Paleodemographic applications are even more problematic: (*a*) There is no provision for distorted prehistoric crania (pre- or postmortem). (*b*) The functions derive nearly all of their power from size effects, which are population specific (see above), resulting in reduced accuracy in collections other than the Terry or the Hamann-Todd collections (Kajanoja 1966). (*c*) Older adults of both sexes display increasingly masculine craniometrics (Meindl et al 1985a) because of remodeling and craniofacial expansion, which occur well into old age (Israel 1973, 1977). This kind of directional error might prove to be the greatest liability in formulating two-sex mortality models in paleodemographic contexts.

Some components of the human skull exhibit hormonally mediated sexual dimorphism. In fact, discriminant functions that incorporate some measure of the prominence of the superciliary arches (brow ridges) and the external occipital protuberance (at the midline of the meeting of the occipital and nuchal planes) perform quite well (Song et al 1992). We suspect that receptor sites may soon be discovered on the supraorbital aspect of the frontal bone and perhaps elsewhere. If so, subjective and statistical sexing of skulls may one day have more to offer in paleodemographic reconstruction.

## AGE ESTIMATION OF SUBADULT SKELETONS

Three kinds of hard-tissue data reflect age in the developing skeleton. These are, starting with the most accurate (and least affected by environmental conditions), dental development and eruption, then longbone epiphyseal closure, and finally linear longbone growth. Linear seriation should be used when working with these data in order to minimize observer error and for other reasons as well (see below).

Several studies have provided chronologies of deciduous and permanent tooth formation and emergence. For all 26 pairs of teeth in the human primary and secondary dentitions, Oliver (1969) presented schedules of stages rather than single eruption times. Moorrees et al (1963a,b) did the same but restricted their analyses to several teeth. Ubelaker (1989) estimated the timing of dental development in Native-American children. Demirjian and colleagues (Demirjian et al 1973, Demirjian & Levesque 1980) predicted a dental age from a composite maturity score based on the radiographs of seven permanent left mandibular teeth. Gustafson & Koch (1974) published a schematic representation of tooth formation and eruption and claimed that comparison of the dental developmental status of any 3 to 13 year old to the diagram will yield an age estimate generally within two months of actual age. Bang (1989) and El-Nofely & İşcan (1989) surveyed the literature on age assessment from developing dentition. White (1991) and Schwartz (1995) provided instructions for using some of these methods.

Tooth formation and eruption varies among populations. For example, some African children tend to develop more quickly than some Europeans and especially Asians; however, while these distinctions are statistically significant owing to the large sample sizes, the average differences are less than a year (El-Nofely & İşcan 1989). Despite these minor geographic variations, there is consensus that dental development is the age indicator most resistant to nutritional deficiencies, hormone imbalances, and any other environmental effect.

Saunders et al (1993) verified the precision of Moorrees's standards with a small sample from the St. Thomas's Church cemetery. Demographers of contemporary nonindustrial societies have pointed out that for their purposes there are no meaningful differences among populations in deciduous tooth eruption; moreover, they now recognize that, in so-called noncounting cultures, dental development in young children is a better predictor of a child's age than is the mother's recall of the date of birth (Townsend & Hammel 1990).

Data on the union of epiphyses are frequently used to establish age at death during the second decade of life; however, environmental stress can retard skeletal age by as much as three years (Johnston & Zimmer 1989). General summaries of the standards available may be found in Stewart (1979), Krogman & İşcan (1986), and Ubelaker (1989). Cemeteries may represent the growth of the population's healthy children (Wood et al 1992); therefore, in paleodemographic applications, age estimation from diaphyseal length and epiphyseal closure may be biased downward.

## ADULT AGE ESTIMATES

Postdevelopmental skeletal aging is a complex product of both genetics and environment. In the third decade of life, variation in the aging process starts to increase, both between individuals and even within a single skeleton. Our work at Kent State University was the most recent in a series of studies, spanning several decades, that used multiple indicators of adult skeletal age in order to partly compensate for this phenomenon (Krogman 1962, Acsádi & Nemeskéri 1970, Lovejoy et al 1985a). Although the indicators of age are reviewed separately here, we do not imply that age assessment of adults can be based on single age indicators. We present in this review those methods appearing to be among the most reliable estimators of age currently available. We allude to other methods of age determination because of their historical importance.

A simple way to reduce observer error in age estimation is to seriate all skeletons for each age indicator (Lovejoy et al 1985a). This procedure has two effects: (a) The intercalation of every osteological specimen into the entire ordered series extracts maximum information about relative biological age, and (b) seriation minimizes observer error by eliminating fatigue and other time-shift effects. The arrangement of a sequence of increasing skeletal age, with the progressive detection and reduction of error, and the final assignment of individual target ages requires long tables and consumes considerable amounts of time and effort. However, it produces final ages for each skeleton that in effect are assigned simultaneously. We recommend this exercise to even the most skilled osteologist for its heuristic effects. The process should be repeated for each age estimator independently. Phase, component, and even regression methods for estimating age can benefit greatly from this approach.

Error in age estimation can be quantified only when methods are tested on individuals of known chronological age. The amount of *bias*[1] and *inaccuracy*[2] of age prediction vary greatly among skeletal aging methods. In most circumstances inaccuracy can be minimized across the age range by including more than one method. Bias, however, is another matter and, in paleodemographic contexts, a more serious one. Most methods exhibit age-related levels of error, for example, small error below a certain age but unacceptably wide error margins afterward. Application of such methods must be limited to those age ranges for which age-related changes are regular. Otherwise, the problem of reference population bias may become pronounced.

A critical problem in paleodemography is the bias that results from poor accuracy in age estimation and its effect in skewing the calculation of demographic profiles. The reversal of the fixed independent regressor (real age) with the "free-to-vary" dependent regressand (age indicator morphology) has always been a problem in the field of skeletal demography (Bocquet-Appel & Masset 1982). Age estimation of a series of skeletons may produce a distribution reflecting the skeletal reference population on which the aging method was originally developed, rather than the age structure of the cemetery being analyzed. Such mimicry tends to be marked when indicators correlate poorly with actual age. Several studies have addressed this issue (Van Gerven & Armelagos 1983; Buikstra & Konigsberg 1985; Mensforth & Lovejoy 1985; Buikstra et al 1986; Siven 1991; Jackes 1985, 1992, 1993).

Bocquet-Appel & Masset (1996) have become convinced recently that the mean age of a cemetery is indeed recoverable. Konigsberg & Frankenberg (1992, 1994; Konigsberg et al 1997) pursue a more useful goal, the demonstration that both the mean and the shape of a cemetery age-distribution can be estimated with minimal bias. They have surveyed paleodemographic reports, explored the fisheries literature on the subject of calibration, and shown the supe-

---

[1]Bias = $\Sigma$ (estimated age − real age)/number of individuals; that is, sign is considered.
[2]Inaccuracy = $\Sigma$ |estimated age − real age|/number of individuals; that is, sign is not considered.

riority of maximum likelihood methods of adult age estimation over Bayesian approaches. If these methods are to be used, future developments in age determination methods will have to include distributions of morphology types by extreme age, and cross-classification of multiple indicator morphologies against known age as well (Konigsberg & Frankenberg 1992). However, there will always be the need to appreciate that no statistical procedure can ever overcome the limitations of an abysmal age indicator (i.e. one that is unrelated to age). Even some of the traditional adult indicators of skeletal age yield virtually no additional information after a certain developmental stage has been attained (see below).

## Gross Morphological Indicators of Age

The gross morphological indicators of age are relatively easy to apply, require no special equipment, and are nondestructive. However, their application requires the observer to have a clear understanding of the anatomy, development, and physiology of the soft tissues associated with the bony/dental landmarks in order to understand normal variation in the age-related features and to discriminate outliers, pathologies, and postmortem damage.

CRANIAL SUTURE CLOSURE   Cranial suture closure has long been used in the estimation of skeletal age. There are now formal aging methods based on both ectocranial and endocranial closure, using different batteries of sutures and different scoring systems (Meindl & Lovejoy 1985, Masset 1989). Employment of sutures as an aging indicator fell into disfavor during the 1950s following widely cited criticisms (Singer 1953, Brooks 1955, McKern & Stewart 1957). The subsequent abandonment of such methods during this period was the result of poor and variable performances of available systems in addition to the expectation that more accurate techniques would soon emerge. However, because no such method has been forthcoming, cranial suture closure is being used once again, but only as one of multiple indicators of skeletal aging.

Acsádi & Nemeskéri (1970) presented one of the most widely used methods for aging the skeletons of young and middle-aged adults (for whom suture closure was still active at the time of death). Subsequent tests of vault suture aging of the endocranium by Masset (1989) and the ectocranium by Saunders et al (1992) revealed poor performance. Most vault closure is simply too early to be of any great help in estimating extreme age, for which new forensic standards are most needed. Meindl & Lovejoy (1985) offered two ectocranial methods, one of which appears to monitor changes at the higher ages more efficiently; nevertheless, error may become large after age 50 (Lovejoy et al 1985a). Schwartz (1995) fully described the application of these techniques.

PUBIC SYMPHYSIS   The pubic symphyseal face (i.e. the surface of the pubic bone where the two innominates most closely approach) has received the most attention of all the anatomical structures in estimating age at death. Todd first described age-related changes in humans (1920, 1921a ) and in other mammals (1921b). His careful characterization of pubic epiphyseal fusion and progressive degenerative changes provided the basis for all such subsequent aging methods (McKern & Stewart 1957, Gilbert & McKern 1973). When used in one of its condensed forms (Meindl et al 1985b, Suchey et al 1986) the pubic symphysis can be a valuable method for estimating young and middle adult age.

The importance of the pubic symphysis in paleodemography is limited to the aging of adults up to about age 40 years (Hanihara & Suzuki 1978; Meindl et al 1985b; Lovejoy et al 1995, 1997). The appearance and fusion of the ventral rampart of the pubic symphysis are nothing more than uniquely human, delayed epiphyseal events, representing the only discrete features that make the pubic symphysis a valuable aging locus. Fusion is typically completed before age 35, marking the end of all developmental activity at this joint. Post-epiphyseal changes are all degenerative, highly variable, and not particularly valuable for age estimation, as confirmed by Saunders et al (1992) and others.

AURICULAR SURFACE OF THE ILIUM    Lovejoy et al (1995, 1997) examined the senescent biology of the auricular surface of the ilium (i.e. the iliac side of the innominate-sacrum articulation) in hominoids. They argued that age changes in the morphology of the sacroiliac joint are a consequence of its highly unusual phylogenetic and embryological development and that the iliac face has a uniquely protracted metamorphosis in both bipedal and quadrupedal hominoids. They demonstrated that, unlike the pubic symphysis, the auricular surface reflects changes well into the sixth decade. The changes from a billowed epiphyseal-like surface to a more coarsely granulated one and especially the late metamorphosis from a smooth dense face to one of increasing degenerative irregularity provide a series of biological events that can be used to assess age (Lovejoy et al 1985b, Meindl & Lovejoy 1989).

This method is not without its critics: Rogers (1990) was not able to replicate our results for older skeletons, and Jackes (1992) cited "constant interobserver disagreement" over the auricular ages of apparently very fragmentary Mesolithic skeletons. Murray & Murray (1991) confirmed that there are neither sex nor geographic differences in auricular aging but were displeased with the method's performance in a forensic setting. Konigsberg & Frankenberg (1992) recognized from the Murrays's account that the auricular surface is valuable to paleodemography because it fits Howell's (1976) "uniformitarian assumption" that both extant and extinct human populations age in similar fashions and at identical rates. Saunders et al (1992) examined a series of older skeletons of known age but failed to adequately test the ability of the auricular surface to predict extreme age: They chose not to seriate, and they curiously assigned unknown specimens to the youngest age class possible despite our explicit directions to the contrary (Meindl et al 1990:353). Still, the auricular surface predicted extreme age better than the other indicators, especially the pubis, in this test (Saunders et al 1992) and in another (Bedford et al 1993). Finally, researchers have noted that the frail pubic symphysis is not nearly as archaeologically durable as the auricular surface (Pfeiffer 1986, Waldron 1987).

COSTOCHONDRAL JOINTS    The potential of costochondral joints (i.e. ventral articular surfaces of ribs) to represent adult age was appreciated as early as the 1950s (McKern & Stewart 1957). İşcan et al were the first to formalize an aging method (by sex) based on the fourth rib (1984a,b). Independent tests of their method have confirmed its utility in age estimation and its acceptably low bias before age 50 (Saunders et al 1992, Russell et al 1993, Dudar et al 1993). The metamorphosis of the joint includes a change from a smooth billowed immature surface to a more concave and irregular surface as a result of remodelling (i.e. periosteal accretion and endosteal resorption). Any geographic differences in the rates of change (İşcan et al 1987) cannot be very large (Russell et al 1993).

OCCLUSAL DENTAL WEAR    Occlusal dental wear is one of the most reliable methods of estimating adult age, as long as the assumption of uniform rates of attrition in the population can be reasonably met. Murphy (1959) and Miles (1963) presented two of the seminal methods for estimating age from dental wear. Murphy (1959) used an ordinal scale in which each cusp was scored independently. Miles (1963) used a single evaluation per tooth. Modifications of such methods were fruitful and can be recommended for age estimation (Smith 1984, Kieser et al 1985, Lovejoy 1985). Even in the heterogenous Hamann-Todd collection, occlusal dental wear was the least-biased single estimator of extreme adult age (Lovejoy et al 1985a); therefore, it is very important for paleodemographic application.

Careful assessment of adolescent tooth wear, consideration of individual variation in dental attrition, and an appreciation of the effects of antemortem tooth loss on the rest of the dentition must all be evaluated for successful application of the methods. We are aware of two sites, both Green River Archaic cemeteries, for which dental wear was too extreme to be useful in aging skeletons: the Carlston-Annis site (Mensforth 1990) and the Ward site (Meindl et al 1998). Certainly the rates of wear changed for the oldest members of these populations when attrition began to involve the buccal roots of the lower molars.

CHANGES IN BONE DISTRIBUTION    Many investigators have observed age-related changes in adult cortical and trabecular (i.e. compact and spongy) bone distribution (Acsádi & Nemeskéri 1970, Singh 1972, Walker & Lovejoy 1985). In the macroscopic methods used for such observations, seriation of radiographs is especially important in fostering the retention of biologically relevant differences among individuals in both bone density and distribution. Because of the dramatic physiological and mechanical factors influencing bone remodeling, the internal macroscopic structure of bone is not an extremely accurate method of age assessment. However, the method can contribute effectively to improving age estimation when used in concert with other aging sites (Lovejoy et al 1985a).

## Histological Indicators of Age

Bone growth and modeling produce a mature cortex with a characteristic structure. Remodeling occurs throughout life in long-lived adult mammals in response to mechanical and physiological activity. The remodeling of osteons provides a quantifiable means of assessing age-at-death from sectioned adult cortical bone. Kerley (1965, Kerley & Ubelaker 1978) provided the first systematic means of quantifying osteons and osteon fragments, circumferential lamellar bone (thin parallel layers of bone), and non-Haversian vascular canals (formed as the cortex increases diameter around peripheral blood vesels) to produce regression equations suitable for estimating age in unknown individuals. Other modifications followed (Ahlqvist & Damsten 1969, Singh & Gunberg 1970, Thompson 1979, Walker 1989).

Since bone continues to remodel under mechanical stress throughout adult life, multiple sampling sites from more than one cross-section are necessary (Stout 1992). Stout & Paine (1992) suggested that non–weight-bearing bones such as the clavicle and sixth rib might be more suitable than the major long bones because they undergo less mechanical remodeling. Frost (1987) and Stout (1992) proposed the calculation of a *mean tissue age.*

Histological aging methods all use linear regression equations, which are notoriously limited (Giles and Klepinger 1988, Maples & Rice 1979, Lucy et al 1996). Confidence intervals are neither small nor equivalent but expand as the regression line moves away from the mean. Histological techniques have been reported which are averages of histological and gross estimators adequate for measuring rib age in individuals under age 60 (Dudar et al 1993). However, they may be no better at indicating older ages than methods using the pubic symphysis (Aiello & Molleson 1993). Walker et al (1994) claimed that for individuals older than age 50, osteon density does not correlate as well with age as it does with geometric properties of femoral cross-sections.

Preservation of microscopic bone structure depends heavily on soil conditions, and macroscopic appearance of a bone may not be a good indicator of its histological preservation (Garland 1987). There can be partial to complete destruction (particularly of periosteal regions) of the bone microstructure, even when gross bone preservation is excellent (Lovejoy et al 1977, Hanson & Buikstra 1987, Pfeiffer 1992, Jackes 1992).

Gustafson presented a detailed method for estimating age from histological changes in individual adult teeth. The method involves assigning ordinal scores to six age-related changes: attrition, periodontosis, secondary dentin formation, cementum apposition, root resorption, and root transparency (Gustafson 1950). Problems with the original method have been well documented (Maples & Rice 1979). Yet the age-related changes first described by Gustafson have generated many useful methods for estimating age at death, even when only one or a few teeth are available per individual (Maples 1978, Condon et al 1986, Lucy et al 1996, Russell 1996). Bias and inaccuracy have been evaluated for a cementum annulation method (Condon et al 1986) and for a combination of attrition, secondary dentin, root dentin transparency, and cementum thickness (Russell 1996).

## A Hierarchical Method of Age Estimation

Acsádi & Nemeskéri (1970) introduced a complex method for determining adult age, composed of estimates from the pubis, the endocranial sutures, and the loss of trabecular bone in both proximal humerus and femur. They suggested dividing the adult portion of the cemetery into three groups on the basis of pubic symphyseal morphology (young, middle, and old). This step would determine a specific portion of the age ranges (low, middle, or high) for each of the three remaining indicators. The final estimate was the arithmetic average of the four.

We have suggested calculating the final age estimates of specimens from a cemetery as a weighted average of all indicators (called the summary age), with the weights determined by the first eigenvector of a principal component analysis of the intercorrelation matrix of the various age indicators used (Lovejoy et al 1977, Meindl et al 1983). We later suggested a modification to eliminate systematic bias in the higher ages: Mean ages should be calculated from all but the lowest estimates, or the lowest two, for the oldest skeletons in the series (Lovejoy et al 1985a). The correlations of the final age estimates with real ages were very high when subjected to blind tests of accuracy. Most important for paleodemographic reconstruction, bias was acceptably low; therefore, unknown age distributions could be approximated quite well by such multifactorial methods as long as actual adult life expectancy is low, that is, $\bar{e}_{15}$ is less than about 30 years (Lovejoy et al 1985a).

This precision was attributed incorrectly to an artificial reduction in variation in the cadaver test population (Cleveland's Hamann-Todd collection) by Katz & Suchey (1986, 1989), and in turn by İşcan (1989a) and İşcan & Loth (1989). We provided a large-sample analysis showing that the Hamann-Todd collection is a superior resource when careful subselection procedures are applied to ensure accuracy of age at death of the specimens used for analysis; in addition, subselection did not result in reduced variation (Meindl et al 1990).

In summary, methods for estimating the age distributions of representative cemeteries can be accurate provided that (a) seriation is applied, (b) biological assessment of each aging site is used, rather than so-called comparison-matching of specimens to a series of discrete morphotypes, and (c) reliance is placed on a battery of proven adult age estimators.

At this time we would also offer the following amendment to our previous research: As before, a weighted average or subjective combination of aging methods should be used for all young and middle-aged adult skeletons. This can be done according to an algorithm (as above) or in a general way, such as the subjective estimation of clinical age (Lovejoy et al 1985a). Furthermore, for those skeletons determined to be older than 40 years, new estimates should be provided from dental attrition (if possible) and especially from the auricular surface. Although these methods remain difficult to learn and apply and do not often satisfy the specific needs of forensic specialists, few alternatives exist at this time for estimating the ages of the oldest decedents in archaeological populations—one of the most important methodological issues in paleodemography today.

## MORTALITY MODELS AND REFERENCE POPULATIONS

A compelling mathematical consistency in the pattern of adult mortality by age has long been recognized, beginning with Gompertz's work early in the nineteenth century. After World War II there was a shift in approach away from functional graduations toward reference sets of life tables (see Brass 1971 for discussion). These tables primarily supplemented incomplete demographic data from developing countries, especially those in tropical Africa.

Conventionally called models or model life tables, such reference tables are based on the same basic assumption that governs mathematical models: A limited number of dimensions of variation exist for the shape of the "curve of deaths." The best known reference set was developed at Princeton's Office of Population Research (Coale & Demeny 1966, 1983). From more than 300 two-sex life tables of the nineteenth and twentieth centuries, there emerged four families of mortality profiles. For instance, life tables representing populations still in the grasp of the European tuberculosis epidemic underlie the North series of models. An East and a South pattern also coalesced. The West family took form as a residual collection after the three other regions were removed. The West reference set has become the regular choice in most anthropological applications.

Many anthropologists have used the models (accessible by a continuum of either intrinsic growth rates or gross reproductive rates) to examine and explain fundamental processes as they might apply to extinct populations (Sattenspiel & Harpending 1983, Gage 1988, Horowitz & Armelagos 1988, Buikstra & Konigsberg 1985, Dumond 1997, Sullivan 1997). However, others have invoked the modern patterns of longevity in efforts to dismiss certain archaeological populations from the study of human demography altogether (Howell 1982, Johansson & Horowitz 1986, Milner et al 1989, Paine 1989). Not only are the survivorship levels of most skeleton-based demographies extremely low, but their patterns stand in marked contrast to the lowest survivorship levels of the West family. Since by modern standards the levels of childhood mortality in paleodemography are low relative to adult mortality levels, some researchers have inferred that paleodemographic tables must be incorrect.

Whether such conclusions are appropriate depends on the nature of the data on which the Coale & Demeny tables were based. The historical mortality profiles that were used had to meet strict standards of accuracy. As a result only 7% of the database populations predated 1870, and of these not one was from outside Europe (Coale & Demeny 1966:7). However, there remained "large variations from the model patterns" especially in the under-10 and over-60 age groups (Coale & Demeny 1966:12). This variation was especially evident in the underrepresented areas of nineteenth-century peasant Europe and in the underdeveloped countries in Asia, Africa, and Latin America. Brass (1971) went on to examine many of the profiles not used in the regional set calculations, such as Mauritius 1942–1946 and Guyana 1945–1947, which had very high adult death rates compared to those expected during childhood. He noted that "social and environmental factors in particular populations could lead to larger deviations from the model experience" (Brass 1971:95).

In any event, these deviations were lost under the mathematical restrictions of the final two-parameter graduations (i.e. region and level). Such modeling may have maximized demographic precision for applications to modern populations, but there remains too little variety in mortality patterns to justify using these models for purposes of generalizing about mortality conditions in anthropological contexts.

Although the vital experiences of European-derived and European-acculturated populations during the past 100 years were recorded accurately, we would argue that they also represented a unique period in human demographic evolution. In particular, human longevity had never been so artificially or rapidly protracted. More important, the extension of the patterns derived from tables with very high life expectancies to populations with much lower values represent extrapolations to levels well beyond the range of observed data (Brass 1971, Weiss 1973). That is, there is no empirical basis to indicate that the shapes of the mortality profiles for, say, Spain in 1900, Taiwan in 1921, or

Sweden in 1851, for which life expectancy at birth exceeded 35 years, actually approximate those of paleodemographic populations with lower life expectancies (Coale & Demeny 1966:29).

Many alternatives are available for smoothing or completing life-table data. Weiss's (1973) tables are a little more flexible; however, they depend to some degree on modern patterns. Gage (1988, 1989, 1998) has developed some hazard models for use in anthropological contexts. These alternatives have some valuable practical and theoretical properties, including the flexibility to smooth life-table data without shoehorning them into modern patterns.

## PREHISTORIC POPULATION GROWTH

A fundamental problem in paleodemography is that for any given prehistoric cemetery (i.e. a distribution of ages at death), each of a continuum of stable populations could have filled it with exactly the same age proportions. These populations may range from high mortality/moderate fertility (with low intrinsic growth or decline) to moderate mortality/high fertility (with high growth), and every gradation in between. The implications are important. For example, what does a very young cemetery age distribution from the period of early adoption of agriculture imply? A moderate increase in fertility signaling the success of a cultigen-based economy and a healthy population growth rate is one possibility. Another is exactly the opposite: a considerable increase in childhood mortality, population decline, and the nutritional limitations of undiversified agricultural products. By itself, the cemetery could be interpreted in either fashion or, more appropriately, in a whole range of fashions.

Bennett (1973), Weiss (1973), and Moore et al (1975) were the first to give archaeologists the practical means under stable population theory for relating the age distribution of a cemetery to a mortality profile through an intrinsic growth rate ($r$, the Malthusian parameter). Weiss (1973) also outlined the calculation of both an age-specific fertility function and the population's age proportions, or pyramid, under assumed conditions of stable growth. The problem is that there is no direct cemetery evidence for fertility, age structure, or intrinsic growth rate. Therefore, in the parlance of elementary algebra, there are more unknowns than equations here, and an exact solution is not possible without more information. A given cemetery does not provide a solution in the sense of one demographic profile but rather a continuum of solutions, each point of which contains a mortality level and a fertility level, with an associated growth level.

Sattenspiel & Harpending (1983) looked at variation in life expectancy and birthrate within several of the Coale & Demeny West models and offered an interesting observation: For stable populations the cemetery age-distribution determines the birthrate but makes no prediction of life expectancy. Mean age at death predicts the reciprocal of the crude birthrate nearly exactly for all (humanly possible) values of the intrinsic rate of growth (i.e. $-1\% < r < +4.0\%$ per year). In other words, the cemetery fixes the crude birthrate, but both mortality and growth are anybody's guess. Johansson & Horowitz (1986) restated this finding and explored more closely the small departures from linearity of the relationships between mean age and life expectancy. Horowitz & Armelagos (1988) showed that the closeness of these approximations is limited to the kinds of conditions that only paleodemographers examine, that is, heavy early mortality.

If fertility is fixed by the cemetery, how can demographers choose a specific mortality level on the continuum of solutions? Bennett's (1973) analysis of Point of Pines, Asch's (1976) approach to Middle Woodland groups in the Lower Illinois Valley, and Muller's (1997) models for the dynamics of late prehistoric populations in the Eastern Woodlands all argued for solutions based on a hypothesized growth rate. However, archaeological support for a single value is exceedingly difficult to find (Horowitz & Armelagos 1988).

Life expectancy at birth ($\bar{e}_0$) is a function of mortality only. By contrast, the crude birth rate ($b$) depends on age-specific fertilities, the age structure of the population, and even the mortality function. We suggest that a hypothesized fertility (or restricted range) be used to complete a demographic reconstruction whenever the use of a growth rate is not feasible. However, as Sattenspiel & Harpending (1983) pointed out, the regression of $b$ on $r$ or on any mortality variable is virtually horizontal. No numerical solution could emerge from a hypothesized crude birth rate; moreover, only one value of $b$ is possible for a given cemetery.

A different fertility measure, one stripped of any influence of maternal mortality or age structure, may be more appropriate. The total fertility rate (TFR) is a measure of completed fertility performance only and has been emphasized in general frameworks by Howell (1976), Roth (1992), Harpending (1997), and Keckler (1997). The TFR represents the average number of live births to women who live to the end of the reproductive span (age 50 years), that is, the sum of the age-specific fertility rates. For purposes of estimation this measure increases too slowly with $r$ in the vicinity of stationarity (i.e. zero growth), but it increases geometrically after growth rates exceed about 1%. Therefore, one problem with this approach is that the only exact solutions possible are high-growth solutions. Another problem is the issue of choosing a value for the TFR, because its variance in anthropological populations is surprisingly large (Wood 1990), an observation that may one day force a reconsideration of the meaning of the term "natural fertility."

An example of this approach is our analysis of the Late-Archaic Ward site cemetery in Kentucky (15McL11), for which we found a mean age of death in the mid-20s (Meindl et al 1998). A hypothesized value of 6.5 children for the

TFR determined both a new life expectancy in the mid-30s and an average nonzero growth rate of 2.5% (It was assumed that only the periods of growth were represented in the cemetery). A value of 2.5% per annum is high but not unusual for well-censused primitive Amerindian populations of the twentieth century (Weiss 1975, Hill & Hurtado 1996). This analysis corresponded to a consensus among Eastern Woodland archaeologists that the first population explosion in Kentucky took place in the Late Archaic (Griffin 1967, Jefferies 1996).

## CONCLUSION

Some of the criticisms leveled recently at osteological paleodemography have been justified. Too many studies had been undertaken using unacceptable skeletal samples. Some demographies were based on skeletal age indicators whose only merit was that they correlated in some way with increasing age. The fundamental observation by modern demographers that fertility changes tend to have far larger impacts on age structure than mortality had gone largely unappreciated by our field. As a result anthropologists had to begin again with what Larry Angel called the "Bases of Paleodemography" (1969).

We have limited our review to the advances in the most fundamental element of this field, the consideration of age-at-death distributions. And while there have been improvements in the field, there is more work to be done. First, skeletal aging methods for the oldest decedents in a cemetery must be further developed and refined, and we must recognize the fact that many traditional aging methodologies will never be able to contribute here. Second, paleodemographers must borrow fertility and growth parameters from living anthropological populations more freely in order to complete their inferences from skeletal age-at-death distributions. And last, paleodemography, a "valid, specialized subfield of demography" (Roth 1992:175), should now assert itself. Its data should not be forced into modern industrialized demographic profiles without some empirical justification. If the demographic patterns of prehistory were fundamentally different, archaeological demographers should reserve the opportunity to detect them.

ACKNOWLEDGMENTS

We thank Owen Lovejoy and Alan Swedlund for critical readings of this manuscript. Henry Harpending gave helpful comments on the "Growth" section. These scholars have been influential in the field of paleodemography and have improved this paper.

Visit the *Annual Reviews home page* at
http://www.AnnualReviews.org.

## Literature Cited

Acsádi G, Nemeskéri J. 1970. *History of Human Life Span and Mortality.* Budapest: Hung. Acad. Soc. 346 pp.

Ahlqvist J, Damsten O. 1969. A modification of Kerley's method for the microscopic determination of age in bone. *J. Forensic Sci.* 14:205–12

Aiello LC, Molleson T. 1993. Are microscopic ageing techniques more accurate than macroscopic ageing techniques? *J. Archaeol. Sci.* 20:689–704

Angel JL. 1969. The bases of paleodemography. *Am. J. Phys. Anthropol.* 30:427–37

Arsuaga JL, Carretero JM. 1994. Multivariate analysis of the sexual dimorphism of the hip bone in a modern human population and in early hominids. *Am. J. Phys. Anthropol.* 93:241–57

Asch DL. 1976. *The Middle Woodland Populations of the Lower Illinois Valley: A Study in Paleodemographic Methods.* Northwest. Univ. Archaeol. Program, Sci. Pap. No. 1. 99 pp.

Bang G. 1989. Age changes in teeth: developmental and regressive. See İşcan 1989b, pp. 211–35

Bedford ME, Russell KF, Lovejoy CO, Meindl RS, Simpson SW, Stuart-Macadam PL. 1993. A test of the multifactorial aging method using skeletons with known ages at death from the Grant Collection. *Am. J. Phys. Anthropol.* 91:287–97

Bennett KA. 1973. On the estimation of some demographic characteristics on a prehistoric population from the American Southwest. *Am. J. Phys. Anthropol.* 39:223–32

Berrizbeitia BA. 1989. Sex determination with the head of the radius. *J. Forensic Sci.* 34:1206–13

Black TK. 1978. A new method for assessing the sex of fragmentary skeletal remains: femoral shaft circumference. *Am. J. Phys. Anthropol.* 48:227–31

Bocquet-Appel JP, Masset C. 1982. Farewell to paleodemography. *J. Hum. Evol.* 11: 321–33

Bocquet-Appel JP, Masset C. 1996. Paleodemography: expectancy and false hope. *Am. J. Phys. Anthropol.* 99:571–83

Brass W. 1971. On the scale of mortality. In *Biological Aspects of Demography,* ed. W Brass, pp. 69–110. London: Taylor & Francis

Brooks ST. 1955. Skeletal age at death: the reliability of cranial and pubic age indicators. *Am. J. Phys. Anthropol.* 13:567–89

Budinoff LC, Tague RG. 1990. Anatomical and developmental bases for the ventral arc of the human pubis. *Am. J. Phys. Anthropol.* 82:73–79

Buikstra JE. 1997. Paleodemography: context and promise. See Paine 1997, pp. 367–80

Buikstra JE, Konigsberg LW. 1985. Paleodemography: critiques and controversies. *Am. Anthropol.* 87:316–33

Buikstra JE, Konigsberg LW, Bullington J. 1986. Fertility and the development of agriculture in the prehistoric midwest. *Am. Antiq.* 51:528–46

Buikstra JE, Mielke JH. 1985. Demography, diet, and health. In *The Analysis of Prehistoric Diets,* ed. RI Gilbert, JH Mielke, pp. 359–422. Orlando, FL: Academic

Coale AJ, Demeny P. 1966. *Regional Model Life Tables and Stable Populations.* Princeton, NJ: Princeton Univ. Press. 871 pp.

Coale AJ, Demeny P, Vaughan B. 1983. *Regional Model Life Tables and Stable Populations.* New York: Academic, 496 pp.

Cohen MN. 1997. Does paleopathology measure community health? A rebuttal of "The osteological paradox" and its implications for world history. See Paine 1997, pp. 242–60

Condon K, Charles DK, Cheverud JM, Buikstra JE. 1986. Cementum annulation and age determination in *Homo sapiens.* II. Estimates and accuracy. *Am. J. Phys. Anthropol.* 71:321–30

Corruccini RS, Brandon EM, Handler JS. 1989. Inferring fertility from relative mortality in historically controlled cemetery remains from Barbados. *Am. Antiq.* 54: 609–14

Demirjian A, Goldstein H, Tanner JM. 1973. A new system of dental age assessment. *Hum. Biol.* 45:211–17

Demirjian A, Levesque G-Y. 1980. Sexual differences in dental development and prediction of emergence. *J. Dent. Res.* 59: 1110–26

Dittrick J, Suchey JM. 1986. Sex determination of prehistoric central California skeletal remains using discriminant analysis of the femur and humerus. *Am. J. Phys. Anthropol.* 70:3–9

Divale W, Harris M. 1976. Population, warfare, and the male supremacist complex. *Am. Anthropol.* 78:521–38

Dudar JC, Pfeiffer S, Saunders SR. 1993. Evaluation of morphological and histological adult skeletal age-at-death estimation techniques using ribs. *J. Forensic Sci.* 38:677–85

Dumond DE. 1997. Seeking demographic

causes for changes in population growth rates. See Paine 1997, pp. 175–90

El-Nofely A, İşcan MY. 1989. Assessment of age from the dentition in children. See İşcan 1989b, pp. 237–54

Falsetti AB. 1995. Sex assessment from metacarpals of the human hand. *J. Forensic Sci.* 40:774–76

Fernández Camacho FJ, Gómez Pellico L, Fernández-Valencia Rodríguez R. 1993. Osteometry of the human iliac crest: patterns of normality and its utility in sexing human remains. *J. Forensic Sci.* 38: 779–87

Frost HM. 1987. Secondary osteon populations: algorithm for determining mean bone tissue age. *Yearb. Phys. Anthropol.* 30:221–38

Gage TB. 1988. Mathematical hazard models of mortality: an alternative to model life tables. *Am. J. Phys. Anthropol.* 76:429–41

Gage TB. 1989. Bio-mathematical approaches to the study of human variation in mortality. *Yearb. Phys. Anthropol.* 32:185–214

Gage TB. 1998. Aggregate patterns of variation in human demography. *Annu. Rev. Anthropol.* 27:197–221

Garland AN. 1987. A histological study of archaeological bone decomposition. In *Death, Decay and Reconstruction: Approaches to Archaeology and Forensic Science,* ed. A Boddington, AC Garland, RC Janaway, pp. 109–26. Manchester, UK: Manchester Univ. Press

Gilbert BM, McKern TW. 1973. A method for aging the female *os pubis. Am. J. Phys. Anthropol.* 38:31–38

Giles E, Elliot O. 1963. Sex determination by discriminant function analysis of crania. *Am. J. Phys. Anthropol.* 21:53–68

Giles E, Klepinger LL. 1988. Confidence intervals for estimates based on linear regression in forensic anthropology. *J. Forensic Sci.* 33:1218–22

Goodman A, Lallo J, Armelagos GJ, Rose JC. 1984. Health changes at Dickson Mounds, Illinois (A.D. 950–1300). In *Paleopathology at the Origins of Agriculture,* ed. MN Cohen, GJ Armelagos, pp. 271–306. New York: Academic

Gordon CC, Buikstra JE. 1981. Soil pH, bone preservation, and sampling bias at mortuary sites. *Am. Antiq.* 46:566–71

Griffin JB. 1967. Eastern North American archaeology: a summary. *Science* 156: 175–91

Gustafson G. 1950. Age determination of teeth. *J. Am. Dent. Assoc.* 41:45–54

Gustafson G, Koch G. 1974. Age estimation up to 16 years of age based on dental development. *Odontol. Revy* 25:297–306

Hamilton ME. 1982. Sexual dimorphism in skeletal samples. In *Sexual Dimorphism in Homo sapiens,* ed. RL Hall, pp. 107–63. New-York: Praeger

Hanihara K, Suzuki T. 1978. Estimation of age from the pubic symphysis by means of multiple regression analysis. *Am. J. Phys. Anthropol.* 48:233–40

Hanna RE, Washburn SL. 1953. The determination of the sex of skeletons, as illustrated by a study of the Eskimo pelvis. *Hum. Biol.* 25:21–27

Hanson DB, Buikstra JE. 1987. Histomorphological alteration in buried human bone from the Lower Illinois Valley: implications for paleodietary research. *J. Archaeol. Sci.* 14:549–63

Harpending H. 1997. Living records of past population change. See Paine 1997, pp. 89–100

Harrison GA, Weiner JS, Tanner JM, Barnicot NA. 1977. *Human Biology.* Oxford: Oxford Univ. Press. 499 pp. 2nd ed.

Hill K, Hurtado AM. 1996. *Ache Life History.* New York: Aldine de Gruyter. 561 pp.

Holland TD. 1991. Sex assessment using the proximal tibia. *Am. J. Phys. Anthropol.* 85:221–27

Holman DJ, Bennett KA. 1991. Determination of sex from arm bone measurements. *Am. J. Phys. Anthropol.* 84:421–26

Horowitz S, Armelagos G, Wachter K. 1988. On generating birth rates from skeletal populations. *Am. J. Phys. Anthropol.* 76: 189–96

Howell N. 1976. Toward a uniformitarian theory of human paleodemography. In *The Demographic Evolution of Human Populations,* ed. RH Ward, KM Weiss, pp. 25–40. New York: Academic

Howell N. 1982. Village composition implied by a paleodemographic life table. *Am. J. Phys. Anthropol.* 59:263–69

Hrdlička A. 1952. *Practical Anthropometry.* Philadelphia, PA: Wistar Inst. Anat. Biol. 241 pp. 4th ed.

İşcan MY. 1989a. Research strategies in age estimation: the multiregional approach. See İşcan 1989b, pp. 325–39

İşcan MY, ed. 1989b. *Age Markers in the Human Skeleton.* Springfield, IL: Thomas

İşcan MY, Loth SR. 1986. Estimation of age and determination of sex from the sternal rib. In *Forensic Osteology: Advances in the Identification of Human Remains,* ed. KJ Reichs, pp. 68–89. Springfield, IL: Thomas

İşcan MY, Kennedy KAR, eds. 1989. *Reconstruction of Life from the Skeleton.* New York: Liss

İşcan MY, Loth SR. 1989. Osteological manifestations of age in the adult. See İşcan & Kennedy 1989, pp. 23–40

İşcan MY, Loth SR, Wright RK. 1984a. Metamorphosis at the sternal rib end: a new method to estimate age at death in white males. *Am. J. Phys. Anthropol.* 65:147–56

İşcan MY, Loth SR, Wright RK. 1984b. Age estimation from the rib by phase analysis: white males. *J. Forensic Sci.* 29:1094–104

İşcan MY, Loth SR, Wright RK. 1987. Racial variation in the external extremity of the rib and its effect on age determination. *J. Forensic Sci.* 32:452–66

Israel H. 1973. Age factor and the pattern of change in craniofacial structures. *Am. J. Phys. Anthropol.* 39:111–28

Israel H. 1977. The dichotomous pattern of craniofacial expansion during aging. *Am. J. Phys. Anthropol.* 47:47–52

Jackes MK. 1985. Pubic symphysis age distributions. *Am. J. Phys. Anthropol.* 68:281–99

Jackes MK. 1992. Paleodemography: problems and techniques. See Saunders & Katzenberg 1992, pp. 189–224

Jackes MK. 1993. On paradox and osteology. *Curr. Anthropol.* 34:434–39

Jefferies RW. 1996. Hunters and gatherers after the Ice Age. In *Kentucky Archaeology,* ed. RB Lewis, pp. 39–77. Lexington: Univ. Press Kentucky

Johansson SR, Horowitz S. 1986. Estimating mortality in skeletal populations: influence of the growth rate on the interpretation of levels and trends during the transition to agriculture. *Am. J. Phys. Anthropol.* 71:233–50

Johnstone FE, Zimmer LO. 1989. Assessment of growth and age in the immature skeleton. See İşcan & Kennedy 1989, pp. 11–21

Kajanoja P. 1966. Determination of Finnish crania by discriminant function analysis. *Am. J. Phys. Anthropol.* 24:29–34

Katz D, Suchey JM. 1986. Age determination of the male *Os pubis. Am. J. Phys. Anthropol.* 69:427–35

Katz D, Suchey JM. 1989. Race differences in pubic symphyseal aging patterns in the male. *Am. J. Phys. Anthropol.* 80:167–72

Keckler CNW. 1997. Catastrophic mortality in simulations of forager age at death: Where did all the humans go? See Paine 1997, pp. 205–28

Kerley ER. 1965. The microscopic determination of age in human bone. *Am. J. Phys. Anthropol.* 23:149–64

Kerley ER, Ubelaker DH. 1978. Revisions in the microscopic method of estimating age at death in human cortical bone. *Am. J. Phys. Anthropol.* 49:545–46

Kieser JA, Groeneveld HT, Preston CB. 1985.

Patterns of dental wear in the Lengua Indians of Paraguay. *Am. J. Phys. Anthropol.* 66:21–29

Kieser JA, Moggi-Cecchi J, Groeneveld HT. 1992. Sex allocation of skeletal material by analysis of the proximal tibia. *J. Forensic Sci.* 56:29–36

Konigsberg LW, Frankenberg SR. 1992. Estimation of age structure in anthropological demography. *Am. J. Phys. Anthropol.* 89:235–56

Konigsberg LW, Frankenberg SR. 1994. Paleodemography: "Not quite dead." *Evol. Anthropol.* 3:92–105

Konigsberg LW, Frankenberg SR, Walker RB. 1997. Regress what on what? Paleodemographic age estimation as a calibration problem. See Paine 1997, pp. 64–88

Krogman WM. 1962. *The Human Skeleton in Forensic Medicine.* Springfield, IL: Thomas. 337 pp.

Krogman WM, İşcan MY. 1986. *The Human Skeleton in Forensic Medicine.* Springfield, IL: Thomas. 2nd ed. 568 pp.

Lazenby RA. 1994. Identification of sex from metacarpals: effect of side asymmetry. *J. Forensic Sci.* 39:1188–94

Leslie P, Gage TB. 1989. Demography and human population biology: problems and progress. In *Human Population Biology: A Trandisciplinary Science,* ed. M Little, JD Haas, pp. 15–44. New York: Oxford Univ. Press

Leutenegger W. 1982. Encephalization and obstetrics in primates with particular reference to human evolution. In *Primate Brain Evolution,* ed. E Armstrong, D Falk, pp. 85–95. New York: Plenum

Lovejoy CO. 1985. Dental wear in the Libben population: its functional pattern and role in the determination of adult skeletal age at death. *Am. J. Phys. Anthropol.* 68:47–56

Lovejoy CO, Meindl RS, Mensforth RP, Barton TJ. 1985a. Multifactorial determination of skeletal age at death: a method and blind tests of its accuracy. *Am. J. Phys. Anthropol.* 68:1–14

Lovejoy CO, Meindl RS, Pryzbeck TR, Barton TS, Heiple KG, Kotting D. 1977. Paleodemography of the Libben site, Ottawa County, Ohio. *Science* 198:291–93

Lovejoy CO, Meindl RS, Pryzbeck TR, Mensforth RP. 1985b. Chronological metamorphosis of the auricular surface of the ilium: a new method for the determination of adult skeletal age at death. *Am. J. Phys. Anthropol.* 68:15–28

Lovejoy CO, Meindl RS, Tague RG, Latimer B. 1995. The senescent biology of the hominoid pelvis: its bearing on the pubic symphysis and auricular surface as age-at-death indicators in the human skeleton. *Riv. Antropol.* 73:31–49

Lovejoy CO, Meindl RS, Tague RG, Latimer B. 1997. The comparative senescent biology of the hominoid pelvis and its implications for the use of age-at-death indicators in the human skeleton. See Paine 1997, pp. 43–63

Lovell NC. 1989. Test of Phenice's technique for determining sex from the *Os pubis. Am. J. Phys. Anthropol.* 79:117–20

Lucy D, Aykroyd RG, Pollard AM, Solheim T. 1996. A Bayesian approach to adult human age estimation from dental observations by Johanson's age changes. *J. Forensic Sci.* 41(2):189–94

Luo Y-C. 1995. Sex determination from the pubis by discriminant function analysis. *Forensic Sci. Int.* 74:89–98

Maples WR. 1978. An improved technique using dental histology for estimation of adult age. *J. Forensic Sci.* 23:764–70

Maples WR, Rice PM. 1979. Some difficulties in the Gustafson dental age estimations. *J. Forensic Sci.* 24:168–72

Marino EA. 1995. Sex estimation using the first cervical vertebra. *Am. J. Phys. Anthropol.* 97:127–33

Masset C. 1973. Influence du sexe et de l'âge sur la conservation des os humains. In *L'Homme, Hier et Aujourd'hui: Recueil d'études en Hommage à André Leroi-Gourhan,* ed. M Sauter, pp. 333–43. Paris: Cujas

Masset C. 1989. Age estimation on the basis of cranial sutures. See İşcan 1989b, pp. 71–103

McKern TW, Stewart TD. 1957. *Skeletal age changes in young American males.* Quartermaster Res. and Dev. Command Tech. Rep. EP–45. Natick, MA

Meindl RS, Lovejoy CO. 1985. Ectocranial suture closure: a revised method for the determination of skeletal age at death based on the lateral-anterior sutures. *Am. J. Phys. Anthropol.* 68:57–66

Meindl RS, Lovejoy CO. 1989. Age changes in the pelvis: implications for paleodemography. See İşcan 1989b, pp. 137–68

Meindl RS, Lovejoy CO, Mensforth RP. 1983. Skeletal age at death: accuracy of determination and implications for human demography. *Hum. Biol.* 55:73–87

Meindl RS, Lovejoy CO, Mensforth RP, Don Carlos L. 1985a. Accuracy and direction of error in the sexing of the skeleton: implications for paleodemography. *Am. J. Phys. Anthropol.* 68:79–85

Meindl RS, Lovejoy CO, Mensforth RP, Walker RA. 1985b. A revised method of age determination using the os pubis, with a review and tests of accuracy of other current methods of pubic symphyseal aging. *Am. J. Phys. Anthropol.* 68:29–45

Meindl RS, Mensforth RP, York H. 1998. Mortality, fertility, and growth in the Kentucky Archaic: the paleodemography of the Ward site, McLean County. In *Hunters-Gatherers to Horticulturalists,* ed. K Vickery. Columbus, OH: Ohio Archaeological Council. In press.

Meindl RS, Russell KF, Lovejoy CO. 1990. Reliability of age at death in the Hamann-Todd collection: validity of subselection procedures used in blind tests of the summary age technique. *Am. J. Phys. Anthropol.* 83:349–57

Mensforth RP. 1990. Paleodemography of the Carlston-Annis (Bt-5) Late Archaic skeletal population. *Am. J. Phys. Anthropol.* 82: 81–99

Mensforth RP, Lovejoy CO. 1985. Anatomical, physiological, and epidemiological correlates of the aging process: a confirmation of multifactorial age determination in the Libben skeletal population. *Am. J. Phys. Anthropol.* 68:87–106

Miles AEW. 1963. The dentition in the assessment of individual age in skeletal materials. In *Dental Anthropology,* ed. DR Brothwell, pp. 191–209. New York: Pergamon

Milner GR, Humpf DA, Harpending HC. 1989. Pattern matching of age-at-death distributions in paleodemographic analysis. *Am. J. Phys. Anthropol.* 80:49–58

Moore JA, Swedlund AC, Armelagos GJ. 1975. The use of life tables in paleodemography. *Am. Antiq.* 40:57–70

Moorrees CFA, Fanning EA, Hunt EE. 1963a. Formation and resorption of three deciduous teeth in children. *Am. J. Phys. Anthropol.* 21:205–13

Moorrees CFA, Fanning EA, Hunt EE. 1963b. Age variation of formation stages for ten permanent teeth. *J. Dent. Res.* 42: 1490–1502

Muller J. 1997. Native Eastern American population continuity and stability. See Paine 1997, pp. 343–64

Murphy TR. 1959. The changing pattern of dentine exposure in human tooth attrition. *Am. J. Phys. Anthropol.* 17:167–85

Murray KA, Murray TM. 1991. A test of the auricular surface aging technique. *J. Forensic Sci.* 36:1162–69

Oliver G. 1969. *Practical Anthropology.* Springfield, IL: Thomas. 330 pp.

Owsley DW, Webb RS. 1983. Misclassification probability of dental discriminant functions for sex determination. *J. Forensic Sci.* 28:181–85

Paine RR. 1989. Model life table fitting by maximum likelihood estimation: a procedure to reconstruct paleodemographic characteristics from skeletal age distributions. *Am. J. Phys. Anthropol.* 79:51–62

Paine RR, ed. 1997. *Integrating Archaeological Demography: Multidisciplinary Approaches to Prehistoric Population.* Carbondale: South. Ill. Univ. 395 pp.

Pfeiffer S. 1986. Morbidity and mortality in the Uxbridge ossuary. *Can. J. Anthropol.* 5:23–31

Pfeiffer S. 1992. Cortical bone age estimates from historically known adults. *Z. Morphol. Anthropol.* 79:1–10

Phenice TW. 1969. A newly developed visual method of sexing the *Os pubis. Am. J. Phys. Anthropol.* 30:297–301

Richman EA, Michel ME, Schulter-Ellis FP, Corruccini RS. 1979. Determination of sex by discriminant function analysis of postcranial skeletal measurements. *J. Forensic Sci.* 24:159–67

Rogers T. 1990. *A test of the auricular surface method of estimating age-at-death and a discussion of its usefulness in the construction of paleodemographic lifetables.* Presented at 18th Annu. Meet. Can. Assoc. Phys. Anthropol., Banff, Alberta

Rogers T, Saunders S. 1994. Accuracy of sex determination using morphological traits of the human pelvis. *J. Forensic Sci.* 39:1047–56

Roth EA. 1992. Applications of demographic models to paleodemography. See Saunders & Katzenberg 1992, pp. 175–88

Russell KF. 1996. *Determination of age-at-death from dental remains.* PhD thesis. Kent State Univ., Ohio

Russell KF, Simpson SW, Genovese J, Kinkel MD, Meindl RS, Lovejoy CO. 1993. Independent test of the fourth rib aging technique. *Am. J. Phys. Anthropol.* 92: 53–62

Sattenspiel L, Harpending H. 1983. Stable populations and skeletal age. *Am. Antiq.* 48:489–98

Saunders SR. 1992. Subadult skeletons and growth related studies. See Saunders & Katzenberg 1992, pp. 1–20

Saunders SR, DeVito C, Herring DA, Southern R, Hoppa R. 1993. Accuracy tests of tooth formation age estimations for human skeletal remains. *Am. J. Phys. Anthropol.* 92:173–88

Saunders SR, Fitzgerald C, Rogers T, Dudar JC, McKillop H. 1992. A test of several methods of skeletal age estimation using a documented archaeological sample. *Can. Soc. Forensic Sci.* 25:97–118

Saunders SR, Katzenberg MA. 1992. *Skeletal*

*Biology of Past Peoples: Research Methods.* New York: Wiley-Liss

Scheuer JL, Elkington NM. 1993. Sex determination from metacarpals and the first proximal phalanx. *J. Forensic Sci.* 38: 769–78

Schulter-Ellis FP, Schmidt DJ, Hayek IA, Craig J. 1983. Determination of sex with a discriminant analysis of new pelvic bone measurements: part I. *J. Forensic Sci.* 28: 169–80

Schwartz JH. 1995. *Skeleton Keys: An Introduction to Human Skeletal Morphology, Development, and Analysis.* Oxford: Oxford Univ. Press. 362 pp.

Scrimshaw SCM. 1984. Infanticide in human populations: societal and individual concerns. In *Infanticide: Comparative and Evolutionary Perspectives,* ed. G Hausfater, SB Hrdy, pp. 439–62. New York: Aldine

Singer R. 1953. Estimation of age from cranial suture closure. *J. Foren. Med.* 1:52–59

Singh IJ. 1972. Femoral cortical trabecular pattern of the upper end of the femur as an index of osteoporosis. *J. Bone J. Surg. A* 52:457–67

Singh IJ, Gunberg DL. 1970. Estimation of age at death in human males from quantitative histology of bone fragments. *Am. J. Phys. Anthropol.* 33:373–82

Siven CH. 1991. On estimating mortalities from osteological age data. *Int. J. Anthropol.* 6:97–110

Smith BH. 1984. Patterns of molar wear in hunter-gatherers and agriculturalists. *Am. J. Phys. Anthropol.* 63:39–56

Song H-W, Lin QL, Jia JT. 1992. Sex diagnosis of Chinese skulls using multiple stepwise discriminant function analysis. *Forensic Sci. Int.* 54:135–40

Steele DG. 1976. The estimation of sex on the basis of the talus and calcaneous. *Am. J. Phys. Anthropol.* 45:581–88

Stewart TD. 1979. *Essentials of Forensic Anthropology: Especially as Developed in the United States.* Springfield, IL: Thomas. 300 pp.

Stini WA. 1985. Growth rates and sexual dimorphism in evolutionary perspective. In *The Analysis of Prehistoric Diets,* ed. RI Gilbert, JH Mielke, pp. 191–226. Orlando, FL: Academic

Stout SD. 1992. Methods of determining age at death using bone microstructure. See Saunders & Katzenberg 1992, pp. 21–35

Stout SD, Paine RR. 1992. Histological age estimation using rib and clavicle. *Am. J. Phys. Anthropol.* 87:111–15

Suchey JM, Wiseley DV, Katz D. 1986. Evaluation of the Todd and McKern-

Stewart methods for aging the male os pubis. In *Forensic Osteology,* ed. KJ Reichs, pp. 33–67. Springfield, IL: Thomas

Sullivan NC. 1997. Contact period Huron demography. See Paine 1997, pp. 327–42

Sundick RI. 1978. Human skeletal growth and age determination. *Homo* 29:228–49

Sutherland LD, Suchey JM. 1991. Use of the ventral arc in pubic sex determination. *J. Forensic Sci.* 36:501–11

Tague RG. 1989. Variation in pelvic size between males and females. *Am. J. Phys. Anthropol.* 80:59–71

Tague RG. 1991. Commonalities in dimorphism and variability in the anthropoid pelvis, with implications for the fossil record. *J. Hum. Evol.* 21:153–76

Tague RG, Lovejoy CO. 1986. The obstetric pelvis of A.L.288-1 (Lucy). *J. Hum. Evol.* 15:237–55

Thompson DD. 1979. The core technique in the determination of age at death in skeletons. *J. Forensic Sci.* 24:902–15

Todd TW. 1920. Age changes in the pubic bone: I. The white male pubis. *Am. J. Phys. Anthropol.* 3:285–34

Todd TW. 1921a. Age changes in the pubic bone: II. The pubis of the male Negro-white hybrid; III. The pubis of the white female; IV. The pubis of the female Negro-white hybrid. *Am. J. Phys. Anthropol.* 4: 1–70

Todd TW. 1921b. Age changes in the pubic bone: V. Mammalian pubic metamorphosis. *Am. J. Phys. Anthropol.* 4:333–406

Townsend N, Hammel EA. 1990. Age estimation from the number of teeth erupted in young children: an aid to demographic surveys. *Demography* 27:165–74

Ubelaker DH. 1989. *Human Skeletal Remains: Excavation, Analysis, and Interpretation.* Washington, DC: Taraxacum. 116 pp. 2nd ed.

Uesugi Y, Taguchi O, Noumura T, Iguchi T. 1992. Effects of sex steroids on the development of sexual dimorphism in mouse innominate bone. *Anat. Rec.* 234:541–48

Van Gerven DP, Armelagos GJ. 1983. Farewell to paleodemography? Rumors of its

death have been greatly exaggerated. *J. Hum. Evol.* 12:353–60

Waldron T. 1987. The relative survival of the human skeleton: implications for paleopathology. In *Death, Decay, and Reconstruction: Approaches to Archaeology and Forensic Science,* ed. A Boddington, AN Garland, RC Janeway, pp. 55–64. Manchester, UK: Manchester Univ. Press

Walker PL, Johnson JR, Lambert PM. 1988. Age and sex biases in the preservation of human skeletal remains. *Am. J. Phys. Anthropol.* 76:183–88

Walker RA. 1989. *Assessments of human cortical bone dynamics and skeletal age at death from femoral cortical histomorphology.* PhD thesis. Kent State Univ., Ohio

Walker RA, Lovejoy CO. 1985. Radiographic changes in the clavicle and proximal femur and their use in the determination of skeletal age at death. *Am. J. Phys. Anthropol.* 68:67–78

Walker RA, Lovejoy CO, Meindl RS. 1994. Histomorphological and geometric properties of human femoral cortex in individuals over 50: implications for determination of age-at-death. *Am. J. Hum. Biol.* 6: 659–67

Weiss KM. 1972. On the systematic bias in skeletal sexing. *Am. J. Phys. Anthropol.* 37:239–50

Weiss KM. 1973. *Demographic Models for Anthropology.* Mem. 27 Soc. Am. Archaeol.; also *Am. Antiq.* 38:2, Part II. 186 pp.

Weiss KM. 1975. The application of demographic models to anthropological data. *Hum. Ecol.* 3:87–103

Weiss KM. 1989. A survey of human biodemography. *J. Quant. Anthropol.* 1:79–151

White TD. 1991. *Human Osteology.* San Diego: Academic. 455 pp.

Wood JW. 1990. Fertility in anthropological populations. *Annu. Rev. Anthropol.* 19: 211–42

Wood JW, Milner GR, Harpending HC, Weiss KM. 1992. The osteological paradox. *Curr. Anthropol.* 33:343–70

Annu. Rev. Anthropol. 1998. 27:401–26
Copyright 1998 by Annual Reviews. All rights reserved

# CONTEMPORARY TRANSFORMATIONS OF LOCAL LINGUISTIC COMMUNITIES

*M. Silverstein*

Department of Anthropology, University of Chicago, Chicago, Illinois 60637-1539;
e-mail: m-silverstein@uchicago.edu

KEY WORDS: language communities, language shift, minority languages, linguistic ideology, language norms

---

## ABSTRACT

An emergent focus of linguistic anthropological research is discernible in the investigation of the causes and consequences of contact of local language communities with forces of the wider polities in which they have become incorporated. This focus can be sketched by surveying a number of its component conceptual approaches, such as anthropological linguistics, ethnography of communication, variationist sociolinguistics, and the sociology and politics of languages. Its consideration of language as a total cultural fact is outlined by reference to studies that differentially emphasize language structure, entextualization/contextualization of language, and language ideology.

---

## INTRODUCTION

This chapter is a status report of a subdisciplinary focus emerging more and more distinctly in the last 10 to 15 years. It is the dynamic linguistic anthropology of what we might term "local language communities" investigated as dialectically constituted cultural forms. This emergent linguistic anthropology reconceptualizes phenomena of language structure and use that have separately and severally long been staples of one or another captioned field of scientific discourse. Partaking of the trends in the larger field of sociocultural anthropology, this linguistic anthropology is refashioning the synchronic structuralisms and functionalisms (both structural-functionalism and reductive functional-

401

0084-6570/98/1015-0401$08.00

ism) of earlier approaches (Williams 1990). It takes literally the proposition that through social action, people participate in semiotic processes that produce their identities, beliefs, and their particular senses of agentive subjectivity. It considers culture to be a virtual—and always emergent—site in sociohistorical spacetime with respect to the essentialisms of which such agents experience their groupness.

Studying cultural process—viewed at whatever temporal scale—thus reveals culture, indexed by people's dialectical working through matters of practical social concern visible in individual, aggregate, and corporate perspectives. In such cultural process, moreover, language is at once an aspect of people's focused concern as agentive subjects, as well as perhaps the very most central semiotic medium or modality through which those cultural processes are, as it were, articulable and articulated. Language seems potentially to bear an inherently double relationship to the larger cultural processes of which it is both emblematic and enabling.

In such fashion, we now understand that entities that are called "languages" are sociocultural constructs for linguistic, as for more general sociocultural, anthropology. Languages are only relatively stable—hence, when perduring, classifiable—outcomes of dialectical valorizing processes among populations of people; like all culture, these processes are semiotic in their essence [see Gal & Irvine 1995; Irvine & Gal 1994; Silverstein 1996a (1987)]. Viewed in this way, the language community also appears in its proper light. We can see that language communities are groups of people by degree evidencing allegiance to norms of denotational (aka "referential," "propositional," "semantic") language usage, however much or little such allegiance also encompasses an indigenous cultural consciousness of variation and/or change, or is couched in terms of fixity and stasis. Such language communities emerge, perdure, and even disappear over the course of sociocultural process affecting aggregate populations. The language community, and hence its language, can be seen as a precipitate of sociocultural process. As so precipitated, moreover, denotational language provides us a route of access to cultural process unmatched by any other.

This view opens to us whole new ways of conceptualizing and investigating traditional problems of linguistics, both synchronic and historical, of sociolinguistics, of the sociology of language, and of the role of language in various phenomena particularly characterizing contemporary human experience. What does it mean in these terms for a group to "lose their language," for a group to change the "functional repertoire" of languages within their overall communicative economy? What does the encounter of two or more "languages" entail for their speakers in a contact community or in a relatively stable plurilingual speech community? What is the genesis of so-called "mixed languages?" Of so-called "pidgins" and "Creole languages?"

For a very long time, these questions have been amply illustrated in various descriptive and even theorizing studies which, however, have cast them neither in sociocultural nor, certainly, in processual semiotic terms. The recent period of ferment in the social sciences of language has been characterized by an emerging shift in our disciplinary consciousness of such problems. In dialogue with issues that have arisen in and have been made acute by earlier studies, exemplary, ethnographically based, and historically informed work has been produced that opens the issues to broader sociocultural debate as it continues to render discursive practice a paradigmatic case for understanding cultural process.

To be sure, disciplinary linguistics during this period, both in its self-styled "formalist" guise and in its self-styled "functionalist" one, has moved more and more to its telos of pure intensionalism centered in the individual mind (sometimes seen in relation to an other; compare so-called "speech act" approaches). Consequently, one must look to the social sciences of language, which are centered in issues congenial to sociology, to anthropology, and to political science. Such approaches worry about the fundamental conceptual terms on which to rest understanding of the aggregate and even collective properties of communication as the presenting phenomena where "language," and everything dependent on it, actually live.

## DEFINITIONAL ISSUES

Let us look at some of the definitional issues of the phenomena we are here concerned with before passing on to the dialogue of linguistic anthropology with other discourses that have focused on one or another of the aspects of the problems of "local" "language communities" and their contemporary transformations.

### Locality

Language communities, relativistically speaking, are "local" when they are perduringly bounded through cultural means in relation to sociopolitical processes on a global scale. As Appadurai (1996) has astutely reminded us, increasingly for populations of people, locality is and must be precipitated as a positive dimension of cultural being, for each person an identity-relevant dimension of belonging to a particular group that otherwise can be defined only residually or negatively. Indeed, "locality" becomes for a group of people an assumed property of self-ascriptions of having a particular "culture." By contrast, such global-scale processes as (a) the formation of empires and then, postcolonially, of nation-states and their internal political orders; (b) the emergence of global economies and communicational patterns, with intensifying commodification of information; and (c) the emergence and consciousness of diasporization or mosaic-like world distributions of people bearing multiple "cultural" allegiances, render the fact of locality problematic or at least threaten a new residualness for those whose consciousness has not been mobilized into these processes. Groups of people are increasingly challenged to have newly active, positive cultural processes emanating from centering institutions, so that what we have here termed the relative and seemingly residual fact of locality gets semiotically turned into a positive attribute of their identity. It is thus the production of a characteristically ethnogeographic and ethnohistorical sense of community boundedness about a "center" that constitutes locality as a cultural fact.

In these processes, we can contrast such "global" language communities as the English language community, the Spanish, the Russian, and the Hindi-Urdu, and such "national" language communities as the Tok Pisin language community, the Modern Hebrew, the Lithuanian, and the Bahasa Indonesia. For these languages are structured as vehicles (emblematic semiotic sites) and mechanisms (codes-over-channels) of encompassing institutionalized projects of their respective mass sociopolitical orders. In relation to such global and national language communities, language communities are thus "local" only to the extent that within a group of communicating people there is a process that produces a contrastive and positive sense of their participation in their own language community. "Locality" of language community is only a relationally produced state in a cultural-ideological order.

Ironically, for hundreds of years nation-states and imperial regimes have sought to borrow from such communities a figuration of their very locality as a mechanism for stimulating in their subjects the "imagination" necessary for hegemony over them; hence, what to do with genuinely local language communities in such national and imperial orders has been a problem of some longstanding duration. In such circumstances, for local language communities, locality must emerge from within, and is inherently only as stable as the processes that produce cultural concepts, semiotically both positive and negative, of anchored, or centered, and graduated inclusiveness of a distinctly imaginable collective experience of using a "language," a denotational code.

Consider, for example, cases wherein dominant cultural notions of "purism" of language constitute the mode of allegiance of people to a denotational code, even in the face of much plurilingualism in a speech community. To the degree such purism is grounded in beliefs about restricted access to a code because of some cosmic essence shared by a restricted population, which essence requires emblematic semiotic propitiation through regimes of purification of language, we have a case of a local language community that has come into being no matter what the state of residualness by which an outsider might recognize a language in some material economic or political institutional orders.

"Local" language communities do not exist in a state of nature; the very concept of locality as opposed to globality presupposes a contrastive consciousness of self-other placement that is part of a cultural project of groupness.

In linguistic terms, scholarly and scientific consciousness of "local" languages has emerged in various projects of mapping diversity on behalf of some (generally politically interested) project. That is, scholarly consciousness has in effect contributed to the production of (cultural) locality in the contemporary world by associating, for particular eras or phases of Western historical imagination, particular, geopolitically conceptualized, bounded swatches of the earth attached to particular labels for "languages"—and their bearers—sometimes in the face of the actualities of communicational patterns. And such mapping has led to formulating and asking questions about phenomena in particular ways: about geographical variants—dialects—within "the same" language community, about migrations of the "bearers" of a particular language, about the (geographical) "spread or contraction" of families of languages over time, and the like. We are certainly familiar with this project of the universal-historical imagination, as ever ready to be renewed by a political cause as by a bit of speculative input from archaeology or biological anthropology. (Greenberg 1987, Nichols 1992, and an immense literature in support and critique come immediately to mind.)

Additionally, where "locality" has been construed from distributions of language use in social space, that is, from language distributed in types of events of communication, scholarly consciousness of language communities has frequently just assumed a parallelism to the widespread European experience of complex speech communities. It has taken account in this way of boundedness of occasions or events of use, relative to an inventory of languages-in-communicative-situations over a population. Here, locality is characteristically recognized as "restrictedness" of use, frequently with a concept of a hierarchy of inclusiveness (greater > lesser) along a functional cline of types such as public > private, institutional-collective > personal-individual, and so forth. Frequently identified by scholarly interests as the codes of home (as opposed to marketplace), of intimate gatherings (rather than public politics), and along other parallel dimensions of contrast, "local" languages are thus always the lesser of the nameable languages on a functional cline assumed to be more or less commonsensically given.

Of course, the way in which a group actually constitutes its cultural modes of allegiance to particular denotational norms may or may not be the same as these traditionally functionalist scholarly assumptions. Precisely which communicative events count as, in effect, ritual centers of authority in which usage is licensed, warranted, and endowed with its cultural dimensionalities of locally understood autonomy? These will determine how the denotational norm is informed by specific genres, voicings, registers, and indexicalities interdiscursively licensed by such contexts, so as to orient people's senses of good vs bad usage and the limits thereto over a population of even part-time and perhaps only partly knowledgeable users of forms encompassed under it. Too quickly, perhaps, an earlier scholarship un-self-reflexively imposed its own norm-presuming values that are clearly identified with regimes of standardization of European languages (and their historically dependent colonial and postcolonial ones) in particular politicoeconomic orders. In this way, local cultural schemata for comprehending functional distributions of usage across events in relation to the licensing of good and bad (denotational) language seem to have been generally masked by us experts as much as by linguistic laypersons such as explorers, missionaries, and their contemporaries.

## Language (Versus Speech) Community

The semiotic-functional analysis of linguistically centered communication has more and more informed linguistic anthropology in recent years. This generalizing use of (Peircean) semiotic to address problems of understanding communication also sharpens our consciousness of the heretofore unproblematized European and colonial conceptualization of things. Here, methodological recognition of "languages" and their structures is based in the European experience of explicitly theorizing denotational usage as encompassed under "grammar" or "structure" and of leaving everything else in the semiotics of verbally mediated interaction to the realm of "rhetoric" or even vaguer notions. (Amplifications of grammar with self-styled linguistic pragmatics, e.g., Levinson 1983, Schiffrin 1994, do no better.)

Of course, there are other, more general group-derived and group-sustaining functions of verbal signs in communication—generally indexical functions which are, in principle at least, independent of the linguistic function of making denotational text. These more general functions yield distinct notions of "structure" in languages, even though native speaker access (even implicitly or tacitly) to these other functions is generally mediated by those very forms of language that are involved in denotation. That is, denotational code does, universally, seem to play a role, however implicit, in the local cultural definition of normatively conforming vs normatively nonconforming use of language. Sometimes this local cultural sense appears in the guise of local doctrines of meaning and paraphrase, as in the European culture of language, while sometimes it appears in the guise of a locally constituted sense of register variation across culturally understood communicative event-types.

So whatever be the local cultural semiotics through which one does, then, manifest allegiance to a determinate denotational code, people give evidence in this way of there being a—perhaps contextually differentiated—norm for using verbal forms that gradiently conform to grammar. This norm-of-allegiance seems, with a high degree of predictability, to be very much in the realm of compatibility with the concept of the "structure" of a language we analytic linguists model under our assumptions of communicative usage's specifically referential-and-predicational relevance. Denotational code structure is, in other words, reasonably assumed to be universally immanent in communication. It is the normativity of usage of this sort that we have in mind when talking about a "language" used—under presupposition of normativity for the users—by a population who communicate with respect to the presupposition of a "shared grammar" of their "language." The people encompassed under this measure of normativity are members of what we have been terming a "language community" (see Silverstein 1996b:127–30 and references therein).

This contrasts with a "speech community," a much more general term. This term indicates that there are perduring, presupposable regularities of discursive interaction in a group or population. When we can recognize an implicit normativity to such indexical semiosis as informs and underlies communicative acts of identity and groupness, we have a speech community. Denotational function—and the degree of successful denotational communication—is not here to the point. Speech communities, even more than language communities, are highly variable in manner and degree of stability and extent over populations, times, institutional formations, places, and other determinants.

As has long been recognized, speech communities are frequently plurilingual, that is, they encompass speakers who belong to more than one language community. Sometimes such plurilingualism is even a normative attribute of individuals within the speech community, so that there will be a regular differentiation of their using one language in some socioculturally defined occasion-type and another language in another occasion-type. The range of such plurilingualisms has been extensively documented in terms of attributes of the occasions normatively associated with use of one or another denotational code. Based on structural concepts of the separateness or integrity of denotational codes as manifested in contexts, a concept of "code switching" or "code mixing" has emerged as an at least descriptive, if not well theorized, concept. It is interesting, however, that in normatively plurilingual communities, denotational codes ("languages") frequently take on the characteristics of register-alternates and hence begin to serve as indexically pregnant modes of performing ("voicing") identities (Myers-Scotton 1993b). This points to the possibility of a new language community incipiently coming-into-being, for which the concept of code switching/mixing would be manifestly inappropriate (cf Urciuoli 1991). Note also, as Bakker (1997) now extensively describes for Michif (Cree-French/French-Cree), the crystallization of a mixed-language norm at a more advanced and structurally regimented stage of such a process.

Such considerations exemplify the fact that the speech community is the context of emergence, sustenance, and transformation of distinct local language communities. Within the various processes of communicative regularities, users of languages in essence construct culturally particular concepts of denotational normativity that bind subsets of them into "language"-bearing groups. The contemporary fate of such language-bearing groups within complex and dynamic speech communities is the topic here reviewed.

## DISCIPLINARY PERSPECTIVES

Our knowledge of the contemporary state of local language communities is based on approaches brought to the topic from a variety of fields. We review here some of the exemplary recent work of various sorts, with a view to characterizing the chief concerns of these different approaches.

### Anthropological Linguistics

Local language communities have been the traditional sites of structure-centered anthropological linguistics. This linguistics of generally otherwise "unwritten" languages has first been descriptive in orientation, with aims of producing scientific and technical grammars, lexicons, and sample collections of running narrative text, a mode of scholarly production that continues. But it has recently turned to incorporating an "applied" component that involves pedagogical grammars or at least nonlinguist-friendly descriptive materials especially for people in and around the language community of a particular language (for a recent sampler on Western Hemisphere indigenous languages, see Reyhner 1997). A great number of the descriptive materials on local languages are being produced with the latter interest in mind, though the framework for making materials on the local language accessible to local people generally has derived from global metalinguistic consciousness as systematized in international—Western—structuralizing linguistics and language pedagogy. The problem of implementation or "application" is generally conceptualized as outside of the expertise that brings grammatical order to the facts of local language use—"normativity," to be sure, in perhaps an unintended and somewhat undertheorized sense! A certain social scientific reflexivity is, of course, really what is called for—note Hofling 1996—to avoid—or at least to face—the ironies of being more an agent of essentially colonial cultural change in local communities, the more one merely desires to play a role in sustaining or fixing a local language structure within the institutional assumptions of the surrounding society.

Anthropological linguistics has, traditionally, been the vehicle of exploration of "exotic" languages in situ (insofar as possible), and has looked at language-in-use in such communities through the lens of sometimes typologically unusual grammatical and lexical resources, especially as these are revealed in language categories. Thus, through the semantic (denotational) and pragmatic (indexical) meanings such categories project, very distinctive use characteristics are discernible in the languages where they are found pointing to distinctive cultural foci of the people who communicate using them. The pages of the several regionally specialized primary data journals are filled with exemplification of new categories in the world's typological inventory from field research on indigenous local languages. And certainly, in terms of the universalizing scientific project of linguistics, preserving and documenting the richness of at least phenomenal variability of systems of grammaticalization and lexicalization among the world's languages, is an important disciplinary goal.

In the contemporary condition of globalizing processes, however, anthropological linguists find themselves in a current of rather fast-moving dynamic cultural processes. When these processes are viewed through the lens of the grammar-centered projects of the discipline, they give impressions of "language death," of less severe "language loss" in one or another respect of structural and lexical and pragmatic richness, and of "language interference" or mixing (see Dorian's benchmark collection of 1989; Fase et al 1992; and regionally focused studies such as Dutton 1992 on Melanesia; Grenoble & Whaley 1998, mostly on the Americas; Schmidt 1990 on Australia).

In much of this literature there lurks a recuperative diachrony that implies its own—generally mythic—horizon of purity and isolation of systems of denotational structure and use, needless to say. Yet on the one hand we must acknowledge the facts that are the foci of "areal linguistics," namely, massive mutual interinfluencing of denotational codes under complex speech-community conditions even in precolonial, predocumentation eras. And on the other hand, we must acknowledge the implicit contrast being drawn with the observed contemporary-period interinfluencing of a local language and a national or transnational one. For surely it is only in terms of the statistical and demographic political apparatus of nation-states and such that "minority languages" (in the sense of denotational codes) become a problem—and one conceptualized from the enveloping framework of state cultural projects. At the level of language system (as opposed to speech community), how should one face issues of "purity" as an anthropological linguist and the transformation of denotational norms? As advocate? As planner?

The issue of "purity" as specifically structural autonomy (grammatical and lexical plenitude) also haunts pidgin and creole language studies, we must note, where linguists have for some generations been caught in a dilemma: to accept and re-theorize the folk-view of these languages as in some sense defective or exceptional ("impure"), or to find a way of understanding them as perhaps gradiently stark examples of processes going on in every language in every speech community. For some recent linguists' views, see Spears & Winford 1997; for some interesting descriptive studies, Thomason 1997.

To be sure, in a variety of studies, typologically comparable recent changes in languages of traditionally local communities have been discerned and described. For example, we have reports of the collapse of systematic vocabulary levels (taboo lexical registers, registers of religious esoterica, and the like); of the decline in categorial richness or delicacy of structural distinctions (gender systems, tense/mode/aspect/voice, superordinate vs subordinate clause-structure systems, and more); these are exemplified in Dorian 1989; cf also Schmidt 1985; Moore 1988; Cook 1989; Craig 1992; Sabino 1994. And we have reports of the transformation of local language forms and/or functions specifically on the basis of apparently nonlocal linguistic models, "super-strates." (See, for example, Mühlhäusler 1996 for a finger-pointing survey of Australia and Oceania; Siegel 1997 for a review-reply, with bibliography.)

Especially for languages that have some depth of documentation over colonial and postcolonial encounter history, these changes, perceptible from the record of linguistic description left by missionaries, linguists, anthropologists, and so on, render problematic the codification of norms of a particular phase of a speech community's recent history as the basis for pedagogical materials for the consciousness of a language community, even a "heritage language" community with no active use of a particular denotational code in any context of interaction. For such materials are, perforce, always standardizing in the usual way, even if for a language in effect standardized after its era of use has passed. [Of course, standardization to inform—sometimes to create—the language community's norm is a paramount colonial as well as ethnonationalist move, as Anderson (1991) elaborates.]

## Event-Centered Studies of Use

The ethnography of communication and interactional sociolinguistics have focused on patterns of language-in-use as a field of typological variation, finding in traditional and exotic locales—i.e., in distinctively local language communities—interesting, non-Western ways that language in use accomplishes the social work of identity- and group-demarcation and (re)production.

New kinds of discursive interaction have been emerging in local communities, generally in increasingly plurilinguistic social fields, and with increasingly technologically mediated communication stimulated from outside. Consequently, new genres of linguistic entextualization have emerged. These include (Christian, Muslim, and other) religious sermons and related speeches and discursive forms (Besnier 1995, Bowen 1993, Keene 1997, Watson-Gegeo & Gegeo 1991), as well as explicit school lessons (Duranti & Ochs 1988, Schieffelin 1995), radio call-in shows and scripted television productions, medical examinations mediated by translators, tourist huckstering in markets, and the like. At the same time, the intensities and forms of other kinds of interactional events have shifted in clearly discernible ways between "tradition" and "(post)modernity," such as disputing and its resolution, curing, taking counsel, and so forth. Event-centered studies have concentrated on questions of transformation of language economies in social life by asking, on the one hand, how the new event genres are assimilated in some respects to local "traditional" forms of one or another sort, and, on the other hand, how these latter are gradually disappearing or diminishing as the interactional practices of "traditional" life are less and less in evidence.

Public events of these kinds particularly become sites not only for social reproduction in the (at least theoretically) homeostatic political organization of a local community; they are increasingly problematic rituals of identity transformation in relation to an expanding field of intersecting cultural allegiances. Special verbal registers and genred textforming knowledge either license, or are necessary to, effective oratorical performance in case after case of documented ethnographies of public talk (see Briggs 1988; Caton 1990). Yet, shifting competence in these realms on the part of would-be participants as a consequence of plurilingualism in speech communities is itself changing the terms of performance and adding new sociopolitical contingencies to the outcomes of such events (Kulick 1992; Merlan & Rumsey 1991; cf Florey 1993). Sometimes even seen locally in essentializing ideological terms of "tradition" and "modernity," these polar(ized) opposites become a processual armature of revalorization of the very language forms with which positioned identities are heard to speak in various public fora.

Hence, results of careful, exegetical study of the shifting conditions of public entextualization and contextualization become, methodologically, indicative of the state of a language community in respect of discursive practice. Such results point to the dynamic processes that a local "language" is swept up into as the fate of its status as focus of normative allegiance can be understood to be part of local politics of culture. Languages and their locally recognized variants become emblems (iconically essentialized indexes) of their users' positions in a shifting field of identities. So, studying the distribution and dynamics of such emblems (tokens of words and expressions in particular languages) in discursive deployment is an important kind of evidence about what is happening in the larger societal matrix (see Woolard 1995). Such studies put the ill-named "code switching" in a completely new light. Here, moreover, is the very ethnographic heart of a theoretically justifiable project of "variationist" sociolinguistic analysis in a population.

## Stratification of Languages in Sociolinguistic Perspective

Variation-centered sociolinguistics has studied the covariation of forms of language with context-instantiated forms of social structure. The prototype model (Labov 1966) has been stratified linguistic registers in normatively standardized language communities. Registers are alternative ways of "saying the same thing" within the same denotational code ("language") with a certain cotextual coherence across the indexically significant elements of text-sentence, which thus bear indexical values of normative contexts of occurrence. As denotational codes, registers in general can themselves have all the fundamental properties of languages, being contextually identifiable ways of communicating. At the same time, the indexical covariations of register frequently are limited to one or another plane or level of analysis, like a phonological register (experienced as "accent"), or a lexical register (experienced as "vocabulary levels"), or a morphological or syntactic one (experienced as word—and sentence—"style"). We can thus see that, in structural features, a "language" is the set-theoretic union of all its registers.

Variationist studies have generally studied statistical samples of language-as-produced, with an eye to degrees of coherence among cooccurring formal "variables" in the record of how people "say the same thing" under different contextual conditions. Observed variable language production data reveal kinds and degrees of stratified enregisterment, most transparently as a function of some aspect of the social (i.e., demographic) identity of the sender (speaker, writer, etc) of the discourse, defined in the light of institutions with an impact on social stratification. Of course, any token or instance of production of discourse can manifest numerous different systems of stratification and social partitioning, brought together as figurations of identity in analogical structures of mutual indexical tropology [Ochs 1992; Silverstein 1995b (1985)]. Furthermore, sociolinguistic variation can be relatively more "dialectal" or "superposed" (Gumperz 1968:383–84) so that as semiotically functioning signs, the variables observed fall along a cline of ideologically informed cultural transparency as "indicator-marker-stereotype" (Labov 1972:237).

For national and global languages, the denotational norms are, of course, informed by a "standard" register, one stipulated for a population over which they might have sway, by authoritative usage and even prescriptive and proscriptive pronouncements of standardizing institutions of one or another sort (see bibliography in Silverstein 1996b:129, 140 n.3) . In such a situation, power and authority in matters of language have been seen to follow the same pyramidical logic as other stratifying and centralizing political, economic, and "cultural" forces of a hegemonic sort. "Authorized language" (Bourdieu 1991), then—in other words, relatively standard usage—is at the neutral (hegemonic) top-and-center of stratified society; any deviations—whether "too much" or "too little" standard—can only be interpreted as marked variants that index the demographic figuration of the producer as also being a correspondingly removed one.

Of course, all of this is premised on a particular state of affairs manifested, in fact, by languages such as English, French, and the like. These languages exist in this condition because the respective language communities are structured through the semiotics of an encompassing politicoeconomic order that has been as central to the mode of essentializing matters of "culture" as to the more obvious expansive projects of ethnonationalism, state-colonialism, and cognate processes. To be sure, languages of local communities have, for a very long time, been drawn into such encompassing politicoeconomic orders, frequently in relation to one or more national or global languages [note Gal's Europe-based analysis (e.g., in Gal 1979, 1987, 1988, 1993)]. The presence of a local language in its "pure" form in these politicoeconomically shaped cultural circumstances increasingly makes of it a polar opposite, in register terms, of the other language(s) in its (their) "pure" form—which in the case of such languages will be the standardized one.

What frequently results is very much like gradient register-based variation within a language community studied by variationist approaches (see Romaine 1992 on Tok Pisin in Papua New Guinea; Romaine 1994 on Hawai'i Creole English; Schieffelin & Doucet 1994 on Haitian Creole). The local language perdures in a symbolic economy of variation-by-degrees over the range of communication situations from "pure" local language usage, whether normatively standardization-informed or not, to "pure" national/global language usage (English in Papua New Guinea and Hawaii, French in Haiti). The range of intermediate usages, bespeaking a register-like gradience of form under stratification, has been conceptualized under the rubrics of "code switching," "code mixing," or "interference" in the literature for some time (or, even worse, as "diglossia with bilingualism!"). Indeed, in such situations investigators have even looked for intralinguistic (grammatical) determinants of where such switching and mixing will take place in discourse (Myers-Scotton 1993a), given two particular denotational codes, as well as for straightforward extra-linguistic—or social—determinants of the sort that focus on demographics of senders and receivers of messages, as in other variationist studies.

Long ago, of course, Blom and Gumperz (1972) discovered (to variationists' methodological chagrin) that as an indexical phenomenon, "code switching" in such circumstances is as frequently context-entailing or performative (their term is "metaphorical switching") as it is context-presupposing or expectable from other, verifiable circumstances (their term is "contextual switching"). Hence, as with any other indexical phenomenon, code switching/mixing must be seen as the socioculturally meaningful creation and transformation of interactional context through the use of entextualized forms. In this case, the social meaning of the various configurations and ratios of language forms in a segment of discourse must be modeled in terms of a scheme of identities that emerge in the flow of discourse by association with graded (stratified) values mediating between polar-opposite denotational code structures.

Such phenomena show how local languages are being incorporated into an increasingly complex system of emblematic stratification, the effects of which can be measured as intensities and trends of contextualized usage of language forms identified as local for some particular group or as non-local for others. The important point is that such "code switching" and related phenomena are indexical, with all the characteristics of such and entailments for methodological approach (problematizing Myers-Scotton 1993a-c, for example, and similar work).

## Institutionally Focused Sociology of Language

Taking units such as languages, dialects, and similar constructs as givens, sociologists of language have studied distributions of such labeled entities over populations in polities. For example, they have studied sociopolitically recognized ethnolinguistic groups within a nation-state, in relation to commonsense institutional sites or "social domains" wherein a language or dialect is used (home, religious and educational institutions, government bureaus, broadcast and other mass-communicational institutions, and the like). Such macrosocial study of already labeled languages has generally assumed as its starting point the framework of national and global language communities associated with political processes in the contemporary world. This metric of differential equivalence presupposes a kind of functional comparability at the level of institutional structures in polities over which languages are seen to be distributed.

Indeed, the field of surveying and inventorying the changes in "status" of local languages (see, for example, Ammon & Hellinger 1992) has generally been carried out within this conception of a sociology of language. Congenial to being a "policy science," such an approach has been an official one of a government, government agency, or similarly interested entity, or an equivalent scholarly-scientific conception that has policy implications when translated into the "applied science" mode. The vitality of local languages can be profiled, it is assumed, by describing the extent of various institutional kinds of usage, and attitudes encompassing such usage, across a demographic base of language users within some sociopolitical entity. And insofar as such data are comparable from one language community to another, languages and their communities of users can be descriptively or even numerically ordered by such criteria. Within polities, these numerical data allow labeling of "majority" and "minority" languages, for example, bespeaking an economistic or market-like conceptualization of power, of political telos, and so on. Macrosociological typologies of languages by status follow upon such work of census, map, and—in this case—data base, as Anderson (1991) has pointed out.

People within local language communities actively position themselves with respect to the political orders of contemporary nation-states and more encompassing international political institutions (e.g., The United Nations [Organization]); i.e., to various extents, they are "mobilized" within the polity. For such interested parties, the data on linguistic "status" are fraught with implication, positive and negative. Countermajoritarian assertions of linguistic and cultural "rights," for example (Skutnabb-Kangas & Phillipson 1994), with respect to national and transnational projects of political entities are obviously bound up with having a developed concept of the trajectory of one's language's status, and probably hence of one's language-based status within a sociocultarally imagined order of interested difference.

As political scientists have long discussed (Inglehart & Woodward 1967, Anderson 1991), when groupness is at issue within Western, market-imaged political frameworks, language becomes a site of struggle—both toward a telos of creating a new language community and, by contrast, in resistive preservation or resuscitation of what once was/is to be still counted as a language community. The various sides of such struggles must share basic cultural principles of an ethnosociology of language to carry them on; hence, for postcolonial local language communities, it has been interstitial cultural brokers to the larger polities that have played formative roles in these processes. For it is such people who mediate the encompassing polity's views of "minority" language and the local language community's construction/construal of its own locality.

In the contemporary world, strongly influenced by Herderian constructions of difference, language becomes essentialized as a necessary condition of ethnocultural identity, too, by groups on one or both sides of an issue of language status and its consequences. Within such a view, such concepts as "heritage languages," i.e., labeled languages only reconstructively identifiable with ancestors of a population of users of some other language or languages, figurate language as a timeless, essential quality of community membership, notwithstanding changes of practical discursive knowledge and practice of it over time.

## INDICATORS OF TRANSFORMATIONAL PROCESS

Observe the three epistemologically distinct phenomena to be engaged in a local language community: (a) language structure as a synchronic abstraction; (b) regularities of entextualization/contextualization of discourse; (c) group-relative reflexive ideological engagement with language-in-culture. From the perspective of seeking to analyze the cultural dynamics of language, these are the principal moments of what is actually a dialectically continuous process of the sociocultural life of languages and language communities. All three moments of abstraction from the dialectical back-and-forth are possible points of methodological entrée into the transformation of local language communities. Studies of these complex processes of necessity frequently highlight one of these moments as the starting point for analysis, treating the others as backdrop or as explanatory framework. Or, they treat in detail one or more of the pair-wise binaries one can abstract so as to engage with the dynamic quality of the processes transforming local languages in relation to their cultural and political ecologies. Here we point out some important studies of recent years.

## Structural Foci of Transformative Processes

In contemporary local language communities, structural and lexical transformation of the very denotational codes is a matter of some interest. Issues such as the following emerge in the contemporary context of the existence of these languages: What is the structural (and especially lexical) integrity of the denotational code in the condition of being a local language with respect to national and international ones? Can it be maintained? Is there massive interinfluencing of morphosyntax and lexicon from "superstrate" national and international languages? Are pidginized and/or creolized forms of such superstrate languages an emergent part of the cultural processes of interinfluencing? What effects in denotational code and register structures seem to emerge in the current condition of communicative technologies and channels of use of the local language—e.g., print media, telecommunication, and the like? With what degree of integrity on occasions of communication is the local denotational code, in its so-called "pure" form, realized, or is there "code mixing" or "code switching" inherent in the denotational-textual real time of communicative events?

In an interesting series of studies stretching over the last two decades, for example, Jane Hill and Kenneth Hill (1978, 1980, 1986; J Hill 1985, 1998) have investigated the structural and functional effects of the stratified envelopment of Mexicano (Nahuatl) language communities by the national language, Spanish. Intersecting the two analogies of "syncretism" of morphological categories in language and "syncretism" of cultural practices in postcolonial societies, the Hills have identified a number of ways in which local Mexicano/Castellano (Spanish) constitutes a space of variant, though hybridly "syncretic," language structures and practices. From the perspectives of two distinct, denotationally normative code structures, a whole range of lexically, morphologically, and syntactically intermixed construction-types comprise the local forms of code observable in the village communities of the Malinche Volcano area of Tlaxcala and Puebla that the Hills studied.

And there is clear stratification of registers, with what they identify as a "power code," highly syncretized, most indexically identifiable with politicoeconomically mobilized and important local men. And in the local economy of usage, the less powerful—women, more "traditional" men, and others—use more of the traditional stylistic range of a less syncretized Mexicano, including especially forms of honorification, which is a point of explicit ideological focus for Mexicano speakers on the value of local culture. Ironically, then, to the degree to which discursively they instantiate non-Hispanized Mexicano, such highly traditional and highly monolingually fluent speakers uphold the explicitly shared ideals of language usage. Yet at the same time, such usage indexically bespeaks their exclusion from the sites of power that are increasingly defined from outside the local language community and locally embodied in the so-called "power code" elite.

In contrast to this syncretistic project of envelopment of denotational norms, we encounter a local language with a very different profile, Arizona Tewa, through the reports of Paul Kroskrity (e.g., 1993, 1998). Living on First Mesa of the Hopi Reservation—itself geographically encompassed by the Navajo Reservation—in a larger society once Spanish-speaking, now predominantly English-speaking, Arizona Tewa speakers present us with asymmetric trilingualism in which their language has been a focus of exclusivity in identity-maintenance for over 300 documented years. Expanding on the results of Dozier (1956) for Tewa-speaking peoples of the Rio Grande pueblos, Kroskrity documents the rigid exclusion of borrowed lexical and grammatical material in Arizona Tewa, whether from Spanish or English, from Navajo, or from Hopi (from which there is a marginal amount of convergent influence and a couple of loanwords).

Echoing Jerrold Levy's recent (1992) reconsideration of the nature of hierarchy and social stratification in the Hopi "egalitarian" society of Orayvi Village, Kroskrity emphasizes that such structural and lexical "purism" of Arizona Tewa may be less a simple function of community-wide rejection of things "foreign" to preserve distinctness than once was thought. Kroskrity suggests that it might be more a function of the centering of norms of Tewa denotational code on the usages emergent from and resonant of the ceremonial center of society, the kiva, the workings of which cosmically grounds the social reproduction of socioeconomic elites who control community resources as much as they do esoteric knowledge (including "kiva talk," the norm-influencing register that provides an ideological model of good Tewa).

A set of studies focused on languages in contact situations in the Pacific—notably, Jeff Siegel's (1987) on multiple bilateral pidginizations in Fiji plantation history; Terry Crowley's (1990) on the rise of Bislama from pidgin to the position of national language of Vanuatu (the colonial New Hebrides Islands); and Suzanne Romaine's (1992) on the depidginization of Tok Pisin in Papua New Guinea from rural to urban code—exemplify also a concern with the structural transformation of grammar as well as the incorporation of lexicon from a variety of sources over the time course of historical formation of a distinct local language community. Each of these works uses historical as well as contemporary field-based study to point out the various phonological, lexical, morphological, and syntactic routes to stabilization of norms within the respective language communities. In the case of Bislama and Tok Pisin, of course, as these have themselves become postcolonial languages of widespread knowledge and use, community norms have more and more been subject to the institutional paraphernalia of print-based standardization (including pedagogical and reference materials, media, and the like), constituting cases of incipient stratification of the type one sees in classic variationist studies, as is made so evident in the Romaine work, for example.

## Shifting Entextualization/Contextualization in the Contemporary World

The actualities of using language result in texts-in-context; the processes underlying are termed entextualization and contextualization (Silverstein & Urban 1996), and are simultaneous semiotic moments of an experientially unitary phenomenon. Insofar as texts are genred, and insofar as such genres are nonuniformly distributed through social space, textuality-in-context can be studied like any other normed cultural fact. Some texts are public and/or ritual in nature, while others arise in less determinately bounded but still recurrent contextual surrounds, such as the flow of daily activities in a household or workplace or service encounter.

In contemporary language communities, such genred textualities are frequently being transformed in interesting ways. There are new genres of text, such as come, for example, with global and national influences and reactions thereto. There are new contexts in which genres of text appear, such as self-consciously demonstrative displays of culture that reconstitute locality of identity in interesting ways. There are explicit new channels of emergence and circulation of texts, such as print or broadcast, that transform the event envelope in which texts exist in respect of tempo, extent of circulation, and other characteristics. There are new modes of text-artifactuality (creation of objectual inscriptions that mediate entextualization/contextualization), such as print, audio/videotape, electronic storage, and the like, that are transforming the roles of senders and receivers of texts in the circulation of culture. All these changes have been noted as aspects of the contemporary linguistic scene in local language communities; several studies even focus on one or another aspect of this multiple set of pragmatic innovations.

Missionary-induced textual activities, whether artifact-focused, as in acquiring scriptural literacy, or nonartifactual, as in participating in new forms of liturgy, devotional discourse, and public speaking (e.g., sermons), has clearly been a ubiquitous force for transforming local language communities. Duranti & Ochs (1988) and Schieffelin (1995), among others, have both written about literacy practices under missionization (in Samoa and among the Kaluli of Papua New Guinea, respectively), discerning aspects of the transformation of epistemologies of language in the learners. Similarly, Keeane (1997a,b) has noted the real conflict that arose between traditional Anakalangese (Sumba, Indonesia) views of the cosmic power of performative control, through ritual texts, of the word-for-thing relationship, and the Dutch Reformed missionary-induced concepts of referentiality and personal intentionality underlying Christian belief and devotional language.

Among Kwara'ae speakers, as noted by Watson-Gegeo & Gegeo (1991), and among speakers of Nukulaelae, as noted by Besnier (1995), the popularity of Christianized modes of speech has resulted in the creation of registers of usage that always make a *renvoi* (gesture of reference) to texts such as scripture and sermon as newer prototypes for public discourse, for example in community meetings. Kulick (1992, 1998) also notes for the village of Gapun on the northeast coast of Papua New Guinea the emergent prestige of such registers, strongly indexing their user's Christian modernity as well as what is traditionally considered mature social wisdom (Tok Pisin, *save*), which has become syncretically identified and gendered as male.

New consciousness of ritual entextualizations emerge in local language communities as a function of transformations of identity in at least traditionally sociopolitical framing. As a case in point, local cultures in Indonesia must negotiate vis-à-vis the demands of the officially Muslim nation-state as, for example, Bowen's series of studies of ritual performances, both of Gayo "tradition" (*adat*) and of Muslim devotion (Bowen 1989, 1991, 1993) demonstrate. Parmentier (1987, 1993) has pointed up the transformation of the very discourse of chiefly politics in Palau, heavily laden as it is with self-locating and self-justifying historical narrative that potentially figurates that which is to be accomplished in the event by invoking its precedent in narration. Such applications of precedential narrative are, in fact, widespread as traditional rhetorical forms of ritualized politics, sometimes poetically sketched through a denotational encompassment of places and routes of origin in what appear to be lists of placenames [as, e.g., among the Weyéwa of Sumba, according to Kuipers (1990)]; and yet, these systems of authoritative performance are being everywhere transformed by the encounter with modernist discourses of politics couched in terms of the denotational referentiality of "rationalized" governance in the modern nation-state orders.

## Ideological Processes of Cultural Valorization of Language and Discourse

Such observations of changing patterns of discursive interaction brings us, of course, to the question of how people from local language communities conceptualize their participation in complex speech communities (cf. the interesting collection of boosterisms in Fishman 1997). That is, such observations of necessity lead us to consider the ideological dimension of the linguistic phenomena noted above. [See Silverstein 1979, 1995a; Woolard & Schieffelin 1994; and the papers in Woolard et al 1992 (also 1998, for overviews of this perspective on language).] Ideologies are socially locatable, to be sure, in the sense that they bespeak interests of the social groups and categories of those who articulate or in other ways give evidence for them. But ideologies are also locatable, particularly at those sites of production of concepts of "locality" in the sense noted above, through which people imagine their participation in a language community. Hence, in each one of the cases of transformation of local language structures, and of the transformation of discursive practices, the ideological aspect of analysis is central and key to understanding how people experience the cultural continuities and interruptions in the particular case.

For example, among the Gapuners of Kulick's (1992, 1993, 1998) series of reports on language shift, a structure of ideologically driven indexical equations seems to constitute the social space in which Taiap, the Papuan language identified with the village, is being lost in favor of Tok Pisin, the language of the nation-state of Papua New Guinea. In the local ideological constructions of the matter, there is a strongly gendered component, where Taiap : Tok Pisin :: female : male. There is an imagined locatability of the difference as well in discursive style associated with a positively and negatively valuated genre of talk: the (male-dominated) civic meeting, at which demonstrations of oratorical skill involve high degrees of strategic indirection on the part of speakers and diplomatic misrecognition on the part of addressees/audiences vs the (ascriptively female) domestic flare-up, the *kros bilong meri*, an insult-, invective-, and obscenity-filled display of one's own id, one's own egocentric *hed*, as it is locally termed—conceived of as basically delivered in Taiap, statistical counts of frequencies notwithstanding. Hence male : female :: *save* : *hed* :: skilled oratory : *kros* :: Tok Pisin : Taiap. It is in this overall ideological space—apparently shared rather widely by both men and women in Gapun village—that the ideological devaluation of Taiap and the hypervaluation of Tok Pisin constitutes the backdrop for the shift of denotational norms. The shift becomes a "natural" consequence to be regretted, perhaps, only when it is too late.

Similarly, there is revealed to be a complex and contested ideological field dialectically regimenting the Mexicano-Castellano [Nahuatl-Spanish] bilingual register cline. On the one hand, as Hill (1998) notes, those so-called "power code" elites who censor anything but "pure" Mexicano and yet ironically use a highly "mixed" register themselves, articulate an ideological "discourse of nostalgia" focused on such prototypical sites of interpersonal social relations as the encounter of *compadres* (as Hill & Hill 1978 show, one of the statistical peaks of honorification in speech). The point is, they summon a time of unquestioned locality, in which everyone knew his or her place, and a clear ground for knowing when to use "T" talk and when to use "V" talk was shared knowledge. On the other hand, various others, especially women and not particularly successful/rich men, revealed to Hill their ideological counterdiscourse, or rather metadiscursive move in dialogic criticism of this attempt to put them in their (traditional) place—namely, at the "T"-receiving end of deference-and-demeanor relations. And this, note, in a double sense: non-power(-code) elites in the contemporary political economy of ethnicity of the Mexican nation-state, and probably asymmetrically less privileged in the traditional local social organization.

Hence, the discourse and counterdiscourse focused in the nostalgic *renvoi* to an era of interpersonal politeness and mutual care, in the ideological field of contestation all about the essential link to using Mexicano, rather than Castellano, can be seen in terms of the stratification of positioned views of the emblematicity of the polar distinction in a rapidly transforming political economy of indigenous vs national culture. Note the parallel in a way to the case of the Arizona Tewas discussed by Kroskrity (1993, 1998), where the ideological struggle of contemporary emblematicity—local, though kiva-elite-centered Tewa vs (inter)national American English—presents itself in terms of two potent identifications, the first a system of stratification that involves local, traditional wealth and position, the second a system of mobilization into the late capitalist imaginary of individual identities. Can locality of thus emblematized denotational norms ("languages") survive in this ideologically presented dichotomization?

We also call attention to the studies of ideologically informed processes of language shift by (*a*) Dorian (1987, 1994) on Scottish Gaelic and other languages; (*b*) Tsitsipis (1988, 1995) on Arvanítika (Albanian) in Greece; (*c*) Lanoue (1991) on Sekani in British Columbia; and (*d*) Gross (1993) on Walloon (Belgium) and Tamazight (Morocco).

## THE DISCOURSES OF LINGUISTS AND LINGUISTIC ANTHROPOLOGISTS

Professional students of these transformative phenomena are, perforce, themselves engaging in a kind of explicit, necessarily ideological discourse about them. In its ideological aspects, to be sure, such discourse manifests a range of sociocultural positionalities of imagined linguistic projects within the global and national orders. With respect to the processes of transformation of languages and communities, that is, such discourse bespeaks views of possible destinies for local languages and their communities—interesting social facts that ought themselves to be reflexively understood.

Discourses about "linguistic rights" on the model of more general notions of human rights, for example, about "endangered languages" on the analogy of endangered species, about "linguistic cultural wealth" suggesting something of an ethnonationality's or nation-state's (or primordial kinship-based group's) collective and corporate property, and so on, are more than mere turns-of-phrase (see Hill 1995). They suggest conceptual analyses of contemporary transformation along lines that are, in fine, completely a function of a politics of particular discursive fields, such as universalizing liberationist individualism, or the current ecopolitics of Western liberal democracies, or the dichotomy of a utopian primitive corporatism distinct from Western capitalist individualism. Hence, such discursive models of complex situations, communicated at least partly ex cathedra *malgré nous* from the edifice of (social) Science, may sometimes be more stipulative (normative) and less based on careful sociocultural and historical analysis of situations than is warranted.

Needless to say, once linguists and linguistic anthropologists start using these analogical terms to model the situations they are engaged with, they have entered the field of study as a subjective agent, perhaps an intentional agent-of-change, with a decidedly formed ideological agenda. They have become in some way players in the process in a qualitatively new way. Of course, being committed to the well-being of a research population or to the causes that the research population espouses has a long tradition in anthropological research and even in professional anthropological ethics. But how such commitment gets played out in terms of one's own politics within one's own political order, in which the researched language community also of necessity constitutes an object of presumptive so-called "scientific" expertise, is not an easy problem to navigate [viz., the set of essays, response, and rejoinder in *Language* during 1992–1993 (Hale 1992a,b; Ladefoged 1992; Dorian 1993)].

As these and other materials show, from linguists who are purveyors of theorizations of language as autonomous formal structures and more-or-less universal cognitive engines, give or take a parameter here and there, one sees in such linguistic literature a biologistic and "species"-focused discourse about "endangerment" of specific languages seen to be near "extinction." We might understand this as "Green" politics metaphorically applied to language. As political position, it may be. But in terms of professional—that is, scientific—self-justification for the applicability of the metaphor, on the other hand, we generally find merely an untheorized folk view. The position is generally rationalized by a most naïve Whorfianism about culture and so-called "world view" (itself an ideological term that bespeaks a lack of contact with serious anthropological, linguistic anthropological, or philosophical discourse since probably 1950!); these are somehow seen to be embodied in each particular language's denotational structure—of all things!—of which "world view" must somehow be a function. This from the same folks who, as theoreticians, value the language-specific only in terms of a universalist and explicitly or implicitly formalist scientific project!

To be sure, one recognizes the interested subjectivity, the self-positioning of the anthropological linguist as archivist-rescuer of collective cultural riches in languages. Indeed one recognizes a kind of secular or even anti-clerical missionary worker on behalf of the mystical telos of "science"-for-the-betterment-of-life on behalf of the benighted who would "give up their language (denotational code)." In many ways, such a subjectivity has all the patronizing attitudes we generally decry in the more traditionally mystified telos of engagement with "exotics," missionaries, civilizers, and the like, with nothing more than a denotational-code-to-"world-view" folk Whorfianism to offer. It takes a broadened and more sociologically and semiotically sophisticated reconsideration of what language is to bring the political-missionary sensibility together with a scientific one. Are anthropological linguists up to the challenge?

To the extent, in other words, to which we combine a scientific engagement with a language and its local linguistic community with a political commitment that may drive our desires for practical amelioration of the fate of languages and their speakers, it behooves us to try to understand something of the dynamics of the local cultural process.

This means reconstituting the framework for one's reflexive self-placement in local language communities so that one can be both "scientist" and "citizen" within a mutually enhancing theorized totality. We owe no less to both science and citizenship, because we all owe much more, as scholars and people, to our fellow humans in local language communities.

ACKNOWLEDGMENTS

I am grateful to Daniel F Suslak, who has served as (paid) research assistant for this project, applying thereto his excellent bibliographic and computer skills, as well as the informed editorial advice of a first-rate linguistic anthropologist in all but dissertation.

> Visit the *Annual Reviews home page* at
> http://www.AnnualReviews.org.

## Literature Cited

Ammon U, Hellinger M, eds. 1992. *Status Change of Languages*. Berlin: Walter de Gruyter

Anderson B. 1991. *Imagined Communities: Reflections on the Origin and Spread of Nationalism*. London: Verso. 2nd ed.

Appadurai A. 1996. *Modernity at Large: Cultural Dimensions of Globalization*. Minneapolis: Univ. Minn. Press

Bakker P. 1997. *A Language of Our Own: The Genesis of Michif, the Mixed Cree-French Language of the Canadian Métis*. New York: Oxford Univ. Press

Besnier N. 1995. *Literacy, Emotion, and Authority: Reading and Writing on a Polynesian Atoll*. Cambridge, UK: Cambridge Univ. Press

Blom JP, Gumperz JJ. 1972. Code-switching in Norway. In *Directions in Sociolinguistics*, ed. JJ Gumperz, DH Hymes, pp. 407–34. New York: Holt, Rinehart & Winston

Bourdieu P. 1991. *Language and Symbolic Power*. Transl. G Raymond, M Adamson. Cambridge, MA: Harvard Univ. Press

Bowen JR. 1989. Poetic duels and political change in the Gayo highlands of Sumatra. *Am. Anthropol.* 9(1):25–40

Bowen JR. 1991. *Sumatran Politics and Poetics: Gayo History, 1900–1989*. New Haven, CT: Yale Univ. Press

Bowen JR. 1993. *Muslims Through Discourse: Religion and Ritual in Gayo Society*. Princeton, NJ: Princeton Univ. Press

Briggs CL. 1988. *Competence in Performance: The Creativity of Tradition in Mexicano Verbal Art*. Philadelphia: Univ. Penn. Press

Caton SC. 1990. *"Peaks of Yemen I Summon": Poetry as Cultural Practice in a North Yemeni Tribe*. Berkeley: Univ. Calif. Press

Cook E. 1989. Is phonology going haywire in dying languages? Phonological variations in Chipewyan and Sarcee. *Lang. Soc.* 18(2):235–55

Craig C. 1992. Language shift and language death: the case of Rama in Nicaragua. *Int. J. Sociol. Lang.* 93(1):11–26

Crowley T. 1990. *Beach-la-Mar to Bislama: The Emergence of a National Language in Vanuatu*. New York: Oxford Univ. Press

Dorian NC. 1987. The value of language-maintenance efforts which are unlikely to succeed. *Int. J. Sociol. Lang.* 68(1):57–67

Dorian NC, ed. 1989. *Investigating Obsolescence: Studies in Language Contraction and Death*. Cambridge, UK: Cambridge Univ. Press

Dorian NC. 1993. A response to Ladefoged's other view of endangered languages. *Language* 69(3):575–79

Dorian NC. 1994. Purism vs. compromise in language revitalization and language revival. *Lang. Soc.* 23(4):479–94

Dozier E. 1956. Two examples of linguistic acculturation: the Yaqui of Sonora and the Tewa of New Mexico. *Language* 32(1):146–57

Duranti A, Ochs E. 1988. Literacy instruction in a Samoan village. In *Culture and Language Development: Language Acquisition and Language Socialization in a Samoan Village*, pp. 189–209. Cambridge, UK: Cambridge Univ. Press

Dutton T, ed. 1992. *Culture Change, Language Change: Case Studies from Melanesia*. Canberra, Aust.: Pac. Linguist.

Fase W, Jaspaert K, Kroon S, eds. 1992. *Maintenance and Loss of Minority Languages*. Amsterdam: Benjamins

Fishman JA. 1997. *In Praise of the Beloved Language: A Comparative View of Positive Ethnolinguistic Consciousness*. Berlin: Mouton de Gruyter

Florey MJ. 1993. The reinterpretation of knowledge and its role in the process of language obsolescence. *Ocean. Linguist.* 32(2):295–309

Gal S. 1979. *Language Shift: Social Determinants of Linguistic Change in Bilingual Austria*. New York: Academic

Gal S. 1987. Codeswitching and consciousness in the European periphery. *Am. Ethnol.* 14(4):637–53

Gal S. 1988. The political economy of code choice. In *Codeswitching: Linguistic and Anthropological Perspectives*, ed. M Heller, pp. 245–64. Berlin: Mouton de Gruyter

Gal S. 1993. Diversity and contestation in linguistic ideologies: German speakers in Hungary. *Lang. Soc.* 22(3):337–59

Gal S, Irvine JT. 1995. The boundaries of languages and disciplines: how ideologies construct difference. *Soc. Res.* 62(4):967–1001

Greenberg JH. 1987. *Language in the Americas*. Stanford, CA: Stanford Univ. Press

Grenoble LA, Whaley LA. 1998. *Endangered Languages: Language Loss and Community Response*. Cambridge, UK: Cambridge Univ. Press

Gross JE. 1993. The politics of unofficial language use: Walloon in Belgium, Tamazight in Morocco. *Crit. Anthropol.* 13(2):177–208

Gumperz JJ. 1968. The Speech community. In *International Encyclopedia of the Social Sciences*, ed. DL Sills, vol. 9, 381–86. New York: Macmillan & the Free Press

Hale K, ed. 1992. Endangered languages. Special section of *Language* 68(1)1–42

Hill JH. 1985. The grammar of consciousness and the consciousness of grammar. *Am. Ethnol.* 12(4):725–37

Hill JH. 1995. *Language death and linguistic markets*. Presented at Annu. Meet. Am. Anthropol. Assoc., 94th, Washington, DC

Hill JH. 1998. "Today there is no respect": nostalgia, "respect" and oppositional discourse in Mexicano (Nahuatl) language ideology. In *Language Ideologies: Practice and Theory*, ed. BB Schieffelin, KA Woolard, PV Kroskrity, pp. 68–86. New York: Oxford Univ. Press

Hill JH, Hill KC. 1978. Honorific usage in modern Nahuatl: the expression of social distance and respect in the Nahuatl of the Malinche Volcano area. *Language* 54(1):123–55

Hill JH, Hill KC. 1980. Mixed grammar, purist grammar, and language attitudes in modern Nahuatl. *Lang. Soc.* 9(3):321–48

Hill JH, Hill KC. 1986. *Speaking Mexicano: Dynamics of Syncretic Language in Central Mexico.* Tucson, AZ: Univ. Ariz. Press

Hofling CA. 1996. Indigenous linguistic revitalization and outsider interaction: the Itzaj Maya case. *Hum. Organ.* 55(1):108–16

Inglehart RF, Woodward M. 1967. Language conflicts and political community. *Comp. Stud. Soc. Hist.* 19(1):27–45

Irvine J, Gal S. 1994. Language ideologies and linguistic differentiation. To appear in *Regimes of Language*, ed. PV Kroskrity. Santa Fe, NM: SAR. In press

Keeane W. 1997a. *Signs of Recognition: Power and Hazards of Representation in an Indonesian Society.* Berkeley: Univ. Calif. Press

Keeane W. 1997b. From fetishism to sincerity: on agency, the speaking subject, and their historicity in the context of religious conversion. *Comp. Stud. Soc. Hist.* 39(4): 674–93

Kroskrity PV. 1993. *Language, History, and Identity: Ethnolinguistic Studies of the Arizona Tewa.* Tucson, AZ: Univ. Ariz. Press

Kroskrity PV. 1998. Arizona Tewa kiva speech as a manifestation of a dominant language ideology. In *Language Ideologies: Practice and Theory*, ed. BB Schieffelin, KA Woolard, PV Kroskrity, pp. 103–22. New York: Oxford Univ. Press

Kuipers JC. 1990. *Power in Performance: The Creation of Textual Authority in Weyewa Speech.* Philadelphia: Univ. Penn. Press

Kulick D. 1992. *Language Shift and Cultural Reproduction: Socialization, Self, and Syncretism in a Papua New Guinean Village.* Cambridge, UK: Cambridge Univ. Press

Kulick D. 1993. Speaking as a woman: structure and gender in domestic arguments in a Papua New Guinean village. *Cult. Anthropol.* 8(3):99–129

Kulick D. 1998. Anger, gender, language shift and the politics of revelation in a Papua New Guinean village. In *Language Ideologies: Practice and Theory*, ed. BB Schieffelin, KA Woolard, PV Kroskrity, pp. 87–102. New York: Oxford Univ. Press

Labov W. 1966. *The Social Stratification of English in New York City.* Washington, DC: Cent. Appl. Linguist.

Labov W. 1972. *Sociolinguistic Patterns.* Philadelphia: Univ. Penn. Press

Ladefoged P. 1992. Another view of endangered languages. *Language* 68 (4):809–11

Lanoue G. 1991. Language loss, language gain: cultural camouflage and social change among the Sekani of northern British Columbia. *Lang. Soc.* 20(1):87–115

Levinson SC. 1983. *Pragmatics.* Cambridge, UK: Cambridge Univ. Press

Levy JE. 1992. *Orayvi Revisted: Social Stratification in an "Egalitarian" Society.* Santa Fe, NM: SAR

Merlan F, Rumsey A. 1991. *Ku Waru: Language and Segmentary Politics in the Western Nebilyer Valley, Papua New Guinea.* Cambridge, UK: Cambridge Univ. Press

Moore RE. 1988. Lexicalization versus lexical loss in Wasco-Wishram language obsolescence. *Int. J. Am. Linguist.* 54(4):453–68

Mühlhäusler P. 1996. *Linguistic Ecology: Language Change and Linguistic Imperialism in the Pacific Region.* London: Routledge

Myers-Scotton C. 1993a. *Dueling Languages: Grammatical Structure in Codeswitching.* New York: Oxford Univ. Press

Myers-Scotton C. 1993b. *Social Motivations for Codeswitching: Evidence from Africa.* New York: Oxford Univ. Press

Myers-Scotton C. 1993c. Common and uncommon ground: social and structural factors in code-switching. *Lang. Soc.* 22(4): 475–503

Nichols J. 1992. *Linguistic Diversity in Space and Time.* Chicago: Univ. Chicago Press

Ochs E. 1992. Indexing gender. In *Rethinking Context: Language as an Interactive Phenomenon*, ed. A Duranti, C Goodwin, pp. 335–58. Cambridge, UK: Cambridge Univ. Press

Parmentier RJ. 1987. *The Sacred Remains: Myth, History, and Polity in Belau.* Chicago: Univ. Chicago Press

Parmentier RJ. 1993. The political function of reported speech: a Belaun example. In *Reflexive Language: Reported Speech and Metapragmatics*, ed. JA Lucy, pp. 261–86. Cambridge, UK: Cambridge Univ. Press

Reyhner J, ed. 1997. *Teaching Indigenous Languages.* Flagstaff: Cent. Excell. Educ., North. Ariz. Univ.

Romaine S. 1992. *Language, Education, and Development: Urban and Rural Tok Pisin in Papua New Guinea.* New York: Oxford Univ. Press

Romaine S. 1994. Hawai'i Creole as a literary language. *Lang. Soc.* 23(4):527–54

Sabino R. 1994. They just fade away: language death and the loss of phonological variation. *Lang. Soc.* 23(4):495–526

Schieffelin B. 1995. Creating evidence: making sense of written words in Bosavi. *Pragmatics* 5(2):225–44

Schieffelin B, Doucet RC. 1994. The "real" Haitian Creole: ideology, metalinguistics, and orthographic choice. *Am. Ethnol.* 21(1):176–200

Schiffrin D. 1994. *Approaches to Discourse.* Cambridge, MA: Blackwell

Schmidt A. 1985. *Young People's Dyirbal: An Example of Language Death from Australia.* Cambridge, UK: Cambridge Univ. Press

Schmidt A. 1990. *The Loss of Australia's Aboriginal Language Heritage.* Canberra, Aust.: Aborig. Stud. Press

Siegel J. 1987. *Language Contact in a Plantation Environment: A Sociolinguistic History of Fiji.* Cambridge, UK: Cambridge Univ. Press

Siegel J. 1997. *Review of Linguistic Ecology: Language Change and Linguistic Imperialism in the Pacific Region,* by Mühlhäusler. *Aust. J. Linguist.* 17(2):219–44

Silverstein M. 1979. Language structure and linguistic ideology. In *The Elements: A Parasession on Linguistic Units and Levels,* ed. R Clyne, W Hanks, C Hofbauer, pp. 193–247. Chicago: Chicago Linguist. Soc.

Silverstein M. 1995a. Indexical order and the dialectics of sociolinguistic life. In *Proc. Annu. Symp. Lang. Soc., 3rd, Austin,* ed. R Ide, R Parker, Y Sunaoshi, pp. 266–95. Austin: Dept. Linguist., Univ. Tex.

Silverstein M. 1995b. Language and the culture of gender: at the intersection of structure, usage, and ideology. In *Language, Culture, and Society: A Book of Readings,* ed. BG Blount, pp. 513–50. Prospect Heights, IL: Waveland. 2nd ed.

Silverstein M. 1996a. Monoglot "standard" in America: standardization and metaphors of linguistic hegemony. In *The Matrix of Language: Contemporary Linguistic Anthropology,* ed. D Brenneis, RKS Macaulay, pp. 284–306. Boulder, CO: Westview

Silverstein M. 1996b. Encountering language and languages of encounter in North American ethnohistory. *J. Linguist. Anthropol.* 6(2):126–44

Silverstein M, Urban G, eds. 1996. *Natural Histories of Discourse.* Chicago: Univ. Chicago Press

Skutnabb-Kangas T, Phillipson R, eds. 1994. *Linguistic Human Rights: Overcoming Linguistic Discrimination.* Berlin: Mouton de Gruyter

Spears AK, Winford D, eds. 1997. *The Structure and Status of Pidgins and Creoles.* Amsterdam: Benjamins

Thomason SG, ed. 1997. *Contact Languages: A Wider Perspective.* Amsterdam: Benjamins

Tsitsipis LD. 1988. Language shift in narrative performance: on the structure and function of Arvanítika narratives. *Lang. Soc.* 17(1): 61–86

Tsitsipis LD. 1995. The coding of linguistic ideology in Arvanítika (Albanian) language shift: congruent and contradictory discourse. *Anthropol. Linguist.* 37(4): 541–77

Urciuoli B. 1991. The political topography of Spanish and English: the view from a New York Puerto Rican neighborhood. *Am. Ethnol.* 18(2):295–310

Watson-Gegeo KA, Gegeo DW. 1991. The impact of church affiliation on language use in Kwara'ae (Solomon Islands). *Lang. Soc.* 20(4):533–55

Williams G. 1990. *Sociolinguistics: A Sociological Critique.* London: Routledge

Woolard KA. 1995. Changing forms of codeswitching in Catalan comedy. *Catalan Rev.* 9(2):223–52

Woolard KA, Schieffelin B. 1994. Language ideology. *Annu. Rev. Anthropol.* 23:55–82

Woolard KA, Schieffelin B, Kroskrity PV, eds. 1992. Special Issue on Language Ideologies. *Pragmatics* 2(3)

Woolard KA, Schieffelin B, Kroskrity PV, eds. 1998. *Language Ideologies: Practice and Theory.* New York: Oxford Univ. Press

*Annu. Rev. Anthropol. 1998. 27:427–49*
*Copyright © 1998 by Annual Reviews. All rights reserved*

# GLOBALIZATION AND THE FUTURE OF CULTURE AREAS: Melanesianist Anthropology in Transition

## R. Lederman

Anthropology Department, Princeton University, Princeton, New Jersey 08544;
e-mail: Lederman@pucc.princeton.edu

KEY WORDS: comparison, marginality, Melanesia, place

### ABSTRACT

In the last decade, anthropology has faced challenges to its self-definition associated both with new worldly circumstances and scholarly trends inside and outside the discipline. Recent interest in globalization has provoked discussion concerning what anthropology should be about, how it might be done, and what its relationships are to other bodies of literature and knowledge practices. Unsettling questions have been raised about working concepts of culture, ethnography, the field, fieldwork, and comparative analysis. Extending the rethinking of "place" in anthropology begun by Appadurai, I consider the future of "culture areas" as discursive frameworks for organizing disciplinary practices. Some characteristics of anthropological regionalism are located by contrasting them to interdisciplinary area studies, insofar as globalization poses apparently similar challenges to each. Because of its iconic disciplinary status as an exemplar of "real" anthropology, Melanesianist ethnography is given extended consideration as a particularly interesting case.

## INTRODUCTION

In the last decade, anthropology has faced a series of challenges to its autonomy and self-definition. Among other sources, journals and conferences provide evidence of a growing interest in cross-disciplinary or "postdisciplinary"

427

0084-6570/98/1015-0427$08.00

orientations such as cultural studies (Hall 1991, Grossberg et al 1992) and various postmodernisms (e.g. Lyotard 1986, Harvey 1989, Jameson 1990). These shifts in attention have been fostered by the pervasive sense that we are witness to a novel historical condition associated with late-twentieth century capitalism: The term globalization refers to this radical intensification of relations between geographically separated places; to a structurally transformative movement of people, things, and ideas across cultural and national borders (e.g. Wolf 1982, Rosaldo 1989, Hannerz 1989, 1996, Kearney 1995).

Both shifting scholarly alliances and an altered sense of the world have provoked discussion concerning what anthropology might be about and how it should be done. Our habitual self-understanding as firsthand observers of the diversely "local" now leaves many anthropologists with a sense of insufficiency: The local appears (only) small-scale, compared with the global, however startling the insights it affords about what is humanly possible, however necessary the commitment it actualizes to take seriously realities marginalized by mainstream EuroAmerican perspectives (Tsing 1993, 1994). Unsettling questions have been raised about the adequacy of our working concepts: culture (e.g. Rosaldo 1989, Gupta & Ferguson 1992), the field (e.g. Gupta & Ferguson 1997b), fieldwork (e.g. Sanjek 1990, Martin 1994), ethnography (e.g. Marcus & Fischer 1986, Clifford 1988, Fox 1991b), and comparative analysis (e.g. Holy 1987, Strathern 1988). The contemporary "world in creolization" (Hannerz 1987)—unbounded transnational flows (whether of labor migrants, refugees, or tourists), globalized markets, media (electronic, televisual), and other public cultural forms moving across national borders and problematizing once salient distinctions between regions and centers/peripheries—all of this appears to demand new scholarly concepts, sites, and methods.

Among our defining, or constitutive, practices, the regional or "culture area" organization of training and research in anthropology has become particularly problematic (e.g. Herzfeld 1984, Fardon 1990, Alvarez 1995). Extending the recent rethinking of "place" in anthropology (e.g. Appadurai 1986, 1988b), I consider culture areas as discursive frameworks for organizing disciplinary practices. The particularity of culture areas is drawn out by comparison with interdisciplinary area studies, themselves recently the objects of serious rethinking.

As culture areas go, Melanesianist anthropology is especially interesting because of its role in the history of the discipline before and after "the ethnographer's magic" (Stocking 1992).[1] This regional literature has offered

---

[1]The term Melanesia is used here to refer both to a geographical/cultural construct (whether heuristic or naturalized) evident in the ethnographic writings of anthropologists working in the southwestern Pacific and to a disciplinary icon: Melanesia as an exemplar of things anthropological both inside and outside anthropology. It has also become a (necessarily contested) local marker of ethnic/cultural identity (see footnote2).

powerful, contradictory visions of the anthropological project: Melanesian communities have been represented as "islands" of localized variation and microevolutionary development and, in the same breath, in terms of unbounded sociocultural and material relationships with near and distant others (e.g. Mead 1938, Schwartz 1963, Rappaport 1968, Watson 1970). Invoked as exemplars both of the different and of the familiar (e.g. Pospisil 1972, Gregory 1982), Melanesian practices have also long inspired important reflexive arguments about cultural analysis, comparison, and translation (e.g. Mauss 1925, Wagner 1975, Strathern 1988).

Often cited as the foundational scene of "real" anthropology [even by Africanists (Fardon 1990)], Melanesia is complexly implicated in contemporary "postexoticist" (Clifford 1997) discourse concerning the fortunes of the discipline as a whole. Although Melanesianist ethnography may now be resituated, throughout the century-long elaboration of metropolitan academic anthropology, it has in fact been vanguard, paradigm, and anachronism all at the same time (although by no means always and everywhere in the same proportions). This chapter is a gleaning of this literature's present-day interest. It outlines the impact of contemporary theory on Melanesian studies and, conversely, the particular critical perspective on the world enabled by regional disciplinary commitments.

## ANTHROPOLOGICAL REGIONALISM

Regional specialization has been a central component of EuroAmerican anthropological training and practice for much of this century. As Fardon (1990:24) pointed out, its importance is evident in the social organization of the field: its professional associations and journals. Knowing (and being known in) your "place" is important in manuscript, hiring, and tenure evaluations. Although over time their power might wane, disciplinary expectations concerning areal specialization are particularly strong early in individual careers (when most field research gets done).

### "Place" in the Background

Nevertheless, only in the last decade have the covertly regional inflections of topical discourses (on, for example, kinship, hierarchy, or historical consciousness) come to be recognized. Appadurai (1986:358) neatly directed attention to the "tendency for places to become showcases for specific issues" and conversely for these issues (or "gatekeeping" ideas) to stand for whole regions—for example, as in the identification of South Asian ethnography with debates about hierarchy (Appadurai 1988a)—even when the concepts derived from parts of those regions or from somewhere else entirely (e.g. Dresch

1988). These homogenizing handles constrain research even as they invite it; carved by our disciplined imaginations from the intricately located experiences we encounter, their graspable, transportable shape makes other possibilities (and their own contingency) hard to hold in mind.

We have also come to recognize how a hierarchy of located topics (or thematized places) has structured research in the discipline as a whole (Herzfeld 1987). The privileging of research in distant, small-scale rural places—particularly insofar as these places were represented as analytically isolatable from trans-local colonial and postcolonial political-economic relations—has been under assault from several directions for some time (e.g. Hymes 1972, Asad 1973, Fabian 1983). We now understand some of the ways in which these locational hierarchies tacitly enacted anthropology's simultaneously critical and collaborative relationship with colonial and state projects (e.g. cf Said 1978; Stocking 1987) and how they have limited our ability to imagine new venues for anthropological practice (Rosaldo 1989, Gupta & Ferguson 1992, Malkki 1995, Passaro 1997, Weston 1997). These understandings have important implications for Melanesian anthropology given its historically central place in disciplinary hierarchies.

## Culture Areas

One reason for the revelatory force of critical arguments such as that on the covert operations of "place" (Appadurai 1988b) is that they reframe understandings we have long had but that, over the past 30 years with the rise of interpretive anthropologies and decline of positivist comparativism, we have ignored (see below). Anthropological expertise has never rested on regional specialization. The distinctive internal (mutually constitutive) relationship between ethnographic locations and comparative/theoretical interests such as personhood or ethnicity is a legacy of the culture area discourses that have motivated anthropological regionalism for a good part of this century.

The term culture area originally referred to regions variously demarcated by turn-of-the-century ethnographic schools in the United States and elsewhere. Credited to Wissler (1917) by Kroeber (1939), the culture area approach was originally used, especially in Germany and the United States, as a framework for classifying museum exhibits. Geographic contiguity implied relationship [if not necessarily homogeneity (cf Thomas 1989:27)]: contact, common history, similar environmental conditions. From this perspective, systematic ethnographic surveys and observations within an area promised to yield evidence of trait diffusion and, thereby, to suggest cultural patterning or culture history (as in Wissler's age-area hypothesis) for anthropologists such as Boas (1896), Kroeber (1939), or Herskovitz (1955) and functional determinacies, cross-cultural typologies, or developmental progressions for anthropologists such as Murdock (1951, 1967) or Sahlins & Service (1960; see also Fox 1991a, Ehrich & Henderson 1968, Winthrop 1991).

The key point is that culture areas were, from the outset, less simply about areas than about culture theories. They operated as heuristic bases for generalization; they organized local ethnographic particulars for theoretical and comparative ends (Ehrich & Henderson 1968:565; cf Winthrop 1991).

If longstanding particularist, functionalist, and neoevolutionary rationales for culture areas have been marginalized in the wake of interpretive and critical styles of anthropology, we still live with versions of the same maps and their associated ethnographic discourses. The relationships of increasing interest to anthropologists now are geographically discontinuous and their contexts cannot usefully be imagined as cultural "islands" (bounded, internally homogeneous, historically stable clusters of traits), nor are they to be found only in certain types of places. Indeed, the range of reference of the term culture has exploded (as it also has outside anthropology) so that it serves poorly as a unit of positivist comparative analysis, although it still serves well in the time-honored Boasian critical fashion (Strathern 1990, Fox 1991a).

Although one might conclude from all this that culture areas are simply relics and ought to be jettisoned, I suggest that anthropological regionalism is more interesting than that judgment allows. The point can best be made by analysis of the historical dynamics of particular regional literatures; however, my interest in culture areas is also founded on general observations. For example, even as culture area constructs tacitly enacted (and often enough directly supported) racial and colonial hierarchies, they were not drawn up to fit national borders and were at odds with (if not actively subversive of) the interests and naturalizing claims of nation-states (unlike area studies; see below). Even while designating the study of certain peoples and topics as more "anthropological" than others, culture area constructs nevertheless motivated and organized systematic consideration of cultural realities marginalized by the urban, metropolitan focus of other disciplines. Finally, in addition to the indisputably local character of classical fieldwork, the discipline has tended to privilege topically focused ethnography with cross-areal (i.e. comparative/theoretical) implications: In anthropology, unlike in economics or politics, theory is mediated by the display of cross-cultural knowledge and, unlike in history or (by and large) literary studies, area specialization for its own sake can become a disability over the course of a career.

## Culture Areas and Area Studies

Another comparison sharpens the point: The peculiarity of anthropological regionalism is more visible when it is juxtaposed to that of interdisciplinary area studies, with which it has been engaged in practical ways—though more so in some places (like East Asia) than in others (like the Pacific)—especially after

World War II. Despite this entanglement, culture areas and interdisciplinary area studies face an only apparently similar crisis in the face of globalization.[2]

The challenge to area studies has recently been explicit and pointed. In the last few years, funding agencies underwriting area-studies programs [not only the Social Science Research Council/American Council of Learned Societies (SSRC/ACLS) but also the National Science Foundation and others (Brenneis 1997)] have been rethinking their support in favor of attention to phenomena that cut across areas.

Post-World War II funding by SSRC/ACLS of area-studies programs was intended to end the parochialism of US social science and humanities scholarship, disciplinarily separated from one another (as well as from scholarly institutions not based in the United States) and substantively focused almost exclusively on EuroAmerican realities (Prewitt 1996c:31–32). The Councils' postwar funding structures aimed to create or elaborate linkages between various disciplines on the model of multidisciplinary Classics programs that had existed prior to World War II (Rafael 1994). It also aimed to demonstrate the compatibility of "disciplinary" and "area" knowledge (Prewitt 1996b: 34) by setting up conditions meant to further the compatibility.

But the practical demands of the resulting institutional structures—notably language training—created new, regionalized separations. Additionally, because of the organizational subordination of area studies programs to disciplinary departments in universities, area knowledge (not to mention cross-areal comparison) remained peripheral to economics, political science, and sociology.

An index of its recent elevation to the mainstream, globalization is the explicit focus of the mid-1990s' reworking of the funding strategies of the SSRC/ACLS. According to SSRC Director Kenneth Prewitt, the Councils are pulling back from the committed regional specialisms associated with area

[2]It has often been pointed out that area studies programs were nurtured by cold war politics, dependent as they were on Title II funding and responsive as their emphases have been to shifting state geopolitical interests. I agree with Gupta & Ferguson (1997a:9) when, referring to university area-studies centers, they assert that "ideas about culture areas in the anthropological literature are refracted, altered, and sometimes undermined by the institutional mechanisms that provide the intellectual legitimacy and financial support for doing fieldwork." They point out that, as the "institutional mechanisms that define areas, fund research, and support scholarship," area-studies programs have helped to define where research will be done.

In any case, one wonders how the discipline-wide prestige of Melanesianist research was shaped by the absence of interdisciplinary area-studies funding for research in Melanesia. The lack of area-studies funding may have encouraged Pacific-area scholars when seeking their funding elsewhere to emphasize the theoretical or comparative rationale for their research over its contribution to regional specialist debates. It is possible that extra-regional topical and theoretical debates within anthropology have played a larger role for Pacific-area ethnographers than they have for anthropologists working in those world areas with vigorous area-studies communities and that this emphasis accounts for a measure of the disciplinary prominence Melanesianist and Pacific anthropology has historically enjoyed.

studies, now seen as undermining the study of transnational and other global processes. At the same time, the Councils aim to continue promoting what Prewitt calls "area-based" knowledge—i.e. knowledge acquired through foreign "field study" in and of particular places but (contra existing area-studies tendencies) this time applied to "processes, trends, and phenomena that transcend any given area" (1996c:31–32). This reorientation is meant to discourage an analytic "globalism" that "floats free of history and place" (Prewitt 1996a:18, 1996c:40).

Anthropologists would appear to be favorably positioned for such research because of the historical legacy of culture-area regionalism (with its contingent and uneven involvement in area-studies programs). Their intertwined commitments both to areas and cross-area topics mean that disciplinary and area knowledge (to use Prewitt's terms) are integral in anthropology in ways they are not in the other social sciences. Nevertheless, because of the ways in which translocal connections have come to be made in and between culture areas, a significant rethinking is needed for globalization to be incorporated into anthropological practice.

## From Armchair to Open Air Comparativism

Rarely has anthropological area expertise not been motivated by comparativist projects of one sort or another: whether positivist projects of typologizing for functional and developmental analysis (emphasizing cross-cultural similarities) or interpretive projects, reflexive or otherwise (emphasizing differences). The early prominence of positivist projects—exemplified most elaborately by the Human Relations Area Files and its various products (e.g. Levinson 1991)—is evident in the tendency of mid-century ethnography to typify observed practices rather than to narrate or contextualize events as such (see Clifford 1988, Rosaldo 1989).[3] From the positivist perspective, interpretive projects have seemed anti-comparative for emphasizing the distinctiveness of cultural practices.[4]

In its positivist modes, anthropological comparison was an "armchair" activity. Juxtaposing cultures and their traits within or between culture areas was one of the things we did with our own and other anthropologists' ethnographic data when we were not doing primary (field) research.[5] But over the last gen-

---

[3]By no means are the results of positivist comparative work necessarily pernicious or uncritical. They figured prominently, for example, in 1970s' feminist and structural-Marxist breaks with then-conventional anthropological arguments (e.g. Ortner 1981, Modjeska 1982, Godelier 1986).

[4]Insofar as they thereby seek to make evident the cultural particularity of our own interpretive media, interpretive projects are comparative in an enlighteningly reflexive, critical way.

[5]An earlier generation sought to do fieldwork in more than one place as an ideal basis for comparative analysis and (as my teachers taught) bulwark against "secondary ethnocentrism." Although this goal may not be entirely out of fashion, it is surely less feasible than it once might have been.

eration armchair comparison has been gradually displaced from its central position in anthropological debate. The very distinction between ethnography and comparison has itself been eroded by an expansion of what many anthropologists now recognize as ethnographic research sources and objects (e.g. refugees, commodities) that themselves traverse areas.

What has expanded around the furniture has been surprisingly close to the Boasian ideal articulated a century ago (Boas 1896; see also Hannerz 1989, Vincent 1990): a historically informed tracing of the connections among peoples—then conceived as "diffusion" within culture areas (and admitting of exogenous influences, e.g. "acculturation") and nowadays encompassing transregional relationships and referred to by a host of politically charged terms.[6] That is, we have a plethora of significant ethnographic, historical, and textual studies of not only transnational media and identities but also colonial and postcolonial political-economic relationships and representations (Sahlins 1985, Cooper & Stoler 1989, Vincent 1990, Stoler 1991, Comaroff & Comaroff 1991, Fox 1991b, Wilmsen & McAllister 1996). Like critical relativism, "open-air" comparativism (that is, inquiry into intercultural entanglements) tends to be viewed by practitioners as a species of the very world-making cultural/political processes it represents rather than (as was the case in positivist projects) a description of them.

Comparison was never a topical specialization in anthropology but one of its defining practices. Therefore, if comparison has largely given way to studies of global processes (in the broad sense above), this is not just a shift in research foci. It means that we have come to a new step in a generation-long transformation of disciplinary means and ends. This step has, as Kearney (1995) put it, entailed a movement away from a "modern world view" of "progressive bipolar time" and its hierarchized "spatial correlate" of centers and peripheries (as in development studies). It has seen the growing persuasiveness of spatially dispersed research open to an eclectic array of sources and the popularity of decentered accounts of the cultural politics of translocal connections.

## Anthropology in the "Savage Slot"?

Recent multidisciplinary scholarship has undermined expectations of a coming homogenous "world system" in favor of testifying to a world of proliferating

---

[6]Gupta & Ferguson (1997a:19–22) frame Vincent's argument about the diffusionist legacy in terms of heterodox alternatives to the canonical Malinowskian functionalist ethnographic style. Perhaps on account of how these things play out in the history of Melanesianist ethnography, I am not convinced the two have not been on a more equal footing all along. For example, even when taking Mead as an exemplar of a post-Boasian turn away from diffusionism and toward the Malinowskian model (Gupta & Ferguson 1997a:21), they cannot avoid footnoting her involvement in acculturation studies (1997a:44). One also wonders where to "place" Malinowski's own kula travels in this picture.

differences, disjunctures, and inequalities (Comaroff 1996). As research markedly "from somewhere," anthropological studies have helped to bring this variously oppressive or liberatory heterogeneity into focus (Appadurai 1990, Appadurai & Breckenridge 1988, Hannerz 1996). At the same time, there is a palpable panic in writings about this subject, as if we are not clear what anthropology, as such, has to do to remain in the game; as if our own working strategies are uncritical and clarity is mostly to be found elsewhere. In self-caricaturing panic, we allow (and actively contribute to) a reduction of what the discipline has been about to some set of fundamental features rather than owning up to a more equivocal, historically negotiated dialectic of places, topics, and methods.

Take, for example, the rhetorical agreement by Carrier (1992a:3) that anthropology may aptly be identified simply "as one of the disciplines by which Westerners study non-Western societies." This may seem an innocuous simplification, but consider the implications. Wallerstein (1996) and Wallerstein et al (1996) recently published an argument for the reorganization of the social sciences based on a series of similar disciplinary caricatures. Their unreferenced myth-history begins with the nineteenth century division of social scientific labor in which anthropology took (or got handed) as its subject matter those parts of the world that were neither "Western" (claimed by sociology, political science, and economics), "past" (claimed by history), or "civilized" (claimed by Oriental Studies). In this account, after the post-World War II institutionalization of area studies, once other disciplines were drawn into the study of the contemporary non-West, anthropology's (apparently sole) reason for being was undermined.[7] By these lights, our day is long gone.

It is bad enough when others construct straw men, but it is particularly debilitating when the caricatures are self-inflicted. A whiff of self-caricature can be detected, for example, in Appadurai's (1991:194–95) suggestion that an adequately "cosmopolitan" reenvisioning of anthropological practice requires that anthropology be situated within cultural studies and that we acknowledge how the "high ground" in debates about "culture" (in the cultural studies sense of the "relationship between the word and the world") "has been seized by English literature...and literary studies in general." But the histories of these fields are no less culturally parochial and complicit with class and imperial power, their self-knowledge no more refined, than anthropology's own. Al-

---

[7]In all fairness, anthropology is not the only discipline to be caricatured in Wallerstein et al's (1996) presentist narrative, which pays scant attention to messy methodological details and is at odds with nuanced disciplinary histories. The policy-driven aim of their argument is to establish a rationale for abolishing the separate social sciences, all of which are, in their account, becoming remarkably sociology-like anyhow. (Indeed, if one follows their story, even the natural and biological sciences and the humanities appear to be spiraling mothlike toward a vaguely sociological oblivion.)

though its New Left sensibilities disengage cultural studies from those histories, its blindness to the rural is still worth noting (Ching & Creed 1997).

It is more productive to acknowledge the simultaneous and particular complicities and subversions in anthropological scholarship as in that of other disciplines, and to maintain a wide-angle and historical perspective on the disciplines' respective types of projects (Vincent 1990, Fox 1991a, Knauft 1994, Gupta & Ferguson 1997a), including their underappreciated methodological complementarities. Our vulnerability to our own doubts and others' criticisms has been as much a matter of these poorly understood methodological differences (between, for example, fieldnotes, social surveys, historical documentation, and literary analysis, and variants thereof) as of our distinctive topics and places. Consequently, to adopt new topics and places is, by itself, not an adequate response to the demands of shifting disciplinary environments.

Ironically, despite their possibilities, globalization studies in anthropology may be as vulnerable to the stereotyping side of culture-arealization as "Borneo" is to "headhunting." It teeters on the brink of becoming routinized as the study of essentially unessentializable peoples (migrants, refugees, gypsies) in inherently postmodern spaces (airports, franchise restaurants).[8] Conversely, despite our best efforts (e.g. Weston 1991, M Strathern 1992), topics like "kinship" are stigmatized by virtue of their canonical (therefore, putatively conservative) status, as likewise are out-of-the-way places like Melanesia (Boon 1982, Herzfeld 1987, Tsing 1993).

Indeed, the whole discipline of anthropology is subject to just such a culture area–like reduction. Trouillot (1991) has warned that the reproduction of the idea of the "primitive," and the identification of anthropology with a "savage slot" (that is, with the practice of reproducing images of a homogenized, Civilization-mirroring Other), is not a matter simply of disciplinary history but also of historically deeper and broader forces (see also Meek 1976, Pagden 1982; cf Kuper 1988).

Without a doubt, anthropology needs to assail being placed in a "savage slot" in this sense; but the question is how best to do this given the diverse ends to which we seek to contribute. I suggest that what Kuper (1988; see also Headland & Reid 1989) calls the "persistence of the primitive" cannot be addressed by marginalizing practices and places within anthropology that have always been invisible in other scholarly precincts. Instead, ideas might be

---

[8]It is easy to imagine how conventional field research might disrupt this. One can imagine fieldwork in which the experience of those passing through (tourists, scholarly convention-goers) is juxtaposed to that of those for whom such places are not nearly so anonymous, standardized, or given (cashiers, baggage-handlers, flight crews). When it comes to cultural meaning, an anthropological project is at least as much a matter of tracking the heterogeneous reception and reworking (consumption) of images (whether in Fiji or at LAX) as of dissecting their aesthetic or unveiling the interests of their authors/producers.

sought by considering what has in fact been going on in the discipline's rhetorical birth place and recurrent touchstone.

## ANTHROPOLOGICAL REGIONALISM IN MELANESIA

The disciplinary viability of anthropology and the fortunes of Melanesian studies come together over charges of exoticism. Insofar as globalization is viewed as a challenge to the field (in both senses), it may be construed as a challenge to whatever anthropologists do, down there, in the southwestern Pacific. The (not strictly academic) image of "Melanesia"—in the figure first of Bronislaw Malinowski (e.g. 1922) and his paradigmatic Trobriands research and then of Margaret Mead (e.g. 1935)—has come to stand for anachronism: field studies of small-scale communities that bracket away historical currents and extra-local influences and that focus literal-mindedly on exotic practices and beliefs of a homogeneous Self-defining Other. But to what degree is this "Melanesia" present in the actualities of Melanesianist anthropology (or, indeed, in Melanesian actualities, as is implied in arguments that our analytical means need now catch up with a worldly reality in which, for example, communities are "no longer" spatially bounded, homogeneous, or historically unaware, implying that they once were so)?

A corollary question might be how Melanesianist anthropology might most productively enact disciplinary self-criticism and redirection. In what ways, in what contexts exactly, has an emphasis on "difference" lost or retained its critical value (compare Boon 1982, Strathern 1988, Appadurai 1990, Comaroff 1996)? Do studies of colonialism, resource exploitation by multinationals, or nationalism in Melanesia necessarily help dislodge disciplinary (not to say regional) stereotypes or will only certain approaches to these topics do? How might studies of mythology or exchange also contribute to this end?

### Globalizing Anthropology in Melanesia

Contemporary Melanesianist ethnography has been struggling with these questions. Recent works on contemporary Melanesia—only a suggestive, arbitrary, and radically incomplete sampling—have included monographs and collections on the history of Western influences (Carrier 1992b); Melanesian historical experiences and representations of regional and global relationships (White 1991; see also Gewertz & Errington 1990, Schieffelin & Crittenden 1991, and Melanesianist contributions to Lindstrom & White 1990); anticolonial movements and the problematics of cultural "resistance" (Keesing 1992); religion, sexuality, and morality in countercolonial discourses (Kelly 1991); self-making and personhood (Battaglia 1995b); the cultural construction and political economy of contemporary gender interests (Gewertz & Errington 1987); the making of national cultures (Foster 1996b); and the cultural politics and experience of socioeconomic transformations (Errington & Gewertz 1995). Regionally focused works (Weiner 1988a,b, Lutkehaus et al 1990, Knauft 1993, Biersack 1995) consistently offer theoretically and topically focused arguments that connect local ethnography with discipline-wide concerns about identities, borders, and voices, as well as our representations of these things. Collections with a Pacific-wide focus—e.g. on the impact of missions and colonialism on domestic life (Jolly & MacIntyre 1989), the politics of cultural identities and ethnicity (Linnekin & Poyer 1990), and socioeconomic transformations (Lockwood et al 1993)—contain important Melanesianist contributions on, for example, the social upheaval attendent on the destruction of material culture and creation of Christian households (MacIntyre 1989), the crisis of legitimacy of the state (Larcom 1990), and contemporary legacies of colonial "racial" hierarchies (Kaplan 1993, 1995). Other recent work has concerned missions (Huber 1990), language shift and loss (Kulick 1992), media and advertising (Sullivan 1993, Foster 1996a), violence (A Strathern 1992, 1993; Kulick 1993), emergent class interests (Errington & Gewertz 1997), and prostitution and the spread of sexually transmitted diseases (Hammar 1992, 1995; Zimmer-Tamakoshi 1993a,b).

Throughout contemporary Melanesian studies, it is common to find detailed ethnographic descriptions elaborated in relation to equally well-developed theoretical and comparative framings. That the ethnography connects itself explicitly with larger disciplinary and interdisciplinary trends is nothing new, however. Melanesianist anthropology has typically been extroverted (Strathern 1990; also see footnote 2). By and large, these works carry on the regional ethnographic habit of contextualized and layered analysis of extended case materials, now integrating face-to-face fieldwork with a range of new sources and research contexts. They seek out the cultural/historical specificities of novel relationships and discourses, the better to understand the contradictory practice of local cultural innovations and erosions (in addition to the foregoing, see Clark 1993, Hyndman 1994, Weiner 1994, O'Hanlon 1995, Robbins 1995, Sykes 1995). In so doing, they articulate newer (perhaps more accessible) topics with long-standing (harder to translate) concerns. These contextualizations make a world of difference.

This literature also takes to heart the criticisms of ethnographic representation at large in anthropology.[9] As Keesing & Jolly (1992) note, recent work has tended to make explicit the position of the observer and to attend to Mela-

---

[9]Melanesianist anthropology has also engaged in a range of textual innovations [going way back (Bateson 1936)]. These have included, for example, intercultural collaborations (Strathern 1979, Kyakas & Weisner 1992), decentered histories of first contact (Schieffelin & Crittenden 1991), contextualized biographies (Keesing 1978), reflections on the use of other anthropologists' fieldnotes (Weiner 1976, Gewertz & Errington 1987, McDowell 1991, Lutkehaus 1995), not to mention unclassifiable efforts to do as one says (M Strathern 1991).

nesian criticism of the anthropological project (e.g. Hau'ofa 1975, Iamo 1992, Waiko 1992). Often critical of the literature to which it is contributing—including its role in reproducing the regional category itself[10]—recent work is engaged directly in a struggle over the contradictory implications of "exoticism."

In that struggle, breaks with the past may legitimately be emphasized over continuities. However, the boundary between newer Melanesianist work inspired by a transdisciplinary focus on globalization and older work on colonial and postcolonial transformations and the dilemmas of development is not actually so clear (e.g. Worsley 1957). Melanesian anthropology has also a venerable history of applied socioeconomic research, much of which is accessible only locally [e.g. the Waigani seminar volumes, *New Guinea Reseach Bulletins*, Research School of Pacific Studies working papers, and the like (e.g. M Strathern 1975, May & Spriggs 1991, Jenkins 1994)].

A notable intervention at the juncture between scholarly critique and activism, and a frontal assault on the "savage slot," is the collection by Foerstel & Gilliam (1992). A commentary on marginalizing objectifications and their historical repercussions, not to say fallout, the collection is integrated by its assessment of Mead's work (rife with objectifications) and its advocacy of a nuclear-free Pacific (made necessary by the political invisibility such representations help to create).

What is extraordinary about this analytically unpretentious collection is its combination of passion and complexity: It makes a challenging model for the critique of anthropology inside and outside Melanesian studies. The editors and their contributors, about half of whom are Melanesian, present an unrestrained diagnosis of Mead's paternalism together with a feminist appreciation of her attention to sociocultural change and her efforts to popularize anthropology as cultural criticism (e.g. Leacock 1992, Gilliam 1992). In equally complex counterpoint, the collection contrasts the invocation by Waiko (1992) on the value of deeply situated "insider" knowledge to the near-universal, Mead-like position of Melanesianist anthropologists. In this essay, Waiko thoroughly relativizes his own insiderhood (as in his account of how he insisted that his history dissertation be evaluated not only by his Australian university committee but also by his Binandere elders) at the same time as he demonstrates how different (mutually "exotic") interests and positionings might be negotiated and articulated.

The active efforts of Waiko and Mead to bridge the chasm between scholarship and lay discourses (whether in Binandere conversations or American

---

[10]Melanesia (the regional category, its boundaries, and subdivisions) has been critically analyzed in interesting ways recently (e.g. Thomas 1989, Keesing & Jolly 1992, Hays 1993). At the same time, local millenial, anti-, and postcolonial movements have invested that category (along with others like "custom") with political significance (e.g. Narakobi 1983; see also Keesing & Tonkinson 1982, Keesing 1992, Lawson 1993).

ones) are steps toward a "postexoticist" world: Their work also enables us to consider the riskiness of such dispersed authority. Waiko's demonstrates the ground to be gained through reflexive engagement whereas Mead's alerts us to the historically shifting valences of an *effective* public voice.

## Conventional Provocations

Melanesianist anthropology has been implicated in heterodox trends since before the beginning, so to speak. Thus, Malinowski's showmanship may have been key to unseating cultural evolutionism in British social anthropology, but the way had already been cleared for him by Rivers (1914), who converted from evolutionism to diffusionism in the analysis of his own Melanesian field materials (Stocking 1987:321ff, Vincent 1990:121–24). Indeed, if nowadays diffusionism is being reclaimed as precursory to contemporary trends, it has deep roots in Melanesianist ethnography.

Translocal microregionalism is an inescapable ethnographic reality in that part of the world. It is apparent in the work of anthropologists of all theoretical persuasions [and subdisciplinary specialties (Foley 1986, Swadling 1990)]: from Mead (1938), for whom the Arapesh were an "importing culture," and Schwartz (1963), who described "systems of areal integration", through numerous studies of trading and exchange systems linking regional populations and village/clan/island communities (e.g. recently Strathern & Sturzenho-fecker 1994, Biersack 1995), to studies of mythic geographies (e.g. Wagner 1967, Munn 1986, Strathern 1995).

The Melanesian literature on regional relationships is closely tied to ethnographic explorations of indigenous comparative discourses (Lederman 1991a) and relational identities. For example, in studies of cosmology and myth (e.g. Wagner 1967, LeRoy 1985, Weiner 1988a,b), the prominence of themes of movement and both "internal" and "external" difference is striking. The syncretic openness (Glasse 1995) or improvisational inventiveness of indigenous discourses (Wagner 1975) is also evident in anthropological histories of first contact, colonial entanglements, political economic articulations, and gender constructions (e.g. Lederman 1986b, Biersack 1991, Schieffelin & Crittenden 1991, Lutkehaus 1995).

Melanesian cultural styles present a disorienting challenge to ideas about knowledge, power, identity, and sociality. These days, social theory is dominated by arguments, for example, about "the modern," a term made visible by contrast with "the postmodern." For all its productivity across disciplines, this polarity helps reproduce "the premodern" (a hodgepodge of the exotic, the rural, the tribal...) as a shadowy, illegitimate, background term, even in anthropology. Melanesianist ethnography presents images that cut across these distinctions (and at the same time force readers to face this otherwise residual category head-on). Indeed, the regional ethnography had a hard time imagining Melanesian cultures as "premodern," even when discovery of developmental progressions *was* fashionable. The ethnographic literature has confronted this conceptual challenge in two (related) ways: through an extreme elaboration of regional comparativism (in the form of endlessly dueling typologies, a cacophony of competing models), and through the pursuit of adequately critical translations (played out in local ethnography but engaging theoretically significant categories).

As far as typology-building goes, rhetorically unstable analogies abound, dismantled sometimes even in the act of construction (Modjeska 1982): For example, local exchange practices and ideas have been called "capitalist" and "entrepreneurial" (Epstein 1968, Pospisil 1972, Finney 1973), or they have looked like capitalism's opposite and then, inevitably, both and neither (Gregory 1982, Weiner 1992). Nowadays, longstanding descriptions of Melanesians' apparently iconoclastic, improvisational cultural style of dealing with novelty is looking oddly familiar in yet another way (as an alternative postmodernism perhaps).

Local ethnography has surely succumbed to—even luxuriated in—the comparativist temptations that such analytically decontextualized handles present, such that both their attractiveness and their limitations are painfully evident (Lederman 1991b). However, in the production of new, ill-fitting cases, and in the argumentative reordering of cases to make new typological models and to identify developmental patterns, these efforts set up another, more contextualizing, approach. Always incomplete (looking at individual works), much more satisfactory (looking at the literature as an extended conversation), Melanesian studies have shifted the language of anthropology to ever more critical translations of local discourses.

One example is the ethnography of Highland New Guinea social organization. This literature opened, in the 1950s, already deep in conversation with Africanist anthropology (Barnes 1962, Meggitt 1965, Kelly 1977, Karp 1978, A Strathern 1982a). Initially about the relevance of "African" segmentary lineage models, local ethnography quickly turned to fielding a variety of new images and debating their adequacy in representing what went on in this or that community: "flexible" structures, "loosely structured" societies, "non-groups" (Watson 1970, Keesing 1971). The reworking of anthropological language in an effort to produce adequate representations of Melanesian sociality (not to mention striking contrasts with existing ethnography) has involved detailed contextualization of local terms and practices (Lederman 1986a, Li-Puma 1988) and the coinage of eye-stopping neologisms (e.g. Strathern 1984, Merlan & Rumsey 1991) that shake loose from Durkheimian presuppositions about "society" and collectivity and their constitutive opposite, "the individual" (see especially Wagner 1974, Strathern 1988).

Never simply ethnographic though always elaborately committed to the detailed documentation of cases, to contextualization, and to storytelling, this regional literature poses a challenge to the presuppositions of Western social theory, a disruption to its recurrently naturalized universalisms. To appreciate how it has done this, the literature is best viewed as a whole, dialogically (rather than in terms of individual ethnographies): as a series of challenging engagements with extra-regional social theory, themselves both motivating and motivated by vigorous internal (intra-Melanesianist) debate over terms, functional relations, and interpretations. Viewed in this way, it has achieved its critical effects for the most part not by means of stereotyping (Us/Them) contrasts, but rather by means of progressively more ethnographically nuanced and constrained—therefore less transparent, more difficult—translations (Boon 1982, Asad 1986, M Strathern 1988). Accessibility is lost, surely (as novice readers can testify); but it would be a serious misreading to conclude that the cause is "exoticist" involution. What is gained is precisely the sort of equivalence and respect for coherence suggested in Trouillot's call for serious attention to diverse (lower-case) others.

The same story could be told about other (necessarily overlapping) topical conversations in the regional literature (on gender, exchange and value, knowledge, and power). The elaboration of critical translation work in Melanesianist ethnography, together with its explicit articulation with transregional social theory, accounts for much of its historical value in the discipline as a whole. And that is why it is still worth the trip (and the reading).

## CONCLUSION

The critical literature that frames this brief discussion of Melanesianist ethnography is full of arguments about the future of anthropology generally. As a cautious contribution to disciplinary futurology, I suggest that culture areas will have a modicum of on-going value not as geographical mappings of placed topics but as situated disciplinary discourses. Culture area discourses remain one of the valuable sociable contexts in which anthropological research is accomplished (as the recent formation of new area-based organizations by North Americanists and Europeanists suggests). The layering of perspectives and cross-purposes engendered by different anthropological observers—oriented Janus-like both to Trobrianders or Malaitans (of different sorts, at different times) and to one another (each with only partly overlapping disciplinary and extradisciplinary interests)—makes for a subtlety and depth not achievable by individual works, no matter how dialogic. That is something to acknowledge and to amplify.

Insofar as our work is "re-search" [as Appadurai (1997) offers, using a George Stocking-ism], it presumes "an organized professional community of criticism": a "prior citational world," a specialized community of readers, and conditions favoring "cross-checking"—all perhaps familiar sociology-of-science contexts for the normalization of ideas. But if Melanesian studies is at all typical, culture area work is not necessarily as homogenizing and conservative as this would imply. In these and other regards, we have a lot to learn about the practices of our various culture area communities, including not only their internal dynamics but also their mutual interrelations, and their respective engagements with non-anthropological specialist colleagues and nonspecialist interlocutors (readers, informant-readers, journalistic representers).[11] In the wake of disciplinary concern over anthropology's global positioning, the present, more limited, consideration of Melanesianist anthropology offers some evidence of the critical value of areal commitments when they are engaged, systematically and in diverse ways, with global discourses.

> **Visit the *Annual Reviews* home page at**
> **http://www.AnnualReviews.org.**

---

[11]A deeper comparative understanding of the various areal ethnographies and their mutual relationships (as Africa/Melanesia) or lack thereof—and, consequently, the dialogic elaboration of our various topical interests—would require explorations into their practical infrastructures. We would need to understand not only matters of funding and the pressures and opportunities afforded by related interdisciplinary area studies programs (as mentioned earlier) but also, for example, their respective journals, organizations, newsletters, academic meetings, and other fora of scholarly communication, not to mention the influence (or lack) of key figures (for example, there is no equivalent in Melanesian studies of Levi-Strauss's influence in Amazonian ethnography). In this context, we also need to explore our teaching practices: largely taken for granted but (anecdotal evidence suggests) likely to be a huge resource for understanding disciplinary trends. An investigation into these matters vis-à-vis Melanesia might (among many other things) include accounts of the Association for Social Anthropology in Oceania and of electronic discussion groups like ASAONET, recently a forum not only for scholarly and practical advice (whether about computers, kava, cultural categories, or class syllabi) but also for political discussion and organizing (around Hagahai genetic property rights, El Niño—related drought conditions and relief, logging, media image, and other issues).

444 LEDERMAN

## Literature Cited

Alvarez A. 1995. The Mexican-US border: the making of an anthropology of borderlands. *Annu. Rev. Anthropol.* 24:447–70

Appadurai A. 1986. Theory in anthropology: center and periphery. *Comp. Stud. Soc. Hist.* 28:356–61

Appadurai A. 1988a. Putting hierarchy in its place. See Appadurai 1988b, pp. 36–49

Appadurai A, ed. 1988b. Place and voice in anthropological theory. Theme issue. *Cult. Anthropol.* 3(1):16–96

Appadurai A. 1990. Disjuncture and difference in the global economy. *Public Cult.* 2(2):1–24

Appadurai A. 1991. Global ethnoscapes: notes and queries for a transnational anthropology. See Fox 1991b, pp. 191–210

Appadurai A. 1997. The research ethic and the spirit of internationalism. *Items* 51(4): 55–60

Appadurai A, Breckenridge CA. 1988. Why public culture? *Public Cult.* 1(1):5–10

Asad T. 1973. *Anthropology and the Colonial Encounter.* London: Ithaca

Asad T. 1986. The concept of cultural translation in British social anthropology. In *Writing Culture: The Poetics and Politics of Ethnography,* ed. J Clifford, G Marcus, pp. 141–64. Berkeley: Univ. Calif. Press

Barnes J. 1962. African models in the New Guinea highlands. *Man* 52:5–9

Bateson G. 1936. *Naven.* Stanford, CA: Stanford Univ. Press

Battaglia D. 1995a. On practical nostalgia: self-prospecting among urban Trobrianders. See Battaglia 1995b, pp. 77–96

Battaglia D, ed. 1995b. *Rhetorics of Self-Making.* Berkeley: Univ. Calif. Press

Biersack A, ed. 1991. *Clio in Oceania: Toward a Historical Anthropology.* Washington, DC: Smithson. Inst.

Biersack A, ed. 1995. *Papuan Borderlands: Huli, Duna, and Ipili Perspectives on the Papua New Guinea Highlands.* Ann Arbor: Univ. Mich. Press

Boas F. 1896. The limitations of the comparative method of anthropology. *Science* 4: 901–8

Boon J. 1982. *Other Tribes, Other Scribes: Symbolic Anthropology in the Comparative Study of Cultures, Histories, Religions, and Texts.* Cambridge, UK: Cambridge Univ. Press

Breckenridge CA, Appadurai A. 1988. Editors' comments. *Public Cult.* 1(1):1

Brenneis D. 1997. New lexicon, old language: negotiating the "global" at the National Science Foundation. In *Critical Anthropology Now,* ed. G Marcus. Santa Fe, NM: SAR

Carrier J. 1992a. Introduction. See Carrier 1992b, pp. 1–37

Carrier J, ed. 1992b. *History and Tradition in Melanesian Anthropology.* Berkeley: Univ. Calif. Press

Ching B, Creed G, eds. 1997. *Knowing Your Place.* New York: Routledge

Clark J. 1993. Gold, sex, and pollution: male illness and mythology at Mt. Kare. *Am. Ethnol.* 20:742–57

Clifford J. 1988. On ethnographic authority. In *The Predicament of Culture: Twentieth Century Ethnography, Literature and Art,* ed. J Clifford, pp. 21–54. Cambridge, MA: Harvard Univ. Press

Clifford J. 1997. Spatial practices: fieldwork, travel, and the disciplining of anthropology. See Gupta & Ferguson 1997b, pp. 185–222

Comaroff JL. 1996. Ethnicity, nationalism, and the politics of difference in an age of revolution. See Wilmsen & McAllister 1996, pp. 162–83

Comaroff JL, Comaroff J. 1991. *Of Revelation and Revolution: Christianity, Colonialism, and Consciousness in South Africa,* Vol. 1. Chicago: Univ. Chicago Press

Cooper F, Stoler A, eds. 1989. *Tensions of Empire: Colonial Control and Visions of Rule.* Special Issue. *Am. Ethnol.* 16(4): 609–765

Dresch P. 1988. Segmentation: its roots in Arabia and its flowering elsewhere. See Appadurai 1988b, pp. 50–67

Ehrich RW, Henderson GM. 1968. Culture area. In *International Encyclopedia of the Social Sciences,* ed. DL Sills, pp. 563–68. New York: Macmillan

Epstein S. 1968. *Capitalism, Primitive and Modern.* Canberra: Aust. Natl. Univ. Press

Errington F, Gewertz D. 1995. *Articulating Change in the "Last Unknown."* Boulder, CO: Westview

Errington F, Gewertz D. 1997. The Wewak Rotary Club: the middle class in Melanesia. *J. R. Anthropol. Inst.* NS 3(2):333–53

Fabian J. 1983. *Time and the Other: How Anthropology Makes Its Object.* New York: Columbia Univ. Press

Fardon R, ed. 1990. *Localizing Strategies: Regional Traditions of Ethnographic Writing.* Washington, DC: Smithson. Inst.

Finney B. 1973. *Big Men and Business: Entrepreneurship and Economic Growth in the New Guinea Highlands.* Canberra: Aust. Natl. Univ. Press

Foerstel L, Gilliam A, eds. 1992. *Confronting the Margaret Mead Legacy: Scholarship, Empire, and the South Pacific.* Philadelphia, PA: Temple Univ. Press

Foley W. 1986. *The Papuan Languages of New Guinea.* Cambridge, UK: Cambridge Univ. Press

Foster R. 1996a. Print advertisements and nation making in metropolitan Papua New Guinea. See Foster 1996b, pp. 151–81

Foster R, ed. 1996b. *Nation Making: Emergent Identities in Postcolonial Melanesia.* Ann Arbor: Univ. Mich. Press

Fox R. 1991a. For a nearly new culture history. See Fox 1991b, pp. 93–113

Fox R, ed. 1991b. *Recapturing Anthropology: Working in the Present.* Santa Fe, NM: SAR

Gewertz D, Errington F. 1987. *Cultural Alternatives and a Feminist Anthropology.* Cambridge, UK: Cambridge Univ. Press

Gewertz D, Errington F. 1990. *Twisted Histories, Altered Contexts: Representing the Chambri in a World System.* Cambridge, UK: Cambridge Univ. Press

Gilliam A. 1992. Leaving the record for others: an interview with Nahau Rooney. See Foerstel & Gilliam 1992, pp. 31–54

Glasse R. 1995. Time belong *mbingi*: religious syncretism and the pacification of the Huli. See Biersack 1995, pp. 57–86

Godelier M. 1986. *The Making of Great Men: Male Domination and Power among the New Guinea Baruya.* Cambridge, UK: Cambridge Univ. Press

Gregory C. 1982. *Gifts and Commodities.* London: Academic

Grossberg L, Nelson C, Treichler P, eds. 1992. *Cultural Studies.* New York: Routledge

Gupta A, Ferguson J. 1992. Beyond 'culture': space, identity, and the politics of difference. *Cult. Anthropol.* 7(1):6–23

Gupta A, Ferguson J. 1997a. Discipline and practice: "the field" as site, method, and location in anthropology. See Gupta & Ferguson 1997b, pp. 1–46

Gupta A, Ferguson J, eds. 1997b. *Anthropological Locations: Boundaries and Grounds of a Field Science.* Berkeley: Univ. Calif. Press

Hall S. 1991. The local and the global: globalization and ethnicity. In *Culture, Globalization and the World-System: Contemporary Conditions for the Representation of Identity,* ed. AD King, pp. 19–39. Binghamton: State Univ. NY Press

Hammar L. 1992. Sexual transactions on Daru: with some observations on the ethnographic enterprise. *Res. Melanesia* 16: 21–54

Hammar L. 1995. Crisis in the South Fly: the

problem with sex and the sex industry on Daru Island, Western Province, Papua New Guinea. PhD thesis. City Univ., New York

Hannerz U. 1987. The world in creolization. *Africa* 57:546–59

Hannerz U. 1989. Notes on the global ecumene. *Public Cult.* 1(2):66–75

Hannerz U. 1996. *Transnational Connections: Culture, People, Places.* New York: Routledge

Harvey D. 1989. *The Condition of Postmodernity: An Enquiry into the Origins of Cultural Change.* Cambridge, UK: Blackwell

Hau'ofa E. 1975. Anthropology and Pacific islanders. *Oceania* 45:283–89

Hays T. 1993. "The New Guinea Highlands": region, culture area or fuzzy set? *Curr. Anthropol.* 34:141–64

Headland T, Reid L. 1989. Hunter-gatherers and their neighbors from prehistory to the present. *Curr. Anthropol.* 30:43–66

Herskovitz M. 1955. *Cultural Anthropology.* New York: Knopf

Herzfeld M. 1984. The horns of the Mediterraneanist dilemma. *Am. Ethnol.* 11:439–54

Herzfeld M. 1987. *Anthropology Through the Looking Glass: Ethnography in the Margins of Europe.* Cambridge, UK: Cambridge Univ. Press

Holy L, ed. 1987. *Comparative Anthropology.* New York: Blackwell

Huber M. 1990. The bishop's progress: representations of missionary experience on the Sepik frontier. See Lutkehaus et al 1990, pp. 197–211

Hymes D, ed. 1972. *Reinventing Anthropology.* New York: Pantheon

Hyndman D. 1994. *Ancestral Rain Forests and the Mountain of Gold: Indigenous Peoples and Mining in New Guinea.* Boulder, CO: Westview

Iamo W. 1992. The stigma of New Guinea: reflections on anthropology and anthropologists. See Foerstel & Gilliam 1992, pp. 75–100

Jameson F. 1990. *Postmodernism or the Cultural Logic of Late Capitalism.* Durham, NC: Duke Univ. Press

Jenkins C. 1994. *National Study of Sexual and Reproductive Knowledge and Behavior in Papua New Guinea.* Monogr. 10. Goroka, Papua, New Guinea: PNG Inst. Med. Res.

Jolly M, MacIntyre M, eds. 1989. *Family and Gender in the Pacific: Domestic Contradictions and the Colonial Impact.* Cambridge, UK: Cambridge Univ. Press

Kaplan M. 1993. Imagining a nation: race, politics and crisis in post-colonial Fiji. See Lockwood et al 1993, pp. 34–54

Kaplan M. 1995. *Neither Cargo Nor Cult: Rit-*

ual Politics and the Colonial Imagination in Fiji. Durham, NC: Duke Univ. Press

Karp I. 1978. New Guinea models in the African savannah. Africa 48:1–17

Kearney M. 1995. The local and the global: the anthropology of globalization and transnationalism. Annu. Rev. Anthropol. 24: 547–65

Keesing R. 1971. Simple models of complexity: the lure of kinship. In Kinship Studies in the Morgan Centennial Year, ed. P Reining, pp. 17–31. Washington, DC: Anthropol. Soc. Wash.

Keesing R. 1978. 'Elota's Story: The Life and Times of a Solomon Islands Big Man. St. Lucia, Queensland, Aust: Univ. Queensland Press

Keesing R. 1992. Custom and Confrontation: the Kwaio Struggle for Cultural Autonomy. Chicago: Univ. Chicago Press

Keesing R, Jolly M. 1992. Epilogue. See Carrier 1992b, pp. 224–47

Keesing R, Tonkinson R, eds. 1982. Reinventing Traditional Culture: The Politics of Kastom in Island Melanesia. Mankind 13: 297–399

Kelly J. 1991. A Politics of Virtue: Hinduism, Sexuality, and Countercolonial Discourse in Fiji. Chicago: Univ. Chicago Press

Kelly R. 1977. Etoro Social Structure: A Study in Structural Contradiction. Ann Arbor: Univ. Mich. Press

Knauft B. 1993. South Coast New Guinea Cultures: History, Comparison, Dialectic. Cambridge, UK: Cambridge Univ. Press

Knauft B. 1994. Foucault meets south New Guinea: knowledge, power, sexuality. Ethos 22:391–438

Kroeber A. 1939/1963. Cultural and Natural Areas of Native North America. Berkeley: Univ. Calif. Press

Kuklick H. 1996. Islands in the Pacific: Darwinian biogeography and British anthropology. Am. Ethnol. 23:611–38

Kuklick H. 1997. After Ishmael: the fieldwork tradition and its future. See Gupta & Ferguson 1997b, pp. 47–67

Kulick D. 1992. Language Shift and Cultural Reproduction: Socialization, Self, and Syncretism in a Papua New Guinean Village. Cambridge, UK: Cambridge Univ. Press

Kulick D. 1993. Heroes from hell: representations of "rascals" in a Papua New Guinea village. Anthropol. Today 9:9–14

Kuper A. 1988. The Invention of Primitive Society. London: Routledge

Kyakas A, Weisner P. 1992. From Inside the Women's House: Enga Women's Lives and Traditions. Burunda, Queensland, Aust: Brown

Larcom J. 1990. Custom by decree: legitimation crisis in Vanuatu. See Linnekin & Poyer 1990, pp.175–90

Lawson S. 1993. The politics of tradition: problems for political legitimacy and democracy in the South Pacific. Pac. Stud. 16(2):1–29

Leacock E. 1992. Anthropologists in search of a culture: Margaret Mead, Derek Freeman, and all the rest of us. See Foerstel & Gilliam 1992, pp. 3–30

Lederman R. 1986a. What Gifts Engender: Social Relations and Politics in Mendi, Highland Papua New Guinea. Cambridge, UK: Cambridge Univ. Press

Lederman R. 1986b. Changing times in Mendi: notes towards writing Highland New Guinea history. Ethnohistory 33:1–30

Lederman R. 1991a. Dialectics of the gift. Book review forum. Pac. Stud. 14:142–56

Lederman R. 1991b. 'Interests' in exchange: Mendi big men in context. In Big Men and Great Men: The Development of a Comparison in Melanesia, ed. M Godelier, M Strathern, pp. 71–91. Cambridge, UK: Cambridge Univ. Press

LeRoy J. 1985. Fabricated World: An Interpretation of Kewa Tales. Vancouver: Univ. B. C. Press

Levinson D, ed. 1991. Encyclopedia of World Cultures. Boston: Hall

Lindstrom L, White G, eds. 1990. Island Encounters: Black and White Memories of the Pacific War. Washington, DC: Smithson. Inst. Press

Linnekin J, Poyer L, eds. 1990. Cultural Identity and Ethnicity in the Pacific. Honolulu: Univ. Hawaii Press

LiPuma E. 1988. The Gift of Kinship: Structure and Practice in Maring Social Organization. Cambridge, UK: Cambridge Univ. Press

Lockwood VS, Harding T, Wallace B, eds. 1993. Contemporary Pacific Societies: Studies in Development and Change. Englewood Cliffs, NJ: Prentice Hall

Lutkehaus N. 1995. Zaria's Fire: Engendered Moments in Manam Ethnography. Durham, NC: Carolina Acad. Press

Lutkehaus N, Kaufman C, Mitchell W, Newton D, Osmundsen L, et al, eds. 1990. Sepik Heritage: Tradition and Change in Papua New Guinea. Durham, NC: Carolina Acad. Press

Lyotard J-F. 1986. The Postmodern Condition: a Report on Knowledge. Manchester, UK: Manchester Univ. Press

MacIntyre M. 1989. Better homes and gardens. See Jolly & MacIntrye 1989, pp. 156–69

Malinowski B. 1922. *Argonauts of the Western Pacific*. New York: Dutton

Malkki L. 1995. Refugees and exile: from "refugee studies" to the national order of things. *Annu. Rev. Anthropol.* 24:495–546

Marcus G, Fischer M, eds. 1986. *Anthropology as Cultural Critique*. Chicago: Univ. Chicago Press

Martin E. 1994. *Flexible Bodies: Tracking Immunity in American Culture from the Days of Polio to the Age of AIDS*. Boston: Beacon

Mauss M. 1925/1967. *The Gift*. Transl. I Cunnison. New York: Norton

May RJ, Spriggs M, eds. 1991. *The Bougainville Crisis*. Bathurst, NSW: Crawford House

McDowell N. 1991. *The Mundugumor: From the Fieldnotes of Margaret Mead and Gregory Bateson*. Washington, DC: Smithson. Inst.

Mead M. 1935/1963. *Sex and Temperament in Three Primitive Societies*. New York: Morrow

Mead M. 1938. The Mountain Arapesh: an importing culture. *Am. Mus. Natl. Hist. Anthropol. Pap. 36*, pp. 139–349

Meek R. 1976. *Social Science and the Ignoble Savage*. Cambridge, UK: Cambridge Univ. Press

Meggitt M. 1965. *The Lineage System of the Mae Enga of New Guinea*. New York: Barnes & Noble

Merlan F, Rumsey A. 1991. *Ku Waru: Language and Segmentary Politics in the Western Nebilyer Valley, Papua New Guinea*. Cambridge, UK: Cambridge Univ. Press

Modjeska N. 1982. Production and inequality: perspectives from central New Guinea. See Strathern 1982b, pp. 50–108

Munn N. 1986. *The Fame of Gawa: A Symbolic Study of Value Transformation in a Massim Society*. Cambridge, UK: Cambridge Univ. Press

Murdock G. 1951. South American culture areas. *Southwest. J. Anthropol.* 7: 415–36

Murdock G. 1967. *The Ethnographic Atlas: A Summary*. Pittsburgh, PA: Univ. Pittsburgh Press

Narakobi B. 1983. *The Melanesian Way*. Suva: Univ. South Pacific

O'Hanlon M. 1995. Modernity and the "graphicalization" of meaning: New Guinea Highland shield design in historical perspective. *J. R. Anthropol. Inst. NS* 1:469–93

Ortner S. 1981. Gender and sexuality in hierarchical societies: the case of Polynesia and some comparative implications. In *Sexual Meanings*, ed. S Ortner, H Whitehead, pp.

359–409. Cambridge, UK: Cambridge Univ. Press

Pagden A. 1982. *The Fall of Natural Man: The American Indian and the Origins of Comparative Ethnology*. Cambridge, UK: Cambridge Univ. Press

Passaro J. 1997. "You can't take the subway to the field!": 'Village' epistemologies in the global village. See Gupta & Ferguson 1997b, pp. 147–62

Pospisil L. 1972. *Kapauku Papuan Economy*. Yale Univ. Publ. Anthropol. 67. New Haven, CT: Hum. Relat. Area File

Prewitt K. 1996a. Presidential items. *Items* 50(1):15–18

Prewitt K. 1996b. Presidential items. *Items* 50(2/3):31–40

Prewitt K. 1996c. International dissertation field research: a new fellowship program. *Items* 50(4):91–92

Rafael V. 1994. The cultures of area studies in the United States. *Soc. Text* 41:91–111

Rappaport R. 1968. *Pigs for the Ancestors*. New Haven, CT: Yale Univ. Press

Rivers WHR. 1914. *The History of Melanesian Society*. Cambridge, UK: Cambridge Univ. Press

Robbins J. 1995. Dispossessing the spirits: Christian transformations of desire and ecology among the Urapmin of Papua New Guinea. *Ethnology* 34:211–24

Rosaldo R. 1989. *Culture and Truth: The Remaking of Social Analysis*. Boston: Beacon

Sahlins M. 1985. *Islands of History*. Chicago: Univ. Chicago Press

Sahlins M, Service E. 1960. *Evolution and Culture*. Ann Arbor: Univ. Mich. Press

Said E. 1978. *Orientalism*. New York: Routledge

Sanjek R, ed. 1990. *Fieldnotes: The Makings of Anthropology*. Ithaca: Cornell Univ. Press

Schieffelin E, Crittenden R, eds. 1991. *Like People You See in a Dream: First Contact in Six Papuan Societies*. Stanford, CA: Stanford Univ. Press

Schwartz T. 1963. Systems of areal integration. *Anthropol. Forum* 1:56–97

Stocking G. 1987. *Victorian Anthropology*. New York: Free Press

Stocking G. 1992. The ethnographer's magic: fieldwork in British anthropology from Tylor to Malinowski. In *The Ethnographer's Magic*, pp. 12–59. Madison: Univ. Wis. Press

Stoler A. 1991. Carnal knowledge and imperial power: gender, race, and morality in colonial Asia. In *Gender at the Crossroads of Knowledge*, ed. M DiLeonardo, pp. 51–101. Berkeley: Univ. Calif. Press

Strathern A. 1979. *Ongka: A Self-Account by a*

*New Guinea Big-Man.* Transl. A Strathern. London: Duckworth

Strathern A. 1982a. Two waves of African models in the New Guinea Highlands. See Strathern 1992, pp. 35–49

Strathern A, ed. 1982b. *Inequality in New Guinea Highlands Societies.* Cambridge, UK: Cambridge Univ. Press

Strathern A. 1984. *A Line of Power.* London: Tavistock

Strathern A. 1992. Let the bow go down. In *War in the Tribal Zone: Expanding States and Indigenous Warfare,* ed. B Ferguson, N Whitehead, pp. 229–50. Santa Fe, NM: SAR

Strathern A. 1993. Violence and political change in Papua New Guinea. *Pac. Stud.* 16(4):41–60

Strathern A. 1995. Ritual movements reconsidered: ethnohistory in Aluni. See Lutkehaus et al 1995, pp. 87–110

Strathern A, Sturzenhofecker G, eds. 1994. *Migration and Transformations: Regional Perspectives on New Guinea.* Assoc. Soc. Anthropol. Oceania Monogr. 15. Pittsburgh, PA: Univ. Pittsburgh Press

Strathern M. 1975. *No Money on Our Skins: Hagen Migrants in Port Moresby.* Canberra: Aust. Natl. Univ. Press

Strathern M. 1988. *The Gender of the Gift: Problems with Women and Problems with Society in Melanesia.* Berkeley: Univ. Calif. Press

Strathern M. 1990. Negative strategies in Melanesia. See Fardon 1990, pp. 204–16

Strathern M. 1991. *Partial Connections.* Savage, MD: Rowman & Littlefield

Strathern M. 1992. *Reproducing the Future: Anthropology, Kinship, and the New Reproductive Technologies.* Manchester, UK: Manchester Univ. Press

Sullivan N. 1993. Film and television production in Papua New Guinea: How media become the message. *Public Cult.* 5: 533–55

Swadling P. 1990. Sepik prehistory. See Lutkehaus et al 1990, pp. 71–86

Sykes K. 1995. *Raising Lelet: education, knowledge, and the crisis of youth in central New Ireland, Papua New Guinea.* PhD thesis. Princeton Univ., Princeton, NJ

Thomas N. 1989. The force of ethnology: origins and significance of the Melanesia/Polynesia division. *Curr. Anthropol.* 30:27–42

Trouillot M-R. 1991. Anthropology and the savage slot. See Fox 1991b, pp. 17–44

Tsing A. 1993. *In the Realm of the Diamond Queen: Marginality in an Out-of-the-Way Place.* Princeton, NJ: Princeton Univ. Press

Tsing A. 1994. From the margins. *Cult. Anthropol.* 9:279–97

Vincent J. 1990. *Anthropology and Politics: Visions, Traditions, and Trends.* Tucson: Univ. Ariz. Press

Wagner R. 1967. *The Curse of Souw: Principles of Daribi Clan Definition and Alliance in New Guinea.* Chicago: Univ. Chicago Press

Wagner R. 1974. Are there groups in the New Guinea Highlands? In *Frontiers of Anthropology,* ed. M Leaf, pp. 95–122. New York: Van Nostrand

Wagner R. 1975. *The Invention of Culture.* Chicago: Univ. Chicago Press

Waiko J. 1992. Tugata: culture, identity, and commitment. See Foerstel & Gilliam 1992, pp. 233–66

Wallerstein I. 1996. Open the social sciences. *Items* 50(1):1–7

Wallerstein I, Juma C, Fox Keller E, Kocka J, LeCourt D, et al. 1996. *Open the Social Sciences: Report of the Gulbenkian Commission on the Restructuring of the Social Sciences.* Stanford, CA: Stanford Univ. Press

Watson J. 1970. Society as organized flow: the Tairora case. *Southwest. J. Anthropol.* 26: 107–24

Weiner A. 1976. *Women of Value, Men of Renown: New Perspectives on Trobriand Exchange.* Austin: Univ Tex. Press

Weiner A. 1992. *Inalienable Possessions: The Paradox of Keeping-While-Giving.* Berkeley: Univ. Calif. Press

Weiner J. 1988a. *The Heart of the Pearlshell: The Mythological Dimension of Foi Sociality.* Berkeley: Univ. Calif. Press

Weiner J, ed. 1988b. *Mountain Papuans: History and Comparative Perspectives from New Guinea Fringe Highlands Societies.* Ann Arbor: Univ. Mich. Press

Weiner J. 1994. The origin of petroleum at Lake Kutubu. *Cult. Anthropol.* 9:37–57

Weston K. 1991. *Families We Choose: Lesbians, Gays, Kinship.* New York: Columbia Univ. Press

Weston K. 1997. The virtual anthropologist. See Gupta & Ferguson 1997, pp. 163–84

White G. 1991. *Identity Through History: Living Stories in a Solomon Island Society.* Cambridge, UK: Cambridge Univ. Press

Wilmsen E, McAllister P, eds. 1996. *The Politics of Difference: Ethnic Premises in a World of Power.* Chicago: Univ. Chicago Press

Winthrop R. 1991. Culture area. In *Dictionary of Concepts in Cultural Anthropology,* pp. 61–63. New York: Greenwood

Wissler C. 1917/1957. *The American Indian: An Introduction to the Anthropology of the*

*New World.* Gloucester, MA: Smith. 3rd ed.

Wolf E. 1982. *Europe and the People Without History.* Berkeley: Univ. Calif. Press

Worsley P. 1957. *The Trumpet Shall Sound: A Study of 'Cargo' Cults in Melanesia.* London: MacGibbon & Kee

Zimmer-Tamakoshi L. 1993a. Nationalism and sexuality in Papua New Guinea. *Pac. Stud.* 16(4):61–97

Zimmer-Tamakoshi L. 1993b. Bachelors, spinsters, and *pamuk meris.* In *The Business of Marriage: Transformations in Oceanic Matrimony*, ed. R Marksbury, pp. 83–104. Pittsburgh, PA: Univ. Pittsburgh Press

*Annu. Rev. Anthropol. 1998. 27:451–72*
*Copyright © 1998 by Annual Reviews. All rights reserved*

# CURRENT ISSUES IN LINGUISTIC TAXONOMY

*Peter A. Michalove*

University of Illinois, 307 S. McKinley, Champaign, IL 61821-3247;
e-mail: peterm@hercules.geology.uiuc.edu

*Stefan Georg*

University of Bonn, Heerstrasse 7, Bonn, D-53111 Federal Republic of Germany;
e-mail: georg@home.ivm.de

*Alexis Manaster Ramer*

Wayne State University, 4225 Walden Drive, Ann Arbor, MI 48105; e-mail:
manaster@umich.edu

KEY WORDS: historical linguistics, comparative linguistics

---

## ABSTRACT

The genealogical classification of languages has been the subject of investigation for more than two centuries, and progress continues to be made in deepening our understanding of language change, both in theoretical terms and in the study of specific language families. In recent years, as in the past, many new proposals of linguistic relationships have been constructed, some promising to various degrees and others clearly untenable. The debate about specific recent proposals is part of the healthy process needed to evaluate proposed relationships, discard those that prove incorrect, and refine those of merit. Rather than evaluating the relative linguistic "distance" between potentially related languages, with temporal distance leading to some point where we cannot distinguish real relationships from chance similarities, we propose a scale of easy to difficult relationships in which temporal distance is only one factor that makes some relationships more recognizable than others.

---

## INTRODUCTION

Linguistic taxonomy, the attempt to group languages by genetic affiliation, has been going on informally for as long as people have noticed that some lan-

451

guages share certain features that do not characterize other languages. But it was Sir William Jones' famous statement in 1786 that not only led to the recognition of Indo-European (which has become the most intensely studied language family in the world, by far), but also put linguistic taxonomy on a solid foundation for the first time:

> The Sanskrit language, whatever may be its antiquity, is of a wonderful structure; more perfect than Greek, more copious than Latin, and more exquisitely refined than either, yet bearing to both of them a stronger affinity, both within the roots of verbs and in the forms of grammar, than could possibly have been produced by accident; so strong indeed that no philologer could examine them all, without believing them to have sprung from some common source, which, perhaps, no longer exists....

Although there were various precursors of Jones, such as Père Gaston Coeurdoux (see Godfrey 1967), it was Jones' statement alone that influenced the development of comparative linguistics. One of the immediate implications of Jones' pronouncement was the concept that all living languages change over time. Thus, the thousands of modern languages spoken in the world today are all later, changed forms of earlier languages and, at least in many cases, they are later, changed forms of the same earlier languages. Thus, by comparing languages that have developed from an earlier common ancestor, we can reconstruct, to varying degrees, the actual features of the ancestral language common to that group of later, attested languages. By the middle of the nineteenth century, many linguists concluded that it might be possible to reconstruct the greater part of such an unattested ancestral tongue language (which came to be known as a "proto-language"), although ever since then opinions have continued to be divided over the extent to which we can hope to know any proto-language.

This view of a discernible genealogical relationship among at least many of the languages of the world paralleled the growth of Darwinian ideas of biological evolution and Linnaean classification in the nineteenth century. Over the past two centuries, however, the study of historical and comparative linguistics has grown vastly more sophisticated, and scholars have profited from the lessons gained in neighboring fields, such as synchronic linguistics, anthropology, and sociology. While the genetic model of linguistic relationships is still the best way to describe the relationships among the majority of languages, more recent insights about language contact have demonstrated that linguistic development is not nearly so simple.

Thus, the lexicon of modern English, a Germanic language, consists more of loan forms (primarily from Latin, French, and Norse, with smaller contributions from a host of other languages around the world) than of native forms. Yet the derivation of its most basic vocabulary, as well as its structure, leave no doubt of its Germanic origins. We can see this clearly by comparing features of

English and German, such as ablaut (vocalic alternations that indicate morpho-logical functions) in the English paradigm *sing, sang, sung* with German *sin-gen, sang, gesungen*; or in suppletive relationships like English *good, better, best* with German *gut, besser, am besten.*

At the same time, the presence of loans in the language makes the need to distinguish native and borrowed elements a key task in historical linguistics. In languages without the long written tradition of English (that is, the majority of languages of the world), this task is all the more crucial and difficult, but not necessarily impossible, as we shall see below.

As the field of historical linguistics matured, a number of language families quickly emerged as clear taxonomic entities, agreed upon by all scholars who worked with them. Some, like the Romance or Germanic languages, were eas-ily recognized as valid families simply because their structure and lexicon were so obviously parallel. Indo-European as a whole, while more diverse and less obviously related, came to be recognized as an uncontroversial grouping, simply because it was subject to greater study, since most historical linguists were native speakers of Indo-European languages.

Still other language groupings, such as Altaic and Na-Déné, have been more controversial and, to some extent, remain so, partly because the evidence is much less clear, and partly because they have received far less scholarly atten-tion than have the classical languages of the Old World. In the meantime, new research continues to modify our views of the taxonomy of even well-recognized families.

Our goal in this paper is to survey some of the better-known current propos-als, and to put them and the discipline of linguistic classification into proper historical perspective. We refrain from discussion of our personal views on each of these proposals, since that is not our goal here, and in fact the three of us do not all agree on the merits of each of these proposals. In addition, some of these proposals involve languages with which we do not all have familiarity and are not competent to judge. Rather, in this survey we hope to convey some of the potential and importance of recent work in language classification.

The study of linguistic classification is twofold: (*a*) It attempts to identify which languages are demonstrably continuations of a common earlier form, and (*b*) it attempts to separate that evidence for common origin from the more recent developments within the individual languages as well as the results of language contact. In these tasks, the discipline of historical linguistics has achieved a number of remarkable successes, both in identifying language families that represent later, changed forms of a common ancestral language, and in identifying spurious matches, common features of attested languages that are not, in themselves, evidence of common ancestry.

Thus, to take a concrete example, we know that forms like Modern English *ten*, Latin *decem*, Greek *déka*, Sanskrit *daśa,* Russian *desjat'*, Lithuanian *děšimt*, and Armenian *tasn* are cognate forms; that is, they represent the subsequent developments of a common Indo-European form, usually reconstructed as \*deƙm̥. A vast number of forms illustrate the correspondences by which English and Armenian initial /t/- correspond to /d/- in the other branches of Indo-European; certain instances of /s/ in Slavic and Armenian, and Lithuanian /š/ correspond to /k/ in the other branches; Greek /a/ and Armenian and Germanic final /n/ correspond to the vocalic \*/m̥/ of Indo-European; Sanskrit /a/ corresponds to Greek and Latin /e/, and so on. Examples of each of these correspondences can be found dozens and, in some cases, hundreds of times among these languages. By the same token, the absence of such correspondences in English forms such as *decade* and *decimal* indicates that we are not dealing with native Germanic forms, but with loan words—in this case, the first from Greek, and the second from Latin.

Similar regularities in morphological constructions are another important clue that we are dealing with descendants of a common earlier language. For example, Latin *es-t* (he is) and *s-unt* (they are), correspond to Sanskrit *as-ti* and *s-anti* (id.), Old Church Slavonic *jes-tŭ* and *s-ǫtŭ* (id.), as well as German *is-t* and *s-ind* (id.) and other Indo-European forms.

## FACT AND MYTH IN LINGUISTIC TAXONOMY

Largely thanks to the work of Greenberg (1955, 1963), but going back at least to Setälä (1913), we also know that many typological features, such as vowel harmony (the restriction on vowels that may co-occur within a given phonological domain), or ergativity (the manner of marking subjects of intransitive verbs and direct objects of transitive verbs) occur in many languages throughout the world and are not probative for linguistic relationship. While most linguists take this point for granted today, it is all too easy to forget that the early surveys of the languages of the world had yet to learn this lesson. While we cannot review the entire history of linguistic classification, we should note that Adelung (1806–1817), a monumental and valuable effort, classified languages according to their geographical locations but, especially in the first volume devoted to the languages of Asia, the top-level subdivision is that into "einsylbige" vs "mehrsylbige Sprachen"; moreover, according to Adelung, the latter are viewed as derived from the former. Typological traits are thus viewed as principally subject to change. Nevertheless, even if sometimes remarkable observations are made that this or that language has some material elements (usually words) in common with another language, Adelung's work rests largely on these isomorphisms of form rather than on material commonalities.

In fact, languages commonly gain or lose typological features in the course of their development. Old Turkic, like most of the modern Turkic languages, exhibits vowel harmony, but this feature has largely been lost in modern urban Uzbek. Most Indo-European languages, including Classical Greek, on the other hand, do not have vowel harmony; however, it has developed relatively recently in the Greek of Asia Minor.

Similarly, ergative morphosyntax is attributed to proto-Kartvelian and is characteristic of Georgian and Svan, but it can be shown to have been lost in Laz and Mingrelian, the other two languages of that family. And while ergativity is not characteristic of most Indo-European languages, it developed relatively recently in Hindi-Urdu and most of the other modern Indic languages. The same diversity of development can be shown to apply to the other typological factors, such as word order, the presence or absence of phonemic tone, morphological structure, and others.

Greenberg (1955, 1963) also clarified (as had again been stated as early as Setälä 1913) that language relationships cannot be determined on the basis of ethnicity. The mistaken notion that languages can be meaningfully classified on the basis of the race or physical type of their speakers is already present in Adelung, especially in Volume 3 on African languages, but reached its epitome in Müller (1876–1887), that other major milestone—for, despite this and other drawbacks, a milestone it was—of nineteenth-century language classification. Here, the very subdivision of the work clearly bespeaks the racial foundation of the whole enterprise. Thus, we find (*a*) "Die Sprachen der wollhaarigen Rassen" ("The languages of the thick-haired races") (Khoisans, Papuans, and Black Africans); (*b*) "Die Sprachen der schlichthaarigen Rassen" ("The languages of the sleek-haired races") (Australians, Native Americans, Oceanians, and Asians—the latter further differentiated into speakers of monosyllabic and polysyllabic languages); (*c*) "Die Sprachen der lockenhaarigen Rassen" ("The languages of the curly haired races") (Nubas and Dravidians); and (*d*) "Die Sprachen der mittelländischen Rasse" ("The languages of the Mediterranean race"), comprising Caucasians, Basques, and the speakers of Indo-European and Afroasiatic languages. Although Müller explicitly subscribes to the principle that language-relationship can only be asserted and demonstrated positively on the basis of regular material correspondences of vocabulary and morphology, his whole work is riddled with this racial perspective, leading to the acceptance of Altaic but an apparent rejection of Uralic (Samoyed plus Finno-Ugric), obviously for racial reasons. Elsewhere, very correct observations on the relationship between Hausa and other "Hamitic" languages are made, but at last attributed to a "profound influence of Hamitic" on one of the languages of Black Africa, again in order not to allow any language grouping to transgress Müller's a prioristic racial groups.

Of course, languages cannot be meaningfully classified on racial bases. Factors such as conquest, migration, and intermarriage can cause speakers of one language to adopt a completely different language. In the United States alone, English is spoken by representatives of probably every ethnicity in the world. At the same time, a child born to English-speaking parents but raised in an environment speaking some different language will grow up as a native speaker of that language.

## RECENT PROGRESS IN LINGUISTIC TAXONOMY

In recent years, the comparison of known language families in a search for more distant relationships has received a great deal of scholarly and (what may be a new factor) public attention. Many of the new proposals have been quite controversial and, unfortunately, the rhetoric has become very strident and increasingly extremist. Coming on the heels of a generation that showed relatively little interest in diachronic work of any sort, this kind of stormy debate may appear to be a new development in historical linguistics. But our thesis here is that current work in linguistic classification is simply the continuation of a longstanding scholarly tradition that, unfortunately, does not proceed in neat, clearly agreed-upon steps, but that, in the long run, has always yielded worthwhile results.

In fact, aside from some of the more controversial current proposals, it is important to note that progress in linguistic classification has been a constant throughout the past two centuries, and recent decades have seen a number of important steps in understanding the position of languages whose affinity had not been previously understood or agreed upon. While the position of a number of languages and families (such as Eskimo-Aleut, Afroasiatic, and Algic) has reached a consensus in recent decades, two examples seem to be especially informative.

The Vietnamese language, which was tentatively linked with Mon-Khmer in the nineteenth century (Logan 1852, Forbes 1881), came under further question in the early twentieth century. Its typological similarities with Chinese (such as the phonemic role of tonal contrasts and its primarily monosyllabic structure), along with the large number of Chinese loans in the language led some scholars to consider Vietnamese a Sino-Tibetan language, or specifically a member of the Diac group, which was considered part of Sino-Tibetan at the time. The great authority of Maspéro (see Maspéro 1912) added considerable weight to this position. But, as we will see shortly, typological similarities can be misleading in genealogical classification, and the matter was not really settled until the decisive array of papers by Haudricourt (1952, 1953, 1954). Haudricourt showed that the system of Vietnamese tones developed from the historical loss of certain consonants, and that regular correspondences could be established between the six phonemic tones of Vietnamese and the position of consonants that had been retained in other Mon-Khmer languages. Thus, Vietnamese was firmly established among specialists as a Mon-Khmer language that had been subject to enormous Chinese influence; Logan's and Forbes' original hypothesis was confirmed a century later, but this time on a more scientific footing.

A different example is that of the Daic languages (of which the best known is Thai). As we mentioned, these, like Vietnamese, were originally classified with Sino-Tibetan, largely on the basis of typological features and extensive Chinese influence. Benedict (1942) showed that the Sino-Tibetan (specifically Chinese) elements were loans from Chinese, and that Daic could not be treated as part of that family, a finding that is almost universally accepted now. Benedict included Daic in a proposed Austro-Thai family (consisting of Austronesian, Kadai (Thai, Kam-Sui, Lati, and some other minor southeast Asian groups), and Miao-Yao (Hmong-Mien), but that conclusion has not found wide support among others. As a result, the Daic family is now seen as an uncontroversial family, but one to which relations with any other families have not been demonstrated. This example shows that "progress" in linguistic classification cannot be measured solely through greater consolidation of previously recognized families; in some cases, it means the removal of languages from families in which they had been wrongly included. In broader terms, "progress" here can only mean deepening our understanding of the relationships among the world's languages.

Moreover, this work of Benedict's, as well as that of other pioneers of linguistic taxonomy (such as Bopp and Rask in the nineteenth century, Sapir and Kroeber earlier in the twentieth century, and Greenberg and Benedict in our time) reveals another important point: the fact that the same linguist quite typically advances a number of proposals of differing quality and probative value. Thus, Benedict included Daic in a proposed Austro-Thai family (consisting of Austronesian, Kadai (Thai, Kam-Sui, Lati, and some other minor southeast Asian groups) and Miao-Yao (Hmong-Mien), but that conclusion remains controversial. As a result, the Daic family is now seen as an uncontroversial family, but one whose relations with any other families are still open to debate.

Perhaps the best-known and most thoroughly argued of the currently debated proposals is the Nostratic theory, first proposed by Holger Pedersen (1903), and worked out in some detail by Vladislav M Illich-Svitych in the 1960s before his premature death (Illich-Svitych 1967, 1971–84). Illich-Svitych's vision of Nostratic proposed a genetic affiliation among the Afroasiatic, Kartvelian, Indo-European, Uralic, Altaic, and Dravidian families. Illich-Svitych worked out specific phonological correspondences among these languages, and his posthumous Nostratic dictionary and other works list close to 700 proposed cognates, with varying distributions among the families.

One reason that work like Illich-Svitych's appeared when it did is that by the early 1960s, comparative grammars and/or etymological dictionaries of these families had been completed. Thus, Illich-Svitych worked from a comparison of reconstructed proto-languages. This procedure struck some observers as a new methodology, but like so much else in recent comparative work, it was really a simple extension of previous methods. The idea of comparing reconstructed proto-languages, however imperfectly we may have reconstructed them, is not new: Indo-Europeanists have always made at least implicit use of Proto-Germanic, Proto-Slavic, Proto-Celtic, and others, since we do not have an attested parent form to represent those families.

Of course the comparison of reconstructed forms can be a somewhat dangerous approach, since our reconstructions are almost by definition incomplete and are always subject to change as new data become available, or new means of analysis are applied. For example, if new languages are discovered or newly described, or if outstanding phonological problems are solved by new analyses, then our reconstructed form will have a different look. In this sense, reconstructions always present a moving target and may appear less reliable a basis for comparison and further, deeper reconstruction.

But a reconstruction is by definition a set of correspondences among attested languages, and the exact phonetic realization of a reconstructed form is not nearly as important to historical linguists as the fact of the attested correspondences. Even with the addition of new data, we still work from the fact that a set of correspondences in one group of languages regularly corresponds to a similar or different set of correspondences in another group. For example, after the development of the laryngeal theory (or theories) (Winter 1965) in the twentieth century, views of Proto-Indo-European phonology were subjected to profound modification. But the geneticity of Indo-European was not affected by the inclusion of laryngeals in reconstruction work; a new set of correspondences simply took the place of some earlier reconstructions.

In the comparison of reconstructed forms then, we must distinguish between well-established language families, such as Dravidian, Uralic, or Uto-Aztecan, in which we are sure that many (although not necessarily all) of the forms we compare are truly cognate, and less well established families like Austro-Thai, North Caucasian, or Khoisan, where further research may well modify our views of what forms are indeed cognate. Comparison of reconstructed forms from these families is naturally much riskier than that of better-established families and must be undertaken with the greatest care. Of the language families that are established on the basis of large numbers of cognate forms, studied by specialists in the various constituent languages, we know of no case in which subsequent findings in reconstruction have altered the model of genealogical affiliation. This achievement of historical linguistics may well be unparalleled in the other empirical sciences.

## WIDER, CURRENTLY DEBATED CLASSIFICATIONS

The exact composition of Nostratic is not agreed on by all scholars who have dealt with it. Some recent work suggests that Dravidian and perhaps Afroasiatic do not belong in this group, and that Chukchi-Kamchatkan and Eskimo-

Aleut do belong here. Joseph Greenberg's (1987) Eurasiatic hypothesis is similar to Nostratic, but excludes Afroasiatic, Dravidian, and Kartvelian—not because Greenberg believes that these families are unrelated to the others, but because he considers their relationship to be more distant, so that they do not form a taxonomic node with the others. Greenberg does include Chukchi-Kamchatkan, Eskimo-Aleut, Gilyak, and Ainu in his Eurasian proposal. Bomhard & Kerns (1994) and Bomhard (1996) accept Greenberg's Eurasiatic grouping (except for Ainu) and see Eurasiatic as a subset of a larger Nostratic family, restoring Afroasiatic, Dravidian, and Kartvelian at the Nostratic level as more distant relatives, and possibly adding Sumerian.

In fact, the question of subgrouping is often more controversial than the establishment of larger affinities. In Indo-European, the textbook example of a language family, for example, the relationships of Slavic and Baltic, or Hellenic and Armenian are still undecided. Thus, while Altaic is part of all of these versions of Nostratic, the unity of that family itself is vigorously debated, while Chukchi-Kamchatkan itself is not accepted by all scholars. Yet smaller configurations of these families (such as Chukchi-Kamchatkan and Eskimo-Aleut) have been proposed by some scholars (Swadesh 1962, Hamp 1976).

Other recent proposals include Déné-Caucasian (Bengtson 1995, 1997), a proposal uniting Basque, North Caucasian, Sino-Tibetan, Burushaski, Yeniseian, and Na-Déné. This proposal is an extension of an earlier one by Starostin (1984) of an affiliation consisting only of North Caucasian, Sino-Tibetan, and Yeniseian. Of these families, North Caucasian is not accepted by all scholars in the field (for example, Klimov 1986), and the inclusion of Eyak, Tlingit, and Haida in Na-Déné is disputed as well. While the Déné-Caucasian hypothesis is also based on a set of phonological correspondences among the various languages, it is not nearly as well worked out as Nostratic, and Trask (1995) in particular has shown that many of the Basque forms proposed are secondary or the result of borrowing. Other currently controversial language families include Austric (uniting Austronesian with Austroasiatic) (Benedict 1942), Pakawan (a group of extinct languages of Texas and northern Mexico) (Manaster Ramer 1996), and several others.

An important sociological point that must be mentioned in this context is that, for many languages of the world, the taxonomic (or indeed, any) work is done by a very small number of specialists (sometimes as few as one). The sparse coverage of many of the world's languages, especially as far as taxonomy (as opposed to description) is concerned, is also probably the reason why it has more than once been possible for a putative language family to be proposed (and to some extent accepted) on the basis of mere assertions by the one linguist knowledgeable in the relevant area and with literally no data being presented (as happened with Swanton's Coahuiltecan and several of Sapir's proposals in the North American arena; see Swanton 1915; Sapir 1913, 1915,

1920, 1921a,b, 1925, 1929). Similar sociological considerations help explain why reference works, textbooks, encyclopedias, and other works of general linguistics have often failed to keep up with the current state of certain proposals (e.g. Altaic in recent decades), sometimes even going so far as to proclaim as fact certain proposals that were far from being generally accepted by specialists in the particular languages (e.g. Ural-Altaic between the world wars) or pronouncing as refuted for all time theories that were (or are) if anything winning increasing acceptance (as with Altaic in the last few years).

Somewhat aside from these and other proposals based on the application of traditional methods in historical linguistics is the work of Joseph Greenberg (whose Eurasiatic proposal was alluded to above), based on the comparison of lexical data from large numbers of languages at once. Greenberg's method of classification by "mass comparison" of lexical data goes back at least to von Strahlenberg (1730), who used lexical lists to produce an actually quite conservative classification of many of the language families of the Russian Empire. (For more discussion of the connection between von Strahlenberg's and Greenberg's work, see Manaster Ramer & Sidwell 1997:155–56).

Greenberg used the approach most successfully to demonstrate the affiliation of the Afroasiatic family and, by the account of some Africanists (Newman 1995), his findings for the other languages of Africa still hold up well. He has applied the technique most ambitiously to the languages of the Americas, where he concludes (1987) that all of the indigenous languages of North and South America, except for Eskimo-Aleut and Na-Déné, are related in an "Amerind" family. However, even this proposal was not entirely new, as it was largely foreseen in Swadesh (1960).

While the process of comparing often modern forms of large numbers of languages without the confirmatory tools of phonological correspondences may seem to be a superficial one, Newman (1993:235) points out that, whatever the validity of its results in individual cases, Greenberg's work is based not on superficial observation, but on a kind of "immersion technique in which after looking at huge quantities of data from language after language, one begins to develop a sense of what is diagnostic for one group as opposed to another." Although some critics (e.g. Campbell 1988:595–96) have claimed that Greenberg considers only lexical parallels to the exclusion of morphological evidence, Newman (1993:235–36) continues, "[a]lthough vocabulary is inevitably given prominence, by Greenberg and others, in methodological discussions on mass comparison, in practice Greenberg has always accorded great importance to grammatical similarities in his works on classification. This was true in his successful African linguistic classification, and his American Indian classification is no exception."

Greenberg often states (1987 and elsewhere) that his goal is classification, not reconstruction, and that classification must necessarily precede reconstruction. He asks how we can reconstruct a language family if we have not first established the genealogical affinity of the languages on which we will base our reconstruction. But it is important to note that, in practice, classification and reconstruction are usually performed in tandem, with (in successful cases) one confirming or refining the other, and it makes little sense to ask which of the two tasks a linguist is working on at a given moment.

On the same basis, although perhaps without Greenberg's depth of insight, his adherent Ruhlen (1994a,b) and others (such as John Bengtson and Václav Blažek) have proposed that all languages of the world can be shown to be related, and they have published claims of a number of "proto-world" etymologies (e.g. Ruhlen 1994a). The claim that it might be possible to recover at least some part of the origins of all (surviving) languages goes back at least to the work of Trombetti (1905, 1922). While the idea of monogenesis of language is an appealing one, and may find some confirmation in anthropology, we should note that this is not the issue here. The issue is what relationships we can establish on the basis of the linguistic forms now available to us, and this is what scholars from Trombetti to Ruhlen, Blažek and Bengtson claim to do. Thus, for these linguists, all problems of classification, then, are really problems of subclassification of a single ultimate family. Few other linguists, however, have accepted their conclusions.

# NEW PROPOSALS AND THEIR CRITICS: BETWEEN SKEPTICISM AND REJECTIONISM

Thus, as we have seen, many new classificatory proposals have been proposed in recent years, and not all of them will stand the test of time. (In fact, not all of them can be correct, since some are mutually exclusive.) In addition, it is likely that any of the new proposals that may turn out to be essentially correct will need significant revision, just as most theories in historical linguistics have always been subject to revision, often radically.

For this reason, detailed critiques of new proposals, particularly by specialists in the various languages involved, are needed and should be welcomed by all parties. The best of recent skeptical work questioning current proposals (such as Vine 1991 on Nostratic, and Trask 1995 on Déné-Caucasian) does just that, by addressing the data. It is only through a rigorous analysis of the data that we can properly evaluate the individual proposals, work to refine those that appear to be promising, and abandon those that do not. Or, put another way, there is a world of difference between controversial groupings such as Altaic, or even Nostratic (which, whether or not they are eventually found to be correct, or even partially correct, are backed up by solid scholarship and a careful consideration of the histories of the languages involved), and groupings such as "Maya-Altaic" (Wikander 1967–71), "Korean as Indo-European" (Eckardt 1965), or "the Dravidian and Manding substratum in Tocharian" (Winters 1988), which can easily be dismissed because they lack just such background. This kind of discrimination, of course, is based on an analysis of the data in the individual proposals being evaluated.

But what is particularly disturbing are the recent claims that linguistic connections beyond some given time limit cannot be recovered, so the data adduced for such proposals is a priori meaningless. For example, Nichols (1992:5–6) states, "The comparative method when applied at time depths greater than its cut-off point of some 8,000 years gives no way of choosing between competing claims of relatedness." Later, Nichols (1992:184) states that,

> Since the comparative method is only valid for time depths up to about 10,000 years, in principle it cannot tell us whether any two stocks of a continent-sized area are related or not, and thus in principle it cannot tell whether features shared by several stocks in a continent are ultimately related....

Hock (1986:566) states of the prospects for long-range comparison,

> Ultimately, this issue is tied up with the question of whether there was a single or multiple origin of Language (writ large). And this question can be answered only in terms of unverifiable speculations, given the fact that even with the added time depth provided by reconstruction, our knowledge of the history of human languages does not extend much beyond ca. 5000 BC, a small "slice" indeed out of the long prehistory of language....

These writers do not explain how they arrived at their figures, but in addition to his claim of a limit on the capability of reconstruction, Hock adds the erroneous claim that proposals going beyond ca 5000 BC represent proto-world, that is, the question of "whether there was a single or multiple origin of Language (writ large)." Certainly there is a huge difference, which should be clarified here, between proposals like Nostratic (which represents only a small fraction of the world's languages) and claims of true proto-world reconstruction. Hock & Joseph also fail to make this distinction clear in their work, where they include a chapter entitled "Proto-World? The Question of Long-Distance Genetic Relationships" (Hock & Joseph 1996:485–506). The very title suggests that they do not distinguish between proto-world hypotheses based on mass comparison and more modest, but controversial proposals like Nostratic based on the traditional comparative method. In this chapter, Hock & Joseph offer some valid (as well as some straw-man) critiques of the proto-world proposal and Greenberg's techniques. But having dismissed proto-world efforts (in the chapter as a whole), they then quickly write off Nostratic and all other proposals of greater time depth with the same broad brush (Hock & Joseph 1996:495–96).

But like so much else in recent work, the claim that the comparative method has gone as far as it can go is not a new one. More than a generation ago, Kroeber (1960:21) said without any references or argument,

> But there comes a point in the past—perhaps 10,000 years ago, perhaps less—at which the [sc. comparative] method no longer yields reliable results....

Similarly, Lehmann (1962:49) wrote,

> Genealogical classification was admirably suited to determine the interrelationships of languages such as the Indo-European for which we have many records from several millennia. For languages attested only today we may be limited to classification based on typology....

Haas (1966:120) specifically addressed Lehmann's argument by pointing out that, "the work of Bloomfield on Algonkian, together with that of Sapir on Uto-Aztecan, Athapaskan, and other linguistic families" show how much can be determined about language families that do not have early written records. In the Old World, the well-established Uralic family, which has been reconstructed to a very large extent, demonstrates the same point. Languages without early written records have played an important role in historical linguistics, and the histories of many of them have been worked out in considerable detail. Early written records are extremely useful, but not always necessary for linguistic classification.

Although all of these claims of ceilings on the capability of the comparative method are intended as approximate, not absolute thresholds, the point to stress here is that even approximate limits, if inherent in the method, must be relative at best. The varying rates of change affecting different features of a language preclude any universal cut-offs in the method, even approximate ones. In addition, there are other factors, such as the number of attested languages in the family, morphological constructions that produce highly recognizable alternations, and the like, that will make some families more amenable to reconstruction than others. Further, it is important to note that some families may be reconstructable to a greater level of detail than others, reflecting the difference in features retained.

In fact, genetic affiliation can be demonstrated on the basis of a very small number of cognate forms if they are truly convincing. Goddard (1986), for example, argues that only 35, or 18%, of the 196 morphemic and lexical comparisons proposed by Sapir (1914) between Algonquian and Ritwan are definitely correct, and another 13, or 7%, are likely to be. Yet, after rejecting between 76% and 82% of Sapir's etymologies, Goddard, like all modern scholars who have considered these relationships, accepts Sapir's demonstration that Algonquian and Ritwan are related, thanks to the work of Haas (1958). Moreover, comparative linguistics, especially the work on linguistic taxonomy, appears to be learned by experience and example rather than from any explicit set of first principles. As a result, the chances of a probabilistic "killer" argument for or against any proposed linguistic classification seem remote. We consider it far more important to attempt an application of the linguistic methods to the data we do have than to pronounce the effort a priori impossible (or, on the other extreme, rendered a priori unnecessary by some probabilistic shortcut).

Furthermore, since very few linguists now accept glottochronology as a reliable means of absolute dating of language splits (see Bergsland & Vogt 1962), it is very difficult to assign any firm dates to the proto-languages we are sure of, much less be confident of a date beyond which valid relationships supposedly cannot be identified.

Another style of rejection of much new work attempts to propose mathematical tests of the number and distribution of the proposed cognates to determine whether a given set of languages can be considered demonstrably related. This is the approach of Ringe (1992, 1995) but his work is based on flawed mathematics, as shown in Manaster Ramer & Hitchcock (1996) and Baxter & Manaster Ramer (1996). In fact, it shows complete disregard of the basic ideas of probability theory: It confuses the notion of a binomial distribution with randomness; it fails to test for significance; and above all it constructs arguments based on the (fallacious) notion that for a given set of languages to be related they must exhibit some *particular* property to a given degree. A glaring example of this reasoning is Ringe's central claim that two languages can only be regarded as related if, given a particular list of 100 meanings, we find the words with these meanings, compare the initial consonants of the words with the same meaning across the two languages, and find more matches between any such consonant in one language and in the other than would be expected by chance. This ignores the possibility of relationships among other words than those in the particular 100-meanings list, relationships between words with somewhat different but relatable meanings (e.g. English *hound* with Dutch *hond,* which means not "a hunting dog" but simply "dog," as the English word did once), as well as relationships involving vowels or consonants in other than word-initial position.

A further argument against the possibility of establishing linguistic affiliations older than those already settled is that recent work in language contact points increasingly to the significance of such contact in the development of languages. The fact of language contact, borrowing, and other factors that make the genetic model messy have always been part of the picture. At the extreme, there are a handful of examples of "mixed languages" (see Bakker & Maarten 1994), such as East Armenian Romany (Armenian and Romany), Copper Island Aleut (Russian and Aleut), Mitchif (French and Cree), and Loshnekoudesh (Hebrew and Yiddish), for which we can identify the principal sources of the elements of each language, but cannot always say which is native and which is borrowed because neither component is clearly dominant. For these cases, although there are very few of them, the simple genealogical model is not a successful means of describing linguistic development. That such factors are receiving more attention now (see e.g. Thomason & Kaufman 1988, Bakker & Maarten 1994) is a positive development in historical linguistics; it helps us to understand the total process of language change, and it helps us to identify spurious relationships or spurious elements in genuine relationships. But it is not a substitute for the study of genealogical developments that underlie most language relationships, even, as we mentioned above, for English, which has undergone such massive influences from Romance and other sources.

## TOWARD AN EVALUATION SCHEME FOR PROPOSALS IN LINGUISTIC TAXONOMY

But what of Greenberg's (and now others') method of mass comparison, intended to demonstrate relationship, not provide reconstruction? As we have observed, the distinction between the two is somewhat artificial, and further, every linguist knows how easy it is to construct word lists of more-or-less similar forms with vaguely similar meanings from randomly chosen languages. As Greenberg himself points out, his findings should be seen as a first step in understanding the relationships of the languages he has dealt with. The relationships he posits are his best guess based on the data he has observed, and they may be refuted by positing a relationship that fits the data better.

As Trask (1996:389) points out, there can be at least three reactions to Greenberg's work: (*a*) Mass comparison is, all by itself, adequate to establish previously undetected genetic groupings; (*b*) Mass comparison is not, of itself, adequate to establish genetic links, but it is none the less valuable in generating promising hypotheses for further investigation by conventional methods; (*c*) Mass comparison is worthless for any purpose, and is indeed pernicious and obstructive of serious work.

In an intellectual environment where, for example, Campbell (in Greenberg et al 1986:488) calls for Greenberg's work to be "shouted down," even before Greenberg (1987) was published, Trask rightly laments that little attention has been paid to the possibilities offered by the second option listed above. Surely, significant further classificatory work can be done in the native American languages, and Greenberg's work, with all its flaws, is at the very least a useful tool in finding possibilities worth further investigation.

Trask's observation that the intellectual climate has pushed too many scholars to the extremes is a valuable one, and the attempts of writers like Ringe (1992, 1995) on Nostratic, Campell (1988) on Amerind, or Doerfer (1973, 1993) on Nostratic have often sought to discredit carefully constructed, if imperfect, hypotheses on the basis of isolated weaknesses. Doerfer's (1963–1975, 1966, and passim) work has addressed Altaic more systematically, but still with excessive prejudice and preconceptions (see Georg et al, manuscript in preparation). This approach has not helped the state of our knowledge in any of these areas. Rather than forcing ourselves to accept or reject each new proposal in toto, it would be more useful to put our efforts into correcting the flaws in the more promising proposals and see what we can build on their stronger points.

Clearly, the problem of how to evaluate the validity of the currently controversial proposals (or any future ones) is far from being solved, but just as clearly, progress is being made. The large-scale agreement regarding methodological issues in Altaic, despite the fact that even the authors of this paper disagree about the likely ultimate resolution of the Altaic issue (Georg et al, manuscript in preparation), is one example. Campbell's (1996) pointed critique of Manaster Ramer's (1996) specific arguments for Pakawan mark a similar turning point, rejecting many of the spurious criteria that have often been invented in the past as the basis for rejecting any and all new proposals regarding language classification, and identifying some of the strongest points of the Pakawan proposal, on which a revised proposal could be (and is being) crafted. Together with such developments as the growing acceptance of several other proposals, notably Penutian, Na-Déné (without Haida, whose membership is still not universally accepted), and Uralo-Yukaghir, these developments point to a possible future of convergence of opinions in a number of significant areas.

It seems essential to us to steer a middle course between these extremes, to grasp that linguistic taxonomy is an ongoing enterprise that is neither finished because we have reached a temporal ceiling that cannot be exceeded for identifying relationships, nor finished because we have solved all the problems. It seems essential to us to find a way to identify the issues that are neither proven nor hopeless, and to work toward their eventual solution. In this light, it may be instructive to plot language affiliations (and proposed affiliations) on a sort of continuum, with decreasing degrees of transparency (and hence acceptability) for observers with different backgrounds and research interests.

At the lowest end of such a continuum, we may place different idiolects of the same speech community, followed by dialects or sociolects of what is still generally agreed on by all members of the community to be the same language. The relationship of such lects is usually obvious, and forms part of the worldview of linguistically untrained speakers of natural languages all over the world. Next to this, we may put the dialect-continuum, where slight differences between adjacent dialects of the same language may lead to mutual unintelligibility at the opposite ends of this continuum, often, if political or other boundaries intervene, leading to the emergence of different standard languages as poles attracting the nonstandard dialects. Good examples are the

Dutch–Low German continuum or East Scandinavian (Norwegian and Swedish). Usually, the nonlinguist understands that these speech forms are somehow related, but not quite the same. The Slavic family illustrates a close-knit relationship with clearer, nongradual, language boundaries—not much mutual intelligibility, but still a transparent relationship. Thus, a speaker of, say, Russian can detect rather easily, without any linguistic background, that even though he or she may not fully understand, say, Czech, the language has many basic words, morphological elements, and processes in common with his own language, and that this relationship does not hold between Russian and German or Czech and Romanian.

Knowledge that the latter languages are after all related, that is, the transition from close-knit Slavic to not-immediately-obvious Indo-European, may be marked as the threshold between relationships detectable by common sense alone and those where the methodology of comparative linguistics must be applied. Thus, the relationship of Hungarian to Finnish had to be detected by the application of linguistic sophistication, rather than forming part of the naive worldview of their speakers. Much the same can be said for the relation between Chuvash and other Turkic languages, Svan and Georgian within the Kartvelian language family, or between Arabic and Tamazight (Berber) within Afroasiatic. In addition, most of the classifications, which have received general acceptance by linguistically trained scholars, have the additional probative criterion that the data from one language or branch can be used to explain or solve etymological questions in other branches. A well-known example is that of Verner's Law (Verner 1877), in which morphological and accentual data from Greek and particularly Sanskrit solved a problem in Germanic phonology that could not be solved on the basis of the Germanic data alone.

The next step in this continuum may be represented by alignments that are worked on intensively by a large number of researchers, but have not yet attained general or unanimous acceptance. Perhaps the best example of this step on the continuum is the still hotly debated question of the genealogical status of the Altaic languages, involving the Turkic, Mongolic, Tungusic, Korean, and, by some accounts, Japanese languages. Disregarding here the generations of debate on the Altaic question that have often revolved around irrelevant typological, ethnic, and political issues (for an account of which, see Georg et al, manuscript in preparation), we may now be at a point where the Altaic question can be investigated as would any other proposal in historical linguistics: on the basis of the data and the objectively based findings of the best researchers who have addressed the issue in the past. Here, proponents of the relationship have worked out phonological correspondences in some detail based on a thorough knowledge of the individual language families involved, and have identified a fair number of common morphological elements. At the same time, the more principled skeptics in this field point to the actual handling of the relevant data by at least some proponents of Altaic, the lack of systematic-ity of the reconstructs proposed so far, the role of contact-induced similarities between the languages (or the lack of a proper distinction between these and the truly genetic material). and the lack of explanatory power of proto-Altaic as it stands for a better understanding of the lower-level languages. The ongo-ing debate on Altaic may currently be regarded as open, without a clear con-sensus in the scholarly community, but capable of solution given a widespread consensus on the methodological apparatus to be employed. Proposals at this stage of the continuum may simply be labeled as "debated."

One step further, proposals such as Nostratic may be posited in this idealized continuum as alignments that, although again based on observations and meth-ods well within the range of generally accepted procedures of comparative lin-guistics, still meet with more reluctance than support. Again, much of the debate so far has focused on unproductive issues, such as preconceptions of what a valid language family must look like, or supposed temporal limits on the com-parative method, as we discussed above. We hope that, like Altaic, the Nostra-tic hypothesis can now be investigated objectively, and purely in light of the data available, whatever conclusions those data may lead us to. Proposals like Nostratic and even the considerably less well supported Déné-Caucasian have the virtue of being debatable or testable. They are argued on the basis of the traditional comparative method and are subject to refutation on the same basis.

This scale, then, ranging from alignments that are obvious to even untrained persons familiar with the language to those that require the greatest depth of study to even begin to form an opinion, is not intended to describe the actual degrees of relationship that (may) obtain between the languages involved (al-though it may at times coincide with it). Rather, it seeks to present an evaluation-scheme for given proposals. Thus, we do not include in this scale the truly absurd and uninformed proposals, lacking any understanding of com-parative linguistics or the known history of the languages involved. Often such proposals are simply impossible, such as those that try to connect Hungarian alone (without the rest of Uralic) to Sumerian, Tungusic, Basque, or any other candidates.

For the proposals that can be taken seriously, then, we propose a continuum from the easiest to recognize to the most difficult. In a Greek mood, the authors of this paper have sometimes called the extremes of this continuum "rhadio-comparison" for the easiest, and "khalepo-comparison" for the most difficult. We feel that this nomenclature has several virtues. For one thing, we hope these terms may replace the often emotion-laden prejudice of a dichotomy be-tween "macro-" versus "micro-"comparison, or between "traditional" versus "long-range" comparison, much less the meaningless distinction of linguists working on language classification into "lumpers" and "splitters."

We also hope these terms will erase the idea that the study of more difficult comparison uses different methods or has different goals than work on the easier forms of comparison. In fact, the application of the comparative method, internal reconstruction, and the examination of early texts, when available, must be the same for comparative work in the most obvious or the most oblique comparisons. In addition, we wish to make it clear that difficulty of comparison is not (necessarily) a function of time depth or even geographic distance: In the case of Altaic, for example, it is precisely the mutual influence of neighboring languages, a factor agreed on by all including those who support the hypothesis, that has made the situation so difficult to interpret. Difficulty of comparison derives from the features of the languages and the amount and quality of information available to us, of which relative time depth is only one possibly relevant factor.

Thus, statements about the placement of a particular grouping on this continuum are statements about our knowledge of the languages, not about their plausibility or the degree of acceptance they have attained, much less about their actual degree of relationship. If comparison of more difficult groupings yields less clear information about the relationships involved, the goal of comparative linguistics is precisely to clarify those relationships to the extent possible.

Heated controversy in historical linguistics is as old as work on linguistic classification. And as we have seen, principled critiques of individual proposals serve a valuable purpose in separating the promising proposals from the misguided ones, as well as in refining those that are of value. In addition, most mainstream linguists have been understandably jaded by generations of uninformed claims of language origins, often based on nationalistic or religious agendas. Thus, despite the polarizing tone of much of the current debate, the goal now, as throughout the history of the discipline, is to consider each proposal on its merits and judge each one on the same standards that we apply to any serious proposal in linguistics.

Linguistic classification today offers exciting visions and challenges, and those who dismiss new proposals all too easily (like those who accept them all too quickly) do not do the field much good. The current controversies in the study of linguistic relationships are only the continuation of historical linguistics as it has always been practised. Above all, it is a slow business. Such now universally recognized linguistic relationships as Algonquian-Ritwan (Algic), Indoeuropean-Anatolian, Mon-Khmer-Vietnamese (as part of Austro-asiatic), Tlingit-Eyak-Athapaskan (Na-Déné), or Aztec-Sonoran-Shoshonean (Uto-aztecan) took anywhere from a decade to a half-century or more between the publication of the first substantive arguments for their validity and the advent of universal recognition. If the current trends toward more acceptance of Hokan, Penutian, Haida-Nadéné, Altaic, Austric, and some other hitherto controversial linkages continue, and they do become universally accepted before the end of the millennium, the record will stretch to something close to a century. The process is difficult, sometimes infuriating, and occasionally truly rewarding as we find new understanding of the developments that produced the languages we find attested today.

> **Visit the *Annual Reviews home page* at**
> **http://www.AnnualReviews.org.**

## *Literature Cited*

Adelung JC. 1806–1817. *Mithridates oder allgemeine Sprachenkunde mit dem Vater Unser als Sprachprobe in bey nahe fünfhundert Sprachen und Mundarten.* 1806 (I); 1809 (II); 1812 (III/1,2); 1816 (III/3); 1817 (IV). Berlin: Vossische Buchhandlung

Bakker P, Maarten M, eds. 1994. *Mixed Languages.* Amsterdam: Inst. Funct. Res. Lang. Lang. Use (IFOTT)

Baxter W, Manaster Ramer A. 1996. Review of Ringe 1992. *Diachronica* 13:371–84

Benedict P. 1942. Thai, Kadai, and Indonesian: a new alignment in Southeastern Asia. *Am. Anthropol.* 44: 576–601

Bengtson JD. 1995. Basque: an orphan forever? *Mother Tongue* (NS) 1: 84–103

Bengtson JD. 1997. Basque and the other Déné-Caucasic languages. In *The Twenty-Third LACUS Forum*, pp. 137–48. Chapel Hill, NC: LACUS

Bergsland K, Vogt H. 1962. On the validity of glottochronology. *Curr. Anthropol.* 3(2): 115–53

Blažek V. 1989. Materials for global etymologies. In *Reconstructing Languages and Cultures*, ed. V Shevoroshkin. Bochum: Brockmeyer

Bomhard AR. 1996. *Indo-European and the Nostratic Hypothesis.* Charleston, SC: Signum

Bomhard AR, Kerns JC. 1994. *The Nostratic Macrofamily: A Study in Distant Linguistic Relationship.* Berlin/New York: Mouton de Gruyter

Campbell L. 1988. Review of Greenberg 1987. *Language* 64:591–615

Campbell L. 1996. Coahultecan: a closer look. *Anthropol. Linguist.* 38.4:620–34

Campbell L, Mithun M. 1979. Introduction: North American Indian historical linguistics in current perspective. In *The Languages of Native America: Historical and Comparative Assessmen*, ed. L Campbell, M Mithun, pp. 3–69. Austin/London: Univ. Tex. Press

Doerfer G. 1963–1975. *Türkische und Mongolische Elemente im Neupersischen, unter besonderer Berücksichtigung älterer neupersischer Geschichtsquellen, vor allem der Mongolen- und Timuridenzeit.* Wiesbaden: Steiner. 4 Vols.

Doerfer G. 1966. Zur Verwandtschaft der altaischen Sprachen. *Indoger. Forsch.* 71: 81–123

Doerfer G. 1973. *Lautgesetz und Zufall: Betrachtungen zum Omnicomparativismus. (Innsbrucker Beitr. Sprachwiss.* 10) Innsbruck: Sprachwiss. Inst. Univ.

Doerfer G. 1993. Nostratismus: Illič &-Svitič und die Folgen. *Ural.-Altai. Jahrb. (*NF) 12:17–35

Eckardt A. 1965. *Grammatik der Koreanischen Sprache (Studienausgabe).* Heidelberg: Julius Groos Verlag

Forbes CJFS. 1881. *Comparative Grammar of the Languages of Further India.* London: Allen

Georg S, Michalove PA, Manaster Ramer A, Sidwell PA. 1998. Telling general linguists about Altaic. *J. Linguist.* In press

Goddard I. 1986. Sapir's comparative method. In *New Perspectives in Language, Culture, and Personality: Proc. Edward Sapir Centenary Conf., Ottawa, 1-3 Oct. 1984*, ed. W Cowan, MK Foster, K Koerner, pp. 191–210. Amsterdam/Philadelphia: Benjamins

Godfrey JJ. 1967. Sir William Jones and Père Coeurdoux: a philological footnote. *JAOS* 87(1):57–59

Greenberg JH. 1955. *Studies in African Linguistic Classification.* New Haven, CT: Compass

Greenberg JH. 1963. *The Languages of Africa.* Bloomington: Indiana Univ.

Greenberg JH. 1987. *Language in the Americas.* Stanford, CA: Stanford Univ. Press

Greenberg JH, Turner CG II, Zegura SL. 1986. Settlement of the Americas. *Curr. Anthropol.* 27:477–97

Haas M. 1958. Algonkian-Ritwan: the end of a controversy. *Int. J. Am. Linguist.* 24:159–73

Haas M. 1966. Historical linguistics and the genetic relation of languages. *Current Trends in Linguistics: Theoretical Foundations,* ed. TA Sebeok, 3:113–54. The Hague: Mouton de Gruyter

Hamp EP. 1976. On Eskimo-Aleut and Luoravetlan. In *Papers on Eskimo and Aleut Linguistics,* ed. EP Hamp, pp. 81–92. Chicago, IL: Chicago Linguist. Soc.

Haudricourt A-G. 1952. L'origine mon-khmer des tons vietnamiens. *J. Asiat.* 240/2:264–65

Haudricourt A-G. 1953. La place du vietnamien dans les langues austroasiatiques, *Bull. Soc. Linguist.* 49:122–28

Haudricourt A-G. 1954. De l'origine des ton en vietnamien. *J. Asiat.* 242:69–82

Hock HH. 1986. *Principles of Historical Linguistics.* Berlin: Mouton de Gruyter. 1st ed.

Hock HH, Joseph B. 1996. *Language History, Language Change and Language Relationship: An Introduction to Historical and Comparative Linguistics. Trends Linguist. Stud. Monogr.* 93. Berlin/New York: Mouton de Gruyter

Illich-Svitych VM. 1967. Materialy k sravnitel'nomu slovarju nostraticheskix jazykov. *Etimologija* 1965:321–73

Illich-Svitych VM. 1971–1984. *Opyt Sravnenija Nostraticheskix Jazykov.* Moscow: Nauka

Klimov GA. 1986. *Vvedenie v Kavkazskoe Jazykoznanie.* Moscow: Nauka

Klaproth J. 1823. *Asia Polyglotta.* Paris: Schubart

Kroeber AL. 1960. Statistics, Indo-European, and taxonomy. *Language* 36:1–21

Lehmann WP. 1962. *Historical Linguistics: An Introduction.* New York: Holt, Rinehart & Winston. 1st ed.

Logan J. 1852. Ethnology of the Pacific Islands. *J. Indian Archipel.* 6:658

Manaster Ramer A. 1996. Sapir's classifications: Coahuiltecan. *Anthropol. Linguist.* 38.1:1–37

Manaster Ramer A, Hitchcock C. 1996. Glass houses: Ringe, Greenberg, and the mathematics of comparative linguistics. *Anthropol. Linguist.* 38:601–19

Manaster Ramer A, Sidwell P. 1997. The truth

about Strahlenberg's classification of the languages of northeast Eurasia. *J. Soc. Finno-Ougr.* 87:139–60

Maspéro H. 1912. Études sur la phonétique historique de la langue annamite: les initiales. *Bull. École Fr. Extrême-Orient.* 12/1:1–127

Müller F. 1876-1887. *Grundriss der Sprachwissenschaft. , I. Band I. Abt. Einleitung in die Sprachwissenschaft 1876. II. Abt. Die Sprachen der Wollhaarigen Rassen 1877. II. Band: Die Sprachen der Schlichthaarigen Rassen, I. Abt. Die Sprachen der Australischen, der Hyperboreischen und der Amerikanischen Rasse 1882. II. Abt. Die Sprachen der Malayischen und der Hochasiatischen (Mongolischen) Rasse 1884. III. Band: Die Sprachen der Lockenhaarigen Rassen. I. Abt. Die Sprachen der Nuba-Rasse und der Dravida-Rasse 1884. II. Abt. Die Sprachen der Mittelländischen Rasse. 1887.* Wien: Hölder

Newman P. 1993. Greenberg's American Indian classification: a report on the controversy. In *Historical Linguistics 1991,* ed. J van Marle, pp. 229–42. Amsterdam/Erdenheim, PA: Benjamins

Newman P. 1995. *On Being Right: Greenberg's African Linguistic Classification and the Methodological Principles Which Underlie It.* Bloomington: Indiana Univ.

Nichols J. 1992. *Linguistic Diversity in Space and Time.* Chicago: Univ. Chicago Press

Pedersen H. 1903. Türkische Lautgesetze. *Z. Dtsch. Morgenl. Ges.* 57:535–61

Ringe DA Jr. 1992. *On Calculating The Factor of Chance in Language Comparison.* Philadelphia: Am. Philos. Soc.

Ringe DA Jr. 1995. 'Nostratic' and the factor of chance. *Diachronica* 12:55–74

Ruhlen M. 1994a. *On the Origins of Language: Studies in Linguistic Taxonomy.* Stanford, CA: Stanford Univ. Press

Ruhlen M. 1994b. *The Origin of Language: Tracing the Evolution of the Mother Tongue.* New York: Wiley

Sapir E. 1913. Southern Paiute and Nahuatl: a study in Uto-Aztecan. Pt. I. Vowels. *J. Soc. Am. Paris* 10:379–425

Sapir E. 1914. Wiyot and Yurok, Algonkin languages of California. *Am. Anthropol.* 15:617–46

Sapir E. 1915. The Na-Dene languages: a preliminary report. *Am. Anthropol.* 17:534–58

Sapir E. 1920. The Hokan and Coahuiltecan languages. *Int. J. Anthropol. Lang.* 1:280–90

Sapir E. 1921a. A bird's-eye view of American languages north of Mexico. *Science* 54:408

Sapir E. 1921b. A supplementary note on Salinan and Washo. *Int. J. Anthropol. Lang.* 2:68–72

Sapir E. 1925. The Hokan affinity of Subtiaba in Nicaragua. *Am. Anthropol.* 27:402–35, 491–527

Sapir E. 1929. Central and North American languages. *Encycl. Britannica* 5: 138–41. 14th ed

Setälä E. 1913. Zur Frage nach der Verwandtschaft der finnisch-ugrischen und samojedischen Sprachen. *J. Soc. Finno-Ougr.* 30(18):1-104

Starostin SA. 1984. Gipoteza o geneticheskix svjazax sinotibetskix jazykov s enisejskimi i severo-kavkazskimi jazykami. *Lingvist. Rekonstr. Drevnejsh. Istor. Vostoka,* 4:19–38. Moscow: Akad. Nauk SSSR

Strahlenberg PJ von. 1730. *Das Nord- und Östliche Theil von Europa und Asia.* Reprinted as *Stud. Ural.-Altai.,* 1975. Vol. 8, ed. JR Krueger. Szeged: Univ. Szeged. Attila Jozsef nomin.

Swadesh M. 1960. On interhemisphere linguistic connections. In *Culture in History: Essays in Honor of Paul Radin,* ed. S Diamond, pp. 894–924. New York: Columbia Univ. Press

Swadesh M. 1962. Linguistic relations across the Bering Strait. *Am. Anthropol.* 64:1262–91

Swanton JR. 1915. Linguistic position of the tribes of southern Texas and northeastern Mexico. *Am. Anthropol.* 17:17–40

Thomason SG, Kaufman T. 1988. *Language Contact, Creolization, and Genetic Linguistics.* Berkeley: Univ. Calif. Press

Trask RL. 1996. *Historical Linguistics.* London/New York: Arnold

Trask RL. 1995. Basque and Déné-Caucasian: a critique from the Basque side. *Mother Tongue* (NS) 1:3–82

Trombetti A. 1905. *L'Unita d'Origine del Linguaggio.* Bologna, Italy: Libreria Treves de Luigi Beltrami

Trombetti A. 1922. *Elementi di Glottologia.* Bologna, Italy: Zanichelle

Verner K. 1877. Eine Ausname der ersten Lautverschiebung. *Z. Vgl. Sprachforsch.* 23:97–130

Vine B. 1991. Indo-European and Nostratic. *Indoger. Forsch.* 46:9–35

Wikander S. 1967–1971. Maya and Altaic. I: *Ethnos* 1967:141–48; II: *Ethnos* 1970: 80–88; III: *Orientalia Suecana* 19/20:186–204

Winter W, ed. 1965. *Evidence for Laryngeals.* London: Mouton de Gruyter

Winters CA. 1988. The Dravidian and Manding substratum in Tocharian. *Cent. Asiat. J.* 32:131–41

*Annu. Rev. Anthropol. 1998. 27:473–502*
*Copyright © 1998 by Annual Reviews. All rights reserved*

# LEGAL, ETHICAL, AND SOCIAL ISSUES IN HUMAN GENOME RESEARCH

*Henry T. Greely*

Stanford Law School, Stanford University, Stanford, California 94305-8610;
e-mail: hgreely@stanford.edu

KEY WORDS: genetics, ethics, law, society, project

---

## ABSTRACT

In the past several decades, biological sciences have been revolutionized by their increased understanding of how life works at the molecular level. In what ways, and to what extent, will this scientific revolution affect the human societies within which the science is situated? The legal, ethical, and social implications of research in human genetics have been discussed in depth, particularly in the context of the Human Genome Project and, to a lesser extent, the proposed Human Genome Diversity Project. Both projects could have significant effects on society, the former largely at the level of individuals or families and the latter primarily at the level of ethnic groups or nations. These effects can be grouped in six broad categories: identity, prediction, history, manipulation, ownership and control, and destiny.

---

## INTRODUCTION

> It has not escaped our notice that the specific pairing we have postulated immediately suggests a possible copying mechanism for the genetic material.
>
> Watson & Crick (1953)

Watson & Crick did not announce the discovery of DNA in their famous, understated paper. Nor did they invent molecular biology or human genetics. But the now-familiar double helix they discovered, with its embedded sequence of nucleotides coding for proteins, has combined with the so-called "Central

473

Dogma"—that genetic information passes from DNA to RNA to protein—to transform biology (Judson 1979). The result has been a vision of DNA molecules, and the genomes they constitute, as the "blueprints" of life with vast consequences for science.

Nor did it escape the notice of others that the science of DNA, when applied to humans rather than bacteria or fruit flies, immediately suggested many and varied applications to human affairs. As the tools for analyzing and understanding the human genome improved, the possible value of those tools for understanding human lives captured the attention of many publics, academic, political, and popular. Forty-five years later, the implications of human genome research for human societies, though still largely in the future, are becoming clearer.

These implications have also become the subject of what is nearly a discipline: ELSI—ethical, legal, and social implications. The social effects of increased knowledge of human genetics probably have been speculated about—and studied—more than those of any ongoing social change in history. Some of this attention derives from the fascination, sometimes tinged with horror, humans have with any technology that offers—fairly or not—to teach us about our pasts, our futures, and our essences. Although substantial scholarly attention was paid to these issues before 1990 (Andrews 1987; Fletcher 1988; Milunsky & Annas 1975, 1980, 1985; President's Comm. Study Ethical Probl. Med. Biomed. Res. 1982, Reilly 1977), some of the attention stems from the decision, apparently made on the spur of the moment by James Watson as director of the United States Human Genome Project, to commit at least 3% of the project's budget to ELSI (Cook-Deegan 1994). The results include myriad conferences, symposia, books, and articles, as well as grants for anthropologists, lawyers, philosophers, physicians, psychologists, sociologists, students of religion, and others (Annas 1992, Cranor 1994, Frankel & Teich 1993, Kevles & Hood 1992, Kitcher 1996, Murray & Lappé 1994, Murray et al 1996, Pollock 1994, Weir & Lawrence 1994, Wertz & Fletcher 1989).

This chapter does not seek to summarize or synthesize all that work. Instead, it seeks to point out the more interesting legal and social issues raised by human genome research and to group them into some analytically useful categories. The Human Genome Project (Natl. Res. Counc., Comm. Mapp. Seq. Hum. Genome 1988; US Congr., Off. Technol. Assess. 1988a; Cook-Deegan 1994) and the proposed Human Genome Diversity Project (Weiss 1998; Natl. Res. Counc., Comm. Hum. Genome Divers. 1997) are especially useful for this effort because their effects fall largely at different levels of social organization. The Human Genome Project (HGP), with its effort to find and understand the full set of human genes, speaks primarily to the implications of genetic knowledge for individuals or families. The more controversial proposed Human Genome Diversity Project (HGDP) (Greely 1997b), with its effort to collect and assess samples of human genomes from throughout the world, speaks primarily to the implications of genetic knowledge for larger human groups (and, of course, for the people within them).

This chapter first examines specific concerns arising from human genetic research, which are grouped into six categories:

1. Human genomes and identity
2. Human genetics and predicting the future
3. Human genetics and revealing the past
4. Manipulating human genomes
5. Ownership and control of human genes and genetic information
6. Genomes, souls, and destiny

The chapter then points out some common strands in many of these issues. Some of those strands point to ways in which human genetic research has social implications similar to those of other kinds of science or technology. Other strands identify ways in which those implications are unique. Both sets are crucial to viewing the possible consequences of human genetic research in perspective.

And perspective is vital. Discussions of the ethical, legal, and social implications of human genetic research are usually alarming. The foreseen social implications are usually threatening to some or all people, and the likelihood that they will occur is unknown. The foreseen benefits, although also largely speculative, fall mainly in the medical and scientific realms. Both the uncertainties and the differences in the nature of these kinds of implications make it difficult to weigh the long-term human benefits against the long-term human costs. Most discussions of the social consequences of human genetic research do not even make the attempt. This chapter is no exception, so, like similar discussions, it could be read as a litany of plausible horrors. That is not my goal. I want to alert the reader to the consequences I think are most plausible and most significant.

## ETHICAL, LEGAL, AND SOCIAL ISSUES: SPECIFIC CONCERNS

The six categories discussed below do not begin to exhaust the implications of human genome research. The possible direct consequences of genome research for medicine are ignored, yet genomics-based interventions that either increase the average life span or decrease morbidity during life could have enormous social implications. Issues arising within the research community itself—corporate, university, and public—are diverse and fascinating (Rabinow 1996, Greely 1995) but are ignored here. Instead, I want to look at the possible implications of these technologies for ordinary people in nonmedical situations.

The following discussion attempts both to expose the reader to many of those implications and to classify them into a few analytically useful categories. The first three categories focus on the effects of information available as a result of genetic research on individuals, groups, and societies. The fourth category deals with the intentional manipulation of human genomes. The fifth deals with issues relating to the acquisition, control, and use of genetic information. The final category deals with the possibly profound implications of human genetic research for our perceptions of ourselves.

## Human Genomes and Identity

The use of genetic information for identification gives rise to concerns in at least three areas: individual identification, cloning, and group membership.

INDIVIDUAL IDENTITY   The use of DNA tests for individual identification has been most discussed in the context of criminal law. DNA testing has been used since the mid-1980s to try to match suspects to DNA-containing residues left at the scene of a crime. The forensic uses of DNA technology for identification have prompted concerns about competence, overimpressiveness, ethnic discrimination, privacy, and implicit coercion (Lander 1989; US Congr., Off. Technol. Assess. 1990a; Billings 1992; Natl. Res. Counc. 1992, 1996).

The first concern is a straightforward fear that the technology may not be effective or that it may not be done well by average practitioners. This concern is similar to that faced with any new forensic procedure, but it is a continuing worry, as new and more sensitive types of DNA analysis are regularly introduced as the technology improves. The second concern is a fear that jurors would be overly swayed by the apparent scientific proof implied by DNA testing.

A third concern has been with ethnic discrimination. The markers used to analyze the DNA may not be distributed randomly across the population. Certainly, when a suspect has an identical twin, the odds of someone matching are good. Similarly, the odds that family members will match are higher than the odds of a random match. And it is possible that the variations that were examined in a suspect's DNA are found more commonly in the suspect's ethnic group than among the rest of the population. Failure to take that into account might produce overly low estimates of the possibility of a random match. This issue was debated extensively in the late 1980s and early 1990s; the controversy appears to have been resolved with the techniques now being used by forensic labs to calculate the odds of a match (Natl. Res. Council 1996).

Another concern revolves around privacy (McEwen 1997; Am. Soc. Hum. Genet., Ad Hoc Comm. DNA Technol. 1988). The possible value of DNA for forensic purposes has led to the creation of databases that could invade privacy. Some states have created databases of DNA "fingerprints" for those imprisoned or those convicted of certain crimes. These databases are used to investigate other crimes. The US military is creating a database of DNA samples for all uniformed personnel for use in identifying remains if necessary. These kinds of databases raise concerns about who may get access to the DNA or its analysis, the uses to which the samples might be put, and the coercive nature of such laws. (Of course, if the database contains only the analysis of DNA samples, checked against a panel of common markers, the possible abuses of the database are much more limited because those markers usually do not have health consequences.)

Finally, coercion may be present apart from mandatory participation in databases. The first use of DNA testing in a criminal context occurred in a rural area of England after a rape and murder. Young men in the nearby villages were asked to volunteer to provide DNA samples to be matched against DNA left on the victim. One man paid an acquaintance to provide a sample in his name; the acquaintance told the police, leading to the suspect's arrest and conviction (Cook-Deegan 1994). It may be worth worrying about how voluntary participation in such a screening program would truly be, when failure to participate could reasonably be expected to draw the attention of the police. Without sympathizing with the guilty, one may be concerned for all those not guilty who are effectively forced to provide a DNA sample.

Convicting the guilty does not normally raise ethical concerns, but the issues raised above can affect the rights and interests of both the guilty and innocent. As the technologies improve and their implementation becomes more routine, some of the concerns about false matches will fade, but that increased accuracy may only increase the pressure for invasions of individual privacy. It is, however, worth noting that DNA testing rules out suspects about as often as it incriminates them—it is much easier to say that there is no match between two samples than to compute the odds that a false match has occurred by chance (US Dep. Justice 1996).

Also, DNA identification has been used for other purposes, such as paternity testing, reuniting separated families, and identifying human remains. The latter two functions have been used in recent years in situations of political interest. DNA analysis has brought together the parents and children of people "disappeared" by the military during the junta's rule in Argentina, and it has been used in Central America to identify the remains of victims of government massacres.

CLONING   The birth of Dolly has made it seem possible that new human babies might be created with genes taken solely from one adult parent. Rather than resulting from the random mixing of genes from mother and father, the child would have the entire nuclear genome of one parent. It remains unclear whether humans can be cloned from adult cells—thus far, no one has even cloned a second sheep from adult sheep cells. But the possibility of human cloning has raised concerns about the physical, and psychological, identity of the resulting child (Silver 1997, Kolata 1998, Pence 1998).

Some of these concerns may have stemmed from a naive, Hollywood understanding of clones as photocopies—one 30-year-old person suddenly becoming five identical 30-year-olds. Clones would begin life as babies. The clone and the "donor" would be no more identical than, at most, identical twins. If the donor nucleus came from an adult cell, the clone would necessarily grow up in an environment different from that of his or her "older twin." Perhaps more important, the clone would develop before birth in a different environment, either an entirely different womb or the same womb but of a much older mother. These are reasons to suspect that clones would be substantially less similar than identical twins, but at this point that remains speculative. That the confusion of identical genomes with identity (Brock 1992)— making a copy of one's self—is a major thread in the negative reaction to cloning seems clear.

GROUP MEMBERSHIP    Population genetics and the HGDP raise another possible concern about identity. It is possible that membership in various tribal or ethnic groups might be defined on the basis of an individual's genetic variations (Cavalli-Sforza et al 1994). Thus, for example, the Basques or Euskadi, who constitute the population with the highest known frequency of the Rh-negative blood type, could conceivably require Rh-negative blood as a condition for recognition as a community member.

Such a method for determining group membership would be extremely arbitrary. Groups generally are defined culturally, frequently with provisions for "adoption" into a group. Even for group members who share recent common ancestry, genetic variations will not provide a sensible method for defining a group. It is highly unlikely that any genetic variation is found, in the entire human species, in only one particular population. It is even less likely that it is found in all members of that population. Population genetics deals, as its name indicates, with populations, not with individuals. Although Basques are the people most likely to be Rh negative, most Rh-negative people are not Basque and most Basques are not Rh negative. The group frequencies, unless they are absolutely 100% or 0%, cannot be used logically to determine whether an individual is a group member.

That a membership criterion is arbitrary does not, of course, mean that it might not be used. The ethical implications of the use of such an arbitrary criterion are likely to hinge on the circumstances—including whether the criterion is chosen by the group or imposed externally—regardless of whether the criterion is genetic. Use of a genetically based group membership criterion could, however, have the negative effect of reinforcing false ideas that ethnic groups or races can be scientifically defined through genetics.

## Human Genetics and Predicting the Future

Probably the most important immediate issues concerning these new technologies revolve around their ability to predict future expressed characteristics. The strength of the link between the human gene sequence, or genotype, and the functioning person, or phenotype, is often exaggerated, but in some cases genotype does determine phenotype and in other cases strongly influences it. Genetic tests look for genotypes that help predict phenotypes. To the extent that such tests allow medical interventions that benefit the tested person, they are rarely controversial. But the predictions from genetic tests can be problematic in at least four respects: (a) through parental decisions about childbearing, (b) through individual and familial reactions to prediction, (c) through private third-party discrimination based on the predictive information, and (d) through government action. Many of these effects could take place as a result of research on either individual or population genetics.

CHILDBEARING   Genetic counseling for any patient raises complex issues (Capron & Lappé 1979; President's Comm. Study Ethical Probl. Med. Biomed. Res. 1983; Rapp 1988; Holtzman 1989; Bosk 1992; Caplan et al 1993; Inst. Med., Natl. Acad. Sci. 1993; Nelkin & Tancredi 1994; Wertz et al 1994), perhaps especially in childbearing. Genetic tests are already in use to predict a couple's chances of having fetuses with particular characteristics or the actual characteristics of an already created embryo or fetus. Pre-conception analysis of the possible parents can lead to decisions about marriage or bearing children; analysis of embryos or fetuses can be used to determine which embryos or fetuses will be allowed to survive to birth.

Prospective parents can be tested to determine if the couple is at risk for bearing a child with some genetic diseases. Such pre-conception testing for the risk of Tay-Sachs disease is common in the Ashkenazi Jewish community. This kind of testing can raise conflicts between an individual's possible duty to disclose genetic risks to a potential partner and his or her own privacy and protection from discrimination.

Prenatal fetal diagnosis evokes a spectrum of responses. At one end, some question whether parents should allow a genetically diseased infant to be born; at the other, some attack the morality of elective abortion. An intermediate position, allowing or encouraging abortions for some kinds of genetic diseases but not others, raises difficult questions of drawing lines. Abortion for Tay-Sachs disease, in which children inevitably die after short, unpleasant lives, might raise fewer concerns than would abortion for late-onset Alzheimer's disease, with which people lead normal lives until old age, or for BRCA1 mutations, which confer a 50–80% chance of a breast cancer diagnosis sometime in life. Although under current US constitutional law the issue would not be whether abortion for a given disease would be allowed, one might regulate whether certain genetic tests could legally or ethically be used for prenatal testing (Capron 1990; Robertson 1990, 1994; Rothenberg & Thomson 1994; Rothman 1986).

One twist on this issue could come from parents with unusual preferences for their children, preferences for what many would view as a genetic disease. Thus, two people with achondroplasia, one of the common forms of very short stature, might want to use prenatal diagnosis to select a fetus with achondroplasia. If society allows prenatal testing for genetic diseases, who defines "disease?"

These latter issues may pose even greater concerns if and when genetic tests can predict phenotypic characteristics that are not generally viewed as diseases. Thus far, only one such characteristic is readily tested—sex. The ethics of parental sex selection by abortion, and the ethics of telling parents fetal sex when sex-selective abortion may be a possibility, are controversial. Some other nondisease characteristics of interest to some parents, such as skin, hair, and eye color and possibly potential height, seem likely to be heavily influenced by genetics and hence eventually testable.

It remains unclear whether other, more complex—and more interesting—traits, such as various aspects of intelligence or personality, will be amenable to genetic testing. If so, they could raise not only issues of the propriety of parents using such traits to abort fetuses (or to decide not to implant embryos), but also broader social issues of "parental eugenics." The ability to select children for particular characteristics may confer on those children cultural advantages. If such selection is allowed but restricted by financial considerations or religious beliefs, some parents—but not others—would be able to give their children a prenatal, genetic advantage or even just a valuable *perception* of genetic advantage. Such a result may have effects significantly greater than the effects of different environments available to children based on their family's wealth, class, or beliefs, but it would be an extension of those kinds of advantages, with possible implications for class structure and distributive justice (Duster 1989).

INDIVIDUAL AND FAMILIAL REACTIONS    The personal, psychological, and familial consequences of predictive genetic information are often overlooked, but they may well raise ethical or legal concerns. Apart from the actual health risks revealed by a genetic test, new knowledge of a risk or a perceived flaw can affect a person's self-perception and happiness (King et al 1993, Natl. Soc. Genet. Couns. 1997). Similarly, genetic tests can have significant effects within a family by affecting relationships with spouses, parents, siblings, and children. Also, when one family member tests positive for a disease-related gene, that person's parents, siblings, and children all have a 50% chance of carrying that version of the gene. Whether a physician or genetic counselor has legal or moral obligations to inform other family members of their risks remains uncertain (Andrews 1997).

PRIVATE THIRD-PARTY DISCRIMINATION   Concerns about discrimination in health insurance and employment are often reported in the United States as major deterrents to genetic testing. These issues have also been raised for disability insurance, life insurance, and adoption (as to genetic tests both of the child and of the potential adoptive parents). Only a few anecdotal cases of employment and insurance discrimination have been reported (Billings et al 1992; US Congr., Off. Technol. Assess. 1988b, 1990b), but concern is nonetheless high.

These situations share the characteristic that private actors seek to use genetic information about a person to make decisions concerning that person. The information may be used in a rational manner, where the genetic information really does provide data significant for the decision. In other situations, the information could be used inaccurately and irrationally, on the basis of misunderstandings about the nature of the genetic condition.

The legal questions surrounding employment and health insurance discrimination are murky (Gostin 1991; Greely 1992; Alper & Natowicz 1993; Rothstein 1993; Task Force Genet. Inf. Ins., Natl. Inst. Health/Dep. Energy Work. Group Ethical, Legal, Soc. Implic. Hum. Genome Res. 1994). First, it is not clear whether the federal Americans with Disabilities Act prohibits employment discrimination on the basis of genetic characteristics. The issue would turn largely on whether a genetic characteristic actually is a disability, defined by the statute as a mental or physical impairment that significantly affects a major life activity, or is merely regarded as a disability by the employer. No judicial decisions have interpreted that language with regard to genetic characteristics; the Equal Employment Opportunity Commission, which has the power to enforce the employment discrimination provisions of the act, has stated that genetic characteristics may be disabilities, but that conclusion does not have the force of law (Equal Employ. Oppor. Comm. 1995). Many states have statutes similar to the Americans with Disabilities Act; the application of these statutes to genetic characteristics generally also remains unclear.

The situation surrounding health insurance is even more confusing. The issue revolves around medical underwriting and  preexisting condition limitations. Insurers and health maintenance organizations medically underwrite consumers when they decide whether to issue coverage based in part on information about consumers' predicted future health (and hence future covered health costs). Most Americans with health coverage are not subject to medical underwriting, as they receive coverage from large employers, who rarely use medical underwriting, or from Medicare and Medicaid, public programs that do not medically underwrite. People purchasing their own health coverage or receiving it from a small employer, however, may be subject to medical underwriting with respect to their past health and known health risks. Similarly, individual coverage, small-employer coverage, and some large-employer coverage can include preexisting condition limitations that exclude, for a fixed period of time or forever, payments for conditions that the insured had at the time the coverage began.

In insurance markets where they are used, medical underwriting and preexisting condition limitations can be used to reject for insurance people with a record of many conditions, such as cancer, hypertension, diabetes, obesity, or smoking. Genetic testing would add another class of factors (and another group of people) to those affected by these practices: genetic factors that predict future illness without causing substantial present symptoms.

Federal law does not generally prohibit either medical underwriting or preexisting condition limitations (Greely 1992, Hudson et al 1995). The Americans with Disabilities Act largely exempts health insurance from its coverage, even when the insurance is related to employment. The recently passed Kassebaum-Kennedy bill, however, prohibits most employers from providing health coverage for some employees but not others based on medical conditions. It does not, however, regulate what prices can be charged and what conditions can be covered. The act also puts a complicated time limit on the length of preexisting condition limitations imposed by most employers and restricts the ability of covered employers to classify genetic characteristics as preexisting conditions.

About 20 states have now prohibited insurers from using genetic information in medical underwriting, although those statutes generally do not deal with genetic characteristics as preexisting conditions. The meaning of "genetic information" in these statutes is variable and somewhat uncertain. The scope of these statutes is limited because state jurisdiction over employer-provided health coverage is, to a large extent, prohibited by a federal statute called the Employee Retirement and Income Security Act (ERISA) (Rothenberg 1995, Greely 1992).

Beyond the surprisingly unclear questions of the current legal status of employment and health insurance discrimination based on genetic information lies the normative question of whether such discrimination should be legal. Employers, insurers, and others discriminate among people on many grounds; are genetic grounds inherently inappropriate? Some argue that they are, analogizing them to other characteristics over which individuals have no control, such as their race, sex, or age. Others argue that the propriety of genetic discrimination depends on the importance of the good that could be denied. Under that kind of analysis, discrimination might be banned in health insurance but allowed in life insurance, which could be seen as less important. One could also point out that singling out genetic characteristics for protection tends to emphasize a view of genetic characteristics as inherently immutable, which is often not true. Thus, a person with a genetic predisposition to a given condition might be able either to avoid the condition altogether or to mitigate its effects, through, for example, using eyeglasses to counteract myopia.

All of these concerns can be the result of either individual or population genetic research. Although individuals carry alleles, some kinds of genetic conditions, and hence some varieties of alleles, are more common in some groups than others. Sickle-cell anemia is found at unusually high levels among people from parts of Africa and the Mediterranean; Tay-Sachs disease is disproportionately common among Jews and French Canadians; cystic fibrosis is unusually frequent in people from northern Europe. Research that revealed a high rate of a particular genetic characteristic in certain populations could be used to stigmatize the entire population, leading insurers to reject all its members without examining the genetic makeup of individuals in that group. Of course, to the extent that this kind of stigmatization of an entire group exists already, based on epidemiological evidence, the development of individual genetic tests could be used to protect individuals from the discriminatory consequences. Even if some individual members of the group escape discrimination, however, the stigma may still have negative consequences for the group as a whole (Duster 1989).

Finally, one must note that these issues will present themselves to different people and in different cultural settings. Americans over the age of 65 almost always can receive health coverage through Medicare, with no medical underwriting. Health insurance discrimination should be of little concern to them, as, if they are retired, should employment discrimination. In the United Kingdom, health coverage is universal through the National Health Service, but medically underwritten credit life insurance is important for those seeking home or automobile loans. The use of genetic tests in health insurance is not a major issue there; the use of genetic tests in life insurance is.

GOVERNMENT ACTION    Governments could also use genetic predictions to make distinctions among individuals or groups. The history of the eugenics movement looms over this issue. This movement viewed with alarm what it considered the increase in "genetically defective" people caused by what it perceived as a greater rate of reproduction among the "genetically inferior" (Kevles 1986, Müller-Hill 1988, Proctor 1988, Paul 1992). Many countries, including the United States, Germany, Sweden, and the United Kingdom forcibly sterilized people on grounds of genetic predispositions to such traits as criminality and feeblemindedness. The US Supreme Court, in an opinion by Justice Holmes, upheld one such statute (Buck v. Bell 1927) with the famous words "three generations of imbeciles are enough," although it later applied constitutional restrictions to a similar statute (Skinner v. Oklahoma ex rel. Williamson 1942). Arguments from the eugenics movement were also used to support immigration legislation that greatly favored northern Europeans.

State-sponsored eugenics is not simply a matter of history. The People's Republic of China recently adopted legislation that requires all couples to receive a medical certificate before being allowed to marry; the legislation also requires prenatal testing for pregnancies involving those with "serious" genetic diseases (Gewirtz 1994). The statute at the very least encourages long-term contraception, sterilization, and abortion for those affected. In other countries, the concern that the genetically less favored are "overreproducing" continues to resonate.

The original eugenics movement collapsed with the revelations of the lengths to which Germany took these arguments during the Third Reich, but its demise was aided by an increased scientific understanding of the complex genetic and environmental roots of the conditions at which eugenicists took aim. As knowledge of genetic influences on those kinds of complex conditions increases, some form of more scientifically based, and hence more limited, eugenics can take shape. Required abortion or sterilization is one extreme, but incentives short of requiring abortion might be imposed, such as a refusal to provide health coverage for infants born after such a prenatal diagnosis. Such efforts would raise constitutional questions in the United States and ethical and moral questions everywhere.

Government action based on the predictive power of genetics would not necessarily be limited to eugenics, however. The press occasionally reports the discovery of a "violence gene." A government might decide to take preventive criminal action against someone carrying that genotype. Similarly, a government might use genetic evidence of low intelligence or learning disabilities to limit the education and life opportunities of certain children. On the other hand, such information might be useful in identifying children who would benefit from special attention.

Finally, although the discussion above has been about government action against individuals, data from population genetics could be used to cast an entire ethnic group as genetically inferior. There is no evidence from existing genetic studies that such an outcome is scientifically plausible. All human populations seem to contain nearly all the same genetic variants, albeit at somewhat different frequencies. Levels of particular genetic disorders higher than the overall species average can be found in almost any group. Nonetheless, the absence of good arguments to be drawn from population genetic data does not mean that bad but politically attractive arguments will not be made. Misused data might be cited to argue that governments should take action against "genetically inferior" peoples, action up to and including genocide.

## Human Genetics and Revealing the Past

The "fortune-telling" aspects of human genetics have received the most attention, but in some circumstances that information can look backward as well, to provide evidence about the past. These uses of genetic data can raise less obvious social concerns, with respect to both individuals and groups.

INDIVIDUAL ANCESTRY   One of the most straightforward uses of human genetic information is to trace family relationships. Parenthood can usually be established readily, as can more distant relationships. Although such analyses have long been done with blood types (based on proteins that are themselves genetically determined), additional genetic data can make the conclusions even more certain.

Whether establishing "true" genetic family ties is a good or bad thing may depend on the circumstances. When used to reunite the children of victims of the Argentinean junta with their grandparents, its advantages seem clear. But if it is used without the consent of those involved, it could have serious implications for their privacy, their social relationships, and even their lives. Genetic counselors can encounter this problem when testing for a familial disorder. They have often discovered that the putative father was not, in fact, the genetic father. In that situation, they had to decide whom, if anyone, to tell about the true parentage. Similarly, use of genetic tests to establish paternity for child-support purposes, though justifiable, would violate the privacy of both a nonconsenting father and a nonconsenting mother, with possibly serious effects on their lives.

HISTORICAL FIGURES   Writers have long speculated on the medical and psychological ailments and characteristics of famous people. DNA testing has provided another method to learn more about individuals who have died. Genetic tests on remains can sometimes be used to determine whose remains they really are, as with the Romanovs and Jesse James. Some have urged that remains from Abraham Lincoln be analyzed to determine whether he had Marfan's syndrome, as has often been speculated. Genetic tests, in such circumstances, provide just one more way of analyzing the past, but one that may garner greater attention because of the high status of genetic information. The spread of such testing has implications for the privacy of the dead historical figures, with surviving family members probably experiencing the strongest effects. It also could have broader social implications, if, for example, the identification and reburial of the Romanov remains were used as weapons in Russian politics.

THE HISTORY OF PEOPLES—AND PEOPLE   The HGDP raises another set of issues about the past, centering on particular populations. With enough data, population geneticists can estimate how closely related different populations of humans are to each other. This information could then be used, with linguistic, anthropological, archeological, and historical analysis, as one line of evidence to help trace the history of human migrations across the globe (Cavalli-Sforza et al 1991, Cavalli-Sforza et al 1994, Weiss 1998).

For some cultures, that evidence might be unwelcome. Many societies have their own creation stories, one of which is the Garden of Eden. Although belief in the literal truth of the Bible's creation story remains strong in the United States in spite of much scientific evidence to the contrary, for some peoples additional inconsistent scientific evidence might disrupt their own historical beliefs or self-image. In some situations, such information could disrupt an entire culture.

Genetically based historical information could have modern political implications. In the American Southwest, for example, the Hopi and Navajo peoples have long disputed ownership of certain land. Genetic evidence as to whether the Navajo are relatively recent immigrants to the region, as the Hopi maintain, could have political consequences for that land dispute. Of course, the genetic evidence would be only one additional strand of evidence, but it could be an important strand.

More broadly, evidence from population genetics could help confirm, or rebut, understandings of overall human evolution. The "out of Africa" and multiregional hypotheses certainly could be affected by more genetic data, which in turn could change scientific and popular views about human creation or evolution.

Even more broadly, one of the most striking findings from research into genomes is how much genetic material is shared by very different kinds of life. Genes found in humans can almost always be found in substantially similar form in mice; they can often be found in fruit flies, nematodes, and even yeast. "Human" genes are often just slight variants on "mammalian" genes or "vertebrate" genes or genes that are universal to all life on earth. A broad public appreciation of this reality might affect our understanding of nature and humanity's place in it. Not only would all humans be cousins, but all life would be demonstrably related.

## Manipulating Human Genomes

Thus far, the implications discussed have arisen from information derived from existing (and inferred past and future) human genomes. The manipulation of human genomes may also raise ethical issues.

Moving DNA bearing genes from one species into another species in order to create chimeras—organisms that, genetically, are part one species and part another—is a mainstay of research in molecular biology and is also used extensively in biotechnology. Moving human DNA into non-human animals strikes some as a profanation of humanity; mixing DNA from non-human species can be perceived as a violation of a perceived natural order. The creation of mixes of humans and other animals that are apparent at a non-molecular level—chimpanzees with near-human brains, humans with feline fur—remains in the realm of science fiction, but if accomplished would raise serious questions about the meaning of "human" for various laws and cultural norms.

Finally, supporters of animal rights would also raise concerns about the purposeful use of members of other species for human ends, especially when the human gene caused harm or discomfort to the animal or when the animal ultimately was killed for human use, as would be the case with organ transplants.

HUMAN GENE THERAPY   Moving genes from one human to another for therapeutic purposes is less controversial. The paradigm of gene therapy, as originally conceived, was to insert a "proper" gene into the relevant cells of a person with a genetic disease so that the gene would produce a protein necessary for health. Thus, gene therapy for cystic fibrosis would provide lung cells with genes making functional copies of the CTFR1 gene (Lyon & Gorner 1996).

Because of its direct connection to human health, gene therapy aimed at inserting functioning genes into the relevant cells of the body has caused little ethical controversy. This approach to treatment, however, has produced little success in spite of major funding; the appropriate level of support has thus become controversial. Some have also questioned the ethics of human gene therapy research in offering highly experimental treatments to often desperate patients.

HUMAN GERM LINE GENE MANIPULATION   The somatic cell gene therapy discussed above would affect only the patient who received it; it would not normally have any effects on the genes of the patients' descendants. Particular variants of genes could also be inserted into eggs and sperm, thus making intentional changes in the genomes of the patients' descendants indefinitely. This could be done for the purpose of avoiding a genetic disease or, possibly, for "enhancing" the characteristics of the child. The alleles that are added might come from the parents or from other humans. In theory, at least, they could also come from other species or come, newly made, from laboratories. It is not clear how realistic these scenarios are. All these technologies would be technically difficult and of uncertain safety for the fetus; the desire for alleles found in the parents or in other humans could also be met by preimplantation diagnosis and sperm or egg donation.

Germ line genetic manipulation raises all the issues of prenatal genetic selection, through preimplantation diagnosis or otherwise. It is not clear whether it raises others. Some might argue that the affirmative act of inserting alleles not otherwise present is different from the sorting through of genetic combinations produced by the merger of eggs and sperm, perhaps paralleling the action/inaction distinction. The social implications of the two technologies, whether voluntarily chosen by parents with the opportunity (and the money) to make the choice or imposed by the state, seem largely identical.

## Ownership and Control of Human Genes and Genetic Information

The next set of issues moves from how human genetic material and information could be used to who should control those materials and their uses. Control might be exercised in several ways: through property rules, through privacy protections, through informed consent, or through direct government regulation.

OWNERSHIP OF HUMAN BIOLOGICAL MATERIALS AND HUMAN GENETIC INFORMATION   Human genetic research raises issues as to appropriate legal and ethical ownership of both human biological materials and the information they contain. Human bodies and their parts have long been subject to special treatment under the law of property. Anglo-American law, at least after the abolition of slavery, does not recognize property interests in human bodies, living or dead. The next of kin of a decedent have a long-recognized quasi-property right over the corpse, but only for the purpose of arranging for its proper disposition. While living, people are viewed as having control over their bodies and bodily integrity, but not as a result of the laws of property. Thus, in the United States, competent adults are not legally able to exercise one of the prime characteristics of a property right with respect to their organs: They are not allowed to sell them.

On the other hand, some kinds of body parts can be sold: human hair, blood and blood products (in some states), and eggs and sperm. Other organs may be donated and, where they come from a living donor, may be designated for donation to a specific person. The donors are entitled to get their expenses but no price for the organs themselves.

Biological materials sought primarily for their genetic information do not fit easily into this framework. Who owns—or should own—chromosomes or genes, or, indeed, cells contained within human tissues, once they have been separated from the person in whom they grew? (US Congr., Off. Technol. Assess. 1987; Knoppers 1997; Knoppers et al 1996a; Gold 1996). Only one court decision has addressed this issue—*Moore v. Regents of the University of California*—and *Moore*'s importance is unclear (Moore v. Regents of the Univ. Calif. 1991). The California Supreme Court in *Moore* rejected a claim that a patient owned a cell line derived from his surgically removed tissue, although it allowed Moore to try to prove at trial a claim that he had not given true informed consent to the procedure. Because of its facts, *Moore* may not apply to anything other than cell lines or other substantially modified human biological materials; in any event, at this point it has not been adopted—or rejected—by any other court. It remains the express law in California only, leaving the property status of human biological materials in other contexts legally uncertain.

The ethical discussion of ownership of human biological materials has two major aspects. The most prominent argument revolves around the effects such ownership would have on our views of humans, on whether humans would become commodities. This view has been expressed forcefully with respect to surrogate motherhood and the selling of organs for transplantation purposes; the connection between individual cells, molecules, or parts of molecules from human bodies to humans seems more tenuous but can still be asserted.

The second argument, raised clearly by John Moore's suit, is the fairness of the distribution of benefits from human tissue: If any profit is made as a result of research with human biological materials, how should it be shared between the source of the materials and the researchers? Individual donors of materials rarely will be able to show that their contributions played a crucial role, as most human genetic research depends on contributions from many individuals. The argument, however, becomes stronger when the entire group that has contributed to the research—extended families, people who share a genetic disease, or communities—asserts such a claim (Greely 1997a; North Am. Reg. Comm., Hum. Genome Divers. Proj. 1997).

The legal status of intellectual property in the *information* in human genetic material seems clear, except at the margins. The ethical status of that kind of property is much more controversial (Eisenberg 1990).

The United States, Europe, and Japan have all issued patents for "inventions" that include human genetic information. These patents follow from the long-standing patent treatment of complex organic chemicals. Even though the chemical might be found in nature, a method for producing a useful compound at greater purity or higher effectiveness than found in nature can be patented. For the patent offices, human DNA has largely been just another complex organic chemical.

Patents issued on human DNA confer on the holder a monopoly on the right to use that invention for a limited amount of time, now usually 20 years from the date of the patent application. The patent holder cannot claim control over naturally occurring DNA with that sequence—it could not demand royalties from all humans for their normal use of "its" DNA—but it can control commercial uses of that DNA sequence during the patent's term. (There is a statutory exception for some research uses in the patent statutes of many countries; the United States has no statutory research exception but there is some unclear support for one in court opinions.)

Some "inventions" involving human DNA, such as expressed sequence tags, may not qualify for patent protection because they lack some of the essential attributes of patentability, notably utility, enablement, and novelty. And in many countries, but not the United States, the patent statutes contain an exception for inventions that are "against public morality;" this might be used against some patents on biotechnology. The core concept that useful stretches of human DNA sequence can be patented is not, however, in substantial legal doubt in the United States, Europe, or Japan.

Whether such DNA patents are ethical is, however, controversial. Patents on human DNA have attracted opposition from many directions. Some opponents object, on religious grounds, to any claim of human ownership to divinely created creatures or their DNA. Others view the human genome, in particular, as a common heritage of mankind that should belong to all humanity. This position, adopted by the UNESCO International Bioethics Committee in its Universal Declaration of Rights in the Human Genome, rejects the idea that some should profit from the human genome. Others object to the possibility of genetic engineering generally and view the elimination of DNA patents as a useful instrument for slowing or stopping the entire technology. Still others, equating parts of the human genome with humans themselves, see gene patents as a commodification of humanity. Finally, even some biotechnology companies and academic researchers object to certain patents or the scope of some patents, such as patents on expressed sequence tags or on single nucleotide polymorphisms, as likely to interfere unduly with research.

Thus far, the movement against gene patents has led to some relatively minor modifications in a European patent directive; otherwise it seems to have had little influence on the constantly increasing number of patents issued on DNA sequences.

PRIVACY   The concept of genetic privacy has great appeal (Andrews & Jaeger 1991; Annas et al 1995a,b; Rothstein 1997; Gostin 1993a). It is the subject of much proposed and enacted legislation throughout the United States, in part as a means of avoiding the kinds of employment and insurance discrimination discussed above and in part as an end in itself. When examined closely, however, genetic privacy becomes complex and difficult (Greely 1998b).

First, privacy itself has many meanings. Privacy can refer to the ability to make particular decisions without governmental intrusion, as in abortion. It can mean a claimed right to choose with whom to associate, as in marriage or certain residential situations. It can refer to a right to avoid unwanted publicity, even if accurate. It can denote a right against unwanted physical intrusion into one's body or one's home, as in the Fourth Amendment's protection from unreasonable governmental search and seizure. Finally, it can mean confidentiality—the right to insist that information, conveyed to one party for a particular purpose, not be retransmitted to another. Most of these forms of privacy are subject to some degree of constitutional or statutory protection in the United States. Discussion of genetic privacy has focused on intrusion and confidentiality, with some discussion of a decisional privacy right in making decisions about childbearing (Robertson 1990, 1994).

Protection against intrusional privacy would involve prohibitions on the collection of genetic information on people without their consent. At one level, this is not difficult. One cannot normally force someone to provide a blood sample, cheek swab, or other source of genetic material. On the other hand, people constantly shed biological materials that contain cells from which DNA can be recovered, in sloughed skin, fallen hairs, saliva, urine, and feces. There seems to be little legal protection for such, often unintentionally, discarded materials; nor does there seem any practical way to enforce a prohibition on the collection of such materials.

The intrusion, however, could be viewed not as the collection of biological materials but their analysis for genetic information. In that case, a ban on analysis for genetic information of materials collected without consent might be plausible. Such a rule would, however, raise problems both in the definition of genetic information and in the situation of partial consent: If a person authorizes the collection and analysis of a blood sample for medical purposes, would all genetic information have to be the subject of specific consent? At least one US court has ruled that testing voluntarily provided blood samples for "intimate" medical information—information on pregnancy, syphilis infection, and carrying an allele for sickle-cell anemia—without specific consent may violate the law (*Norman-Bloodsaw v. Lawrence Berkeley Lab. 1998*).

That kind of limitation on the unconsented genetic analysis shares a second problem with attempted protection of the confidentiality of genetic information. "Genetic information" may be a meaningless term because a great deal of information, medical and otherwise, provides evidence, conclusive or weak, about genes. For example, a person's ABO blood group is determined by a test of certain molecules found on the surface of red blood cells. Those molecules are determined by the variations in specific genes; knowing that a person is blood type O gives an observer specific information about the person's genetic sequence. Knowing that a couple had a child with sickle-cell anemia provides the observer with definite knowledge of the sequence of a hemoglobin gene found in each parent. Even knowing that people are male or female provides information about their genomes. If genetic information is defined narrowly, as the result of analyses of a gene's sequence, it misses family history or protein tests that would provide strong evidence about the person's genome. If genetic information is defined broadly, it encompasses nearly all medical information.

Medical information is currently protected by various legal doctrines, but that protection is generally considered woefully inadequate (US Congr., Off. Technol. Assess. 1993; Gostin 1993b, 1995). The difficulty of defining "genetic information" could argue for more effective protection of all medical information. Unfortunately, trends in both medicine and the financial management of health care in the United States are pushing for broader collection and easier dissemination of medical information. The practical scope for legisla-tion improving the privacy of medical information is unclear (Holtzman 1995, Reilly 1995, Greely 1998b).

Genetic privacy also has a corollary in population genetics. Communities studied by population genetic researchers may not want to be identified for fear of various negative consequences, such as discrimination or weakening a political argument. It may be possible to blur the identity of such groups by re-ferring to them only as members of a broader group of people. Thus, instead of identifying research as being done in a particular village of a particular Apache nation, published accounts might speak of research in an Apache village or, more broadly, a village of speakers of a language in the Na Dene language family. This technique, if chosen by the group, is feasible to some extent, but the greater the imprecision in the description of the group, the less useful the published data would be for fine-scale research.

INFORMED CONSENT   In the past 40 years, the requirement of informed con-sent of a patient to medical intervention has become an important part of US law governing the doctor-patient relationship. During the same period, the principle of requiring informed consent of human participants in research has become enshrined in international and US law. Both kinds of informed consent have important implications in human genetics.

In the clinical setting, the law of informed consent may well be insufficient to protect patients adequately with respect to genetic testing. States have taken two approaches to determining when informed consent is necessary. In some states, informed consent is required only when the standards of professional practice require it—that is, doctors have to get their patients' informed consent for a particular intervention only if doctors usually get informed consent in that situation. Other states have adopted a "reasonable patient" standard: Doctors have to get their patients' informed consent when the intervention involves risks that a reasonable patient would want to know about.

Under either standard, it is not clear that informed consent would be re-quired for genetic tests. There is no established standard for most genetic tests, and most kinds of clinical tests are not currently the subject of informed con-sent. More fundamentally, the risks to a patient from genetic tests are not the kinds of direct medical risks, such as death or paralysis, that informed consent usually covers. Indeed, the risks of the "procedure" could be said to be limited to the trivial risks of drawing a blood sample.

If informed consent were required, what kind of information should be given? The main risks of genetic tests are usually the risks of psychological consequences, familial disturbances, and employment and insurance discrimi-nation that test results might bring. These are not the kinds of risks that physi-cians normally view as the consequences of medical interventions, but they could well be much more important to patients than a minute risk of a negative medical effect of, for example, a spinal tap.

Beyond the legal and ethical questions about the existence and scope of any informed consent obligation in the clinical use of genetic tests lies the question of *whose* informed consent. Should informed consent be required from the patient or the entire family that might be affected by the information? Knowledge of the genetic status of one relative provides powerful, sometimes conclusive, information about the genetic status of parents, siblings, and children. It could be argued that the obligation of clinical informed consent should be expanded to encompass all those strongly affected by the resulting information. Such an expansion might give other family members a veto over the patient's decision or merely give them information about the test and an opportunity to discuss the decision with the patient.

For research, US law generally requires informed consent from human subjects participating in research at institutions receiving federal funding or in research that will be used in a submission to the Food and Drug Administration (FDA). These rules, and similar rules in other countries, raise at least four important legal and ethical issues.

One currently heated battle involves the use of previously collected human biological materials for genetic research. Hospitals, universities, blood banks, states, and others have vast collections of human tissue samples, some with associated clinical information. These kinds of samples are potentially invaluable resources, particularly when tied to clinical data. On the other hand, the patients involved did not give informed consent for this kind of research use, and where their identities could be linked to the sample, the analysis could harm them—for example, by identifying them as at high risk for a disease (Clayton et al 1995). The US National Bioethics Advisory Commission is currently studying this issue; it is expected to report on it during 1998.

A second concern deals with the scope of uses that may permissibly be requested through informed consent. Some argue that research subjects can give consent only to research on specific and narrowly defined topics. Subjects could not be fully informed of the risks and benefits of research with their samples unless the research plan has been formulated. This position would arguably make it impossible for subjects to agree to allow their samples to be used as general resources for genetic studies, as the HGDP contemplates, or even, perhaps, to be part of the sequencing of the entire genome planned by the HGP. The research that might be conducted with that information, and the possible consequences for the subject, cannot be specified in advance.

A third issue focuses on the use of informed consent to restrict, in a binding way, the uses made of a research subject's samples. Research subjects, as part of informed consent, might be able to authorize use of their samples for research into diabetes but forbid their use for research into alcoholism. They might require the destruction or return of their samples within a specified period or might put conditions, including financial conditions, on any subsequent use of their samples for commercial purposes.

It is not clear under existing law whether the informed consent process, as currently constituted, leads to a binding contractual agreement between the researcher and the subject. There seems no reason, however, to think that binding contracts could not be achieved in connection with informed consent. Such contracts could provide research subjects with potentially valuable ways to control the use of their samples, as long as the subjects had the ability, as well as the legal right, to enforce such contracts (Greely 1997a,b; North Am. Reg. Comm., Hum. Genome Divers. Proj. 1997).

Finally, for some kinds of research, as for some kinds of clinical genetic tests, one might ask whose informed consent should be required. This is particularly true for population genetics, where the object of the study is primarily the population as a whole and not the individual participants, but it could also apply to research with individuals or families affected with genetic diseases. When a group is the actual subject of the research, it might be appropriate to require the informed consent of the entire group, acting through whatever authorities it recognizes. A study of the genetic constitution of Icelanders, for example, affects all people from Iceland, whether they are among the individual research subjects or not.

If there are entities that the group recognizes as having authority over them as a group, such as a national or tribal government or an important religious or cultural body, such group consent might be demanded. This consent would have the beneficial effect of allowing the group, as a whole, to determine whether to run the risks of genetic research to their history, political standing, insurability, and so on. It would also, of course, be difficult to implement: What are the boundaries of a group, and what are the culturally appropriate authorities that speak for them? It could also be viewed as infringing on individual liberty by preventing willing group members from participating in research that they found worthwhile (North Am. Reg. Comm., Hum. Genome Divers. Proj. 1997).

SOCIAL REGULATION    Apart from rules of property, privacy, and informed consent, other forms of regulation could be imposed on genetic technologies through, among other possibilities, professional organizations, governments, or international organizations. These regulations could cover many kinds of human genetic research or its applications. For example, many of those groups have already attempted to ban human cloning. Perhaps the most interesting case, at least in the United States, is the commercial availability of genetic testing.

In the United States, neither drugs nor biologicals can legally be sold or used without FDA permission, which is based on strong proof of their safety and efficacy as well as close monitoring of the conditions under which they are produced. The FDA also limits the advertising, marketing, and labeling of drugs. Medical devices are subject to similar, though somewhat less stringent, regulation. The practice of medicine, however, is subject to no such limitations. While a new drug, vaccine, or device can be used commercially only after government permission, a physician can use a new medical procedure at any time, with fear largely of only possible malpractice litigation.

Depending on how they are offered, genetic tests may be treated like medical procedures and not like drugs or medical devices. If the test is being offered as a service, by a clinical laboratory, the FDA has not asserted jurisdiction over it as a medical device. If, however, the test is packaged for resale to clinical laboratories, physicians, or individuals, it is a medical device and must be shown to be safe and effective before it can be sold. Not surprisingly, firms marketing genetic tests have chosen to market them as services and not as test kits, thus avoiding the stringent FDA approval process or real review of the value of test. The Clinical Laboratory Improvement Act Amendments of 1988 regulate the credentials and working conditions of the technicians who perform clinical laboratory analyses and provides for regular tests of laboratory competence, but it does not limit what tests can be performed. Some states have imposed more stringent limitations on clinical laboratories, but they have not required rigorous proof of the safety and efficacy of genetic tests. The extent to which the state or federal governments should, or will, impose such regulation remains in doubt.

## Genes, Souls, and Destiny

The most important social implications of human genetic research may lie in its possible deep cultural effects. Two consequences seem particularly plausible: the "sacralization" of human DNA and an increasing belief in determinism. Both derive from attaching a seemingly exaggerated importance to a set of very long molecules.

It has been argued that, for some people, a human's genome has taken on attributes of the traditional Christian soul. It is uniquely individual (except in identical twins), it is a person's essence, and it is, at least in the form of information, potentially immortal. Nelkin & Lindée even note an effort to sell bits of celebrity DNA, which, they point out, parallels medieval practices with Christian relics (Nelkin & Lindée 1995).

In some cultures, the sacred nature of human biological materials already imposes some constraints on genetic research; for example, when DNA samples may be taken from cheek swabs or other tissues but not from blood. A broadening sense that human DNA is somehow sacred has implications for research, for genetic manipulation, and for privacy. At the same time, the demonstrably close connections between human genes and non-human genes could diffuse some of this sense of sacredness to other life.

The second possible consequence is a greater belief that individuals' abilities, and fates, are determined by their DNA. Reports of "gay" genes or "risk-seeking" genes, like phrenology, astrology, and other variants of fortune-telling, attempt both to predict and to provide explanations for human behavior and human outcomes (Hamer & Copeland 1998). The war between free will and determinism has been played out in different contexts during different eras in Western culture (and probably many other cultures as well), but the tension remains (Degler 1991). Increasing associations of genetic variations with particular traits may well increase the appeal—and the perceived "scientific truth"—of determinism.

In fact, much human genetic research does not support such a deterministic view (Lewontin et al 1984, Lewontin 1992, Hubbard & Wald 1993). Only a few, usually rare genetic conditions are solely and completely determined by a known gene or genes. Variation in the severity of the phenotype exists for many major genetic disorders, such as cystic fibrosis and sickle-cell anemia. Variation in the penetrance of other disease-related genotypes, the percentage of people with the genotype who will get the disease phenotype, is common, with examples from Alzheimer's disease to breast cancer to colon cancer. Many conditions with strong genetic components, such as phenylketonuria, and weaker ones, such as myopia, can be treated successfully. And most human traits, disease-related or otherwise, seem to be a result of a complex interaction of many genes and many environments, including perhaps prenatal environment. For some unfortunate humans, such as children born with Tay-Sachs disease, genes are destiny. For most of us, they are only one more influence in the contingent histories of our lives.

I believe that the paragraph above is correct. I also want to live in a society that believes it is correct. The possible serious undercutting of such a belief by research in human genetics would be, to me, its most negative consequence.

## ETHICAL, LEGAL, AND SOCIAL ISSUES: COMMON STRANDS

Three common strands run through most of the issues discussed above. First, much human genetic research simultaneously raises many quite different issues. Second, the social consequences of human genetic research are similar to those of many other kinds of research. Third, the *perception* that genetic research is different is powerful. These latter two themes are important in themselves and combine to create a policy dilemma.

This chapter has carefully assigned different concerns arising from human genetics research to one of six categories, yet any given research project is likely to raise many issues from different categories. For example, research on genetic links to some forms of intelligence would spark concerns about, among other things, discrimination, prenatal testing and abortion, eugenics, germ line genetic manipulation, genetics, property, and determinism.

The proposed HGDP, whose North American ethics subcommittee I chair, provides another example. This proposal for collection, storage, and analysis of DNA samples from a broad spectrum of human populations has been attacked as "biopiracy," as reinforcing racism, as violating informed consent principles, as breaking down culturally important myths, and as leading to discrimination against ethnic groups (if not biological warfare), among other things (Mead 1996; Rural Advancement Found. Intl. 1993, 1995, 1997; Cultural Survival Q. 1996). The breadth of the issues involved both confuses the analysis and guarantees that there will be something for almost anyone to worry about. The resulting debates have led to some working out of ethical principles (Human Genome Diversity Project 1994, UNESCO Intl. Bioethics Comm., Subcomm. on Bioethics and Population Genetics 1995, Human Genome Organisation 1996, Knoppers et al 1996b, North Am. Reg. Comm., Hum. Genome Divers. Proj. 1997, Natl. Res. Council, Comm. Hum. Genome Divers. 1997) and, perhaps, to some improved understanding between, and among, the researchers, activists, and populations involved. But the very breadth of the issues involved has made those understandings more difficult to reach, as well as underlining the necessity of some continuing ethical oversight of this and other such endeavors. The issues are too complex, the individual contexts are too important, and the participants are too human to create "the" solution to the issues this kind of effort raises; only a continuing and vigilant process can minimize negative consequences from such research.

The second common strand is that the issues discussed above do not arise uniquely from genetic research. They are consequences of information about people or peoples; in some respects, human genetic research just makes possible another kind of information.

Thus, the forensic use of DNA raises issues largely identical to the earlier introduction of fingerprints or blood group tests. Genetic tests merely extend the reach of discrimination in employment and individually underwritten health insurance from, for example, people with a history of breast cancer to people with a genetically high risk of getting breast cancer in the future. Any advantages wealthy parents could confer on their children from genetic selection are probably dwarfed by the educational and cultural advantages money buys during their lives. The historical use of population genetics just adds one more line of evidence to findings that may undermine common beliefs about ethnic, national, or human origins. Privacy is threatened whenever information people care about has value to others, whether it is genetic information, medical information, or credit information. Many clinical tests and not just genetic tests should probably have expanded informed consent, as a "mere" test is not necessarily an entirely benign procedure.

The consistent thread is a new sort of information of value. Even some of the wilder issues, such as part-human chimeras, have parallels outside genetics, as in speculation about the legal and moral status of truly intelligent computers.

The third strand is that genetic information is often different from other kinds of information in its scientific origins and is always different in its perceived "essential" nature. Genetic information comes from examining invisible molecules. It is the result of the work of high-status scientists, laboring in clean laboratories in major universities. It is threatening (Rifkin & Howard 1981, Rifkin 1998), and it comes from one's "blueprint," the "Code of Codes," the stuff that "makes us what we are." And, perhaps as a result of those facts, research in human genetics, whether speculative or confirmed, is often on the front page of newspapers and the cover of news magazines (Nelkin & Lindée 1995).

This elevated status for the human genome is not only deeply inappropriate but also dangerous. At the same time, as a social phenomenon, it is very real. This sets up a serious dilemma that runs through many policy issues in genetics. Greater public knowledge of, interest in, and concern about genetic research gives this kind of research unusual power. Whether genetic information gives insurers anything more than medical information may be unclear, but if insurers believe it is powerful, it will have a greater effect on people's lives. And if people believe that, their anxiety concerning the uses of genetics will rise.

Thus, the mere perception of a peculiar power in human genetics may cause heightened risks that could justify special intervention for genetic information. Or, alternatively, the heightened concern might provide enough political support to ban, for example, medical underwriting for genetic susceptibilities even though sufficient support does not exist to ban medical underwriting for current or past health conditions.

But, on the other hand, providing special legislation or regulation may just feed the cultural belief that genetics truly *is* special. If that is the case, one might win a small tactical victory against the misuse of genetics in ways that harm people while reinforcing dangerous misperceptions of the power of genetics (Wolf 1995). This deep dilemma is perhaps the greatest ethical, legal, and social challenge posed by human genetic research.

## CONCLUSION

This article is an attempt to forecast the major ethical, legal, and social implications of ongoing research into human genetics. It is, necessarily, a somewhat idiosyncratic vision of those implications. Only two conclusions seem certain. The first is that the implications will be important, leading to changes in day-to-day matters like medicine and in concepts of our world and our humanity. This revolutionary expansion in our knowledge of the molecular biology of life, especially human life, will have major effects on all cultures that partake of it. The second conclusion is that this article's discussion will prove to be, in some important parts, wrong. Issues will not play out as expected, unforeseen problems will arise, and time and chance will have their effects. Most of the effects of DNA on human society will prove to be no more predetermined than most of its effects on individual humans.

> Visit the *Annual Reviews home page* at
> http://www.AnnualReviews.org.

## Literature Cited

Alper JS, Natowicz MR. 1993. Genetic discrimination and the public entities and public accommodations titles of the Americans with Disabilities Act. *Am. J. Hum. Genet.* 53:26–32

Am. Soc. Hum. Genet., Ad Hoc Comm. DNA Technol. 1988. DNA banking and DNA analysis: points to consider. *Am. J. Hum. Genet.* 42:781–83

Andrews LB. 1987. *Medical Genetics: A Legal Frontier.* Chicago: Am. Bar Found.

Andrews LB. 1997. Gen-etiquette: genetic information, family relationships, and adoption. In *Genetic Secrets: Protecting Privacy and Confidentiality in the Genetic Era,* ed. MA Rothstein, pp. 255–80. New Haven: Yale Univ. Press

Andrews LB, Jaeger AS. 1991. Confidentiality of genetic information in the workplace. *Am. J. Law Med.* 17:75–108

Annas GJ, ed. 1992. *Gene Mapping: Using Law and Ethics as Guides.* New York: Oxford Univ. Press

Annas GJ, Glantz LH, Roche PA. 1995a. Drafting the genetic privacy act: science, policy and practical considerations. *J. Law Med. Ethics* 23:360–66

Annas GJ, Glantz LH, Roche PA. 1995b. *The Genetic Privacy Act and Commentary.* Boston: Boston Univ. Sch. Health

Billings PR, ed. 1992. *DNA on Trial: Genetic Identification and Criminal Justice.* Plainview, NY: Cold Spring Harbor Lab.

Billings PR, Kohn MA, Decuevas M, Beckwith J, Alper JS, Natowicz MR. 1992. Dis-

crimination as a consequence of genetic testing. *Am. J. Hum. Genet.* 50:476–82

Bosk C. 1992. *All God's Mistakes: Genetic Counseling in a Pediatric Hospital.* Chicago: Chicago Univ. Press

Brock DW. 1992. The human genome project and human identity. *Houston Law Rev.* 29: 7–22

Buck v. Bell. 1927. 274 U.S. 200, 47 S.Ct. 584, 71 L.Ed. 1000

Caplan AL, Bartels DM, LeRoy BS, eds. 1993. *Prescribing Our Futures: Ethical Challenges in Genetic Counseling.* New York: Aldine de Gruyter

Capron AM. 1990. Which ills to bear? Reevaluating the "threat" of modern genetics. *Emory Law J.* 39:665–96

Capron AM, Lappé M, eds. 1979. *Genetic Counseling: Facts, Values and Norms.* New York: Liss

Cavalli-Sforza LL, Menozzi P, Piazza A. 1994. *The History and Geography of Human Genes.* Princeton: Princeton Univ. Press

Cavalli-Sforza LL, Wilson AC, Cantor CR, Cook-Deegan RM, King MC. 1991. Call for a worldwide survey of human genetic diversity: A vanishing opportunity for the human genome project. *Genomics* 11: 490–91

Clayton EW, Steinberg KK, Khoury MJ, Thomson E, Andrews L, et al. 1995. Informed consent for research on stored tissue samples. *JAMA* 274:1786–92

Cook-Deegan R. 1994. *The Gene Wars: Sci-*

*ence, Politics, and the Human Genome.* New York: Norton

Cranor CF, ed. 1994. *Are Genes Us? The Social Consequences of the New Genetics.* New Brunswick, NJ: Rutgers Univ. Press

Degler CN. 1991. *In Search of Human Nature: The Decline and Revival of Darwinism in American Social Thought.* New York: Oxford Univ. Press

Duster T. 1989. *Backdoor to Eugenics.* New York: Routledge

Eisenberg RS. 1990. Patenting the human genome. *Emory Law J.* 39:721–45

Equal Employ. Oppor. Comm. 1995. *Order 915.002, Definition of the Term "Disability."* Reprinted in *Daily Labor Report.,* March 16, 1995, pp. E1, E23

Fletcher JC. 1988. *The Ethics of Genetic Control: Ending Reproductive Roulette.* Buffalo, NY: Prometheus

Frankel MS, Teich AH. 1993. *The Genetic Frontier: Ethics, Law, and Policy.* Washington, DC: Am. Assoc. Adv. Sci.

Gewirtz DS. 1994. Toward a quality population: China's eugenic sterilization of the mentally retarded. *NY Law Sch. J. Int. Comp. Law* 15:147–62

Gold ER. 1996. *Body Parts: Property Rights and the Ownership of Human Biological Materials.* Washington, DC: Georgetown Univ. Press

Gostin LO. 1991. Genetic discrimination: the use of genetically based diagnostic and prognostic tests by employers and insurers. *Am. J. Law Med.* 17:109–44

Gostin LO. 1993a. Genetic privacy. *J. Law Med. Ethics* 23:320–30

Gostin LO. 1993b. Privacy and security of personal information in a new health care system. *JAMA* 270:2487–93

Gostin LO. 1995. Health information privacy. *Cornell Law Rev.* 80:451–527

Greely HT. 1992. Health insurance, employment discrimination, and the genetics revolution. In *The Code of Codes: Scientific and Social Issues in the Human Genome Project,* ed. DJ Kevles, L Hood, pp. 264–80. Cambridge, MA: Harvard Univ. Press

Greely HT. 1995. Conflicts in the biotechnology industry. *J. Law Med. Ethics* 23: 354–59

Greely HT. 1997a. The control of genetic research: involving "the groups between." *Houston Law Rev.* 33:1397–430

Greely HT. 1997b. The ethics of the Human Genome Diversity Project: the North American Regional Committee's proposed model ethical protocol. See Knoppers 1997, pp. 239–56

Greely HT. 1998a. Informed consent, stored tissue samples, and the Human Genome Diversity Project: protecting the rights of research participants. In *Ethical Issues in Stored Tissue Samples,* ed. RF Weir. Iowa City: Univ. Iowa Press. In press

Greely HT. 1998b. Problems in protecting "genetic privacy." *Chicago-Kent Law Rev.* In press

Hamer D, Copeland P. 1998. *Living with Our Genes: Why They Matter More Than You Think.* New York: Doubleday

Holtzman NA. 1989. *Proceed with Caution: Predicting Genetic Risks in the Recombinant DNA Era.* Baltimore, MD: Johns Hopkins Univ. Press

Holtzman NA. 1995. The attempt to pass the Genetic Privacy Act in Maryland. *J. Law Med. Ethics* 23:367–70

Hubbard R, Wald E. 1993. *Exploding the Gene Myth.* Boston: Beacon

Hudson KL, Rothenberg KH, Andrews LB, Kahn MJE, Collins FS. 1995. Genetic discrimination and health insurance: an urgent need for reform. *Science* 278:391–93

Human Genome Diversity Project. 1994. *Summary Document.* Available at http://www.stanford.edu/group/morrinst/HGDP. html.

Human Genome Organisation. 1996. HUGO statement on the principled conduct of genetics research. *Genome Digest* 2 (May 1996). Also available at http://hugo.gdb. org:90/conduct.htm.

Inst. Med., Natl. Acad. Sci. 1993. *Assessing Genetic Risks: Implications for Health and Social Policy.* Washington, DC: Natl. Acad. Press

Judson HF. 1979. *The Eighth Day of Creation: The Makers of the Revolution in Biology.* New York: Simon & Schuster

Kevles DJ. 1986. *In the Name of Eugenics: Genetics and the Uses of Human Heredity.* Berkeley: Univ. Calif. Press

Kevles DJ, Hood L, eds. 1992. *The Code of Codes: Scientific and Social Issues in the Human Genome Project.* Cambridge, MA: Harvard Univ. Press

King M-C, Rowell S, Love SM. 1993. Inherited breast and ovarian cancer: what are the risks? What are the choices? *JAMA* 269:1975–80

Kitcher P. 1996. *Lives to Come: The Genetic Revolution and Human Possibilities.* New York: Simon & Schuster

Knoppers BM, ed. 1997. *Human DNA Sampling: Law and Policy—International and Comparative Perspectives.* The Hague: Kluwer Law Int.

Knoppers BM, Caulfield T, Kinsell TD, eds. 1996a. *Legal Rights and Human Genetic Material.* Toronto: Montgomery Publ.

Knoppers BM, Hirtle M, Lormeau S. 1996b. Ethical issues in international collaborative research on the human genome: the HGP and the HGDP. *Genomics* 34: 272–93

Kolata G. 1998. *Clone: The Road to Dolly and the Path Ahead.* New York: Morrow

Lander ES. 1989. DNA fingerprinting on trial. *Nature* 339:501–5

Lewontin RC. 1992. *Biology and Ideology: The Doctrine of DNA.* New York: Harper Collins

Lewontin RC, Rose S, Kamin LJ. 1984. *Not in Our Genes.* New York: Pantheon Books

Lyon J, Gorner P. 1996. *Altered Fates: Gene Therapy and the Retooling of Human Life.* New York: Norton

McEwen JE. 1997. DNA data banks. See Rothstein 1997, pp. 321–51

Mead A. 1996. Genealogy, sacredness, and the commodities market. *Cult. Surviv. Q.* 20(Summer):46–52

Milunsky A, Annas GJ, eds. 1975. *Genetics and the Law.* New York: Plenum

Milunsky A, Annas GJ, eds. 1980. *Genetics and the Law II.* New York: Plenum

Milunsky A, Annas GJ, eds. 1985. *Genetics and the Law III.* New York: Plenum

Moore v. Regents of the Univ. Calif. 1990. S. Cal. 3d, 120,793, p. 2d 479. 271 Cal. Rptr. 146

Müller-Hill B. 1988. *Murderous Science: Elimination by Scientific Selection of Jews, Gypsies, and Others 1933–1945.* Oxford: Oxford Univ. Press

Murray TH, Lappé M, eds. 1994. *Justice and the Human Genome Project.* Berkeley: Univ. Calif. Press

Murray TH, Rothstein MA, Murray RF, eds. 1996. *The Human Genome Project and the Future of Health Care.* Bloomington: Ind. Univ. Press

Natl. Res. Counc. 1992. *DNA Technology in Forensic Science.* Washington, DC: Natl. Acad. Press

Natl. Res. Counc. 1996. *DNA Technology in Forensic Science: An Update.* Washington, DC: Natl. Acad. Press

Natl. Res. Counc., Comm. Hum. Genome Divers. 1997. *Evaluating Human Genetic Diversity.* Washington, DC: Natl. Acad. Press

Natl. Res. Counc., Comm. Mapp. Seq. Hum. Genome. 1988. *Mapping and Sequencing the Human Genome.* Washington, DC: Natl. Acad. Press

Natl. Soc. Genet. Couns. 1997. Predisposition genetic testing for late-onset disorders in adults. *JAMA* 278:1217–20

Nelkin D, Lindée MS. 1995. *The DNA Mystique: The Gene as a Cultural Icon.* New York: Freeman

Nelkin D, Tancredi L. 1994. *Dangerous Diagnostics: The Social Power of Biological Information.* Chicago: Univ. Chicago Press. 2nd ed.

Norman-Bloodsaw v. Lawrence Berkeley Lab. 1998. 135 F.3d 1260 (9th Circuit)

North Am. Reg. Comm., Hum. Genome Divers. Proj. 1997. Proposed model ethical protocol for collecting DNA samples. *Houston Law Rev.* 33:1431–73

Paul D. 1992. Eugenic anxieties, social realities, and political choices. *Soc. Res.* 59: 663–83

Pence GE. 1998. *Who's Afraid of Human Cloning?* Lanham, MD: Rowman & Littlefield

Pollock R. 1994. *Signs of Life: The Language and Meanings of DNA.* Boston: Houghton Mifflin

President's Comm. Study Ethical Probl. Med. Biomed. Res. 1982. *Splicing Life: A Report on the Social and Ethical Issues of Genetic Engineering with Human Beings.* Washington, DC: The Commission

President's Comm. Study Ethical Probl. Med. Biomed. Res. 1983. *Screening and Counseling for Genetic Conditions: A Report on the Ethical, Social, and Legal Implications of Genetic Screening, Counseling and Education Programs.* Washington, DC: The Commission

Proctor R. 1988. *Racial Hygiene: Medicine Under the Nazis.* Cambridge, MA: Harvard Univ. Press

Rabinow P. 1996. *Making PCR: A Story of Biotechnology.* Chicago: Univ. Chicago Press

Rapp R. 1988. Chromosomes and communication: the discourse of genetic counseling. *Med. Anthropol. Q.* 2:143–57

Reilly PR. 1995. The impact of the genetic privacy act on medicine. *J. Law Med. Ethics* 23:378–81

Reilly PR. 1977. *Genetics, Law, and Social Policy.* Cambridge, MA: Harvard Univ. Press

Rifkin J. 1998. *The Biotech Century: Harnessing the Gene and Remaking the World.* New York: Tarcher/Putnam

Rifkin J, Howard T. 1981. *Who Should Play God? The Artificial Creation of Life and What It Means for the Human Race.* New York: Dell

Robertson JA. 1990. Procreative liberty and human genetics. *Emory Law J.* 39: 697–719

Robertson JA. 1994. *Children of Choice: Freedom and the New Reproductive Technologies.* Princeton, NJ: Princeton Univ. Press

Rothenberg KH. 1995. Genetic information

and health insurance: state legislative approaches. *J. Law Med. Ethics* 23:312–19

Rothenberg KH, Thomson EJ, eds. 1994. *Women and Prenatal Testing: Facing the Challenges of Genetic Technology.* Columbus: Ohio State Univ. Press

Rothman BK. 1986. *The Tentative Pregnancy: Prenatal Diagnosis and the Future of Motherhood.* New York: Viking

Rothstein MA. 1993. Genetic discrimination in employment and the Americans with Disabilities Act. *Houston Law Rev.* 29: 23–84

Rothstein MA, ed. 1997. *Genetic Secrets: Protecting Privacy and Confidentiality in the Genetic Era.* New Haven, CT: Yale Univ. Press

Rural Advancement Found. Intnatl. 1993. *Communiqué: Patents, Indigenous People, and Human Genetic Diversity* (May 1993). Also available at http://www.rafi.ca

Rural Advancement Found. Intnatl. 1997. *Communiqué: The Human Tissue Trade* (Jan../Feb 1997). Also available at http://www.rafi.ca

Rural Advancement Found. Int. 1995. *Indigenous Person from Papua New Guinea Claimed in US Government Patent* (Oct. 4, 1995). Available at http://bioc09.uthscsa.edu/natnet/archive/nl/hgdp.html.

Silver LM. 1997. *Remaking Eden: Cloning and Beyond in a Brave New World.* New York: Avon Books

Skinner v. Oklahoma ex rel. Williamson. 1942. 316 US 535, 62 S. Circuit. 1110, 86 L. Ed. 1655

Task Force Genet. Inf. Ins., Natl. Inst. Health/Dep. Energy Work. Group Ethical, Legal, Soc. Implic. Hum. Genome Res. 1994. *Genetic Information and Health Insurance.* Bethesda, MD: Natl. Inst. Health

UNESCO Intnatl. Bioethics Comm., Subcomm. on Bioethics and Population Genetics. 1995. *Bioethics and Human Population Genetics Research.* Available at http://www.biol.tsukuba.ac.jp/~macer/PG.html

US Congr., Off. Technol. Assess. 1987. *New*

*Developments in Biotechnology: Ownership of Human Tissues and Cells.* Washington, DC: US Gov. Print. Off.

US Congr., Off. Technol. Assess. 1988a. *Mapping Our Genes—The Human Genome Project: How Big, How Fast?* Washington, DC: US Gov. Print. Off.

US Congr., Off. Technol. Assess. 1988b. *Medical Testing in the Workplace.* Washington, DC: US Gov. Print. Off.

US Congr., Off. Technol. Assess. 1990a. *Genetic Witness: Forensic Uses of DNA Tests.* Washington, DC: US Gov. Print. Off.

US Congr., Off. Technol. Assess. 1990b. *Genetic Screening in the Workplace.* Washington, DC: US Gov. Print. Off.

US Congr., Off. Technol. Assess. 1992. *Cystic Fibrosis and DNA Tests: Implications of Carrier Screening.* Washington, DC: US Gov. Print. Off.

US Congr., Off. Technol. Assess. 1993. *Protecting Privacy in Computerized Medical Information.* Washington, DC: US Gov. Print. Off.

US Dep. Justice. 1996. *Convicted by Juries: Exonerated by Science: Case Studies in the Use of DNA Evidence to Establish Innocence After Trial.* Washington, DC: Natl. Inst. Justice

Watson JD, Crick FHC. 1953. A structure of deoxyribose nucleic acid. *Nature* 171: 737–38

Weir RF, Lawrence SC, eds. 1994. *Genes and Human Self-Knowledge.* Iowa City: Univ. Iowa Press

Weiss KM. 1998. Coming to terms with human variation. *Annu. Rev. Anthropol.* 27: 273–300

Wertz DC, Fanos JH, Reilly PR. 1994. Genetic testing for children and adolescents: who decides? *JAMA* 272:875–81

Wertz DC, Fletcher JC, eds. 1989. *Ethics and Human Genetics: A Cross-Cultural Perspective.* New York: Springer-Verlag

Wolf SM. 1995. Beyond "genetic discrimination": toward a broader harm of geneticism. *J. Law Med. Ethics* 23:345–53

*Annu. Rev. Anthropol. 1998. 27:503–32*
*Copyright 1998 by Annual Reviews. All rights reserved*

# THE POLITICS AND POETICS OF DANCE

## Susan A. Reed

Department of Anthropology, University of California at Berkeley, Berkeley,
California 94720-3710; e-mail: sreed@qal.berkeley.edu

KEY WORDS: performance, embodiment, movement, identity, folklore

### ABSTRACT

Since the mid-1980s, there has been an explosion of dance studies as scholars
from a variety of disciplines have turned their attention to dance. Anthropologists have played a critical role in this new dance scholarship, contributing comparative analyses, critiquing colonial and ethnocentric categories,
and situating studies of dance and movement within broader frameworks of
embodiment and the politics of culture. This review highlights ethnographic
and historical studies that foreground dance and other structured movement
systems in the making of colonial cultures; the constitution of gender, ethnic
and national identities; the formation of discourses of exoticization; and the
production of social bodies. Several works that employ innovative approaches to the study of dance and movement are explored in detail.

## INTRODUCTION

It has been 20 years since Adrienne Kaeppler's review of anthropology and
dance in this series (Kaeppler 1978). At that time, given the marginal status of
dance, Kaeppler wondered about the propriety of devoting an *Annual Review*
article to such an "esoteric aspect" of anthropology. But in the intervening decades, the anthropology of dance has gained greater legitimacy as a field of inquiry, even as it is being reconfigured within the broader framework of an anthropology of human movement (Farnell 1995b, Kaeppler 1985). As Lewis
(1995) has argued, this shift to "movement," motivated by a critique of
"dance" as a universally applicable category of analysis, parallels develop-

0084-6570/98/1015-0503$08.00

ments in other fields of expressive culture such as music and theatre. In ethnomusicology, for example, Feld (1990b, 1991) has argued for a shift from the category of "music" to sound, while the creation of "performance studies" by Victor Turner and Richard Schechner was, in part, a reaction to the ethnocentrism implicit in the use of the term "theater" to refer to non-Western performance forms (Lewis 1995:223).

Concurrent with the growing interest in dance and movement within anthropology, "dance history" has transformed into "dance studies," an interdisciplinary field focusing on the social, cultural, political and aesthetic aspects of dance (Daly 1991b). Three recent collections (Desmond 1997, Foster 1995a, Morris 1996) chart this emerging field, while the long-awaited *International Encyclopedia of Dance* (Cohen 1998) includes several related entries. The expanding interest in cultural studies of dance is evidenced by the fact that more than a third of the works cited in this article were published since 1995. This new dance scholarship has made significant contributions to our understandings of culture, movement and the body; the expression and construction of identities; the politics of culture; reception and spectatorship; aesthetics; and ritual practice.

Although the study of dance and other "structured movement systems" (Kaeppler 1985) has expanded within anthropology, such work remains on the margins of the discipline. There are at present only a few anthropologists who specialize in dance and movement analysis, and many are located outside of anthropology, in departments of music, dance, or performance studies. The field of anthropology needs more specialists in movement and dance; additionally, movement analysis should be included as part of the general anthropology graduate curriculum. It is indeed ironic that, despite the considerable growth of interest in the anthropology of the body (Lock 1993), the study of moving bodies remains on the periphery.

Though the emergence of the anthropology of dance as a distinct subfield can be traced to the 1960s and 1970s, dance has been the subject of anthropological study since the discipline's inception. Early anthropologists including Tylor, Evans-Pritchard, Radcliffe-Brown, Malinowski and Boas all addressed aspects of dance in their writings, predictably emphasizing the social functions of dance, with little attention to the specifics of movement. Williams (1991) provides a comprehensive survey of these early anthropological analyses of dance, while Spencer's theoretical survey (1985b), Ness's analysis of selected anthropological works (1996), and review articles by Kaeppler (1978, 1991) and Giurchescu & Torp (1991) outline developments in dance studies to the late 1980s. Youngerman (1998) and Quigley (1998) provide succinct histories of dance anthropology and ethnology, while the contributions of ethnomusicologist John Blacking to the development of dance studies within the United Kingdom are discussed by Grau (1993b).

In the 1960s and 1970s, a small group of scholars—Adrienne Kaeppler, Jo-ann Kealiinohomoku, Anya Peterson Royce, Judith Hanna, and Drid Wil-liams—laid the groundwork for an anthropology of dance. They examined dance within theoretical paradigms inspired by Boas and Herskovits (Kealii-nohomoku, Royce), Chomsky and Saussure (Kaeppler, Williams), ethnosci-ence (Kaeppler), and communications theory (Hanna). These studies thus stressed the form and function of dances, the deep structures of dance, and dance as nonverbal communication. Dance anthropologists also critiqued the ethnocentrism implicit in much standard dance scholarship. For example, Kealiinohomoku's article on ballet as "ethnic dance," originally published in 1970, took to task several classic works of dance scholarship published from the 1920s to the 1960s. Kealiinohomoku demonstrated how dance scholars' blanket categorization of non-Western dances as ethnic, folk, or primitive was based on an evolutionary paradigm in which Western theatrical dance, espe-cially ballet, emerged as "...the one great divinely ordained apogee of the per-forming arts" (Kealiinohomoku 1983; see also Friedland 1998).

Since the 1980s, the most significant developments in dance anthropology have been in studies of the politics of dance, and the relations between culture, body, and movement. Studies in these areas, which draw from semiotics, phe-nomenology, postcolonial, poststructural, and feminist theories, reflect the dramatic changes that occurred in anthropology in the 1980s. In this review, I focus on studies that address these two dimensions of dance and movement, giving particular attention to studies that exemplify original and insightful syntheses of them. Although I focus primarily on ethnographic and historical analyses by anthropologists, I also discuss the works of many non-anthro-pologists whose studies speak to anthropological issues.

## THE POLITICS OF DANCE

Dance as an expression and practice of relations of power and protest, resis-tance and complicity, has been the subject of a number of historical and ethno-graphic analyses in recent years. These analyses complicate issues raised in earlier works on the politics of dance (Brandes 1979, Hanna 1979, Royce 1977), particularly in the areas of ethnicity, national identity, gender and, less commonly, class.

Desmond's anthropologically informed article (1993) on how social identi-ties are "signaled, formed and negotiated" through bodily movement is par-ticularly useful for its detailed attention to the complex ways in which dance and movement styles are transmitted across class, ethnic, and national lines. Desmond makes a powerful case for attending to movement as a primary so-cial text: complex, polysemous, and constantly changing, signalling group af-filiation and difference. Desmond shows, for example, how issues of class and locality can be embodied in changing lexicons of movement, resulting in a form of "bodily bilingualism" (1993:46). While acknowledging that the concepts of resistance, appropriation, and cultural imperialism are useful for understanding changes in dance across time and place, Desmond stresses that an overemphasis on these concepts may only highlight formal properties, while ignoring contextual meanings and processes of hybridization.

## Colonialism

Dance studies have much to contribute to recent scholarly debates and discussions in colonialism and culture (Cooper & Stoler 1997, Dirks 1992), demonstrating the importance of dance in the "civilizing process," the control and regulation of "disorderly" practices, and the profound refigurations of both local and European culture.

The suppression, prohibition and regulation of indigenous dances under colonial rule is an index of the significance of dance as a site of considerable political and moral anxiety. Colonial administrations often perceived indigenous dance practices as both a political and moral threat to colonial regimes. Local dances were often viewed as excessively erotic, and colonial agents and missionaries encouraged and sometimes enforced the ban or reform of dance practices (Comaroff 1985, Kaspin 1993). However, dance was also a site of desire, and colonial accounts record that male colonists were often captivated by "native dancers," sometimes even joining them in dances. Thus, in many colonial arenas, dance tended to generate multiple and contradictory policies and attitudes.

In some colonized areas, dance practices posed a genuine threat of political resistance or rebellion, particularly in societies where dance was a site of male collective performance, in which a sense of unity and power was heightened, potentially spawning uprisings against colonial rulers or slave masters. In Hazzard-Gordon's analysis of dance on slave plantations in North America, it is evident that while attitudes toward and regulation of plantation dance varied widely across time and region, dance was very often perceived as a significant threat (Hazzard-Gordon 1990:3–62). In some states, legislation banning dance and drumming was enacted as dances came to be seen as likely sites for plotting insurrections, or even the occasions for the insurrections themselves (Hazzard-Gordon 1990:32–34).

Poole's analysis of the choreography and history of Andean ritual dance focuses on the complex ways in which convergences between Spanish Catholic and Andean conceptions of dance as "devotion" allowed the dance to be sustained over centuries, in part because of the uncomprehending cultural "blindness" of the Spanish to "non-religious" political meanings of the dance (Poole 1990). Employing vivid descriptions, diagrams, and photographs of Andean dance movements and patterns, Poole shows how, despite transformations in costumes, props and gestures, Andean dance retained characteristic movement patterns that embedded concepts of social hierarchy and social time fundamentally distinct from those of Europeans. While Andean dance was forced to work within the space of Catholicism and the church, where it was largely conceptualized as an acceptable "devotional" practice akin to Christian church dances, for the Andeans the dance retained much of its significance as a means of gaining individual status and power. Taking the dance into the present, Poole argues that, like the colonial Spanish, some contemporary "outside" observers (mis)read the dance within their own interpretive schemes, viewing the dance as a symbol of an essentialized Andean identity.

Representations of dance under colonial rule played a critical role in their transformation. Udall's analysis of the impact of Euro-American image-makers (photographers, painters, illustrators) on the practice of the Hopi snake dance explores the transformative and intrusive aspects of colonial (and post-colonial) visual representations on ritual practice (Udall 1992). Representations of Javanese performances by the Dutch and the legacies of colonialism in contemporary performance scholarship are explored by Schechner (1990), who argues that scholars who establish "normative expectations" for "traditional" performances perpetuate colonial thinking by valorizing one version of performance as "true" while dismissing others as corrupted.

The most sustained, and historically and theoretically rich research on dance under colonial rule has been done on *bharata natyam* and the dances of the *devadasis* of India, the object of several recent anthropological and historical studies (Allen 1997; Kersenboom-Story 1987; Marglin 1985; Meduri 1988, 1996; O'Shea 1997, 1998; Srinivasan 1984, 1985, 1988). The *devadasis*—female temple dancers of South India—are something of a celebrated case in the colonial history of India, well known because their practices of dance and ritual were banned during the Anti-Nautch social reform movement of the 1890s, which was implemented as part of a series of other reforms designed to "civilize" practices of Indian women. Moreover, *bharata natyam*—a dance form that emerged in the 1930s and is ostensibly derived from the dances of the *devadasis*—has now migrated to Europe and the United States, gaining legitimacy as a form of "world dance" (Meduri 1996).

Meduri's study of the construction of the *devadasi* in the 19th and 20th centuries shows the ways in which identities of indigenous dancers shifted as they became implicated in changing discourses of colonialism, nationalism, and Orientalism (Meduri 1996). While Kersenboom-Story and Srinivasan present comprehensive, detailed accounts of the *devadasi* under precolonial and colonial rule, from which Meduri draws, Meduri's focus is on demonstrating the ways in which the *devadasis* became implicated in larger debates about sexuality, womanhood, and the nation as these developed from the 19th century to the present. She keeps the focus of her research on the perspectives of the *devadasi*s, insofar as these are made visible in documents such as ritual texts and protest letters, and in the "visible body" of the dancer. Meduri traces the transfiguration of the *devadasi* from her precolonial practice as a temple ritual performer to her naming, in the 19th century, as temple "prostitute" or "dancing girl" and finally, in the 20th century, to emblem of the nation.

Allen's (1997) work focuses on the complex processes involved in the re-contextualization of the *devadasi* dance during the late colonial period. Allen discusses the multiple influences on the development of *bharata natyam* in the 1930s and 1940s, and his work illustrates the complex process by which a ritual dance form was extracted from its original context and then domesticated, reformed, and resanctified for middle-class consumption. Illluminating the many transformations that are masked by the term "revival," Allen shows how this celebratory and seemingly innocent term obscures several processes, which he succinctly glosses as re-population (one community appropriating a practice from another), re-construction (altering elements of repertoire and choreography), re-naming (from *nautch* and other terms to *bharata natyam*), re-situation (from temple and court to the stage), and re-storation (the splicing together of performances to invent a seemingly ancient practice) (Allen 1997: 63–64).

The dynamic exchanges that occurred between colony and metropole are the heart of Erdman's (1987) study of the Indian oriental dancer Uday Shankar (Erdman 1987) and her critical analysis of the ways in which nationalism has affected the construction of the history of Indian dance (Erdman 1996). Erdman shows that the important place of "oriental dance"—the dances first developed in Europe and based on oriental themes—in histories of Indian dance has long been overlooked for political reasons. After Independence, only two genres of Indian dances were recognized by nationalists: the "classical" dances based on regional styles, and the numerous "folk" dances derived from regional and local contexts (Erdman 1996:296). Because histories of Indian dance were constructed as nationalist histories—thus erasing the influences of Europeans and Americans, such as Anna Pavlova and Ruth St. Denis (Coorlawala 1992), as well as European-influenced Indian dancers like Shankar—Erdman argues that a "new history of Indian dance" is required, a critical history that questions long-held tenets about the alleged authenticity and antiquity of classical dance.

Erdman's critique of Indian dance histories has many implications for the development of a critical dance scholarship, and in calling for new, politically aware histories of dance, Erdman is keenly aware of the difficulties of the task, and leaves open-ended the forms that such histories might take. In the Indian case, she argues, they certainly should include the many contemporary developments in the art, the new choreographies of inventive Indian dancers that are both "Indian *and* modern" (Erdman 1996:297). But Erdman even questions whether the categories of "Indian dance" or "oriental dance" will necessarily be the most salient ones, emphasizing that regional, caste, or religious identities may be more relevant for understanding the ways in which dance practices are understood by the people themselves (Erdman 1996:299). Her critique raises serious issues about how colonial categories, including the often naturalized classifications of "folk" and "classical" dances, may enact an exclusionary history as well as reify particular politically motivated social identities. Erdman's call, in fact, is an opportunity for dance scholars to intervene in the often-divisive reification of ethnic and national identities, an area in which dance scholarship has sometimes been complicit.

Exoticization takes many forms, and the representation of the exotic Other, especially women, has been an important feature of both dance performances and visual representations of dance since at least the 18th century. Dance also played a critical role in the ethnological exhibitions of the 19th century. Franz Boas, for example, brought Kwakiutl Indians to perform dances at the Chicago's World Columbian Exposition in 1893 (Hinsley 1991), while "native dancers" featured prominently in Carl Hagenbeck's profitmaking ethnological displays in 19th-century Europe.

Dances of the colonized were often appropriated and refigured as adjuncts to the civilizing mission, variously reinforcing stereotypes of mystical spirituality and excessive sexuality. In the early 20th century, European and American dancers, including Maud Allan, Ruth St. Denis, Ted Shawn, and Anna Pavlova, appropriated aspects of non-European dance into their performances, creating the exotic in a myriad of ways. Dance historians of European and American theatre dance have made significant contributions to rethinking issues of appropriation in their representation of the Other in theatrical dance, locating these within discourses of imperialism, racism, Orientalism, masculinity, and nationalism, among others (Desmond 1991, Koritz 1994, Strong 1998).

Anthropological studies from the early 1970s stressed the ritual reversals, parody, and satire inherent in festivals and ritual dramas of many societies. Embedded in many of these studies were brief descriptions of danced parodies of European and nonlocal "Others," and several of the studies cited above include such descriptions. But local peoples also adapted, imitated, and transformed the dances of colonizers, and many contemporary dances are social texts that embed long and complex histories of intergroup relations.

Szwed & Marks (1988) describe how African Americans in the Americas and the West Indies took up European court dances of the quadrille, the cotillion, and the contradance, arguing that these dances were both "Africanized" and adapted for sacred purposes, as well as restructured to become the basis of popular culture in the New World (Szwed & Marks 1988:29). Some of these hybrid dances, such as the cakewalk, became phenomenally popular in North America in the late 19th and early 20th centuries, even becoming an international dance craze (Malone 1996). Ranger documents how the Beni-ngoma or "drum band" complex of East Africa, a caricature of the European military parade, became incorporated into social practices that predated colonialism (Ranger 1975). The *matachines* dance, performed widely in Native American and Hispanic communities throughout the Americas, derives from medieval European folk dramas and was brought to the New World by the Spanish (Rodriguez 1996:2; see also Poole 1990:114). Most scholars, according to Rodriguez, agree it was brought for the purpose of "Christianizing the Indians," and as it is performed today it "symbolically telescopes" centuries of Iberian-American ethnic relations as interpreted within individual communities (Rodriguez 1996:2).

In some colonized societies, imitations of European dances became a means of upward mobility, much as the speaking of European languages and the wearing of European dress could become markers of prestige and status. Ness, for example, shows how a Phillipine dance, the troupe *sinulog*, developed in the late 19th century by incorporating features from Hispanic performance forms such as the war dance/drama, *comedia,* and the dances of Spanish Catholic boy choristers (Ness 1992). Ness argues that this process was part of a wider movement towards Europeanization among Cebu elites in the 19th century, in which elements of European, especially Spanish, culture were considered marks of cosmopolitanism.

## Nationalism and Ethnicity

Since at least the 19th century, dance and music have emerged as potent symbols of identity for ethnic groups and nations worldwide. Studies of dance, ethnicity, and national identity have explored the "objectification" of dance as national culture (Handler 1988), the politics of the category of "art" (Hughes-Freeland 1997), the reconstruction of tradition (Kaeppler 1993b), the reinforcement and contestation of gender, ethnic, and class stereotypes (Daugherty & Pitkow 1991, Mendoza 1998, Mendoza-Walker 1994, Reed 1998), the role of competitive dance in transforming tradition (Stillman 1996), the multiple resonances of dance and national identity (Taylor 1987), and the practices of dance as complex social commentaries on interethnic relations (Rodriguez 1996; Sweet 1980, 1985). European dance scholars or "choreologists" have long focused on documenting the structure of folk dances of ethnic minorities in a rather decontextualized manner (Giurchescu & Torp 1991), although more recently, several European scholars have turned to the study of the politics of folk dance as nationalist practice (Quigley 1993). Vail has examined how Balkan folk dance in a New England community was constituted as a site for middle-class white Americans to play both an idealized egalitarian American "self" and an exotic Old Country peasant "Other" (Vail 1996).

Dance is a powerful tool in shaping nationalist ideology and in the creation of national subjects, often more so than are political rhetoric or intellectual debates (Meyer 1995). The role of state institutions in the promotion and reformation of national dances has been documented in a number of studies (Austerlitz 1997; Daniel 1991, 1995; Manning 1993, 1995; Mohd 1993; Ramsey 1997; Reed 1991, 1995; Strauss 1977). The appropriation of the cultural practices of the rural peasantry or of the urban lower classes by the state is a pervasive strategy in the development of national cultures throughout the world, whether as indications of the dominance of one ethnic group or as displays of cultural pluralism.

In many postcolonial nations, the dancer of the valorized national dance comes to be idealized as an emblem of an authentic precolonial past. Where necessary, dancers come to stand in for the nation at local, regional, national, and international festivals and other occasions. As an embodiment of cultural heritage, the dancer becomes inscribed in nationalist histories and is refigured to conform to those histories, yet ambivalence about the dancers and their practices is often evident because the practices themselves often resist being fully incorporated into nationalist discourses. Indeed, the very aspects that make dances appealing and colorful as representations of the past may be precisely the things that do not easily fit into the self-representation of the nation. Vestiges of folk religion (Reed 1991), eroticism (Meduri 1996), and social critique in the performance of dances may sometimes be a source of discord in the presentation of an idealized national image.

Political ideologies play a critical role in the selection of national dances. Strauss's study examines the ideological reasons for the adoption of ballet during China's Cultural Revolution, emphasizing its narrative possibilities, movement vocabularies that stressed strength and action, and its flexibility in expressing gender equality through movement (Strauss 1977). Daniel's studies of the Cuban rumba represent a particularly striking case in which a national dance form was selected almost exclusively for ideological reasons related to its identity with a particular community—the lower-class, dark-skinned workers of Cuba (Daniel 1991, 1995). Although there were two other legitimate contenders for the position—the conga, an easier, more participatory form, and the son, the most popular social dance of Cuba—the rumba was selected by the government because it was viewed as most closely supporting the ideals of a socialist, egalitarian state, and because it expressed an identification with African-derived aspects of Cuban culture (Daniel 1995:16). In Cuba, the Ministry of Culture was the key agent in the organization of rumba (indeed, of all the performing arts), directing amateur dances at neighborhood cultural houses (*casas de cultura*) and overseeing three professional folkloric dance companies.

In the context of state institutions, recontextualization of dance usually entails the domestication of dance, the taming of its potentially disorderly elements. For example, while in the early postrevolutionary period rumba was associated with drinking, public revelry, and even fighting, Daniel suggests that subsequent government support for the dance promoted its shift from this rather unruly atmosphere to the more contained, controlled sites of the culture house and the stage (Daniel 1995:61). Indeed, today the dance is highly regulated, particularly in the Conjunto Nacional troupe, where no innovations or "mixed" dances are allowed. Artistic freedom is limited by the state, and the original spontaneous character of rumba has been suppressed.

Regulating purity and authenticity in folkloric dance in a patriarchal and protective mode is a common feature of state and elite interventions, often indexing notions of a defensive culture under seige. In Ireland, such an authoritarian approach to dance is evident in the regulations of the Gaelic League's Irish Dancing Commission that "controls virtually every aspect of Irish dance from transmission to performance" and forbids the teaching, learning, and performing of Irish dance without the approval of the Commission (Meyer 1995:31; see also Hall 1996). Although occurring outside the parameters of state control, the "ossification" and standardization of the Catalan *sardana* is cited by Brandes as an indicator of the legitimate defense of the Catalans against the threat of Castilian cultural hegemony in Spain (Brandes 1990).

The domestication and regulation of a ritual dance form is exemplified in Ramsey's study of the relationships between nationalism, Vodou, and tourism in postoccupation Haiti of the 1930s through the 1950s (Ramsey 1997). Ramsey illustrates how the state transformed the powerful ritual practice of vodou into a symbol of Haitian identity. Vodou in Haiti was a potent symbol in two distinct senses, both of which, from the point of view of the state, necessitated its domestication. First, while Vodou had been a site of resistance for over two centuries in Haiti, in the West it had been an object of sensationalist fascination for nearly as long (Ramsey 1997:347). This exotic image, however, which had proved quite successful in drawing tourists also caused considerable concern for the state, whose efforts to control culture through standardization of dance, were, as Ramsey argues, only partially successful. The process by which the state attempted to contain culture is a familiar one of sanitization and desacralization, attempting to separate dance from ritual, and magic and superstition from more appropriate aspects of folklore. The attempts at state control over dance were extraordinary; in 1949, for example, when Jean-Leon Destine, Haiti's premier dancer, was asked to organize a national folklore troupe, state ethnologists attended his performances every night to monitor his representations of Haitian identity (Ramsey 1997:365).

National dances are derived from the practices of specific communities, but the dynamics of the appropriation of these practices and the effects they have on the communities of origin have often been overlooked in the literature on "invented traditions." Reed's ethnographic studies of the Kandyan dance of Sri Lanka focus on the central role of traditional ritual dancers in the recontextualization of dance from a specialized ritual practice to popular secular form (Reed 1991, 1995). While acknowledging the critical role of the state in this refiguration, which has resulted in an almost entirely secular form of the dance, Reed explores the means by which traditional dancers fought to retain some semblance of the dance's ritual meaning, even as it became increasingly simplified and standardized within the structures of state bureaucratic practices. Tracing the development of Kandyan dance since the colonial period, Reed also shows how the cultural politics of Tamil and Sinhala rivalries made dance a focal point for the reification of ethnic identities. In state-sponsored dance seminars and programs and in dance history texts, for example, oppositional categories of Sinhala and Tamil are reinforced, despite the quite obvious family resemblances between the Kandyan dance and its Tamil counterpart, *bharata natyam*.

The emotional power of dance as national symbol is evoked in Shapiro's studies of Cambodian court dance in contemporary refugee communities (Shapiro 1994, 1995). Refugee Cambodian dancers are seen as emblems of the Cambodian nation as it existed prior to the Khmer Rouge, and the sustenance of the elaborate and difficult court dance form, with its more than 4500 gestures and postures, is experienced by Cambodians as a continuity with a place and a past from which they have been severed. During the brutal repressions of Pol Pot, in which scores of dancers and other artists were killed, dancers had to deny their own identities to survive, and they kept the dance alive by practicing the gestures and movements in the darkness of night (Shapiro 1995). After the devastations of Cambodian culture by the Khmer Rouge, the court dance traditions came to stand for all that was lost, "the soul of the Khmer," and the burden of healing the body politic is now in the hands of master dancers.

With few exceptions (Daniel 1996, Kaeppler 1977), tourist dances, although often discussed in passing in the context of other concerns, have received surprisingly little attention from anthropologists, despite their obvious importance in constituting ethnic and national representations of self and Other. This may well reflect anthropology's continued attachment to authenticity, and the taints of impurity and corruption often associated with tourism. Malefyt's study of the traditional and commercial forms of the Spanish flamenco places tourist performances in a wider context of gendered conceptions of culture and authenticity (Malefyt 1998). Malefyt explores how aficionados of the dance deploy discourses of purity and impurity, "inside" and "outside," to create exaggerated distinctions between the public (masculine), commercialized performances and the closed, private, and intimate (feminine) sphere of private flamenco clubs. Malefyt's work thus echoes other studies that show how protection of the feminine is linked to the defense of purity in cultural traditions.

## Dance in a Global Context

The study of dance within contemporary global/transnational contexts is an arena ripe for anthropological investigation. The influences of migration and media, especially electronic media (Appadurai 1996), on the production and reception of dance have only recently received attention from dance and movement analysts.the ways in which ballet has been "indigenized" and transformed is the subject of Ness's study of the *Igorot*, a Philippine transnational ballet (Ness 1997). Arguing against a simple view of appropriation as "cultural imperialism," Ness demonstrates how *Igorot* is produced as an original and creative form that selectively references both ethnic and balletic styles. The result is neither entirely Filipino nor Western, but rather a complex hybrid that produces contradictory effects. On the one hand, the *Igorot* is, Ness argues, a "decolonizing" dance that employs a complex movement vocabulary to create a form of Philippine self-representation (1997:68). On the other hand, the dance has the effect of reifying an identification of the *Igorot* with all Filipinos, thus promoting a conservative agenda that denies the internal ethnic diversity and hierarchy of the Philippine nation state (1997:80).

Marta Savigliano's complex text on the tango is a major work that engages feminist, postcolonial, and poststructuralist theories to produce a provocative account of the Argentinian national dance (Savigliano 1995). Savigliano presents tango as a complicated, contradictory practice that has been produced and continues to be reproduced through multiple processes of exoticization. With historical and ethnographic documentation and nuanced movement analyses, accompanied by a score of illustrations of dancers, publicity flyers, programs, and dance manuals, Savigliano details the very complex lives the tango has led in Argentina and in the cultural capitals of London, Paris, and Tokyo. As a symbol of the passionate Other and of exotic culture in a global capitalist economy, Savigliano shows the many ways in which the tango has been commodified for "imperial consumption." In addition, she demonstrates how the tango has become the object of a process of "auto-exoticization" by the colonized themselves.

Savigliano's focus on the global context of the production and appropriation of tango is among the book's most significant contributions. As she tells us, the imperial, bourgeois classes of Europe constituted the exotic as both desirable and repulsive, fascinating and scandalous. Unlike other exotic dances (such as the African American cake-walk and the Brazilian maxixe), the tango did not have a clear-cut class or race identity, and its erotic character was displayed as a process of controlled seduction, not instinctive or wild sexuality. Tango, in short, was highly malleable, an "exotic dance that could easily be stretched in various directions" (Savigliano 1995:114). In order to make the exotic palatable as a European practice, however, elements of its raw and passionate "primitiveness" had to be reshaped to suit cosmopolitan aesthetic sensibilities. Dance masters in early 20th century Paris played a key role in standardizing the dance, simplifying its improvisational characteristics into a morally acceptable set of steps, while tango manuals and congresses contributed to its domestication, "a choreographic transformation suited to French manners and good taste" (Savigliano 1995:122).

Of considerable import for anthropologists is Savigliano's discussion of "auto-exoticization," the process by which the colonized come to represent themselves to themselves through the lenses of the colonizers. Globally, dance has come to play this role in many postcolonial nations, and Savigliano's description of how tango played back home after its incorporation into the exotic dance repertoire of Europe is relevant for analyzing more generally the role of the arts in constituting national identities. Although tango originated among the low working-class sectors of Argentina's Rio de la Plata region in the 1880s, it was only after it achieved fame in the world's cultural capitals in the 20th century that it became popular throughout Argentina. Moreover, this reintroduction of tango also brought with it new ideas about the social and moral meanings of dancing—ideas that were culturally dependent on the colonizers (Savigliano 1995:137). Savigliano's analysis maintains the tension between two key effects of exoticization: one that is empowering, granting local recognition to certain social groups and their practices, the other co-opting and binding, reifying a "tasteful" exotic that served to maintain the (neo)colonized population's dependent status. As Savigliano points out, the (neo)colonizers maintain the upper hand in this process, the threat of withdrawal of recognition always being in their power.

The role of media and mediating images in the representation and presentation of bodily practices is explored by Zarrilli in his study of the Indian martial art form *kalarippayattu* (Zarrilli 1998). Zarrilli, who situates *kalarippayattu* within the contemporary transnational zone of late 20th century "public culture" (Appadurai & Breckenridge 1988), examines how "an increasingly diverse group of culture producers and their audiences" are using mass media to shape martial practices (Zarrilli 1998: 4). Zarrilli's interest is in "the dynamic and shifting relationship between body, bodily practice[s], knowledge, power, agency and the practitioner's 'self' or identity, as well as the discourses and images of the body and practice created to represent this shifting relationship" (Zarrilli 1998: 4). He outlines a model for the study of these various domains as a complex of four interactive arenas: (*a*) the "literal" arenas of practice, such as the training ground, competitions, and the public stage; (*b*) the social arenas of the school, lineage, and formal associations; (*c*) the arena of "cultural production" that generates live or mediated presentations or representations such as films; and (*d*) the arena of experience and self-formation—the individual's experience of embodied practice in the shaping of a self (Zarrilli 1998:9).

The impact of media images on popular reception and practices of dance is explored in Franken's historical account of the changing image of female dancers in Egyptian film and television (Franken 1996). Franken argues that the emergence of a "respectable" female dance form in Egypt and other parts of the Arab world can largely be attributed to the enormous popularity of the cinematic dance performances of a single dancer, Farida Fahmy. While Fahmy danced in a style that was recognizably Egyptian, her modest costumes and the de-eroticized context of her dancing projected an image of a "sweet Egyptian girl who was a true daughter of the country—the antithesis of the image of the belly-dancer who appeared in cabarets and films" (Franken 1996:279). Though Fahmy's films were made in the 1960s, they are still shown on television throughout the Middle East, and thus continue to popularize ideas about dancing and respectability far beyond Egypt (Franken 1996: 282).

## DANCE AND GENDER

If we accept as a given that gender is not an essential quality or characteristic but one that is largely performative, it is evident that dance studies have much to contribute to research on gender identities. In comparison to other performance forms such as theatre (Senelick 1992), dance has been in many societies one of the few sites where women can legitimately perform in public (Thomas 1993:72). While there have been many studies of male and female dances as evidenced in Hanna's crosscultural survey (1988), surprisingly few have engaged with the larger debates in the anthropology of gender and sexuality as they have developed in recent decades.

Dance is an important means by which cultural ideologies of gender difference are reproduced. Through movement vocabulary, costuming, body image, training, and technique, discourses of dance are often rooted in ideas of natural gender difference, as Daly describes for the classical ballet (1987/88). Movement lexicons of males and females often demonstrate the ideals of gendered difference in action. In the Cuban rumba, for example, male dancers use dance as an arena for exhibiting strength, courage, and bravado, while women's dance is generally softer, subtler, more cautious, and graceful (Daniel 1995).

However, dance performances are also sites of gender-crossing, mixing, and reversal (Grau 1993a, 1995). There are numerous examples of males performing in the costumes and manners of the stereotypical female, some as parodies of female dancing, others as homoeroticism or provocations to same-sex erotic encounters (Hanna 1988:57–59). The meaning of role reversals is highly complex and not at all self-evident. In Africa, where women adopting "male traits" in collective dances is fairly widespread, Spencer notes the wide-ranging meanings that anthropologists have ascribed to these types of dances, including temporary release from subservience, veiled protest against male domination, competitiveness between women, and fulfillment of traditional roles in rites of passage (Spencer 1985:3).

## Women, Sexuality, and Dance

Prohibitions on and regulation of dance practices are often accurate indices of prevailing sexual moralities linked to the regulation of women's bodies. In her historical account of American adversaries of dance from the 17th century to the present, Wagner argues that opposition to dance, propagated mostly by white, male Protestant clergy and evangelists, was largely based on a fear of women, the body and the passions (Wagner 1997). Over the centuries, the most extensive opposition to dance focused on the alleged or actual sexual immorality of dancing or its environment. Dance opponents cast women as either "pure and pious"—in need of protection from dance—or "fallen and sinful," and therefore either victims or perpetuators of the evils of dance. Opposition to dance was also related to Protestant clerics' emphasis on strict rationality and the devaluation of the body. As a "merely" physical activity, dancing was dismissed as a waste of time because "neither mind nor spirit was edified" (Wagner 1997: 395). Dance is often an ambivalent and problematic performance site for women as it demonstrates contradictory and ambivalent attitudes about female sexuality. Cowan discusses how female sexuality is regarded in northern Greece as both pleasurable and threatening. In dancing, women are encouraged to display their beauty, energy, skill, sensuality, and even seductiveness, while they are simultaneously viewed with suspicion for drawing too much attention to themselves or failing to maintain self-control (Cowan 1990:190). Because of the inherent ambiguity of bodily actions, there is often no consensus on what distinguishes "a 'legitimately' sensual and pleasing gesture from one that 'goes too far,'" and thus, for women, the pleasures of dance are often ambiguous (Cowan 1990:190–91).

Furthermore, dance performances can exhibit and generate gender/class conflicts regarding the appropriateness of sexually provocative dance movements for women. In urban Senegal, women's dances range from bawdy and explicitly sexual to highly restrained movements (Heath 1994). While traditional dancing is considered to be "women's business," dancing is also considered risky for a woman's reputation, particularly after marriage. Yet their performances are required for public ceremonies, and men's reputations even depend on them. However, upper-class men often try to control the dancers—insisting on restraint, rather than sexual expressivity. Women, however, often resist, testing the limits of appropriateness by sneaking in risque movements, thus attempting to defy total control by males (1994:93).

A number of studies illustrate the contradictions and ambiguities of dance for women in Islamic societies (al Faruqi 1978). In the "Iranian culture sphere," which includes diaspora communities, Shay (1995) argues that the *bazi-ha-ye nameyeshi*, a women's theatrical dance-play performed only for women, is simultaneously a site of bawdy, erotic expression and also a social critique that reinscribes a patriarchal system in which women are defined primarily through their husbands. Deaver's study of Saudi Arabian belly dancing (a term used by her informants) echoes this interpretation, as women dance for each other in a competitive way, displaying their wealth, social status, and sexual desirability (Deaver 1978). Outside the safety of the feminine private sphere are professional female dancers. Van Nieuwkerk's historical and ethnographic account of professional female belly dancers and singers in Cairo explores the way in which these performers negotiate their identities within religious and classed discourses of honor and shame, while also showing how Orientalist stereotypes of the dancers still persist in contemporary Egypt (van Nieuwkerk 1995). A key contribution of Buonaventura's lavishly illustrated book on *baladi* (belly dance) is her documentation of Orientalist representations of dancers in 19th and early 20th century paintings, photographs, and other media (Buonaventura 1990).

Kapchan's analysis of the many "bodies" of *shikhat*, Moroccan female performers who represent the quintessential transgressive female in Moroccan society, highlights the complexity of dancers' identities and both the costs of marginality and its freedoms (Kapchan 1994). As exemplars of the quality of matluqat—free, unlimited and unrestricted—*shikhat* are admired as "lively, animated, spirited," embodying features of "exhilaration and flowing movement" (1994: 94). At the same time, the "loose language" of the shikha, both corporeal and linguistic, is seen as inseparable from her shameful moral character (1994: 86). Describing the multiple "bodies" of the dancers, Kapchan evokes the complex meanings of these performers. The "competent body" of the dancer denotes her as an artist of the physical, exemplifying her sexual prowess, while the "nonsense body" is an expression of subversion and the carnivalesque (1994: 93–95). However, these more pleasurable bodies come at the cost of the "exiled body" (1994: 96). *Shikhat* may be independent and fun-loving, but the majority have been rejected by their families and thus uprooted from place, a state which Kapchan describes as "...the greatest hardship possible" in Moroccan society (1994: 97). Critiquing "resistance" as a limited construct for understanding the role of the *shikhat*, Kapchan notes how, despite their independence, *shikhat* also internalize "...the dominant value system that degrades their material and spiritual worth" (1994: 96).

## Dance and Feminist Theory: Gaze and Reception

As dance historian Ann Daly has indicated, the common interests of feminist scholarship and dance studies would suggest a natural alliance (Daly 1991a), although as yet, few anthropological studies of dance have drawn explicitly on feminist theories. Daly's study of Isadora Duncan and American culture (1995) provides an important model for interpreting the cultural significance of theatrical dance and the importance of audiences. Daly presents a complex and fluid model for understanding the ways in which dancers mirror, contest, and transform gender, ethnic, and class identities. One of Daly's primary points is her definition of the body as a complex, contradictory, and ever changing cultural site of "discursive intercourse" which is constructed dialogically by the dancer and her audiences (1995:17). Daly's extensive research into primary sources of Duncan's audience of mostly upper-class white women (dance reviews, articles, and memoirs) provides the basis for her analysis. In foregrounding the importance of reception as co-creation, Daly's analysis is highly suggestive for anthropologists who, with few exceptions (Hanna 1983), have tended to focus primarily on performers or the contexts of performance.

While the "male gaze" (Kaplan 1983, Mulvey 1975) and the gendered reception and reading of dances has been the subject of considerable critical discussion by dance historians and sociologists (Coorlawala 1996, Daly 1992, Manning 1997, O'Shea 1997, Thomas 1996), there has been little ethnographic research on dance reception and spectatorship. Miller's study of same-sex female sexual dancing in the Trinidadian carnival underscores the critical importance of exploring gender in the interpretation of dance (Miller 1991), although one wishes he had further explored this dimension of analysis. In Trinidad, lower-class women's dance groups perform in a sexually expressive way, often parodying men. Indeed, in the Carnival of the late 1980s, same-sex female dancing had become so conspicuous that the Trinidadian men Miller interviewed deemed it an expression of "lesbianism gone rife" (1991:333). This interpretation was considered incomprehensible by Miller's female consultants, who, according to Miller, did not care with whom they danced. Situating his interpretation within the wider contexts of cross-gender relations among the lower classes, Miller argues that this form of sexual dancing, known as "wining," is not homoerotic, but actually a dance of "autosexuality," a sexuality not dependent upon men (1991:333).

## MOVEMENT, BODY, AND CULTURE

In the last ten years, anthropologists and dance scholars have made significant contributions to cultural analyses of bodies in motion, situating their studies in relation to broader issues of social and philosophical theory (Farnell 1994, 1995a,b; Foster 1992, 1995b; Lewis 1992, 1995; Novack 1990, 1995). The works of Bourdieu, Foucault, Merleau-Ponty, and Peirce, in particular, have provided analysts opportunities for critique and reflection. Anthropologists Lewis and Farnell, for example, have demonstrated how the legacies of Cartesian mind/body dualism permeate the language and categories of theories of embodiment, providing difficulties for movement analysis (Lewis 1992, 1995; Farnell 1994, 1995b). Farnell shows how these categories have resulted in an "absence of the person as a moving agent" in the Western philosophical tradition and suggests that the "new realist" philosophy of science espoused by Harré holds much promise for transcending materialist/immaterialist categories (Farnell 1994). Lewis proposes that a dialogue between the phenomenological approaches of Peirce and the continental phenomenologists, such as Merleau-Ponty, can contribute greatly to clarifying cross-cultural issues of embodiment (Lewis 1995: 228).

The body as a conceptual object has been the subject of much debate among dance scholars, and the interventions of Cynthia Jean Cohen Bull[1] have played a critical role in reconceptualizations of the body in dance studies. Bull was one of the pioneers of a phenomenological approach, and her untimely death from breast cancer in 1996 left an enormous gap in the world of dance scholarship. Fortunately, Bull's considerable body of writings remain a rich source of insight and analysis on the cultural study of dance; Deirdre Sklar has provided an elegant summary of her life and work (Sklar 1997).

In an article on "the body's endeavors as cultural practices," Novack critiques some dominant conceptualizations of the body as they have been formulated in anthropology, as well as in the field of dance studies (Novack 1995). Citing a call for papers for a 1990 anthropological conference on the body, Novack notes how the categories listed in the notice "posited the body as an object, manipulated by external forces in the service of something: religion (body as icon), the state (the discipline of the body), gender (the feminine body), and so on" (1995:179). Novack argues that while these categories articulate some

---

[1]Most of the works of Cynthia Jean Cohen Bull were published under the name of Cynthia Novack. In the last months of her life, Cynthia requested that her name be changed.

aspects of social experience, they do not capture the full experiential significance of the body as a responsive and creative subject (1995:179–80). In addition, Novack also cautions against reifying "the body" as the primary analytic
category in dance studies. In some contexts, she argues, it may be that ideas
about sound, movement and social ethics are more culturally relevant for understanding "bodily endeavors" (1995:183). This perspective resonates with
Turner's emphasis on the utility of studying "bodiliness" and "productive activity" rather than isolated individual and bounded bodies (Turner 1995:150),
and his insight that the social body is produced as an "ensemble of bodily activities" (Turner 1995:166).

"Dance, perhaps more than any other body-centered endeavor, cultivates a
body that initiates as well as responds ..." (Foster 1995b:15). Foster's essay on
the body in dance includes an important critique of Foucault and emphasizes
the agency of the body as a vital counterbalance to the neglect of agentive bodies in traditional dance studies: "The possibility of a body that is written upon
but that also writes moves critical studies of the body in new directions. It asks
scholars to approach the body's involvement in any activity with an assumption of potential agency to participate in or resist whatever forms of cultural
production are underway" (Foster 1995b:15). Like Novack and Turner, Foster
does not posit a stable category of the body, but rather considers such questions
as "What bodies are being constructed here?" or "How do these values find
embodiment?" or "How does this body figure in this discourse?" (Foster
1995b:12).

The agentive nature of dance has often linked it to notions of resistance
(Martin 1990) and control (Limon 1994), although recent criticisms of the use
of the resistance concept (Abu-Lughod 1990, Ortner 1995) will undoubtedly
lead to refinements in future dance studies. Paradoxically, while some aspects
of the experience of dance may engender kinesthetic sensations of power, control, transcendence, and divine union, other aspects may locate it within paradigms of ideological repression or subordination. This stress on the paradox of
agency in dance was early formulated by ethnomusicologist John Blacking,
who argued that "ritual may be enacted in the service of conservative and even
oppressive institutions...but the experience of performing the nonverbal
movements and sounds may ultimately liberate the actors...Performances of
dance and music frequently reflect and reinforce existing ideas and institutions, but they can also stimulate the imagination and help to bring coherence
to the sensuous life..." (Blacking 1985:65). This quality of dance as simultaneously productive and reproductive is echoed by Novack, who remarks that
"Dance may reflect *and* resist cultural values simultaneously," noting the example of the ballerina who "embodies and enacts stereotypes of the feminine
while she interprets a role with commanding skill, agency and a subtlety that
denies stereotype" (Novack 1995:181).

Novack's major ethnographic work on contact improvisation (1990), a modern communal danced "art-sport" that focuses on the physical sensations of "touching, leaning, supporting, counterbalancing, and falling with other people" (Novack 1990:8), located this form within "American culture" (a term she unfortunately did not adequately problematize). Novack provides a comprehensive analysis of several aspects of contact improvisation, following her notion that in order to understand any dance form, one must take into account the interplay of its different facets: (*a*) the "art" (choreographic structures, movement styles, techniques of dance); (*b*) the institutions (local, national, global) in which it is practiced and performed; and (*c*) those who participate in it as performers, producers, spectators and commentators (Novack 1995:181). In her study, Novack addresses each of these, situating the dance in relation to particular historical circumstances and showing how the meanings of movement and constructions of the body changed over two decades, from the 1960s to the 1980s. Drawing on her own long-term experience in learning contact improvisation, Novack provides a rich, sensual interpretation of movement that is sensitive to the centrality of the body, as well as to the ways in which culture shapes and is shaped by it.

Novack's attention to historicizing the body in culture is one of her main contributions to dance scholarship. In a discussion of theatrical dance forms in 20th century America, for example, Novack articulates the differences between the ways in which bodies are conceptualized in ballet ("as an instrument which must be trained to conform to the classical movement vocabulary"), in modern dances of the 1930s and 1940s ("a more expressionist view of the body...in which internal feelings were realized in external movement"), and in dances of the postwar period (a model of the body that was "more abstract, or objective, and more phenomenological") (Novack 1990:31). But Novack also looks beyond theatrical dance to other cultural influences on the body, exemplified by rock dancing, experimental theatre, and bodily based therapies such as Alexander technique, yoga, and meditation. In taking this broad perspective, Novack situates contact improvisation in relation to wider currents of change in the 1960s regarding conceptualizations of the body.

Both the sensual/sensible experience of dance and its cultural meanings are the focus of a comparative article by Bull that draws on Paul Stoller's formulation of "sensibility" and "intelligibility" (Bull 1997; Stoller 1989). Exploring how ballet, contact improvisation, and West African dance stress the senses of sight, touch, and sound, respectively, Bull argues that the particular characteristics of each dance form, as well as its modes of transmission and performance, encourage "priorities of sensation that subtly affect the nature of perception itself" (1997:285). Bull thus hypothesizes that dance "finely tunes" culturally variable sensibilities, raising important questions about the transmission of dance from one cultural setting, or historical period, to another (Bull 1997:285).

Body, space, movement, culture, and history are explored in Sally Ness's ethnography of the *sinulog*, a dance form of the Philippine port city of Cebu (Ness 1992). Through her interpretations of the varieties of *sinulog* dancing, Ness connects a number of issues in the field of dance and movement in an original way. Ness's key conceptual innovation is the use of a category she calls "choreographic phenomena." By deploying this category in contexts where the term dance would be too narrow or confining, Ness both draws attention to a wider array of patterned body movements—such as those found in ritual practices—and provides linkages between these more public and formal structures and the more commonplace moves of walking or handholding. Through the use of analogies, Ness demonstrates how both the visual and the sensory qualities of movement can be expressed in language. Her description of the opening move in the ritual *sinulog* is typical: "Imagine gentle currents of energy, flowing freely through and beyond your body, forming warm pools of movement in the space just around you. Your hands are brought to life in this softly pulsing current. They wave around in the watery space, leaving invisible traces of their movement in the air. The current spreads down your legs, which begin to bear your body's weight alternately, subtly shifting your body from side to side through the liquid space in a slight sway..." (Ness 1992:1).

Interpreting movement, however, also requires a sensitivity to cultural space. As Ness shows, space is not an inert backdrop for movement, but is integral to it, often providing fundamental orientation and meaning. In an analysis of the urban environment of Cebu, Ness ranges from a description of the street plans and built environment to a discussion of the structured movements of walking, traffic, and ritual dance, drawing out patterns of continuity between all of these. These patterns she identifies as off-verticality, resiliency, and surface values, all of which manifest themselves in a wide variety of contexts and constitute the fluidity of life that Ness notes as characteristic of Cebuano culture.

Williams draws attention to the importance of locating movement in space through an examination of a "bow" in three movement systems—tai chi, a Latin Mass, and a modern ballet (Williams 1995). In her discussion, drawing on ideas derived from Hertz and Dumont, Williams attends to the cultural meanings of movements and directions such as up/down, right/left, front/back, and inside/outside. Employing Dumont's idea of a hierarchy of structural oppositions, she notes, for example, that in European culture movements forward and backward correlate with temporal ideas of the future and the past. Williams argues that understanding bodies, spaces, and objects in terms of these structural oppositions is essential for conceptualizating human movement as intentional action.

Lewis's study of the Brazilian capoeira—a complex cultural genre that includes elements of martial art, dance, music, ritual, and theatre—combines detailed analysis of movement with incisive commentaries on its social and cultural significance (Lewis 1992). In his study, Lewis draws on the insights of Peircean semiotics and context-sensitive sociolinguistic theories (see also Urciuoli 1995) to illuminate capoeira as a kind of discourse, a "physical dialogue" or "conversation" between two partners, a conversation that takes place through action, not talk. Viewing his primary project as a contribution to a general theory of signs in culture, Lewis attends to both the formal and contextual aspects of the capoeira. The voices of capoeira masters, as well as that of the anthropologist, are present throughout the text.

One of the key contributions of Lewis's study to dance and movement analysis is his use of a Peircean semiotic perspective that emphasizes the polysemy of sign systems, the multiplicity of interpretations, and the negotiated and unstable nature of cultural production. While language has long been the privileged site of analysis in semiotic approaches influenced by Saussure, Lewis shows how Peirce's attention to the iconic and indexical features of signs may prove more illuminating for analyses of extralinguistic sign systems such as dance and music (see also Feld & Fox 1994). While stressing the conditioned and highly contextualized nature of such systems, the Peircean perspective provides a broad view that allows the analyst to make links with other sign complexes within a society. Like Ness, Lewis demonstrates that the relationships between everyday movements and movements in performance are continuous, though not identical, relating to what Lewis calls a "cultural style" linking everyday life with art (1992:132). Cultural styles, in Lewis's view "are composed of signs which are semiotically related but functionally and pragmatically diverse: able to function in many ways, mean many things, but all in the same 'way'" (1992:132). As Lewis indicates, cultural style is often embedded in physical habits and rarely articulated—thus dependent on the keen eye and body of the participant/observer.

Attention to the multiple and contested interpretations of movement in history, and the dilemmas of the anthropologist in sorting out these contested histories, is yet another important aspect of Lewis's project. Throughout his analysis, Lewis relates the movements in capoeira to practitioners' accounts of their links to the culture of Brazilian slavery, and by extension, to Africa. While acknowledging the political meanings that such links may have in contemporary culture, Lewis does not refrain from casting doubt on some prominent oral traditions explaining the origins of capoeira and he attempts to sort out and examine its multiple influences—Amerindian, African, and European. In his discussions of the "multiple semiotic channels" of capoeira—movement, music, and speech—Lewis frequently comments on the African and European influences that are in evidence, or are meaningful to capoeira masters. He also shows capoeira's links to other Afro-Brazilian movement systems, such as the samba, and to African music and ritual aesthetics, making again a case for a distinctive cultural style (see also Lewis 1995:226).

The thread that binds this complex semiotic system together and links it to other facets of Afro-Brazilian culture is the theme of liberation, escape, and freedom: freedom from slavery, from class domination, from poverty, and even from the constraints of the body (Lewis 1992:2). Deception is a key means of achieving liberation, a trait that Lewis suggests evolved under slavery as a "weapon of the weak" and has now become a central value in contemporary society. In capoeira, many moves are made to deceive—a blessing that results in a kick (Lewis 1992:32), or the set of movements Lewis classes as "pretend to run away," in which a player initially feigns fear, only to turn and attack (1992:130). These tactics of deception, along with a host of other pretend movements (pretend to lose sight of the opponent, pretend to be injured, pretend to be angry, and so on), Lewis argues, are viewed as a necessary and valued aspect of life, both in and out of the capoeira ring. In capoeira, however, unlike in everyday life, deceptive tactics are revealed, and thus, truths about society are unmasked (1995:194).

Barbara Browning's exploration of the Brazilian samba employs vivid language to inscribe the "bodily writing" of dance, drawing the reader into the worlds of samba, candomblé, and capoeira of Bahia and New York City (Browning 1995). In Brazil, Browning writes, "I began to think with my body" (1995:xxii), and it was through her experience of Brazilian dancing that Browning conceived "entirely different ways of thinking about language, writing, representation, narrative, even irony" (1995:xxi). Browning conceives of her project as neither purely historical nor purely semiotic analysis, but an account that would "allow for a synthesis of time and signs, which would be the only way to account for the complex speaking of the body in Brazil" (Browning 1995:9). The circle or *roda* of samba, candomblé, and capoeira stands as a metaphor through Browning's analysis; there is no linear progression, but rather expansion and always return. While Browning discusses the "secular" samba, the "religious" candomblé, and the "martial dance" of capoeira in separate chapters, she makes clear that the boundaries between them are not at all clear, and that references to one may be encoded in another.

The centrality of dance in trance and healing has long been acknowledged by anthropologists (Bourguignon 1968), and a number of insightful studies have stressed body-centered or phenomenological approaches (Deren 1970; Drewal 1989, 1992; Devisch 1993; Friedson 1996; Kapferer 1983; Katz 1982). In her discussion of the dances of the syncretic Afro-Brazilian Catholic-Yoruba religion of candomblé, Browning explores a critical issue of representation in describing what anthropologists have generally classified as "possession." What does it mean to be "mounted" by the gods, and how can one describe its "divine choreography"? Like other writers who describe African trance dance as a manifestation of divine powers, Browning shifts from reading the body as the central object of analysis, to the orixás—the principles of nature—that stand outside of, and before, human creative potential (1995:42). In making this shift, Browning alters her analytic focus from the individual body to more culturally salient notions. But how is divinity represented in dance?

Browning answers this question by undertaking a semiotic analysis of the ways in which "orixá choreography" is danced. The invocative dances of the orixás, subdued and subtle dances that are performed prior to their descent, are not evocations or imitations of the orixás, but a "prayer of significance" and offering to them (Browning 1995:70). For male gods, the dances are performed in reference to the metonymic, physical objects that are associated with them; for goddesses, the dances tend to be embodied in relation to their principles. The lightning god Xangô, for example, is invoked in a manner in which the body of the dancer comes to resemble his implement, the thunder axe, while in dancing Yemanjá, the goddess of salt waters, the dancer pulls her outstretched arms inward as if drawing the waters in at low tide (Browning 1995:65). Browning's conclusion is that representations of divinity in candomblé can be made contiguously or metonymically, but not mimetically, and grasping this essential principle enables one to interpret the choreography of candomblé.

Among the many stereotypes that Browning counters in her book is the cathartic theory of dance and ritual (see Spencer 1985:3–8) that argues that the dances of the marginal and lower classes are a means to cope with the oppression of their lives by using dance as a temporary "escape" from everyday suffering. Browning provides an alternative reading to this, asserting that dance is not a retreat but rather a means of remembering, a mode of "cultural record keeping" and a form of "cultural inscription" (Browning 1995:xxii), a "language in response to cultural repression" (1995:174). As she concludes in her final chapter, "the insistence of Brazilians to keep *dancing* is not a means of forgetting but rather a perseverence, an unrelenting attempt to intellectualize, theorize, understand a history and a present of social injustice difficult to believe, let alone explain" (Browning 1995:167).

As Ness, Lewis, and Browning all demonstrate, patterning and principles of continuity exist across domains of movement, space, material objects, music, and verbal play. Though still a minor theme in dance scholarship, there is a small but important body of work that explores the connections between dance and other modes of expressive culture. Kaeppler's studies of Tongan and Hawaiian dance, music, and poetry, for example, illustrate how key aesthetic principles are manifested in verbal, visual, and musical forms (Kaeppler 1993a, 1995, 1996). Feld's analysis of the Kaluli ceremonial dance of gisalo explores how the Kaluli concept for style and aesthetics, "lift-up-over-sounding," reverberates in sound, text, face painting, costume, and dance movements (Feld 1988, 1990a). Kersenboom highlights how dance is integral to an understanding of the Tamil language (muttamil, literally "three Tamil") which, by definition, includes dance, music, and text (Kersenboom 1995). Other studies examine aesthetic and stylistic relationships between dance and music (Chernoff 1983, Erlmann 1996, Thompson 1966), dress (Kealiinohomoku 1979), mime (Royce 1984), and sculpture, painting, mythology, and literature (Gaston 1982, Thompson 1974, Vatsyayan 1968).

## CONCLUSION

Since the mid-1980s, there has been an explosion of dance studies as scholars from a variety of disciplines have turned their attention to dance. Anthropologists have played a critical role in this new dance scholarship, contributing comparative analyses, critiquing ethnocentric categories, and situating studies of dance and movement within broader frameworks of embodiment and the politics of culture. Countering theories of the body which view it primarily as a site of inscription, dance scholars have demonstrated how performers invent and reinvent identities through movement. Dance scholars have also refuted notions of the body as an isolated entity by showing how a multiplicity of bodies is produced through dance.

As scholars of dance and movement explore new ways of thinking through and with the body, there is no doubt that they will continue to challenge conventions, undermining entrenched dualisms (e.g. mind/body, thinking/feeling), critiquing evolutionary, colonial, and nationalist typologies (e.g. classical, folk, ethnic), exposing the limits of conceptual categories (e.g. dance, art), and revealing dimensions of dance experience (e.g. the sensual, the divine) that have often been neglected in scholarly inquiry.

ACKNOWLEDGMENTS

I would like to express my thanks to those friends and colleagues who provided much encouragement and critical commentary on this review: E Valentine Daniel, Mary Des Chene, Jeanne Marecek, and Elizabeth Tolbert. I am grateful to J Lowell Lewis, Bill Smith, and Faye Harrison for useful suggestions in the final stages. Adrienne Kaeppler, Janet O'Shea and the late Cynthia Jean Cohen Bull generously provided numerous references.

Visit the *Annual Reviews home page* at
http://www.AnnualReviews.org.

# Literature Cited

Abu-Lughod L. 1990. The romance of resistance: tracing transformations of power through Bedouin women. *Am. Ethnol.* 17(1):41–55

al Faruqi LI. 1978. Dance as an expression of Islamic culture. *Dance Res. J.* 10 (2): 6–13

Allen MH. 1997. Rewriting the script for South Indian dance. *Drama Rev.* 41(3): 63–100

Appadurai A. 1996. *Modernity at Large.* Minneapolis: Minn. Univ. Press

Appadurai A, Breckenridge C. 1988. Why public culture? *Public Cult.* 1(1):5–9

Austerlitz P. 1997. *Merengue: Dominican music and Dominican identity.* Philadelphia: Temple Univ. Press

Blacking J. 1985. Movement, dance, music and the Venda girls' initiation cycle. See Spencer 1985a, pp. 54–91

Bourguignon E. 1968. Trance dance. *Dance Perspect.* 35:6–60

Brandes SH. 1979. Dance as metaphor: a case from Tzintzuntan, Mexico. *J. Lat. Am. Lore* 5(1):25–43

Brandes SH. 1990. The sardana: Catalan dance and Catalan national identity. *J. Am. Folk.* 103(407):24–41

Browning B. 1995. *Samba: Resistance in Motion.* Bloomington, IN: Indiana Univ. Press

Bull CJC. 1997. Sense, meaning and perception in three dance cultures. See Desmond 1997, pp. 269–87

Buonaventura W. 1990. *Serpent of the Nile: Women and Dance in the Arab World.* New York: Interlink

Chernoff J. 1983. *African Rhythm and African Sensibility: Aesthetics and Social Action in African Musical Idioms.* Chicago: Univ. Chicago Press

Cohen SJ, ed. 1998. *International Encyclopedia of Dance.* 6 Vols. Oxford, UK: Oxford Univ. Press

Comaroff J. 1985. *Body of Power, Spirit of Resistance: The Culture and History of a South African People.* Chicago: Univ. Chicago Press

Cooper F, Stoler AL, eds. 1997. *Tensions of Empire: Colonial Cultures in a Bourgeois World.* Berkeley, CA: Univ. Calif. Press

Coorlawala U. 1992. Ruth St. Denis and India's dance renaissance. *Dance Chr.* 15(2): 123–52

Coorlawala U. 1996. *Darshan* and *abhinaya*: an alternative to the male gaze. *Dance Res. J.* 28(1):19–27

Cowan J. 1990. *Dance and the Body Politic in*

*Northern Greece.* Princeton: Princeton Univ. Press

Daly A. 1987/1988. Classical ballet: a discourse of difference. *Women Perform.: J. Fem. Theory* 3(2):57–66. See Desmond 1997, pp. 111–19

Daly A. 1991a. Unlimited partnership: dance and feminist analysis. *Dance Res. J.* 23(1): 2–3

Daly A. 1991b. What revolution? The new dance scholarship in America. *Ballett Int.* 14(1):48–53

Daly A. 1992. Dance history and feminist theory: Isadora Duncan and the male gaze. See Senelick, 1992, pp. 239–59

Daly A. 1995. *Done into Dance: Isadora Duncan in America.* Bloomington, IN: Indiana Univ. Press

Daniel YP. 1991. Changing values in Cuban rumba: a lower class black dance appropriated by the Cuban revolution. *Dance Res. J.* 23(2):1–10

Daniel YP. 1995. *Rumba: Dance and Social Change in Contemporary Cuba.* Bloomington, IN: Indiana Univ. Press

Daniel YP. 1996. Tourism dance performances: authenticity and creativity. *Ann. Tour. Res.* 23(4):780–97

Daugherty D, Pitkow M. 1991.Who wears the skirts in Kathakali? *Drama Rev.* 35(2): 138–56

Deaver S. 1978. Concealment and display: the modern Saudi woman. *Dance Res. J.* 10(2):14–18

Deren M. 1970. *Divine Horsemen: The Living Gods of Haiti.* New York: Dell

Desmond JC. 1991. Dancing out the difference: cultural imperialism and Ruth St. Denis's "Radha" of 1906. *Signs* 17(1): 28–48

Desmond JC. 1993/1994. Embodying difference: issues in dance and cultural studies. *Cult. Critique* 26:33–63. See Desmond 1997, pp. 29–54

Desmond JC, ed. 1997. *Meaning in Motion: New Cultural Studies of Dance.* Durham, NC: Duke Univ. Press

Devisch R. 1993. *Weaving the Threads of Life: The Khita Gyn-Eco-Logical Healing Cult Among the Yaka.* Chicago: Univ. Chicago Press

Dirks NB. 1992. Introduction: colonialism and culture. In *Colonialism and Culture,* ed. NB Dirks, pp. 1–25. Ann Arbor, MI: Univ. Mich. Press

Drewal MT. 1989. Dancing for Ogun in Yorubaland and in Brazil. In *Africa's Ogun: Old World and New,* ed. S Barnes, pp.

199–234. Bloomington, IN: Indiana Univ. Press

Drewal MT. 1992. *Yoruba Ritual: Performers, Play, Agency*. Bloomington, IN: Indiana Univ. Press

Erdman JL. 1987. Performance as translation: Uday Shankar in the West. *Drama Rev.* 31(1):64–88

Erdman JL. 1996. Dance discourses: rethinking the history of "oriental dance." See Morris 1996, pp. 288–305

Erlmann V. 1996. *Nightsong: Performance, Power and Practice in South Africa*. Chicago: Univ. Chicago Press

Farnell B. 1994. Ethno-graphics and the moving body. *Man* (NS) 29:929–74

Farnell B, ed. 1995a. *Human Action Signs in Cultural Context: The Visible and the Invisible in Movement and Dance*. Metuchen, NJ: Scarecrow

Farnell B. 1995b. Introduction. See Farnell 1995a, pp. 1–28

Feld S. 1988. Aesthetics as iconicity of style, or 'lift-up-over-sounding': getting into the Kaluli groove. *Yearb. Tradit. Music* 20:74–113

Feld S. 1990b. *Sound and Sentiment: Birds, Weeping, Poetics and Song in Kaluli Expression*. Philadelphia: Univ. Penn. Press. 2nd ed.

Feld S. 1990a. Aesthetics and synesthesia in Kaluli ceremonial dance. *UCLA J. Dance Ethnol.* 14:1–16

Feld S. 1991. Sound as a symbolic system: the Kaluli drum. In *The Varieties of Sensory Experience: A Sourcebook in the Anthropology of the Senses*, ed. D Howe, pp. 79–99. Toronto: Univ. Toronto Press

Feld S, Fox A. 1994. Music and language. *Annu. Rev. Anthropol.* 23:25–53

Foster S. 1992. Dancing bodies. In *Incorporations*, ed. J Crary, S Kwinter, pp. 480–95. New York: Zone Books. See Desmond, 1997a, pp. 235–57

Foster S, ed. 1995a. *Choreographing History*. Bloomington, IN: Indiana Univ. Press

Foster S. 1995b. An introduction to moving bodies. See Foster, 1995a, pp. 3–21

Franken M. 1996. Egyptian cinema and television: dancing and the female image. *Vis. Anthropol.* 8(2-4):267–85

Friedland L. 1998. Folk dance history. See Cohen, 1998, 3:29–38

Friedson SM. 1996. *Dancing Prophets: Musical Experience in Tumbuka Healing*. Chicago: Univ. Chicago Press

Gaston A-M.1982. *Siva in Dance, Myth and Iconography*. New York: Oxford Univ. Press

Giurchescu A, Torp L. 1991. Theory and methods in dance research: a European approach to the holistic study of dance. *Yearb. Trad. Music* 22:1–10

Grau A. 1993a. Gender interchangeability among the Tiwi. See Thomas 1993a, pp. 94–111

Grau A. 1993b. John Blacking and the development of dance anthropology in the United Kingdom. *Dance Res. J.* 25(2):21–32

Grau A. 1995. Dance as part of the infrastructure of social life. *World Music* 37(2):43–59

Hall F. 1996. Posture in Irish dancing. *Vis. Anthropol.* 8(2-4):251–66

Handler R. 1988. *Nationalism and the Politics of Culture in Quebec*. Madison: Univ. Wis. Press

Hanna JL. 1979. *To Dance is Human: A Theory of Nonverbal Communication*. Austin: Univ. Texas Press

Hanna JL. 1983. *The Performer-Audience Connection: Emotion to Metaphor in Dance and Society*. Austin: Univ. Texas Press

Hanna JL. 1988. *Dance, Sex and Gender: Signs of Identity, Dominance, Defiance and Desire*. Chicago: Univ. Chicago Press

Hazzard-Gordon K. 1990. *Jookin': The Rise of Social Dance Formations among African Americans*. Philadelphia: Temple Univ. Press

Heath D. 1994. The politics of appropriateness and appropriation: recontextualizing women's dance in urban Senegal. *Am. Ethnol.* 21(1):88–103

Hinsley C. 1991. The world as marketplace: commodification of the exotic at the World's Columbian Exposition, Chicago, 1893. In *Exhibiting Cultures: The Poetics and Politics of Museum Display*, ed. I Karp, S Lavine, pp. 344–65. Washington, DC: Smithson. Inst. Press

Hughes-Freeland F. 1997. Art and politics: from Javanese court dance to Indonesian art. *J. R. Anthropol. Inst.* (NS) 3:473–95

Kaeppler AL. 1977. Polynesian dance as "airport art." In *Asian and Pacific Dance: Selected Papers from the CORD Conference and SEM Conference, 1974 CORD Annual.* 8:74–84. New York: Comm. Res. Dance

Kaeppler AL. 1978. Dance in anthropological perspective. *Annu. Rev. Anthropol.* 7:31–49

Kaeppler AL. 1985. Structured movement systems in Tonga. See Spencer 1985a, pp. 92–118

Kaeppler AL. 1991. American approaches to the study of dance. *Yearb. Tradit. Music* 23:11–21

Kaeppler AL. 1993a. *Poetry in Motion: Stud-*

*ies of Tongan Dance.* Nuku'alofa, Tonga: Vava'u Press

Kaeppler AL. 1993b. *Hula Pahu Hawaiian Drum Dance,* Volume 1. *Ha'a and Hula Pahu: Sacred Movements.* Honolulu: Bishop Mus.

Kaeppler AL. 1995. Visible and invisible in Hawaiian dance. See Farnell 1995a, pp. 31–43

Kaeppler AL. 1996. The look of music, the sound of dance: music as visual art. *Vis. Anthropol.* 8(2-4):133–53

Kapchan DA. 1994. Moroccan female performers defining the social body. *J. Am. Folk.* 107(423):82–105

Kapferer B. 1983. *A Celebration of Demons: Exorcism and the Aesthetics of Healing in Sri Lanka.* Bloomington, IN: Indiana Univ. Press

Kaplan EA. 1983. *Women and Film: Both Sides of the Camera.* London/New York: Methuen

Kaspin D. 1993. Chewa visions and revisions of power: transformations of the Nyau dance in central Malawi. In *Modernity and Its Malcontents,* ed. Jean Comaroff, John Comaroff, pp. 34–57. Chicago: Univ. Chicago Press

Katz R. 1982. *Boiling Energy: Community Healing among the Kalahari Kung.* Cambridge, MA: Harvard Univ. Press

Kealiinohomoku J. 1979. You dance what you wear, and you wear your cultural values. In *The Fabrics of Culture,* ed. JM Cordwell, RA Schwarz, pp. 77–83. The Hague, Netherlands: Mouton

Kealiinohomoku J. 1983. An anthropologist looks at ballet as a form of ethnic dance. In *What Is Dance? Readings in Theory and Criticism,* ed. R Copeland, M Cohen, pp. 533–49. Oxford, UK: Oxford Univ. Press

Kersenboom S. 1995. *Word, Sound, Image: The Life of the Tamil Text.* Oxford, UK: Berg

Kersenboom-Story S. 1987. *Nityasumangali: Devadasi Tradition in South India.* Delhi: Motilal Banarsidas

Koritz A. 1994. Dancing the orient for England: Maud Allan's *The Vision of Salome. Theatre J.* 46:63–78. Reprinted in Desmond, 1997a, pp. 133–52

Lewis JL. 1992. *Ring of Liberation: Deceptive Discourse in Brazilian Capoeira.* Chicago: Univ. Chicago Press

Lewis JL. 1995. Genre and embodiment: from Brazilian capoeira to the ethnology of human movement. *Cult. Anthropol.* 10(2): 221–43

Limon JE. 1994. *Dancing with the Devil: Society and Cultural Poetics in Mexican-*

*American South Texas.* Madison, WI: Univ. Wis. Press

Lock M. 1993. Cultivating the body: anthropology and epistemologies of bodily practice and knowledge. *Annu. Rev. Anthropol.* 22:133–55

Malefyt T. 1998. "Inside" and "outside" Spanish Flamenco: gender constructions in Andalusian concepts of Flamenco tradition. *Anthro. Q.* 71(2):63–73

Malone J. 1996. *Steppin' on the Blues: The Visible Rhythms of African American Dance.* Urbana/Chicago: Univ. Illinois Press

Manning S. 1993. *Ecstasy and the Demon: Feminism and Nationalism in the Dances of Mary Wigman.* Berkeley, CA: Univ. Calif. Press

Manning S. 1995. Modern dance in the Third Reich: six positions and a coda. See Foster 1995a, pp. 165–76

Manning S. 1997. The female dancer and the male gaze: feminist critiques of early modern dance. See Desmond 1997, pp. 153–66

Marglin F. 1985. *Wives of the God-King: The Rituals of the Devadasis of Puri.* Delhi: Oxford Univ. Press

Martin R. 1990. *Performance as Political Act: The Embodied Self.* Westport, CT: Greenwood

Meduri A. 1988. Bharatha natyam—what are you? *Asian Theatre J.* 5(1):1–22

Meduri A. 1996. *Nation, Woman, Representation: The Sutured History of the Devadasi and Her Dance.* PhD. thesis. New York Univ., New York

Mendoza Z. 1998. Defining folklore: mestizo and indigenous identities on the move. *Bull. Lat. Am. Res.* 17(2): In press

Mendoza-Walker Z. 1994. Contesting identities through dance: mestizo performance in the southern Andes of Peru. *Repercussions: Crit. Altern. Viewpoints Music Scholarship* 3 (2):50–80

Meyer M. 1995. Dance and the politics of orality: a study of the Irish *scoil rince. Dance Res. J.* 27(1):25–39

Miller D. 1991. Absolute freedom in Trinidad. *Man* (NS) 26(2):323–41

Mohd AMN. 1993. *Zapin: Folk Dance of the Malay World.* Singapore: Oxford Univ. Press

Morris G, ed. 1996. *Moving Words: Rewriting Dance.* London: Routledge

Mulvey K. 1975. Visual pleasure and narrative cinema. *Screen* 16(3):6–18

Ness SA. 1992. *Body, Movement and Culture: Kinesthetic and Visual Symbolism in a Philippine Community.* Philadelphia: Univ. Penn. Press

Ness SA. 1996. Observing the evidence fail: difference arising from objectification in cross-cultural studies of dance. See Morris 1996, pp. 245–69

Ness SA. 1997. Originality in the postcolony: choreographing the neoethnic body of Philippine ballet. *Cult. Anthropol.* 12(1): 64–108

Novack CJ. 1990. *Sharing the Dance: Contact Improvisation and American Culture.* Madison: Univ. Wis. Press

Novack CJ. 1995. The body's endeavors as cultural practices. See Foster 1995a, pp. 177–84

Ortner S. 1995. Resistance and the problem of ethnographic refusal. *Comp. Stud. Soc. Hist.* 37(1):173–93

O'Shea J. 1997. *Darshan, drishti and the devadasi:* bharata natyam *and the male gaze(s).* Presented at Conf. Re-Presenting Women: Women Vis., Lit. Perform. Arts India, Berkeley

O'Shea J. 1998. "Traditional" Indian dance and the making of interpretive communities. *Asian Theatre J.* 15(1):45–63

Poole DA. 1990. Accommodation and resistance in Andean ritual dance. *Drama Rev.* 34(2):98–126

Quigley C. 1993. Report on International Council for Traditional Music Study Group on Ethnochoreology, 17th symposium. *Dance Res. J.* 25(1):51–54

Quigley C. 1998. Methodologies in the study of dance: ethnology. See Cohen, 1998, 4: 368–72

Ramsey K. 1997. Vodou, nationalism and performance: the staging of folklore in mid-twentieth century Haiti. See Desmond 1997, pp. 345–78

Ranger TO. 1975. *Dance and Society in East Africa 1880–1970.* Berkeley: Univ. Calif. Press

Reed SA. 1991. *The Transformation of Ritual and Dance in Sri Lanka: Kohomba Kankariya and the Kandyan Dance.* PhD thesis. Brown Univ., Providence, RI

Reed SA. 1995. *The politics of aesthetic production in Kandyan dance.* Presented at Sri Lanka Conf., 5th, Durham, NH

Reed SA. 1998. *Between Purity and Respectability: Women Dancers in Postcolonial Sri Lanka.* Presented at South Asia Conf., 13th, Berkeley

Rodriguez S. 1996. *The Matachines Dance: Ritual Symbolism and Interethnic Relations in the Upper Rio Grande Valley.* Albuquerque: Univ. NM Press

Royce AP. 1977. *The Anthropology of Dance.* Bloomington: Indiana Univ. Press

Royce AP. 1984. *Movement and Meaning: Creativity and Interpretation in Ballet and Mime.* Bloomington, IN: Indiana Univ. Press

Savigliano M. 1995. *Tango and the Political Economy of Passion.* Boulder, CO: Westview

Schechner R. 1990. Wayang Kulit in the colonial margin. *Drama Rev.* 34(2):25–61

Senelick L. 1992. Introduction. In *Gender in Performance: The Presentation of Difference in the Performing Arts,* ed. L Senelick, pp. ix–xx. Hanover/London: Univ. Press New England

Shapiro T. 1994. *Dance and the Spirit of Cambodia.* PhD thesis. Cornell Univ., Ithaca, NY

Shapiro T. 1995. The dancer in Cambodia. *Asian Art Cult.* 8(1):8–23

Shay A. 1995. *Bazi-ha-ye Nameyeshi*: Iranian women's theatrical plays. *Dance Res. J.* 27(2):16–24

Sklar D. 1997. In memoriam: Cynthia Jean Cohen Bull. *Dance Res. J.* 29(1):111–15

Spencer P, ed. 1985a. *Society and the Dance.* Cambridge, UK: Cambridge Univ. Press

Spencer P. 1985b. Introduction: interpretations of the dance in anthropology. See Spencer, 1985a, pp. 1–46

Srinivasan A. 1984. *Temple "prostitution" and community reform: an examination of the ethnographic, historical and textual context of the Devadasi of Tamil Nadu, South India.* PhD thesis. Cambridge Univ., Cambridge, UK

Srinivasan A. 1985. Reform and revival: the *devadasi* and her dance. *Econ. Polit. Wkly.* 20(44):1869–76

Srinivasan A. 1988. Reform or conformity? Temple "prostitution" and the community in the Madras Presidency. In *State, Community and Household in Modernizing Asia,* ed. B Agarwal, pp. 175–98. New Delhi: Kali for Women

Stillman AK. 1996. Hawaiian hula competitions: event, repertoire, performance, tradition. *J. Am. Folk.* 109: (434)357–80

Stoller P. 1989. *The Taste of Ethnographic Things: The Senses in Anthropology.* Philadelphia: Univ. Penn. Press

Strauss G. 1977. Dance and ideology in China, past and present: a study of ballet in the People's Republic. *Asian and Pacific Dance: Selected Papers for the CORD and SEM Conference, 1974, CORD Annual* 8:19–54. New York: Comm. Res. Dance

Strong T. 1998. Orientalism. See Cohen 1998, 5:44–47

Sweet JD. 1980. Play, role reversal and humor: symbolic elements of Tewa Pueblo Navajo dance. *Dance Res. J.* 12(1):3–12

Sweet JD. 1985. *Dances of the Tewa Pueblo Indians.* Santa Fe, NM: Sch. Am. Res.

Szwed JF, Marks M. 1988. The Afro-American transformation of European set dances and dance suites. *Dance Res. J.* 20(1):29–36

Taylor J. 1987. Tango. *Cult. Anthropol.* 2(4): 481–93

Thomas H. 1993. An-other voice: young women dancing and talking. In *Dance, Gender and Culture,* ed. H Thomas, pp. 69–93. London: Macmillan

Thomas H. 1996. Do you want to join the dance?: Postmodernism/poststructuralism, the body and dance. See Morris 1996, pp. 63–87

Thompson RF. 1966. An aesthetic of the cool: West African dance. *Afr. Forum* 2(2): 85–102

Thompson RF. 1974. *African Art in Motion.* Berkeley, CA: Univ. Calif. Press

Turner T. 1995. Social body and embodied subject: bodiliness, subjectivity and sociality among the Kayapo. *Cult. Anthropol.* 10(2):143–70

Udall SR. 1992. The irresistible other: Hopi ritual drama and Euro-American audiences. *Drama Rev.* 36(2):23–43

Urciuoli B. 1995. The indexical structure of visibility. See Farnell 1995a, pp. 189–215

Vail JA. 1996. Balkan tradition, American alternative: dance, community and the people of the pines. See Morris 1996, pp. 306–19

van Nieuwkerk K. 1995. *A Trade Like Any Other: Female Singers and Dancers in Egypt.* Austin: Univ. Texas Press

Vatsyayan K. 1968. *Classical Indian Dance in Literature and the Arts.* New Delhi: Sangeet Natak Akad.

Wagner AL. 1997. *Adversaries of the Dance: From the Puritans to the Present.* Urbana: Univ. Ill. Press

Williams D. 1991. *Ten Lectures on Theories of the Dance.* Metuchen, NJ: Scarecrow

Williams D. 1995. Space, intersubjectivity, and the conceptual imperative: three ethnographic cases. See Farnell 1995a, pp. 44–81

Youngerman S. 1998. Methodologies in the study of dance: anthropology. See Cohen 1998, 4:368–72

Zarrilli P. 1998. *When the Body Becomes All Eyes: Paradigms, Discourses and Practices of Power in Kalarippayattu, a South Indian Martial Art.* Delhi: Oxford Univ. Press

# AUTHOR INDEX

Camak L, 317
Cambell C, 97
Campbell BC, 359, 360
Campbell KL, 208, 209, 354
Campbell L, 460, 465, 466
Campbell TN, 39, 40
Canclini NG, 130, 141
Candido A, 116, 121, 122
Candland DK, 313
Canizares R, 262
Cann RL, 6, 7, 9, 12, 13, 155, 286
Cantor CR, 289, 485
Capistrano FH, xix
Caplan AL, 479
Cappenberg M, 365
Capron AM, 479, 480
Cardew G, 279
Cardoso R, 121
Cardoso de Oliveira LR, 118, 119, 133
Cardoso de Oliveira R, 121
Carmack RM, 53, 54
Carman J, 331, 337
Carneiro da Cunha M, 118, 119
Caro TM, 322
Carpenter M, 306
Carr C, 331
Carr SM, 13
Carretero JM, 380
Carrier J, 435, 437
Carstenuto L, 11, 12
Carvalho JJ, 132, 136, 147
Casanova J, 85, 87, 89, 99
Caselli G, 260
Caspari R, 3, 10, 11, 18
Cassman V, 44
Castells F de P, 49
Castillo ED, 46
Castillo LJ, 332, 333
Castro Faria L, 121
Castrucci MR, 263
Caton SC, 411
Cattani J, 260
Caughly G, 199, 206
Caulfield T, 488
Cavalcanti ML, 121
Cavalli-Sforza LL, 9, 11, 12, 156, 161, 162, 164, 165, 282, 283, 285, 286, 288, 289, 322, 478, 485
Cave MD, 260
Cavell S, 173, 176, 180, 183, 186, 187, 189
Cetron MS, 261
Chace PG, 47
Chadwick D, 279
Chagnon NA, 364
Chakrabarti D, 237

Chakraborty R, 12, 163, 282, 283
Chakravarti A, 290, 291
Chambers DB, 71
Chambers R, 253
Champion T, 76, 224, 225
Chang B, 7
Chapman CA, 311
Chapman LE, 258
Chapman RW, 333, 338
Charles DK, 388
Charnov EL, 357
Chasiotis A, 352, 365
Chatterjee P, 94, 225
Chatterji R, 174
Chaturvedi R, 184
Cheney DL, 306, 314
Chernoff J, 527
Chernykh EN, 225
Chesser RK, 158
Chestnut RA, 97
Cheverud JM, 388
Chinery WA, 259
Ching B, 436
Chippindale C, 335
Chisholm JS, 352, 361, 365
Chowdhury AI, 357
Chowdhury M, 363
Christian WA, 93
Claassen C, 340
Clark AG, 12, 158, 285, 364
Clark DN, 95
Clark GG, 259, 331
Clark J, 333, 438
Clark TW, 312
Clasteres P, 172
Clay DC, 356
Clayton EW, 493
Clendinnen I, 53
Clifford J, 111-13, 179, 428, 429, 433
Clifford SL, 9, 161, 164
Cliquet RL, 351
Clottes J, 336
Clutton-Brock TH, 197, 362
Coale A, 198, 206
Coale AJ, 198, 213, 215, 389
Cockburn TA, 248, 250
Cohen JE, 217, 263
Cohen ML, 261, 340
Cohen MN, 52, 252, 253, 376
Cohen SJ, 504
Cohen-Williams AG, 51
Cohn BS, 84, 93, 94
Collins C, 262
Collins F, 275, 290, 291
Collins FS, 482
Coluzzi M, 259
Colwell RR, 248, 259

Comaroff Jean, 28, 29, 84, 88, 96, 434, 506
Comaroff John, 28, 29, 88, 96
Comaroff JL, 28, 434, 435, 437
Condon K, 388
Conkey M, 331, 332, 335, 340
CONKLIN HC, xiii-xxx
Connors M, 257
Conrad C, 368
Conrad G, 333
Cook E, 410
Cook SF, 46
Cook-Deegan RM, 275, 276, 289, 296, 474, 477, 485
Cooper D, 68
Cooper F, 434, 506
Cooper R, 85
Coorlawala U, 509, 519
Copeland P, 496
Copet-Rougier E, 118
Corbin JE, 39, 40, 42, 43
Cordell LS, 34-36
Cornelissen E, 165
Cornplanter JJ, xvi
Correa G, 53
Corrêa M, 121
Corruccini RS, 378-80
Cortés de Brasdefer F, 49
Cossar JH, 263
Costello JG, 43, 44, 47
Course J, 286
Cowan J, 518
Cowgill G, 333
Cox MJ, 13, 156, 160, 285, 287
Craig C, 410
Craig J, 380
Cramer JS, 165
Cranor CF, 474
Crapanzano V, 112
Crawford CB, 355
Crawford JT, 262
Creed G, 436
Creveling MC, 69, 76, 77
Criado F, 333
Crick FHC, 473
Crick M, 109
Critescu M, 351
Crittenden R, 437, 438, 440
Crofton J, 248
Cronk L, 352, 362
Crosby AW, 262
Crow JF, 12
Crowley T, 417
Cruxent JM, 27
Csanaky A, 365
Cumming DC, 354
Curtin PD, 66
Curtis GH, 154

# SUBJECT INDEX

## A

Abstract identities
  where to find Africa in the
  nation, 134
Adaptability
  evolutionary reproductive
  ecology and, 347, 365–67
Advantage
  perception of human
  human genome research
  and society, 480
Afghanistan
  nationalism and archae-
  ology, 228, 242
Africa
  genetic architecture of
  modern populations,
  154–55, 163–67
  genetics of modern human
  origins and diversity,
  1–11, 14, 18–19
  globalization and culture
  areas, 441
  human genome research
  and society, 486
  multiple modernities and
  world religions, 95, 97
  nationalism and archae-
  ology, 225, 234, 236
  paleodemography and,
  389–90
  where to find Africa in the
  nation, Brazilian ethnic
  paradigm, 142–49
  where to find Africa in the
  nation
  ethno-racial paradigm,
  135–49
  localizing influence,
  129–31
  national constructions of
  race, 135–37
  North American ethnic
  paradigm, 137–42
  North American myth of
  separation and its critics,
  131–35
  racisms, 135–49
  reciprocating gaze,
  137–42
  repatriating gaze, 142–49

African diaspora
  archaeology of
  African identity, 66–69
  beginnings, 64–66
  freedom from slavery,
  69–73
  introduction, 63–64
  race, 73–76
  relevance, 76–78
Afro-Americans
  where to find Africa in the
  nation, 129–49
Afro-Brazilians
  where to find Africa in the
  nation, 129–49
Afro-European hybridization
  model
  genetics of modern human
  origins and diversity, 2–3
Age estimation
  paleodemography and,
  375–93
Agency
  archaeology of symbols
  and, 329–42
Akowe clan
  Wittgenstein and anthropology, 184
Albania
  local linguistic communities and, 421
Algiers
  nationalism and archae-
  ology, 228
*Al-nizam-al-islami*
  multiple modernities and
  world religions, 91
Altaic language
  linguistic taxonomy and,
  453
Alterity
  anthropology at home and,
  116–22
  where to find Africa in the
  nation, 130
*Alu* insertion polymorphisms
  genetic architecture of
  modern populations,
  160–61
  genetics of modern human
  origins and diversity,
  9–13, 15

American English
  local linguistic communities and, 421
Amerindians
  paleodemography and, 393
American Southwest
  Mission archaeology and,
  34–38
Americas
  Christianization of, Mission
  archaeology and, 25–54
Among-group variation
  genetics of modern human
  origins and diversity, 12,
  16
Anakalangese
  local linguistic communities and, 419
Ancient society
  archaeology of symbols
  and, 329
Antagonistic pleiotrophic effects
  comparative demography
  of primates and, 217
Anthropological linguistics
  local linguistic communities and, 401–23
Anthropology
  history of research,
  xiii–xxviii
Anthropology at home
  alterity, 116–22
  alternative viewpoint,
  115–16
  antecedents, 107–8
  anthropology of anthropology, 110
  Brazil, 116–22
  conferences of 1970s,
  109–10
  contact with otherness,
  118–19
  doing, 110–12
  introduction, 105–7
  nearby otherness, 120–21
  otherness in context, 122
  perspectives, 122–23
  post-exotic anthropology,
  112–14
  radical otherness, 117–18
  radical us, 121

# CUMULATIVE INDEXES

## CONTRIBUTING AUTHORS, VOLUMES 19–27

# CHAPTER TITLES, VOLUMES 19–27